TRAYNER'S LATIN MAXIMS

Lord Trayner
Senator of the College of Justice 1885-1904

This portrait by Sir George Reid, RSA, which was acquired
by the University of Dundee in 1970 from the estate of Lord Trayner's grandson
hangs in the entrance hall to the Scrmygeour Building, Faculty of Law,
and is reproduced with their kind permission.

TRAYNER'S LATIN MAXIMS

collected from
The Institutional Writers
on the Law of Scotland
and Other Sources
with
translations and illustrations

Fourth Edition

with a foreword by
A.G.M. DUNCAN, M.A., LL.B., W.S.

W. GREEN/Sweet & Maxwell
EDINBURGH
1993

Published by W. Green, The Scottish
Law Publisher, 21 Alva Street,
Edinburgh EH2 4PS.

First published by W. Green & Son in 1861
        Second edition   1876
        Third edition   1883
        Fourth edition   1894
        Reprinted   1993

This edition © 1993
W. Green & Son Ltd.

Reprinted in paperback 1998

Cased: ISBN 0 414 01061 2
Paper: ISBN 0 414 01294 1

A catalogue record for this book
is available from the British Library

Printed in Great Britain by
Antony Rowe Ltd, Chippenham, Wiltshire

FOREWORD

IN the preface to the first edition of this work, published in 1861, the author, then a junior member of the Scottish bar, explained that his chief aim had been to combine correctness of statement with clearness of expression by endeavouring to offer the most intelligible explanation of the maxims and phrases and to give the most apposite illustration of their meaning and application; he hoped that the work might be useful to students and others in assisting them to acquire a knowledge of the technical import and application of the Latin maxims and phrases which in many cases could not be acquired by a mere knowledge of classical Latin. In fact no knowledge of Latin is required by the reader, an important consideration today with Latin largely disappearing as a subject of study in schools and colleges.

The success of the work was evidenced by its reaching its fourth edition in 1894, when the author had been some nine years on the Court of Session bench. As updated and expanded, the fourth edition is almost twice the size of the first. It received very favourable reviews in the legal press, the *Scots Law Times* of 1894/5 describing it as a work invaluable to the whole legal community, scientific jurists, practitioners and students. Unfortunately, although the author remained on the bench for a further 10 years and survived in retirement for another 25 years to become the father of the bar, no further editions appeared. The format was, however, followed on a reduced scale but without conspicuous success in *Select Scots Law Maxims* by Connolly and Brown published in 1934 to meet, as it was said, a need arising from Lord Trayner's work being out of date and out of print.

The reprinting of the fourth edition of Trayner after an interval of almost a century may be said to raise the question of the significance of Roman law in Scots law today. In an English case of *Sinclair* v. *Brougham* ([1914] A.C. 398 at p. 432) Lord Dunedin, in a passage quoted by Professor James Mackintosh in the introduction to his *Roman Law in Modern Practice* (1934), spoke of going to the Roman Law not as an authority, for such it is not, but for instruction on how matters should be dealt with and for suggestions of the true answers to the difficulties of a case. More recently, Professor Peter Stein, writing in the *Juridical Review* for 1963 at pages 244–245, indicated that Roman law was probably spent as a source of new law in Scotland, it being rare for the *corpus juris* to be cited in the Court of Session. He added, however, that the Roman notions introduced into Scots law in its formative period were embedded so firmly in its structure that many parts still bear an unmistakably Roman stamp and cannot be comprehended without a knowledge of the Roman institutions from which they are derived.

While, as Professor Stein indicates, citation of the *corpus juris* in the Court of Session is now rare there is a very recent instance, in the case of *Stirling* v. *Bartlett*, 1992 S.C.L.R. 994 where Lord Coulsfield included, in his judgment at page 997, a quotation from Justinian's *Institutes* for the rules of law applicable where, by avulsion or alluvion, change occurs in the course of a river forming the boundary between properties.

The lasting importance of maxims such as those collected in Trayner's work is well expressed by Lord Cameron in an article on "Maxims," in Green's *Encyclopaedia of the Law of Scotland* (vol.9, para. 1201) where he says:

> "In legal discussions reference is constantly being made to certain principles of common sense and justice, which are necessarily the same in the legal systems of all nations. Many of these fundamental principles and rules, founded on experience and reason, have found expression in the legal maxims, most of which are derived directly or indirectly from the Roman law. Nowhere is the faculty of clear and terse statement of legal principles more conspicuously exhibited than in the texts of the civil law. Accordingly, while the legal systems of modern civilised nations differ greatly in

their technical rules and forms, all of them recognise the value of the simple and apposite statements of fundamental principles embodied in the maxims of Roman jurisprudence."

Reprints have recently become available of some works of the institutional writers and other distinguished authors long out of print. It seems most appropriate that in the same way there should be made available to the profession and other interested persons this work of an eminent judge and distinguished scholar generally acknowledged to be the best of its kind.

A.G.M. Duncan,
Edinburgh,
February 1993

PREFACE TO FOURTH EDITION.

IN preparing the present Edition for the Press, such alterations have been made in the text as were rendered necessary by recent changes in the law. Decisions bearing upon, or illustrative of, the different questions dealt with in the text, pronounced since the Third Edition was issued, have been added; as also have a few phrases not contained in former Editions.

EDINBURGH, *October*, 1894.

PREFACE TO SECOND EDITION.

THIS work was originally undertaken for the purpose of aiding students of law to acquire a knowledge of the technical import and application of the Latin law maxims and phrases in common use, a knowledge which in many cases could not be acquired by a mere acquaintance with classical Latin. The author has been glad to learn that his work has, in some measure at least, accomplished the purpose it was designed to fulfil.

The First Edition having been for some time out of print, and the book being still in demand, the author has taken advantage of the opportunity afforded by the publication of a Second Edition, to endeavour to make his work a more complete repertory than it formerly was of legal maxims and phrases, and he hopes that in its present state it will be found more useful, both to the student and practitioner, than heretofore. Many phrases and maxims have been added in the present Edition, and many of the original articles have been altered or rewritten, where changes in the law have rendered this necessary.

The present Edition has been prepared in the midst of other engagements, and in such leisure hours as the Spring and Summer Vacations of the Court during the past two years have placed at the author's disposal. It was carefully revised in manuscript by his friend Mr. W. F. Hunter, Advocate, who made many important corrections and suggestions, which have contributed largely towards any value which this volume may be found to possess.

EDINBURGH, 1*st June*, 1876.

LIST OF ABBREVIATIONS.

Abbott . . . . . . Abbott's Law of Merchant Ships and Seamen, 12th ed.
Addison on Con. . . . Addison on Contracts, 8th ed.
Addison, Torts . . . Addison on the Law of Torts, 5th ed.
Arnould . . . . . Arnould on Marine Insurance, 5th ed.

B. & C. . . . . . Barnewall & Cresswell's Reports of Cases determined in the Court of King's Bench.
Bac. Max. . . . . Maxims of the Law, by Lord Bacon.
Bankton . . . . . Bankton's Institute of the Law of Scotland.
Bell . . . . . . Bell on the Law of Arbitration.
Bell . . . . . . Bell's Reports of Scotch Cases decided on Appeal in the House of Lords.
Bell C. C. . . . . Bell's Crown Cases Reserved.
Bell's Dict. . . . . Bell's Law Dictionary. Edited by G. Watson.
Bell's Com. . . . . Bell's Commentaries on the Law of Scotland, 7th ed.
Bell's Prin. . . . . Bell's Principles of the Law of Scotland, 7th ed.
Benjamin . . . . Benjamin on Sales, 3rd ed.
Blackstone . . . . Blackstone's Commentaries on the Laws of England. Edited by R. M. Kerr. 3rd ed.
Broom . . . . . Broom's Selection of Legal Maxims, 5th ed.
Broun . . . . . . Broun's Justiciary Reports.
Burrow . . . . . Burrow's Reports of Cases determined in the Court of King's Bench.

C. . . . . Code (Corpus Juris, vol. ii.)
C. B. . . . . . . Common Bench Reports.
Campb. . . . . . Campbell's Nisi Prius Reports.
Cl. . . . . Clark's House of Lords Cases.
Cl. & F. . . . . . Clark and Finnelly's House of Lords Cases.
Coke . . . . . . Coke's Institutes of the Laws of England.
Connell . . . . . Connell on Tithes.
Couper . . . . . Couper's Justiciary Reports.
Cox . . . . . . Cox's Equity Cases.

D. . . . . Reports of Cases in Court of Session, reported by Dunlop and others, from 1838 to 1862.

LIST OF ABBREVIATIONS.

D. or Dig.	Digest or Pandects.
Dickson	Dickson on Evidence, 2nd ed.
Dodson	Dodson's Admiralty Reports.
Dow	Dow's Reports of Decisions on Appeal in the House of Lords.
Duff's Feud. Con.	Duff's Treatise on the Deeds and Forms used in the Constitution, Transmission, and Extinction of Feudal Rights.
East	East's Reports of Cases determined in the Court of King's Bench.
Ersk.	Erskine's Institutes of the Law of Scotland, edited by Lord Ivory.
Ersk. Prin.	Erskine's Principles of the Law of Scotland, edited by J. Guthrie Smith.
F. C.	Faculty Collection.
Fergusson	Fergusson's Consistorial Cases.
Fraser	Fraser's Treatise on Husband and Wife according to the Law of Scotland, 2nd ed.
Fraser, Par. & Ch.	Fraser on the Law of Parent and Child, and Guardian and Ward, 2nd ed.
Fraser, Mas. & Ser.	Fraser on the Law of Master and Servant, 3rd ed.
Gaius	Institutes of Gaius.
H. Bla.	Reports of Cases determined in the Courts of Common Pleas and Exchequer Chamber, by Henry Blackstone.
Hume	Hume's Commentaries on the Law of Scotland, respecting Crimes. 1844.
Hunter	Hunter on the Law of Landlord and Tenant, 4th ed.
Irvine	Irvine's Justiciary Reports.
Jarman	Jarman on Wills, 4th ed.
Just. Inst.	Institutes of Justinian.
Kames' Eq.	Principles of Equity, by Lord Kames, 4th ed.
L. J.	Law Journal Reports. New Series. The different Reports are distinguished thus: Q. B., Queen's Bench; C. P., Common Pleas; Exch., Exchequer; Ch., Chancery.

LIST OF ABBREVIATIONS.

L. R.	Law Reports issued by the Incorporated Council of Law Reporting for England and Wales. The different Reports are distinguished thus: Q. B., Queen's Bench; Q. B. Div., Queen's Bench Division; C. P., Common Pleas; Eq., Equity Cases; Ch. Ap., Chancery Appeals; Ad. & Ec., Admiralty and Ecclesiastical; Sc. Ap., Scotch Appeals, &c.; App., Appeal Cases.
M.	Morrison's Dictionary of Decisions.
M. & S.	Maule & Selwyn's Reports.
M. & W.	Meeson & Welsby's Reports.
M. P. C.	Moore's Privy Council Cases.
M'Laren	M'Laren on the Law of Wills and Succession.
Macdonald	Macdonald's Treatise on the Criminal Law of Scotland, 2nd ed.
Mackenzie Rom. Law.	Studies in Roman Law, by Lord Mackenzie.
Maclachlan	Maclachlan's Treatise on the Law of Merchant Shipping, 3rd ed.
Macp.	Reports of Cases in Court of Session, reported by Macpherson and others, from 1862 to 1873.
Macq.	Macqueen's House of Lords Reports.
Maude & Pollock . .	Maude & Pollock on the Law of Merchant Shipping, 4th ed.
Maxwell	Maxwell on the Interpretation of Statutes.
May	May on the Law of Insurance, 2nd ed.
Menzies' Lect. . . .	Menzies' Lectures on Conveyancing, 3rd ed.
Montesquieu . . .	Montesquieu, De l'Esprit des Lois.
More's Notes . . .	More's Notes on Stair's Institutes.
Murdoch	Murdoch on Bankruptcy, 4th ed.
Napier	Napier on the Law of Prescription.
Paterson's Compend. .	Paterson's Compendium of English and Scotch Law.
Paton	Paton's House of Lords Cases.
R. & M.	Russell & Mylne's Reports.
Raym.	Raymond's (Lord) Reports of Cases determined in the Courts of King's Bench and Common Pleas.
R.	Reports of Cases in Court of Session, reported by Rettie and others, from 1873.
Roper	Roper on the Law of Legacies, 4th ed.
Ross, L. C.	Ross's Leading Cases in the Law of Scotland; L. R., affecting Land Rights; and C. L., on Commercial Law.

LIST OF ABBREVIATIONS.

Ross's Lect.	Ross's Lectures on the Practice of the Law of Scotland.
Russ. & Ryan	Russell & Ryan's Crown Cases Reserved.
S.	Shaw, and Shaw & Dunlop's Reports of Cases in the Court of Session from 1822 to 1838.
S. & M'L.	Shaw & M'Lean's Reports of Cases determined on Appeal in the House of Lords.
Sandars' Just.	Institutes of Justinian, by Sandars, 7th ed.
Scot. L. Rep.	Scottish Law Reporter.
Shand	Shand's Practice of the Court of Session.
Sh. Ap.	Shaw's Reports of Cases determined on appeal in the House of Lords.
Smith's Dict.	Dictionary of Greek and Roman Antiquities, by Dr. Smith, 2nd ed.
Smith L. C.	Smith's Leading Cases in the Law of England, 8th ed.
Smith on Rep.	Treatise on the Law of Reparation, by J. Guthrie Smith.
Smith on R. and P. Prop.	Smith's Law of Real and Personal Property, 5th ed.
Smith's Mer. Law.	Smith's Mercantile Law, 9th ed.
Stair	Stair's Institutes of the Law of Scotland, edited by Brodie.
Stark.	Starkie's Nisi Prius Cases.
Stephen's Com.	Stephen's Commentaries on the Laws of England, 7th ed.
Story, Con. Law	Story's Conflict of Laws.
Sugden	Sugden on Powers, 8th ed.
Swinton	Swinton's Justiciary Reports.
Taunt.	Taunton's Reports.
Taylor	Taylor on Evidence, 7th ed.
Thomson	Thomson on Bills, edited by J. Dove Wilson.
W. & S.	Wilsons & Shaw's House of Lords Reports.
Weightman	Weightman's Law of Marriage and Legitimacy.
Wharton	Wharton's Law Lexicon, 6th ed.
Williams	Williams on Executors and Administrators, 8th ed.
Williams on R. Prop.	Williams's Principles of the Law of Real Property, 14th ed.

LATIN MAXIMS AND PHRASES,

WITH

TRANSLATIONS AND ILLUSTRATIONS.

———◆———

A

A cœlo usque ad centrum.—From the heavens to the centre (of the earth). This phrase is used to denote the extent of the right of a proprietor of land, who, on his feudal investiture in the land, becomes entitled to everything pertinent or belonging to it, whether above or below ground, such as houses, trees, minerals, &c. It includes also the proprietor's power of using his property as he may think fit, and preventing any other person encroaching thereon, above or below the surface. He may erect any kind of building on it, and to any height, or he may work the minerals to any depth. See *Corbett* v. *Hill*, L. R. 9, Eq. 671; *Goodson* v. *Richardson*, L. R. 9 Ch., Ap. 221; *The Glasgow C. and D. Ry. Co.* v. *MacBrayne*, 10 R. 894; *Wandsworth Board of Works*, L. R., 13 Q.B.D. 904.

A contrario sensu.—Literally, in the opposite sense or view; equivalent to the common expression, on the other hand. (Stair, B. 4, T. 50, § 10.)

A fortiori.—By a stronger argument; so much the more.

A jure suo cadunt.—They fall from (or lose) their right. This refers to the loss of right in a subject, by loss of possession or abandonment. When property has in this way passed from the right of the last possessor, it is confiscated as caduciary, and belongs to the Crown, or others deriving right therefrom, and does not, as in the case of subjects never before appropriated, become the property of the finder or first subsequent possessor. "Things already appropriated, but lost, forgotten, or abandoned, fall under a different rule from that which regulates things that have never been appropriated. The rule is *quod nullius est fit domini regis.*" (Bell's Prin. § 1291.) Wrecks, prizes taken in war, treasure-trove, and waif and stray goods, all fall to the Crown as caduciary. See *Res nullius.*

A libello ut libellatur.—From the libel as laid. The terms used long ago in interlocutors of the court, dismissing an action and pronouncing decree of absolvitor in favour of a defender.

A me de superiore meo.—From me, of my superior. This forms that part or clause of a conveyance of lands which indicates the nature of the tenure by which they are to be held, and whereby it is declared that when the feudal title is completed the grantee is to hold of the granter's superior. This is commonly known as an *a me* holding as opposed to a holding *de me*. The former (*a me*) is now called a public holding, while the latter (*de me*) is termed, base. These significations did not always attach to the respective phrases; and it may not be out of place to notice here very briefly how the change occurred. Originally all lands in Scotland were held directly of the Crown Prince. He was the immediate superior of the lands, and the barons to whom the lands were gifted were his vassals. Their holding was *de me*, and necessarily so, because they could hold of no higher superior, and this, therefore, was originally the nobler of the two holdings. But when the crown lands were, for the most part, gifted, and the barons in their turn began to give grants of lands to their followers, the character of the tenures in this respect underwent a change. A *de me* holding from a baron was a holding permanently subordinate to him and his successors, while the holding *a me* enabled the disponee or grantee, to whom lands were conveyed on that tenure, to pass over the baron, and, by resignation, obtain an entry with the Crown, whereby the grantee became a Crown vassal, holding directly of the Crown, without any interjected subject superior. Thus the *de me* holding, originally the nobler, became the baser, while the *a me* holding, formerly the baser, became the public, and the nobler holding of the two. The *a me* holding being one of the superior of the disponer, the disponee required to enter with that superior before his feudal title could be made complete. This, formerly could only be done in the one way, namely, by resignation *in favorem*, as the superior was not bound to enter a singular successor as his vassal by confirmation. Notwithstanding this, the practice of entering vassals by confirmation is a very old one ; and as entry by this mode had become a matter of daily practice, it was rendered obligatory on superiors so to enter vassals by the Transference of Lands Act (10 & 11 Vict. cap. 48). The holding most frequently to be found in practice is the alternative one, *a me vel de me*. On this, the disponee could formerly either infeft as the disponer's vassal, and thus save an entry with the superior, or, by resignation or confirmation, enter at once with the over superior. The former course was most frequently followed, as subsequent confirmation acted *retro* (as to which see *Duke of Buccleuch* v. *Johnstone*, 18 R. 587, affd. H.L. 19 R. 39), and had the effect, in the event of a competition, of making a holding, originally base, a public one, as from the date of the infeftment on the *de me* precept. The effect, practically, of such procedure was, to save the expense of an entry, while the holding could be rendered public and indefeasible at any time by confirmation. By the Act 37 & 38 Vict. cap. 94, it is declared that every proprietor duly infeft in lands shall be held to be, as at the date of the registration of his infeftment, duly entered with the superior ; and renewal of investiture is abolished. As to the effect of this implied entry with the superior, see *Ferrier's Trs.* v. *Bayley*, 4 R. 738 ; *Lamont* v. *Rankine's Trs.*, 6 R. 739, affd. H.L. 7 R. 10 ; *Stuart* v. *Hamilton*, 16 R. 1030 ; *Stuart* v. *Jackson*, 17 R. 85 ; *Duke of Athole* v. *Stewart*, 17 R. 724 ; and *Duke of Buccleuch, supra cit.*

A mensa et thoro.—From bed and board. This is a judicial separation of husband and wife, which may be obtained at the instance of either spouse, on the ground of adulterous practices, cruelty, &c. A decree of separation in such an action can only proceed upon proof of the facts alleged. The effect of such a decree, when obtained by the wife, was, formerly, to put an end to the husband's powers over the wife's person, but not otherwise to interfere with his marital rights. But a very material change was made upon the law by the Conjugal Rights Act (24 & 25 Vict. cap. 86), which provided (§ 6) that after a decree of separation *a mensa et thoro* had been obtained at the instance of a wife, all property acquired by, or which devolved upon her, should be considered as property belonging to her, from which the *jus mariti* and right of administration were excluded; that such property might be disposed of by her as if she were unmarried; and on her death, if she died intestate, her heirs and representatives succeeded thereto, as if her husband had been dead. If the wife cohabit again with her husband, all property possessed by her, or to which she was entitled at the date of such cohabitation, is to be held to her separate use, exclusive of the *jus mariti* and right of administration. During her separation, the wife may sue and be sued, may incur obligations, and be liable for wrongs and injuries as if she were not married. Further changes have been made by recent legislation on the law regulating the rights of husband and wife, for which see *Communio bonorum*. A separation *a mensa et thoro* may be the result of a voluntary contract between the parties. But such a contract, as a general rule, may be revoked or resiled from by either party at will, and in no case has voluntary separation the effect, as regards the wife's property, which, as above explained, follows from a decree of separation. (Bell's Prin. §§ 1541-44.) Until the year 1858, a separation or divorce *a mensa et thoro* was the only kind of separation which could be decreed by the law courts of England, a divorce *a vinculo* not being obtainable, except under an Act of Parliament. This is now altered (20 & 21 Vict. cap. 85), and the law of England has become almost the same as that of Scotland on this point.

A morte testatoris.—From the death of the testator. A legacy or bequest does not vest in the legatee or beneficiary until this event takes place; and therefore, where the legatee predeceases the testator, the legacy lapses, and the legatee's successor takes no benefit under the bequest, unless there be a conditional institution of the legatee's heirs. See the opinion of the Lord President (Inglis) in *Finlay* v. *Mackenzie*, 2 R. 909. Legacies to a class of persons do not lapse if any of the objects survive. This phrase is used to distinguish between those rights under a settlement which vest upon the death of the testator, and those of which the vesting is postponed to a later period.

A non domino.—From one who is not the proprietor. A conveyance by such a one, with infeftment thereon, and consequent possession and acts of ownership for forty years, renders the possessor's title unassailable, except on the ground of falsehood, Act 1617, cap. 12 : the prescriptive period has been reduced to twenty years by the Act 37 & 38 Vict. cap. 94, § 34. Within the prescriptive period, the objection that the title proceeded *a non domino* is fatal.

A non habente potestatem.—From one not having power. This is akin to the preceding phrase, and may be illustrated by reference to a practice in conveyancing often resorted to in former times, as a means of saving expense. If A. disponed ground, which he held on a personal title, to B., he could not grant warrant for the infeftment of B., himself being uninfeft ; but he could assign to B. the unexecuted precept of sasine in his (A.'s) own favour, and on it B. could complete his feudal title. If, instead of thus assigning a valid precept, A. himself granted a precept for the infeftment of B., such a precept was *a non habente potestatem*, and ineffectual. This was a defect, however, which was remedied by prescription.

A pari.—Equally ; In like manner. (Stair, B. 2, T. 2, § 12.)

A quo invito aliquid exigi potest.—From whom something may be exacted against his will. This is given by Erskine (B. 3, T. 1, § 5) as a definition of a debtor in a perfect obligation. In obligations merely natural, fulfilment is voluntary ; a civil obligation, being "that tie of positive law by which one is bound without any foundation in equity," although founding action, may be successfully resisted on many grounds, as, for instance, fraud ; but mixed obligations, where law and equity combine, are prestable, and fulfilment may be enforced, whether the obligant is willing to fulfil or not.

A rubro ad nigrum.—Literally, from the red to the black. Acts of Parliament formerly had their titles printed in red, which thus obtained the name of "rubrics;" and this phrase means that the title, as a part of the statute, may be considered in construing the Act itself: "Where the title of a statute is either framed by the Legislature itself, or hath received its tacit approbation in any succeeding enactment, it ought to be accounted part of the statute; and of course an argument may be properly drawn, in that case, *a rubro ad nigrum*, from the title to the Act itself." (Ersk. B. 1, T. 1, § 49.) The title of an Act is not, however, always regarded as forming part of the Act, nor necessarily to be considered in construing any passage in it which is doubtful or ambiguous. (Maxwell, 34.) See *Nigrum nunquam*, &c.

A verbis legis non est recedendum.—No departure is permitted from the words of a statute. Where the language of a statute is plain and unequivocal, it must be read according to its necessary meaning, and so enforced. In such circumstances, the statute is not open to construction. See *Argumentum ab inconvenienti*, &c.

A vinculo matrimonii.—From the bond of marriage. A divorce *a vinculo* sets the parties as free from each other as if they had never been married, and entitles each to marry again, even during the lifetime of the previous spouse. A separation *a mensa et thoro* has not this effect. See *A mensa*.

Ab agendo.—From acting. A person is said to be *ab agendo* when incapacitated for business or transactions of any kind, through old age, mental weakness, or any other cause.

Ab ante.—Before; previously.

Ab antiquo.—From ancient time; of old.

Ab identitate rationis.—By identity of reason; for the same reason.

Ab inconvenienti.—From inconvenience. See *Argumentum ab inconvenienti*, &c.

Ab initio.—From the beginning.

Ab intestato.—From a person dying intestate. The property of any one dying without disposing of it by a valid deed, is distributed, according to certain fixed legal rules; and property so acquired is said to be derived *ab intestato*.

Absentia ejus qui reipublicæ causa abest, neque ei, neque alii damnosa esse debet.—His absence, who is absent on account of the State, ought not to be injurious to him, or to another; or (less literally) no one should take injury or disadvantage from an absence occasioned by the service of the State. An illustration of the application of this maxim may be found in the case of a soldier, who having a residential settlement in this country, and being absent with his regiment from the parish of his settlement for more than four years, is, nevertheless, held not to have lost his settlement by absence. This has never been purely decided, but there are *dicta* which go this length. In the case of *Hay* v. *Croll*, 20 D. 507, the Lord Justice-Clerk (Hope) said :—" When a man is absent—not from voluntary departure from his family, but in the service of the country as a soldier—his settlement continues in the parish where he had acquired one, and in which he left his wife and family. Hence, when he returns on his discharge, that settlement continues, and he or his wife and children must be maintained, if they become paupers, by the parish in which he had acquired a settlement at the date of his enlistment." See also the opinions delivered in the case of *Masons* v. *Greig*, 3 Macp. 707. Absence in the service of the State does not, of itself, interrupt the currency of prescription. (Napier, 534 *et seq.*) As to whether a soldier leaving this country to join his regiment abroad is bound to sist a mandatory, see the case of *Simla Bank* v. *Home*, 8 Macp. 781.

Absoluta sententia expositore non indiget.—An absolute (or unequivocal) sentence needs no expositor. When a sentence or phrase is ambiguous, either in a private deed or in an Act of Parliament, it is, in legal parlance, open to construction; the ambiguity may be removed, and the real meaning discovered, by reference to the context or otherwise. But where no ambiguity exists, and the phrase is clear and absolute in its terms, no construction is admitted beyond that which the words employed usually bear. In such a case no expositor is needed; the words clearly enough expound themselves. The *sententia* of this maxim does not, primarily, include the *sentence* or decree of a judge, although the rule expressed by the maxim would apply to a judicial order, as well as to any other, if there was room for its application.

Absque ipsius regis speciali licentia.—Without the special authority of the king himself. This forms part of an enactment passed in the reign of David II. cap. 24, which prohibited the Crown vassals from alienating their lands without first having obtained such special warrant for doing so. A subsequent statute (Robert III. cap. 17) declared such alienations, without previous license, to be a ground of recognition, or forfeiture of the fee.

Abundans cautela non nocet.—Extreme caution does no harm. This maxim finds its application generally in cases where the granter of a deed, as, for example, a testator, adds words descriptive of the person or class of persons he means to favour, beyond what are necessary for the purpose of mere description, in order to make his intention more clear. Or again, where the granter of a deed, as an entailer, adds words beyond what are absolutely necessary, to express the conditions of the entail, or the consequences which are to follow the violation of certain conditions. In such cases the superfluous words do no harm, as the deed can be read without them, and still be a good and valid deed. At same time it has happened, that a conveyancer, by introducing unnecessary words, has caused great harm to his clients or their representatives; as an example of which, reference may be made to the case of *Adam* v. *Farquharson*, 2 D. 1162, and particularly to the opinion of Lord Gillies in that case. See *Superflua*, &c.

Acceptilatio.—A mode, under the civil law, of extinguishing a verbal obligation. It consisted in the creditor declaring, in a prescribed form of words, that he had received from his debtor that which was due, when in reality he had received nothing. It was the form adopted by a creditor who wished gratuitously to release the debtor from his obligation. The same name is given to a gratuitous discharge in our law. (Ersk. B. 3, T. 4, § 8.) See *Stipulatio*.

Accessorium principale sequitur.—An accessory follows the principal to which it is an accessory. Where two things stand in such intimate connection, that the one depends upon, or is derived from the other, the accessory belongs to him who has right to the principal subject. So the proprietor of land is, on this principle, also the proprietor of any buildings erected on it, and of the fruits it yields (there being an exception in certain cases as regards industrial fruits); the owner of vested capital has right to its interest and profits ; and the owner of cattle to their offspring. The same principle applies to accessory obligations, as, for example, to cautionry. The cautioner's obligation being accessory to that of the principal debtor, is discharged on the extinction of the principal obligation.

Accessorium sequitur naturam rei cui accedit.—An accessory follows the nature (or acquires the character) of the subject or right to which it accedes. Erskine illustrates this by quoting a case where "one who had, in security of a purchase of lands, acquired right to the escheat of the seller, was not allowed to ascribe his possession to the gift of escheat, but was obliged to apply it to the minute of sale, because that was the principal and the sovereign right." (B. 2, T. 1, § 30.) The right, as donee of the Crown, in the escheat, became thus a mere corroboration, and partook of the character of the antecedent singular title. A further illustration may be taken from the case, where an additional moveable security is taken for a debt already heritably secured. The taking of the moveable security does not make the debt moveable, but, being an accessory, would partake of the nature of its principal, and would consequently, in a question of succession, descend to the heir and not to the executor. But the most familiar illustration of this maxim is to be found in the case of fixtures, which, though in themselves moveable, become heritable by accession. (Bell's Prin. § 1473.)

Accidentalia.—Accidents of a contract, in opposition to the *essentalia*,—essential parts of it ; as in a contract of sale the right of pre-emption may be added, which is an accident of the contract ; but the agreed-on price is an essential of it. There may be a contract of sale without the former, but there cannot be such a contract without the latter.

Accidentalia feudi.—"All provisions in the feudal contract which are neither of the essence nor of the nature of a feu." (Ersk. B. 2, T. 3, § 11. Such, for example, as the condition that within a certain period subjects of a fixed value shall be erected on the land feued, or conditions restrictive of building.

Accipe ecclesiam.—Receive this church or living. The form of words sometimes used by a patron in presenting an incumbent to a vacant cure. *Trado tibi ecclesiam* (I deliver the living or church to you) was also a form of expression sometimes used.

Accumulando jura juribus.—By adding rights to rights. This phrase will be found in deeds, as expressing the intention of the maker or granter of it that the right thereby conferred on the grantee is not to be regarded as coming in place of other rights which the grantee has or may acquire otherwise, but as an addition thereto : the rights conferred are not prejudicial to other rights existing or future. A good illustration of this phrase will be found in the case of *Dalyell*, 17th January, 1810, F.C.

Accumulatio actionum.—Accumulation of actions. It is not permitted in practice to accumulate several actions in one; and therefore "two or more persons, unconnected as partners, &c., cannot, in one action, conclude against the same or different persons for payment of sums due to the pursuers separately." (Shand, I. 203.) Persons, however, who have a joint interest in the matter libelled, or who have been aggrieved by the same act, may sue jointly. A frequent instance of the last-mentioned case is found where a widow and her children sue jointly for damages on account of the death of the husband and father, caused by the fault of another. A pursuer may, however, convene six separate and unconnected defenders in one summons (Shand, I. 204), although this is now unknown in practice. On the whole subject, see Ersk. B. 4, T. 1, § 65.

Accusatio suspecti tutoris.—Accusation of a suspected tutor. This was an action under the civil law against a tutor, arising out of certain circumstances. If he was unfaithful in performing his duties, such as failing to have alimony decreed to the pupil, or was of bad character, he might be removed from his office as *suspectus*, on an application to the Prætor, at the instance of any citizen. Such an application with us can only be made to the Court by one of the minors' or pupils' next-of-kin, or by a co-tutor, or co-curator of the *suspectus*. By the Pupils' Protection Act (12 & 13 Vict. cap. 51), it is made competent to the Lord Advocate, where he has reasonable grounds for suspecting "malversation or misconduct on the part of" the tutor, to apply to the Court for his removal.

Acquisita et acquirenda.—Things acquired, and to be acquired. Some forms of diligence affect both these classes of subjects, while others only affect the *acquisita*. Arrestment only attaches what is acquired or due at the time of its being used. Inhibition formerly affected both subjects acquired at the time of inhibiting, and those acquired subsequently, so long as the inhibition remained undischarged; but by the Act 31 & 32 Vict. cap. 101, § 157, inhibition was declared to be ineffectual against *acquirenda*, except in the case of a person succeeding to lands which, at the time the inhibition was used, were destined to him by a deed of entail or other indefeasible title. The adjudication of a bankrupt's estate to the trustee in his sequestration affects both, until the bankrupt be discharged and reinvested.

Acta exteriora indicant interiora secreta.—External acts reveal the internal secret purpose; or, more shortly, acts indicate the intention. Thus the crime of murder consists in the depriving another of life intentionally; but the intention in the general case can only be gathered from the acts of the person committing the crime. The nature of the assault which ended in death; the weapon, if any, used; and the whole surrounding circumstances or *res gestæ*, are taken into account in ascertaining the intention of the person charged with the crime. To take another illustration from the common law: in cases for damages for slander, the essence of the pursuer's case is that the defender uttered the slander maliciously, and such malice is presumed (where there is no privilege) from the fact that the slanderous statement is untrue. But in cases where malice has to be proved, the actings and expressions of the defender are the best and indeed the only evidence of his malicious intention or purpose. Again, in actions for damages on account of wrongous diligence, malice is inferred from the defender's having acted with undue zeal in the exercise of his right without having regard to the rights of others—such undue zeal indicating an intention on his part to do more than merely exercise the right which the law confers upon him. On the subject of this maxim, see the observations of Lord Ardmillan in the case of *Cameron* v. *Mortimer,* 10 Macp. 469.

Acta in uno judicio non probant in alio nisi inter easdem personas.—Things done in one action cannot be taken as evidence in another unless it be between the same parties. The deposition of witnesses in one suit cannot, as a rule, be given as evidence in a different suit; and the tendency of modern decisions has been to extend this rule to cases even where the second action is between the same parties. The deposition of a witness who has died is admissible, however, because his re-examination being impossible, secondary evidence is admissible, and a deposition formally emitted is better than mere hearsay. The reader will find the law on this subject stated in Dickson, § 1930 *et seq.,* and in the cases there cited.

Actio.—An action; that is, the means which one person employs for obtaining, from a properly-authorised judge, a sentence upon another person, ordaining him to fulfil some obligation under which he lies. The various kinds of action under the civil law were numerous and complicated. They arose from four chief sources—namely, contracts, quasi-contracts, delicts, and quasi-delicts, each of which had several divisions and subdivisions; and the modes of procedure in raising and prosecuting these actions were different, at different periods in the history of the Roman law. Some actions were private and personal, which could only be raised by the person having interest, such as the action *ex stipulatu* (arising from a stipulation or verbal contract); while others were popular, and could be sued by any citizen. The latter were regarded as affecting the public interest, and therefore could be raised by any one; as, for example, the *accusatio suspecti tutoris.* Some contracts gave rise to two different actions, which were respectively termed *directa* and *contraria,* the former being that which arose directly and necessarily from the contract, and the latter being an action not necessarily arising, but which had arisen from circumstances attendant upon the contract, and in connection with its fulfilment. To illustrate the character of these counter-actions, take the contract of deposit, under which the depositary received something belonging to the depositor, to be kept by him, and restored when the depositor required delivery. The contract gave rise to an action at the instance of the depositor, to enforce delivery of the subject deposited, and this was called the *actio directa depositi;* and it might also give rise, although not necessarily so, to another action. If the depositary had expended any sum in the preservation of the deposit; if he had been at the expense of nourishing it, as in the case of a living deposit, cattle, &c., or had incurred damage through the deposit having been made—upon all or any of these grounds an action arose at his instance against the depositor for reimbursement of the sums expended, or for indemnification on account of the damage sustained. Such action was called the *actio contraria depositi.* The right of the depositor to the redelivery of the subject being an essential part of the contract, it gave rise to the *actio directa;* but the *actio contraria* arose from circumstances not essential to the contract, and circumstances which might never have arisen. It would be irrelevant to the purpose of this work to enumerate and explain all the different actions under the Roman law, but such of them as have been referred to by the institutional writers on Scotch law will now be adverted to. And first, may be noticed five different *classes* of action, viz.:—

ACTIONES BONÆ FIDEI.—Actions of good faith. This term was applied to those actions in which the judge was entitled to decide, not simply according to the strict civil law, but according to equity or good faith; and under this class fell actions arising from the contracts of sale, location, partnership, deposit, pledge, &c. Actions of good faith were opposed to

ACTIONES STRICTI JURIS.—Actions of strict law, where the judge could only regard the strict terms of the contract and decide according to the rules of law affecting it, without regarding the equity of the question at issue.

ACTIONES POPULARES.—Popular or public actions. This class of actions has already been alluded to. They arose out of circumstances affecting the public interest or welfare, and could be raised and prosecuted by any citizen.

ACTIONES REI PERSECUTORIÆ.—Actions for the recovery of something belonging to the pursuer of the action. These actions were used where the pursuer had a right to, and insisted on delivery being made to him of the *ipsum corpus* of the subject sought; but they were also used for the recovery of something *due* to the pursuer. *Actiones in rem* were chiefly for recovery of the *ipsum corpus*, and arose from a *jus in re*, although they might also include a demand for indemnity or penalty.

ACTIONES PENALES.—Penal actions, or actions having penal conclusions. Under these actions the pursuer not only sought for the fulfilment of some obligation incumbent on the defender, but also for a pecuniary penalty, on account of its non-fulfilment. The action competent against a vitious intromitter was of this class, as he was bound not only to make good to a just claimant what he had acquired through his intromission, but was bound for the whole debts of the deceased with whose effects he had intromitted, even where these were not of value equivalent to the debt. The same action is applicable in our law to the recovery of violent profits from a possessor in *mala fide*.

We proceed now to notice such of the particular actions of the Roman law as are referred to by Scotch institutional writers:—

ACTIO COMMODATI.—The action arising from the contract of commodate,—a contract under which one person gratuitously lent to another a certain subject, the borrower undertaking to return it to the lender when the purpose for which it had been lent was accomplished. This contract gave rise both to the *actio directa* and *contraria*, the former being that by which the lender enforced the redelivery of the subject lent, and the latter being the action competent to the borrower for the recovery of any extraordinary expenses required to be outlaid on the preservation of the subject.

ACTIO COMMUNI DIVIDUNDO.—An action for the division of a subject held by several proprietors in joint property. When one of the joint proprietors gathered the fruits of the subject, he was bound to account for them to the others, who, in their turn, were bound to relieve him of a share of the expense of management. These obligations gave rise to this action, which is similar in principle to that known in Scotland as an action of division of commonty.

ACTIO CURATELÆ.—See *Actio tutelæ.*

ACTIO EMPTI.—This action, as well as the *actio venditi*, arose from the contract of sale, and were both *actiones directæ*. The *actio venditi*, competent to the seller, was the action by which he recovered payment of the stipulated price. The *actio empti* was that competent to the purchaser under which he could compel delivery of the subject sold, or, where the subject was *extra commercium* and could not be delivered, could obtain indemnification for any damage he had sustained. These actions are sometimes called *ex empto*, and *ex vendito*.

ACTIO EXERCITORIA.—See *Actio institoria.*

ACTIO EXPILATÆ HÆREDITATIS.—An action for recovering the penalties of a pillaged heritage or succession. This action, among the Romans, was nearly equivalent to the action in Scotch law against a vitious intromitter. Any one who took away, without right or authority to do so, any part of the succession or estate, was held guilty of the *crimen expilatæ hæreditatis*, which was regarded as theft. This action could be brought against almost every person guilty of the *crimen*, but it could not be brought against the widow of the deceased whose estate was pillaged. The punishment attached to this crime was reckoned *extraordinaria*, and was in the discretion of the judge who decided the case; like all thefts, however, the sentence in this action inferred infamy.

ACTIO FAMILIÆ ERCISCUNDÆ.—An action under which the succession (*hæreditas*) was divided among the heirs. This action only differed from that *communi dividundo*, in respect of the peculiar character of the subject divided.

ACTIO FINIUM REGUNDORUM.—An action for fixing the boundaries of adjoining lands. This action was competent to either proprietor when the landmarks had been fraudulently removed, or where they had decayed, and the judge was entitled to mark out the boundaries, when he had ascertained that his intervention was necessary. In fixing the boundaries, the judge was invested with considerable discretionary power, and could, for the purpose of making the boundary more clear, adjudge part of the land belonging to one, to belong to the other, sentencing the latter to pay the former the price of land so adjudged, which price the judge himself fixed. The effect of such adjudication was to transfer immediately the property to the person in whose favour it was made. Sheriffs, and other judges-ordinary in Scotland, are vested with a somewhat similar power. By the Act of 1669, cap. 17, they are authorised, " where a landlord proposes to inclose any part of his grounds, to appoint, at his suit, a visitation of the marches between him and the adjacent proprietors ; and where they are crooked, or otherwise improper for a fence, to adjudge such part of the grounds as occasion the inconveniency, from one proprietor to the other, for grounds of equal value, so that the fence to be made, according to that adjudication, shall be reputed the common march for the future. This power is not limited by the intendment of the statute to small parcels of ground, but reaches to that quantity which produces the inconveniency, though it should amount to several acres." (Ersk. B. 1, T. 4, § 3.) This proceeding is known in our law as the straightening of marches.

ACTIO INSTITORIA.—An action against a master or a father who had respectively given a slave, or a child *sub potestate*, charge of a certain business, to enforce liabilities incurred by the slave or child in reference to the business which each had been appointed to conduct. There is a similar ground of action in our law. A husband is liable for the obligations incurred by a wife in a business in which he has placed her, or which she superintends with his acquiescence; a principal is bound by the acts of his agents, where they do not exceed the ordinary powers of such an agent, and "the person who has the management of a shop has a presumed general authority to bind his principal by his proper acts of administration as shopkeeper." (Bell's Prin. § 231.) The *actio exercitoria* is of a like character, but refers only to the acts of a shipmaster, which are binding upon the shipowner. These actions derive their names from the person charged with the management of a business being called *institor*, and the person to whom the ship's daily profits belong being called *exercitor*. (Just. Inst. B. 4, T. 7, § 2.)

ACTIO PAULIANA.—This was an action given to creditors by which they could recover property alienated by their debtor in fraud of their rights, and was competent against persons acquiring the property by a title importing clear gain, but not against a purchaser for a valuable consideration, unless he was aware of the fraud. This action could either be brought as a real action, for recovery of the property itself, or as a personal action for its value, the former proceeding upon the fiction that the property had never been duly delivered, and had therefore always remained among the goods of the debtor, into possession of which the creditors had been put. This action acquired its name from the Prætor Paulus who introduced it.

ACTIO PIGNERATITIA.—This arose out of the contract of pledge, and was either *directa* or *contraria*. The action *directa* was at the instance of the debtor who had pledged the subject, against the creditor with whom it was pledged, to compel restoration of the pledge after the debt was discharged in security for which it had been given; or to compel the creditor to pay over the balance in his hands after deduction of his debt, if in virtue of his right he had sold the pledge. The action *contraria* was at the instance of the creditor, by which he could obtain reimbursement of any necessary expense he had been put to in preserving the pledge; or indemnification, where he had been dispossessed of the pledge, which might occur where the debtor had pledged something not his own.

ACTIO QUANTI MINORIS.—This action, as well as the *actio redhibitoria,* arose from the contract of sale. If the purchaser, after delivery, discovered some latent fault in the subject purchased, he was entitled by the *actio redhibitoria* to have the seller ordained to take back the subject and restore the price; or, if the purchaser was so disposed, he might retain the subject, and under the action *quanti minoris* (which was also called the *actio æstimatoria*) recover as much of the price as exceeded what he might reasonably have given for the subject had he known of the defect. The *actio redhibitoria* could be raised any time within six months of the sale, and the *actio æstimatoria* within a year, but of these actions the purchaser had merely an alternative choice, for the raising of one of them excluded the other. The *actio quanti minoris,* in so far as it proceeds upon the ground of the value of the subject being disproportioned to the price paid, is rejected by the Scotch law, but the *actio redhibitoria* is allowed in those cases where the purchaser was not bound to, and could not, satisfy himself of the soundness of the subject bought, as, for example, in the case of purchase by sample. The subject, however, in such case, cannot, as under the Roman law, be retained for six months. The examination of it must be made with all due speed, and undue delay in objecting to the character or quality of the subject will bar all action for restitution of the price.

ACTIO REDHIBITORIA.—See above.

ACTIO TUTELÆ VEL CURATELÆ.—An action (*directa*) competent to a minor or his heirs against his tutor or curator when his guardianship came to an end, to compel him to render accounts of his intromissions, and pay over the estate to the minor. The tutor or curator had the *actio contraria,* under which he might obtain indemnification for all expenses incurred and engagements contracted by reason of the guardianship, as well as a discharge of his office and administration.

ACTIO VENDITI.—See *Actio empti.*

Actio contra defunctum coepta, continuatur in hæredes.—An action commenced against a person deceased transmits against his heirs. This rule is not universal, because there are actions properly personal which do not transmit either to or against heirs. Such are all actions for recovery of penalties arising *ex delicto,* which do not transmit against the heir, who is not liable for his ancestor's delict. Penal actions do not transmit, but it is otherwise as regards actions for civil reparation and damage. Some actions (as, for example, actions for damages on account of defamation, &c.) being in a measure personal and not transmissible in the ordinary case, do nevertheless transmit to and against heirs, if there has been litiscontestation.

Actio personalis moritur cum persona.—A personal right of action dies with the person. It has been seen, in dealing with the immediately preceding maxim, that there are some actions which transmit to and against an heir: the present maxim expresses the rule of law with regard to another class of actions which do not transmit, but die with the person who had the right to bring the action, or against whom it had been brought. All penal actions are of this character, as well as those in which the cause of action arises from delict. An action for assythment is not an infringement of this rule, although at first sight it might appear so. In such an action the representatives of a deceased person claim damages from the person through whose delict or crime the death was occasioned. They do not, however, claim damages as representatives or executors of the deceased, but claim in their own right, not for injury done to the deceased, but for injury done to themselves through his death. Actions for divorce are strictly personal to the offended spouse, and are "barred, or after being commenced the action falls, by death, and cannot competently be commenced or continued by the heir or representative of the injured party" (Bell's Prin. § 1534). This rule seems, however, to be subject to some modification. In the case of *Ritchie* v. *Ritchie*, 1 R. 826, a husband had obtained decree of divorce, before the Lord Ordinary, against his wife, who reclaimed, but before the reclaiming note was heard the husband died. The Court held that the deceased husband's trustees and executors were entitled to sist themselves as respondents in the reclaiming note in room of the husband, to the effect of supporting the judgment obtained by him. The authorities on the question will be found fully cited in the report of that case. In the case of *Auld* v. *Shairp*, 2 R. 191, it was held that a widow was entitled to sue for damages on account of a slander uttered against her husband during his lifetime, and on account of which he had raised no action himself. In that case it was observed by the Lord Justice-Clerk that the rule expressed in the maxim under consideration is not a rule in the law of Scotland. This judgment was not unanimous; but it proceeded upon a very full discussion and careful consideration of the question. Whether that judgment can now be regarded as sound is very doubtful after the decision pronounced in the case of *Bern's Executor*, 20 R. 859. On the subject of this maxim see Broom, p. 904 *et seq.*

Actio pœnalis in hæredem non datur, nisi ex damno locupletior hæres factus sit.—A penal action does not lie against an heir unless he has been made wealthier (or taken advantage) by the act (or delict) out of which the action arises. Even in the exceptional case where an action lies against an heir for the consequences of his author's delict, it is plain that no penalty can be exacted from the heir,—the action against him is limited *ad civilem effectum*. Thus, if the author had stolen something of which the heir got possession, any action against him could only be for restitution of the thing stolen; he could not otherwise be made liable for his author's crime.

Actor.— Pursuer or plaintiff. *Reus.*— Defender or defendant.

Actor debet sequi forum rei.—A pursuer must follow the forum or court of the defender; that is, a pursuer raising an action against his debtor or obligant, must do so before the forum or court to the jurisdiction of which the defender is subject at the time. The rationale of this rule is obvious; for if the defender be outwith the jurisdiction of the Court before which he has been cited, he is not bound, and cannot be compelled to answer before that Court; and any decree of that Court will be valueless, there being no way of enforcing it.

Actor sequitur forum rei.—A pursuer follows the forum or court of the defender. Another and more frequently adopted form of the preceding phrase.

Actore non probante absolvitur reus.—A pursuer not having proved his case, or established his claim, the defender is assoilzied. It lies with the pursuer to substantiate any claim which he advances, and until he does so, the defender cannot be required to refute it. Thus, where the question is a right of possession of a subject held by the defender, he (the defender) is not bound to show any title to the possession until the pursuer has shown a sufficient title to call that possession in question. Nor can he be dispossessed until the pursuer shows a better title than that on which the defender holds.

Actori incumbit probatio.—Proof (of his case) is incumbent upon the pursuer. Another form of the preceding phrase.

Actum et tractatum.—Done and transacted. See Ersk. B. 3, T. 4, § 22.

Actus.—One of the chief rural servitudes of the Roman law, which conferred upon the dominant owner the right of driving cattle or a vehicle along the road or way burdened with the servitude. It included the servitude of mere right of passage, called the *jus eundi*. The right of *actus* was the *jus agendi*. Similar to the *actus* are the Scotch servitudes of horse road, coach or cart road, and loaning for cattle.

Actus animi.—An act of the mind; intention. The *animus* enters into many questions of law as an essential element. Thus, for example, in acquiring a domicile, mere residence is not sufficient, if there be not the intention to acquire it, as domicile can only be acquired *animo et facto*. Again, consent, which is essential to all contracts, is an *actus animi*, and is presumed in all cases where the contract is *ex* *facie* regular. But this presumption may in certain cases be redargued, as in the reduction of a deed, on the ground of force or fear. In such cases, however, the burden of proving lies upon the person challenging the contract or deed. As to the effect of intention in criminal cases see *Actus non facit*, &c.

Actus curiæ neminem gravabit.—An act of the Court shall prejudice no man. No litigant is responsible for the acts of the Court, and can take no prejudice by obeying its orders, which he is bound to obey. If, for example, in a multiplepoinding the Court should order payment to be made to a claimant, and payment is made under that order, the holder of the fund cannot be required to repeat the amount in the event of its being shown that the claimant preferred had no title to the sum paid, or that another had a better title than he. Again, certain acts by a litigant outwith the *cursus curiæ* might be sufficient to bar a subsequent appeal, but if these acts are performed not voluntarily, but under the orders of Court, the appeal will not be barred.

Actus Dei nemini facit injuriam.—The act of God does injury to no one. The *injuria* of this maxim is different from what is usually meant by the term injury: there may be great injury inflicted or suffered, and yet no *injuria*, which means only the injury arising from such a wrongous or culpable act as renders the doer of it responsible for the consequences. This being kept in view, the truth of the maxim is obvious, and its application made easy. See *Damnum sine*, &c.

Actus legis nemini est damnosus.—The act (or operation) of the law is injurious to no one. Laws which are enacted for the benefit or advantage of the State generally, may sometimes operate to the disadvantage or detriment of some of the subjects of the State. But for such detriment there is no remedy, because it must be regarded as *Damnum absque injuria*. This maxim is sometimes rendered as follows :—

Actus legis nemini facit injuriam.—The act or operation of the law does injury to no one. See *Executio juris*, &c.

Actus legitimus.—A legal act—*i.e.*, an act requiring legal solemnity in its performance. The solemnity may consist in the form of the procedure, or the persons present at its performance. Such acts were numerous under the civil law, including *mancipatio, acceptilatio, tutoris datio,* &c. The old ceremony of giving sasine in our law was such an act, requiring the observance of certain solemnities in its performance, as—*ex. gr.*, the presence of the disponer or his bailie upon the ground, with the notary, witnesses, and attorney of the disponee, the delivery of the requisite symbols, taking instruments, &c.

Actus me invito factus, non est meus actus.—An act done against my will is not my act. Those acts alone can be said to be done by the person performing them which proceed from his own will and intention. Accordingly, when the act is performed unwillingly, under force, intimidation, or fear, it is not regarded as the act of the performer, and he is not bound by it. A deed executed under such circumstances may be reduced. It is, however, to be borne in mind that the force referred to must be illegal or improper. For, take the case of a person who, legally bound to convey certain subjects to another, declines to do so, and yet is compelled to grant the conveyance under a judicial decree. That conveyance, however unwillingly granted, would be regarded as the act of the granter, and could not be set aside on the ground stated in the maxim. In the supposed case, the act was one which the granter of the deed was bound to perform; the acts referred to in the maxim are those which a person is not bound to perform, and has only performed against his will.

Actus non facit reum, nisi mens sit rea.—The act does not make (the performer of it) a criminal, unless there be also criminal intention. The essence of all crime is the felonious or criminal intention with which the act has been committed: what would be criminal if the intention was present, might not be so if that intention did not exist. To take the property of another without or against his will is theft, if the felonious intention be present, and prompting the act; but to take the property of another in mistake, in ignorance, or in mere heedlessness, would not be theft. The overt act in both cases is the same, but the will or intention is different. In like manner, a person may offer counterfeit coin in ignorance or in error, and commit no crime; but another doing the same act, in the knowledge that the coin offered is counterfeit, is criminal, because of the criminal intention to utter base coin. This maxim must, however, be read and applied with caution, for the want of intention is not always a sufficient defence; there are some cases in which intention is presumed by the law, and in which the defence of want of intention would be entirely unavailing. For example, if one man attacks another with a lethal weapon, or in such a manner as to show that he is utterly regardless of the consequences of his act, and death ensues, the crime will be that of murder, although the intention to kill was not present when the attack was made, the law presuming intention from the fact that the person committing the offence was regardless of the consequences of his act. Again crime may be committed and infer punishment although there is no intention on the part of the culprit to do wrong, as in the case of culpable neglect of duty on the part of officials (*ex. gr.* railway officials, engine-drivers, pointsmen, &c.), whose neglect results in bodily injury to others. In such cases (which form an exception to the rule of this maxim, or at least an important qualification of it), the crime consists not in doing something wrong with a bad intention, but in omitting to take sufficient care to do right. Where anything is positively forbidden by statute, the commission of that thing, even ignorantly, may in some cases infer punishment or penalty, without the existence of any corrupt motive whatever. "For instance, it has been held that a dealer in tobacco, having in his possession adulterated tobacco, although ignorant of the adulteration, is liable under the statute 5 & 6 Vict. cap. 93, § 3, to the penalties therein mentioned, and this decision merely affirms the principle established in previous cases, and shows that penalties may be incurred under a prohibitory statute without any intention on the part of the individual offending against the statute law to infringe its provisions" (Broom, p. 307). In further illustration of this maxim, and in support of what has just been said, reference may be made to the case of *Watt*, decided in the High Court of Justiciary on 26th July, 1873 (2 Couper, 482). That was a prosecution under the provisions of the Act 34 & 35 Vict. cap. 110, § 11, which provides that every person who, having authority as owner or otherwise to send a ship to sea, sends her to sea in an unseaworthy state, so as to endanger the life of any person belonging to her or on board the same, shall be guilty of a misdemeanour, unless he proves that he used all reasonable means to make and keep the ship seaworthy, and was ignorant of such unseaworthiness, &c. Watt, as owner of a certain vessel, was charged with having sent her to sea in an unseaworthy condition, whereby she was lost, and all on board perished. At the trial it was contended for him that the essence of the offence was the sending the ship to sea in an unseaworthy condition, and that in order to obtain a conviction it was necessary for the prosecutor to prove that the panel knew this, as without guilty knowledge there was no crime. It was laid down by the presiding judge, that if the ship was sent to sea in an unseaworthy condition, a conviction would follow unless the panel established his innocence by proving his ignorance of her condition, and that he had used all reasonable means to make and keep her seaworthy. This ruling (which proceeded upon the words of the statute) was not contradictory of the rule laid down in the maxim, but it put upon the panel the *onus* of proving the want of guilty intention, whereas, in the general case, the prosecutor is bound to prove the existence of that guilty intention. According to the provisions of that statute, as interpreted by the presiding judge, the *mens rea* is presumed, and it lies upon the panel to redargue the presumption. See *Furiosi nulla*, &c.

Actus proximus.—The direct or immediate act by which something has been done, or some crime committed, as distinguished from an act which was merely mediate or preparatory to the immediate act. (Hume, i. 151.)

Ad auctoritatem præstandam.—For interposing or adding their authority. Interdictors and curators *ad litem* are appointed for this purpose merely, and incur no personal liability through the performance of the duties of their office. Tutors and curators, the one given as a guardian of the pupil's person, the other of the minor's estate, are liable for the exercise of a care and diligence, in which persons of the class we are dealing with are not bound. Interdictors give their consent to the deeds of the person interdicted, and by such consent incur no responsibility in warrandice, &c.; while curators *ad litem*, by their becoming parties to a suit in that character, incur no liability for expenses, &c. Such persons are appointed merely to their respective offices *ad præstandam auctoritatem*.

Ad captandum lucrum.—For the purpose of making gain. (Stair, B. 2, T. 4, § 54.)

Ad captum vulgi.—Suited to the common understanding; easily understood. The phrase is used by Erskine, B. 1, T. 1, § 51 (quoting from the aphorisms of Bacon), as expressive of the manner in which statutes treating of matters "concerning which persons do not usually advise with lawyers, but trust to their own judgment," should be framed. This phrase is equivalent to the more ordinary one, *ad captandum vulgus*.

Ad civilem effectum.—As to the civil effect. The civil effect referred to in this phrase is the effect or result of an act at common law, as distinguished from the effect or result of the same act before a criminal tribunal. Many acts have this double effect. A person charged with culpable homicide may be sentenced to be punished for his criminal act by the Justiciary Court, but that does not exclude the civil effect of his act, which still exists in the shape of an action for assythment at the instance of the next-of-kin of the deceased. A thief is liable at common law for the value of the goods stolen, even although he has been punished for the theft. The civil effect of the crime of perjury was formerly to render the person guilty of it incapable of bearing testimony in a court of justice. The decision of the one court on the civil effect of an act does not in any case rule the decision of the other court. The Court of Session may find that a bill alleged to be forged is a valid document of debt, and give decree on it, but that will not prevent a criminal prosecution, nor the punishment of the forger, if his crime is made clear before the Court of Justiciary; while, on the same principle, should the alleged forger be acquitted on the criminal charge, the Court of Session may, nevertheless, hold the bill to be a forgery, and assoilzie the defender, who has been sued upon it.

Ad consimiles casus.—To similar or analogous cases.

Ad convincendam conscientiam judicis.—Sufficient to satisfy the moral conviction of the judge. (Stair, B. 4, T. 45, § 11.) This refers to questions of probation, where direct proof of acts alleged cannot be obtained, and where the judge is entitled to accept of less than such direct evidence. This used to occur frequently in cases of affiliation, where the judge might be satisfied of the paternity without direct proof of connection, although in such cases the proof required to amount to more than affording a ground merely for suspicion. When the mind of the judge had thus been convinced, an oath in supplement was allowed to complete the otherwise defective proof : but the oath in supplement is not now known in practice, as by the Act 16 & 17 Vict. cap. 20, parties are allowed to be examined as witnesses for themselves in almost all cases. On this point, see the opinions given in the case of *Scott*, 19 D. 119 ; *M'Bayne*, 22 D. 738 ; *M'Kinven*, 19 R. 369 ; and *Young*, 20 R. 768.

Ad ea quæ frequentius accidunt jura adaptantur.—The laws are adapted to those cases which most frequently occur. See Broom, p. 43.

Ad factum præstandum.—For the performance of a certain act. In popular language almost all obligations may be said to be of this class, but there are obligations of a peculiar character which alone are denoted by the legal signification of this phrase. The obligation of a debtor is clearly one for the performance of a certain act, namely, the payment of his debt ; but a decree at the instance of his creditor would not be termed a decree *ad factum præstandum*. An obligation *ad factum præstandum* is one for the performance of an act within the power of the obligant, and thus a decree of the Court, ordering delivery of certain writs, would be so termed, as also would a decree charging a superior to enter a vassal to whom he had refused an entry. The difference between an ordinary decree and one *ad factum præstandum* was in former times very considerable. For recovery of a debt the creditor could attach the debtor's estate, real and personal, but an obligation *ad factum præstandum* could be made effectual by letters of horning. Under that form of diligence, if a person was put to the horn for non performance, he was held to be a rebel, his goods were escheat, and for putting him to death no one could be punished. Letters of horning were afterwards (1584) granted for payment of debt, but the effects formerly resulting from this kind of diligence were abolished by the Act 20 Geo. II. cap. 50. By the Act 1 & 2 Vict. cap. 114, letters of horning are declared to be still competent, but it is provided that a creditor adopting that form of diligence shall not be entitled to recover expenses incurred by it, unless he can show that it would have been incompetent to have proceeded under the simpler form of diligence introduced by that statute. There is still this important difference between an ordinary debtor and a debtor *ad factum præstandum*, that whereas by the Act 43 & 44 Vict. cap. 34, imprisonment for civil debt has been (in the ordinary case) abolished, such personal diligence is still competent under a decree *ad factum præstandum*, and a debtor in such an obligation is denied the benefit of the act of grace, the privilege of sanctuary, and the *cessio bonorum*. As to what is considered a decree *ad factum præstandum*, on which imprisonment may still follow, see *Mackenzie* v. *Balerno Paper Mill Co.*, 10 R. 1147.

Ad fundandam jurisdictionem.—For the purpose of founding jurisdiction. See *Arrestum*, &c.

Ad infinitum.—Without limit.

Ad informandum judicis.—For the information of the judge; to inform the mind of the judge.

Ad levandam conscientiam.—For the purpose of easing or disburdening the conscience. Confessions so made, when proved, are evidence against the person confessing, in regard to the subject-matter of the confession. It sometimes happens that such confessions are made by criminals on their apprehension, and if so, they may be adduced in support of the prosecution against them. But if a person charged with a certain crime has been apprehended on that charge, and in answer to certain questions put by the apprehending officer admits or confesses to certain points material to the prosecution, the substance of the prisoner's answers cannot be received as evidence against him. It is *ultra vires* of the officer to interrogate the prisoner; this can only be done by the proper authority, in the presence of a magistrate, whose duty it is to warn the prisoner that any statement he makes may be used against him and to see any such statement, when made, fairly taken down. This is an established rule. See the cases of *Hay*, 3 Irvine, 181 ; and *Millar*, 3 Irvine, 406.

Ad litem.—As regards the action. When persons of tender years are pursuers in any action, the Court appoints a curator *ad litem*, to watch the progress of the action, and see that everything is done for the interest, and nothing to the disadvantage of the ward to whom he has been appointed curator. See *Ad auctoritatem præstandam.*

Ad longum.—At length.

Ad medium filum.—To the middle line. Proprietors of land bounded by a private river have a right of property in the *alveus* or bed of the river *ex adverso* of their lands up to the *medium filum*, that is an imaginary line or *thread* drawn down the centre of the river. But although the *alveus* of the stream is thus divided between the two proprietors of the opposite banks, and is held by each up to the *medium filum* in sole property on either side, their interest in the water is a common interest. *Morris* v. *Bicket*, 2 Macp. 1082.

Ad omissa vel male appretiata.—As regards things omitted or undervalued. Every executor confirmed before the Commissary is bound to give up an inventory of the whole moveable estate of the deceased to whom he has been confirmed executor ; but in the event of his afterwards discovering that he has omitted to give up part of the estate, or has undervalued that which has been given up, he may rectify this by expeding an eik to the inventory ; or failing his thus rectifying the inventory, any one having an interest may apply to have the executor compelled to do so, or to have himself confirmed executor to the things omitted or undervalued. Should the executor die before the executry has been administered, the next-of-kin after the deceased executor may obtain confirmation *quoad non executa*—*i.e.*, in reference to those parts of the estate not administered, or those duties of executor not performed.

Ad paratam executionem.—For execution on completed diligence. See an instance of the use of this phrase in the judgment pronounced in *Lourie* v. *Earl of Dundee*, M. 911.

Ad pares casus.—To similar cases.

Ad perpetuam rei memoriam.—For a perpetual record of the matter. By the statute 1685, a register-book is appointed to be kept, in which entails are to be recorded, with the name of the maker, the heirs, the provisions and conditions of the entail, "all to remain in the said register *ad perpetuam rei memoriam.*"

Ad perpetuam remanentiam.—To remain for ever. Resignation, one of the oldest forms of transmission of a feudal right, was of two kinds—viz., resignation *ad perpetuam remanentiam*, and resignation *in favorem*. The former was used when the vassal surrendered to the superior the right of property which he held, that it might be reincorporated with the right of superiority, and remain with the superior; the latter when the vassal, having sold his right of property or feu to another, resigned it into the hands of the superior *in favorem* —*i.e.*, in favour of the purchaser, "in order that it might be conferred by the same power upon the new vassal, and carry with it the same assurance of protection" (Menzies' Lectures, 615). By the resignation *ad remanentiam*, the rights of property and superiority, formerly separated, became consolidated in the person of the superior. The possession of a procuratory of resignation *in favorem* entitled the disponee to demand and enforce an entry with the superior. The mode of making up a title by an instrument of resignation *in favorem* was abolished by the Act 8 & 9 Vict. cap. 35; and resignation *ad perpetuam remanentiam* has been superseded by a simpler form, under which the rights of superiority and property are consolidated, 37 & 38 Vict. cap. 94, § 6.

Ad pristinum statum.—To the former condition.

Ad quæstionem facti non respondent judices; ad quæstionem legis non respondent juratores.—Judges do not answer questions of fact, nor juries questions of law. This maxim expresses the respective duties of a judge and jury in the determination of any case which comes before them. In civil causes which have been sent for trial to a jury, the jury determine what has or has not been proved as matter of fact, by their verdict, which is an answer to the question put to them in the form of an issue. In our practice, the issue is essentially a question of fact, from which questions of law are rigidly excluded. On the other hand, all questions of law arising at the trial are determined by the judge, whose statement of the law the jury are bound to accept and adopt. In criminal trials this maxim is of universal application, and neither the determination of the jury on the facts, nor the decision of the judge upon the law, is, in Scotland, subject to appeal. In civil cases, the maxim has a more limited application with us than in England, and can only have reference to cases which are tried before a jury, for under other forms of procedure questions of fact are constantly being answered by judges. This is not only so according to the practice of the common law, but also under statutory provision. By the Act 13 & 14 Vict. cap. 36, it is provided (§ 46) that, of consent of parties, the Lord Ordinary may try an issue without a jury, and his findings in fact are declared to be final; and by § 48 of the same statute it is provided that the Lord Ordinary, without adjusting any issue, may pronounce an interlocutor, stating specifically what question or questions of fact he wishes investigated; and on proof being led as to the question so stated, "the Lord Ordinary shall find on each such question separately, and his finding upon such questions shall be final." In both of these cases the judge is required to answer questions of fact; and, indeed, since the passing of the Act (29 & 30 Vict. cap. 112) abolishing the taking of proofs by commission, and appointing them to be taken by the Lord Ordinary, almost all questions of fact are answered or determined by judges. The cases enumerated in the 28th section of the Judicature Act (6 Geo. IV. cap. 120), as appropriate to jury trial, are not now invariably submitted to a jury, and for the most part (except actions where damages are to be assessed for personal wrongs or injuries, actions of reduction, or actions for nuisance, 13 & 14 Vict. cap. 36, § 49) are decided by the judge, both as regards the facts and the law. There are some cases in which it appears to be considered advisable that the judge should answer or determine the question of fact at issue, not only without the aid of a jury, but even without the aid (at least, in the first instance) of witnesses; as, for example, where the question at issue is whether or not a deed produced has been erased; regarding which, see the observations made in the case of *Hamilton* v. *Lindsey-Bucknall*, 8 Macp. 323.

Ad reprimendam improbitatem hoc genus hominum.—To repress the dishonesty of this class of men. Innkeepers, shipmasters, and others, to whose care goods of considerable value are often committed, were supposed to possess great facilities for committing theft, with less than usual probability of detection. With the view of checking the dishonesty of such persons, peculiar responsibilities were imposed upon them regarding the careful preservation of things placed in their charge, and they were made liable for the full value of the subject lost. The edict of the Roman prætor, *nautæ, caupones, stabularii* (to be noticed hereafter), was issued to repress this dishonesty.

Ad rimandam veritatem.—For the purpose of investigating the truth. Although as a general rule writings cannot be cut down or explained by parole testimony, yet in some cases, on the principle expressed by the phrase, such testimony is admitted. A deed may be reduced on the parole testimony of the testamentary witnesses, if they swear that they were not present at the subscription, and did not hear the signature acknowledged; a decree on a bill or bond may be refused, if it can be proved that the document of debt was obtained through fraud; and parole testimony is admitted, to remove any doubt which may arise from latent ambiguity in a deed.

Ad similes casus.—To like cases.

Ad sustinenda onera matrimonii.—To bear the burdens or expenses of the married state. The dowry brought by a wife at her marriage is given to the husband for this purpose, and he is not liable for his wife's debts after her decease, unless the dowry has been excessive, for otherwise he is not accounted *lucratus* by the dowry, it having been given for the onerous cause of meeting the expenses of the married state, and presumed to have been so expended. Dowry being given for this purpose, should the marriage be dissolved by divorce on account of the husband's delict, the husband is bound to restore it, there being no room for its intended application; in which case, not only can the wife recover her dowry, but also all her legal and conventional rights, in the same way as if her husband had died. Should the divorce proceed upon the delinquency of the wife, the husband retains the dowry as if the wife had died, and it had been expended during the subsistence of the marriage.

Ad tentandas vires hæreditatis.—For the purpose of testing the strength of the succession. Ross, L. C. (L. R.) I. 368.

Ad valorem.—According to value.

Ad vindictam publicam.—For the maintenance and defence of the public interest. For this purpose the Lord Advocate of Scotland, or those to whom he delegates his authority, are the public prosecutors of all criminals, and although a crime committed has been condoned or discharged *ad civilem effectum* by the person entitled so to do, this does not preclude the prosecution of the criminal, as the public interest demands that all criminals should be punished.

Ad vitam aut culpam.—For life or till fault; said of an office so held, where the tenure of the possessor is determinable only by his death or delinquency. The equivalent of this phrase generally used in England is *Dum* (or *quamdiu*) *se bene gesserit:* whilst (or, so long as) he conducts himself properly; during good behaviour.

Ad vitandum perjurium.—For avoiding perjury. Stair, B. 3, T. 1, § 41. See *Ob metum perjurii.*

Addictio in diem.—A condition or agreement sometimes added to the contract of sale under the civil law, by which the seller reserved right to himself to annul the sale, if within a certain fixed time he met with a better offer. Such a condition is not known in our law, but there was a practice very much similar to it before ward holdings were abolished. Before that time superiors were entitled to the casualty of recognition, which implied a forfeiture on the part of the vassal of his fee, on alienation of more than one-half thereof without the superior's consent. To avoid the forfeiture, it was common to insert in the deed of conveyance a clause to the effect that the disponee should have no right to the property until the superior's consent was obtained, and this operated like the *addictio in diem*, as a suspensive clause, preventing the transmission of any real right until the condition was purified.

Ademptione.—By ademption. Special legacies are held to be revoked when (1) the specific thing bequeathed has ceased to exist, or (2) has ceased to belong to the testator at the time of his death, or (3) although in effect still belonging to the testator, has been changed in character so as no longer to be the specific thing described in the bequest. In all such cases the legacy is said to have been revoked by ademption. The doctrine of ademption, or implied revocation of legacies, is derived from the civil law, but is adopted with us subject to a very important modification. According to the civil law, if the subject of the specific bequest had ceased to exist at the date of the testator's death, the legacy was held to have been adeemed; but if, still existing, it had been alienated by the testator, or had been changed in its character, ademption did not follow, unless it appeared that by the alienation or change the testator had intended to operate a revocation. According to the law of Scotland, the testator's intention in such questions is not regarded, it being enough to operate revocation if the specific thing bequeathed is no longer in a condition falling within the description of the bequest. *Pagan*, 16 S. 383; *Chalmers*, 14 D. 57; *Anderson*, 4 R. 1101. The same rule (disregarding the testator's intention) prevails in England. In the case of *Stanley* v. *Potter*, 2 Cox, 180, Lord Thurlow observed: "The idea of proceeding on the *animus adimendi* has introduced a degree of confusion into the cases which is inexplicable, and I can make no precise rule from them upon that ground. . . . It will be a safer and clearer way to adhere to the plain rule before mentioned, which is to inquire whether the specific thing remains or not." This rule, and the decisions giving effect to it, have been characterised (*Anderson, supra*) as "utterly at variance with any principle of jurisprudence." "The term *ademption*, which was used in the civil law to denote the implied revocation of legacies, has in England been employed in a more restricted sense, to express the satisfaction of one provision by a subsequent provision of a different nature—*e.g.*, the satisfaction of a legacy by a marriage portion, or the satisfaction of a debt or portion by a legacy. In that sense it has lately come into use in Scotch practice" (M'Laren, i. 441).

Aditio hæreditatis.—The entering upon, or taking up, a succession, and that whether in moveables or heritage.

Adjectio dominii per continuationem possessionis.—The addition of the right of property by continued possession.

This is the effect of the positive prescription. Ross, L. C. (L. R.) III. 516, 532.

Adpromissor.—Cautioner. The *adpromissor* of the Roman law is to be carefully distinguished from the *fidejussor*. The obligation of the former was one which could only be undertaken by a Roman citizen, was limited to verbal contracts, was only binding for two years, and did not transmit against heirs. The latter (*fidejussor*) could be added to any kind of contract; his obligation was not limited to any precise period, and not only bound himself, but his heirs. The *Senatus-consultum Velleianum* forbade women binding themselves as cautioners for another person.

Adscriptitii.—A class of slaves who were attached to certain lands, neither of which could be sold separately, and so called because they were *adscripti glebæ*, joined to the land. They were entitled to retain for their own use all they could gain from the land beyond the value of a yearly payment which they had to make to the owner of the soil: they enjoyed also all the family rights of freemen. "Their situation was very similar to that of the workmen employed in collieries and salt-works in Scotland, before the passing of the Stat. 15 Geo. III. cap. 28" (Bell's Dict. *h.v.*).

Advocatus ecclesiæ.—The patron of a benefice or living.

Ædificatum solo, solo cedit.—That which is built upon the ground accrues to the ground. See *Inædificatum solo*, &c.

Æmulationis causa.—For the purpose of annoying or injuring. See *In æmulationem*, &c.

Affectus sine effectu.—A design without effect—*i.e.*, a purpose or intention not carried into effect, or expressed in action.

Affinitas affinitatis.—Affinity of affinity. This constitutes no relationship. The brother of a husband is no way thereby related to the sister of the wife; but this is the kind of tie known as *affinitas affinitatis*.

Affirmanti incumbit probatio.—The burden of proof lies with the party affirming. Negatives cannot be proved; they are presumed and need no probation, but any one alleging a fact, is bound, when it is disputed, to prove it. The *onus probandi* in the ordinary case lies with the pursuer of an action, when the defender denies the obligation on which he is sued; yet, when the defender admits the obligation, but objects to its fulfilment, or alleges facts and circumstances purging the obligation, the burden of proving his defence lies with him.

Ager arcifinius.—Enclosed or bounded land. This phrase applies to land, the boundaries of which are given, for the purpose of identifying or describing the subjects, and not as expressing their limit or extent; and differs from—

Ager limitatus.—Bounded land; where the boundaries given are the limit of the right conveyed. Under the former the disponee may acquire certain privileges, and even rights of property, over the other lands adjoining or discontiguous, by prescriptive possession, the new right thus acquired, passing along with his own proper lands, as parts and pertinents, although not specified. Under the latter (commonly called with us a bounding charter) no additional right of property is ever acquired by mere possession, for nothing attaches to it as part and pertinent, by prescription, outwith the specified boundaries. *Reid* v. *M'Coll,* 7 R. 84. The *agri limitati* of the Roman law were lands detached from the public domain, and converted into private property, by sale or grant, beyond the limits of which the owners could claim nothing. Any addition around or beyond them was public property.

Alibi.—Elsewhere. This is the name given to the special defence sometimes put forward by a panel in a criminal prosecution, to the effect, that at the time libelled as the time when the criminal act was committed, he was in a different place from that specified in the indictment. An *alibi* is the best defence which can be stated in such cases, if it can be clearly proved, but it is always regarded with great suspicion, and is very rarely successful.

Alienatio feudi.—Disposition or conveyance of a feu right. Such dispositions are not now restricted, unless by special arrangement, or condition, as in a deed of entail. Formerly it was not so, for under the feudal system, no vassal could convey his right, without the consent of the superior. Fidelity and service being the inherent conditions of a vassal's right, " the very nature of the contract exempted the superior from having vassals imposed upon him, who were not selected by himself." (Menzies' Lectures, 608.) Sub-infeudation was not regarded, however, as an alienation, for, although this gave the *dominium utile* to the sub-vassal, it did not divest or discharge the original vassal, from whom the subaltern right flowed, of the duties and services owing to his superior, for which he was still liable. Such sub-infeudation did, notwithstanding, expose the rights of the superior to great risk, as they were necessarily rendered in some measure insecure, by the divestiture of the immediate vassal, and it was as a protection against such risk that the superior was entitled, by the casualty of recognition, to resume the entire feu if the vassal alienated more than half of it. "It is a remarkable evidence of the firmness of the grasp, in which the landrights of Scotland were held by the feudal rules, that these restraints were not subjected to any mitigation until the latter part of the fifteenth century—that, until the middle of the last century, the superior's power of refusal could only be obviated by a legal device—and that it was not entirely relaxed until, by the Lands Transference Act of 1847, the last traces of the superior's power to refuse entries to purchasers were removed." (Menzies, *ut supra.*) The restrictions on alienation were abolished at an earlier period in England, for, by the Act 18 Edward I. cap. 1 (called the statute *Quia Emptores*, from its introductory words), sub-infeudation was abolished, and the disponee, upon infeftment, was constituted, by force of law, the vassal of his author's superior. It has been said that the Scotch Act, 2 Rob. I. cap. 24, enacted similar provisions for Scotland, but the authenticity of that Act has been seriously doubted, and, even if authentic, there is every reason to believe that its provisions were disregarded.

Alienatio feudifirmæ feudifirmarum.—The name given to an old form of conveyance introduced for the purpose of evading the prohibition of alienation of crown lands; to prevent which, so far as the Crown was concerned, the Act 1597, cap. 239, was passed, which declared all such conveyances null.

Alieni juris.—Dependent upon or subject to the power of another. Under the Roman law all persons were divided into two great classes, those *sui juris*, who were independent and not under the power of any other person, and those *alieni juris*. Children were *alieni juris* because they were subject to the *patria potestas*, and a wife (if the marriage had been contracted by one of the strict forms of the older law) was so, being under the power of her husband. In Scotland there is no such thing as the *patria potestas* of the Roman law; but pupils who can of themselves perform no valid act, and enter into no binding obligation, are called *alieni juris*, while minors who may enter into contracts, and whose deeds (except those diverting the succession to their heritable estate) are valid, are termed *sui juris*.

Alioqui successurus.—Otherwise entitled to succeed; or, succeeding under a different title. In the general case, an heir who succeeds to an estate, incurs by his succession liability for the debts and obligations of his ancestor. As he takes the estate of the deceased, with all its advantages, he is burdened also with its disadvantages. But if the heir succeeding to the estate can take it up in a different character from that of heir of the last proprietor, if he be *alioqui successurus*, such liability is not incurred. Thus, if a son, on the death of his father, succeeds to an entailed estate, in terms of the destination of the entail, he does not, by making up his title thereto, render himself liable for his father's private debts. He incurs no representation, because he succeeds not as his father's heir-at-law, but *alioqui successurus*, namely, as heir of entail. Or, again, if a father dispones to his son heritage burdened with certain conditions, to which that son was entitled to succeed simply under the terms of a deed granted by a previous ancestor, or, it might be, of the antenuptial marriage-contract of his parents, he may disregard the conveyance executed by his father, and elide the conditions imposed by it, by making up his title under the other deeds which gave him the right. If he could only take the heritage under his father's conveyance, he would be bound by the adjected conditions, but being *alioqui successurus*, he can disregard them, because he can disregard the deed which creates them. Under the old law, the casualty of recognition was not inferred where the vassal disponed his lands to one who was *alioqui successurus*, although such a conveyance to one who had not, and could not have any other than the singular title, inferred that casualty.

Aliqualis probatio.—Any kind of proof whatever, although not strictly in accordance with legal rules, and not resorted to when any other better evidence can be adduced. (Ersk. B. 1, T. 7, § 36.) See *Prout de jure*.

Aliud est celare, aliud tacere.—It is one thing to conceal, another thing to be silent. Where a subject is sold that is defective or imperfect, the buyer can in some cases be restored against his purchase, and in some he cannot. If the seller warrants the subject sold to be sound or perfect, the buyer is of course entitled to reject the article on discovery of the defect, and recover the price if this has been paid. But where the subject sold is submitted to the inspection of the buyer, and no art is used to conceal the defects, then the buyer's eye is his merchant, and if he buys a defective subject, he must himself bear the loss. On the other hand, if anything is done to conceal the defects, the buyer has his remedy against the seller. Concealment, however, is very different from mere silence. A seller is not legally bound to proclaim the defects of the subject offered for sale: he may remain silent and allow the buyer to inspect the article and satisfy himself before concluding the transaction, whether it is defective or not. Such silence does not amount either to implied warranty, or to concealment. In the case of *Keates v. Earl of Cadogan* (10 C. B. 591), it was held that there was no implied duty on the owner of a house which was in a ruinous and unsafe condition to inform a proposed tenant that it was unfit for habitation. In that case Jervis, C. J., said: "It is not pretended that there was any warranty, express or implied, that the house was fit for immediate habitation; but it is said that, because the defendant knew that the plaintiff wanted it for immediate occupation, and knew that it was in an unfit and dangerous state, and did not disclose that fact to the plaintiff, an action of deceit will lie. The declaration does not allege that the defendant made any representation, or that he had reason to suppose the plaintiff would not do what any man in his senses would do—viz., make proper investigation, and satisfy himself as to the condition of the house before he entered upon the occupation of it. There is nothing amounting to deceit." On the other hand, see the case of *Hill* v. *Gray* (1 Stark, 434), which was distinguished from the case above referred to, as containing the element of "aggressive deceit" or misrepresentation. "It is only where a party is under some pledge or obligation to reveal facts to another that mere silence will be considered as a means of deception" (Benjamin on Sales, p. 387 *et seq.*). Concealment of facts, therefore, which ought to be disclosed, will vitiate the contract or obligation which has thus been entered into or obtained. In *Railton* v. *Matthews* (6 D. 536, reversed H.L. 3 Bell, 56), it was decided that the non-disclosure of facts concerning material irregularities on the part of an agent previous to the granting of a bond of caution for his future intromissions vitiated the bond of caution, without regard to the motive from which the non-disclosure arose. In *Dempsters* v. *Rae*, 11 Macp. 843, an agreement was set aside on the ground of concealment of important facts by one of the parties which he was bound to have disclosed. The cases of *Broatch* v. *Jenkins*, 4 Macp. 1030, and *French* v. *Cameron*, 20 R. 966, may also be referred to on this subject. The non-disclosure of material facts is fatal to a contract of insurance. In such a contract it is the duty of the insured "carefully and diligently to review all the facts known to himself bearing on the risk proposed to the insurers, and to state every circumstance which any reasonable man might suppose could in any way influence the insurers in considering and deciding whether they will enter into the contract. Any negligence or want of fair consideration for the interest of the insurers on the part of the insured leading to the non-disclosure of material facts, though there be no dishonesty, may therefore constitute a failure in the duty of disclosure which will lead to the voidance of the contract." Per Lord President Inglis in *Life Association of Scotland* v. *Foster*, 11 Macp. 359 ; *Ionides* v. *Pender*, L. R. 9 Q.B. 537. Arnold, i. 549. May, 245. See *Caveat emptor*.

Aliud est possidere, aliud esse in possessione.—It is one thing to possess, another to be in possession. In common parlance, to possess and to be in possession are synonymous terms, but they have a widely different meaning in legal phraseology. To possess implies the right of property ; to be in possession, mere custody. Thus a landed proprietor possesses the farm of which his tenant is in possession; the lender possesses the subject of which the borrower is in possession; the owner of a lost or stolen article still possesses it when it is in the possession of a finder, or honest and onerous purchaser. This difference is not altogether illustrated by the division of possession into natural and civil known in the Scotch law. For natural possession implies both property and custody, while *possidere* only necessarily implies the former, but civil possession is equivalent to *in possessione esse*.

Aliud simulatum, aliud actum.—One thing pretended, another thing done.

Aliunde.—Otherwise. Proof of the resting-owing of a debt falling under triennial prescription, can only be made by writ or oath of the party; an ordinary debt not falling under that prescription can be proved *aliunde*. " The husband is not liable for any debt contracted by his wife after inhibition, except for such furnishings suitable to her quality, as he cannot prove he provided her in *aliunde*." (Ersk. B. 1, T. 6, § 26.)

Allegans contraria non est audiendus.—He is not to be heard who alleges things contradictory of each other. For example, no one can be heard to maintain that a deed is invalid as regards some obligation which it imposes upon him, and yet valid in so far as it confers upon him a right. A landlord cannot sue for rent on the ground that the defender is his tenant in certain subjects, and at the same time sue the same defender for damages in respect his possession of the subjects is an intrusion or trespass. A person cannot claim exemption from personal liability under a contract on the ground that he entered into it as agent for another, and thereafter sue on the contract for its performance on the ground that he was himself really the principal. In other words, no one is permitted at the same time to approbate and reprobate. It must be kept in view, however, that this does not militate against what is fair alternative pleading. Thus it is quite permitted to a defender in an action for damages to allege that the pursuer has not sustained any injury whatever and at same time to allege that, even if that be otherwise, the damage was occasioned by the pursuer's own act or fault, or the act of his fellow-servant, or arose under circumstances which exempted the defender from liability. Such alternative pleading does not fall within the maxim, for the things alleged are not (as in the other instances above given) contradictory of each other.

Allegans suam turpitudinem non est audiendus.—He is not to be heard who alleges things disgraceful or discreditable to himself. This maxim is not of frequent use, nor of wide application. An instance of its use and application will be found in the case of *Minet* v. *Gibson*, Ross, L. C. (C. L.) I. 88. As a general rule, a person who alleges or confesses something to his own discredit, is heard, and his statement accepted, because no one readily acknowledges what is discreditable to himself. The rule of the maxim finds its application where one alleges his own fraud or other discreditable conduct in answer to some obligation, and with the view of avoiding its fulfilment. Even this is liable to exception; as, for example, where one pleads that he is not liable for payment of a bill, because it was given in payment of a gambling debt, or as the price and reward of illicit intercourse. These defences involve allegations of conduct discreditable to the person making them, but they are not the less heard on that account; if proved, they are sustained as sufficient defences to the claim.

Allegatio falsi.—The statement of what is untrue. See *Expressio falsi*.

Alluvio.—This signifies the addition made to the lands of a riparian proprietor by the natural operation of the stream, whether by the slow retiring of the river itself and thus leaving a greater bank, or by the successive accumulation of soil brought down by it, washed from other lands. Such addition accresces to the owner of the land to which the addition is made. This gradual addition is to be distinguished from *avulsio*, which is the violent tearing away of ground belonging to one proprietor by a torrent or inundation or any convulsion of nature, and subsequent depositation of it along the bank of another's land. In such case the land thus added does not accresce, but remains the property of the original proprietor. It is also to be distinguished from *alvei mutatio*, which is the change occasioned when a river bounding the lands of conterminous proprietors, changes or deviates from its course. Any addition thus made to the lands of one of the proprietors does not accresce, but, as in *avulsio*, remains the property of him to whom it originally belonged. *Mather* v. *Macbraire*, 11 Macp. 522.

Alternis vicibus.—Alternately, by turn. The right of presentation to a benefice was directed to be thus exercised by the Act 1617, cap. 3, where two churches formerly belonging to different patrons were united.

Alterum non lædere.—To injure no one. This is one of the three fundamental maxims, or first principles, laid down by Justinian, as those upon which all rules of law are based. The other two were *honeste vivere*, to live morally, and *suum cuique tribuere*, to give every one that which is his due.

Altius non tollendi.—Literally, of not raising higher. This was one of the Roman law servitudes, by which the owner of the servient tenement was held bound not to raise his building to a height which would be prejudicial to the dominant tenement. Some writers on the civil law mention a servitude *altius tollendi*, but the majority of writers agree that this could not, properly speaking, be a servitude. Most probably the term was used as a means of extinguishing the servitude *altius non tollendi*, and thus restoring to the owner of the servient tenement the natural power of a proprietor to raise a house or other building on his own land to whatever height he pleased.

Alvei mutatio.—A change in the course or of the bed of a stream. See *Alluvio*.

Alveus.—The bed or channel of a river.

Ambigua responsio contra proferentem est accipienda.—An ambiguous answer is to be taken (or interpreted) against the person making it. In pleading, where a pursuer avers something as having been done or said by the defender, or in his presence, or generally, where the subject of his averment is a matter that should be within the knowledge of the defender (a *factum proprium*), such an averment must be met with an admission or denial. If, in such a case, the defender resorts to the answer, "not admitted," which is neither admission nor denial, the answer will be construed against him, and be regarded as an admission. In like manner, under a reference to oath, if the matter referred "is a *factum proprium et recens*, which the party cannot be supposed to have forgotten, his oath of *non memini* will show an attempt to shirk or evade the reference, and he will be held as confessed, in the same way as if he had refused to depone." (Dickson, § 1624.)

Ambiguitas latens et ambiguitas patens.—Latent and obvious ambiguity. The ambiguities here mentioned are those which arise from the terms in which a deed or instrument is expressed. The difference between these two kinds of ambiguity is important, and they are treated differently in the cases where they respectively arise. A latent ambiguity is that which does not appear from the face of the deed, but which arises from some extraneous circumstance or collateral fact. In this case a proof is allowed to clear up the ambiguity, and take away the doubt it gives rise to. For example, if A. dispones, by *mortis causa* deed, to B., his tenement in Princes Street, Edinburgh, and on his death is possessed of two tenements in that street, there arises an uncertainty as to which of the two tenements it was intended should become the property of B. There is no ambiguity on the face of the deed, which clearly enough dispones a tenement situated in a certain street; but the ambiguity arises from the fact external to the deed, that there are two tenements falling under the same description. To remove this doubt proof of the intention of the disponer would be allowed. A patent ambiguity, on the other hand, is that which appears *ex facie* of the deed. As if a destination was expressed thus:—"To A. and B. and heirs;" or, "to A. and B. jointly, and his heirs." The doubt here arises, to whose heirs does the destination carry the subjects on the death of the disponees. In this case the law allows no proof of intention beyond what can be gathered from the deed itself, and the Court will deal with the right of succession, regarding which the doubt exists, as the general tenor of the deed seems to warrant. See Lord Bacon's Maxims of the Law, Reg. 25; Lord Chancellor's opinion in *Morton* v. *Hunter*, 4 W. & S. 379; and Wigram on the admission of

Extrinsic Evidence in aid of the Interpretation of Wills (4th Ed.), p. 74 *et seq.*

Ambiguum placitum contra proferentem interpretare debet.—An ambiguous agreement ought to be interpreted against the person putting it forward (*i.e.*, maintaining or pleading upon it). The word *placitum* includes order, decree, opinion, plea, as well as agreement; and with reference to this maxim, the reader is referred to what is said under *Ambigua responsio*, &c., and *Verba sunt*, &c. For an instance of an ambiguous clause in a contract of insurance construed *contra proferentem*, see *Foster*, 11 Macp. 358. See also *Dryer* v. *Birrell*, 10 R. 585, revd. (H.L.) 11 R. 41. For further illustration of the maxim, reference may be made to the case of *Cockburn* v. *Alexander* (6 C. B. 814), where it was observed in reference to a charter-party that "generally speaking, where there are several ways in which the contract might be performed, that mode is adopted which is the least profitable to the plaintiff, and the least troublesome to the defendant."

Ambulatoria est voluntas defuncti usque ad vitæ supremum exitum.—The will of the deceased is ambulatory (*i.e.* admits of change, is revocable) even to the last moment of his life. For the law on the subject of a testator's right and power to revoke his will or deed or settlement at any time, see M'Laren, i. 249.

Amicus curiæ.—Literally, a friend of the Court; the name given to any bystander, who, without having any interest in the cause, of his own knowledge makes a suggestion on a point of fact or law, for the information of the Court, or to correct a mistake.

Amittit legem terræ.—He loses or forfeits the law of the land; that is, he loses or forfeits all the protection afforded, and privileges conferred, by the law of the land. This is said to be the effect of a sentence of fugitation or outlawry. Hume, ii. 270.

Animo defamandi.—With the intention of defaming. This enters as an element into every action for damages or solatium on account of verbal injury. It is that malice which is essential in such cases, and may be either actual or implied. *Macdonald* v. *Rupprecht*, 21 R. 389. Such malice is presumed in ordinary cases of slander (there being no question of privilege) when the slander is proved to be untrue in point of fact.

Animo differendi.—For the purpose of obtaining delay; a presumption against the proceedings of the defender in a cause, according to Stair. (B. 4, T. 40, § 12.)

Animo donandi.—With the intention of giving as a donation. This is rarely presumed, and only so when the act can bear no other construction. A debtor is never presumed to give in donation; but where spouses enter into contracts with each other, which are either gratuitous or without equivalent consideration, a different rule is observed, for there the law presumes donation; allowing the presumption to be redargued by proof. (Bell's Prin. § 1616.)

Animo et facto.—By act and intention. In certain cases acts only take legal effect where they are induced or accompanied by positive intention. Thus, domicile is acquired only where actual residence in a place is accompanied by the intention of remaining and acquiring a domicile there. A Scotchman having his domicile in Scotland may reside, even for a lengthened period, in another country on a visit, or for the transaction of business, or for some temporary purpose, but such residence will not take away his Scotch domicile, nor give him a domicile where he is residing. (*Patience* v. *Main*, L. R. 29 Ch. Div. 976.) It would be otherwise if the residence abroad had been taken up with the intention of remaining and acquiring a domicile there, and in such a case length of residence is not necessary to obliterate the old, and constitute the new domicile. To acquire a domicile, therefore, requires both the fact of residence and the intention of remaining. There is an exception to this rule in the case of a Scotchman domiciled abroad, who has abandoned his foreign domicile with the view of returning to reside permanently in Scotland. In that case the domicile is held to be in Scotland, although the person so intending to return should never return in point of fact, but die *in itinere.* These observations apply to questions of domicile as to succession, not to domicile for the purposes of jurisdiction. The mere fact of residence in Scotland, without any intention to remain there, will constitute a domicile, rendering the persons so residing liable to the jurisdiction of the Scotch Courts. Such residence in itself has also been held sufficient to constitute jurisdiction *ratione domicilii* in the sense of the Bankruptcy (Scotland) Act, 1856, § 13. See *Joel* v. *Gill*, 21 D. 929.

Animo indorsandi.—With the intention of indorsing. Every one who indorses a bill or promissory-note becomes liable for the amount contained in it to the subsequent indorsee and holder, except, of course, in the case where he indorses "without recourse." But the rule is not so absolute in reference to the indorsation of bank cheques. In the greater number of cases, the indorsation of the payee's name or the name of the person actually receiving payment of the cheque from the bank, is merely made by way of receipt or acknowledgment, and imports no obligation to make good the amount of the cheque in the event of its not being honoured, or there being no funds to meet it. Such indorsation is generally resorted to only as a means of identifying the person to whom the money was paid. But it may be otherwise; and if any one indorses a cheque *animo indorsandi*, with the intention of becoming a proper indorser and obligant, he will be liable for the amount of the cheque, in the event of its dishonour. *Macdonald* v. *Union Bank*, 2 Macp. 963. As to whether indorsation of a cheque makes it the writ of the person indorsing, sufficient to prove *scripto* a loan to him of the amount of the cheque, see the case of *Haldane* v. *Speirs*, 10 Macp. 537, where it was held that the alleged loan was not instructed by the indorsed cheque.

Animo obligandi.—With the intention of entering into an obligation. Certain words uttered with this intention would complete an obligation, while the same words, used merely in jest, would not. "To a perfect obligation, it is necessary that there shall be a deliberate and voluntary consent and *purpose* to engage." (Bell's Prin. § 10.)

Animo remanendi.—With the intention of remaining. Said of a person leaving a country without meaning to return; or, of a person resident in a foreign country with the intention of remaining there and not returning to settle in his native country.

Animo revertendi.—With the intention of returning.

Said of a person leaving a country merely for a temporary purpose; as, for example, a sailor in following out his occupation, but with the intention to return.

Animo ulciscendi.—With the intention or purpose of taking revenge. (Hume, i. 429.)

Animus.—Will; intention.

Animus adimendi.—The intention of adeeming. See *Ademptione*.

Animus contrahentium.—The intention or purpose of the contracting parties.

Animus gerendi.—See *Gestio pro hærede*.

Animus immiscendi et adeundi hereditatem.—The intention of meddling with and taking up a succession. It is of importance to show, by his acts, that an heir acted with this intention, in a question whether he has incurred representation to the deceased by intromission.

Animus injuriandi.—The intention or desire of injuring. See *Animo defamandi*.

Animus occidendi.—The intention of killing. (Hume, i. 238.)

Anni continui.—Years successive, continuous, without break or interruption.

Anni utiles.—Literally, years which can be used; years in which a right can be exercised.

Both these phrases are most frequently to be met in cases where a question of prescription is at issue. Against any one fully able, during the whole period, to assert and defend his right, the years of prescription are *anni continui;* but as the loss arising from the currency of prescription is considered as the penalty of negligence, the prescriptive years are not so regarded in the case of one under a legal incapacity to sue. If a heritable right is being acquired by prescription against the proprietor of lands, or if a title, questionable in itself, is becoming valid through prescription, and a minor becomes entitled to that right against which prescription is running, the currency of the prescriptive period ceases, until the minor is *valens agere*—*i.e.*, in a position to defend his right on attaining majority. Although, therefore, the prescriptive period may in reality have expired, yet as there were some years which were not *anni utiles* to the minor, prescription does not take place. On the succession of the minor the currency of prescription ceases, and only resumes when he has become *valens agere*.

Annus deliberandi.—The year for deliberating; being the year allowed to an heir to deliberate whether he will take up the succession devolving upon him, and represent his ancestor. This year commences as at the date of the ancestor's death; and should the apparent heir die during his year of deliberation, the next heir has a year from the death of the apparent heir. The time for deliberation has now been reduced to six months. 31 & 32 Vict. cap. 101, § 61. See *Damnosa*, &c.

Annus inceptus pro completo habetur.—A year begun is held as completed—a rule of very limited application. See Stair, B. 2, T. 8, § 34.

Ante litem motam.—Before an action has been raised. Any stranger intromitting with the estate of a deceased person without title, incurs by such intromission a passive title, rendering him generally liable for the deceased's debts. Such vitious intromission is purged, and the passive title not incurred, if the intromitter confirms himself executor, before any creditor has raised an action against him on the passive title. If the intromitter has an antecedent title, such as next-of-kin, or relict, a passive title is not incurred if confirmation is expede within a year of the deceased's death, even although an action has been raised by a creditor before that time.

Ante omnia.—Before any other thing is done or considered; first of all. A preliminary defence objecting to the pursuer's title, or to the jurisdiction of the Court, is discussed *ante omnia*, because, if sustained, all further procedure is barred.

Ante redditas rationes.—Before accounts are rendered, or given up. On the expiry of a tutory or curatory, no action can be raised against the pupil or minor for payment of advances made, or relief from obligations undertaken on his behalf, at the instance of the tutor or curator, until he has rendered accounts of his intromissions with the ward's estate. In a word, until this is done he cannot insist in the *actio contraria tutelæ vel curatelæ*.

Antiqua et nova.—Old and new rights. The technical terms in our law equivalent to these Latin terms are, heritage and conquest; heritage (*antiqua*) being that estate to which any one succeeds as heir; conquest (*nova*) that which he succeeds to or acquires by purchase, gift, or any singular title. The distinction between heritage and conquest is now abolished, 37 & 38 Vict. cap. 94, § 37.

Antiquus et novus extentus.—Old and new extent. Extent is the name given to the ancient valuation put upon all lands in Scotland, for the purpose of regulating the proportion of public subsidies and taxes which each should bear, as well as for fixing the rights of a superior under his different casualties. It is conjectured by Lord Kames that the old extent is the value of lands ascertained about the year 1280, and that subsequently, the lands having been much deteriorated by the frequent wars of the period, several such valuations were made, which were designated the new extent. Under the old form of special service, one of the inquiries directed to be made by the brieve of inquest was, " *Quantum valent dict. terræ* NUNC *per annum et quantum valuerunt* TEMPORE PACIS ?" (*i.e.*, How much is the yearly value of the said lands now, and how much in time of peace?) "It was extremely natural to characterise the old extent by the phrase *tempore pacis*, not only as made in a peaceable reign, but also in opposition to the new extent, occasioned by the devastation of war." (Kames' Law Tracts.) The new extent, properly so called, was introduced by the statute 1474, cap. 55.

Apices juris non sunt jura.—The subtleties of law are not laws. This maxim (not much used in Scotland) is of frequent occurrence in the English law books, and there chiefly in reference to questions of pleading. It expresses the rule on which the Courts proceed in disallowing "curious and nice exceptions tending to the overthrow or delay of justice" (Broom, 188). Perhaps among the *apices juris* may be mentioned the former practice in our Courts of refusing to allow a pursuer to make amendments on his record after it had been closed; or to give him decree, in respect that the strictly legal ground on which he was entitled to succeed had not been formerly pleaded before the closing of the record; a practice now happily at an end, under the provisions of the Court of Session Act, 1868.

Apocha trium annorum.—Receipt (or discharge) for three years. Receipts granted by a creditor to his debtor for three consecutive termly or periodical payments raises the presumption that all such sums previously due have been discharged. It is not necessary that the receipts should be for annual payments; they may be for half-years or quarters, provided they are periodical payments. The presumption does not arise from the creditor *receiving* three termly payments, but from his granting written discharges therefor. Ersk. B. 3 T. 4, § 10; Bell's Prin. § 567.

Applicando singula singulis.—Literally by applying each to each; that is, to apply each special condition, provision, declaration, &c., as the case may be, to the particular subject to which it is referable. This is a well-known rule adopted in the construction of deeds—an instructive illustration of which will be found in the case of *Bontine,* 13 S. 905.

Approbans non reprobat.—One approbating cannot reprobate. See *Qui approbat, &c.;* and *Allegans contraria, &c.*

Apud acta.—Literally among the acts; in the course of procedure. This expression refers to orders judicially pronounced in open Court in presence of parties, and to which obedience must be paid without further notice or requirement. Thus, in a criminal process, the Court may adjourn the trial to a specified day, and this being intimated *apud acta* to witnesses, assizers, and parties, is sufficient to require their attendance without further citation. This mode of citing parties is not uncommon in the procedure before Church Courts.

Aquæductus.—The rural servitude of aqueduct, being a right to conduct water through the servient tenement by means of pipes, canals, &c.

Aquæhaustus.—Another rural servitude conferring right upon the dominant owner of watering his cattle at any stream, well, pond, &c., in the servient lands.

Argumentum ab inconvenienti plurimum valet in lege.
—An argument drawn from inconvenience has much force in law. In certain cases an argument *ab inconvenienti* has great weight; and such an argument generally arises in questions of

construction, either of a private writ or of an Act of Parliament. If in a private deed (as, for example, a deed of settlement) there be equivocal expressions, and great inconvenience must necessarily follow from the adoption of one construction of them, this will go far to show that such a construction is not according to the true intention or meaning of the granter, and will lead to the adoption of some other construction which will not be followed by such inconvenience. If, however, the words be plain and admit fairly of only one construction, that construction must be adopted, although resulting in inconvenience, because it is plainly the intention of the granter of the deed. In like manner in construing an Act of Parliament, if the language be equivocal, or its meaning doubtful, that construction of it will not readily be adopted, which would necessarily entail great inconvenience in carrying out the provisions of the Act: another construction, not attended with inconvenience, would be preferred. But, as in the case of a private deed, if the language of the statute has a necessary meaning, it must be construed accordingly, no matter what the inconvenience may be arising therefrom, because *a verbis legis non est recedendum.*

Arma in armatos sumere jura sinunt.—The laws permit arms to be used against the armed; or, to resist violence by violence. If anyone attempts by violence to disposses another of a subject in his possession, the possessor may use violence to *maintain* his possession, but not to *recover* that of which he has been so deprived.

Arrestum jurisdictionis fundandæ causa.—An arrestment used for the purpose of founding jurisdiction. The effect of this arrestment is to render the person against whom it has been used amenable to the jurisdiction of the Scotch Courts, but does not operate as an arrestment in security; nor can a jurisdiction be thus founded in questions of *status.*

Arrhæ.—Earnest or Arles. A small sum of money or other commodity delivered and received in token of the completion of a bargain. The practice of giving arles, formerly very common, is not now much observed.

Arrhæ sponsalitiæ.—A pledge or earnest given, under the Roman law, after betrothal, by the man to his betrothed, which he forfeited if he afterwards, without cause, declined to fulfil the engagement entered into. If the bride resiled from the engagement, she was, in the general case, obliged to return the pledge thus given, and as much more; but in certain cases she was merely bound to restore the pledge itself.

Assignatus utitur jure auctoris.—An assignee exercises the right of his cedent. The assignee not only becomes entitled to the right or subject assigned, but also to the actions at law by which the right may be enforced. In some cases such action must be specially assigned, as in the case of an assignation of a bill, on which diligence has been done, where, unless specially assigned, the diligence does not pass to the assignee, although at common law he may otherwise enforce payment. Exceptions competent to the debtor against the cedent are for the most part effectual against the assignee, although in the case of bills (which are peculiarly favoured), no exception pleadable against the original creditor, if merely personal and not inferring inherent nullity, can be maintained against an indorsee, if he become indorsee and holder before the date when the bill fell due. But any one taking a bill by indorsation, after the date when it became payable, is now "deemed to have taken the same subject to all objections or exceptions to which the said bill or note was subject in the hands of the indorser." 19 & 20 Vict. c. 60, § 16. The case of *The Scottish Widows' Fund* v. *Buist*, 3 R. 1078, will be found instructive on the subject of the principle set forth in this maxim.

Asyla.—Sanctuaries; places of refuge. Such, for example, as the Abbey at Holyrood Palace. The privilege of sanctuary, according to the law of Scotland, was merely a refuge from personal diligence on account of civil debt; but imprisonment for civil debt having been abolished (43 & 44 Vict. c. 34, and 45 & 46 Vict. c. 42), the privilege of sanctuary no longer exists. Under the Roman law *asyla* were chiefly founded for the purpose of protecting slaves from the severity of their masters, and they afforded protection also to any who had been guilty of minor delinquencies.

Auctor in rem suam.—One who acts for his own behoof. A tutor or curator cannot so act in reference to the estate of his ward, either by purchasing (except at public auction, Ersk. B. 1, T. 7, § 19) any part of the ward's estate, or by giving his consent to any deed granted by the minor, in which he, the curator, has a substantial interest.

Auctore prætore.—With the sanction of the Judge; at the sight of the Court.

Auctoritate judicis.—By judicial authority.

Avizandum.—To be looked into or considered. A process is said to be at avizandum when the judge, after debate, is considering it with the view of pronouncing a decision. When a Lord Ordinary transmits or reports a case to the Inner House, that parties may be heard, and decision pronounced there, he is said to make "great avizandum" with the cause.

Avulsio.—The violent separation of a portion of land by a torrent or inundation or any convulsion of nature, from the property to which it originally belonged, and the depositing of it on, or beside, the property of another proprietor. See *Alluvio*.

B

Baratriam committit qui propter pecuniam justitiam baractat.—He commits baratry who perverts justice for a bribe. This practice, although quite unknown in Scotland now, was at one time so general as to call for an Act for its suppression. By the Act 1540, cap. 104, it was provided that judges who, through wilfulness, corruption, or partial affection, used their authority as a cover for injustice or oppression, should be punished with the loss of honour, fame, and dignity. *Baratria* was also used to signify simony. It is so used in the Act 1427, cap. 107, where it denotes the crime of clergymen, who went abroad or exported money for the purpose of purchasing benefices from the see of Rome. But baratry is only used now to signify any illegal and fraudulent act on the part of the master and crew of a ship, to the prejudice of its owners. See *Crimen repetundarum*.

Bastardus non potest habere hæredem nisi de corpore suo legitime procreatum.—A bastard can have no heir except one lawfully begotten of his own body. A bastard is regarded by the law as *filius nullius*. "Not only has he no father, but no proof can give him a father; nothing can do that but marriage between his mother and his putative father" (*Corrie* v. *Adair*, 22 D. 900). A bastard, therefore, can have no relations in the collateral or ascendant degree, and his only possible heir-at-law is one procreated of his own body: and failing such heir, the estate of a bastard who dies intestate falls to the Crown. It has been the subject of controversy whether, in such a case, the estate falls to the Crown, as the bastard's heir, or as arising from escheat: but the right of the Crown has been settled to be that of an heir (Fraser, Par. & Ch. 121). As a bastard, however, has now the right to dispose of his property, heritable and moveable, as he pleases, he may so convey or bequeath it that others may succeed to him in the character of heir of provision or heir of tailzie. Prior to the Act 6 Will. IV. cap. 22, a bastard without lawful issue could not make a testament to the prejudice of the Crown's right. A bastard's widow is entitled to claim terce and *jus relictæ*.

Bellum inter duos.—A hostile meeting between two persons; a duel. If death ensues to either of the principals in a duel, however fairly the combat may have been conducted, the survivors and the seconds are held guilty of murder. By the Act 1696, cap. 35, it was enacted, that whatever person, principal or second, should give a challenge to fight a duel, or should accept a challenge, or otherwise engage therein, should be punished by banishment and escheat of moveables, although no fighting should ensue.

Benedicta est expositio quando res redimitur a destructione.—That exposition (or construction) is to be commended by which the matter is rescued from destruction. This maxim expresses a rule to be observed in the construction of deeds or contracts. When the writing is ambiguous and open to construction, that construction of it is to be preferred which will make it of avail, rather than that which, if adopted, would make it of no avail. The contract or writing having been executed presumably with the view of having some effect, no construction of it will readily be adopted which would result in making it a dead letter. The intention of parties will rather be sought for, and given effect to.

Beneficium.—The name at one time given to a feudal grant. Originally the grants of land made by the chiefs to their followers, as rewards for past services, and to ensure fidelity and future service, were called *munera*, and were revocable at the pleasure of the granter. In the seventh and eighth centuries, however, these became grants for life, and acquired the name of *beneficia;* and afterwards, when feudal rights had attained what Craig calls their manhood, they received the title of *feuda*, became descendible to heirs, and transmissible to collaterals deriving right from a vassal in the fee. "This last character was conferred by the Emperor Conrad in 1026, on the eve of an important military expedition, which shows that the spirit of conquest retained in fidelity by the original precarious grants had become so tamed down by the lapse of centuries as to require a boon which made those grants the absolute property of the vassals, to rouse it to sufficient exertion." (Duff's Feud. Con. 39.)

Beneficium cedendarum actionum.—The benefit or privilege of assigned actions. This was a benefit or right conferred upon a co-cautioner by the civil law, entitling him to demand from the creditor an assignation to the actions competent to him against the principal debtor in respect of the debt due, on payment thereof being made. Under the civil law, co-cautioners each became bound by *stipulatio* for the whole debt, and there was no obligation or ground of action on which they could operate reciprocal relief. This *beneficium* was introduced as an equitable remedy, whereby any one of the co-cautioners, having paid the debt, could demand an assignation to the creditor's action *ex stipulatu*, under which (suing rather in the character of creditor than as co-cautioner) he could compel his co-sureties to repay him the shares respectively due by them, or enforce payment of the whole from the principal debtor. This is not necessary under the Scotch law, where co-cautioners have right of relief at common law; but a cautioner making payment of the debt may require the creditor to assign his right to him, along with the documents or grounds of debt.

Beneficium competentiæ.—The benefit of a competence. This was also a benefit or right conferred by the civil law, under which the granter of a gratuitous obligation, whose circumstances had become embarrassed prior to its fulfilment, was entitled to decline such fulfilment, except to the extent of his ability to do so, after retaining what would be sufficient for his own maintenance. Thus, in an action at the instance of a wife against her husband for restitution of her dowry, the husband was entitled to plead this *beneficium*, and was only condemned to pay that which his means could afford. This plea was allowed in all cases between husband and wife, except where the claim made was grounded on delict; and also in cases where one brother sued another; but this privilege was personal, and did not avail heirs or sureties. The law of Scotland confers this privilege on fathers and grandfathers as against children and grandchildren, for the obvious reason that if the former were held bound to fulfil their obligations to the latter to the extent of depriving themselves of the means of livelihood, the children could take no benefit by such fulfilment, as they would then be liable for the support of their indigent parents. This privilege does not extend to the case of strangers, or to collateral relations, or even to the case of a brother against a sister. According to Erskine, a debtor who acquires any estate after having obtained the benefit of cessio, is entitled, as against his creditors, to retain out of such new acquisition " as much of it as is necessary for his own maintenance" (Ersk. B. 4, T. 3, § 27). But this doctrine is not supported by any reported decision ; on the contrary, it appears to be settled that in such a case a debtor is not entitled " to have any part of his effects set aside to him for his maintenance," *Reid* v. *Donaldson*, M. 1392. See also *Gassiot*, 12th November, 1814, F. C. and Bell's Com. ii. 483.

Beneficium divisionis.—The benefit of division. Under the old Roman law, co-cautioners were each liable to the creditor for the whole debt, it being in the power of the creditor to enforce payment of the whole from any one of the co-cautioners, whom he might choose to sue. But this privilege was introduced by a rescript of the Emperor Hadrian, by which the surety against whom the creditor sought an action, might require the Prætor, in granting one against him, not to grant it for the whole debt, but only for his portion, so as to compel the creditor to sue each of the sureties for their portions respectively. This is a privilege competent to a co-cautioner under the law of Scotland, where he has bound himself simply as a cautioner, along with another, for the principal debtor. If, however, the co-cautioners bind themselves, conjunctly and severally, for and with the principal debtor, the benefit of division is lost, and the creditor may recover the whole debt from any one of the co-obligants.

Beneficium inventarii.—The benefit of inventory. This is also borrowed from the civil law. By taking up a succession, the heir made himself liable for the whole obligations of the deceased ; but if he undertook the succession *cum beneficio inventarii*, he was only liable for such obligations to the extent of the deceased's estate. Justinian provided, however, that if an heir demanded a period for deliberation, he should forfeit his right to this *beneficium*. In Scotland the same privilege was conferred by the Act 1695, cap. 24, whereby an apparent heir, within a year and a day after his predecessor's death, was permitted to take up the succession on inventory, according to the practice in moveable succession. Decrees of special service, or of general service with specification, were declared by statute 31 & 32 Vict. cap. 101, §§ 47 and 49, to infer only a limited passive representation to the deceased, to the extent or value of the lands embraced by the service. By the Act 37 & 38 Vict. cap. 94, § 12, it is provided that an heir shall not be liable for the debts of his ancestor beyond the value of the estate to which he succeeds.

Beneficium ordinis.—The benefit of discussion. A right which formerly every cautioner had at common law to insist upon the creditor's using all proper diligence to recover the debt from the principal debtor, before claiming it under the cautionary obligation. This right was presumed to be reserved unless specially renounced by the cautioner; but by the Mercantile Law Amendment Act (19 & 20 Vict. cap. 60) this rule was altered, and the creditor is now entitled to proceed at once against the cautioner, unless the benefit of discussion has been specially reserved.

Benigne faciendæ sunt interpretationes ut res magis valeat quam pereat.—Liberal constructions are to be given, so that the matter (*i.e.* the deed or writing construed) may be made of avail rather than be destroyed. This is another rule of construction, which, although differently expressed, has the same meaning and effect as the maxim *Benedicta est*, &c.

Benignior sententia in verbis generalibus seu dubiis est preferenda.—Of general or doubtful words, the more liberal opinion or interpretation is to be preferred. Another rule of construction importing that when the words of the writing are vague, general, or doubtful, they are to be interpreted liberally, so as to give effect to the intention of the granter or parties to the deed. This and the preceding rules have especial application in the construction of wills, where the maker of the deed is no longer alive to state his intention in other and less doubtful words. As an example of the application of the present maxim, reference may be made to the case of *Scott* v. *Sceales*, 2 Macp. 613, where the expression of the testator's "consent" that a legatee should receive a certain subject was held to be equivalent to a bequest of that subject.

Billa vera.—A true bill ; the words endorsed by the grand jury in England on any bill of indictment, when they are of opinion that the evidence laid before them is sufficient to warrant a trial. If they entertain an opposite opinion, they formerly indorsed the word *ignoramus* (we are ignorant, or we ignore) upon the bill. They now use the words "no true bill," or "not found," which stops further proceedings, and procures the discharge of the suspected criminal.

Bona castrensia et quasi castrensia.—These were the goods which a filius-familias, under the Roman law, was entitled to bequeath by will, or otherwise dispose of without the consent of the pater-familias. Being under the power of his father, all property which he acquired, generally speaking, became the property of his father ; but, in course of time, the Emperors allowed sons to acquire certain goods of their own, which were called *peculia*. These were four in number. The *peculium profecticium* comprised everything derived by the son out of the estate of the father, but in this the father acquired the absolute property. The *peculium castrense*, being property acquired by the son on account of military service (thence deriving its name), as well as the *peculium quasi castrense*, comprising all presents from the Emperor, and everything acquired in the exercise of civil and ecclesiastical duties, were the absolute property of the son, of which he could dispose by will or otherwise. The *peculium adventicium* comprised everything coming to the son, except in the three ways already stated ; but this was subject to the management of the father, and of which he enjoyed the usufruct or liferent. On the father's death, but only then, this *peculium* became the absolute property of the son.

Bona fide perceptio et consumptio.—Gathering and consumption in good faith. Fruits gathered and consumed by a *bona fide* possessor, are regarded as his own : he is not bound to account for them, even although it should afterwards appear that he had no right to the possession held by him, and is evicted from the possession by the true owner.

Bona fide possessor facit fructus consumptos suos.—A possessor in good faith makes the fruits consumed his own. Where one holds a subject in the reasonable belief that it is his own, and gathers and consumes the fruits, he cannot be called upon to repeat or restore these fruits, on his being evicted from the subjects by one having a better title thereto. His *bona fides* protects him from such a claim, and the fruits so gathered and consumed are deemed the property of him who has gathered and consumed them. This equitable rule is said to be based "not only on the hardship of subjecting a person who has lived in the belief that the property was his own, to a claim for repetition of what he has drawn from it, but also on the negligence of the real proprietor, who has himself to blame for his delay to vindicate his property." (Bell's Dict., *h. v.*) The fruits consumed may either be the natural fruits of the earth, the rents paid by tenants, or the interest paid by debtors. But such fruits, to fall within the protection of the maxim, must be not merely gathered during the *bona fide* possession, but must also be fruits arising or falling due during that period. This distinction, at least, was drawn in the case of *Oliphant* v. *Smith*, M. 1721, where a *bona fide* possessor was held bound to repeat arrears of teind-duties received by him, which were due at the time when his possession commenced. What is sufficient to put an end to *bona fides* in the possessor is, in most cases, a question of circumstances. In some cases, where the defect of the possessor's title becomes at once apparent, the execution of the summons challenging its validity will be a sufficient interruption of the *bona fides*, while, in other cases, where the question of right is attended with difficulty, the interruption of *bona fides* will not be held to have taken place until decree has been pronounced. But *bona fides* always ends when the possessor becomes aware that his title is insufficient or invalid, however this knowledge has been acquired.

Bona fide possessor, in id tantum quod ad se pervenerit tenetur.—A possessor in good faith is only liable for that which he himself has obtained. He is a *bona fide* possessor who possesses a subject on a title which he honestly believes to be good; and so long as he possesses in that character the fruits he gathers and consumes cannot be claimed from him. Fruits not gathered, however, go, with the property, to the real owner. A possessor *in mala fide*, who knew, or might have known, that he had no right or title to the subjects, is not only liable to restore what he has actually gathered or received, but also all that which the subjects were capable of yielding, whether yielded or not, known in Scotland by the name of violent profits.

Bona fides.—Good faith.

Bona fides non patitur ut bis idem exigatur.—Good faith (honesty or fair dealing) does not allow the same thing to be exacted twice. An obligation once fulfilled, or a debt once paid, cannot be again enforced, provided the debt or obligation was paid or performed to the person having the title to demand performance or payment; accordingly it is a good defence to an action for payment of money, that the pursuer is not the creditor in the obligation, and cannot validly discharge it; for if payment was made to him, the real creditor might afterwards enforce payment, and thus the debtor might have to pay the same debt twice, which is contrary to fair and honest dealing. On the same principle, no one can be punished twice for the same delict or crime. But it will be borne in mind that a crime may give rise to two distinct obligations, the fulfilment of one of which will not discharge the other. For example, if A. commits an assault on B., he may be fined or imprisoned on account of it, and still be liable to B. in damages. The fine or imprisonment is paid or undergone *ad vindictam publicam*, while the damages are due to B. in his individual capacity for the injury or wrong done to him. In this case A. does not pay the same thing twice, but rather he once discharges the several obligations imposed upon him by his own act. There is an exception to this rule. Where A. murders B., and suffers the extreme penalty of the law for his offence, no claim for assythment can be made against his estate by the representatives of B. for the civil wrong they have suffered. But if A., after committing the offence, has fled and been fugitated, or if after condemnation his sentence has been commuted, or a pardon has been granted, the claim for assythment will lie against his estate.

Bona gratia.—Out of goodwill, voluntarily.

Bona vacantia.—The goods of persons dying without successors. Such goods become the property of the Crown, as *ultimus hæres*.

Boni judicis est ampliare jurisdictionem.—It is the duty of a judge to extend or amplify his jurisdiction ; is a literal translation of this maxim, but does not accurately express what the maxim is intended to state. In the first place, *jurisdictio* does not here mean what is generally understood by jurisdiction : it rather means justice or the administration of justice ; and accordingly Lord Mansfield once suggested that the proper reading of the maxim should be *justitiam* instead of *jurisdictionem* (1 Burrow, 304). To extend his jurisdiction in the ordinary sense of the term would be anything but the act or duty, of a good judge. But in administering the law it is the duty of the judge " to amplify its remedies, and, without usurping jurisdiction, to apply its rules to the advancement of substantial justice" (per Lord Abinger in *Russell* v. *Smyth*, 9 M. and W. 818) ; and this appears to be the true meaning and import of this maxim. To illustrate this maxim, reference may be made to the practice of our Courts, prior to the passing of the Act, 45 & 46 Vict. c. 61, to allow proof *prout de jure* that a bill, although bearing to have been granted for value, was not so granted in point of fact, where it was alleged that the bill was obtained through fraud, or that the holder of it obtained possession thereof in the knowledge that it was so obtained. The ordinary rule was that the allegation of want of value could only be proved by the writ or oath of the holder, but this rule gave way in the case supposed. The Courts in such a case amplified the legal remedies or rules, in order to get at the real facts and do substantial justice.

Bonorum possessor.—Possessor of goods. This name was given under the civil law to the person put in possession of the goods or estate of a deceased person by the Prætor. The proceeding before the Prætor under which the *bonorum possessio* was given was one more of equity than law. For example, if a man died intestate, whose child was precluded from being *hæres* by the civil law, on account of *capitis diminutio*, or otherwise, the Prætor overlooked the strict rule of law, and gave possession to the child; or, again, if the deceased left no heir, at least no relative which the civil law regarded as legal heir, the Prætor gave the possession of goods to relations, whom the law thus passed over.

Breve testatum.—The writing anciently delivered by a superior to his vassal, as an attestation of the fact that he, the superior, had conferred upon the vassal a grant of lands, and given possession of them. The *breve* was more the record of what had already taken place, than itself the grant; and was attested by the seals of the superior, and *pares curiæ*. At a later period the *breve testatum* was signed by the superior, wherever he happened to be, and possession was given separately by the superior's bailie.

Brevi manu.—Summarily, without a legal warrant. The expression is used to signify the performance of an act by a person on his own authority. Thus, a landlord, who ejects a tenant refusing to remove from the property when the legal term of his occupancy has ceased, without any warrant for such ejection, is said to act *brevi manu*. Such a power, by the older law of Scotland, was competent to the landlord; but it is not so now, and any such unwarranted proceeding would subject him in damages. Among the Romans, the phrase *brevi manu* was generally applied to a kind of constructive delivery. Thus, if a subject already pledged for debt, or deposited for security, was sold by the owner to the then holder of it, it was said to be transferred by *brevi manu* tradition. Delivery was essential to pass the property in the subject; but the act of delivery, in such a case, upon the new contract (that of sale), was dispensed with, or rather held to have been performed, to save the necessity of delivering up the subject to the owner, and again receiving it.

Brevitatis causa.—For the sake of brevity. A phrase used in law papers, where a document important to the cause is only referred to and not quoted. The reference has the effect of importing the document into the case, as completely as if it had been copied at length.

C

Cadit quæstio.—The question is at an end; the dispute falls to the ground.

Cæteris paribus.—Other things being equal; in similar circumstances.

Canon.—A yearly payment in return for a grant of land, as in feus; and under the Roman law, for the right of *emphyteusis*.

Canon emphyteuticus.—The yearly payment made by the *emphyteuta* for his lands. If such payment was in arrear for three years, the *emphyteuta* forfeited his right to the subject; he did so if the yearly duty was in arrear for two years, where the right was derived from the Church. A somewhat similar provision was introduced into the Scotch law by the Act 1597, cap. 246 (in some editions of the Scotch Act, cap. 250), whereby it was provided that all vassals by feu-farm, failing to pay their duty for two years, should lose their right, in the same way as if an irritant clause to that effect had been specially engrossed in their charter.

Capax doli.—Capable of wrong-doing; able to commit fraud. Under the feudal system, when the vassal was in minority, the superior exercised the right and enjoyed the casualty of ward, until (in male heirs) the vassal attained majority. The right of ward ceased sooner than this if the vassal committed treason, on which the lands fell by forfeiture to the Crown. Persons were considered capable of treason when they were "*capaces doli*, that is" (says Erskine), "according to the general opinion, at the age of sixteen." In our criminal courts, culprits are judged to be *capaces doli*, and are punished for their misdeeds long before they have attained that age. In the civil courts, also, the acts of children, even of tender years, have been considered and dealt with as being of material importance, and it may be convenient under this head to notice what has been laid down as law on the subject of a child's capacity to be guilty of fault or contributory negligence, so as to affect the civil claim for damages arising out of the accident or injury to which that fault or negligence has contributed. In the case of *Campbell* v. *Ord & Maddison*, 1 R. 149, damages were claimed for injury done to a child of four years of age, whose right hand had been crushed by a machine called an oil-cake crusher belonging to the defenders. The machine had been exhibited for sale, with several other agricultural implements, in an open market-place, where such exhibitions had been usual. The child who was injured and his brother (aged seven years) had been playing together about the machine, and having meddled with it, the injury was sustained. The defenders maintained that if the child had not wrongously meddled with the machine, no injury could have been sustained; and that as the child had himself occasioned the injury, or at all events materially contributed thereto, they were not liable. At the trial the defenders asked the presiding judge to direct the jury that the child was to be held in law as capable of contributing to the accident which resulted in the damage libelled; but this direction the judge refused to give. At advising a bill of exceptions, the Lord Justice-Clerk (Moncreiff) said that what he had been asked to lay down was "a proposition not of law but of fact. It would be as unsound to say as a proposition in law that this child was not capable of negligence as to say that he was. Negligence implies a capacity to apprehend the duty, obligation, or precaution neglected, and that depends to a large degree on the nature of that which is neglected, as well as on the intelligence and maturity of the person said to have neglected it. The capacity to neglect is a question of fact in the individual case, as much so as negligence itself, which is always a question of fact." With regard to the question whether the child did contribute to the accident, his Lordship said: "It is contended on one side that a child of this age could not be guilty of contributory negligence, on the other that his acts must be judged of without regard to his tender years. I do not agree with either proposition. This is a question of fact, to be decided on the evidence. There is no doubt that if the child had been a man the act would have amounted to contributory negligence. But he was not a man. It is said he must be dealt with as if he had been a man. He must in my opinion be held to be nothing but what he was." An entirely different view was taken in England, in the case of *Mangan* v. *Atterton*, L. R. 1 Exch. 239, the particular circumstances of which were strikingly similar to those in the case of *Campbell*—where the contributory negligence of a child of four years of age was held sufficient to absolve the defenders from the consequences of an accident. Some doubt has been thrown on the soundness of that decision, by Cockburn, C. J., in *Clarke* v. *Chambers*, L. R. 3, Q. B. Div. 339. It is difficult, however, to distinguish between the law laid down in *Mangan* v. *Atterton*, and that given effect to in *Abbot* v. *Macfie* and *Hughes* v. *Macfie*, 33 L. J. Exch. 177. The authority of the last-mentioned cases has never been questioned; and they appear to have been decided on similar grounds to those on which the Court of Session proceeded in the case of *Grant* v. *Caledonian Railway Company*, 9 Macp. 258. In that case the pursuer claimed damages on account of his child having been run over by a train and killed. The child, who was about six and a-half years of age, crossed the defenders' line of railway in full daylight, at a level crossing where the public crossed the line, but without observing that a train was coming. The Court held that the defenders were not liable in damages, the child having by her own rashness contributed to the accident. In giving judgment Lord Ardmillan said: "It is said that the little girl was between seven and eight years of age. Now, the fact that she was a young child is, in my opinion, of no importance. Either she was so young as not to be able to take care of herself, in which case she should not have been permitted to be there, and in that case the railway company are not liable; or she was, when accompanied by an elder brother, in a position to take care of herself; and if so, she was on an equal footing with other passengers crossing the line. We must deal with her just as if she was of full age." In the same case Lord Neaves observed: "I think that the death of this child was occasioned by such conduct as would be plainly rash and reckless in a grown-up person. In a legal point of view, such conduct on the part of a child must be regarded in the same light." The Lord President (Inglis) said: "I agree with your Lordships that the child must be dealt with in this case precisely as if she had been a grown-up person; and if there be recklessness on her part materially contributing to the accident, that will be a sufficient defence to the railway company." "If I could arrive at the conclusion that the railway company are more responsible for a child than for an adult, my decision might be different." It is difficult, to say the least, to reconcile the opinions in the case of *Campbell* with those in the case of *Grant*, but the law of Scotland is probably more in accordance with the decision in the latter case. The views expressed by the Lord Justice-Clerk in the case of *Campbell* appear, however, to have received some support from two of the judges who took part in the decision of the case of *Fraser* v. *Edinburgh Tramway Company*, 10 R. 264. See also the case of *Gibson* v. *Glasgow Police Commissioners*, 20 R. 466. The more important authorities bearing on this question will be found cited in the cases to which reference has now been made.

Capiendo securitatem pro duplicatione feudifirmæ.—By taking caution for the payment of a double of the feu-duty. This was a clause formerly inserted in precepts from Chancery for entering an heir, by which it was enjoined that caution should be taken for payment of a double of the feu in name of relief-duty, where this had not been expressly stipulated for in the investiture. It was at one time a question whether relief was exigible in feu-holdings, unless specially stipulated; and this clause was inserted to ensure the payment of relief to the Crown. "The casualty of relief is (now) payable by an heir, both in Crown holdings and in feus held of subject superiors, whether stipulated in the investiture or not" (Menzies' Lectures, 525).

Capitis diminutio.—A change or diminution of status. Three elements went to make up the status of a Roman citizen—viz., liberty, citizenship, and family. To lose the first, by being taken captive in war, or otherwise becoming a slave, involved the loss of the whole three; for a slave was not a citizen, and belonged to no family. This was therefore called the *maxima* (or greatest) *diminutio capitis*. The loss of the second, called the *media* (or lesser) *diminutio capitis*, took place when the rights of citizenship were withdrawn, or when a citizen was sent into exile; this involved the loss of the second and third but left the first untouched. The third was lost when a person changed his family, by adoption, adrogation, or otherwise, and as this did not affect his liberty or citizenship, it was called the *minima* (or least) *capitis diminutio*. It is not within the purpose of this work to explain how such loss might, in certain cases, be retrieved; or the civil effects of the different *diminutiones;* otherwise such explanations might have been entered upon, as being not without interest. The reader, however, may consult Just. Inst. B. 1, T. 16, and the Dig. B. 4, T. 5.

Cardo controversiæ.—The hinge of the controversy; the point on which the controversy turns.

Casus amissionis.—The occasion or circumstances of the loss. Where a writ has been lost or destroyed, its contents may be proved by an action brought before the Court of Session for that purpose, called an action for proving the tenor, a decree in which comes into the place of the lost document. Two points require to be proved in such action —namely, the particular accident by which, or the special circumstances under which, the document was lost or destroyed (termed technically the *casus amissionis*), and, the contents of the document; the nature and extent of the explanation and evidence necessary under the first point being somewhat different in different cases. If the lost document be, for example, a sasine, or other deed necessary to give a complete title to a purchaser, the Court will not require the same strict evidence as it would in a case where the lost document was a bill or bond, the obligation under which would be restored by the decree of proving the tenor. In the former case a more general statement of the *casus* would be received —it has been thought that to libel a mere *casus fortuitus* would be enough—but in the latter the evidence must be very explicit, because the document of debt might have been destroyed by the creditor with the view of discharging the obligation, which he subsequently attempted by this action to restore.

Casus fortuitus.—An accident. If an article is hired for a special purpose, and while being used for that purpose is deteriorated or destroyed, the lessor must bear the loss; but if the lessee uses it for another purpose, he becomes liable for any loss or deterioration, even when occasioned by accident.

Casus improvisus.—An unforeseen case; and therefore a case not provided for. This phrase is of frequent occurrence, and admits of varied illustration. Thus, if an Act of Parliament has been passed for the removal of some inconvenience, or the suppression of some evil, and specifies the circumstances or cases in which it is to have application, and a case occurs which is not specified by the Act, in which, nevertheless, the application of the Statute would be beneficial, this is a *casus improvisus*, and neither the procedure nor the provisions of the Act can be applied to it. The Statute cannot be strained so as to be made applicable to a case for which it does not provide. Statutes, however, which are purely remedial are construed liberally, and are often extended to cases similar to those mentioned in the Act, although such cases do not fall within the letter of the enactment. (*Robb v. School Board of Logiealmond,* 2 R. 422.) This is perhaps the most frequent sense in which the phrase is used, but it is equally applicable to many others. Thus in a clause of reference the parties may stipulate to have their differences settled by arbiters; but if a difference should arise between them which is not specified or held as included in the specification made, this is a *casus improvisus*, and such a difference must be settled by a court of law, the clause of reference not having provided for its settlement. An example of this will be found in the case of *Blaikie,* 13 D. 527, as reversed in the House of Lords, 1 Macq. 461. Again, it is usual in charter-parties to stipulate that if the ship is detained in loading or discharging beyond a certain number of days, demurrage shall be due at a certain rate per day. To recover the demurrage, the owners merely require to prove the detention. But if this clause were omitted, the owners of the vessel would have no claim for demurrage under the charter-party, however long the vessel was detained, that being a *casus improvisus*. Their claim would then resolve itself into a claim of damages for the wrongous or undue detention of their vessel, in which they would require to prove that the detention of the vessel had been unreasonable, and that the damage they had suffered thereby amounted to the sum claimed. When a *casus improvisus* occurs, it must be disposed of according to the rules of the common law.

Casus incogitati.—Circumstances unthought of, unprovided for. Where questions arise regarding which there is no rule of law, they are decided according to rules drawn by analogy, or on equitable grounds (Stair, B. 1, T. 1, § 6).

Casus insolitus.—An unusual circumstance or event.

Casus omissus et oblivioni datus dispositioni communis juris relinquitur.—A case omitted and forgotten is left to be disposed of according to the rules of the common law. On the subject of this maxim, reference is made to what has been said above (see *Casus improvisus*), and to what immediately follows.

Casus omissus pro omisso habendus est.—A case (or class of cases) omitted is to be held as (intentionally) omitted. This is a rule to be observed in the construction of statutes, and in considering whether they are applicable to certain cases analogous to the cases therein provided for. An illustration of this phrase will be found in Stair, B. 3, T. 2, § 49. See *Enumeratio unius*, &c.

Causa causans.—The immediate cause; that which directly produces the effect; as distinguished from the *causa causæ causantis*—a proximate but not an immediate cause. This distinction will be found taken by Lord Neaves in the case of *Moss* v. *Cunliffe*, &c., 2 R. 662. See *Causa proxima*, &c.

Causa cognita.—The case having been inquired into; the facts being ascertained. Some orders of Court are pronounced without any inquiry, others are only pronounced when the facts are before the judge. Formerly, inhibitions were not granted except *causa cognita* (although a different rule now prevails), because they imposed a restraint on the full exercise of the rights of property; and in our own time decrees of divorce or judicial separation are not granted, except on inquiry into the facts, and cause shown warranting such orders.

Causa data causa non secuta.—The consideration having failed. Where a sum of money has been paid in consideration of something to be done or procured by the receiver of it, it may be recovered on this ground, where the act is not performed, or the thing not procured, in consideration of which the payment was made. Thus, provision made, or money paid in contemplation of a marriage, must be restored if the event does not take place; or money paid in purchase of a certain subject can be recovered on this ground, if the seller fail in delivery.

Causa debendi.—The grounds of debt.

Causa et modus transferendi dominii.—The title and the manner of transferring property. The chief mode by which property in the possession of one person is acquired by another, is tradition or delivery. Tradition, to be effectual in passing the property, must contain two elements: it must contain the intention of the owner to convey, which is technically termed the *causa*, or the *titulus*, and the actual delivery, which is termed the *modus*. Without the first there could be no effectual tradition, because the owner had no intention of depriving himself of the property—he had given no valid consent: without the second, there was no passing of the property, according to the maxim *Qui cedit et retinet nihil agit.* With regard to the question whether delivery is now necessary in order to pass the property in moveables, see *Dans et retinens,* &c.

Causa proxima et non remota spectatur.—The near and not the remote cause is regarded. This maxim is frequently cited in reference to questions arising out of marine insurances, but the principle of it is not only quite applicable, but often applied in other cases. In reference to marine insurances, it is a well-settled rule that to entitle the policy-holder to recover, he must show that the loss for which he claims was a direct and not a remote consequence of some of the perils insured against; but if this is shown, it will not render his claim less valid that that particular peril was encountered in the endeavour to escape another not covered by the policy. Thus if a ship (the policy over which does not cover war risk) in endeavouring to escape capture by an enemy, runs ashore and becomes a wreck, the owners will be entitled to recover, the direct cause of loss being the stranding, which was covered by the insurance, although the remote cause was the endeavour to escape capture, which was not covered. On the other hand, if the ship was driven by stress of weather into a hostile port, and there seized and condemned as a prize, the owners could not recover for their loss, the proximate cause being the condemnation, which was not insured against, although the remote cause was one of those covered by the policy (*Livie* v. *Jansen*, 12 East, 648). So also under a marine policy covering the ordinary risks, including barratry of the master, but warranted free " from capture and seizure," where the vessel was seized in consequence of the barratrous act of the master the underwriters were held not liable for the loss or expense occasioned by the seizure—the loss having directly arisen from a cause excepted, although that again was the direct consequence of a cause covered by the policy (*Cory* v. *Burr*, L. R. 8, Q. B. Div. 313, Affd. L. R. 8, App. C. 393). Again, if a ship has been compelled to put into port to repair damage caused by the perils of the sea, and the master, in order to pay for the repairs, has sold part of his cargo, and applied the proceeds in paying for such repairs, the underwriter on the cargo will not be liable, as the direct cause of the sale was the necessity the master was under of providing funds for payment of the expenses of repairing, and not the perils which had rendered the repairs necessary (*Powell* v. *Gudgeon*, 5 M. & S. 431). But if a ship is damaged by the perils of the sea, and on putting into port for repairs it is found that the cargo has also been damaged, and the cargo as unfit for further transit is sold for the benefit of all concerned, the underwriter on the cargo will be liable for the loss, as one arising directly from the perils insured against. A very full explanation of this maxim, with illustrations of different cases in which it may be applied, will be found in the opinion delivered by Erle, C. J., in the case of *Ionides* v. *Universal Marine Insurance Co.*, 32 L. J. C. P. 170. The reader may also be referred to the case of *Montoya* v. *London Assurance Co.*, 20 L. J. Exch. 254 (where the cases upon this question are collected), and the decision in *Marsden*, L. R. 1 C. P. 232. See, further, some important observations on the application of this maxim in *Inman Steamship Co.* v. *Bischoff*, L. R. 7, App. 670. In ordinary claims for damage on account of injury, the rule of this maxim is also observed, although not with the same strictness as in the class of cases just considered ; and when the cause of damage libelled is too remote, the claim will not be sustained. See as an example of this the observations made by Martin, B., in the case of *Mangan* v. *Atterton*, L. R. 1 Exch. 240, and by Kelly, C. B., in *Bailiffs of Romney Marsh* v. *Trinity House*, L. R. 5 Exch. 208. Consequential damages are not, in the general case, allowed on the same principle—namely, that the cause of the damage averred is too remote from the consequence which ensued. The maxim is also applied in criminal cases. Where a person commits an assault upon another which results in death, it is no valid defence that the person assaulted was at the time labouring under a fatal disease which was only aggravated by the assault with the result of accelerating the death. The assault was the direct cause of the death at the time it happened, and that, not the more remote cause of the existing disease, will be regarded. But in an English case, where fireworks, kept by the prisoner in contravention of a statute, exploded through accident or the negligence of his servants, setting fire to an adjoining house, and thereby occasioning a person's death, it was held that the illegal act of the prisoner in keeping the fireworks was too remotely connected with the death to support an indictment for manslaughter (*Regina* v. *Bennet*, Bell C. C. 1).

Causa scientiæ.—Cause or means of knowledge. See *Ratio scientiæ*.

Cautio Muciana.—A kind of security given by legatees under the Roman law, deriving its name from its author. When a legacy was bequeathed, on condition that the legatee should abstain from doing some particular act, he received the legacy, on finding caution (the *cautio Muciana*) that he would observe and fulfil the condition, or failing which, that he would restore all that he had received, with its fruits or interest. Such a condition would have had the effect of suspending the vesting of the legacy until the legatee's death, because until then it could not be made certain that he would abstain from the specified act; and this *cautio* was introduced for the purpose of securing the fulfilment of the suspensive condition, and at same time allowing the legatee to derive some benefit from the legacy during his life.

Cautio usufructuaria.—The caution given by a usufructuary to the heir, that he would enjoy the subject without abusing or injuring it, and restore it at the expiration of the usufruct. A right of usufruct was something similar to the right known in our law as liferent, but there are some differences between the two rights; for example, a usufruct might be conferred for a certain number of months or years, or any time short of the life of the usufructuary, whereas a liferent, as its name implies, is a benefit conferred for the whole period of the liferenter's life; again, a usufruct was lost by the usufructuary undergoing the *maxima* or *media diminutio capitis*, while with us the loss of liberty or citizenship would not extinguish a liferent right.

Caveat emptor.—Let the buyer beware. Where a purchaser has himself seen and examined the subject of his purchase, he will not be entitled afterwards to repudiate the transaction on the ground of patent fault, unless he can prove fraud on the part of the seller; the purchaser being bound to satisfy himself, in the ordinary case, of the quality of the subject bought. If the defect be latent, and such as he could not have discovered by examination, the rule does not apply; nor, of course, does it apply where the buyer has not seen the subject, as in the case of purchase by sample. Further, this rule does not apply in the case of goods sold for a specified and particular purpose, for in that case there is an implied condition that the goods are fit for that purpose (56 & 57 Vict. cap. 71, § 14). See *Aliud est celare*, &c.

Census.—A subsidy or tax. This name was also given to the valuations of lands, made in Scotland at different times, with the view of ascertaining the proportion they should respectively bear of the taxes imposed, and for ascertaining the rights of superiors under their casualties. See *Antiquus et novus extentus*.

Certans de damno vitando.—Striving to avoid a loss.

Certans de lucro captando.—Striving to make a gain, or to obtain an advantage.

Certiorari.—An English writ, by which a cause is removed from an inferior to a superior court, equivalent to a Scotch advocation or appeal.

Certum an et quantum debeatur?—Is there a debt due at all, and what is its amount? These two things must be clear with regard to an alleged debt before it can be pleaded in compensation. In legal phraseology, the debt must be liquid before it can found such a plea. See the case of *Monro*, 2 S. 263, where the plea was repelled on the ground of its not being certain whether the defender was entitled to that on which the plea was founded; and the case of *Mowat*, 7 S. 88, where the extent of the claim not having been ascertained, the plea was also repelled. See Bell's Prin. §§ 573-4, and also *De liquido*, &c.

Certum est quod certum reddi potest.—That is certain which can be made certain. This may be illustrated by a reference to the law applicable to the contract of sale. It is essential to that contract that there shall be a certain price agreed upon for some specific subject, but it is not necessary that such price shall be fixed at the time by the parties. It is enough if that price can be made certain and definite by a reference to some determinate standard, by which it may be fixed beyond question, such as the fiars-prices, or the award of a third party; or the price may be sufficiently fixed by arranging it at so much per pound, the subject being unweighed, or so much per foot, the subject being unmeasured.

Cessante ratione legis cessat ipsa lex.—When the reason for a law ceases, the law itself ceases; or when the grounds or reasons which gave rise to a law cease to exist, the law itself ceases to exist. It is obvious that if the circumstances which rendered the passing of a law necessary cease to exist, the law itself will cease to be operative. But it can scarcely be said that the law ceases to exist, for if the same circumstances again emerge, the law does not need to be re-enacted, but may at once be put into force: unless in the meantime it should have been repealed, or have fallen into desuetude. The maxim must therefore be read in this limited sense,—

that when the necessity for the law has ceased, the law is for the time inoperative, just as if it did not exist at all. "For instance, a member of Parliament is privileged from arrest during the session, in order that he may discharge his public duties and the trust reposed in him; but the reason of this privilege ceases at a certain time after the termination of the parliamentary session because the public has then no longer an immediate interest in the personal freedom of the individuals composing the representative body' (Broom, 159). This maxim, if read literally, and in its widest signification, is erroneous and misleading.

Cessio bonorum.—A surrender of goods or estate. This is the name of a legal process well known in Scotland. Originally it was introduced as a remedy for the evils necessarily consequent upon a lengthened imprisonment, and could only be pursued by one in actual confinement; for (says Erskine), "it is in itself incongruous, and might be of bad example, that one should claim the privilege of personal liberty who is not truly deprived of it." It is not now necessary that a debtor shall have suffered imprisonment to entitle him to the benefit of this process, because imprisonment for civil debt has been abolished; it is enough that the debtor shall be notour bankrupt. Formerly a decree of cessio only protected the person of the debtor, and did not operate as a discharge of his debts, any property he acquired after the cessio being subject to the diligence of those who were creditors when the cessio was granted. This, however, has now, to some extent, been altered, and cessio, in its effects, assimilated to bankruptcy. Any creditor of a notour bankrupt may now sue a process of cessio against his debtor. The proceedings under this process are now regulated by the Act 6 & 7 Will. IV. c. 56, as altered and amended by 43 & 44 Vict. c. 34, and 44 & 45 Vict. c. 22.

Cessio fori.—The giving up business (Bell's Com. ii. 154). *Cedere foro*, to quit the market, was the equivalent of our expression to become bankrupt, to stop payment.

Chirographum.—A bond, bill, or other written document of debt.

Chirographum apud debitorem repertum presumitur solutum.—A bond, &c., found in possession of the debtor, is presumed to have been settled or discharged. "This presumption holds not only where the ground of debt is personal—*ex. gr.*, a bill or moveable bond, but in heritable bonds, even when they are perfected by seisin" (Ersk. B. 3, T. 4, § 5).

Chirographum non extans presumitur solutum.—A bond, &c., not existing is presumed to have been discharged. Where a creditor claims or sues on a written obligation which he cannot produce, the law presumes that the obligation has been discharged and the document of debt returned to the debtor, or otherwise that the creditor has destroyed the document of debt with the view of extinguishing the obligation. See the Lord Ordinary's note in the case of *Ryrie*, 2 D. 1214. The only mode in which the creditor can overcome this presumption is by a proving of the tenor, a decree in which will be equivalent to the original obligation. "This presumption strikes at the existence of the deed as a ground of obligation; but does not impair the subsistence of the debt on other and independent grounds" (Dickson, § 382). In the general case a creditor can always refer the subsistence of the debt claimed to the oath of his debtor.

Circum sacra.—About or concerning sacred things. The civil court has a certain jurisdiction in sacred (or rather, and more correctly, ecclesiastical) matters, as in questions of presentation by a patron; but it has no jurisdiction *in sacris*—*i.e.*, such questions as ecclesiastical discipline, or questions of doctrine. In such questions the church has supreme jurisdiction. See the case of *Lockhart*, 13 D. 1296.

Citra causæ cognitionem.—Without investigating the cause. Formerly all interdiction was judicial, and proceeded upon an investigation of the facts and on its necessity or expediency being made out to the satisfaction of the Court. No other kind of interdiction was allowed, but voluntary interdiction, without such investigation, was afterwards admitted.

Civilis ratio civilia jura corrumpere potest naturalia non vero utique.—Civil or legal rights, obligations, or laws, may be abrogated for a civil or legal reason, but never natural ones. Civil or legal rights are those founded on legal obligations which may be enforced by an action, while natural obligations are based upon the law of nature only, or arise from natural equity. The obligation of a father to support his children is a legal obligation, so long as the children are unable to support themselves; but that obligation is limited to what is necessary for support, *Maule*, 1 W. and S. 266; *Smith*, 13 R. 126. The obligation to provide children with an education suitable to their station in life, or to provide them with means to enable them to hold a social position consistent with the father's rank and fortune, is only a natural obligation which cannot be enforced. A child is under legal obligation in his turn to support his indigent parent; he is under natural obligation to reverence and obey them. A brother is under a natural obligation to support his brother or sister, where such support is needed; but there is no legal obligation binding a brother to do so. Modern scientific jurists repudiate the distinction between civil and natural obligations, holding that only to be an obligation which can be legally enforced.

Civiliter mortuus.—Civilly dead; dead to civil rights. An outlaw is said to be in this position. Further, if a husband is divorced by his wife, he is regarded as *civiliter mortuus* to the effect of entitling her to claim and recover all that she would have been entitled to under her marriage-contract, or otherwise through her marriage, in the event of his natural death. See the cases of *Johnstone-Beattie*, 5 Macp. 340, and *Harvey* v. *Farquhar*, 8 Macp. 971, aff. 10 Macp. (H. L.) 26. Where the spouses are each divorced at the instance of the other, they are held mutually to have forfeited all rights arising out of the marriage. *Fraser* v. *Walker*, 10 Macp. 837.

Civitas.—A state having power to make and enforce laws for the government of its subjects. This is the name also given in the civil law to the second of the three elements (citizenship) necessary to the complete status of a Roman citizen.

Civitatis amissio.—Loss of citizenship. See *Cap. diminutio.*

Clare constat.—It clearly appears. This is the name of a writ granted by a superior in favour of the heir of a deceased vassal, granting warrant for his infeftment and entry in the lands, deriving its name from the declaration with which it opens, that from authentic documents laid before the superior, it *clearly appears* that the grantee is the heir. A superior can grant such a writ in favour of no one but an heir, and the warrant it contains for infeftment is so purely personal that it cannot be assigned unexecuted. The superior may grant this precept upon his own knowledge of the heirship, or in his option may require production of a service to show this.

Clausula codicillaris.—A codicillary clause. Under the Roman law, wills or testaments, to be valid, required certain solemnities, which were not necessary to the validity of codicils, and it was, therefore, not unusual for the testator to add to his testament an express clause to the effect that if his testament should be held invalid as a testament, it should take effect as a codicil. This is what commentators call the codicillary clause. The chief difference between a testament and codicil was this, that in the latter an heir properly so called could not be nominated. For a historical narrative of the introduction of codicils, see Just. Inst. B. 2, T. 25, Pr.

Clausula tenoris.—The clause of the tenure. The name formerly given to the clause in a charter setting forth the nature of the tenure, now called the *tenendas*.

Clausulæ inconsuetæ semper inducunt suspicionem.— Unusual clauses always excite suspicion. This maxim does not admit of much being said by way of illustration. In *Todd* v. *Mackenzie*, 5th February, 1875 (not reported), a deed was sought to be reduced on the ground that the granter was facile, and that the defender, in whose favour the deed was granted, had taken advantage of that facility, and procured the deed by fraud or circumvention. The deed was a *de presenti* conveyance of the granter's whole heritable estate, burdened with the payment of some legacies. With regard to the legacies, a power was reserved to reduce or cancel them, but no power to increase them; and as regards the rest of the deed, it was declared irrevocable. The granter reserved his liferent of the lands, and also a power to feu; but this power was limited to the effect that in feuing the granter could only feu at a fair rate of annual feu-duty, and forbade him taking a grassum (or slump sum paid at once in place of a yearly feu-duty). The effect of this clause was to prevent the granter of the deed from burdening his estate beyond the extent of the specified legacies, or doing anything whereby the value of the estate could be lessened. It was put to the jury by the judge who presided at the trial, whether the deed was likely to have been executed by a man capable of managing his own affairs, or whether the peculiar and unusual terms of it (and especial reference was made to the clause giving power to feu) did not indicate the presence of some influence operating on the granter in such a way as to make the deed other than his spontaneous act. The unusual character of the deed and its clauses was put to the jury along with the other evidence adduced, as matter from which they might arrive at a conclusion on the question whether the defender had used fraud or circumvention in procuring the deed. The verdict was against the defender. While clauses unusual in themselves may excite suspicion, the appearance of a clause in itself usual, but in a part of the deed where such a clause is not usually placed, is not attended with the same result. In *Johnstone* v. *Coldstream*, 5 D. 1297, a husband executed a settlement in the body of which it appeared as his deed alone, and no mention was made of his wife as a consenter to it. The testing clause, however, bore that it had been subscribed by the granter, and also by his wife, " in token of her consent to and approval of this deed and all the clauses therein contained," &c. In a competition which arose between the relations of the husband and the wife, it was maintained on the part of the latter that they were not bound by the consent introduced in the testing clause, that no part of said settlement was the deed of the wife, and that she had not *habili modo* become a party to it. The Court held that the settlement hàd been validly and regularly executed by the wife as well as by the husband, and was probative in law as her deed.

Cogitationis pœnam nemo patitur.—No one suffers (or is punished) for his thought. No one is punished for thought or intention alone, unless it be followed up by some act: both act and intention are necessary to constitute an offence or crime. The act may not be successful—may be a mere attempt, but an attempt to commit crime is punishable: and as a general rule, when the act is criminal, the wicked intent is presumed from the act. The Act 36 Geo. III. c. 7, makes it treason "to compass, imagine, invent, devise, or intend death or destruction, or any bodily harm tending to death or destruction, maim or wounding, imprisonment or restraint of the person of the sovereign." But notwithstanding of the terms of this statute, the crime of treason is not committed unless the intention or device is accompanied or followed by some overt act. See *Actus non facit*, &c.

Cognitionis causa tantum.—For the purpose merely of ascertaining or constituting a debt against the estate, not against the person. This is the name given to an action raised by the creditor of a deceased debtor for the purpose of constituting his debt. Decree in such an action is necessary before the creditor can adjudge the heritage of his debtor, or compel his executor to make payment of the amount. It derives its name from the purpose which it is intended to effect—namely, to have the amount of the debt ascertained or cognosced.

Collatio bonorum.—Collation of goods. Collation is a provision of the Scotch law whereby an heir, on renouncing his right to the heritage of the deceased, and allowing it to form a part of the general estate, becomes entitled to an equal share of that estate with the next-of-kin. The heir cannot be compelled to collate, but when the heritable succession is small, and the moveable succession large, it is his interest, and he cannot be prevented from doing so. In collation, the heir is bound to give up whatever heritage he succeeds to through his ancestor; but where he succeeds to property as heir of provision, not being *alioqui successurus*, he can claim a share of the moveables without collating property so derived. Neither is the heir bound to collate presents given, or advances made to him by the deceased during life. Under the Roman law, the heir desiring to collate required to bring into hotchpot whatever he had received by gift out of the estate during the deceased's lifetime.

Collegium.—A corporate body, such as a guild of a trade; cities were also called *collegia* in the Roman law. Such corporate bodies, duly constituted, can acquire and administer property like individuals, and their endurance never ceases. In England there is a kind of corporation known as corporation-sole, of which the highest example is the sovereign, who is supposed never to die, *Rex nunquam moritur*. A corporation is sometimes termed an *universitas*.

Colonus partiarius.—A *colonus* was a farmer or husbandman holding his land as tenant for a money payment; a *colonus partiarius* was a tenant who, instead of money, paid in return to his landlord a certain stipulated proportion of the produce of the lands.

Comes.—An Earl; an ancient Crown officer holding territorial jurisdiction similar to that of a Sheriff.

Comitas legum.—Comity of laws; being that courtesy which the laws of one country show to the laws of another in questions in which the laws of either may be involved. This comity is not, however, extended to any case where the laws of the foreign country are contrary to the known policy, or prejudicial to the interests of the country in which the question arises and has to be decided. Still less will such comity be given effect to where the foreign law pleaded is opposed to the Statute law of the country where the question at issue is being decided. *The "Halley,"* L. R. 2 P. C. 293. *The "Leon,"* L. R. 6 Prob. Div. 148.

Commixtio.—Commixture. Property is sometimes acquired by accession, and commixtion is one of the forms in which it may be so acquired. Commixtion is the term properly applied to the commingling of solids, where the particles of the different substances do not amalgamate; confusion is the term applicable to the mixture of liquids.

Commodatum.—Commodate; a species of loan in which the identical thing lent is to be returned to the lender. It is called commodate, because it is *commodo datum*, given as a convenience or favour. See *Actio commodati. Mutuum*.

Commodatum æstimatum.—A valued commodate. In the ordinary case the borrower was not liable for the subject lent if it perished without his fault; it perished to the owner. But in *commodatum æstimatum*, a value was put on the subject, and the borrower, if unable to return the subject itself, was bound to pay the valued price.

Commodum ex injuria sua nemo habere debet.—No one should take advantage by his own wrongful act. *Injuria* includes any act that is illegal or wrongful. Accordingly, where one has obtained a deed in his favour by fraud or circumvention, the deed is set aside, and the grantee precluded from taking benefit under it, because it is the offspring of his own illegal act. In like manner, where a person has induced another wrongfully to enter into a contract, he cannot enforce the contract to which his fraud or other illegal act gave rise. Another illustration of the maxim may be found in the law of bankruptcy, which prevents a creditor taking any advantage from any illegal preference which he may have induced the bankrupt to grant. In some cases of illegal preference the creditor obtaining it is not only prevented taking any advantage thereby, but is punished for having entered into such a transaction. See *Carter* v. *M'Laren*, 8 Macp. 64, revd. 9 Macp. (H. L.) 49.

Commune forum.—The common forum; the Court having general jurisdiction, as, in Scotland, the Court of Session.

Communes reipublicæ (civitatis) sponsiones.—The obligations common to all the members of a State, and which constitute its laws.

Communi dividundo.—See *Actio com. div.*

Communia.—Commons, common muirs. These properties are generally the property of one person or corporation, in which many people have a right of servitude. This right of servitude differs from a right of commonty, inasmuch as the holder of the latter right has a title to sue for the division of the common subject, which the holder of a mere servitude has not. (*Gall*, 31st May, 1810, F. C.)

Communia precepta.—Common precepts or rules, which constitute the laws of a State, and are binding upon all its subjects.

Communibus annis.—On an average of years; taking one year with another.

Communio bonorum.—Community of goods. These words were formerly descriptive of the whole moveable estate belonging to a husband and wife at the time of their marriage or acquired during its subsistence, except the wife's *paraphernalia*. Of these goods the husband had during the marriage the uncontrolled administration—indeed of such goods he was the owner, the marriage operating in his favour as an assignation of the wife's whole moveable estate, except where otherwise provided by antenuptial contract. On his wife's death, the husband was bound to make over one-half of the goods in communion to her representatives until the passing of the Act 18 Vict. cap. 23, which declared that the representatives of a predeceasing wife should have no right to any share of such goods. Latterly it was questioned whether the law of Scotland recognised any communion of goods between husband and wife (*Fraser* v. *Walker*, 10 Macp. 837); and the reader will find a very able and instructive disquisition on this subject in Lord Fraser's work on Husband and Wife (i. 648 *et seq.*), who regards the term as "quite out of place in the legal nomenclature of Scotland." There is no such thing now as communion of goods between husband and wife in Scotland. The marriage no longer operates as a conveyance of the wife's moveable property in favour of the husband to any extent, for all property acquired by a wife before or during marriage remains her own as separate estate, not subject to the *jus mariti* or right of administration. The only restraint upon the wife's power over such estate is that she may not assign the prospective income thereof, or, unless with her husband's consent, dispose of it. On the other hand, a husband's liability for his wife's antenuptial debts is limited "to the value of any property which he shall have received from, through, or in right of his wife at, or before, or subsequent to the marriage;" and a husband now takes by operation of law "the same share and interest in her moveable estate which is taken by a widow in her deceased husband's moveable estate" (40 & 41 Vict. c. 29, and 44 & 45 Vict. c. 21). As to the husband's right to succeed to a part of his wife's estate, the last-mentioned Act has already been the subject of judicial construction, *Poë* v. *Paterson*, 10 R. 356.

Communis error.—Common or general error. When an erroneous practice has become general, and prevailed for a considerable period, and especially where the parties to some transaction have depended upon the prevailing practice as correct, the Court will not give effect to any objection or defence founded upon it as error. It is necessary, however, that the error be general and of long standing. See as an instance of this the case of *Beattie*, 8 S. 784.

Communis error facit jus.—Common error makes a rule or law. It has been seen under the preceding phrase, that inveterate practice, although erroneous, will be regarded as a sufficient answer to an objection founded upon the error, and that for the reason expressed in this maxim. The long-continued and general observance of what is erroneous, makes the error the rule. But beyond questions of practice this maxim cannot be extended. Erroneous views of the law, however widely held and acted upon, and even where indorsed by decisions, are no answer to the enforcement of the law when the error has been discovered and clearly ascertained; otherwise an error as to the law or a misconception of it would destroy the law (*Anderson* v. *M'Call*, 4 Macp. 765). In like manner, *communis error* and a long course of local irregularity, have been found to afford no protection to one who was answerable for skill in his profession. In the case of *O'Connell* v. *Regina*, 11 Cl. & F. 372, it was remarked by Lord Denman, in giving judgment in the House of Lords, that a large portion of the legal opinion which has passed current for law falls within the description of "law taken for granted," and that, "when in the pursuit of truth, we are obliged to investigate the grounds of the law, it is plain and has often been proved by recent experience, that the mere statement and restatement of a doctrine—the mere repetition of the *cantilena* of lawyers—cannot make it law, unless it can be traced to some competent authority, and if it be irreconcilable to some clear legal principle."

Communis patria.—The common country. Under the old diligence of apprising, directed against heritable rights, the messenger executing the diligence held his court in the head borough of the shire where the lands lay, but afterwards it became the practice to hold these courts in Edinburgh as *communis patria* to all Scotland.

Comparatio literarum.—A comparison of handwritings.

This is resorted to as a mode of proof where it is essential to the question at issue to ascertain whether a certain document is, or is not, in the handwriting of a certain person. Thus, in an action for libel, it would be admitted to show by the handwriting that the libel was written by the defender. It is also resorted to in cases of deeds sought to be reduced on the ground that the signature to the challenged deed is not the signature, or not the unaided signature of the party who bears to have subscribed it. This kind of proof was, formerly, most frequently adduced in cases of forgery, for the purpose of proving that the forged signature was not that of the person whose signature it bore to be : and to this effect such evidence used to receive great weight. It was not considered so conclusive when adduced to prove that the forged signature was the handwriting of the panel. Such evidence does not now receive much weight, if otherwise unsupported, in cases of forgery. It was found that any prisoner could get as many witnesses to express an opinion favourable to his case, as the prosecutor could adduce in support of his view, and the conflicting testimony so procured, while negativing itself, only led to difficulties which were rather to be avoided. Besides, as such evidence was at the best but a matter of individual opinion, it was not thought satisfactory on such slender ground to convict a prisoner of a charge involving consequences so serious. Accordingly, the evidence of engravers, &c., on this point is not now received, nor is any one's evidence received which is based on a mere comparison of letters. This is left to be judged of by the Court or the jury, along with the whole other circumstances of the case. In the case of *Forster* v. *Forster*, 7 Macp. 797, the pursuer sued for a declarator of marriage, founding upon a mutual and unequivocal declaration in writing by the parties accepting of each other as husband and wife. The defender denied that the declaration or the signature thereto was in his handwriting, and the first question came to be whether the writing was authentic. In giving judgment, Lord Ardmillan observed : " I leave altogether out of view the testimony of engravers, who were not previously acquainted with the writing of the defender, and spoke only to their opinion on comparison of handwriting. It has been for some years past the opinion and practice of the Court that evidence by comparison of writing given by persons not acquainted with the handwriting of the party is most unsatisfactory. I do not say that it is in all cases absolutely incompetent, but I am clearly of opinion that it cannot be relied on. If comparison of writing is to be considered as an element of proof, which I do not dispute, then it must either be comparison by those who know the handwriting of the party, or comparison by the Court according to the best of their judgment on personal examination. The testimony of engravers or men of skill, suggesting minute points for comparison or for distinction, is, in my opinion, not only an unsatisfactory, but a dangerous species of evidence. Accordingly, I leave it out of view." See also the cases of *Beveridge*, 3 Irvine, 625, and *Hamilton*, 8 Macp. 323. The law of England on this matter will be found in Taylor on Evidence, p. 1549, et seq.

Compensatio injuriarum.—The compensation of wrongs: or the plea of set-off on account of mutual injuries. Upon this subject, see "Smith on Reparation," p. 36; Bell's Dict. *h. v.*; and *Bertram* v. *Pace*, 12 R. 798.

Conatus.—An endeavour or attempt. The mere attempt to commit certain crimes is punished by our law, although not generally with the same severity, as if the crime attempted had been perpetrated. It more frequently takes the form of an aggravation of a charge, as where assault is libelled with intent, or attempting, to commit murder, in which case the attempt, if established by the acts or words of the panel, will have the effect of increasing the punishment for the assault. The administration of drugs with the intent to procure abortion is a statutory crime, and punishment follows, even though the attempt proved unsuccessful. Attempt to commit crime is to be distinguished from mere intention or purpose, concerning which see *Actus non facit*, &c., and *Cogitationis pœnam*, &c.

Concilium cum ope.—Counsel with aid: aiding and abetting. See *Ope et*, &c.

Concursus debiti et crediti.—A concourse or concurrence of debt and credit. This is necessary to found a plea of compensation, for the parties must be debtor and creditor, each in his own right and at the same time. Thus, If A sue B for payment of a debt due by him, B may plead in compensation a debt due to him by A, and here there is the necessary concurrence. But, if the firm of which A is a partner suing B for a debt due by him to them, be met by the plea of compensation by B, on the ground of a private debt due by A, the plea will not be sustained, for there is no *concursus*; a company being regarded by the law as a separate person. When, however, the company is dissolved, a debt due to it becomes the property of the partners as individuals, and to the extent of any partner's share may be compensated by a debt due by such partner to the company's debtor. *Mitchell*, 7 Macp. 480.

Condictio.—A personal action was so called in the Roman law, as opposed to the *vindicatio* or real action. This personal action arose from a *jus ad rem*, and could only be brought against the person underlying the obligation. Thus if the same subject had been sold to two different persons, each had a *jus ad rem*, and on its delivery to one of them, the other had an action personal against the seller for the value, but no claim against the other purchaser who held possession. A *vindicatio*, was for the recovery of the thing itself, arising from a *jus in re*, and was always directed against the holder of the subject. So, if anything was stolen, its property could be vindicated as against the holder, even if an onerous purchaser; and although a *condictio* was competent against the thief, the *vindicatio* could only be brought against the person in actual possession of the stolen property.

Condictio indebiti.—A personal action adopted by the Scotch from the Roman law, for repetition of that which has been paid under an erroneous belief of obligation. If in the belief that a debt is due, one person pays to another a sum of money, it may be recovered on showing that no such debt existed, and if there be no bar to the recovery, such as a natural obligation. It is necessary to distinguish between money paid through an error in fact, and an error in law. *Condictio indebiti* may be founded on the former, but (although it has been allowed in Scotland) it is scarcely thought can be founded on the latter. See the case of *Wilson*, decided in the House of Lords, 4 W. & S. 398; and the case of *Dickson*, 16 D. 586. Bell's Prin. § 534.

Condictio ob turpem causam.—A personal action for recovery of money paid on account of a dishonourable act. This action is mentioned by Erskine, but is scarcely otherwise known in our law. It will not lie at the instance of a person who was himself involved in the turpitude; for as turpitude bars action for implement of an obligation, so likewise does it bar action for restitution when implement has been made.

Conditio illicita habetur pro non adjecta.—An illegal condition is held as not added. Illegal conditions can only be dealt with in one or other of two ways: the condition itself disregarded, or the deed or contract to which it is attached entirely set aside. In the civil law impossible conditions (which included illegal conditions), if attached to a contract, had the effect of annulling the contract, while in wills or settlements such conditions did not annul the will, but were held in themselves *pro non scriptis*. The same distinction is followed in our law, of which some examples may be given. If a father by his will makes a certain provision in favour of a child, on condition that he or she will never marry, or that he or she will marry a particular person, this is regarded as an illegal condition, being a restraint upon marriage, and will not receive effect. The child will be entitled to the provision although he or she may have contravened the terms of the condition. In *Fraser* v. *Rose*, 11 D. 1467, a father having by his settlement made a provision in favour of his daughter beyond that to which she would have been entitled *ex lege*, added the condition that the daughter should forfeit the provision if she resided with her mother. This condition was held *pro non scripto*, and the daughter, in disregard of the condition, held entitled to the provision. It is not, however, an illegal condition to stipulate either in a marriage-contract or mutual settlement that a liferent to be enjoyed by the surviving spouse shall terminate on that spouse entering into a second marriage (*Kidd* v. *Kidd*, 2 Macp. 227). Nor does it seem to be illegal to make a legacy payable on condition that the legatee shall *not* marry a particular person (M'Laren, i. 589 ; *Forbes*, 9 R. 675). With regard to contracts, the rule, as has been already observed, is different; for if there be an impossible or illegal condition attached to a contract, the contract is thereby annulled. Thus a contract by which one binds himself to pay the grantee a sum of money on condition that the grantee brings about a particular marriage is void, it being considered contrary to public policy to permit marriage to be made the subject of mercenary speculation. A contract by which one binds himself generally not to practise a certain profession or carry on a particular trade is void, " whether with or without a consideration given for it, on the ground not only of injury to the one party by loss of livelihood and the subsistence of his family without a corresponding advantage to the other, but of injury to the public by depriving it of a useful member " (Bell's Com. i. 322). Such a contract, however, would be valid and binding, if the restraint thereby imposed, instead of being general, was limited to a certain trade or business in a particular place, an example of which will be found in the case of *Watson* v. *Neuffert*, 1 Macp. 1110. See also the cases of *Palmer*, L. R. 36, Ch. Div. 411 ; *Baker*, L. R. 39, Ch. Div. 520 ; *Natl. Prov. Bank*, L. R. 40, Ch. Div. 112.

Conditio si sine liberis decesserit.—The condition, if he (the testator) should have died childless. See *Si sine liberis*.

Conditiones præcedentes stricte interpretandæ sed non ita de subsequentibus.—Conditions precedent are strictly interpreted, but it is not so with conditions subsequent. Conditions precedent are those without fulfilment of which the contract of which they form a part is not binding or enforceable. Thus, if one sells to another for cash, payment of the price is a condition precedent, without fulfilment of which the purchaser cannot enforce his contract or demand delivery of the subject sold. Or, if a merchant purchases a cargo coming by a certain vessel, on condition that the vessel arrives on or before a specified date, that is a condition precedent, and he will not be bound to take delivery of the cargo if it only arrives after the time fixed. " In determining whether stipulations as to the *time* of performing a contract of sale are conditions precedent, the Court seeks simply to discover what the parties really intended, and if time appear, on a fair consideration of the language and circumstances, to be of the essence of the contract, stipulations in regard to it will be held conditions precedent" (Benjamin, p. 584). The rule is general and uniform that conditions precedent must be fully and strictly performed before the party on whom their fulfilment is incumbent can call on the other to fulfil his part of the contract. *Bowes* v. *Shand*, L. R. 2 App. 455. Conditions subsequent are of a different character, and do not prevent the contract taking immediate effect. Accordingly, if one sells to another for payment in three months, he cannot refuse delivery of the subject sold (the buyer being solvent), until he sees whether payment will be duly made; the purchaser is entitled to and may enforce immediate delivery. Or, again, if a merchant purchases a cargo coming by a certain vessel, without making any stipulation as to the time of the arrival, he cannot withhold payment (unless he so stipulate) until the vessel's arrival, but must make immediate payment, as he can cover his risk by insurance. This class of conditions is not strictly construed. For example, if in the case last supposed, the purchaser of the cargo bought it as the cargo in a certain vessel, "expected to arrive in the month of June," or "expected about the 15th of June," the non-arrival of the vessel for some time after the date specified would not free him from his obligation to take delivery, but the arrival of the vessel within a reasonable time thereafter would be sufficient fulfilment of the condition. On the other hand, if the arrival of the vessel "on the 15th June" was made a condition precedent, the purchaser would not be bound if the vessel did not arrive till the day after. In charter-parties it is frequently stipulated that the charterer shall be entitled to cancel the charter, if the vessel does not arrive at the port named on or before a certain date. In such a case, the arrival of the vessel on or before the specified date is a condition precedent.

Conductor.—Lessee. In a contract of hiring, the conductor is he who pays the stipulated consideration for the subject let.

Confessio facta in judicio omni probatione major est.— Judicial admission is stronger than any proof. This maxim holds good both as regards criminal and civil procedure. If in the former the panel confesses the crime with which he is charged, or in the latter, the defender admits the obligation which is sought to be enforced against him, such confession or admission is better than any proof which can be adduced, as it renders proof unnecessary. So important is the confession on the part of a criminal, that the law will not allow it to be used against him unless it has been made voluntarily. If it has been induced by threats or promises, such confession cannot be admitted against the prisoner. In regard to civil procedure, it may be noticed that if one party founds upon an admission made by his opponent, he must take that admission exactly as it is given. If the admission has been accompanied with explanation or qualification, these cannot be separated, so as to take advantage of the admission without its qualification. *Picken* v. *Arundale*, 10 Macp. 987 ; *Gelston* v. *Christie*, 2 R. 982. But the party founding on the qualified admission may disprove the qualification, and then found on the admission when freed from it. It only remains to be observed that there are some cases in which judicial admission does not dispense with the necessity for proof, as, for example, in actions for divorce on the ground of adultery, where the averments of the pursuer must be proved, whether admitted or not, to entitle the pursuer to decree. So, also, in actions of separation *a mensa et thoro*: in such cases decree can only be pronounced *causa cognita*, and not on the mere admission of the defender.

Confirmatio ad omissa vel male appretiata.—Confirmation by an executor to subjects omitted or undervalued in an inventory previously given up. See *Ad omissa*.

Confirmatio est nulla ubi donum præcedens est invalidum.—Confirmation is of no avail where the original gift or grant is invalid. There are some deeds, originally invalid, which may be rendered valid by the subsequent acts or deeds of the parties thereto, while some deeds do not admit of being so validated. Of the latter class (to which only this maxim refers) an example may be found in a conveyance of heritage wanting in some of the statutory solemnities. Such a deed is radically defective and null, and no subsequent deed or act confirmatory thereof will make that conveyance good or valid. Again, in the case of an illegal contract, the same rule holds. If one grants a bond obliging himself to pay to another a specified sum on the latter agreeing to withdraw his opposition to the discharge on composition under the Bankruptcy Act of the granter of the obligation, such a contract or obligation being a transaction of preference is *ab initio* invalid, and cannot be enforced. It will not make the grantee's claim any better, that he subsequently receive from the granter a bill for the amount of the preference, for that is equally invalid with the original bond. So much so, that if the grantee has endorsed such a bill to a *bona fide* indorser, who obtains payment of the amount of the bill from the granter, under diligence, the latter may recover the sum so paid from the original payee. *Arrol* v. *Montgomery*, 4 S. 499; *Macfarlane* v. *Nicoll*, 3 Macp. 237.

Confirmatio omnes supplet defectus licet id quod actum est ab initio non valuit.—Confirmation supplies all defects, although that which had been done was not originally of avail or valid. The distinction between this and the preceding maxim is this: the preceding maxim applies to writs which are from the commencement radically null and void, and which cannot be made valid or binding by subsequent acts or homologation; the present refers to such writs or deeds as are through defect rendered unavailing, so long as the defect continues, but which may be remedied and rendered binding by subsequent confirmation. In illustration of this latter class, take the case of an offer to purchase or sell heritage, with an acceptance following thereon, where neither the offer nor the acceptance is holograph or tested. Such offer and acceptance do not constitute a contract which can be made available or enforced by either party, as all contracts relative to the sale or purchase of land must be holograph or tested, and, in the words of the maxim, *id quod actum est non valet*. But if, following upon the defective offer and acceptance, and in consequence thereof, something material is done or allowed to be done, such subsequent acts as confirmatory of the defective bargain, are held sufficient to validate it *ab initio*. Thus, if the intending purchaser is put in possession of the subjects, or in the knowledge, and with the sanction of the seller, expends money in improving the subject, or commences to build on the land, or takes down existing buildings, all these are acts which would be held as confirmatory of the bargain, and would cure its original defect. See the case of *Gall* v. *Bird*, 17 D. 1027, where the distinction was drawn between the homologation of a deed which was null, and one which was merely reducible. This maxim finds farther illustration in the law relating to testamentary writings, which also require to be holograph or tested. A will or settlement which is neither holograph of the testator nor tested is of no avail, and will not receive effect : and if the testator dies without doing anything more, he will be regarded as having died intestate, and his estate will be distributed according to the laws regulating intestate succession. But if by a subsequent holograph writing the testator refers to and adopts the previously-executed settlement which was ineffectual, that, as a confirmation or homologation of the settlement, will confer upon it the privilege of a holograph document. One of the leading cases upon this subject is *Macintyre* v. *Macfarlane*, 1st March, 1821, F. C. For an example of what does not amount to such homologation or adoption, see the case of *Keith* v. *Maitland*, 10 Macp. 79.

Confusio.—Confusion ; a kind of specification, and properly applicable to the commingling of liquids. See *Commixtio*. Confusion is also one of the modes in which an obligation is extinguished. Thus, if a debtor succeeds to, or otherwise acquires the right of his creditor, his debt is extinguished *confusione*, because he then unites in his own person both debtor and creditor. Again, if the proprietor of the servient becomes also the proprietor of the dominant tenement, the servitude is extinguished *confusione*.

Conjectura pietatis.—A presumption or conclusion arising from natural duty : a conclusion or conjecture that something was done or intended to be done, on account of a natural duty to do it.

Conjunctio animorum.—The conjunct consent of parties, essential to the contract of marriage.

Conscientia illæsa.—Literally, an unhurt or unviolated conscience, but in legal phraseology, synonymous with *bona fides*.

Conscientia rei alienæ.—The knowledge that the subject possessed is the property of another. Such knowledge puts the actual possessor in *mala fide*, and renders him liable for violent profits; and it is immaterial whence this information has been derived. In the ordinary case, the possessor's knowledge is presumed to commence when the proprietor raises action to vindicate his right, for, by this measure, the possessor is called upon to consider carefully the nature and strength of the title on which he holds possession.

Conscius fraudis.—Aware of the fraud.

Consensus facit jus.—Consent makes law. This maxim must be read in the limited sense, that the parties have made that to be law for themselves to which they have consented, or by which they have agreed to be bound. The common law lays certain obligations on persons in certain circumstances, but these common law obligations as well as the corresponding rights may be increased or diminished according as the creditor and debtor therein may agree between themselves: and such rights and obligations will be enforced, according to the terms of the agreement or contract of the parties, no matter how much these may vary from what at common law they would have been, had no agreement been made. The parties thus, by their own consent, have made a law for themselves, which they are bound to observe. For example, a feuar is entitled at common law to vertical and lateral support for his feu and the buildings thereon, and may interdict his superior from working the minerals in the feu in such a manner as will deprive it of such support. But it is quite lawful for the superior, in giving the feu, to stipulate that he shall be entitled to work the minerals in the land feued, regardless altogether of the effect of such working on the feu, and if the feuar accepts his feu on such conditions, his common-law right to support is gone, the common-law right having been displaced by the consent of parties. (*Buchanan* v. *Andrews*, 9 Macp. 554; revd. H. L. 11 Macp. 13.) In Articles of Roup, Leases, and other deeds, it is quite usual to insert a clause of arbitration, by which the parties thereto agree to submit any differences that may arise between them to the final decision of an arbiter. Without such a clause these differences would have been determined by the ordinary courts of law, but the parties having by consent agreed to substitute another tribunal by which their differences are to be determined, such agreement excludes any appeal to the courts of law, nor can the decision of the arbiter be reviewed on the ground that he has taken an erroneous view either of the law or of the facts; for the parties by their submission have made the opinion of the arbiter the law by which their rights are to be determined. Again, the indorser of a bill is at common law bound for the amount contained in the bill to any subsequent indorsee: but if any one indorses a bill "without recourse," this is a stipulation on his part that he shall not be so liable, and any one taking the bill subsequently by indorsation is held to have consented or agreed to this stipulation, and cannot claim payment of the bill from him whose indorsation was so qualified. So also, under the contract of location, the conductor is not at common law liable for damage sustained by the subject let in the course of its use. Such damage falls to be borne by the owner. But parties may agree that such loss shall be borne by the conductor, in which case the consent and agreement of parties makes the law of their contract. Lastly, at common law a creditor is entitled to interest on his debt from the time when it is due and payment has been demanded; but he may consent that the loan or debt should not bear interest, in which case he cannot recover any. Just as the debtor may consent to pay interest on a loan or debt at the rate of twenty per cent., and will be liable for interest at that rate on account of his consent; whereas, if no such consent had been given, or no stipulation as to the amount of interest had been made, the creditor would not have recovered beyond five per cent. It is frequently said that parties may do anything by consent—which is just a popular mode of expressing this maxim—and so long as their consent or agreement is not to a contract or bargain in itself illegal, the agreement will be enforced, as that rule or law by which the parties have bound themselves.

Consensus in idem placitum et conventio.—Consent and bargain agreed upon touching the same thing. Some contracts are completed by consent alone, and these are called consensual contracts. To make the contract binding, however, the consent must have been freely given by one capable of consenting, and not induced by force, fraud, or fear. In addition to this, the consent must be *in idem*, for if there be any error or mistake in regard to this, the result is that there is no contract. For example, if one party intends to give something on loan to another in return for a certain sum as hire, and the other thinks or intends for that sum not to hire but to purchase the subject, there is no contract: the one party consenting to a contract of hire, while the other is consenting to a contract of sale, they are not consenting *in idem*. This is an error regarding the nature of the contract itself. But if both parties are agreed that it be a contract of sale, but are yet not agreeing about the same subject, or about the price, or any other essential of the contract, there is no bargain. "It is the essence of a contract that there should be a concurrence of intention between the parties as to the terms. It is an agreement, because they agree upon the terms, upon the subject-matter, the consideration and the promise" (*Davis* v. *Haycock*, L. R. 4 Exch. 381). The reader will find various cases illustrative of this cited in Benjamin on Sales, 41 *et seq.*

Consensus non concubitus facit matrimonium.—Consent, not sexual intercourse, constitutes marriage. Marriage by the law of Scotland, is a consensual contract, which may, like any other contract depending only upon consent for its constitution, be validly entered into and completed by the interchange of consent, without the addition of any religious or other ceremony. The consent must not merely be freely given, but must be given seriously, and with the intention of thereby entering into the contract of marriage. Mere idle or jesting words importing consent to marry are as ineffectual to constitute marriage as idle bargaining with a tradesman for his wares is ineffectual to constitute sale. The consent must be given by persons capable of consenting. So, a pupil cannot contract marriage any more than a person who is already married: the one being prevented by his nonage, the other by the impediment of an existing marriage. Bigamy is said to be the crime of marrying a second wife while the first is still alive; but this is merely popular language: a man who is already married cannot marry a second wife, although he may deceive a woman by a ceremony of marriage, and thus incur the penalties attached to bigamy. There are four modes in which, by the law of Scotland, marriage may be contracted—viz., (1) by the solemn interchange of consent *in facie ecclesiæ* after proclamation of banns, which is the only regular marriage; (2) by *de presenti* words of consent and acceptance of each other as husband and wife; (3) by cohabitation with habit and repute; and (4) by promise *subsequente copula*—the last three being called irregular marriages. In each case the marriage is constituted by consent, in the first and second the consent is expressed, and in the third and fourth is presumed from the actings of the parties. It has been stated on high authority that marriage is not constituted in either of the two ways last mentioned; and that in the latter case especially, the promise followed by *copula* constitutes only a binding pre-contract which requires a judicial sentence before it can become an actual marriage. On this subject the reader may consult the Report of the Royal Commission on the Laws of Marriage (1868), p. 19 *et seq.*, and Fraser, i. 172 *et seq.* The general current of opinion and authority, however, is in favour of the view that marriage is constituted in all the modes above enumerated. The case of marriage by promise *subsequente copula* is peculiar, however, and differs somewhat from the others. For although a promise to marry in the ordinary case only founds an action for damages in the event of its being unfulfilled, yet, where upon such promise there follows carnal intercourse, the law presumes the consent to marriage to have been then given. But it must be shown that the intercourse was dependent on the promise, and that in reliance on it alone the woman yielded her person. The promise must be absolute, and not dependent upon any contingent event, and such promise can be proved only by writ or oath. See a careful review of the whole cases on this point in the case of *Monteith*, 6 D. 934, and *Maloy* v. *Macadam*, 12 R. 431. The presence of witnesses to the contract, or interchange of consent, is not at all necessary to the constitution of the contract itself. The want of witnesses may render proof difficult or impossible, but if the interchange of consent is admitted, or proved by the writ or oath of party, the contract will be enforced as a completed contract, although there were no witnesses present when it was entered into. The complete constitution of the contract is in no way dependent upon subsequent intercourse. See the opinion of the Lord President in *Palmer* v. *Russell*, 10 Macp. 188. The principal difference between marriage and other consensual contracts is this, that in the case of all other consensual contracts, as they have been constituted by consent, so they may be dissolved or abandoned by consent: in marriage it is not so. Marriage can only be dissolved by death, or by decree of divorce pronounced by a competent tribunal.

Consensus tollit errorem.—Consent takes away (the effect of) error; or, the effect of erroneous proceeding. Prior to the passing of the Court of Session Act, 1868, an error in pleading, such as the omission of an important or material plea, was almost without remedy; a pursuer or defender could not succeed on a plea which he had omitted to state. But such an error could always be remedied by consent, as it can now by leave of the Court without consent under the provisions of the Act above mentioned. By the Act of 1850 (13 & 14 Vict. c. 36), a Lord Ordinary is required, in cases which are to be tried before himself and a jury during session, to fix a day for trial not later (except on special cause shown), than twenty-one days from the date of fixing. To fix a later day in the ordinary case would be an error; but any later day may be fixed by consent of parties, which takes away the effect of the error, and bars any objection to the regularity of the proceeding. Or, if in charging the jury, the presiding judge gives them a direction in law which is erroneous, but to which no exception is then taken, no exception can afterwards be admitted, as, however erroneous the direction, the parties not excepting will be held to have consented to take the direction as correct, for *qui tacet consentire videtur*. Again, an Englishman not subject to the jurisdiction of the Scotch Courts, is not bound to appear and discuss in Scotland a claim or question in an action raised against him there, and any decree obtained against him in such an action would be worthless on account of its having been pronounced in an action, erroneously raised in Scotland. But the Englishman may appear and defend such an action if he pleases, and his appearance, without objecting to the jurisdiction, would take away the effect of what would otherwise be a fatal irregularity. It must be observed, however, that consent has not always the effect ascribed to it in the maxim. For example, no consent of parties can confer on a judge the power of deciding in the Small-Debt Court a claim exceeding in amount the sum of £12, the statute having prescribed that amount as the limit of the judge's jurisdiction in that Court. But in matters regulated by the common law, and in questions of practice the rule stated in the maxim is applicable, and will have effect.

Consortium vitæ.—Cohabitation; a mutual obligation undertaken by the parties entering into a marriage to live together, which may be enforced by an action of adherence.

Constat de persona.—It is evident as to the person meant. A false designation will not always vitiate a writing where there is no doubt as to the person designed (*Muir*, 7 D. 1009). Such designation, however, must be merely expository, for in other circumstances the rule will not apply. See *Falsa demonstratio*, &c.

Constat de subjecto.—It is clear as to the subject-matter (of a deed or transaction).

Constructio legis non facit injuriam.—Legal construction inflicts no wrong. As the legal construction of an Act of Parliament, a deed, or contract, that is, the construction put upon it by the Courts of law, must always be regarded as right, at least till that construction has been set aside by a later judgment, or the decision of a superior Court, it is obvious that such construction can inflict a wrong on no one, as injury is only inflicted by an illegal or wrongous proceeding, not by mere error in judgment or opinion. Legal construction may often be injurious in the popular sense to a litigant, but that is not *injuria*.

Consuetudines feudorum.—A compilation made in the twelfth century of the various rules and customs by which all differences between vassals and their superiors were decided. The work is also known as the Book of the Feus.

Consuetudo debet esse certa, nam incerta pro nullis habetur.—Custom ought to be fixed (or settled), for if variable, it is held as of no account. In construing mercantile and other contracts, and determining the rights and obligations of parties arising from mercantile dealings, it is very important to keep in view the effect which the custom or usage of a particular place or a particular trade has upon such questions. To have any effect, however, the custom must be inveterate and uniform, and generally known in the particular trade, for if it be otherwise—if it be recent, and only occasional or local in its application, it cannot, as custom, be binding, unless specially brought before the notice of the contracting parties (*Kirchner* v. *Venus*, 12 M. P. C. 399; *Holman*, 5 R. 657). "The known and received usage of a particular trade or profession, and the established course of every mercantile or professional dealing, are considered to be tacitly annexed to the terms of every mercantile or professional contract made in the ordinary course of business in which the usage prevails, if there be no words therein expressly controlling or excluding the ordinary operation of the usage, and parole evidence thereof may consequently be brought in aid of the written instrument" (Addison on Contracts, 203). Accordingly, where it was the practice to compress bales of cotton by machinery to improve their stowage, a contract to load a full and complete cargo of cotton was held to imply that it should not be stowed in uncompressed bags (*Benson* v. *Schneider*, 7 Taunt. 272). Again, where an insurance was effected "to any port in the Baltic," evidence was admitted to show that the Gulf of Finland was considered by universal custom and consent amongst merchants and in mercantile contracts to be within the Baltic, although the two seas were treated as distinct by geographers (*Uhde* v. *Walters*, 3 Campb. 15). It must be kept in mind, however, that while proof of custom will be allowed to explain or add to a contract, it is inadmissible for the purpose of contradicting the written contract. As to the effect of custom on the construction of charter-parties, see Abbot, p. 210. Upon the whole question, reference may be made to Bell's Com. i. 456; Bell's Prin. § 83; *Anderson* v. *M'Call*, 4 Macp. 765; and Smith's Leading Cases, i. 606 *et seq.*

Consuetudo est optima legum interpres.—Custom or usage is the best interpreter of laws. A custom or usage following upon a statute is the best interpreter of what the statute was meant to enact, as showing what was regarded as the meaning and purpose of the statute among those by whom, or for whom, the Act was passed. In Scotland custom not only interprets laws, but can constitute or abrogate a law, for "as a posterior statute may repeal or derogate from a prior, so a posterior custom may repeal or derogate from a prior statute, even though that prior statute should contain a clause forbidding all usages which might tend to weaken it" (Ersk. B. I. T. 1, § 45, with Lord Ivory's notes, 11 and 12). Custom, to have this effect, must, however, be inveterate and uniform. See *Consuetudo debet*, &c.

Consuetudo loci est observanda.—The custom or usage of a place is to be observed. While a custom to be generally binding must be one of long standing, and generally known in a trade or country, yet a custom purely local may be binding on those in the locality. Thus in *Gardiner*, 6 S. 693, it was held that an uniform usage as to the mode of the election of magistrates, contrary to the terms of the set, must form the rule of election, and that a deviation from that usage was fatal to the election. Again, contracts of service were formerly affected by local usage. In some parts of the country servants were engaged by the old terms, and consequently their service did not commence or terminate at the ordinary terms of Whitsunday and Martinmas, but was regulated by local usage. This, however, has been altered by the Act 53 & 54 Vict. cap. 36.

Consuetudo pro lege servatur.—Custom is observed as law. All law (not being statute law) is founded upon custom, and obtains thus the name of consuetudinary or common law.

Contemporanea expositio est optima et fortissima in lege.—A contemporaneous exposition (or construction) is regarded in law as the best and strongest (most prevailing). The view which was taken at the time an Act of Parliament was passed, as to its meaning, or the construction which was then or soon after put upon its provisions, by those acquainted with the circumstances which called for the enactment or made it expedient, is more likely to be correct (where a difference of opinion arises) than the construction put upon it long after by those who can only gather its purpose from the terms in which it is expressed. A contemporaneous exposition is therefore always preferred to a later one. "Great regard ought, in construing a statute, to be paid to the construction which the sages of the law who lived about the time or soon after it was made put upon it, because they were best able to judge of the intention of the makers at the time when the law was made" (Coke, 2 Inst. 11, 136, 181). So, also, in construing old deeds and writings, care must be taken to expound their words according to the meaning which the words bore at the time when they were used, and not according to what these words have come to mean in later times.

Contra bonos mores.—Against morality. All contracts or obligations which are given for an immoral consideration, or which arise out of an immoral transaction, are ineffectual, and cannot be enforced. Thus a bond given for payment of the wages of prostitution, or as an inducement to commence or continue improper intercourse, cannot be enforced; but a bond given after the immoral intercourse has ceased, as a reparation or compensation for injury done, will be sustained (*Johnstone*, 14 S. 106). A bond or bill granted for money lost or won at gambling, betting, &c., cannot be enforced against the granter by the grantee; but if the granter has paid the amount to the grantee, he cannot claim repetition (*Paterson*, 4 Macp. 602). On the other hand, if the granter has been obliged to pay the amount to an onerous holder of the bond or bill, he is entitled to recover the amount so paid from the original grantee, the distinction being that in the latter case the payment was not voluntary on the part of the granter (Bell's Prin. § 36, 4). In like manner bonds granted in consideration of the grantee bringing about a certain marriage are regarded as *contra bonos mores*, and cannot be enforced. According to the civil law, the sale by an heir of his hope of succession during his ancestor's life (which was termed the *pactum corvinum*) was *contra bonos mores*, and ineffectual; but it is not so regarded in the law of Scotland, under which a *spes successionis* may quite legally be made the subject of sale. On the subject of immoral contracts, see Bell's Prin. § 37, and cases there cited.

Contra executionem.—Against execution. All decrees are granted with an implied reservation in favour of the defender of all objections competent to him against the manner and extent of execution to follow upon them.

Contra fidem tabularum nuptialium.—Against the good faith of the marriage-contract. An antenuptial marriage-contract is regarded by our law as an onerous deed, the terms of which cannot be altered or infringed except with the consent of the parties thereby interested. Provisions in favour of the husband or wife may be altered, reduced, or altogether renounced by the spouse in whose favour such provisions have been conceived (except perhaps in the case of an alimentary liferent secured by a trust, *Duthie's Trs.*, 5 R. 858; *Hughes*, 19 R. (H. L.) 35): and the same may be said of provisions in favour of children, provided the children at the time of the alteration or renunciation are capable of legally consenting. But without such consent the parents cannot effectually interfere with the provisions in favour of children, and any deed executed by them having the effect of diminishing or restricting such provisions is reducible: and such provisions are protected from the diligence of creditors against the parents. Where the provisions in favour of children are made quite fixed and specific, both as regards extent and character, few questions arise as to the effect of such provisions, the distinct terms of the marriage-contract making it plain what the child is entitled to demand. But it is quite usual to have in such deeds a power of apportionment reserved to the spouses, and upon the exercise of such power many nice and difficult questions have been raised. To make this matter clear, suppose that the parents by their marriage-contract bind themselves to provide a certain sum for their children, to be divided equally among them, or otherwise according to a certain rule, or in a fixed proportion, with the declaration that it shall be competent to the spouses by their joint deed, or by the deed of the survivor, to give and determine what each child shall receive; this is called the power of apportionment or of appointment. When such power is exercised, it must, in order to be effectual, be exercised in strict conformity with the terms of the clause conferring it. If the power is to be exercised by the spouses jointly, neither of them can exercise it separately; it must be by their joint deed. Where, as is generally the case, the provision is in favour of "children of the marriage," an appointment which confers any right upon grandchildren is invalid, because it confers benefit upon persons who were not objects of the power (Sugden on Powers, p. 664). So also where the original provision is to "pay and divide" among the children, it is not within the power of the parents to limit the right of a child to a liferent giving the fee to his or her children. The terms of a clause such as we have been dealing with are always strictly construed, and any exercise of the power thereby conferred jealously regarded. The effect of an invalid appointment, is to throw the whole fund for division back upon the terms of the marriage-contract as if no appointment had been attempted: and if the marriage-contract makes no provision for the distribution of the fund, the children will take equally. Although the parents may not go beyond the power conferred upon them, nor do that which the clause has not authorised, yet they may validly exercise the power in part. Thus the parents may by deed of appointment validly allot and apportion a certain sum as the share of the provided fund which is to fall to their child A, without making any allotment in favour of B, C, and D: in which case A takes the portion allotted to him, while B, C, and D will take their shares either according to the terms of the marriage-contract, or equally, if the marriage-contract has made no provision for distribution failing allotment (*Anstruther's Trs.*, H. L. 10 Macp. 39). But if the parents proceed by one deed to exercise their power with reference to the whole fund, and that deed is held in part to be a bad appointment, the whole deed is thereby vitiated, and the fund falls to be divided as if no appointment whatever had been made, for the reason "that you cannot tell what appointment the party intrusted with the power would have made had he known that what he attempted to do was to some extent at least inept" (*per* Lord Curriehill in *Baikie's Trs.* v. *Oxley*, 24 D. 589). The whole question as to the exercise of power of appointment, and the invalidity of a partial appointment, was discussed in the case of *M'Donald's Trs.*, 1 R. 794 (reversed H. L. 2 R. 125), where the leading authorities, both in the English and Scotch law, on the subject will be found cited.

Contra hereditatem jacentem.—Against a succession which the heir has not taken up. A creditor of the deceased is so entitled to proceed. When an heir takes up a succession devolving upon him, he renders himself liable for his ancestor's debts to the extent of the value of the succession; but in the event of his not doing so, the law provides a mode (by adjudication, &c.) by which the creditor may proceed against the estate of his deceased debtor for payment of his debt.

Contra libertatem matrimonii. — Against freedom of marriage. According to the law of Scotland, marriage ought to be free, and restraints put on marriage are regarded as illegal and null. Accordingly, if a father leaves his daughter a provision on the condition that she will never marry, or on condition that she marries a certain person, the condition is ineffectual, and the daughter will be entitled to her provision, and the condition will be disregarded. See *Matrimonia debent*, &c.

Contra non producta.—Against things not produced. In actions of reduction the defenders are called upon to produce the challenged document, that it may be reduced and cancelled, and an order is always pronounced upon the defender to do this, or, as it is technically called, to satisfy production. If he fails to do so, decree of certification *contra non producta* passes against him, the effect of which is that the challenged deed is held to be void.

Contra non valentem agere non currit præscriptio.—Prescription does not run against one who is not able to act in defence of his rights. Prescription (and any loss arising therefrom) is considered as the penalty of negligence, and therefore it does not run against a minor or pupil, nor against an insane person, nor one who is prevented from claiming or defending his rights by imprisonment abroad. But mere absence abroad for business or pleasure does not bar the currency of prescription; nor does the absence of an outlaw, for an outlaw has lost all his legal privileges by his outlawry. This maxim is properly applicable to the long prescription, for it has no application in the shorter prescriptions, such as the triennial prescription of debts or sexennial prescription of bills. The term prescription is used by modern jurists in a general sense, so as to apply either where by lapse of time the former owner's right is extinguished and transferred to the possessor, or where it merely bars the remedy of the former owner against the possessor. As to the distinction between prescription and limitation, see Bell's Prin. § 586 et seq. See *Anni utiles.*

Contra omnes mortales.—Against all mortals; the form in which absolute warrandice is sometimes expressed. There are three kinds of personal warrandice—viz., absolute, from fact and deed, and simple. Absolute warrandice is when the seller of the subject warrants it to the purchaser "at all hands and against all mortals," or " against all deadly as law will," and under this he is liable to the purchaser if eviction takes place from any cause whatever. Warrandice from fact and deed is a warranty given merely against the acts of the seller, either past or future, and he is only liable in the event of eviction on account of something done by himself. Simple warrandice only regards the future acts of the seller, and means that the seller will do nothing in prejudice of his conveyance to the purchaser; but this kind of warrandice is now almost unknown in practice. The short clause, "I grant warrandice," now common in conveyances of land, was first introduced by the Act 10 & 11 Vict. c. 48, and was then declared, unless specially qualified, " to imply absolute warrandice as regards the lands, and writs and evidents, and warrandice from fact and deed as regards the rents." That Act was repealed by the Act 31 & 32 Vict. c. 101, by which, however, the provision as to the import of the short clauses was re-enacted.

Contra pietatem.—Contrary to natural duty. *Pietas* is generally used to denote filial duty.

Contra proferentem.—Against the person from whom it proceeds (as in the case of a deed); or against the person advancing it (as in the case of a plea). See *Ambiguum placitum*, &c.

Contra spolium.—Against the spoil. Things spuilzied, that is, moveable goods stolen from a person, or otherwise illegally removed from his possession against his will, can be recovered by him wherever he may find them, even if that should be in the hands of a *bona fide* purchaser. The owner has not only a personal action for damages against the person who deprived him of the possession, but a real action for recovery of the thing itself. This latter is the action *contra spolium*.

Contractus bonæ fidei, et strictijuris.—Contracts of good faith and of strict law. Such a distinction was drawn between contracts by the Roman law, but it is a distinction scarcely regarded by the law of Scotland. Contracts of good faith were those in which the extent of each party's obligation was determined by equity and good faith; in contracts of strict law, the obligations of parties were determined by the strict terms of the agreement. In Scotland, while contracts will be decided upon according to their terms, yet these terms always receive a fair and equitable construction.

Contrectatæ.—Things meddled with; as by a thief, who feloniously intermeddles with the property of another.

Contrectatio rei alienæ, animo furandi, est furtum.— Meddling with (to the effect of removing) the property of another, with the intention of stealing it, is theft. Theft is generally defined as the felonious taking and appropriation of property without the consent of the person to whom it belongs, or in whose possession it is. But the act of theft may be completed without any appropriation; for, as stated in the maxim, if one meddles with the property of another with felonious intention, that of itself is theft. Thus, if the till of a shop be taken out of the counter, the theft of the till and its contents is fully accomplished, although the thief may not appropriate any of the money or remove it from the shop. So, also, if the thief has put his hand in at a window, and either with his fingers or a stick has drawn articles towards him from where they were lying, that constitutes theft. The meddling, however, must have amounted to removal of the subject, however slight. See Macdonald, *voce* "Theft." Hume, i. 70 *et seq.*

Contributio lucri et damni.—Distribution of, or sharing in, profit and loss. Spoken of as a test of partnership. Bell's Com. ii. 544. But sharing in the profits of a business does not necessarily imply partnership (28 & 29 Vict. c. 86).

Conventio privatorum non potest publico juri derogare.—A private agreement cannot derogate from public law. Laws which have been enacted for the protection or benefit of the people generally cannot be set aside or derogated from by the agreement of private individuals, for otherwise the public laws would be in danger of being rendered inoperative whenever it appeared to private individuals to be for their advantage to make them so. To illustrate this, take the case of a forged bill. The person whose name has been forged may submit to the wrong done to him, may adopt the forgery so as to make himself liable for the amount, and may agree with the forger never to question the authenticity of the bill. But no agreement of this kind will free the forger from the pains which the law attaches to the crime he has committed: and the public law, passed to protect the public from forgeries, will be enforced on proof of the crime having been committed. Again, in the ordinary case, a proprietor of land may either use it himself or let it on lease to another, for any purpose, and on any terms which may be agreed. But if under such lease the tenant proceeds to erect works, or carry on a trade which falls within the legal definition of nuisance, the public law, passed for the protection of the public health, will be enforced, and the nuisance suppressed, notwithstanding of the private agreement between the landlord and the tenant that the subjects let should be used for that particular purpose. Whatever laws exist under which the public, as public, take rights, advantage, or interest, can only be derogated from by the public voice, expressed by an Act of Parliament repealing the law, the continuance of which is no longer desired. In Scotland it is still theoretically held that laws may be repealed by such immemorial custom contrary thereto as sufficiently indicates the will of the community to alter the law; but practically the mode in which laws are repealed or altered is the same in all parts of Great Britain.

Conviciandi animo.—With the intention of reviling, or insulting, or bringing into contempt. Hume, i. 350.

Copulatio verborum indicat acceptationem in eodem sensu.—The coupling of words shows that they are to be understood in the same sense. Where an expression, or a phrase, or even single words, occurring in a deed are ambiguous, or their meaning obscure, the meaning and intention of the maker of the deed may be ascertained by looking at the same words or expression elsewhere used in the same deed, where the meaning attached to them is clear and free of ambiguity, their conjunction or juxtaposition leading to the inference that the words or expression were intended to bear the same interpretation. Thus in *Adam* v. *Farquharson*, 2 D. 1162, which was an action for the purpose of setting aside an entail, the question was whether the resolutive clause struck at a contravention of the restrictions, as distinguished from the conditions, of the entail. The Court repelled the reasons of reduction and assoilzied the defender, on the ground that in the deed of entail the terms "condition" and "restriction" were indiscriminately used, and that the general words "condition and provision of the entail" covered also what might more correctly have been designated "restriction." In the ordinary case these terms have a very distinct and different signification. A condition of the entail is that which, as proprietor, the heir of entail would not be bound to do except for the condition, such as bearing the arms and name of the entailer; while a restriction restrains the heir from doing that which, as proprietor, he would be entitled to do except for the restriction, as, for example, burdening the estate with debt or selling it. But in the case referred to, the coupling and indiscriminate use of the terms led the Court to hold that the entailer meant the term condition to include restriction, and they decided the case accordingly. So also, in a clause of arbitration which contains a reference of disputes between the parties relative to certain particular matters specified, and also submits generally all disputes between the parties, the general clause being thus coupled with a particular, it is a settled rule of law that the general clause only embraces matters which are *ejusdem generis* with the particulars enumerated. "The express enumeration of certain particulars affords a distinct indication of the class of subjects which were actually present to the mind of the parties at the time of their agreeing to submit. There is a strong presumption, therefore, that the general clause was truly intended only to include any matters of a similar class which might have been omitted in the special enumeration." Bell, 66.

Coram non judice.—Before one who is not a competent judge; which is in effect the same as if the question had not been brought before a judge at all.

Corpus delicti.—"In the criminal law of Scotland, the *corpus delicti* is the substance or body of the crime or offence charged, with the various circumstances attending its commission, as specified in the libel." Bell's Dict. *h.v.*

Correi credendi.—Joint creditors. When a bill or bond is granted in favour of two or more persons, or where two or more succeed to the right of some obligation, as, for example, heirs-portioners, they have each a right to a share. The debt cannot be sued for, or discharged, or assigned by any one of them, although each of them may adopt either of these measures as regards his own proportion. This last statement must, however, be read subject to some limitation. Where the right is conferred by a contract under which the whole creditors have a *pro indiviso* claim, the whole creditors must concur (or their interest at least be represented) in any action or proceeding adopted for the purpose of enforcing the right. Thus, for example, the whole of the owners of a ship have a *pro indiviso* right in the profits earned by the ship, or in any claim arising from charter-party or other contract of affreightment, and it is not competent to any one of them to sue on the contract, apart from the others, for his own share (Abbott, p. 69). In the case of *Scotland* v. *Walkinshaw*, 9 S. 25, a part-owner sued for demurrage alleged to be due for detention of the ship; but the general rule was applied that a part-owner cannot *per se* insist in an action for debts due to the whole owners, and the action was dismissed. In that action, however, the pursuer (being only a part owner) sued originally for the whole of the damage due, although he afterwards restricted the conclusions of his summons to one-half of the sum claimed; and therefore the decision scarcely went the length of settling that a part-owner might not competently sue for his own share of a claim of demurrage. Another specialty in that case also was that there was nothing in the circumstances of the co-owner which prevented his concurrence being obtained to the action. In the case of *Robinson* v. *Breysig* (December, 1871, not reported), a part-owner sued for the proportion of a claim of demurrage effeiring to the extent of his ownership, and the defender pleaded, on the authority of *Scotland's* case, that the action could not be sustained without the concurrence of the other owner. The pursuer explained that his co-owner was then insane and incapable of giving authority to sue for his proportion, or of concurring in the action, and that no curator or guardian had been appointed to look after his affairs. In these circumstances the Lord Ordinary (Jerviswoode) repelled the defender's plea, in which judgment the defender acquiesced. This rule, requiring all the owners of a ship to concur in claims for freight or demurrage (see *Andersen* v. *Harboe*, 10 Macp. 217), seems to rest rather on the inequity which would be involved in compelling the defender to state the same defences several times, which would be necessary if each owner sued separately for his share, than upon any radical want of right in each owner so to sue. (A shipmaster may always sue for freight, but he cannot sue in his own name for demurrage unless it has been mentioned in the bill of lading. Maude & Pollock, i. 413.) A distinction has been drawn between the cases where the claim sought to be enforced arises upon contract, or upon delict or fault. Accordingly, in *Lawson* v. *Leith and Newcastle Steam-Packet Co.*, 13 D. 175, it was held that a part-owner of a ship was entitled to pursue in his own name for recovery of his share of the value of the vessel, and of the damage occasioned by her loss through the fault of the defenders. Where there are several creditors in the same obligation, a full right to sue, discharge, or assign the claim, may of course be vested by agreement in each of the co-creditors.

Correi debendi.—Co-obligants for a debt. Under the

Roman law the co-obligant was entitled to the privileges of a cautioner, except where the obligation was for the delivery of a special subject. He could adject conditions to his obligation which were binding upon the stipulator if accepted. In Scotland, if one person binds himself, not as cautioner, but as principal debtor and co-obligant with another, he forfeits the rights of a cautioner, except as in a question between him and the person for whom he became bound. As regards the creditor, the co-obligant stands in the same position as the principal debtor.

Crassa negligentia.—Gross negligence.

Creditor dominii.—The creditor of the subject; the person having the right of property in it. In commodate the lender is creditor of the subject, and on the bankruptcy of the borrower may vindicate his right of property and recover the subject itself, whereas in *mutuum* the lender is merely a personal creditor of the borrower, and is only entitled to rank with his other creditors, and obtain a dividend on the value of the subject lent.

Crimen dolo contrahitur.—Crime is contracted (or committed) through dole. Dole, which is the evil or felonious intention, is essential to crime, and where this is wanting there can be no crime and no punishment. To destroy life is not murder where it has been accidental or unintentional; nor is the mere occupancy of a neighbour's goods theft, unless there be felonious intent. Dole is presumed in a greater or less extent from the circumstances of each particular act. See *Actus non facit*, &c.

Crimen falsi.—The crime of falsehood; a generic term including several crimes known to our law, which consist in falsehood, or fraudulent imitation, or suppression of the truth to the prejudice of another. Under this class may be ranked forgery, falsehood, fraud and wilful imposition, perjury, conspiracy, use of false weights and measures, &c. Under the Roman law, such crimes as fell within this class were punished by loss of citizenship, which was regarded by it as capital punishment; some of them were punished capitally by the law of Scotland until recently.

Crimen majestatis.—Crime committed against the crown; **treason.**

Crimen repetundarum.—The crime of taking money unjustly for an unjust purpose when in office. Under the Roman law, all judges and magistrates who accepted bribes to pervert judgment, or the due administration of justice, were said to be guilty of this crime ; the punishment of which was generally banishment, but was sometimes, according to the circumstances, more severe. In Scotland the offence is known as baratry or bribery. See *Baratriam*, &c.

Crimina extraordinaria.—Extraordinary crimes. This name was given, in the Roman law, to those acts done in violation of a law to which no fixed penalty was annexed, the penalty or punishment being in the discretion of the judge. Although in Scotland there is no class of crimes bearing this name, there are acts of a similar character visited by penalties, and regarded as crimes. Such, for example, are breaches of interdict and sequestration.

Crimina morte extinguuntur.—Crimes are extinguished by the death of the criminal. His death will not, however, extinguish them *ad civilem effectum*, for any claim thence arising will transmit in most cases against his heirs. See *Actio personalis*, &c., and *Actio pœnalis*, &c.

Cui licet quod majus non debet quod minus est non licere.—He who may lawfully do the greater (or more important) act, is not debarred from doing the less. This maxim finds its most frequent application in cases involving questions as to principal and agent. Where an agent is intrusted with a general power or mandate to carry on either any business or negotiations on behalf of his principal, such mandate is held to cover all the acts necessary for the accomplishment of the purpose for which the mandate was granted. Mercantile mandates are held to be extended, restrained, or qualified according to the settled rules and usage of trade. A law-agent authorised to do diligence for the recovery of a debt, has thereby authority to receive payment of the debt and discharge it. As to whether he has thereby an implied authority to grant the debtor delay, see *Cameron* v. *Mortimer*, 10 Macp. 461.

Cuicunque aliquis quid concedit, concedere videtur et id sine quo res ipsa esse non potuit.—He who makes a grant in favour of another appears also to grant that without which the grant itself would be unavailing. To make a grant and yet refuse that without which the grant could not be made effectual, would be simply to reduce the grant to a nullity; and as it could never be supposed that a grant was made except for some purpose, or to confer some right, all that is essential to the exercise or use of the subject of the grant is presumed to have been given along with the grant itself. This principle was applied in the case of *Bald, &c., v. Alloa Colliery Co., &c.*, 16 D. 870, where the facts were shortly these: The Earl of Mar as proprietor feued certain lands to which the pursuers acquired right by purchase. In the feu-right the minerals were reserved by the superior, and they were subsequently leased by him to the defenders, who in the course of working them materially injured the buildings on the lands belonging to the pursuers. The pursuers claimed damages for the injury so done, and the defence was that as the minerals were reserved, so was the power of working them, and that the pursuers could not claim damages for injury arising from the lawful acts of the defenders. That defence was repelled on the ground that with the grant of the feu there was also an implied grant of support, without which the grant of the feu itself would be rendered unavailing. A similar point was decided in the case of *Caledonian Railway Co. v. Sprot* (H. L.), 2 Macq. 449, where the defender, having conveyed certain lands to the railway company for the purpose of the railway, reserving the minerals, raised an action to have it declared that he was entitled to work the minerals so reserved. This was resisted by the company on the ground that the working of the minerals as proposed would injure the railway, and that under the conveyance from Mr. Sprot they were legally entitled to necessary support. The House of Lords gave judgment in favour of the railway company, on the ground that the pursuer's proposed operations would be a derogation from his own grant, and that the grant would be unavailing unless the necessary support to the railway was given. So also in the case of the *Clarence Railway Co. v. Great North of England Railway Co.*, 14 L. J. Exch. 137, it was held that where an Act of Parliament empowered a railway company to cross the line of another company by means of a bridge, the first-mentioned company had consequently the right of placing temporary scaffolding on the land belonging to the latter so far as that was necessary for the purpose of constructing the bridge. A private riparian proprietor who lets his fishings in a river to a tenant, is held to confer on the tenant a right of access to his grounds and the use of the bank so far as is necessary to enable him to exercise his right. In like manner a right to water cattle at a certain place, or to take water from a certain reservoir, implies the right of access to the water, which is necessary to the exercise or enjoyment of the right. "If you grant anything, you are presumed to grant to the extent of your power that also without which the thing granted cannot be enjoyed." Per Sir J. T. Coleridge in the case of *Lord,* 12 M. P. C. 499.

Cuilibet in sua arte perito est credendum.—Credit is to be given to any one skilled in his own art or profession; that is, weight or consideration is to be given to the evidence of one skilled in his own art or profession concerning things falling within or connected with that profession. The general rule undoubtedly is that witnesses are called to speak to facts and not to give opinions; but that rule is subject to exceptions, one of which is expressed in the present maxim. When the question at issue involves matters of scientific knowledge, witnesses are admitted to speak to matters of opinion. Thus in criminal trials medical witnesses are frequently asked whether in their opinion a blow from a certain weapon or instrument would produce the injuries they had observed; and in civil trials involving questions of sanity, medical witnesses are in like manner asked whether, assuming certain acts, or a certain course of conduct, the person committing these acts was in their opinion of sound mind. As to the value of the kind of evidence last mentioned, reference may be made to the observations of the Lord Justice-Clerk (Inglis) in *Morrison* v. *Maclean's Trs.,* 24 D. 631. Thus, also, artists and picture-dealers may be asked as to the value, in their opinion, of a certain picture (*M'Lellan,* 5 D. 1032); or whether in their opinion it is genuine—that is, the work of the master whose work it is represented to be. So, upon a question of sea-worthiness, experienced shipwrights are admissible to prove whether in their opinion a ship in a state in which the one in question was sworn to be on a certain day during the voyage, could have been sea-worthy when she sailed (Taylor, 1194, and cases cited). Chemists also are admitted to state their opinion as to whether certain chemical substances discharged from a manufactory into a stream could have the effect of polluting the stream, so as to render the water unfit for domestic or other purposes. The same principle is applied where the courts of our country have occasion to ascertain what is the law of another country on a particular question, and remit a case for the opinion of foreign counsel: the opinion thus obtained being regarded as conclusive of the question. See *Schultz*, 24 D. 120, which was a question under the laws of shipping, and *Goetze*, 2 R. 150, which was a question in bankruptcy. Formerly in cases involving a question as to the authenticity of handwriting, engravers were admitted to state whether in their opinion it was authentic, but of late this evidence has not been received with favour, and has been in some cases entirely rejected. See *Comparatio literarum*.

Cuique licet juri pro se introducto renunciare.—Every one may renounce a right conceived in his own favour. Parents cannot deprive children of rights conferred on them by the marriage-contract, but the children may validly discharge or renounce their rights. Any creditor in an obligation may renounce his right and relieve the obligant, and that whether the right is one conferred by the common law, or by private agreement or contract. As was seen in reference to a preceding maxim (*Cuicunque aliquis*, &c.), a feuar or purchaser of land is entitled at common law to the right of support; but the reader will find an instance of what was held to be a renunciation of that right in the case of *Buchanan*, 11 Macp. (H. L.) 13. A liferenter whose right has been declared strictly alimentary and not assignable may renounce his right in the sense of declining to take any benefit under the provision made in his favour, although he cannot assign it or disburden the estate over which it is made a charge. *White's Trustees* v. *Whyte*, 4 R. 786; *Hughes*, 19 R. (H. L.) 35. See *Invito beneficium*, &c.

Cujus contrarium est verum.—The contrary of which is the truth.

Cujus est commodum ejus debet esse periculum.—He who reaps the advantage should bear the risk. On this principle the risk of a subject purchased, but still in the hands of the seller, formerly lay with the purchaser. As he reaped any advantage to be derived from the subject, either by accretion or otherwise, so he had to bear the risk of loss through deterioration or accident, *Hansen* v. *Craig & Rose*, 21 D. 432. See *Periculum rei venditæ*, &c. This principle was not, however, of universal application, for in commodate, the borrower, who has all the advantage, bears none of the risk attendant upon the subject. Its deterioration, or accidental loss, falls upon the lender, the owner of the subject, according to the maxim *Res perit suo domino*.

Cujus est dare, ejus est disponere, or (as it is sometimes written) **ordinare.**—He who can give, can also dispose or regulate. The import of this maxim is, that one who is the full and unrestricted proprietor of a subject, and can give it away as he pleases, may attach what conditions to the grant, or regulate its descent or distribution, as he thinks fit. Thus the proprietor of a landed estate may give it to his heir or to a stranger : he may make such conditions in reference to the subsequent succession as he pleases : or may burden it with legacies, annuities, &c. A landlord may let his land to a tenant, under such conditions as to cropping, &c., as he thinks best. Such conditions being a part of the grant, must be observed, and may be enforced by any one having interest, provided, of course, the conditions are legal : for illegal conditions are null. It must be kept in view, however, that this maxim only applies to cases where the granter has not only the power to give, but has the unlimited power of giving and regulating. An example of a case which does not fall within the maxim may tend to make its application clearer. Suppose the case of a power of appointment given to a parent under a marriage-settlement or other deed, whereby he is authorised to apportion a certain fund among certain persons in such proportion as he pleases : in such a case the parent has undoubtedly the power *to give*, but he cannot give to any one not an object of the power, and he cannot adject to his gift or distribution conditions which are not authorised by the power under which he is acting. He is not the unrestricted proprietor of the subject, although he has the power of distributing or giving it away to certain persons. In *Churchill* (L. R. 5 Eq. 44), a parent who had power to apportion a fund among his children, by deed appointed a certain sum to each, but directed that the liferent thereof alone should be paid to the children, and the fee held in trust for their issue. This was held to be an ineffectual condition as not authorised by the power: and the allotment to the children held good as if no such condition had been adjected. This case proceeded on the authority of several decisions, the leading case being *Carver* v. *Bowles*, 2 R. & M. 301.

Cujus est dominium ejus est periculum.—The risk lies upon the owner of the subject. In commodate, in deposit, in pledge, in location, and other contracts, the risk lies with the owner, who bears the loss accidentally occasioned, or any deterioration arising from accident or ordinary use. Injury done to the subject, through the fault of the person in actual possession, must be made good to the owner; for such injury is not one of the risks which he runs, he being entitled to rely on the care and ordinary skill of the actual possessor. This is now the rule of law with regard to the risk attaching to goods sold but not delivered, 56 & 57 Vict. cap. 71, § 20.

Cujus est instituere ejus est abrogare.—He who institutes or ordains can abrogate. In a general sense this maxim holds good, but it is not of universal application: there are cases in which the person from whom a right proceeds cannot recall the right conferred, and where he cannot abrogate that which he has once settled or determined. To take the exceptions first: parents who have by marriage-settlement conferred upon the children of the marriage certain rights cannot, either separately or together, abrogate what they have thus done, so as to lessen the children's rights: nor can any one who has made a gift of his estate to another by a delivered deed, recall or alter that gift at will. Without multiplying instances, it may be stated generally that this maxim does not apply in those cases, where, by the thing settled or ordained, a *jus quæsitum* is conferred upon a third party. On the other hand, consensual contracts may be abandoned or altered by the consent of those who made them, except in the case of marriage, where society has an interest in seeing that such contracts are not dissolved merely of consent. An Act of Parliament may be repealed by the same power as that which enacted it, that is, by the will of the people: in England, however, that will must be expressed by an Act of Parliament, while in Scotland it may be expressed by lengthened contrary usage. A testator may at any time alter the terms and provisions of his will, even when the will has been published, or delivered, because a will is ambulatory, and can have no effect and confer no right until the testator's death. In the case of *Waterston*, 1 R. 470, it was decided that the granter of a cheque was entitled to countermand it, and that on notice of such countermand, the bank upon which it was drawn was entitled to refuse payment upon presentment. On this subject, however, the reader should compare *Waterston's* case with *The Clydesdale Bank* v. *M'Lean*, 10 R. 719.

Cujus est solum, ejus est usque ad cœlum.—He who is proprietor of land is proprietor also of everything on it. All buildings, all natural fruits, and everything above as well as below the surface, belong to the owner of the land. See *A cœlo*, &c.

Cujus hæredibus maxime prospicitur.—Whose heirs are chiefly regarded. This is a rule of construction to be attended to in ascertaining from the terms of a destination, in whom the fee of a property is vested, the ordinary rule being, that he is the fiar whose heirs are preferred. Thus, a conveyance to "A and B jointly, and the heirs of B," gives A merely a joint right of liferent, and gives B the fee. Under such a destination, B is so absolutely the fiar that his rights cannot be impaired by any acts, even onerous, of A, who is held, as we have said, to be a liferenter. In construing destinations to husband and wife, this rule must be applied with care, or rather, care must be taken in ascertaining from the terms used, according to their technical signification, whose heirs are preferred; for if the heirs of either be preferred in a manner inconsistent with any doubt, then the rule may be as surely applied in the case of such deeds as in any other. But where a husband, for example, dispones his own property to himself and to his wife in conjunct fee and liferent, and their heirs in fee, the husband remains sole fiar, and his wife has merely a liferent, "their heirs" being understood as the husband's heirs only. Under a similar destination, if the property was that of the wife and not of the husband, he merely obtains a liferent while she remains absolute fiar; for in these cases, unless the presumption is elided by express provision, the fee is presumed to be in the spouse from whom the subject proceeded.

Culpa.—Fault; negligence. Of this there are three degrees—viz., *culpa lata*, gross fault or carelessness, which the law regards as dole; *culpa levis*, that degree of negligence which a person may be guilty of, even when ordinarily attentive to his own affairs; and *culpa levissima* the slightest degree of fault or negligence, which may be fallen into by one who manages his affairs with the greatest attention and prudence. The degree of diligence for which persons are liable depends upon the nature of the contract under which the obligation for the diligence arises. Thus, in the contract of deposit, which is purely for the benefit of the depositor, and confers no advantage upon the depositary, the latter is only liable for *culpa lata*. Whereas, in the contract of commodate, the borrower, who has the sole advantage by the loan, is liable for *culpa levissima*; and in contracts where both parties reap an advantage—as in location, where the one has the use of the article lent, and the other the hire paid for such use—each party is liable for the middle degree of diligence, *culpa levis*, or (as it is often termed) *culpa*. The general rule in regard to diligence is, that where both parties to the contract are advantaged, each is liable for the middle degree of diligence; and where only one of the parties is advantaged, that person must bestow the greatest care and attention, and will be liable for the least neglect, *culpa levissima*. Where a person is in possession of a subject under a contract, from which he derives no advantage, he is only liable for *culpa lata*. (Ersk. 3, 1, 21.) Whether *culpa levissima* was recognised as a ground of liability under the civil law has been a question much controverted. The import of the different views maintained in this controversy is very clearly stated in Lord Mackenzie's "Studies in Roman Law," p. 186 *et seq.*, to which the reader is referred. It would rather appear that the only degrees of negligence now recognised in the law of Scotland are *culpa lata* and *culpa levis*. *Mackintosh,* 2 Macp. 1357.

Culpa caret qui scit sed prohibere non potest.—He is free from fault who knows but cannot prevent. If one stands by and sees a rape committed without rendering assistance to the person assaulted, he may be indicted as guilty of the crime, actor or art and part (*Kerr,* 2 Couper, 336); but if he is himself overpowered and unable to render assistance, he is free from fault. So also a soldier ordered by his superior officer to fire upon a mob, may know that the order is wrong, and yet incur no fault by firing, as his first duty is obedience, and he cannot prevent the order being carried out.

Culpa lata dolo æquiparatur.—Gross fault is equivalent to bad intention or fraud. This maxim is generally applied to questions of civil liability: the term *dolus* being then understood as equivalent to bad intention or gross fault. The person guilty of such fault is liable for the consequences of it, provided the person injured thereby has not himself been also guilty of contributory negligence or fault. Thus the lessees or owners of a coal-pit, who neglect the duty incumbent upon them of supplying good and sufficient machinery or apparatus, whereby the workings may be safely conducted, are liable for any injuries sustained by the workmen arising from such insufficient apparatus. In a civil action this neglect of duty involves a liability as extensive as if the owners or lessees had intentionally supplied bad and insufficient apparatus. So, again, trustees who have through their gross fault or negligence allowed the property entrusted to them to be lost or deteriorated, are liable to the beneficiaries in restitution or compensation, just as if they had fraudulently disposed of the estate. An instructive illustration of this maxim will be found in the judgment of Lord Ardmillan, in the case of *Faulds* v. *Townsend,* 23 D. 437. In criminal actions gross fault or neglect of duty is regarded as equivalent, to some extent, to criminal intention. As, for example, in the case already supposed of the owner or lessee of a coal-pit, if the gross neglect of his duty to supply proper apparatus should result in the death of workmen, he would be liable to criminal prosecution for culpable homicide, the *mens rea* being presumed from his neglect or fault. Regarding the different degrees of *culpa* recognised in our law, and the diligence or care for which certain persons are responsible, see *Culpa*.

Culpa præcederat casum.—Fault had preceded the calamity.

Culpa tenet suos auctores.—A fault or delict binds its authors; so that a husband, although bound in many cases by the acts of his wife, is not responsible for the consequences of any crime or delict committed by her, nor is he liable for her *quasi* delict. *Barr* v. *Neilson*, 6 Macp. 651. On the other hand, if any one commits a crime through the agency of another, the agent being ignorant that any offence is being committed, the former, not the latter, will be responsible. For example, if A sends B to utter a forged bill or note, B being ignorant of the forgery, A is guilty of uttering, and as the author of the delict will incur the consequences of the crime, although he did not personally commit it. As to the application of this maxim to civil claims for damage, see *Qui facit per alium*, &c.

Cultura.—Culture, tillage. Industrial fruits are said to be so derived, in contradistinction to natural fruits, which are said to spring up *sponte*, without artificial or human labour.

Cum aliquis renunciaverit societati, solvitur societas.—When any partner renounces the partnership, the partnership is dissolved. Bell's Com. ii. 521.

Cum astrictis multuris. — With astricted multures. Multures are a proportion of grain paid to the miller for grinding the rest; astricted multures were those paid by the holders of lands which were astricted or thirled to a certain mill, and the right to them was conveyed in the words of the phrase to the purchaser of the mill. Multures paid under thirlage were termed insucken or astricted, and those paid by persons who voluntarily brought their grain to the mill, but who were not thirled to it, were called outsucken. "Thirlage," says Professor Bell, "being devised originally as an expedient for indemnifying the builder of a mill for extraordinary outlay in a rude age, has degenerated, in times of more improved manufacture, into a burdensome and inexpedient tax on the produce of land, and is now in a state of gradual extinction." Bell's Prin. § 1017.

Cum aucupationibus, venationibus et piscationibus.—With fowlings, huntings, and fishings. Salmon fishing is the only fishing in the sea of which there is an undoubted monopoly, and as salmon are *inter regalia*, the right must flow from the Crown. The clause *cum piscationibus*, followed by possession of salmon fishing, is sufficient to establish a right to such fishing. Such a right may be conferred without any grant of adjoining lands. See *Cum piscariis*.

Cum beneficio inventarii.—With the benefit of inventory. See *Beneficium inventarii*.

Cum columbis et columbariis.—With doves and dovecots. The building of pigeon-houses was put under certain restraints by the Act 1617, c. 19. These words are not to be found in any modern charter, and but few of the old pigeon-houses now remain extant in Scotland.

Cum communi pastura.—With common pasturage. This is a mere right of servitude, and not a right of commonty. See *Communia*.

Cum cuniculis cuniculariis.—With rabbits and warrens.

Cum curiis earumque exitibus.—With courts, and the results or profits of the same. The courts of the Barons had this difference from the courts of the Sheriffs and Stewards, which were King's Courts, that the former received all the amercements and other profits of the court, while the latter were responsible for such profits to the king. A conveyance *cum curiis* carried a right to the profits, although they were not specially mentioned.

Cum curiis et bloodwitis.—If a baron disponed part of his barony *cum curiis*, this conferred a limited jurisdiction on the purchaser, empowering him to judge of questions of debt between tenant and tenant, &c. ; but if the conveyance was *cum curiis et bloodwitis*, it entitled the purchaser to fine for blood. The jurisdiction thus conferred was cumulative only, and did not exclude that of the baron, whose jurisdiction continued over the whole barony.

Cum decimis inclusis et nunquam antea separatis.—With the teinds included, and never before separated. Lands disponed with such a clause as this are exempt from the payment of teinds. Such conveyances seem originally to have flowed from churchmen in right both to the lands and teinds, so that the teinds, being a burden on the lands, became extinguished, as it were, by confusion, when combined in the person of the purchaser, who became, by the same deed, proprietor of the lands and titular of the teinds. As to the origin and history of these rights, the reader may be referred to Ersk. B. 2, T. 10, § 16. Connell on Tithes, ii. 25 *et seq.* A conveyance *cum decimis inclusis* only will not support the claim of exemption, unless it bear *nunquam antea separatis*, or words of similar import. *Beatson*, 5th February, 1812. F. C., *D. of Atholl*, 2 Macp. 1133. *E. of Dalhousie*, 2 Macp. 1349.

Cum domibus, ædificiis.—With houses, buildings. These words are held to include every erection upon the lands conveyed, but they are not essential; for the conveyance of the lands carries all that is erected upon them, unless specially excluded or reserved.

Cum duo inter se pugnantia reperiuntur in testamento ultimum ratum est.—When two clauses (or provisions) are found in a will, contradictory of, or inconsistent with, each other, the last is confirmed (sustained). This maxim has reference to the construction of wills, and is based upon the idea that the "position of the clauses in the instrument may with some reason be held to correspond with the order of development of the testator's intentions in point of time" (M'Laren, i. 338). This rule of construction, which involves the sacrifice of one of the clauses of the will, is not resorted to where it can be avoided: and sometimes, where, of two contradictory provisions, one is consistent with the general scheme of the testator's deed, and the other is at variance with it, the former will prevail though it should be the first in local position. "I think it may be taken as clearly established that this rule must not be acted on so as to clash with another paramount rule, which is, that, before all things we must look for the intention of the testator as we find it expressed or clearly implied in the general tenor of the will; and when we have found that on evidence satisfactory in kind and degree, to that we must sacrifice the inconsistent clause or words, whether standing first or last, indifferently: and this rests upon good reason; for although, when there are repugnant dispositions, and nothing leads clearly to a preference of one, or rejection of the other, convenience is strongly in favour of some rule, however arbitrary; yet the foundation of this rule, as of every other established for the interpretation of wills, obviously is, that it was supposed to be the safest guide, under the circumstances, to the last intention of the testator." Per Coleridge, J., in *Morall* v. *Sutton*, 14 L. J. Ch. 272. See also Jarman on Wills, i. 472 *et seq.* In dealing with Acts of Parliament the same rule is applied. If the clauses are contradictory, and one must yield, the general rule is that the latter clause prevails, and the former is sacrificed: but this only, as in the case of wills, where the clause retained is consistent with the general purpose of the enactment (Maxwell, 46, 133). In contracts where there are clauses repugnant to the general purpose of the contract, and which, if sustained, would render the contract nugatory, they are disregarded: but they will be retained if on any fair construction they can be made conditions or provisions of the contract without destroying it. Where a clause is capable of two interpretations, one consistent with, and the other repugnant to, the purpose and intention of the deed or contract in which such a clause appears, the former construction is preferred. See the case of *Dixon's Trs.*, 21 R. 441, where the relative position of certain clauses in a lease was held not to confer a right to certain rents contrary to what, had the position of the clauses been alone, or chiefly regarded, might have been held to be the import of the lease.

Cum effectu.—With effect. Prescription does not run against any one, as we have seen above, unless he is able to act in defence of his right *cum effectu.* (See *Contra non valentem*, &c.) Under the old feudal system the casualty of ward was not incurred except where the vassal alienated his lands *cum effectu.* Thus, if the vassal was interdicted and disponed without the consent of his interdictors, his conveyance being reducible was not effectual, and the casualty was not incurred.

Cum excessu moderaminis.—Literally, in excess of the limits. This refers to the limits of that violence which one may use in self-defence, without being responsible for the consequences. See *Moderamen inculpatæ*, &c.

Cum fabrilibus, brasinis, et brueriis.—With forges, malt-kilns, and breweries. Anciently, no vassal could erect such works on his lands, without the permission of his superior, but there is now no such restriction on the right of property, unless it be a matter of bargain between the parties, and be inserted in the original charter or feu-contract; or be prohibited by the Acts passed for the protection of the Public Health.

Cum fossa et furca.—With pit and gallows; the expression used in conferring upon Barons the right of pronouncing capital sentence in the Baron Courts. It signified a jurisdiction over felons to punish men by hanging, and women by drowning.

Cum herezeldis.—With herezelds. This expression, to be found occasionally in old charters, gave the landlord a right to the best horse, ox, or cow, of which a deceased tenant was possessed at the time of his death. The herezeld was not exigible from feuars, but from tenants only; but such a right has been long unknown in practice.

Cum libera et plena administratione.—With full and free power of management or administration; such as is given to a factor, an attorney, or a mandatory, entitling him to act for his constituent as he may deem most suitable and advantageous.

Cum libero exitu et introitu.—With free ish and entry.

Cum maritagio.—With the casualty of marriage. This was a casualty of wardholding (now abolished) under which the superior was entitled to payment of a certain sum on the marriage of his ward. When the heir was a female, the superior selected for her a husband, whom she could not refuse except on forfeiture of her property, or as much thereof as was estimated to be the value of the match. When the heir was a male, the consent of his superior to his marriage was required. If such consent was given, it operated as a renunciation of the right of casualty. This consent was often used as a means of extortion, and large sums were paid by the heir for liberty of choice.

Cum molendinis et multuris.—With mills and multures of the same.

Cum nota.—With a mark, or reservation. Formerly when witnesses were disqualified by reason of agency, or partial counsel, &c., it was a frequent practice to admit persons as witnesses who were in some measure chargeable with the disqualification, and especially so where there happened to be a *penuria testium*. They were admitted, however, *cum nota*, that is, with a mark to call the attention of the Judge to the extent of agency, &c., which had been proved against them, and with a reservation to him to give such weight to their evidence as under the circumstances he should think proper. In effect, the evidence of a witness admitted *cum nota*, generally received as much weight as the evidence of those who were not so distinguished.

Cum omni causa.—With every profit or advantage. A depositary is bound to deliver up the subject deposited, with every profit, such as fruits or accessions, to the depositor when demanded. So also is the pledgee bound to deliver the pledge with all its fruits when his claim against the pledger has been satisfied.

Cum onere debitorum defuncti.—Under burden of the deceased's debts. An executor or heir incurs this liability when he enters upon the succession which has opened up to him.

Cum pertinentis.—With pertinents. This includes everything belonging to the lands conveyed; and on such a clause and possession for the prescriptive period, the right of property in ground adjoining may be acquired, except where the original charter containing these words is a bounding charter.

Cum piscariis.—With fishings. The difference between this phrase and *cum piscationibus* is this: that while the latter, with forty years' possession thereon of salmon fishing, will constitute a right thereto, the former (*cum piscariis*) is held as equivalent to an express grant *salmonum piscationibus*, without such prescriptive possession.

Cum satis furore ipso puniatur.—Since he is sufficiently punished by the insanity itself. Hume, i. 44. See *Furiosus solo*, &c.

Cum silvis.—With woods.

Cum sua causa et labe.—With its advantages and its defects.

Cum suo onere.—With its burden. Lands resigned *ad remanentiam* remain burdened with any burden legally imposed upon them by the vassal before resignation, and they must be accepted by the superior *cum onere*.

Cum titulo.—With a title.

Cum virginitas vel castitas corrupta restitui non possit.—Since chastity once violated cannot be restored. On this account, because no sufficient recompense can ever be made to a woman who has been violated, and who can never be restored to her inviolate condition, the punishment of rape is proportionately severe. This phrase, quoted from the civil law, gave rise to the question whether rape could be held to have been committed unless complete connection had taken place. It is now settled that such connection is not essential to the crime.

Cumulatio criminum.—The accumulation of crimes; that is, the charging several distinct and different crimes in the same indictment against an accused person. Hume, ii. 171 *et seq.*

Cura animarum.—The cure of souls; a curacy or cure.

Curator bonis.—The name given to an officer, appointed by the Court on application to that effect, for the preservation or management of an estate, the owner of which at the time is unable to manage or superintend it. Most frequently such curators are appointed to the estates of those persons who through minority or insanity are incapable of attending to their own affairs; but they are also appointed under other circumstances, as, for example, to manage a trust estate where the trustees have declined to act, or to manage the estate of a person who is abroad. In the last-mentioned cases, however, the officer appointed by the Court is called a judicial factor, or factor *loco absentis*.

Curator (datur) rei.—A curator is appointed to the estate; and is in this respect different from a tutor, who is (*datur personæ*) appointed to take care of the person of his ward.

Curia Christianitatis.—A name given to the Ecclesiastical Courts, and especially to the Commissary Court, at the time when it was presided over by the bishops or their vicars.

Curiosus debet esse creditor quo vertatur.—The creditor should inquire how (the money) is applied. This refers to the duty of a creditor who lends money to the tutors of a pupil, or to a minor. He is bound to satisfy himself that the money is applied to the benefit of the pupil or minor; for if it turns out afterwards that the money lent by him was embezzled by the tutors, or squandered by the minor, he will not recover. On this subject see Fraser, Par. & Ch. 408.

Currente termino.—During the currency of the term; a phrase used in reference to leases. A poinding of the tenant's effects during the currency of the term may be stopped by the landlord, as it would interfere with his preferable right of hypothec, to preserve which he may sequestrate *currente termino*, in security for the payment of his rent when it becomes due.

Cursus curiæ est lex curiæ.—The course of the Court (that is, the course of procedure or practice) is the law of the Court. The ordinary practice or course of procedure is the law of the Court in a double sense. In the first place, it is the law of the Court in the sense that it is the law enacted by the Court, either by long usage, or, as in the Supreme Court, by Act of Sederunt, or, as in the Inferior Courts, by order of the principal judge presiding there; for every Court has power over its own forms of process and practice, where these are not specially regulated by the higher authority of an Act of Parliament. In another sense the course of procedure is the law of the Court, because that course of procedure is the law or rule by which procedure is to be regulated. In so far as the procedure has been enacted by the Court itself, or depends merely upon usage, the Court may make such alterations upon such procedure as it deems fit or expedient. In so far, however, as the procedure has been enacted by the legislature, it can only be altered by the same authority, except in the case where, in enacting the procedure, the legislature has conferred the power upon the Court itself to alter or amend such procedure. The ordinary course of procedure ought always to be observed, because if any litigant of consent departs from the *cursus curiæ*, it may bar his right of appeal. On this point, see the cases of *Dudgeon* v. *Thomson*, 1 Macq. 714, and *Robin* v. *Hoby*, 2 Macq. 478.

Custodiæ causa.—For the purpose of keeping or preserving. Interference with the estate of a deceased, if merely for this purpose, will infer no passive title against the custodier. This is the sole purpose of the contract of deposit, and if the depositary uses the subject (further than is necessary for its preservation), he will be liable to the depositor for such use. Such use is called in the Roman law *furtum usus* (the theft of use).

D

Damnosa aut lucrosa.—Injurious or advantageous. As an heir (prior to 1874), in the ordinary case, incurred a general responsibility for the debts and other obligations of the ancestor to whom he succeeded, it was a question of great importance for the heir to consider whether he would take up the succession which had devolved upon him. If the obligations were greater in extent than the value of the succession, it was to the disadvantage of the heir to enter upon it, while it was otherwise if the succession was large and the obligations small. To enable the heir to gain information as to the condition of the succession, and to consider whether he would take it up or renounce it, a year was formerly allowed him, called the *annus deliberandi*, during which period no proceedings could be taken against him as representing his ancestor. That period was reduced to six months by the Act 21 & 22 Vict. c. 76, and, although that Act has been repealed, the provision on this matter has been repeated in the repealing Statute 31 & 32 Vict. c. 101, § 61. The *annus deliberandi* has now, however, no such practical importance as once attached to it; for by the Act 37 & 38 Vict. c. 94, § 12, it is provided than an heir shall not be liable for the debts of his ancestor beyond the value of the estate of such ancestor to which he succeeds; and that, when an heir intromits with his ancestor's estate, and thereafter renounces the succession, he shall be liable for the ancestor's debts to the extent of such intromission, but no further. As to the heirs *jus deliberandi*, see Bell's Com. i. 748-9.

Damnum.—Harm, injury, loss. Under the Roman law this word implied only accidental damage, or damage not the result of a legal wrong.

Damnum absque injuria.—Damage inflicted without legal wrong. Damage so inflicted gives rise neither to prosecution *ad vindictam publicam*, nor to action at the instance of the person injured for compensation. Such is damage arising from accident, or from an act lawful in itself, and not performed with any intent or desire to injure. This is distinguished from the *damnum injuria datum* (damage inflicted wrongously), which gives rise in many cases both to civil and criminal prosecution, and always to the former. *Injuria* includes any act that is illegal or unwarrantable, and therefore damage is said to be inflicted wrongously, where it arises from fault or neglect. Damage may thus be inflicted by an animal not kept with due care by its proprietor, and for such damage the proprietor is liable. It is sometimes a matter of difficulty to determine whether the damage complained of is *absque injuria* or *injuria datum;* but the reader will be materially helped in the solution of such a difficulty, when it arises, by a consideration of the cases on this subject collected in Smith's Leading Cases, ii. 297 *et seq.* With regard to these cases, however, it must be borne in mind that the decisions pronounced in some of them proceed upon principles of English law which have no place in the law of Scotland. The reader, however, will easily distinguish between the cases which proceed upon English law, and those which proceed upon principles common to the law of both countries.

Damnum et interesse.—The loss and interest; or, as the words may also be translated, damage, and its issues or consequences. The words are used by Erskine in treating of the liability of cautioners who become bound to see a specific act performed. Failing performance, the cautioners are liable to the creditors for the *damnum et interesse*—that is, the actual and consequential damage suffered through non-performance on the part of the debtor.

Damnum fatale.—Loss arising from inevitable accident, which human means or prudence could not prevent. All loss occasioned by the acts of God is so called, and must be borne by the person on whom the loss or damage has been inflicted.

Damnum infectum.—Damage not yet occasioned, but

apprehended. Such is damage threatened to buildings from mining operations below them; or violence threatened against the person. The former may be stopped by interdict, the latter provided against by a petition for law-burrows. As regards law-burrows, the reader will note the changes made in our law and practice, by the provisions of 45 & 46 Vict. c. 42. *Damnum infectum* is used in contrast to *Damnum factum*—damage or injury already done.

Damnum injuria datum.—Damage or injury culpably inflicted. See *Damnum absque injuria*.

Damnum sine injuria esse potest.—There may be damage or injury inflicted without any wrong being done. This maxim embodies the distinction between damage wrongously or culpably inflicted, for which the perpetrator is liable, and that damage which is accidental, unintentional, and without fault, on account of which no action for compensation will lie. On the subject of this distinction, reference may be made to Sandars' Justinian, p. 412 *et seq.* See *Damnum absque*, &c.

Dans et retinens nihil dat.—One who gives and yet retains, does not give effectually. The principle of this maxim found frequent application in questions arising out of the contract of sale. The principle of the common law of Scotland prior to the year 1856 undoubtedly was, that goods sold but not delivered (which, in the words of the maxim, was the seller giving the right to the goods but retaining the goods themselves) remained the property of the seller; they were subject to the diligence of the seller's creditors, and passed to the trustee on his estate in the event of his bankruptcy. By the law of England it was otherwise, for by that law the completed contract of sale passed the property in the thing sold to the buyer, leaving the seller only the right of retention for the price. This essential difference between the laws of England and Scotland led to frequent disputes and great inconvenience, with the view of remedying which, and for the purpose of assimilating the law of Scotland to that of England, the Mercantile Law Amendment Act (19 & 20 Vict. c. 60) was passed. That purpose does not seem to have been absolutely effected by the provisions of the statute, for it was stated in one of the earliest cases in which that statute was presented for judicial construction, that "the principle of the common law, that undelivered goods still remain the property of the seller, is untouched by the statute" (*Wyper* v. *Harvey*, 27th February, 1861, 23 D. 612). By the first section of the statute above cited, it was provided not only that goods sold but not delivered, and remaining in the custody of the seller, should not be subject to the diligence of the seller's creditors, nor be affected by the seller's bankruptcy; but also, that such goods should be subject to the diligence of the creditors of the buyer. Practically, therefore, the property in the goods was transferred to the buyer, although still remaining in the custody of the seller. There remained still a "nominal difference between the law of England and the law of Scotland, but for all practical purposes the law of Scotland, where there has been a contract of sale, though no delivery, is made identical with the law of England in the actual result." Per Lord Blackburn in *M'Bain* v. *Wallace*, 8 R. (H.L.) 112. The Mercantile Law Amendment Act of 1856 has (so far as concerns the law of sale) been repealed, and the law of sale for both countries is now regulated by the provisions of the Sale of Goods Act, 1893 (56 & 57 Vict. c. 71). As showing the effect of the Act of 1856 on the law of Scotland, reference may be made to the following cases—*Robertson*, 9 R. 772; *Allan's Trs.*, 10 R. 997; *Seath & Co.*, 12 R. 260, affd. H.L. 13 R. 57; *Scott*, 16 R. 504. There are cases, however, in which the principle of the maxim now under notice is not affected by the provisions of the statutes above referred to. The statutes only apply to contracts of sale; and, accordingly, if the transaction is one, not of sale, but of security merely, then the maxim applies. An assignation of moveables in security, without delivery to the assignee, confers no preferential right on the assignee — the moveables remain the property of the debtor, subject to the diligence of his creditor, and pass to his trustee in the event of bankruptcy. This is so even where the transaction (if really one of security) takes the form of a sale. *M'Bain*, *sup. cit.*, per Lord Watson, p. 115; *Pattison's Tr.* v. *Liston*, 20 R. 806; Sale of Goods Act, 1893, § 61, subsection 4.

Datus bonis.—Appointed to manage an estate. See *Curator bonis.*

De alode parentum.—Lands descending by inheritance from parents were said to be so acquired, in contradistinction to lands held in feu (*de munere regio*), and to those acquired by a singular title. Subsequently the phrase acquired a more comprehensive signification, as all lands were, in process of time, termed allodial, in which the holder had a right of absolute property, without rendering any service therefor, or recognising any superior therein, and of which he had an unlimited power of disposal. "The term is applied—1. To the property belonging to the Crown; 2. To the superiorities reserved by the Sovereign; and 3. To churches, churchyards, manses, and glebes, the right of which does not flow from the Crown. To these may be added the udal lands of Orkney, which are held by natural possession, provable by witnesses, without any title in writing." Bell's Dict. *v.* Allodial.

De calumnia.—Of calumny. An oath (called the oath of calumny) was at one time administered to all suitors, under which they were required to affirm their belief that the statements set forth by them in their libel or defences were just and true. This oath was derived from the Roman law, where it was introduced at a very early period with the view of checking reckless or vexatious litigation. At first it was required of every suitor to take this oath, but latterly it was only administered at the request of either of the parties. It derived its name from the meaning attached to the word *calumnia*, which Gaius defines as the offence committed by a man, who, in the knowledge that he is acting unjustly, yet institutes an action for the purpose merely of annoying his adversary. (*Qui intelligit non recte se agere, sed vexandi adversarii gratia actionem instituit.*—GAI. iv. 174.) In our law, as under the civil law, this oath was at one time required of all suitors, but subsequently it was only administered when the adverse party demanded it; and at the present time it is almost unknown in practice, being confined to cases of divorce and declarator of nullity of marriage, in which the pursuer is required still to emit it. See an interesting case on this subject, where the question was raised whether the oath of calumny still exists in our law; *Paul* v. *Laings,* 17

D. 604. See also the case of *Paterson* v. *Kilgour*, 3 Macp. 1119.

De causa in causam.—From one cause to another. This is a kind of prorogation of jurisdiction, intended to confer on a certain judge a jurisdiction, which, without the consent of parties, he could not possess. Such prorogation is necessarily very limited in extent. "Prorogation of jurisdiction, from causes of one description to those of a totally different description, is inadmissible. Yet, where the cause is of the same nature with those to which the judge is competent, prorogation is admitted. Thus, where the proper jurisdiction of the judge is confined to causes amounting to a certain value, parties may prorogate the jurisdiction to causes above that value, unless the statute conferring the jurisdiction prohibits it, or expressly limits the jurisdiction." Bell's Dict. *v.* Prorogation of Jurisdiction.

De die in diem.—From day to day; daily.

De essentia.—Of the essence; essential.

De facto.—According to the fact; in point of fact. This is antithetical to *de jure*.

De fide et officio judicis non recipitur quæstio, sed de scientia sive sit error juris sive facti.—No question is permitted as to the good faith of a judge, or the honest performance of his duty, but touching his knowledge (or skill) it may be questioned whether he has erred in law or fact. This translation, which aims at being as nearly literal as possible, may be taken along with that given by Mr. Broom, which is as follows :—"The *bona fides* and honesty of purpose of a judge cannot be questioned, but his decision may be impugned for error either of law or of fact" (Broom, p. 85). This maxim, while it states a sound principle undoubtedly, is calculated to mislead if its terms are taken absolutely, and without qualification. A judge being a public officer, charged with the performance of a public duty, is no more free from public criticism than any other. His skill or knowledge may be impugned in reference to any judgment he has pronounced, and any one is entitled, within the bounds of fair criticism, to show that the judgment is erroneous, and proceeds upon ignorance, error, or misconception, either as regards the facts or the law involved. So far as this goes the maxim is quite unambiguous. But a judge's honesty may also be impugned; and he is subject to punishment for acting corruptly under the Act 1540, c. 104. Any complaint, however, against a judge, on account of corruption, oppression, or other improper use of his office, must be made to the Sovereign (and this may be through the Secretary of State for the Home Department) or to Parliament, and the person making the complaint, if he "provis not the samin sufficientlie," is liable to the same punishment as that which would have fallen on the judge had the complaint been proved. To understand the maxim in the sense that a judge's honesty or uprightness cannot be called in question at all, by any authority, however high, or in any circumstances however clamant, would be quite wrong; but what the maxim intends to convey is this —that while the soundness of a judge's decisions may be freely questioned and criticised, the purity of his motives must not be impugned in the same way. The reader may consult on this subject the case of *Robertson*, 1 Couper, 404; and on the subject of a judge's liability for acts done or words spoken in the exercise of his judicial functions, reference may be made to the case of *Haggart's Trs.*, 2 Shaw (H. L.) 125.

De fide instrumentorum.—As to the genuineness or truthfulness of instruments. This is a question raised frequently in actions of reduction of instruments on the ground of forgery, &c., the proof in which requires to be very ample and distinct. On this point see Menzies' Lectures, 118.

De fideli administratione.—Of faithful administration. An oath bearing this title is emitted by certain public functionaries, by judges of the Supreme Court, sheriffs, &c. (and formerly also by officers appointed by the Court, such as curators and tutors), under which they engage to be faithful in the performance of all the duties of their office. A declaration has now been substituted in most cases for the oath (31 & 32 Vict. c. 72). A breach of this oath or declaration, although it gives rise to a civil action for remedy against the consequences, does not involve the penalties of perjury.

De futuro.—Regarding the future; at a future period. This phrase is antithetical to the phrase *de presenti*. A consent to marriage *de presenti* constitutes marriage in itself; a consent *de futuro* does not constitute the contract of marriage, but only gives rise to an action of damages in event of the non-fulfilment of the promise.

De industria.—Designedly; as distinguished from *per incuriam*, by mistake or oversight.

De integro.—As regards the whole; entirely. This phrase is equivalent to the one more commonly used, *in integrum*.

De judicio sisti.—See *Judicio*, &c.

De jure.—According to law; or in point of law. This is antithetical to *de facto*.

De jure communi.—According to the provision of the common law. The phrase is similar in import to the preceding one.

De lana caprina (rixari).—Literally, to contend about a goat's hair; a phrase signifying, to contend or dispute about trifles. (Hor. Ep. i. 18, 15.) An instance of the use of this phrase will be found in *Strang* v. *Steuart*, 2 Macp. 1029.

De libero homine exhibendo.—For the exhibition or production of a free man. This was a part of the Roman law (Dig. B. 43, T. 29), under which a question of false or illegal imprisonment or detention was determined. If any one detained another as his slave, or deprived him of that liberty of action which was the inherent right of every free man, the detainer, under this law, could be compelled to exhibit and produce the person detained in open court, where his status as freeman or slave was at once determined; and if the detention was declared illegal, he was set at liberty. The application to the judge (the Prætor) for production of the person detained was one of the class *actio popularis*, and could be brought by any citizen, whether immediately interested or not. Somewhat analogous to this is the writ of *habeas corpus* in England, when resorted to by a prisoner to have the legality of his imprisonment determined. Under the *Habeas Corpus* Act (31 Charles II. c. 2, amended by 56 Geo. III. c. 100) a prisoner may also obtain his release on bail, where the offence with which he is charged is bailable, or his complete discharge, if he has been unduly detained without trial. The *Habeas Corpus* Act does not apply to Scotland; but by the Act 1701, c. 6, provision was made whereby a prisoner could force on his trial within a hundred days of his committal, by running his letters. By this Act, according to Hume, "the inhabitants of this part of the United Kingdom now enjoy a security and protection in this interesting article (*i.e.*, the matter of their personal liberty) in nowise inferior to that which their fellow-subjects of England have, under the *Habeas Corpus* Act of Charles II." (Hume, ii. 99). So much of the Act of 1701 as related to the prevention of undue delay in trials, other than trials for treason, was repealed in 1887 by the Act 50 & 51 Vict. c. 35, which enacted (§ 43), other provisions in lieu of those repealed. It may be noticed that the provisions of the *Habeas Corpus* Act, and of the Act of 1887, only apply where the imprisonment complained of proceeds upon a judicial warrant, and not, as in the Roman law, where the false imprisonment was by a fellow-subject, without any warrant at all. This latter kind of wrong has its remedy at common law, both in England and Scotland.

De liquido in liquidum.—Of a liquid claim against a liquid claim; having reference to the extinction of a claim by compensation or set-off. By the Act 1592, c. 141 (given in some editions of the Scots Acts as c. 143) it was provided "that any debt *de liquido ad liquidum* instantly verified be writ, or aith of the party, before the giving of the decreete, be admitted be all Judges within this realm, be way of exception; Bot not after the giving thereof, in the suspension, or in reduction of the same decreete." Prior to the passing of that Act compensation could not be pleaded by way of exception; and it will be observed, that even now it can only be pleaded before decree is pronounced: whether it can be pleaded by a defender who has been reponed against a decree obtained in absence pronounced against him, is a point on which Erskine expresses doubt (B. 3, T. 4, § 19). The general rules of compensation are stated in Bell's Prin. § 573 *et seq.*, where the reader will find in what cases, and with reference to what debts, compensation may be successfully pleaded. A difficulty sometimes arises as to whether a defender is entitled to plead by way of compensation a claim for damages arising out of the non-fulfilment of a contract or undue delay in its fulfilment, in answer to the demand for the contract price. To illustrate this, suppose a case: A contracts to do certain work for B for a certain sum named in the contract, and does the work sufficiently, but is guilty of undue delay in the execution of it. A thereupon claims the contract price, payment of which is refused by B, on the sole ground that he has suffered damage to the full extent of the contract price or more, through the undue delay of A. In the action at the instance of A for the contract price, can B plead his claim of damages in compensation? In the case as put, the plea of compensation could not probably be maintained, and the defender would be under the necessity of making good his claim for damages in a separate action. But if the contract had been that A was to finish the work by a certain day, and he had failed to do so, B would be entitled to meet the demand for payment of the contract price by his claim of damages. This, however, would not be, strictly speaking, a plea of compensation, but would be a plea of non-liability, or a right of retention, on the ground that A had not fulfilled his part of the contract, and was therefore not entitled to enforce it against his co-contractor B. In such cases the plea of compensation and that of retention run so closely together that difficulty has been felt in separating them. As examples of the difficulty just adverted to, the reader may be referred to the following cases:—*Taylor* v. *Forbes*, 9 S. 113; *S. N. E. Ry. Co.* v. *Napier*, 21 D. 700; *Johnston* v. *Robertson*, 23 D. 646; *Macbride* v. *Hamilton*, 2 R. 775.

De lucranda dote.—Of being enriched by the dowry: a paction sometimes made between spouses under the Roman law, whereby a husband became entitled to retain the dowry after his wife's decease, which, in the ordinary case, and without such paction, he was not entitled to do.

De me.—Of me. The technical name given to a base holding. See *A me*.

De medietate linguæ.—Of a moiety of tongue; or moiety of voices. In England, formerly, an alien put upon his trial for a criminal offence, was entitled to demand that the jury should consist, to the extent of one-half, of aliens, if so many could be found in the town or place where the trial was to proceed, and if not, then of so many as could be found there.

This was called a jury *de medietate linguæ*. The right to demand such a jury is now abolished, 33 Vict. c. 14, § 5. Such a right appears never to have existed in Scotland. *Itansen*, 3 Irvine, 3.

De minimis non curat Prætor.—The Prætor does not concern himself about trifles; or (as the maxim may be interpreted), the Prætor does not apply his equitable remedies in matters of small moment. This maxim, so long as it is retained in the form here given, is not likely to lead either to error or misapprehension; but latterly, in England, it has been common to read the maxim as *De minimis non curat lex*, which is certainly calculated, at least in its literal meaning, to mislead. It is not correct to say that the *law* does not concern itself about matters of small amount, or of comparatively trivial importance, either in its civil or criminal courts. In the latter, for example, theft is theft, whether it concerns the felonious abstraction of a loaf of bread or a thousand pounds; while, in the former, every legal wrong, however slight, has its appropriate remedy, and every right, no matter of what value or extent, may be enforced. This might be illustrated by a reference to many cases reported in our books, but it may suffice to give the following. In the case of *Meikle* v. *Sneddon*, 24 D. 720, the pursuers sought damages for the unwarrantable arrestment of their vessel, and while they claimed "£500 as *solatium* for the loss, injury, and damage sustained by them in their feelings, character, trade, and business," the actual loss libelled being the expenses occasioned in getting the arrestment loosed, was less than £10. The arrestment proceeded upon an action for payment of coals actually supplied to the vessel, but it appeared that the vessel being under charter, the coals had been supplied to the master as servant of the charterer and not of the owners. The defenders denied all knowledge of the charter, and pleaded that the pursuers had suffered no loss or damage of any kind, and put the pursuers in this dilemma: if the ship was in the hands of the owners when the coals were supplied, they are liable for the price of the coals, and cannot complain of the arrestment; but if the ship was in the hands of the charterer, then her detention occasioned no loss to the pursuers, as they were being paid for the use of the vessel during the time of her detention by the charterer, who was not complaining of the arrestment. The action was obviously based upon a legal wrong, which had not inflicted any material damage; but, in granting the pursuers an issue, the Lord Justice-Clerk (Inglis) observed—"It is of no consequence whether the pursuers have sustained any substantial damage. Suppose the damage to be such that one farthing is recovered, that will show that a wrong has been done by the defenders to the pursuers." Again, in *Strang* v. *Steuart*, 2 Macp. 1015, the Lord Justice-Clerk (Inglis) observed—"We are not indeed bound to adjudicate *de lana caprina*; but if there be a pecuniary or patrimonial interest, however small, depending upon the determination of the question, the parties have a right to invoke the aid of a court of law to decide their difference." It may be said, therefore, that there is no case of which the law can take cognisance, which it refuses to regard merely because the question raised, or the amount involved, is of small moment; in this respect the law does not distinguish between important and unimportant cases. The importance of a case does not depend solely on the pecuniary amount affected by its decision, and if the *law* assumed the right of determining, in the first place, what was and what was not of sufficient importance for the application of its principles, and declined to adjudicate upon questions which it deemed unimportant, it is clear upon the slightest reflection that the result in many cases would be the infliction of positive injustice. But while it is erroneous to say that the "*law* does not concern itself about matters of small moment," the maxim in its proper reading expresses a rule which was acted upon in the law of Rome, and is now observed in the law of Scotland. The Prætor represented what may be termed remedial equity, but his equitable remedies were only resorted to in cases where the common law afforded no remedy, and where the importance of the occasion rendered it fitting and proper that such remedies should be applied. For example, if a minor entered into a contract, he was by the law required to fulfil it; but if the contract was decidedly to the minor's lesion, the Prætor, in exercise of his power, and to remedy the injustice that would follow from an enforcement of the contract, set it aside. At the same time, if the lesion was of a trifling character (*ex. gr.* if the minor had paid a large price for the subject bought, and such as a merchant with more prudence would hardly have given), the contract was allowed to stand : the case was not of sufficient importance to call for the exercise of the remedial power. In like manner, in Scotland, as stated by Erskine (B. 1, T. 7, § 36)—"As to the minor's lesion, if it be inconsiderable, restitution is excluded, for actions of reduction are extraordinary remedies, not to be applied but on great and urgent occasions ;" and Stair (B. 1, T. 6, § 44), dealing with a minor's right to be restored against deeds granted by him to his lesion, says—" But this remeid is not competent for every small lesion, but it must be enorm, which is *in arbitrio judicis.*" Again, the *actio redhibitoria* was a prætorian remedy by which a purchaser, on discovering a latent defect or fault in the subject bought, could have the contract of sale rescinded, and the seller ordained to take back the subject : but this remedy was not allowed for every trifling fault or defect that was discovered after purchase. If the defect was trifling, the maxim applied, and the sale stood (D. 18, 1, 54). For a fuller exposition of this maxim, and an enumeration of the cases in which it did, as well as those in which it did not apply under the Roman law, the student is referred to *Barbosæ Thesaurus locorum communium jurisprudentiæ,* Lib. XI. cap. 38, Ax. 4 : and for the views entertained in reference to the meaning and application of this maxim in England, reference may be made to Broom, p. 142. It may be remarked that the power vested in the Court of Session, known as the *nobile officium,* resembles that which was vested in and exercised by the Prætor, in so far as it affords equitable remedy, not obtainable otherwise. On this subject reference may be made to Stair, B. 4, T. 3, §§ 1 and 2. In cases which turn upon the question whether statutory requirements or provisions have been complied with, this maxim has no application ; and of this the reader will find a notable example in the case of *Thomson v. M'Crummen's Trs.,* 18 D. 470, affd. 21 D. (H.L.) 3. In that case a bond and disposition in security was reduced because each page was not marked "by the number first, second, &c.," although the testing-clause bore that the deed was written on that and the six preceding pages (a correct statement of the number of pages of which the deed consisted), and there was a regular catchword connecting each page with that which followed. This would have been considered, popularly, as sufficiently trivial to entitle the law to disregard it. No one suffered through the want of the figures 1, 2, 3, &c., in the corners of the pages of the deed; there was no allegation that the deed did not represent an honest transaction, or that the money had not been duly advanced, in security of which it had been granted; there was no objection to it except that it was written on two sheets of paper, and was not paged. The objection was thus of the most technical character, and was not entitled to any favour. But as the pagination of a deed was by statute (1696, c. 15) essential, the Court held itself bound to give effect to the objection, and set aside the deed. In that case, the question before the Court was not and could not be, whether the matter was of sufficient importance for the law to deal with; it was a question whether the requirement of the law had been complied with. To prevent the recurrence of such a case the Act 19 & 20 Vict. c. 89, was passed in the same year in which the above decision was pronounced.

De momento in momentum.—From moment to moment. The years of minority are thus computed; and, until the last moment of the twenty-one years, any deeds granted or acts done, are done in minority, and liable to all the objections competent on that head. So also are the years of prescription computed. "Prescription runs *de momento in momentum*, and the interruption may be on the last moment of the fortieth year" (Bell's Prin. § 622).

De morte antecessoris.—Concerning the death of the ancestor. The brief of inquest, under the old form of service, inquired concerning this, and was therefore called the brief of mortancestry. This name, however, properly and originally belonged to a brief used by the heir for calling into Court, the possessor of the ancestor's property, with the view of trying the title under which he possessed. The brief of mortancestry "was purchased by the undoubted heir, even though he had been already served, against the superior of the lands, or against others who had been seized in them upon a title preferable to that of the heir. This last was therefore the ground of a proper action, in which it behoved the heir to cite the person who held the possession from him as a party to the suit." (Ersk. B. 3, T. 8, § 62.)

De munere regio.—By royal gift. Lands held under feudal tenure were generally described by this phrase, in contradistinction to lands acquired by inheritance or singular title ; the name being derived from the fact that all lands held feu were originally gifted by the Crown to the Barons, in reward for past and in view of future services.

De non alienando.—Concerning the non-alienation of the lands. This clause, prohibiting the sale or alienation of the particular lands specified, was a clause in entails essential to their validity, as without it the purpose of the entail could be defeated. The prohibitions against sale, against burdening the entailed lands with debt, and against altering the order of succession, are called the cardinal prohibitions of an entail. These, in order to render the entail effectual, required not only to be expressly stated, but also to be properly fenced with irritant and resolutive clauses. But by the Act 31 & 32 Vict. c. 101, § 14, it was provided that " where a deed of entail contains an express clause authorising registration of the deed in the register of tailzies, it shall not be necessary to insert" the clauses of prohibition, or the irritant and resolutive clauses above mentioned.

De non alienando sine consensu superiorum.—Concerning the non-alienation of the lands without the consent of the superior. This clause, in effect, was at one time common to all charters granted to vassals, and the breach of it incurred the casualty of recognition. But being regarded as hostile to the free use of property, and as a restraint upon the exercise of the just right of alienation, it was abolished by the Act 20 Geo. II. c. 50. This enactment, however, does not appear to strike at the clause of pre-emption, which " is intended, not for preserving the feudal influence of the superior (the abolition of which was the object of the Act), but for conferring upon him a valuable right to the purchase of the estate, and is legitimate and effectual." Bell's Prin. § 865. See also Duff's Feud. Con. 69 ; Menzies' Lectures, 608, and the cases cited by these authors respectively.

De non apparentibus et non existentibus eadem est ratio.—The same rule is applied to things which do not appear, and to things which do not exist; or, things which do not appear (*i.e.*, are not produced or proved) are regarded as non-existent. This rule is of frequent application, and in various forms. Thus, if a litigant requires for the purposes of maintaining his right to the possession of some lands, to found upon a deed or document, it (or such equivalent as the law permits, as, for example, a decree of proving the tenor) must be produced or recovered by him, as otherwise the Court must decide the question before it as if the deed or document never existed; the Court cannot assume that the deed existed, or that its terms were as averred, if these matters are disputed. So, again, if parties have entered into a written contract, the party seeking to enforce it must produce it (or its equivalent) before he can succeed. Further, if parties have entered into a bargain which has been reduced to writing, the terms of the bargain can only be ascertained from the writing itself, which cannot be modified or affected by previous communings or negotiations. As the written bargain is considered the expression and statement of the ultimate agreement of the parties, what does not appear there is treated as if it had never been suggested, or had not existed. Indeed, everything of which the Court can take no notice judicially is regarded, for the purposes of the particular case, as non-existent. Thus in a discussion on a bill of exceptions, the Court can take no notice of anything which occurred at the trial which does not appear on the bill itself; and in like manner, on a motion for a new trial on the ground that the verdict is contrary to evidence, the Court can only judge of that on consideration of the judge's notes of evidence. What does not appear there must be regarded as non-existent.

De non contrahendo debitum.—Against the contraction of debt. A clause inserted in entails, to prevent the heir burdening the entail lands with debt, whereby, through the diligence of creditors, the entail might be rendered ineffectual. See *De non alienando*.

De novo.—Of new.

De novo damus.—We give of new. The charter (or clause) of novodamus is granted (or inserted in a charter by progress) by the superior in favour of his vassal, where the latter, by loss or otherwise, is unable to produce a sufficient legal title to demand entry. As such charters proceed on no resignation, and in obedience to no warrant, they are ineffectual, if challenged, until the years of prescription have run. *Grieve* v. *Williamson*, M. 3022.

De plano.—Immediately, summarily, without attention to forms.

De praxi.—According to practice : sometimes written, but rarely, *De practica*.

De presenti.—At present, now. See *De futuro*.

De recenti.—Recently, recent. In cases of theft before the Justiciary Courts, in which recent possession of the stolen property affords a strong presumptive proof of the prisoner's guilt, the question occasionally arises as to what period of time should be considered *recent*. This has never been positively fixed; but it has been held, that stolen property found in possession of the prisoner two months after the theft had been committed, was not such recent possession as to infer guilt. *John Hannah*, 1 Swinton, 289.

De rei gestæ veritate.—Of the truth of the thing done ; or of the transaction. In an action of proving the tenor of a lost deed, the instrumentary witnesses may be not only witnesses to the existence of the deed, but also to its nature, and sometimes to the truth of its statements. Thus, a witness insert and subscribing to an instrument of sasine under the old form, would be a witness, not only to the existence of the lost instrument, but also to the contents, and the truth of the *res gesta*—*i.e.*, the act or ceremony of giving sasine narrated by it.

De solemnitate.—As a solemnity. Formerly there were certain requisites in deeds called solemnities, the want of which invalidated the deed; while there were other parts of a deed which, although commonly inserted, were not essential to validity. Thus the date of a deed was not a solemnity,—it was not essential to validity. But the name and designation of the writer of the deed required, as a solemnity, to be given in the testing-clause. The names and designations of the attesting witnesses were also by general opinion regarded as essential, although it has been held that the designation of the witnesses only, and not their names, were essential. (*M'Dougall* v. *M'Dougall*, 2 R. 814.) The law regarding the solemnities of deeds has been most materially changed by the provisions of the Act, 37 & 38 Vict. c. 94, to which the reader is referred. See especially §§ 38 and 39.

De statu defunctorum.—Concerning the status of the deceased. The older authorities in our law lay it down, that where a person, during his life, enjoyed the status of legitimacy, it should be incompetent to question this judicially after his death (Stair, B. 3, T. 3, § 42, and cases there cited); but modern practice has differed from this, and it appears competent to any one, having interest, to question the legitimacy of the deceased at any time. See Fraser, Par. & Ch. 20, and authorities cited.

De ventre inspiciendo.—For inspection of the womb. "Where a widow alleges that she is left pregnant, an application may be made to the Court (if there be any suspicious circumstances to warrant such an unusual proceeding) *de ventre inspiciendo*. This is authorised by express statute, has been sanctioned by decision, appears to have been borrowed from the Roman law, and is in accordance with English practice" (Fraser, Par. & Ch. p. 2). A similar inspection is ordered where a woman, convicted of a capital offence, pleads her pregnancy in bar of immediate sentence (Hume, ii. 471 ; Macdonald, 527). As to the admissibility, in the general case, of evidence founded upon an *inspectio corporis*, see the observations of Lord Fraser at the passage above cited, and also the opinions delivered in the case of *Davidson* v. *Davidson*, 22 D. 749.

Debile fundamentum fallit opus.—A weak foundation destroys the superstructure. This maxim is not much used, if at all, in Scotland, although frequently cited in England. Its meaning is obvious, but its application may be shown by one or two illustrations. Thus, if one claims a right as heir of his father, and it be shown that the claimant is not the heir, his claim will be repelled, he being shown not to have that character in which alone he maintained his right. Or, if in the character of heir, one has entered upon possession of certain subjects, and it be shown that he is not the heir because he is illegitimate, or because there is a nearer heir to the deceased than he, he will be deprived of his possession—the foundation on which his right rested having been insufficient, and failed, the right itself cannot be maintained. Again: Letters patent are granted for the protection, to the inventor, of a new invention which is in itself useful, has not been previously published, or used by the public. If these conditions fail, being the foundation on which the patent right has been granted, the protection which would otherwise have existed comes to an end. This maxim is used by Justice Blackburn in the *Mersey Docks* case (L. R. 1 Eng. & Ir. App. 116) while criticising the judgment in another case, in the sense of "the premises being disproved, the conclusion falls." See Broom, p. 180.

Debita fundi.—Debts attaching to the soil; such as feu-duties, ground-annuals, debts heritably secured, &c.

Debita sequuntur personam debitoris.—Debts follow the person of the debtor. According to this rule all debts and personal obligations require to be sued for and enforced before the Court of the debtor's domicile. This rule holds even where, by the contract or obligation sought to be enforced, the *locus solutionis* has been fixed at some place where the debtor is not, nor never has been domiciled. In this country there is an exception to the rule, where funds belonging to a foreign debtor have been arrested in Scotland for the purpose of founding jurisdiction. When such arrestment has been used, the debtor is as much amenable to the jurisdiction of the Scotch Courts as if he were domiciled in Scotland. Another exception to the rule arises when jurisdiction is founded *reconventione*.

Debiti et crediti contributio.—A reckoning of debit and credit. The phrase is used in some parts of the civil law as a definition of compensation or set-off.

Debito tempore.—In due or proper time.

Debitor non præsumitur donare.—A debtor is not presumed to make a gift to his creditor. So long as the debtor's obligation is unextinguished, any payment made, or money given, or bond or assignation granted by him to his creditor, is not presumed to be in gift, but is presumed to be towards the extinction of the existing obligation. In applying this maxim, care must be taken to distinguish between what is a proper obligation on the part of the debtor, and what is promised or given by him by way of gratuitous provision, a distinction which the reader will find carefully brought out in the case of *Darley* v. *Kippen*, 18 D. 1137, and particularly in the opinion of Lord Chancellor Chelmsford in the House of Lords, where that case was taken on appeal (3 Macq. 203). In that case, a father by his marriage-contract bound himself to make certain provisions for the children of the marriage, and by subsequent trust-settlement executed by him, he made certain provisions for his unmarried daughters, greater in amount than those which by his marriage-contract he was bound to make. Thereafter one of his daughters married, and in her marriage-contract her father bound himself to pay her a sum of £5000; but there was no renunciation on the part of the daughter of her legal or other rights, nor stipulation that the £5000 should be accepted in full of legitim, &c. On the death of the father, the daughter claimed not only the £5000 provided to her under her marriage-contract (so far as not already paid), but also—(1) the provision made to her as a child of the marriage under her father's marriage-contract, as well as (2) the provision which had been made for her under her father's settlement. This claim was resisted by the residuary legatees of the father, on the ground that the £5000 was given in full of all claims competent to the daughter, and in support of this, they pleaded the presumption of this maxim. The Court held the maxim to apply in so far as regarded the sum claimed, under the terms of the marriage-contract of the father, that being a proper obligation on his part, amounting to a debt, and therefore repelled the daughter's claim to that extent; but they sustained the claim *quoad ultra*, holding that the maxim did not apply to gratuitous provisions such as those made under the settlement, which were not debts or obligations, but voluntary acts on the part of the father, which he might have altered or revoked. This judgment was affirmed; the result being, as we have seen, that the maxim was held to apply in so far as the father could be shown to be his daughter's debtor, but no further. The case of *Balfour*, 4 D. 1044, is also an important case, as an example of circumstances in which the Court did not apply the maxim, although the person from whom the donation (by way of legacy) proceeded was the debtor of the donee in a proper obligation, it appearing in the whole circumstances that the debtor's intention was to give a donation, and not to pay his debt by the legacy he bequeathed. In that case it was observed that the maxim now under consideration "is too broadly stated, and that, although not to be laid aside as irrelevant in the case of legacies, each case in which it is sought to be applied falls to be decided on a view of the whole circumstances indicating the testator's intention." The maxim, at the best, only deals with a presumption which of course may be redargued by proof that the debtor intended donation, and not payment of a debt. In the more recent case of *Bryce*, 4 Macp. 312, the Court held a cheque given by a debtor who was moribund to his creditor, to have been given partly in payment of his debt, and partly in donation.

Debitorem locupletem esse.—That the debtor is solvent, or sufficient for the debt. In assigning a debt, the cedent does not warrant (except under special arrangement) that the debtor is able to pay it, but he is always held to warrant *debitum subesse*, that the debt is legally due.

Debitorum pactionibus creditorum petitio nec tolli nec minui potest.—A creditor's claim (or right to recover) can neither be taken away nor diminished by bargain among his debtors. This is the application to a particular case of the more general maxim that no one can be deprived of property or right of any kind possessed by him except of his own consent. If a creditor holds several persons bound to him for payment of a sum of money or fulfilment of a certain obligation, his right to enforce payment or performance from all or any of the obligants cannot be lessened by an agreement among the debtors themselves that one of them shall take the whole burden on himself. For example, the onerous holder of a bill is entitled to recover the amount contained in it either from the acceptor or any of the indorsers; but the indorsers are not freed from their obligation to pay, nor is the holder's right to recover from them in any degree affected by the acceptor (or any of the obligants on the bill) undertaking to free the other obligants of their liability. Such an arrangement would entitle the co-obligant who had been compelled to pay to relief against the person who had undertaken the whole responsibility; but could in no way affect the creditor's right, who was no party to the arrangement. So, a cautioner is not relieved from his liability to the creditor by obtaining security from some one else that he will be held free of loss. If the creditor consents to accept one debtor in place of all the others, or one cautioner instead of another, the result would be different. That, however, would not be a paction among the debtors, but a paction between the debtors and the creditor, by the terms of which the creditor would be bound.

Debitum et contractus nullius sunt loci.—Debt and contract are not of any particular place—*i.e.*, neither debt nor contract is limited to any particular locality, but may be sued for or enforced before any court which has jurisdiction over the debtor. This may be said of all personal obligations; but claims upon, or which are sought to be made good out of real estate, must be enforced in the country where the estate is situated.

Debitum fructuum.—A debt forming a burden on the fruits of the lands, such as teinds. Arrears of such debts do not affect singular successors.

Debitum in diem.—A debt which is due, but the term of payment of which has not yet arrived. See *Dies cedit*, &c.

Debitum in presenti solvendum in futuro.—A debt now due, but not payable (that is, not prestable) until a future time. Thus a legacy may be due, that is, may vest in the legatee so as to transmit to his representatives, and yet not be demandable out of the estate of the testator until a time long subsequent. Such debts are called *future debts* in our law, but the term future properly applies to the date of payment alone. See *Dies cedit*, &c.

Debitum reale.—A real debt; a debt affecting lands, as opposed to that which is merely a personal obligation; a debt heritably secured.

Debitum subesse.—That the debt is due. See *Debitorem*, &c.

Decennalis et triennalis possessor non tenetur docere de titulo.—A possessor for thirteen years is not bound to instruct his title. The benefit of this rule of law is confined to churchmen holding a benefice or living, and partakes more of the character of a legal presumption than of prescription. A clergyman who for thirteen years holds possession of a subject as part of his benefice, is presumed to be the rightful possessor, without producing any written title to the subject; but if it can be shown, from his own title or otherwise, that the subject so possessed is outwith the bounds of his title, his possession will be restricted. The thirteen years' possession gives him no actual title, but only raises a presumption in his favour, that the possession is legal, and throws the *onus* of showing that the possession is unwarranted on the challenger. The presumption, as we have said, may be redargued by a contrary proof.

Deceptis non decipientibus, jura subveniunt.—The laws help or succour persons who are deceived, not those deceiving. The laws afford peculiar protection to minors, on account of their youth and inexperience, and as a check upon others who might take advantage of that inexperience. Accordingly, a minor may set aside all deeds granted or ordinary contracts entered into by him during his minority, on proof that such deed or contract was to his lesion; and he may do so either during his minority or during the first four years of his majority, called the *quadriennium utile*. There are two exceptions to this general rule which must be borne in mind —(1) a minor cannot set aside a marriage contracted by him, however much his inexperience may have been taken advantage of; and (2) he cannot question mercantile obligations entered into by him, because "when a minor acts as a trader, and holds himself out to the world as such, his dealings are on the same footing with a major." (Bell's Com. i. 345.) But where the minor gives himself out to be major, or acts as if he were, and having incurred liabilities, pleads his minority in defence, and as a ground on which his liability should not be enforced, such defence will not be sustained. *Wilkie*, 12 S. 506.

Decimæ debentur parocho.—Teinds are due to the parish minister. A minister's stipend is not regarded as of the nature of a fund purely alimentary; it is held to belong to him *pleno jure,* and is therefore arrestable. In *Learmonth* v. *Paterson,* 20 D. 418, it was held by Lord Mackenzie (Ordinary) "that the stipend payable to a minister of the Established Church, and the right he has to the glebe during his incumbency, are attachable by the diligence of creditors, and by sequestration under the Bankrupt Act, subject always to the condition that the minister shall receive from the emoluments of his office such an allowance as may be necessary for his subsistence, and to enable him to discharge his parochial duties." A minister can assign his stipend in security of debt, and his right to grant a lease of his glebe during the period of his own incumbency has been recognised for centuries. How far a minister has the power of letting his manse, will be seen from the decision in the case of *Heritors of Aberdour* v. *Roddick,* 10 Macp. 221. A minister cannot grant any deed or conveyance affecting his stipend, glebe, or manse which would be prejudicial to his successor. Although, as above mentioned, a minister was allowed to grant a lease of his glebe during his incumbency, he had no power to feu it. But considerable alterations were made on the law concerning the rights of ministers over their glebe lands by the Act 29 & 30 Vict. c. 71, the principal of which were—(1) a right to lease the glebe, reserving the five acres nearest and most convenient to the manse, for a period not exceeding eleven years, for such rent and on such conditions as should be approved of by the heritors and presbytery, and under the special condition that if the reserved five acres were included in the lease, such lease, so far as they were concerned, should cease at the first term of Martinmas after the termination of the incumbency of the minister granting the lease; and (2) a right to feu the glebe, or grant building leases thereof, for a term not exceeding ninety-nine years, on obtaining authority so to do from the Court of Session as Commissioners of Teinds.

Decimæ garbales.—Teind sheaves—*i.e.,* the tenth sheaf of the cut corn, to which the rector of the parish had a right.

Decimæ inclusæ.—See *Cum decimis,* &c.

Decimæ rectoriæ.—Parsonage teinds: which may be

described as a tenth of every species of grain raised by culture upon the lands out of which the teinds are payable. They are due to the rector or parson, and the right to levy them cannot be lost by prescription.

Decimæ vicariæ.—Vicarage teinds; commonly called the lesser teinds, because payable, not out of grain, but out of the minor products of the land, such as fowls, eggs, butter, wool, &c. These are not drawn, as are parsonage teinds, according to any fixed and general rule, but according to the usage and custom of each benefice or parish. The right to them may be lost *non utendo*.

Decreta.—The name given in the civil law to those decisions pronounced by the Emperor, as supreme judge, in cases brought before him. There were three kinds of imperial ordinances or constitutions: 1. *Decreta;* 2. *Rescripta*, instructions, or answers by letter, given by the Emperor to questions put to him on cases which had arisen; and 3. *Edicta*, rules voluntarily made by the Emperor, to meet cases which might arise.

Deductis debitis.—The debts being deducted. This must be done before the extent of any estate or succession can be ascertained. It is for the amount of the estate, less the debts, that trustees or executors are liable to representatives; and it is on the amount of the estate thus ascertained that inventory duty is paid.

Del credere.—An Italian mercantile phrase. It is similar in import to the English word *guarantee*, and with us is understood to express the obligation undertaken by an agent, who not only sells his principal's goods, but who also guarantees the solvency of the buyer. On account of this guarantee he receives a higher remuneration or percentage on his transactions, which is called a *del credere* commission.

Delectus personæ.—Choice of person to the exclusion of others. This is a right, either express or implied, which the law recognises in those who place themselves in relationship with others, where mutual trust and confidence are necessary to the carrying out of the purpose for which the relationship was formed. Thus, under the contract of partnership, the partners have this right, whereby they can prevent the admission of any one to the firm as a partner who has not been selected or agreed to by all the existing partners: consequently the heir of a deceasing partner cannot insist on being admitted to the firm of which his father (or ancestor) was a partner, unless such admission has been stipulated for expressly in the contract of copartnery, nor can a partner assign or sell his place in the copartnery, to the effect of making the assignee or buyer a partner. Again, in leases of land the landlord is supposed to have selected the tenant, or granted him the lease, having in view his (the tenant's) personal qualifications; and accordingly, in leases of ordinary length the *delectus personæ* has full operation. This right, at one time, went so far as to exclude the heir-at-law of the tenant, but that is no longer so. Sub-tenants and assignees are, however, in the general case excluded, even where there is no clause of express exclusion in the lease; but if there be no express clause of exclusion—(1) a creditor adjudging his debtor's lease is not excluded, and (2) sub-tenants or assignees are not excluded if the lease be of more than ordinary duration. This right is not presumed in reference to the letting of urban tenements, where the rule is that the tenant has the power to assign, or sub-let, unless expressly prohibited. Bell's Prin. § 1216. Ersk. B. 2, T. 6, §§ 31-33, and notes by Lord Ivory.

Delegata potestas non potest delegari.—A delegated power cannot be delegated; that is, a delegated power cannot be conferred by the delegate upon another. This rule applies equally where the delegated power has been conferred by public or private authority, and proceeds to a great extent upon the principle that in conferring the power there has been a *delectus personæ*, which would be entirely defeated, if the delegate, chosen on account of his own particular position or qualifications, were entitled to transfer the power so delegated to another of his own choosing. A variety of cases may be used as illustrations of this important maxim. And, first, as regards power delegated by public authority. All persons who are intrusted or charged with the performance of judicial functions, whether in the Supreme or Inferior Courts, must perform these duties in person, and cannot delegate their authority to another, except in such cases and to such extent as is expressly authorised by statute or the common law. The appointment of a substitute by the sheriff of a county (while such appointments were made by the sheriff; they are now made by the Crown, 40 & 41 Vict. cap. 50) was no exception to this rule, although at first sight it might so appear. The sheriff did not and could not delegate to his substitute any power or duty expressly conferred on himself personally; and while he had the power of nominating the person who was to fill the office of sheriff-substitute, the acts performed by the latter after his appointment were performed on the same authority as that which authorised the acts of the sheriff. A forcible illustration of this maxim will be found in the case *Lord Advocate* v. *Sinclair*, 11 Macp. 137. That was an application to the sheriff under the Act 1669, cap. 17, which provides that when a proprietor intends to enclose his ground by a dike or ditch upon the march between his lands and those of the conterminous proprietor, it shall be lawful to him to require the sheriff or other Judge Ordinary " to visit the marches alongst which the said dike or ditch is to be drawn : " and the sheriff is thereupon authorised to do certain things with a view to the equitable adjustment of the march. In the application referred to, the sheriff was not asked to visit the march, but the petition prayed for a remit to a person named to report upon the proper line of march, &c. : and it appeared that "in respect of the sheriff-substitute's knowledge of the locality, his visiting the proposed march had been dispensed with by both parties." The judgment of the sheriff having been appealed to the Court of Session, it was there held that the visiting of the marches by the sheriff required by the statute was imperative, and could not be supplied by a remit to a man of skill, even of consent. The power thus delegated by the legislature to the sheriff could not be delegated by him to another. The same principle, though not made the ground of judgment, will be found applied in the case of *Gillespie* v. *Young*, 23 D. 1357. That was an action for the reduction of letters-patent, and by statute (15 & 16 Vict. cap. 83, § 43) required to be brought with the concurrence of the Lord Advocate, " which concurrence Her

Majesty's Advocate is authorised and empowered to give upon just cause shown only." It will be seen from the report of the case that the concurrence had been written on the summons by the Lord Advocate's clerk in the mode adopted generally in those cases where the concurrence of the Lord Advocate was necessary ; but the Court, after inquiry, held that there had been no concurrence, the Lord Advocate not having applied his mind to the case, which was accordingly dismissed. A more apt illustration than is afforded by the case just quoted will be found in the case of *Miles* v. *Bough*, 12 L. J. Q. B. 74. That was an action for recovery of calls made by the Trustees under a local and personal Act, which provided that necessary notices should be signed by three or more of the Trustees or their clerk for the time being. It was objected that the notices of the calls were not so signed, but were signed by the clerk or partner of the clerk to the Trustees, and this was held to be insufficient, Coleridge, J., remarking that this was "signature by a deputy's deputy." One or two illustrations of the application of this maxim may now be given where the power is conferred or delegated, not by public, but private authority. In the ordinary case of mandate, the mandatory cannot devolve upon another the power or authority conferred on himself by the mandant ; but a law agent in the country authorised by a client to adopt proceedings before the Supreme Court was not, formerly, regarded as violating this rule when he, in turn, instructed a practitioner in town to adopt such proceedings, because, as the country agent could not himself practise before the Supreme Courts (which the mandant was presumed to know), his mandate was held to authorise all steps necessary to carry out the mandant's instructions. Whether this would now be held, seeing that all law agents are qualified to practise before the Supreme Courts, is not so clear. An arbiter, also, is bound by this maxim to apply his own mind to the question submitted to him, and cannot delegate his power ; and so, in *Gillon* v. *Simpson*, 21 D. 243, an opinion was expressed that an award consisting of statements by one of two arbiters, as to his own knowledge of the matters referred, and agreeing, on behalf of one of the parties, to take a certain sum in full of all claims, countersigned by the other, "The above decision I agree to," was an incompetent award. There is no difference between the law of Scotland and that of England in reference to the subject of this maxim. "Whatever a man has power to do in his own right, he may (except in one or two very peculiar cases) appoint an agent to do for him. I say *in his own right,* for one agent cannot nominate another to perform the subject of his agency." Smith's Mer. Law, 104.

Delegatio.—Delegation ; one of the modes of extinguishing obligations, by the substitution of a new debtor for the old. The new debtor was, in the civil law, called *delegatus* where the substitution took place with consent of the original debtor ; but, where this was done without the consent of the original debtor, the new debtor was called *expromissor* (Sandar's Just. 396). Delegation is never presumed, and therefore where it is not clear that this was intended, the new obligation will be considered as in corroboration, not extinction, of the old one. The reader will find the law upon this subject discussed and illustrated in the following cases :—*Pearston* v. *Wilson,* 19 D. 197 ; *Muir* v. *Dickson,* 22 D. 1070 ; *Pollock* v. *Murray,* 2 Macp. 14.

Delegatus non potest delegare.— A delegate cannot devolve the duty or power delegated to him upon another. This is another mode of expressing the same principle as that contained in the maxim, *Delegata potestas, &c.*

Derivativa potestas non potest esse major primitiva. —A derived right cannot be greater than that from which it springs. As a general rule, it is quite true that no one can confer upon another a greater right than that which he himself possesses : the right of a cedent is generally the measure of the right of the assignee. But there is certainly one class of cases where the derived right is greater than that from which it springs. The right of an onerous indorsee of a bill is not limited to the right either of the drawer or indorser, from whom his right has been derived. Suppose a bill granted without value, or granted for an immoral consideration, or for a gambling debt, in any of these cases the original holder of the bill to whom it was granted could not recover the amount of the bill from the acceptor. But if the bill be indorsed for value by the drawer to a *bona fide* holder, these grounds would form no defence to the demand for payment by the latter, and the indorsation would thus confer upon the indorsee a right greater than that possessed by the indorser. This, however, is to be taken subject to the limitation imposed by the Mercantile Law Amendment Act (1856), § 16, which provides that where a bill is indorsed after it has become payable, the indorsee shall be deemed to have taken it subject to all the objections or exceptions to which it was subject in the hands of the indorser. See *Craig & Rose* v. *Delargy* (a case which turned upon the terms of the Bills of Lading Act, 18 & 19 Vict. c. 111), 6 R. 1269.

Destinatione.—By destination, or intention. There are two distinct meanings to the term destination, the one popular, the other technical. The first is sufficiently explained by the following passage from Erskine :—" One's collecting of timber, stone, slate, or other materials, for raising any fabric or edifice, is not sufficient to make them heritable *destinatione* till they be united to the surface of the ground by actual building." (B. 2, T. 2, § 14.) The intention of the proprietor, and the purpose for which he destines the material, is here referred to. Technically, that part of a dispositive deed or conveyance which contains the names, or points out the class of persons who are called in a certain order to the succession, is termed the destination, and an heir *destinatione* is one who succeeds by virtue of that clause.

Dicis causa.—For form's sake. Ersk. B. 3, T. 8, § 89.

Diebus feriatis.—On holidays. This includes Sunday, fast-days, or other days which by lawful authority are set apart from business, and which are regarded by the law as *dies non*.

Dies cedit, et dies venit.—These words are borrowed from the civil law, and are defined by Ulpian (Dig. B. 50, T. 16, l. 213) as follows :—" *Cedere diem* signifies that the money has commenced to be due ; *venire diem* signifies that that day has arrived on which the money may be demanded." In Scotch law phraseology, it may be said that *dies cedit* signifies that the right has vested ; *dies venit*, that it has become prestable. Where performance of an obligation is postponed to a fixed and certain day, it is said, *Dies cedit, sed non venit* (the obligation exists, but is not yet prestable); but where the performance is postponed to an uncertain day, and is thus conditional, *Dies nec cedit nec venit nisi conditio extiterit* (it is neither due nor prestable until the condition shall have existed—*i.e.*, been purified).

Dies dominicus non est juridicus.—Sunday is not a day for judicial or legal proceedings. It is in this respect that Sunday is spoken of as not being a *lawful* day. On that day no judicial act is performed, and all proceedings taken on that day, which proceed *auctoritate judicis*, are null. Thus no arrestment or inhibition used on a Sunday is effectual, and caption for civil debt (while that was competent) on that day was illegal. (Bell's Com. ii. 460.) Criminal warrants may, however, be executed on a Sunday, as may also a warrant granted against a person in *meditatione fugæ*, the latter being regarded as *quasi* criminal, and proceeding on the averment that the debtor contemplates flight for the purpose of defrauding his creditor; and it has been held that it is no objection to the legality of the proceedings in a criminal prosecution that the trial extended beyond the end of the week into Sunday morning. (Macdonald, 455.) A distinction has been drawn between judicial and private acts performed on Sunday, for the latter, unlike the former, are not null. A bond or bill granted on Sunday forms a good obligation (Thomson on Bills, 39), and bargains or engagements made on that day are binding. (Bell's Prin. § 44.) Ordinary trading, however, and "using of handy labour on Sunday," are declared illegal by various Acts of Parliament, and these, although of ancient date, are still in force; and the plea that they had fallen into desuetude was repelled in the case of *Bute* v. *More*, 1 Couper, 495. See also on this subject the opinions delivered in the case of *Phillips* v. *Innes* in the House of Lords, 2 S. and M'L. 465, reversing the judgment of the Court of Session, 13 S. 778. The law in England with regard to the legality of acts performed or bargains made on Sunday, is not materially different from that of Scotland; it will be found stated in Addison on Contracts, 1163.

Dies inceptus pro completo habetur.—A day commenced is held as completed. This phrase, expressing one of the rules of our law as to the computation of time, is not of universal application. Thus, where a question of prescription is at issue, it would not be sufficient that the last day of the forty years had begun, to make it complete. The years of prescription, like the years of minority, are computed *de momento in momentum*; and in such a case, therefore, the principle of the maxim would not apply. While, however, it has not universal, it has very general application, and one or two instances of its application may be merely mentioned. The plea of deathbed (before reduction on that ground was abolished by the Act 34 & 35 Vict. cap. 81) was elided if the deceased survived until the morning of the sixtieth day after executing his settlement; a deed granted by a bankrupt cannot be reduced as a preference, if his estate be not sequestrated, until the morning of the sixtieth day after granting it; and in all cases where the law requires the lapse of "year and day," the period is held to be completed if the "day." has begun. On the question of computation of time, see *Ashley*, 11 Macp. 709. See also Bell's Com. I. 759, ii. 168. In cases of demurrage, a fraction of a day counts as a day. *Boulton*, L. R. 10, Q. B. 346; *Hough* v. *Athya*, 6 R. 961.

Dies incertus pro conditione habetur.—An uncertain day is regarded as a condition—*i.e.*, an obligation prestable only on a day which may never come, such as, on a certain person's attaining majority, is regarded as a conditional obligation, which only comes into effect when the condition is purified. See *Turner* v. *Donald*, 2 Macp. 922.

Dies interpellat pro homine.—Literally, the day interferes or demands for the man. Where fulfilment of an obligation is due on a certain day, the occurrence of the day is of itself deemed a sufficient demand on the part of the creditor to the effect of putting the debtor *in mora*, and rendering him liable in all its consequences, should he fail on that day in fulfilment.

Dies non.—A day which is regarded by the law as one on which no judicial act can be performed, or legal diligence used. See *Diebus feriatis*.

Diligentia media.—The middle degree of diligence or care, being that which a man of ordinary prudence usually bestows upon his own affairs. See *Culpa*.

Dissimulatione tollitur injuria.—Injury (or, wrong), is removed by being passed over or forgiven. Any injury, however slight, or however serious, may be, as regards its civil consequences, completely removed by the forgiveness of the person injured; but if the injury amounts to crime, no forgiveness of the injured person can exclude the criminal consequences, or that which is done *ad vindictam publicam*. Ersk. B. 4, T. 4, § 108.

Do ut des, do ut facias.—I give that you may give; I give that you may do. The Roman jurists divided all innominate contracts (that is, all contracts not distinguished by special names) into these four heads—1. *Do ut des*. 2. *Do ut facias*. 3. *Facio ut des* (I do that you may give). 4. *Facio ut facias* (I do that you may do). In the first and second, something is given that something may be received or done in return; and in the third and fourth, something is performed that something may be given or done. It is evident that the division is not exhaustive, as there might be, 5. *Do ut non facias* (I give that you may abstain from doing something); and 6. *Facio ut non facias* (I do something that you may abstain).

Docendo discimus.—In teaching we learn. See Fraser Mas. and Serv. 456.

Dolo circumventus.—Overreached by fraud. Any one fraudulently taken advantage of will not be bound by the contract to which the fraud gave rise. A deed granted under such circumstances can be reduced. Distinction, however, must be made between this and *errore lapsus*,—between actual fraud, and a mistake on the part of one of the parties not corrected or pointed out by the other. A seller is not bound to point out defects in the subject sold by him, if the purchaser has an opportunity of inspecting it for himself—in that case the buyer's eye is his merchant, and he has no redress if he afterwards discovers that the subject bought is not so good or so valuable as he thought it, or not fit for the purposes to which he intended to apply it. But it will be otherwise if the buyer has been misled by the representations of the seller (not being mere commendation of his goods), or if the seller has done anything to conceal defects or turn attention away from them. Mere error will be sufficient, however, to set aside a deed or contract, if the error be an essential one. Thus, in the contract of sale, if the parties are not at one as to the subject to be sold (as, for example, where the seller means to sell oats, and the purchaser thinks he is buying wheat), there is no contract, for the parties are not *ad idem*; and the same result would follow from a difference as to the price, which is an essential of the contract of sale. The error may also be as to the nature of the contract itself supposed to be entered into, as where one party intends to lend a subject on hire, and the other thinks he is purchasing it, or *vice versa*; in such case there is no contract at all. So, again, where one conveys a right or discharges an obligation under essential error as to the extent of his legal rights, the deed so granted may be set aside on this ground. See Bell's Prin. § 11. See also, for the law of England as to the effect of error on a contract, Addison on Contracts, 1181, and Benjamin on Sales, 56.

Dolo facit qui petit quod redditurus est.—He acts unfairly (or with guile) who claims that which he has to restore. See *Frustra petis*, &c.

Dolose.—Deceitfully, fraudulently.

Dolus.—Fraud. In the civil law this is defined to be "every trick, falsehood, or device employed for the purpose of circumventing, cheating, or deceiving another" (Dig. 4, 3, 1, § 2). This is a definition of *dolus* in its most comprehensive sense, generally termed in the civil law *dolus malus*. Any contract or agreement brought about by such means could not be maintained (*dolo malo pactum se non servaturum*, Dig. 2, 14, 7, § 9). The same principle prevails in our law, and any one who has been induced to enter into a contract, or grant a deed or obligation, through fraud or misrepresentation of this kind, may have the contract or obligation set aside upon that ground. There was, however, a distinction recognised in the civil law, which is also recognised in our law, between *dolus malus* and *dolus bonus* or *solertia*. The latter is not regarded as fraud, but merely as that craftiness, skill, or adroitness which a seller may safely use in order to effect a sale, either more immediately, or on better terms than he would otherwise probably obtain. Accordingly the eulogies bestowed by a trader upon his goods with the view of securing a better bargain, or the taking advantage of the buyer's ignorance of any change in the market prices of which he should have been aware, with a view of obtaining a better price,—these, and such like acts, amount merely to *dolus bonus* or *solertia*, and do not vitiate the contract. But a false statement, either as to the character or quality of the goods, made with the intention of deceiving, on which the buyer is to rely, and in reliance on which he enters into the contract, amounts to *dolus malus*.

Dolus auctoris non nocet successori, nisi in causa lucrativa.—The fraud of the author does not affect the successor, except where the latter acquires by a lucrative title—*i.e.*, gratuitously. Where the fraud is inherent, such as in stolen property, even an onerous holder is affected by the author's fraud; but where the fraud is not so, it does not affect an onerous purchaser or holder. An heir, however, who succeeds gratuitously to his ancestor's estate, represents his ancestor in that fraud *quoad* its civil effects.

Dolus circuitu non purgatur.—Fraud is not purged by circuity or indirect procedure. It has already been said that *dolus* vitiates any contract or obligation which was entered into or granted in consequence thereof. The present maxim enunciates the principle that the same consequences will follow where the fraud has been indirectly perpetrated, and that the fact that the person using the fraud did so by some indirect or underhand procedure makes no difference in the result; the indirectness of the means used does not purge the act from the taint of fraud. Thus it is clear, that if A makes false and fraudulent representations as to the character and quality of the goods which he wishes to sell to B, and, in reliance on such representations, B purchases, the contract may be set aside by B on the ground of fraud. In such a case the fraud is the direct act of A. But if, instead of making the false representations himself, he gets another to make them to B, and thereupon B purchases the goods, B may still set aside the contract, and A cannot successfully plead in defence that he did not make the false representations, but that they were made by somebody else. It was not the less fraud on the part of A, because instead of doing it, he procured it to be done. In *Thomson* v. *Hopper*, 27 L. J., Q. B. 441, a question was raised whether the owners of a ship could recover for loss under their policy, or whether in the circumstances they had not knowingly sent the ship to sea in an unseaworthy state, or exposed the ship to the peril through which the loss arose; and in giving judgment on a motion for a new trial on the ground of misdirection, Bramwell, B., observed—"*Dolus circuitu non purgatur* means, you cannot fraudulently do that indirectly which you cannot do directly; and I agree that if a man send his ship to sea with a false compass, in order that she might be lost, and she was lost in consequence, he could not recover." See also some observations made upon this maxim by Willes, J., in *Jeffries* v. *Alexander*, 31 L. J. Chan. 20.

Dolus dans causam contractui.—Fraud giving rise to the contract. If the fraud be such as that without it the engagement would not have taken place, it voids the contract.

Dolus incidens.—Fraud incidental; that is, not affecting the *essentialia* of the contract, but incident to, and as an accompaniment of it, independently of which the parties were engaged. This does not void the contract, " but it will always void what is affected by the *dolus*." Per Lord Mackenzie in *Watt*, 8 D. 529.

Dolus latet in generalibus.—Fraud or deceit lurks in generalities.

Dolus præsumitur contra versantem in illicito.—Dole (fraud, or bad intention) is presumed against one engaged in an illegal act or transaction.

Dolus versatur in generalibus.—Fraud deals in generalities. Where the statements of parties are specific there is less chance of their being fraudulent, or intended to deceive, than where they are of a general character. A specific statement is easily tested, or, at all events, is more easily tested than a vague and general statement. Where, again, the conditions of a contract are specific, it is comparatively easy to ascertain what they are, as well as to prove whether they have been fulfilled. But it is otherwise where the conditions are expressed in broad and general terms. In the latter case it is in the power of that contracting party who wishes to take advantage of the other, to contend that the conditions of the contract mean what is most for his advantage. Where there is an intention to deceive or act unfairly, there is greater opportunity for carrying out that intention in those cases where general statements or expressions are used: one who does not wish to bind himself to that which he pretends he is binding himself to do, will adopt vague and general terms in expressing his obligation, to afford him the greater chance of subsequently getting rid of his obligation.

Dominium.—The name given in the civil law to the right of absolute ownership.

Dominium directum.—The name given to the right vested in a superior; the superiority of lands. It is so called, because at one time it was considered the direct and paramount right in the lands, the vassal's right being regarded as merely a burden upon it. This is a view not now entertained.

Dominium eminens.—The supreme power over property vested in the people, in virtue of which they can, for the purposes of public necessity or utility, compel any proprietor to part with his lands. This is the right exercised in Acts of Parliament, which authorise the purchase of lands by compulsory sale, for the purposes of railways, canals, &c. *Dominium eminens* is sometimes used as equivalent to *dominium directum*.

Dominium non potest esse in pendente.—A fee or right of property cannot be in suspension—*i.e.*, it must always be vested in some one. See the rules of law adopted for preventing the right of property being thus in suspension. Bell's Prin. §§ 1711-15, 1951.

Dominium utile.—The right of property enjoyed by the vassal, as distinguished from the superiority, and so called because the vassal has the useful enjoyment of the subjects and its fruits.

Dominus aliquando non potest alienare.—An owner has sometimes no power to alienate or convey. This maxim is rarely used. It may be illustrated by the case of an heir of entail, who, although the owner of the entailed estate, has no power to alienate or convey it, or otherwise alter the order of succession.

Dominus directus.—The superior. Ersk. B. 1, T. 7, § 46.

Dominus litis.—The person to whom a suit belongs, and who has the real interest in its decision, deriving the benefit of a favourable, and suffering the consequences of an adverse judgment. One may be *dominus litis* whose name does not appear in the proceedings either as pursuer or defender; and he will be liable in the expenses of process, if these are found due by the person under cover of whose name he has been litigating. *Corsan* v. *M'Lauchlan*, 6 S. 505; *Hepburn* v. *Tait*, 1 R. 875.

Dominus omnium bonorum.—Proprietor of all moveable goods. This phrase is used by Stair (B. 3, T. 8, § 46) as descriptive of a husband who was the owner of the goods in communion. The description is no longer applicable since the husband's ownership in such goods has been abolished. 40 & 41 Vict. c. 29, and 44 & 45 Vict. cap. 21.

Domitæ naturæ.—Of a tamed nature: animals which have been *tamed* or are by nature tame, as distinguished from animals *feræ naturæ* which are still wild and untamed—which have not been captured or made the subjects of private property.

Dona clandestina sunt semper suspiciosa.—Clandestine gifts are regarded with suspicion. The rule expressed by this maxim is applicable to other grants besides those which are, properly called, donations; and finds its practical application, perhaps, most frequently in questions which arise under the bankruptcy of the granter. Thus in *Anderson* v. *Guild*, 14 D. 866, the vote of a mother-in-law was disallowed in a competition for the office of trustee on the sequestrated estates of her son-in-law, her claim being founded on a promissory note, dated about eighteen months before the bankruptcy, and payable sixty days after sight, but which had not been operated upon until three days before the bankruptcy. The vote was rejected on account of the suspicions which attached to such a document, not merely as being granted to a person conjunct and confident, but because, in addition thereto, the claimant was not in business, no explanation was given as to the consideration for, or the circumstances under which it had been granted, and no evidence showing its existence until a few days before the bankruptcy occurred. So, also, a latent assignation by a bankrupt or insolvent, of his whole estate to a creditor does not bar the diligence of other creditors (*Fraser*, 8 S. 982); while a trustee in bankruptcy is in competition preferred to latent trusts or latent claims of any kind in all cases of property with a registered title. (Murdoch, 79, and cases cited.) Gifts made by a person who is moribund, by cheque or endorsed deposit receipt, to those who are attending him, and of which no one is made aware until after the donor's death, are always regarded with suspicion, and as donation is never presumed, it falls upon the person claiming the gift to show clearly that donation was intended. See *Bryce*, 4 Macp. 312, where a cheque given in such circumstances was held good. In that case, the Court was satisfied on inquiry of the intention of the granter, and the gift was not in any way clandestine or concealed. Examples of the application of this maxim in England will be found in the cases cited by Broom, pp. 288-90.

Donatio inter virum et uxorem.—Donation between husband and wife. Such donations are in themselves valid, but may be revoked by the donor at pleasure at any time during his or her life, and that without the knowledge of the donee. The revocation may be express, as by a deed recalling the donation; or implied, as by the subsequent conveyance of the subject of donation to another person. The creditors of the donor, in the event of his bankruptcy, have the same right of revoking or setting aside the donation as the donor. Provisions mutually made in an antenuptial contract, do not, of course, fall within the legal rules relative to donations between husband and wife, because such provisions are made before that relationship commences. But provisions or gifts made by postnuptial contracts fall within these rules. (*Dunlop* v. *Johnston*, L. R. 1 Sc. Ap. 109.) With reference to them, however, it is to be observed that a postnuptial contract cannot be set aside on the ground of donation merely because it confers benefits on husband or wife, *stante matrimonio*. Where there has been no antenuptial contract, the husband may make reasonable provision for his wife by a postnuptial contract, and the latter will not be revocable ; but if the provision so made is unreasonable, which will depend upon the circumstances of the donor, it may be revoked or set aside, so far as it is considered excessive. Where there has been an antenuptial contract, all postnuptial deeds increasing or diminishing the provisions made by the former contract are regarded as donations, and are revocable in so far as they do not proceed on onerous considerations. A wife therefore who, during the marriage, renounces her legal rights, or rights conferred on her by an antenuptial contract, for an inadequate consideration, is entitled to revoke her renunciation as donation, and that even after her husband's death. *Dickson* v. *Hunter*, 5 S. 248, affd. 5 W. & S. 455. *Rae* v. *Nielson*, 2 R. 676. But where by mutual settlement or other mutual deed, provisions are granted by both spouses which are rational and proportionate, these considerations will render the deed onerous and not revocable by either party without the consent of the other : if the consideration be reasonable, the Court will not weigh in nice scales whether it is or is not too much. *Hepburn*, 2 Dow, 342. See also *Kidd* v. *Kidd*, 2 Macp. 227. For circumstances in which a husband was found entitled to revoke a mutual settlement after his wife's death, see *Moffat's Trs.*, 1 S. 184. Where the deed sought to be reduced confers a benefit upon a third party, *quoad* that benefit the deed is not revocable : but where the deed nominally confers a benefit on a third party, as on an heir, yet is in reality a gift or benefit to the spouse, it is revocable. If the donor die without revoking, his or her representative cannot revoke, and the right of the donee becomes absolute, for *morte dantis donatio confirmatur*.

Donatio mortis causa.—A donation made in the view of, and to take effect after, the donor's death. This kind of donation, "little known in our practice" (Ersk. B. 3, T. 3, § 91), is borrowed from the Roman law. The essential conditions of such a gift were that it should be made with the view of meeting the case of death, and that it should take effect only if death occurred ; the donor could therefore revoke the gift at any time during his life, and if he survived the donee, the thing given reverted to the donor. According to Justinian (Inst. 2, 7, 1), that was a donation *mortis causa* " where the donor wishes that the thing given should belong to himself rather than the person to whom he gives it, and to that person rather than his own heir." The law of Scotland, with regard to donations of this kind, is very amply stated in the opinions delivered in the case of *Morris* v. *Riddick,* 5 Macp. 1036. In that case the Lord President (Inglis) said—" *Donatio mortis causa* in the law of Scotland may, I think, be defined as a conveyance of an immoveable or incorporeal right, or a transference of moveables or money by delivery, so that the property is immediately transferred to the grantee, upon the condition that he shall hold for the granter so long as he lives, subject to the power of revocation, and, failing such revocation, then for the grantee on the death of the granter. It is involved, of course, in this definition, that if the grantee predecease the granter, the property reverts to the granter, and the qualified right of property which was vested in the grantee is extinguished by his predecease." In the opinion delivered by Lord Deas in the same case, the reader will find stated the respects in which such a donation resembles a legacy, and in what they differ, the principal difference being that a donation *mortis causa* can be proved by parole, while a legacy to be effectual, requires writing, if of a value exceeding £100 Scots. See also *Lord Ad.* v. *Galloway,* 11 R. 541. Different opinions have been expressed as to the necessity for delivery to make a *mortis causa* donation effectual, regarding which reference may be made to the following cases : *Crosbie's Trs.,* 7 R. 821 ; *Milne,* 11 R. 887 ; *Blyth,* 12 R. 674 ; and *M'Nicol,* 17 R. 25.

Donatio non præsumitur.—Donation is not presumed. " No deed is presumed a donation if it can bear another construction ; for no person is presumed to do what, in place of bringing him profit, must certainly be attended with some pecuniary loss." (Ersk. B. 3, T. 3, § 92.) Accordingly, it has been held that the mere possession of an indorsed deposit receipt does not afford any presumption of donation in favour of the indorsee or holder, for it may have been indorsed and delivered in order that the money should be uplifted and paid over to the indorser. *Allan* v. *Munnoch*, 23 D. 417 ; *Durie* v. *Ross*, 9 Macp. 969 ; *M'Nicol*, 17 R. 25 ; *Dawson*, 19 R. 261. So also an acknowledgment of the receipt of money, on which interest was to be paid "if demanded," was held to import a loan, and to raise no presumption of donation. *Robertson*, 20 D. 371. In this case it was decided that donation could only be proved by the writ or oath of the alleged donor. But it has been laid down in later decisions that pure donation (equally with donations *mortis causa*) may be proved by parole. *Wright's Executors*, 7 R. 527 ; *Thomson*, 9 R. 911.

Donatio perficitur possessione accipientis.—Donation is completed by the possession of the donee. So long as the subject of the gift remains in the possession of the donor, there is no effectual donation ; there may be promise to give on the part of the donor, or expectation on the part of the donee, but no donation. But when the donor has delivered the subject of the gift to the donee *animo donandi*, the donation is completed, and the subject remains irrevocably with the donee, for a pure donation cannot be revoked. Mere possession of a subject, however, does not raise any presumption of donation, and if donation is denied, the burden of proving donation lies on the person claiming to be donee. As to the question whether delivery is essential to make a donation *mortis causa* effectual, see the cases referred to under *Donatio mortis causa*.

Donatio propter nuptias.—A donation on account of the marriage. This was the provision made by a husband, under the civil law, as the counterpart of the dowry brought to him by his wife, given partly by way of jointure for the wife in the event of her survivance, and partly as security for the return of the dowry to the wife's heirs in the event of her predecease. During the marriage, the husband had the management and administration of both the dowry and his own *donatio*, but he had no power of alienating either during the subsistence of the marriage. On the death of the wife, the *donatio propter nuptias* reverted in full property to the husband, and, in the general case, the dowry was returned to the wife's heirs, although it was competent to stipulate in the marriage-contract that the husband should retain the dowry on his wife's death. The *donatio propter nuptias*, in our law, is the provision or settlement made by the husband for his wife, in the event of her survivance; and any such provision made in an antenuptial contract, may with us, as under the later civil law, be increased by postnuptial contract. Such postnuptial addition with us, however, is regarded as donation between husband and wife, and therefore subject to revocation.

Donatio velata.—A veiled gift; a gift under pretence of being something else. "All deeds granted by the wife to third parties, in trust for the use of the husband"—" are truly *donationes velatæ*," and as such may be revoked. Ersk. B. 1, T. 6, § 35. For cases in illustration of this, see Fraser, ii. 920 *et seq.*

Dubii juris.—Of doubtful law; an unsettled point.

Dum se bene gesserit.—During good conduct. This is equivalent to *Ad vitam aut culpam*, which see. The latter is the form in which the phrase is most commonly used in Scotland; the former is most frequently used in England.

Dummodo constet de persona.—Provided it be evident who is the person meant. A legacy is valid, although there may be an error in the name or designation of the legatee, if from the whole deed or circumstances connected with it, it is sufficiently plain who is the person meant. See the cases of *Keiller*, 3 S. 279; *Keiller*, 4 S. 730; *Scottish Missionary Society*, 20 D. 634; and *Donald*, 2 Macp. 922. See *Constat de persona*.

Dummodo vassalli conditio non sit deterior.—Provided the vassal's condition be not made worse, or deteriorated. The superior's right of disposing of his superiority is restricted by this rule. He is thereby prevented from interjecting a mid superior between himself and the vassal, and also from conveying the superiority in divided portions, so as to subject the vassal in performance of the services to more than one superior. This rule being designed to guard the vassal's interest, an objection founded upon it is competent to him alone, and may be barred by his acquiescence.

Duo non possunt esse domini ejusdem rei in solidum.—Two persons cannot have the full property of the same thing at the same time. This maxim is sometimes written as follows :—

Duo non possunt in solido unam rem possidere.—Two persons cannot each have the entire right to one thing. In either form, the meaning of the maxim is that there cannot co-exist titles to the same subject or right in two persons at the same time. There may, of course, be many joint rights in the same subject at the same time, such as superiority and property, right of property and right of servitude, commonty, *pro indiviso* rights, &c., but in all these cases each joint proprietor's right is to something properly his own, which is not covered by the title in the person of any of the other joint proprietors. The meaning of the maxim will perhaps be made clearer by considering what are the respective rights, in a subject which has been stolen, of the owner who has been deprived of it, and the person who has in *bona fides* bought it after the theft. The right of the one is that of original ownership of which he was never divested, the other's right is acquired by purchase. But as two persons cannot at the same time have the undivided right to the same subject, the original owner's right prevails over that of the purchaser, since the former was never divested of his right, and the latter, therefore, could not acquire it.

Duorum pluriumve in idem placitum consensus et conventio pactum est.—A contract is the consent and covenant of two or more persons, agreed concerning the same thing. See *Consensus in idem*, &c.

Durante bene placito.—During good pleasure; at will. Any office or appointment, from which the holder of it may be dismissed at the pleasure of the person or authority making the appointment, is said to be held *durante bene placito*, and differs from those appointments which are held *ad vitam aut culpam*, from which the holder cannot be dismissed, except upon the commission of such fault as disqualifies him from holding that office longer. For example, prior to the passing of the Education (Scotland) Act, 1872, the office of parochial schoolmaster was held *ad vitam aut culpam;* but that statute declares (§ 55) that all appointments of teachers in public schools (who now take the place of parish schoolmasters) shall be made by the School Boards, and that such appointments "shall be during the pleasure of the School Board." The reader will find the different natures of the appointments above referred to contrasted in Hume, ii. 18.

Durante furore.—While the fatuosity or insanity endures. Insane or furious persons cannot be tried in a criminal court while they continue in that state, even for crimes committed before they were deprived of reason, because no criminal trial can proceed unless the accused is capable of making his defence. Insanity is therefore a good plea in bar of trial.

Durior sors.—" That debt which bound the debtor fastest, or to which a penalty was adjected." (Ersk. B. 3, T. 4, § 2.) Under the civil law, an indefinite payment made by the debtor was applied *in duriorem sortem.* By our law, indefinite payments are, on the contrary, allowed to be applied by the creditor to his least secured debt.

E

E contra.—On the contrary ; on the other hand ; conversely.

E converso.—Conversely. Another form of the preceding phrase.

Ea quæ commendandi causa in venditionibus dicuntur si palam appareant venditorem non obligant.—Those things which are said by way of commendation in the course of a sale, if they appear openly (*i.e.*, if they refer to such things as the purchaser can check for himself), do not bind the seller. See *Caveat emptor ; Simplex commendatio* &c.

Ea quæ dari impossibilia sunt, vel quæ in rerum natura non sunt, pro non adjectis habentur.—These things which cannot possibly be given, or which do not exist, are held as not added. This expresses a rule universally observed in the construction of wills or other testamentary writings. If a testator leaves as a bequest something which does not belong to him, knowing that it is not his to bequeath, this is still a good legacy, and imposes on the executor the obligation of procuring the thing so bequeathed, and delivering it to the legatee, or otherwise satisfying the legatee therefor. But if the thing bequeathed was a thing which it was not possible for the testator to give, or a thing which had no existence, such a legacy is held as not added to the will, and is disregarded just as if it had never been expressed. These rules are adopted by our law from the Roman law. " A testator may not only give as a legacy his own property, or that of his heir, but also the property of others. The heir is then obliged to purchase and deliver it, or if it cannot be bought, to give its value. But if the thing given is not in its nature a subject of commerce, or purchasable, the heir is not bound to pay the value to the legatee ; as if a man should bequeath the

Campus Martius, the palaces, the temples, or any of the things appropriated to public purposes, for such a legacy is of no effect." Just. B. 2, T. 20, § 4. The difference in effect of an impossible condition (which includes unlawful conditions) attached to a legacy, and of such a condition attached to a contract, must be kept in view. In the case of a legacy the impossible condition is regarded as *pro non scripto*, and the will read as if the condition had not been adjected, whereas an impossible condition adjected to a contract voids the contract altogether. Bell's Prin. § 49.

Eadem persona cum defuncto.—The same person with the deceased. An heir succeeding by universal title to his ancestor, and thereby becoming possessed of all his property, with the rights and privileges attaching thereto, is held liable in payment of his ancestor's debts and fulfilment of his obligations. As the heir thus represents his ancestor in his rights and obligations, he is regarded in law as the same person as the deceased. The different modes in which an heir succeeds and makes up his title carry with them a varied extent of obligation. Thus, one who enters upon the succession *cum beneficio inventarii*, is only liable for the deceased's debts in so far as he is himself *lucratus;* while another, incurring a general passive title, is liable for the whole debts, whether he be *lucratus* to that extent or not. This statement, however, is to be taken subject to the restriction of an heir's liability introduced by the Act 37 & 38 Vict. c. 94, § 12.

Edicta.—Edicts, or the imperial rules issued under the civil law by the Emperor, to provide for the decision of questions which might arise. See *Decreta*.

Edictum perpetuum.—Perpetual edict. The law by which Roman citizens were governed, and their rights and obligations fixed, was originally that of the Twelve Tables. These constituted the first written code of laws among the Romans, and formed the basis of their law until the time of Justinian. They applied exclusively to Roman citizens, and could only be made available by those possessed of the privilege of citizenship, in enforcing their rights before the Prætor. As the Romans advanced in conquest, and in civilisation, the principles of these Tables were found to be too narrow and rigorous, because, as many had come to reside within the Roman territory, for the purposes of commerce or protection, questions arose, not as formerly, between citizen and citizen, but between citizen and stranger. A new magistrate was appointed to deal with such cases, called the *Prætor peregrinus*, who, instead of confining himself to the strict municipal law of Rome, adopted the broader basis afforded by the principles of the law of nations. The wisdom of such a course soon commended itself to the Romans. What had been done for strangers it soon became necessary to do for themselves; and while the Twelve Tables were retained in all their integrity, it became the custom for Prætors, on their assuming office, to publish an edict setting forth the principles on which they would administer justice, in those cases for which provision was not fully made in the Twelve Tables. The authority of each edict expired with the office of its author; but it was generally termed *edictum perpetuum*, signifying that it should continue as the general rule on which its author would proceed during the whole of his prætorship, and as distinguished from the *edictum repentinum*, which was an edict or rule issued during the Prætor's term of office to meet some case unforeseen and unprovided for which had arisen. In the time of Hadrian, however, the name (*edictum perpetuum*) acquired a different signification, for that Emperor directed Salvius Julianus, an eminent jurist, to draw up an edict, partly from existing edicts, and partly according to his own opinion of what was necessary, which would serve as the guide of all subsequent Prætors. This edict was termed *perpetuum*, signifying that it was perpetual and unchangeable, and it became a permanent part of the civil law.

Ei abest.—Literally, it is wanting to him. This refers to the proper disbursements made by one person on account of another, and for recovery of which he may raise action, generally the *actio contraria*. Thus a depositary is entitled to recover from the depositor any disbursements he may have made for the preservation of the deposit. So also is a *negotiorum gestor* entitled, not only to payment of that which he has paid on behalf of the person for whom he interfered, but also to relief from all obligations incurred on his account. Any such payment is *ei abest*, because the payer is *minus* their amount.

Ejusdem generis.—Of the same class, or kind.

Ejusdem negotii.—Part of the same transaction.

Ejus est interpretari cujus est condere.—It belongs to him to interpret (or explain) who enacts; the right of interpreting belongs to him who enacts. This was a maxim of the civil law (belonging to the later period of the Roman Empire), which set forth that the Emperor, to whom alone belonged the right of enacting laws, had alone the right of interpreting them. Where ambiguities in the laws rendered interpretation or construction necessary, the Roman judges might not take upon themselves to put a construction upon the doubtful law, but had to refer the difficulty for explanation or construction to the Emperor. "But should any enactment be considered ambiguous, let the judges refer it to His Imperial Majesty, and it will be made clear by august authority, to whom alone it belongs both to enact and to explain laws" (C. B. 1, T. 17, § 21). In this, its original and proper sense, the maxim has no place either in Scotch or English law. An Act, once passed by the legislature, admits of no explanation by the authority which enacted it; any ambiguity or difficulty must be construed or explained by the judges appointed to administer the law. "The province of legislature is not to construe but enact, and their opinion, not expressed in the form of law, as a declaratory provision would be, is not binding upon Courts, whose duty it is to expound the statutes they have enacted." (Per Parke, B., in *Russell* v. *Ledsam*, 14 L. J. Exch. 358.) In a less technical sense, however, the rule expressed in the maxim is recognised by our law, which permits any one who executes a deed or grants an obligation (and thus enacts or establishes the deed or obligation) to put what interpretation he pleases upon the terms used by him, provided he makes it clear, if he uses terms in other than their ordinary sense, what meaning he attaches to the terms actually used. There is no restriction upon any one using what terms he pleases, with whatever meaning he chooses to attach to them, provided the deed is his own voluntary act, and he is not under obligation to use any specified form of expression. But to affect others by his peculiar expression or meaning, it must appear clearly what the expression used is meant to convey. To illustrate this, suppose that A gives a guarantee to B in the following terms:—" I hereby become security to you for the due payment of any debt which C may owe you, to the extent of £500, that is, any debt incurred by him to you through his intromissions as your agent." The original terms of the guarantee would cover "any debt" incurred by C to B, however incurred; but the interpretation of these terms is, any debt incurred in a certain way, and beyond the terms of the interpretation, the guarantee would not be binding. Or again, if A bequeathes to B "my best and most valuable piece of silver-plate, that is, my epergne," the legacy would be a legacy of the epergne whether it was the best and most valuable piece of the testator's plate or not, because he had so interpreted the general terms used by him. In like manner the legislature may, by an interpretation clause, enact that certain words used in an Act shall bear a certain signification, and if the interpretation clause puts a specified meaning upon a word or expression used in the Act, that word or expression can receive no other interpretation than that put upon it by the power which has used or enacted it. Thus the terms "Justice of the Peace" and "Magistrate" are well known, and are popularly applied in England and Scotland alike to persons holding the same office. But in the Industrial Schools Act (1866), by the interpretation clause, the former of these titles is defined to be applicable only to persons who are Justices of the Peace in England; while the term "Magistrate" is defined as applying only to Scotland, and is interpreted as including the Sheriff, Sheriff-Substitute, and Justice of the Peace, as well as Judges in the Police Court and Provost or Bailie of a city or burgh. In Scotland the term "Magistrate" would not, in the ordinary use of that term, be applied to the persons holding any of the first three offices, which are here held as included in it; but the legislature having used the term "Magistrate" as a convenient one, might have declared it to include and mean any one holding judicial office, or not holding judicial office, or might have attached what meaning to it they pleased. The legislature may either enact their interpretation by a clause in that statute, the terms in which are being interpreted, or by a separate statute. Of the latter kind the reader has an example in the Act 13 Vict. cap. 21 (sometimes known as Lord Brougham's and sometimes as Lord Romilly's Act). But it is obvious that this is not an explanation or interpretation of a previous Act which is doubtful, but a substantive enactment that a certain word shall bear a certain meaning.

Ejus est nolle qui potest velle.—He may be unwilling who can be willing—*i.e.*, he who can consent may object.

Ejus est periculum cujus est dominium—aut commodum.—His is the risk to whom the property belongs, or who reaps the advantage. See *Cujus est*, &c.

Ejus nulla culpa est cui parere necesse sit.—He is not guilty of fault who necessarily obeys; that is, no one incurs fault or blame through the performance of an act which he is under the necessity of performing. Thus one who, in self-defence, having no means of escape, kills another who had attacked him and put his life in danger, will not be responsible for his act, because it was induced by the necessity of preserving his own life. A soldier who in the course of his duty acts on the order of his superior officer is held blameless, for he is not entitled to question the propriety of any order so given, but is bound to render implicit obedience: the fault, if any, resting on the officer who gave the order. An officer in the execution of a criminal warrant is not responsible if the person whom he seeks to apprehend offers resistance, and there remains no alternative but to kill him or allow him to escape. It appears that an officer executing a civil warrant has the same protection. "If, therefore, he is reduced to the alternative of killing the opposer or abandoning his warrant, the law cannot in justice refuse to hold it for a homicide done from constraint of duty, and in nowise reprehensible." (Hume, i. 203.) A wife, formerly, was not held responsible for criminal acts committed by her under the order of her husband, as she was regarded as bound to obey her husband even in that: the husband being responsible for the act committed. But the subjection of a wife is not now regarded as an excuse for her act, but rather as a plea in mitigation of punishment, the effect to be given to which depends upon the circumstances of each case. (Hume, i. 49.)

Electio est debitoris.—The debtor has the election or choice. Where there is an alternative in the mode of fulfilling an obligation, the debtor or obligant can adopt which he pleases. Thus, if there be an obligation to do a certain thing, or pay a certain sum, at a determined time, the obligant may fulfil his obligation, either by performance of the act, or by payment of the money. As to the choice or election which a debtor has to appropriate payments made by him to a creditor whose debtor he is in several obligations, the reader is referred to what is said under the following phrase.

Electio est creditoris.—The creditor has the election or choice. This has reference to a creditor's right to apply indefinite payments, made by his debtor, to that debt or obligation which is least secured; but where the debtor at the time of payment appropriates the sum paid, towards extinction of a particular debt, it must be so applied. The rules as to such payments, to state them generally, are these —(1) the debtor may appropriate the payment at the time of making it; (2) if he does not do so, the creditor may appropriate the indefinite payment towards extinction of any of the several obligations or debts due to him by the debtor, or to interest due rather than to principal; and (3) if there be no appropriation of the payment by either party at the time, the creditor may afterwards, before action, appropriate it according to his election. Where there is an account current between the parties, and no appropriation is made by either party at the time of payment, the law makes an appropriation according to the order of the items in the account, applying the first item on the credit side in extinction of the first item on the debit side, and so on. *Lang* v. *Brown*, 22 D. 113; *Craig* v. *Jackson*, 8 Macp. 408; *Scott's Trustees*, 11 R. 407; *Cuthill*, 21 R. 549. The reader will find the law on this subject stated, and the relative cases fully collected, in Bell's Prin. § 563. See *Durior sors*.

Emphyteusis.—A right of property well known in the civil law, and analogous to the feu-holding of Scotland. It was said to be a lease in perpetuity, under which the tenant (called the *emphyteuta*) had all the rights of property, except the bare ownership, in return for which he became bound to the *dominus* or proprietor in the payment of a yearly sum, called *canon* or *pensio*. The emphyteuta's right descended to his heirs. For a full explanation of the right of *emphyteusis*, and of the analogy between it and our feu-right, see Ersk. B. 2, T. 4, § 6.

Emptio rei facta a pluribus ementibus.—A purchase made by many buyers. Where several persons join in the purchase of a certain subject, they do not thereby become partners, nor incur the responsibilities of partnership. *Neilson*, M. 14551; Bell's Com. ii. 544. The result would be different if the joint purchase was made in pursuance of a partnership, or joint adventure, in which they were engaged. As bearing upon this, see *Lockhart* v. *Moodie*, 4 R. 859.

Emptio venditio.—Purchase, sale. The name given by the Romans to the contract of sale, being the two elements of which the contract was composed. The purchaser's rights were said to be *ex empto*, and the seller's *ex vendito*.

Emptor emit quam minime potest, venditor vendit quam maxime potest.—A purchaser buys as cheaply as he can, a seller sells as dearly as he can. It is upon this view of the conflicting interests of a seller and purchaser that the law forbids any one to purchase what he is intrusted or authorised to sell for the interest of another. Thus a bondholder selling under the powers contained in his bond, cannot purchase the subjects over which the bond has been granted, otherwise he might purchase the subjects at a low price to the disadvantage of the granter of the bond. The more the subjects bring, so much the better for the granter of the bond; his obligation is extinguished, and a balance remains over; or at all events, his obligation is so much reduced; whereas, the smaller the price obtained, so much the better for the bondholder, who, by purchasing at a low price, would get the subjects as his own, leaving the personal obligation of the granter extinguished only to the extent of the small price obtained. The leading case upon this subject is *York Building Co.* v. *Mackenzie*, 3 Paton, 378. On the same principle a trustee in bankruptcy cannot purchase any part of the sequestrated estates (as to whether the law agent in the sequestration can so purchase, see *Rutherfurd,* 18 R. 1061); nor testamentary trustees any portion of the estate they have to administer. M'Laren, ii. 346 *et seq.*

Enixa voluntas.—Anxious wish ; earnest desire ; exerted will disclosed by words or deeds.

Enumeratio unius est exclusio alterius.—The special mention of one thing implies the exclusion of another ; or, the special mention of one thing operates to the exclusion of anything different from that expressed. This is a rule observed in the construction of writs, or Acts of Parliament, and its meaning will be best explained by giving several instances of its application. In a deed of entail it is sufficient if the entailer in the irritant and resolutive clauses declares the forfeiture of the right of the heir in possession to arise in the event of his contravening any of the cardinal conditions or limitations of the entail, and so long as the clauses remain general in their terms, the deed will be effectual and binding on the heirs. But if the entailer proceeds in these clauses to enumerate the several conditions and limitations, and omits any of them, the entail will be ineffectual, the expression of some of the cardinal conditions, on the principle of this maxim, operating as an exclusion of those not mentioned. The case of *Rennie* v. *Horne,* 3 S. & M'L. (H. L.) 142, affords a good example of this. In that case, the cardinal conditions were all set forth, but the irritant clause ran thus : " And in case the said A. H., or any of the heirs of tailzie before mentioned, shall contravene or fail in performing any part of the premises, particularly by," &c., and then followed an enumeration of the conditions of the entail, but omitting special mention of the prohibition against selling. The entail was held to be ineffectual, because the special enumeration of cases in which forfeiture was to follow did not contain any reference to a sale by the heir, and the enumeration excluded the effect of the general clause which preceded it, and which would certainly have been sufficient if it had not been followed, and therefore governed by the particular enumeration. On the other hand, see the case of *E. of Kintore,* 4 Macq. 520, where the general provision was held not to be restricted by the special enumeration on the ground that the words relied on as inferring restriction were used as words of reference, and operated as a repetition of the general clause. Again, in deeds of submission, where parties refer to an arbiter in general terms all differences or disputes between them, but couple the general clause with a particular enumeration of certain disputes, the arbiter will not be entitled to deal under the general reference with any claim which is not *ejusdem generis* with those specially mentioned. " It is a maxim universally received, that in all deeds which contain both general and particular clauses ascertaining their extent, whether conveyances, discharges, bonds of arbitration, &c., the general clause is not to be extended to subjects or claims of a different kind, or of a greater importance than any of the particulars mentioned in the special." (Ersk. B. 3, T. 4, § 9.) This rule applies also, as has been mentioned, to the construction of statutes, where a general rule will be controlled and restricted in its application by a special enumeration of the cases to which it is intended to apply. Thus, the Act 4 Geo. IV. c. 34, relative to the desertion of servants, applies to "any servant in husbandry, or any artificer, calico-printer, handicraftsman, miner, collier, keelman, pitman, glassman, potter, labourer, *or other person.*" The ordinary interpretation of the last words of this clause would include every servant, but the legal interpretation limits it, in respect of the preceding enumeration, to " other persons" *of the same description* as those specified. Accordingly, it has been held that that Act does not apply to domestic servants. *Normant* v. *Wilson,* 2 Broun, 375. In *Henry* v. *M'Ewan,* 7 W. & S. (H. L.) 432, Lord Brougham in construing the provisions of a statute (5 George IV. c. 74, § 15) which declared null certain contracts " for any goods, wares, merchandise, *or other thing* to be sold, delivered, done or agreed for," &c., said : " But an observation has been made upon the words 'or other thing' which follow 'goods, wares, and merchandise.'" Generally speaking, there can be no doubt that the rule is inflexible, that if, after an enumeration of particular things, words of that kind are added, they must be taken by reference to the preceding enumeration to be things *ejusdem generis.*" One further illustration may be given by a reference to a more recent statute. Before the passing of the Infeftment Act (8 & 9 Vict. c. 35), it was necessary to give infeftment separately in each plot of ground, where they lay discontiguous, or being contiguous, were held under different titles, or of different superiors, or by different tenures, &c., even where the whole lands, so situated or held, were conveyed by the one deed. That statute was intended, doubtless, to abolish the necessity for such separate infeftments. It provided that the one instrument should be sufficient, "whether the lands lie contiguous or discontiguous, or are held by the same or by different titles, or of one or more superiors." It made no provision, however, for the case of lands held by different tenures; and although the question was never tried, it can scarcely be doubted (and this was the view adopted in practice), that on the principle of the rule now under illustration, separate instruments would in such case have been necessary, the special enumeration of the cases to which the Act was intended to apply excluding its application to cases not mentioned. "The Titles to Land Act" (1858) put any question to rest which might have arisen on this subject, by abolishing the instrument of sasine altogether.

Eo instanti.—At that moment; the very moment that, &c.

Eo intuitu.—In that prospect; with that view; with that intention.

Eo ipso.—By the thing itself. Thus, a deed by a minor disposing of his heritage, or diverting the course of his succession, is *eo ipso* null, and requires no reduction.

Eo nomine.—In that name, or in that character. A trustee, suing for a debt due to the trust, must sue *eo nomine*, as under any other character the debtor owes him nothing, and cannot be compelled to fulfil his obligation.

Eodem modo quo quid constituitur, eodem modo dissolvitur.—Any obligation is solved or extinguished in the same manner as that by which it was constituted. If an obligation has been constituted verbally, it may be verbally discharged: and it is a general rule (although not without exception) that rights constituted by writing should be extinguished by writing. "The same solemnities that are requisite to a deed which creates an obligation are necessary in a written discharge of it." (Ersk. B. 3, T. 4 § 9.)

But see the opinions delivered in the case of *Leith* v. *Leith*, 10 D. 1137, also given in 1 Ross, L. C. (L. R.) 691. In treating of the extinction of obligations constituted by written instruments, Mr. Menzies says—" At a former period it was the practice, upon performance of an obligation, to rest satisfied with the cancellation of the instrument instructing it. This is not to be relied upon, however, as an effectual discharge. In a bond for money, the fact of payment cannot be proved by parole evidence, and there is, therefore, no available proof of the payment, while, although the bond be destroyed, the tenor of it may be proved ; and however improbable such a thing may appear at the time, a change of circumstances may arise producing effects not now anticipated." (Menzies' Lectures, 269.) In practice, bills, promissory notes, and letters of guarantee, are not generally discharged in any other way than by delivery thereof to the obligant or cautioner ; but with the exception of these, all other written instruments, constituting obligation, are not only delivered up, but are accompanied by a written discharge of the obligation, when that has been fulfilled or departed from. Among the Romans, the rule expressed by this maxim was very strictly applied ; so much so, that the very same words were used in discharging an obligation (where it was one constituted *verbis*) as those which were made use of in its constitution. Rights constituted by use are discharged or extinguished by non-use. So, for example, vicarage teinds, the right to which is constituted by usage, may be extinguished by non-usage, " or by disuse in payment." (Ersk. B. 3, T. 7, § 13.) Servitude rights, such as a right of way acquired by use for more than forty years, may be lost in like manner by a discontinuance of the use for a like period. In England this maxim is sometimes used in this form : *Eodem ligamine quo ligatum est dissolvitur*, but this form is not used by Scotch writers.

Error calculi.—A mistake or error in the calculation.

Errore acerrimo non affectato insimulatove.—Through error of the most pointed or positive character, not merely pretended or feigned. Fraser, Par. & Ch. 29.

Errore lapsus.—A mistake through error. Such mistake will not invalidate a deed or contract, unless where it has been induced by the deceit or dole of the other party to it, or be an error *in substantialibus.* See *Dolo circumventus.*

Essentialia feudi.—The essential qualities of a feu-right; which include the right of superiority, and all those rights inherent in the *dominium directum* which remain in the superior without special reservation. Such, for example, are the superior's right to sell the superiority, and also his right to challenge encroachments and operations of third parties injurious to the feu, whether the vassal interferes or not. *Breadalbane,* 13 D. 647.

Et sequentes paginæ.—And following pages. Generally written *et seq.*

Et sic de anno in annum quamdiu ambabus partibus placuerit.—And so, from year to year, so long as both parties please, or are agreed. A description of tacit relocation. Fraser, Mas. & Ser., 17.

Etiam causa non cognita.—Even where the cause has not been inquired into; without investigation. Some judicial acts are only performed after an inquiry into the facts on which they are to proceed (see *Causa cognita*), but there are others requiring no such investigation. In an ordinary petitory action, decree will pass against the defender if he does not appear to defend, without any inquiry into the soundness of the pursuer's claim; but in actions of divorce, and separation and aliment, no decree passes in the defender's absence, or even on his admission, without inquiry into the grounds of action alleged.

Etiam in articulo mortis.—Even at the point of death. A man's will being ambulatory, may be recalled by him at any time during life, and therefore even at the point of death. He may also, at such a time, execute a settlement disposing not merely of his moveable estate, but also of his heritage, the law which forbade any one executing on death-bed a conveyance of his heritage to the prejudice of the heir-at-law having been abrogated by the Act 34 & 35 Vict. cap. 81. But if a man execute a deed on death-bed of a character which presumably he would not have executed if left to the free exercise of his own will, it will tend to increase the suspicion attaching to such a deed that it was executed when the granter was near his death, and therefore impaired both in bodily and mental strength. But that a deed was executed at the point of death is not in itself any ground for reducing it or refusing to give effect to its provisions.

Etiam in lecto.—Even upon death-bed.

Ex abundanti.—Superfluous.

Ex adverso.—Opposite to ; over against.

Ex æquitate.—On the ground of equity.

Ex animo.—Willingly ; intentionally.

Ex antecedentibus et consequentibus fit optima interpretatio.—The best interpretation (of a word or clause) is to be obtained by a consideration of what goes before and what follows. This is a rule of construction by which a difficulty may be solved relative to the meaning and intention of a word or clause in a deed, where the word or clause is ambiguous or doubtful. If the difficulty arises from the use of a word or expression, it is material to see in what manner, and with what apparent meaning, the same word or expression has been used in other parts of the deed, where no ambiguity or doubt exists, and the same meaning will be attached to the word or expression regarding which the difficulty has arisen, as that which the same word or expression bears where it is unambiguous and clear, for parties will not be presumed to have used the same word or expression in the same deed in a different sense; the contrary presumption will hold in case of doubt. Where the difficulty concerns the meaning or purpose of one of the clauses or provisions of a deed, the same mode is followed, and the clause or provision will be construed in such a manner as will make it consistent or in harmony with the obvious scope and purpose of the deed of which it forms a part, such purpose being ascertained from a consideration of the whole context. *Findlay* v. *Mackenzie*, 2 R. 909. Where two constructions are possible, one consistent with the purpose of the deed, and the other repugnant thereto, the former will be preferred. On this subject the reader may consult the case of *Andrew*, 9 Macp. 554, reversed in the House of Lords, 11 Macp. 13 ; also the observations of Kelly, C. B., in *Morton* v. *Woods*, L. R. 4 Q. B. 305. The same rule is applied in construing Acts of Parliament, where in the case of a clause of doubtful meaning, the Court will consider the other clauses, and even the preamble, and adopt that interpretation of the clause in dispute which is most consistent with the intendment and policy of the statute. *Galloway* v. *Nicolson*, 2 R. 650. It need scarcely be added, that construction is only permissible where the language used admits of doubt, for " if the words of the statute are in themselves precise and unambiguous, then no more can be necessary than to expound the words in their natural and ordinary sense. The words themselves alone do, in such case, best disclose the intention of the lawgiver." (Per Tindal, C. J., in the Sussex peerage case, 11 Cl. & Fin. 143.) " If the precise words used are plain and unambiguous in our judgment, we are bound to construe them in their ordinary sense, even though it do lead, in our view of the case to an absurdity or manifest injustice. Words may be modified or varied where their import is doubtful or obscure." (Per Jervis, C. J., in *Abbey* v. *Dale*, 20 L. J. C. P. 235.) The observations just quoted are equally applicable to the construction of writs or contracts.

Ex auditu.—By hearsay, or report. As a general rule, evidence founded upon hearsay, that is, something which the witness was told, and of which he had no other knowledge, is not admissible. But it is quite competent to prove what a person now dead said during his lifetime. To this, however, there is an exception : it is not competent to prove what a person, now dead, said during lifetime on precognition by an agent. *Macdonald*, 2 Macp. 963. In criminal prosecutions on account of rape, the prosecutor is allowed to prove the statements made by the woman *de recenti*, both as to the circumstances attending the commission of the crime, and the person by whom it was committed, and such evidence is allowed to go to the jury in support of the charge. But it is doubtful whether such evidence is admissible in a civil action for damages at the instance of the woman assaulted, against the person who committed the assault ; and such evidence was rejected in *Hill* v. *Fletcher*, 10 D. 7. It is competent to examine witnesses as to the notoriety of a certain fact, or as to a certain rumour or report being prevalent, although these matters comprehend a number of hearsay statements ; but such evidence is only of use to prove the existence of the rumour, and does not prove that the rumour is true in point of fact.

Ex bonis maternis.—Out of the goods succeeded to through the mother.

Ex bonis paternis.—Out of the goods succeeded to through the father.

Ex bono et æquo.—According to what is right and just ; according to equity.

Ex capite doli.—On the ground of dole or fraud. Where fraud has given rise to a contract, or the granting of a deed, either can be reduced on that ground ; and this phrase is the technical mode of setting forth such a reason for reduction. See *Dolus*.

Ex capite fraudis.—On the ground of fraud. Another form of the preceding phrase.

Ex capite inhibitionis.—On the ground of inhibition. Inhibition is a kind of diligence competent to creditors under our law (which they may use either on an extracted decree or the dependence of an action), whereby they are secured against the alienation of their debtor's heritable estate. This diligence prohibits the debtor from alienating, and interdicts third parties from taking conveyances to such estate to the prejudice of the inhibiting creditor. If, notwithstanding such diligence being used, the debtor grants a conveyance while the inhibition stands unrecalled or undischarged, the creditor can have such conveyance reduced *ex capite inhibitionis*. Inhibition does not now, as formerly, affect *acquirenda*, 31 & 32 Vict. c. 101, § 157.

Ex capite interdictionis.—On the ground of interdiction. Interdiction, now scarcely known in practice, was a means formerly adopted for the protection of those who were weak, facile, and easily imposed upon, and also for the protection of those who, being reckless and profuse, were unable to manage their estate with care and prudence. Interdiction was either judicial or voluntary : and in whichever of these modes the interdiction was effected and imposed, any disposition of heritage thereafter by the interdicted, without the consent of his interdictors, was liable to reduction on the ground of interdiction, except where the conveyances were onerous and rational.

Ex capite lecti.—On the ground of death-bed. Prior to the passing of the Act 34 & 35 Vict. c. 81, deeds disposing of heritage to the prejudice of the heir-at-law, executed within sixty days of the death of the granter, and while he was labouring under the disease of which he died, were reducible on the ground of death-bed. But if the granter survived for sixty days, or attended at kirk or market, after the granting of the deed, the plea of death-bed was elided. If the deed was onerous, it might still be reduced; but in that case the heir had to reimburse the consideration paid. This plea was only competent to the heir, and only competent to him where he had an interest; so that, if the reduction of the deed granted on death-bed had the effect of reviving a former deed which excluded the heir, he had no interest, and therefore could not pursue the reduction. *Wyllie*, 18 R. 218. The donatory of the Crown could reduce any deed prejudicial to his interest on this ground, because he represented the Sovereign, who is *ultimus hæres*. To fall under the provisions of the law of death-bed the deed required to be strictly voluntary, and such as the deceased could not have been compelled to grant; for a deed executed in performance of an obligation undertaken in *liege poustie* was not struck at by the plea of death-bed. But reduction on the ground of death-bed was abolished by the Act above cited.

Ex capite metus.—On the ground of fear. Any deed or obligation obtained from the granter through fear may be set aside upon that ground. But the fear must be not merely "vain or foolish fear" (Bell's Prin. § 12), but such as would overcome a mind of ordinary firmness. Threats of what would be only vexatious or inconvenient would not be sufficient. See *Ex vi, &c.*

Ex capite minorennitatis et læsionis.—On the ground of minority and lesion. A minor, on this ground, can be restored against all deeds granted by him in minority, and that whether they have been granted with consent of his curators or not. To entitle a minor, however, to set aside a deed on the ground of lesion (or injury) it must be shown that the lesion was substantial or material; in the language of the older writers, the lesion must have been *enorm.*

(Stair, B. 1, T. 6, § 44.) "As to the minor's lesion, if it be inconsiderable, restitution is excluded, for actions of reduction are extraordinary remedies, not to be applied but on great and urgent occasion." (Ersk. B. 1, T. 7, § 36.) Those deeds which are null, such as a deed granted by a minor having curators, but without their consent, can be challenged at any time; but those granted with consent of curators, or by a minor who has none, must be challenged within four years after attaining majority, and in the latter class of cases lesion must be proved.

Ex causa lucrativa.—From a lucrative source; gratuitously. An heir who receives from his ancestor a gift, during lifetime, of that to which he would succeed after his ancestor's death, does not thereby avoid the liability of representation. He possesses it under a lucrative title, and is liable for his ancestor's debts contracted prior to the gift. If the transaction between the ancestor and the heir be an onerous one, no liability for debts attaches, because there is no *preceptio hereditatis*, but an onerous purchase.

Ex causa mandati.—On account of the mandate; or by reason of the mandate. A mandatory is entitled to claim from the mandant reimbursement of all moneys disbursed, as well as relief from all obligations incurred, *ex causa mandati* —*i.e.*, on account of the matter which the mandate authorised to be done or performed. On the subject of the claims competent to a mandatory against the mandant, see Bell's Com. i. 534, note 1.

Ex certa scientia.—From certain knowledge.

Ex comitate.—From courtesy. "*Comitas*, as used in international law, signifies the courtesy of nations, by which effect is given in one country to the laws and institutions of another, in questions arising between the natives of both." Bell's Dict. *v. Comitas.* See *Comitas legum*.

Ex consulto.—Deliberately; as the result of deliberation.

Ex continenti.—At once, without interval of time. If any one be violently dispossessed of that which is his, he may recover it by violence if done at the time; but if an interval of time elapses, possession can only be legally recovered by an application to the proper judge. See *Spoliatus,* &c.

Ex contractu.—Arising from a contract; this may either refer to a right or an obligation so arising.

Ex culpa levissima.—On account of the least fault. See *Culpa*.

Ex debito justitiæ.—On account of justice; a claim, the refusal of which would involve an injustice, and therefore one which justice owes it to the claimant to recognise and allow. Dickson, § 1660.

Ex debito naturali.—Arising from natural obligation. Natural obligations are those which arise only from the law of nature, or from equity; and they differ from civil obligations in this, that while the latter can, the former cannot be enforced at law. On this subject see Ersk. B. 3, T. 1, § 4.

Ex defectu juris.—From a defect in the right. A seller is bound to warrant a purchaser against eviction. He does not grant warrandice against eviction by violence or accident, but only against eviction on account of a defect in his own right to the subject sold.

Ex defectu natalium.—From defect of parentage. Formerly, by our law, bastards who died without lawful issue, were incapable of making a testament, and this was said by some to proceed from their defect of parentage; on which Erskine remarks (B. 3, T. 10, § 6): "It is hard to discover a reason why a disability to test should be one of the consequences of illegitimacy." The disability was removed by the Act 6 Will. IV. cap. 22.

Ex delectu familiæ.—From choice of a certain family. Titles of honour, &c., conferred by the patent of the Sovereign, are said to proceed from such choice on his part. They are not transferable; but a grant of lands along with the title gives the recipient the full right of property in them, and they may be disponed, or may be attached by diligence of creditors.

Ex deliberatione Dominorum Concilii.—After consideration by the Lords of Council. Formerly all writs which passed the signet were procured by presentation of a bill (or petition) for such writ. The bill was perused and considered by the Lord Ordinary on the Bills, and if he was satisfied, the bill was passed and the writ issued: the latter bearing the words *ex deliberatione Dominorum Concilii* to signify that the bill had been considered. These words are still appended to almost all writs which pass the signet, but they are now only words of style, since the writs are now passed *periculo petentis* without being submitted to the Lords. Stair, B. 4, T. 3, §§ 4, 32 ; Bankton, B. 4, T. 7, § 9.

Ex delicto.—On the ground of, or arising from, delict. Delicts give rise to civil claims, as well as subjecting the person guilty of the delict to the punishment attached thereto. Thus assault gives rise to a civil claim of damages, and murder to a claim of assythment.

Ex diuturnitate temporis omnia præsumuntur rite et solenniter esse acta.—(In transactions of old date) all things are, on account of the length of time which has elapsed, presumed to have been performed rightly and in the usual manner, or with the necessary solemnities. It is a presumption of law that all things are regularly and duly performed, and that, where certain solemnities are necessary to give the act effect, these solemnities have been duly observed. Such a presumption may be redargued, but it gains force by the lapse of time. See *Omnia præsumuntur*, &c.

Ex diverso.—Conversely ; on the other hand.

Ex dolo.—Arising from dole or fraud. See *Ex capite doli*.

Ex dolo non oritur actio.—A right of action does not arise out of fraud. No one can enforce an obligation or contract whose fraud led to the obligation being granted or the contract entered into: the fraud vitiates that to which it gave rise, so that even where both parties to it were participating in the fraud, it cannot be enforced. For example, where an insolvent, with the view of carrying through a private composition contract, agrees with one of his creditors that if he will accept the composition offered he will grant bills to him for the balance of his debt, and thus give him payment in full, and accordingly grants such bills, the creditor cannot enforce payment of the bills, as these were granted in pursuance of an agreement which was a fraud upon the other creditors of the insolvent. See the case of *Macfarlane* v. *Nicoll*, 3 Macp. 237, where the cases on this subject are all collected. In like manner a preference promised by a bankrupt to one of his creditors cannot be enforced; it is a fraud on the other creditors. Where the parties have been equally guilty of the fraud, the one who has ultimately suffered by it cannot obtain relief from the other, the rule in that case being *In pari delicto potior est conditio defendentis.* But this rule is only applied where the parties have been equally guilty, and voluntarily entered into the fraudulent transaction: a distinction which the reader will find drawn very clearly in the case of *Macfarlane* above cited, and in the opinion of Lord Ellenborough in *Smith* v. *Cuff,* 6 M. & S. 165. Where only one of the parties has been guilty of the fraud, it is at his rights alone that the fraud strikes. If A by fraudulent misrepresentations induces B to purchase certain goods, A cannot enforce the contract, for his fraud gives him no right of action. But B may either enforce the contract, or raise an action for its reduction, or plead the fraud by way of defence when A seeks to enforce it. In the same way, to take the converse of the last case, if A has induced B to sell by fraudulent misrepresentations or concealment, he cannot compel B to fulfil the contract, but B may either enforce the contract or set it aside as he chooses. Again, no contract can be enforced which had for its object the defeating of the revenue laws, and a smuggler cannot recover the price of goods smuggled, from the receiver of them.

Ex eo quod plerumque fit.—From that which generally happens.

Ex equitate.—In equity; according to equitable rule.

Ex eventu.—After the event, or occurrence.

Ex facie.—On the face of it; evidently. This is said of what appears from the face of a writing. For example, a deed may be invalid or null on many grounds, such as fraud, that the person granting it was not in sound mind, &c.; but these do not appear from a mere perusal of the deed; whereas a deed which is erased *in essentialibus,* without any mention of the erasure in the testing clause, is *ex facie* null, the essential defect appearing from the face of the deed itself without any inquiry whatever.

Ex facto jus oritur.—Out of fact the right arises. Many a right, properly so called, arises out of matter of fact; such as a right of property acquired by prescriptive possession, or a servitude arising out of prescriptive use. So also do the respective rights of upper and lower heritors on a stream arise from the fact of their relative position. This maxim may also be, as it is sometimes rendered : The law arises from the fact. The law applicable to a case depends upon the state of the facts. For example, a deed regularly executed and tested is valid and binding if the granter knew what he was doing, and did it voluntarily, and such a deed receives a certain legal effect. It is presumed to be the granter's deed until the contrary be shown. But if it appears that the granter was incapable of executing a deed through mental incapacity, that it had been extorted from him through fear, or obtained by fraud, the deed will receive no effect. Again, a shipmaster signing a bill of lading is presumed to be acting for the owner ; but if the fact appears that the ship had been chartered and handed over to the charterer—if there has been a demise of the ship—the master then acts as the servant of the charterer, and binds him, not the owner : the law as to the enforcement of the obligation depends upon the fact. *Mitchell* v. *Burn*, 1 R. 900.

Ex figura verborum.—By the form of words used. A deed granted *mortis causa*, although in the form of a conveyance *de presenti*, if ineffectual in its real character, will not be improved by the character which it assumes from the form of words used. See Bell's Prin. § 1563.

Ex fraude creditorum.—On the ground of fraud towards creditors. Preferences granted within sixty days of bankruptcy are reduced on this ground.

Ex incommodo.—On account of inconvenience. An argument *ex incommodo* is an argument founded on the inconvenience which would follow if the argument is not sustained or given effect to. See *Argumentum ab*, &c.

Ex incontinenti.—Summarily, without delay.

Ex ingenio.—According to the judgment of any one. Ersk. B. 1, T. 1, § 49.

Ex instrumentis de novo repertis.—On account of documents newly or recently found. Stair says that it is "much controverted whether solemn and formal decreets can be altered" on this ground. There can be little doubt that a decree would now be reduced, however solemnly pronounced, if it could be shown, by documents subsequently discovered, that the party obtaining the decree had no right to it ; as, for instance, if a discharge was found of the debt or obligation for which the decree had been granted.

Ex intervallo.—At some interval ; at some distance of time.

Ex jure naturæ.—According to the law of nature. Many of the duties incumbent on man to man are dependent upon this natural law, some of which, beside being natural, are also civil obligations. Thus the civil obligation of a parent to maintain his children proceeds originally from the law of nature, and becomes a civil obligation, from its being imported into the common law. Those obligations which arise from the law of nature alone cannot be enforced by the common law.

Ex jure representationis.—According to the law of representation. An heir who succeeds to the estate of his ancestor is said to represent him ; and having taken the estate, he becomes liable on the ground of representation for all his ancestor's obligations. In heritable succession this liability might be limited prior to 1874 in either of two ways—(1) By a special service which involved representation only to the extent of the value of the lands embraced in the service ; or (2) by a general service (which involved general representation) with specification annexed ; 31 & 32 Vict. c. 101, §§ 47, 49. By the Act 37 & 38 Vict. c. 94, § 12, it was provided that an heir should not be liable for the debts of his ancestor beyond the value of the estate to which he had succeeded ; and that where an heir had intromitted with the ancestor's estate, and afterwards renounced the succession, he should be liable to the extent of such intromission, but no further. A vitious intromitter with moveable succession incurs general representation ; but it is otherwise with an executor, who gives up an inventory of the deceased's estate for confirmation, who is only liable to the extent of the inventory. Representation includes, not only liability for the deceased's obligations, but also title to the deceased's rights. Thus, the son of the eldest son succeeds in heritage before the second son, not because he is nearer to the ancestor than the second son, but because he represents the eldest son, who was. There was no representation in this sense in regard to moveables prior to the Act 18 Vict. c. 23 ; but representation in moveables was by that Act introduced to a certain extent. On the meaning and construction of that Act see the following cases : *Ormiston* v. *Broad*, 1 Macp. 10 ; *Nimmo* v. *Murray*, 2 Macp. 1144 ; *Turner* v. *Couper*, 8 Macp. 222.

Ex justa causa.—For a just cause, or sufficient reason.

Ex justitia.—Justly ; according to justice.

Ex lege.—Legally ; according to law. Thus, interest on a bill, or money lent, is due to the creditor, from the day when payment should be made, *ex lege;* that is, according to the provision of the common law thereanent, although there may have been no paction on the subject between the creditor and his debtor.

Ex locato.—Arising from the contract of location. For the two actions to which this contract gives rise, and their nature, see *Actio*.

Ex maleficio non oritur contractus.—No contract arises from crime, or from an act which is contrary to law. The law cannot recognise or enforce as a contract any agreement which is based upon crime or upon an illegal act. Thus, if a person charged with a criminal offence engages to pay a sum of money to one of the witnesses against him, provided he will go out of the way and not appear as a witness at the trial, or provided he will appear and commit perjury, so that the accused may obtain an acquittal, such an obligation cannot be enforced ; it is not a contract which the law could recognise, being based upon a consideration contrary to law and vicious in itself. In like manner, an obligation to pay money, provided information be not given to the authorities of a crime committed by the obligor, cannot be enforced. On the same principle a bond or obligation granted as an inducement to continue an illicit connection, or as the wages of prostitution, is not effectual or binding ; because it arises *ex maleficio*, from wrong-doing. But if a bond or other obligation is granted after the illicit intercourse has ceased, and as a reparation for the injury done to the woman, such an obligation is valid, because it does not arise from wrong-doing, but from the desire to repair a wrong, and the law can recognise that as a good ground or consideration for the obligation. A further illustration of this maxim will be found in the case of *Nicholson* v. *Gooch*, L. J. 25 Q. B. 137.

Ex malo regimine.—From bad or wrong treatment. Hume, i. 185.

Ex mandato.—According to the mandate; arising from the contract of mandate. Anything done by a mandatory in terms of the powers conferred upon him by the mandate, is said to be done *ex mandato*. This phrase may also refer to the rights and obligations arising respectively to the mandant and mandatory under their contract. The contract of mandate gives rise to the actions *directa* and *contraria*.

Ex metu carceris.—From fear of imprisonment.

Ex mora debitoris.—On account of the debtor's delay. *Mora* signifies not only delay, but undue or culpable delay, which subjects any person guilty of it in its consequences. Thus a debtor's delay in making payment of his debt renders him liable for interest; and undue delay on the part of one of the parties to a contract, will subject him in the consequences, or entitle the other party to resile. In *Sharrat* v. *Turnbull*, 5 S. 335, the defender was found liable in the price of goods sent to him, as he alleged by mistake, because of his delay in notifying this to the sender. *Mora* on the part of the creditor may result in his losing his right to recover; as examples of which reference may be made to the cases of *Cook* v. *Falconer*, 13 D. 157; and *Jack* v. *Simpson*, 2 Macp. 1221.

Ex multitudine signorum colligitur identitas vera.—From a number of marks the identity of the subject is gathered or ascertained. This maxim, which is not much used, may be explained thus: where a testator leaves a certain article as a bequest, describing it by a number of marks or qualities by which it may be recognised and distinguished from the rest of his property, the bequest will not be rendered invalid if the article does not possess all the marks or qualities by which the testator described or designated it. If from a number of such marks, the identity of the article with the subject of the bequest can be established, the bequest will hold good. On this subject, see Broom, p. 638. See also *Falsa demonstratio*, &c.

Ex natura.—Naturally ; according to nature.

Ex natura feudi.—According to the nature of the feu, or feudal right.

Ex natura rei.—According to the nature of the thing, or of the transaction.

Ex necessitate.—Necessarily.

Ex nobili officio.—On account of, or by virtue of the *nobile officium;* which is the name given to the equitable power vested in the Court of Session, whereby it may, to a certain extent, abate or modify the rigour of the law, and afford an equitable remedy in cases where strict law would afford none.

Ex nudo pacto non oritur actio.—No right of action arises from a bare bargain or promise. A *nudum pactum* under the civil law was a bargain, promise, or engagement undertaken or given without consideration, and did not constitute an obligation which could be enforced. (Dig. 2, 14, 7, 4.) The same rule has been followed in the law of England, which will be found stated at length in Addison on Contracts, 2 *et seq.* The maxim has no application in the law of Scotland, under which promises and engagements may be enforced, although granted gratuitously and without consideration. Bell's Prin. §§ 8 and 64. See *Nudum pactum.*

Ex officio.—Officially ; by virtue of the office.

Ex pacto illicito non oritur actio.—No right of action arises from an illegal bargain or agreement. Every agreement, bargain, or contract is illegal in the meaning of this maxim, the purpose of which is to do or carry out something opposed to the law of the land, or which is opposed to sound policy or morality. Of the first class (those which are in opposition to the rules of law, and forbidden) may be instanced the *pactum de quota litis*, a bargain between agent and client to the effect that the former will receive a part of the subject of the lawsuit instead of his ordinary fees. Contracts for the smuggling of goods in defraud of the revenue, and obligations for gaming debts, are of the same class, and give rise to no action. Trustees are not allowed to purchase the property of the trust, because that would be opposed to sound policy, enabling them to enrich themselves at the cost of those whose interests they as trustees are bound to protect. Contracts or agreements whereby one is to receive a sum of money for bringing about a certain marriage, or contracts or obligations imposing a restraint on marriage, are regarded also as inconsistent with sound policy, and are ineffectual. Obligations granted as the wages of prostitution, or for money given as an incentive to commit crime, or to conceal crime, are illustrations of agreements *contra bonos mores*. None of these contracts can be enforced: they give rise to no action. Bell's Prin. § 35 *et seq.* Addison on Contracts, 1135 *et seq.*

Ex paritate rationis.—By parity of reasoning.

Ex parte.—From one side; one-sided. Thus a statement made by one of the parties to a suit, which his opponent had no opportunity of answering, is termed an *ex parte* statement; and appeals decided in the House of Lords on the appellant's statement, the respondent not having appeared, are said to be decided *ex parte*.

Ex pietate.—From natural affection and duty.

Ex post facto.—From something done afterwards. Any act performed to affect some right or demand brought into question before the performance of that act is called *ex post facto*. A law is called *ex post facto* which has been enacted to rule a case which has already arisen.

Ex proposito.—Intentionally; of design.

Ex proprio motu.—Of his own accord. Without any motion on the subject being made by any of the litigants, the judge may in the course of a process order certain things to be done. He may order a more articulate statement, a more express answer, the addition of certain pleas, or may order the deletion of a part of the record which in his opinion is irrelevant. Such orders are said to be pronounced *ex proprio motu*.

Ex qua persona quis lucrum capit, ejus factum prestare debet.—He who derives advantage from any one, should bear that person's obligations, or make good his deeds. Thus an heir is liable for the debts and deeds of the ancestor to whom he succeeds, and whom he represents; but such liability on the part of an heir is limited to the extent to which he has been made *lucratus* by the succession. 37 & 38 Vict. cap. 94, § 12.

Ex quasi contractu.—Arising as if from a contract, or (as it is technically termed) arising from *quasi* contract. Obligations and rights arise from *quasi* contracts as well as from those that are express. A *quasi* contract is one constituted not by express consent, but by the circumstances out of which it arises. Thus an heir is bound by *quasi* contract for his ancestor's debts; and where goods are thrown overboard for the purpose of saving the ship and remainder of the cargo, the owners of the ship and of the cargo saved are liable, *quasi ex contractu*, for the value of the goods that have so perished. In such cases there could be no express contract, but the rights and relative obligations emerged from the circumstances.

Ex quasi delicto.—From *quasi* delict. A *quasi* delict is that which nearly amounts to crime, but without doing so or inferring criminal prosecution, yet involves such *culpa* as to give rise to civil action for reparation, &c.

Ex quasi maleficio.—Another form of the preceding phrase.

Ex re.—Arising out of the thing, the transaction, or the circumstances. *Quasi* contracts arise *ex re*.

Ex reverentia maritali.—Out of reverence or respect for the husband.

Ex solemnitate.—On account of its being required as a solemnity. See *De solemnitate*.

Ex sua natura.—In its own nature or character.

Ex turpi causa non oritur actio.—No right of action arises from a disgraceful or immoral consideration—that is, no action can be maintained on a contract or obligation, the consideration of which was disgraceful or immoral. Explanation and illustration of this maxim will be found already given under the maxims *Ex maleficio*, &c., and *Ex pacto illicito*, &c. See also *Ob turpem causam*.

Ex vi aut metu.—On the ground of force or fear. Any deed granted under coercion may be reduced on this ground, because consent under such circumstances is not free, and cannot therefore be binding. The degree of force or fear used may be varied, and its degree will be inquired into as material in deciding whether the deed is valid or not. The fear induced must be *justus metus*, a just or sufficient fear, such as would overpower a mind of ordinary firmness; or such as applied to the mind of a person of weaker age or sex, would have that effect. Thus a threat of death, or infamy, will be regarded as sufficient to render the deed invalid, but the mere threat of annoyance, or a lawsuit, will not. Force may also be varied in degree, and it will always be a question of circumstances whether it was a force which could not have been resisted. *Vis major*, in regard to this subject, signifies actual personal violence.

Exceptio falsi est omnium ultima.—The exception of falsehood is the last of all. In our law *falsehood* includes not only the popular meaning of want of truth, but also deception of every kind, whether in word or act, and also what is not genuine. Thus forgery, which is the making of a false writ, falls within the legal definition of falsehood, and the term *exceptio falsi* means generally that the deed or writ to which the exception is taken is a forgery. This expression is seldom if ever used in any other sense. It is said to be the last exception of all, because it may be pleaded after all other defences on the merits have been pleaded and failed.

Exceptio firmat regulam in casibus non exceptis.—An exception confirms the general rule in those cases not excepted. The exception expressed infers that there are no other exceptions. For example, according to the general rule of law, a shipmaster has authority to hypothecate the ship for necessaries, except in a home port. This exception confirms the rule as to the master's authority so to hypothecate the ship in a foreign port. By introducing this exception, the authority of the master to hypothecate is made clear in every case in which the exception does not apply. This maxim is frequently expressed *Exceptio probat regulam*, &c. See *Enumeratio unius*, &c.

Exceptio litiscontestatæ.—The exception or defence of litiscontestation. This exception (which was not known as a defence in the Roman law, although the name is borrowed from it) seems, as explained by Stair (B. 4, T. 40, § 18), to be that known in our time as the exception *lis alibi pendens*.

Exceptio non numeratæ pecuniæ. — The exception or defence that the money was not paid. This was one of the exceptions of the Roman law, and could be pleaded by any one, who had undertaken a certain obligation in the expectation of receiving a certain sum of money in return, which was never paid him. The exception was only available for two years from the date of the obligation. In Scotland, if a person has granted a bond for a certain sum of money, and in it acknowledged its receipt, and become bound for its repayment, he will be entitled to resist any action or diligence raised upon the bond by the grantee, upon the exception that he had never received the money. Such an exception is available at any time against the grantee or his representatives, but is not pleadable against an onerous assignee. The acknowledgment in the bond that the money has been received is not so absolute as to prevent its being redargued by competent evidence in any question with the grantee.

Exceptio quæ firmat legem exponit legem.—An exception which confirms a law, expounds (or explains) the law. It has been seen above that an exception to a rule confirms the rule itself, except in the excepted cases. This maxim teaches that such an exception not only confirms but explains the law which it qualifies. Taking the illustration already given, it is plain that the exception to the general authority of a shipmaster to hypothecate the ship for necessaries, which prevents him doing so in a home port, expounds the law clearly that he may legally and effectually do so in a foreign port. The introduction of the exception being the introduction of a limit, explains not only the extent but the application of the general rule.

Exceptio rei judicatæ.—The exception that the question now raised has already been decided. If the question at issue between the litigants has already been decided by any competent judge, a new action to try the same question would be thrown out of court upon this exception. Even if the question was first decided in an inferior Court, a new action would not be competent before the

Supreme Court; the competent course being to bring the decision of the inferior Court under review. See *Res judicata.*

Excludendo fiscum et relictam.—To the exclusion of the rights of the Crown, and of the widow. Stair, B. 3, T. 4, § 24.

Excusat aut extenuat delictum in capitalibus quod non operatur idem in civilibus.—That which excuses or extenuates a delict involving capital punishment will not operate with the same effect in a civil action or claim. "For instance, the law makes a difference between killing a man upon malice aforethought, and upon present heat and provocation, *in maleficiis voluntas spectatur non exitus;* but if I slander a man, and thereby damnify him in his name and credit, it is not material whether I do so upon sudden choler or of set malice: but I shall be, in either case, answerable for damages." (Broom, p. 324.) With reference to the latter part of the preceding quotation, it has to be observed that, according to the law of Scotland, general passionate words of abuse or reproach, spoken in the heat of a quarrel, are not actionable, where there has been no repetition of the words after the parties have cooled down. Smith on Reparation, 192.

Executio juris non habet injuriam.—The carrying out of the law inflicts no wrong: that is, no wrong for which damages can be recovered. On the dependence of an action a pursuer may arrest his alleged debtor's money and goods, to abide execution in the event of the pursuer succeeding in establishing his claim, but should the pursuer fail in his action he will not be responsible for damages for the use of such arrestment, even although their effect should have been utterly to ruin the credit of the defender. The pursuer was only using the right which the law gave him, and he is not responsible for the consequences of using his legal right. If the defender can show, however, that the claim was, in the pursuer's knowledge, utterly groundless, and that the arrestments were used maliciously, he will be entitled to recover damages, for in that case the pursuer was not legitimately using the legal process adopted by him, but using it merely as a cloak or cover for his illegal acting. In such cases the mere form of legal process affords no protection. As to the meaning of the word *injuria,* see *Damnum absque injuria.*

Exempla non restringunt regulam, sed loquuntur de casibus crebrioribus.—Examples do not restrict the rule, but speak of the cases which most frequently occur. To refer to a number of cases in which a certain rule has been applied, shows the kind of cases which most frequently occur to which the rule is applicable, but that does not prevent the rule being applied (if otherwise applicable) to a class of cases different from that from which the examples have been taken. The rule is not limited, by examples of its application, to the cases given as examples.

Exempli gratia.—For example. Usually written, *ex. gr.*, or *e.g.*

Exercitor.—The person "to whom the daily profits of a ship belong." (Just. Inst. B. 4, T. 7, § 2.) This name (although it includes a freighter or hirer) is generally given to the master of a ship, who has power by his acts to render the owners of it bound for the obligations undertaken by him in connection therewith. As to the powers and authority generally of a shipmaster, in exercise of which he binds the shipowner, see Maclachlan, p. 131 *et seq.* See *Actio institoria.*

Expedit reipublicæ ne quis re sua male utatur.—It concerns the public good that no one should misuse his own property. See *Interest reipublicæ,* &c.

Expressio eorum quæ tacite insunt nihil operatur.—The expression of those things which are implied without expression has no operative effect. This maxim may be illustrated by contrast. If A contract with B that the latter shall make and furnish certain machinery by a day specified, that is a condition binding upon B, to the effect of subjecting him in damages if he fail in performance by the specified time. The condition of delivery by a certain day, however, requires expression, as it is not and cannot be implied. But if, on the other hand, B was only taken bound to make and furnish the machinery "with all reasonable despatch," such a condition has no special or operative effect, for it is implied in all contracts that they shall be so executed. The consignee of a cargo is bound to take delivery and discharge the vessel without undue delay, but this need not be expressed in the charter party or bill of lading, for it is always implied, and the duty of reasonable despatch in discharging the vessel is equally binding whether expressed or not. If the obligation is intended to be more stringent, as, for example, that the ship shall be discharged in so many days, it must be expressed. So, again, where a testator leaves his property "to his heirs," such a destination is mere surplusage, and leaves the estate to be given or distributed practically as an intestate succession, it being presumed that a man leaves his estate to his heirs as pointed out by law, in the event of his not directing it to go in some other direction.

Expressio falsi.—A false statement. The fraud or misrepresentation, on the ground of which a contract can be reduced, may be either positive or negative. It is either the making of a false statement, knowing it to be untrue, or the concealment of a material fact which should have been disclosed. The latter is called the *suppressio veri.*

Expressio unius est exclusio alterius.—The special mention of one thing operates as the exclusion of things differing from it. See *Enumeratio*, &c.

Expressum facit cessare tacitum.—A thing expressed puts an end to tacit implication. This is a rule of general application in the construction of deeds or contracts. Thus (as in the illustrations given above under *Expressio eorum*, &c.) the tacit condition that a contract shall be fulfilled within a reasonable time, is excluded if a fixed time be expressed by which the contract must be fulfilled; the ship must be discharged by the day named, whether the time so allowed is adequate or not for that purpose, the implied condition of a reasonable time being excluded by the express terms of the contract. The implied obligation on a debtor to make payment of his debt at once, is excluded by the parties naming a day on which payment shall be made, or before which it shall not be demandable; and a special warranty that a subject has certain qualities, or is fit for a special purpose, excludes all implied warranty.

Expromissor.—The name given in the civil law to a person who undertook the debt of another, by substituting himself as principal debtor, in place of the former obligant who was thereby freed from his obligation in so far as regarded the creditor. See *Delegatio.*

Exterus non habet terras.—A foreigner or alien holds no lands. An alien is a person born outwith the dominions of the Queen, of parents who are not themselves natural-born subjects. Formerly, by the law of Scotland, an alien was incapable of acquiring heritage either by purchase or succession; he could not even hold a lease for years. By the Act 7 & 8 Vict. cap. 66, it was, however, provided that on compliance with certain requirements, an alien might obtain letters of naturalisation which conferred on him "all the rights and capacities of a natural-born British subject." By a later Act, 33 & 34 Vict. cap. 14, it is provided that an alien may acquire, hold, and dispose of real property of every description within the United Kingdom in all respects as if a natural-born subject. Such property, however, does not qualify an alien for any office, or for any municipal, parliamentary, or other franchise.

Extra commercium.—Beyond commerce. This is said of things which cannot be bought or sold, such as public roads, rivers, titles of honour, &c.

Extra curtem domini.—Beyond the domain or jurisdiction of the superior. When a vassal's service was a money payment, or delivery of a quantity of grain for the superior's use, he was not bound, except on special conditions, to carry or deliver it beyond the superior's domain.

Extra familiam.—Outwith the family. A child is said to be outwith its father's family when it is forisfamiliated. It is *intra familiam* before this takes place.

Extra ordinem.—Out of the usual rule. Judgments *extra ordinem* under the civil law were those pronounced by the magistrate in certain cases without sending them to a *judex.* In such cases the magistrate was said *extra ordinem cognoscere,* and his jurisdiction was termed *extraordinaria.* Among other cases in which the magistrate exercised this jurisdiction, were those in which he restored a person suffering from something from which by law he ought not to suffer, to the same position as that which he had occupied before the wrong was inflicted; as, for example, when a minor was freed from a contract into which he had entered to his lesion, or had rashly taken up a succession which instead of being lucrative was injurious and burdensome.

Extra paterna familia.—Outwith the father's family. As to whether children not residing in family with their father are still subject to his curatorial power, see Fraser, Par. & Ch. 348.

Extra præsentiam mariti.—Outwith the presence of the husband. The ratification of all deeds executed by spouses is made by the wife outwith the presence of her husband, the object being to give her an opportunity of declaring (if such be the case) that she acts under the coercion of her husband, and not voluntarily. It was held at one time that the execution of such a ratification barred the wife at any time thereafter from reducing the deed on the ground of force or fear. Whether it would have such an effect now is a matter of controversy and doubt. In support of the former view, see Brodie's Stair, Note by Editor, B. 1, T. 4, § 18; Bell's Com. i. 138; *Grant*, M. 16483; while in support of the latter, see Ersk. B. 1, T. 6, § 34; Menzies' Lectures, p. 41; *M'Neill*, 8 S. 210. Whether such a ratification would bar a reduction at the instance of the wife making it, of a deed conferring right upon a third party, or not, it is certain that such ratification would not bar her revoking a deed which was of the nature of a donation *inter virum et uxorem*.

Extra quatuor maria.—Beyond the four seas. A child born by a married woman is presumed to be the child of her husband according to the rule *Pater est quem nuptiæ demonstrant:* and this presumption, according to the older law, could only be redargued by proof of the husband's impotency, or of the impossibility of his access to his wife at the time of conception. According to the older English law, the presumption could only be redargued by proof of the husband's absence beyond seas or of his impotency. Neither in England nor in Scotland is it now required to prove absence beyond seas or impossibility of access to redargue the presumption. The whole circumstances of the parties and their conduct are taken into account with the view of determining the question of the child's paternity, and such judgment is pronounced as the circumstances warrant. On this subject, see Fraser, Par. & Ch. 4 *et seq.;* and the decision in *Brodie* v. *Dyce,* 11 Macp. 142, which has been frequently followed.

Extra territorium judicis.—Beyond the territory of the judge—*i.e.*, beyond the territory over which he has jurisdiction.

Extra territorium jus dicenti impûne non paretur.—The law (of a certain territory) may be safely disregarded outwith that territory : or, the order or decision of a judge may be disobeyed with impunity outwith the limits of his jurisdiction. The supreme power in a state can only enact laws for those who are subject to its authority. It cannot enforce those laws against persons not subject to its authority, or who are, by residence outwith the territory, beyond the reach of its power. A person, therefore, who is not within the territory where a certain law is binding, may safely disregard or disobey that law, because in such circumstances, his disobedience infers no penalty which can be enforced. An Englishman may not by the law of his country commit bigamy, and if he does so, will be punished. But if being married in this country, he goes to another country where polygamy is permitted, he may disregard the law of England on this point, and marry a second wife, without fear of punishment on account of that breach of English law. A curious illustration of this maxim will be found in the case of *Lolly,* reported in Fergusson's Consistorial Cases, 269, and Russell and Ryan's Crown Cases, **237.** Lolly having married in England, came to Scotland, where he was divorced at the instance of his wife, on account of adultery, and believing this divorce to be effectual, he returned to England, and there entered into a second marriage. On account of this second marriage, he was tried for bigamy and convicted, because at that time the law of England did not permit of divorce *a vinculo* except by Act of Parliament, nor did it recognise any decree of a foreign court as effectual to dissolve an English marriage. In Scotland, where the divorce was granted, it was undoubtedly effectual, and Lolly might have married again with impunity, had he remained out of England, because the law of England could not have reached him so long as he was absent from that country. But having returned to England, obedience to the law there prevailing was obligatory ; and being in the view of that law still a married man, notwithstanding of the divorce, his second marriage was bigamy, and the punishment due to that crime was incurred. Taking the maxim in reference to the effect of an order or decision pronounced by a judge, it is obvious that such an order is ineffectual beyond the limits of the judge's jurisdiction. A warrant to arrest money, or to cite witnesses, granted by a sheriff, is only effectual when executed within his own county ; and requires, if it is to be executed in another county, to be indorsed by the proper authority in the latter. A witness residing in the county of A cannot be cited to appear before the sheriff of the county of B on the warrant of the latter alone, because the sheriff of B has no jurisdiction over persons outwith his own county. Nor can a decree of the Supreme Court of Scotland be executed in England, unless the authority of the English Courts is interponed. In the case of *Cookney* v. *Anderson*, 32 L. J. Chan. 427, it was held, that an order to cite defenders resident in Scotland, to answer in a suit instituted against them in the Court of Chancery in England, was beyond the power of the Court. In that case Lord Westbury observed: " The Courts of civil judicature in every country sit to administer the municipal law of that country, and their jurisdiction therefore is limited and territorial. It is true that the duty of yielding obedience to the law of his native country may follow the native subject of that country wherever he resides ; for every nation has a right to bind its own natural-born subjects by its own laws in every place. Municipal law, therefore, may provide that judgments and decrees may be lawfully pronounced against natural-born subjects when absent abroad, and may also enact that they may be required to appear in the Courts of their native country, even whilst resident in the dominions of a foreign sovereign. If a statutory jurisdiction be thus conferred, Courts of justice in the exercise of it may lawfully cite, and on non-appearance give judgment in civil cases against, natural-born subjects whilst they are absent beyond seas in a foreign land.

This jurisdiction depends on the statute or written law of the country. Where it is not expressly given it cannot be lawfully assumed. If such a law does not exist, the general maxim applies, *Extra territorium jus dicenti impune non paretur.*"

Extremis probatis præsumuntur media. — Extremes being proved, those things which fall within or between them are presumed. Thus in a reduction of a deed on the ground of deathbed, where it was necessary to show that the deceased at the time he executed it was labouring under the disease of which he died, it was sufficient to prove that the deceased was attacked by that disease, and that within sixty days of executing the deed the granter of it died; the fact of the disease, and the subsequent death being proved, the Court presumed the continuance of the disease between these two periods. So also in questions of right depending on prescriptive possession, it is not necessary to prove use or possession for every day or month of the prescriptive period. It is sufficient to show acts of possession at intervals of time, from which the law will presume that the possession continued throughout the whole period. Again, where an article has been proved to have been stolen, and is also proved to have been found *de recenti* in the possession of a certain person, the law presumes the act of theft of the article by the person in whose possession it is so found.

F

Faciendo domino superiori quod de jure facere tenetur.
—By performing that to the superior which by law he is bound to perform. This refers to the duties of the vassal. He is bound, on claiming an entry, to perform the service or pay the non-entry duties, relief, &c., which under his title the superior has a right to demand on such an occasion; and formerly a charge by the heir upon the superior, charging the latter to enter him as vassal, could be suspended on the ground of the failure in such performance or payment. Renewal of investiture is now abolished, and every proprietor of land duly infeft is held to be entered with the superior as at the date of the registration of such infeftment. 37 & 38 Vict. cap. 94.

Faciendo vobis quod de jure facere debet.—On his performing that to you which he is bound by law to perform. These are the terms of the old precept of Chancery granted to an heir on which he charged the superior for an entry, ordaining the superior to give the entry on all his legal rights being satisfied.

Facio ut des, facio ut facias.—I do that you may give, I do that you may do. For an explanation of these phrases, see *Do ut des*.

Factio testamenti.—The power of making a testament, or of acquiring under a testament made by another. Under the civil law, this was a power at one time vested only in the Roman citizen, although it became more general in the time of Justinian. The *testamenti factio* was necessary to any participation whatever in a testament. Without it, no one could make a will, or take a legacy, or even be a witness to the execution of a will. Every testamentary tutor appointed by the testator required to have the *testamenti factio*, or their appointment was void. In Scotland, prior to the passing of the Act 6 Will. IV. cap. 22, a bastard dying without lawful issue had no *testamenti factio*, and his property passed to the Crown ; but, by that Statute, such persons were empowered to dispose of their moveables by testament in the same manner as others. A bastard can now dispose of his estate, heritable and moveable, as he pleases. In Scotch law, this phrase can only signify the power of making a will, as any one may be a beneficiary under another's settlement.

Factum a judice quod ad officium ejus non pertinet ratum non est.—Anything done by a judge which does not belong to his office (that is, does not fall within his official authority) is not valid. Acts done or orders pronounced by a judge must, in order to be valid, be within his competency ; and if he goes beyond the powers vested in him by virtue of his office, his acts or orders are ineffectual. Thus, if a sheriff in exercise of the jurisdiction conferred by the Small Debt Act decerned against a defender for payment of a sum exceeding £12, the decree would be invalid, because in granting it the judge had exceeded his powers. If a sheriff, in the exercise of his summary jurisdiction in criminal matters, sentenced a prisoner to imprisonment for three months, the sentence would be invalid, as in summary trials a sheriff cannot pronounce a sentence of imprisonment for a longer period than sixty days. So again, if an arbiter decides upon a question not submitted to him, or decerns for more than is claimed, his award is invalid. *Napier* v. *Wood*, 7 D. 166. For an instance of the application of this maxim in England, see *Watson* v. *Bodell*, 14 L. J. Exch. 281.

Factum imprestabile.—An act that cannot be performed : an impossibility.

Factum infectum fieri nequit.—A thing done cannot be undone. An illustration of this maxim is found in the case of a thief, who, after having completed the act of theft, abandons the thing stolen, or returns it to the owner or the place from whence he took it : the theft having been committed cannot be undone, nor its consequences avoided, by the subsequent act of the thief. In *Carter* v. *M'Laren*, 8 Macp. 64 (reversed H. L., 9 Macp. 49), a creditor obtained a preference in consideration of his abstaining from further opposition to the acceptance of an offer of composition made by the bankrupt. It was averred that the creditor did not know he was doing anything illegal in accepting the preference, and that after he became aware of the illegality of his proceeding he returned the preference obtained, and did all in his power to restore matters to the condition in which they were before the preference was granted. It was held that by accepting the preference he had incurred the statutory penalties, and that his subsequent acts did not avoid the consequences of what he had previously done: the preference having been accepted was a thing done which subsequent acts on the part of the creditor could not undo. While the maxim holds good in most cases in so far as the doer of the act is concerned, it does not hold so absolutely against other persons affected by the act done: there are many cases in which a person may be restored against an act done to his prejudice by another. When a thing has been done which cannot be undone, the person wronged thereby has only a claim of damages for the wrong he has sustained; but where it is possible to rescind the thing wrongously done, the Court will set it aside, and give damages also where these have been sustained. To take materials belonging to another, and build them into your own house, is an instance of the former case; to take a conveyance fraudulently from another of his property is an instance of the latter.

Factum proprium et recens.—One's own act recently performed.

Falsa demonstratio non nocet.—An erroneous description does not injure. Where the description is merely expository, an error in it will not vitiate, if there be no doubt as to the identity of the person or thing intended to be specified. Thus if a testator left a bequest "to my nephew William, son of my brother John," and the testator had a nephew William, but his brother John had no children, the bequest would still be a valid bequest to the testator's nephew, for the person intended to be benefited was quite certain, while the erroneous description of him as the son of a certain brother, being merely description, would be innocuous. Or, if the bequest was to my nephew William, "residing in Queen Street," whereas the residence of the legatee was in

George Street, this again being merely erroneous description, would not void the legacy. Again, where the false description is of the thing bequeathed, the same rule holds. A bequest of "my diamond ring, which is locked up in my desk," is a good bequest of the ring, although not found as described; and a conveyance of "my house in Queen Street occupied by A B," would be a good conveyance, although the house was not occupied, and had never been occupied by the tenant named. As illustrative of what has been said, reference may be made to the following cases:—*Bruce*, 2 R. 775; *Bryce*, 5 R. 722; and *Macfarlane's Trs.*, 6 R. 288. See also *Dummodo constet*, &c., and cases there cited.

Falsa demonstratione legatum non perimi.—A legacy is not rendered void by a false description. "For instance, if the testator were to say, I give as a legacy Stichus, born my slave, the legacy is effectual, although the slave had not been a born slave, but bought, if it is clear as to the slave meant. And so if the slave be pointed out thus: 'Stichus, my slave, whom I purchased from Seius,' the legacy is effectual, although he had been bought from some other person, provided there be no doubt as to the slave intended to be given." Just. Inst. B. 2, T. 20, § 30. See also what has been said under the preceding maxim.

Falsa grammatica non vitiat chartam.—False or bad grammar does not vitiate a deed. If a deed or clause sufficiently expresses the purpose or object it was intended to express, it will not be rendered nugatory simply because it is not expressed grammatically. The clause must, however, be intelligible, and its meaning clear. A good illustration of this maxim will be found in the case of *Gollan*, 4 Macq. 585, and the reader may also consult the case of *M'Donald*, 1 R. 858, affirmed on appeal, 2 R. (H. L.) 28. See *Mala grammatica*, &c.

Falsum in uno falsum in omnibus.—False in one thing, false in all. If a witness makes a statement on oath in giving evidence which is manifestly false, the effect of it undoubtedly will be, and most properly so, to cast a doubt over the whole of his evidence. His credibility will thereby be so affected as to make his evidence of little or no value. At same time it would be rash to reject the whole testimony of a witness because in one part of it he has been guilty of falsehood; there may be motives inducing the witness to falsehood on one branch of the case in which he is being examined which do not operate in regard to other parts of it. The whole evidence given will be weighed by the judge or jury, and that which a witness says which appears to be true will receive weight, although he may have also told something which is false; his whole evidence is not necessarily to be disregarded because it is not all true. A person convicted of perjury was formerly held to be inadmissible as a witness, but that is no longer so. 15 & 16 Vict. c. 27, § 1.

Familia.—Family. The word *familia*, as used in the civil law, had a much more comprehensive signification than that which it has in our law. In the latter it is used as signifying merely the members of one household—*i.e.*, the husband, with his wife and children, and very often signifies the children alone; while in the former it signified all who were in any way under the power (*in potestate*) of the *paterfamilias*, including wife, children, and their wives and children, slaves, &c. *Familia* was also used as a name for the whole property of the *paterfamilias*, and hence the name of the action for division of that property, *familiæ erciscundæ*. For the various meanings which attached to the word *familia* in the Roman law, the reader is referred to the Digest, B. 50, T. 16, § 195. In Scotland a legacy to a person and his "family" has been construed as if it had been to him and his "children." *Fyffe* v. *Fyffe*, 3 D. 1205. See also M'Laren, i. 726. In England a legacy to a family is differently construed according to the circumstances of the case. Sometimes it means the heir, sometimes it includes the husband, wife, descendants, and (where there are no descendants) the relations. See the cases collected in Jarman, ii. 90 *et seq.*; Williams, 1129; Roper, i. 137.

Fatetur facinus qui judicium fugit.—He confesses the crime who flees from trial. The maxim is too broadly stated; for although it be alleged in an indictment in the usual language, "that you, the said A B, being conscious of guilt in the premises, did abscond and flee from justice," the proof of such flight will not be regarded in itself as an admission of guilt. Any one might be so overwhelmed with a sense of danger, arising from the mere charge of a crime, as to induce him to flee, while perfectly innocent. The flight, with attendant circumstances, such as disguising the person, &c., would doubtless be elements for the consideration of a jury, but in themselves would not warrant a conviction.

Favorabiliores rei potius quam actores habentur.—Defenders are held to be in a more favourable position than pursuers. See Bankton, B. 4, T. 45, § 124. See also *Melior est conditio*, &c.

Fecit quod non potuit et quod non fecit potuit.—He did that which he had no power to do, and did not that which he had power to do. Ross, L. C. (L. R.) ii. 420.

Feræ naturæ.—Of a wild nature. Animals are so described which are still in their wild or natural state, never having been captured or made the subjects of private property. See *Domitæ naturæ*.

Feuda—The name given to feudal grants of land, when these grants were made absolute. Previously they were termed *munera*, and were then only grants for life, but as *feuda* they were made descendible to heirs, and transmissible to collaterals. See *Beneficia*.

Feuda ad instar patrimoniorum sunt redacta.—Lands held feu are reduced to the character of a patrimony or succession. The meaning of the phrase is, that lands held feu have now lost their strictly feudal character, and are become like any other succession which may devolve upon the heir. Under the old feudal system, where lands were held in return for military services, a woman could not have succeeded; but having lost that character, she may now succeed to heritage equally as to moveables.

Feuda pecuniæ.—A kind of fee, or heritable right in money, sometimes called *feuda nominis*. Erskine explains, that although "there is no proper *feudum* of money, or of bonds, yet, as a yearly profit arises from money as well as land, lawyers have admitted a *quasi feudum* in bonds, which gets the name of *feudum nominis*." (B. 3, T. 8, § 34.) The personal bonds here referred to were held heritable after the term of payment was past; but they were made moveable by the Act 1661, c. 32, except as regards the fisk, and the rights of husband and wife. See the case of *Gray*, 21 D. 709. Heritable securities are now regarded as moveable in so far as succession is concerned, unless executors are expressly excluded. Such securities, however, remain heritable *quoad fiscum*, and as regards the rights of courtesy and terce competent to the husband or wife of the creditor in the security; and they are not treated as part of the creditor's moveable estate in computing the amount of a child's legitim. 31 & 32 Vict. c. 101, § 117.

Feuda soldata.—This is described in the *Consuetudines Feudorum* (B. 2, T. 10) as "a certain yearly gratuitous payment, which transmits on neither part to the heir; for it is put an end to by the death of either the giver or receiver. It is called *soldata*, because for the most part it consists in a donation of *solidi;* although sometimes consisting in a gift of wine, corn, or other produce of the land."

Feudum antiquum.—The name given to land acquired by succession in contradistinction to that (*novum*) acquired by conquest; a distinction which is now abolished. See *Antiqua et nova*.

Feudum burgale.— Lands held by burgage-tenure. "Burgage-holding was introduced for the benefit and protection of the trading and mechanical portion of the community, who were driven to take refuge in towns from the dangers of the open country during the barbarous period of feudal warfare." (Duff, Feud. Con. 49.) The return for lands so held was watching and warding within burgh, or as it is generally expressed in charters, "for service of burgh, used and wont." The distinction between burgage-tenure and lands held feu, was abolished by the Act 37 & 38 Vict. c. 94, § 25.

Feudum ex camera aut cavena.—"In feudal law, was an annual sum of money, or supply of corn, wine, and oil, paid out of the lord's possessions to a soldier, or other well-deserving person. It resembled a pension." Bell's Dict. *h.v.*

Feudum francum.—One of the kinds of feudal tenures, called free fee. It was so called because the vassal was free of all feudal services, and was only bound to the superior by an oath of fealty. "It arose when the feudal manners began to give place to a certain degree of industry and civilisation, and superiors who were in want of money were willing to give lands to their vassals at nominal or quit rents, in consideration of a large sum advanced in a single payment." (Duff's Feud. Con. 49.) This holding in modern phrase is termed blench-holding.

Feudum militare.—A feu held in return for military services. Wardholding, the military tenure of this country, was abolished by the Act 20 Geo. II. c. 50.

Feudum nominis.—See *Feuda pecuniæ*.

Feudum novum.—Land acquired by conquest—*i.e.*, by any singular title, such as purchase, gift, &c. See *Antiqua et nova*.

Feudum rectum.—The name given by the feudalists to lands held by military tenure, called *Feudum militare* in the *Regiam Majestatem*. The vassal holding by this tenure, and liable in the military service it imposed, was called *miles*.

Feudum simplex.—A fee-simple, or one under which the lands descended to heirs whomsoever, in contradistinction to an entailed fee, under which heirs-male alone succeeded.

Feudum talliatum.—A tailzie, or entailed fee, under which heirs-male alone succeeded. This was also called a male fee, and was called *talliatum*, because under tailzies females were generally *cut off* or excluded.

Fiat ut petitur.—Let it be done as prayed for. These are the words used in certain cases when granting the warrant sought for. Thus under the Personal Diligence Act, after a charge has expired, and the creditor seeks a warrant for the imprisonment of his debtor, such warrant, when granted, is expressed in these terms, *Fiat ut petitur*.

Ficta traditio.—Fictitious delivery. By the law of Scotland, delivery was necessary to pass the property in moveables forming the subject of a sale, from the seller to the buyer. The law of England being different (for by it the completed contract of sale transfers the property in the thing sold to the buyer without delivery), the Mercantile Law Amendment Act (1856) was passed for the purpose of assimilating the law of the two countries, a purpose which it does not seem to have quite accomplished. See *Dans et retinens*, &c. But in cases where the buyer of a subject was already in possession of it (either as lessee, depositary, or in some other character), and actual delivery could not take place under the sale, the law presumed a delivery under the contract of sale, although the possession remained undisturbed, and such delivery was called *ficta traditio*. The Mercantile Law Amendment Act, 1856, so far as it related to the law of sale, has been repealed. Delivery of the thing sold is not now in all cases necessary to pass the property. 56 & 57 Vict. c. 71.

Fictio brevis manus.—Another name for the presumed delivery above mentioned.

Fictio juris.—A fiction of law. This is a legal presumption, grounded on equity, that a certain thing is true, which may be false, and which, it may be, is as likely to be false as true. Thus by legal fiction an executor is *eadem persona cum defuncto*, and a wife *eadem persona* with her husband. Again, as some hold, a child legitimated by the subsequent marriage of its parents, is legitimated because, by a fiction of law, that marriage is supposed to have been contracted at the time when the child was begotten; if the parents at that time could not have been lawfully married, a subsequent marriage would not legitimate the offspring. It has been the subject of controversy whether the doctrine of legitimation *per subsequens matrimonium* proceeds upon the legal fiction above mentioned, or whether it is based solely on views of expediency. The reader will find the subject discussed in Fraser, Par. & Ch. 34 *et seq.*, and in the case of *Kerr* v. *Martin*, 2 D. 752, where the view that the doctrine proceeds on the fiction is negatived. A promise of marriage followed by *copula* constitutes marriage, because by legal fiction the consent to marriage which is necessary to its constitution, is presumed to have been given before the woman surrendered her person. By a fiction of law, also, the whole moveable estate of a deceased person is held to be situated in that place in which the deceased had his domicile at the date of his death, although, in point of fact, such moveables might be situated in another country. Such fictions are not frequently had recourse to in Scotch law. They are not applied or given effect to where their application would inflict a wrong, for *fictio legis inique operatur alicui damnum vel injuriam* (a legal fiction operates unfairly when it causes damage or inflicts a wrong). "The court would not endure that a mere form or fiction of law, introduced for the sake of justice, should work a wrong, contrary to the real truth and substance of the thing." (Per Lord Mansfield in *Johnson*, 2 Burr, 963.) "Wherever a fiction of law works injustice, and the facts, which by fiction are supposed to exist, are inconsistent with the real facts, a court of law ought to look to the real facts." (Per Bayley, J., in *Lyttleton* v. *Cross*, 3 B. and C. 325.) See further on this subject, and as an illustration of the rule that the legal fiction has to give place to the real facts where otherwise a wrong would be done, the case of *Whitaker* v. *Wiseby*, L. J. 21, C. P. 116.

Fideicommissa.—Trusts; that is, trusts for carrying out the last wishes of a deceased person. By the civil law, no one could take any benefit under a will or testament unless he had *testamenti factio* with the testator. But as it often happened that a testator desired to benefit some one under his will, who had not this *testamenti factio*, the plan was adopted of appointing some one as the heir who had it, enjoining him at the same time to transfer to the person really to be benefited the legacy or property, whatever it might be, which the testator wished to leave to him. Such injunctions the heir was not bound by the civil law to regard; and as they were entrusted thus to his honour and good faith, and could not be enforced by law, they were called *fideicommissa*. At a later period the heir could be compelled to fulfil the purposes of any trust reposed in him, but there was nothing like an action at law to enforce *fideicommissa*. The *fideicommissarius* (the person who took benefit under the trust), applied for aid as having equity on his side, and if the magistrate chose to interfere in the exercise of his equitable jurisdiction, the trust was enforced. Nothing is more common in the practice of our law, than for testators to dispose of their estate by trust-deed, and the trustee, once accepting, is bound to carry out all its purposes; and all such purposes may, under our law, be enforced by any one having an interest to enforce them.

Fideicommissarium feudum.—A fee in trust; a fiduciary fee. Craig gives this name to the right in the person of a superior, into whose hands lands had been resigned *in favorem.*

Fidejussor.—Cautioner. This kind of cautioner could be added to any contract, and his obligation transmitted against his heirs. It was different with the *Adpromissor*, which see.

Fidelitatis sacramentum.—Oath of fealty, given by vassals to their over-lords.

Fidem facere judici.—Literally, to make faith to the judge. The equivalent for this phrase, in technical language, is to bear faith in judgment—*i.e.*, to afford competent proof of the statements made or claim advanced.

Filiæ-familias : Filii-familias.—All the children in a *familia*, who were subject to the power of the *paterfamilias*, including those who were his own descendants, and those who had become subject to him by marriage or adoption.

Filius constat esse in familia patris et non matris.—A son appears to be in the family of the father and not of the mother. On this principle the father, and not the mother, is liable for the son's alimentary debts. But after the father's death "the principle is equally applicable to the mother, grandfather, and other ascendants in their order." Fraser, Par. & Ch. 99.

Finium regundorum (actio).—An action for defining and fixing the boundaries of lands lying contiguous. See *Actio.*

Fiscus.—The fisk. Among the Romans this was the name given to the private treasury of the emperor, and was distinct from *ærarium*, the public one. By the writers on Scotch law, this word is used to denote the revenue of the Crown; and also (as in the Act 1661, c. 32) the Crown's right to the moveable estate of persons denounced rebels.

Fit occupantis.—It becomes the property of the captor, or the person who first appropriates or takes possession. See *Quod nullius est*, &c.

Flagranti crimine.—In the act of committing the crime, or immediately after the commission. Ersk. B. 1, T. 4, § 4. This is sometimes written *flagranti delicto.*

Flumen.—In our law this word is used in reference to the servitude of stillicide, and signifies the water falling from the roof when collected in a spout. When not so collected it is called stillicide or eaves-drop.

Fœnus nauticum.—Marine interest, or the rate of interest which a person gets in return for money advanced on a ship, or on bottomry. The rate depends upon the terms of the contract, and will vary according to circumstances,—such as the length of the voyage, the sum advanced, and the risk incurred. It is always much higher than ordinary interest, because if the ship perishes the lender has no claim for the sum advanced.

Forma verborum.—The form or tenor of the words.

Formula.—A form in law. The *formula* of the civil law was that writ containing the directions from the Prætor to the *judex*, to be followed in deciding a certain disputed question. It consisted of three parts :—1. The *demonstratio*, which set forth the allegation of the plaintiff on which the suit was founded. 2. The *intentio*, containing the precise claim advanced; and 3. The *condemnatio*, directing the judge to find the defendant liable, or absolve him, according to the circumstances. The system of *formulæ* was abolished before the time of Justinian.

Fortior et potentior est dispositio legis quam hominis. —The disposition of the law is stronger and more efficacious than that of the man. The rules of law sometimes override the will of the individual, and render his act ineffectual, and the expression of his intention of no avail. For example, if a man leaves a will by which he directs a certain small sum of money to be paid to his children or his widow, and the bulk of his moveable property to some one else, such a will is ineffectual, because the law has ruled that a widow and children are entitled to succeed to certain portions of the moveable estate of the husband and father, and of these legal provisions they cannot be deprived by the will of the testator. The widow's *jus relictæ* and the children's legitim are by force of law preferable to any disposition of his moveables which the husband or father can make by *mortis causa* deed. A donation between husband and wife is revocable by law, and the donor cannot by any act or disposition of his own render it irrevocable, and accordingly such a donation may be revoked by the donor's creditors against the wish of the donor. In like manner, all *mortis causa* deeds are revocable during life, and no words or undertaking by the maker of the deed (such as declaring his will to be irrevocable, or putting it on record) can prevent him exercising the power of revocation.

Forum competens.—A competent court, or one to the jurisdiction of which that person is amenable who is brought before it. Thus, in the ordinary case, the court in one county is not *forum competens* in the case of a person residing in a different county, but the Court of Session is *forum competens* in any question between persons residing in Scotland, and even in cases against foreigners, where jurisdiction has been founded by arrestment for that purpose.

Forum non competens.—Literally, an incompetent court; a court not having competency, through want of jurisdiction or otherwise, to adjudicate upon the question submitted for decision. This phrase, however, is rarely used in any other sense than that of *forum non conveniens;* an inconvenient court for trying and deciding the question. In practice, this plea is generally stated by defenders domiciled in a foreign country against whom jurisdiction has been founded by arrestment, and who desire to have the case raised against them, or the claim thereby maintained, decided in the courts of their domicile rather than in the courts here. This plea is more frequently stated than sustained. As the jurisdiction founded by arrestment is as ample and complete in all questions of mercantile law as a jurisdiction founded upon domicile, the courts are bound to exercise their jurisdiction, unless it is clearly shown that in the special circumstances, not only the convenience of the parties, but the justice of the case, render it expedient to send the question for trial before another tribunal. It lies entirely in the discretion of the court whether the plea should be sustained or repelled. " The cases in which the plea of inconvenient forum has been sustained are chiefly of two classes.—1st, Where foreign executors have been sought to be called to account in this country for the executry estate situated in a foreign country. In these cases the question always was, whether it was more for the true and legitimate interest of the executry estate and all the claimants, that the distribution should take place where the executors have had administration. There is, of course, in most cases, a strong presumption in favour of that consideration, and accordingly the plea is generally sustained in such cases. The law of the executry estate is the law of the country where administration is had : and there generally are the papers, the property, and the parties concerned. Another class of cases relates to partnerships. Here, again, there is a manifest expediency in trying all questions at the partnership domicile, where the books and the property may be expected to be, and where the partners themselves concurred in carrying on business. In that class of cases, also, the court is always willing to listen to this plea. It has regard to the interest of the whole parties generally." Per L. J.-C. Inglis in *Clements* v. *Macaulay*, 4 Macp. 592. See also on this subject the following cases : *Brown's Trs.* v. *Palmer*, 9 S. 224. *Tulloch*, 8 D. 657. *Longworth* v. *Hope*, 3 Macp. 1049. *Macadam*, 11 Macp. 860. *Adamson's Exrs.*, 20 R. 738.

Fovere consimilem causam.—To favour or maintain a similar case. A judge may be declined if he has a personal interest in a case the decision of which may be ruled by the decision of the one in which he is declined.

Fractionem diei non recipit lex.—The law does not regard (or take into account) the fractional part of a day. This does not mean that the law will not take into account a fraction of a day in any circumstances ; but rather, that the law will in most cases consider a fraction of a day as a whole day, disregarding the fact that it is merely a fraction. An illustration of this will be found in the case of the *Com. S. S. Co.* v. *Boulton*, L. R. 10 Q. B. 346 (followed in *Hough* v. *Athya*, 6 R. 961), where damage was claimed for the detention of a vessel, and the court regarded a fraction of a day as a whole day in fixing the amount to which the pursuer was entitled. See *Dies inceptus*, &c.

Frater fratri uterino non succedet in hæreditate paterna.—A brother does not succeed a brother-uterine in the heritage of the father. Relations of half blood are either consanguinean or uterine : the former are descended from the same father but a different mother ; the latter are descended from the same mother but a different father. According to the law of Scotland a brother-uterine does not succeed to any heritage derived from the former or subsequent husband of his mother; he is no blood relation of such husband, and does not succeed as heir to him or his descendants. (Bell's Prin. § 1665.) Formerly, a brother-uterine did not succeed to any part of the moveable estate of his brother, but this was modified by the Act 18 & 19 Vict. c. 23, which provides (§ 5) that where an intestate dies without issue, predeceased by his father and mother, and without leaving a brother- or sister-german or consanguinean, or descendants of such brother or sister, his brothers and sisters uterine, or their descendants, shall have right to one-half of the moveable estate. The law of England as to the succession of uterine relations is different from the law of Scotland. As to this see Paterson's Compend. §§ 745 and 762, and also the Act 3 & 4 Will. IV. c. 106.

Fraus auctoris non nocet successori.—The fraud of the author or ancestor does not injure his successor. See *Dolus auctoris*, &c.

Fraus et dolus nemini patrocinari debent.—Fraud and deceit should protect no one. This is another form of stating the maxim that no one can take any advantage by his own fraud. Fraud gives rise to no right of action, nor can it be pleaded in defence by the party who has been guilty of it. An obligation obtained through fraud cannot be enforced by him whose fraud led to the obligation being granted; nor can a discharge similarly obtained be pleaded in answer to a demand for fulfilment of that to which the discharge relates. See *Nullus commodum*, &c.

Fraus est celare fraudem.—It is fraud to conceal fraud. If any one to obtain a personal advantage conceals (and thus takes benefit by) the fraud of another, the fraud becomes his own; the concealment of another's fraud in such a case is fraud on the part of the person concealing.

Fraus latet in generalibus.—Fraud lurks in general statements. Because specific statements as to the particular character or quality of a subject may easily be tested, fraudulent misrepresentations are most frequently made in general terms which admit more readily of different construction or meaning. General expressions therefore of the value, character, or quality of a subject are to be regarded with some suspicion; and the best safeguard for a purchaser is a particular warranty. General terms of commendation on the part of a seller do not amount to warranty, nor will it vitiate the contract that the subject is not conform to the general commendation thus given. See *Simplex commendatio*, &c.

Fructus civiles.—Civil fruits; which are the rents and profits arising from subjects producing no proper or natural fruits, such as rents of lands or houses, interest on money, &c.

Fructus pendentes.—Fruits still hanging, or not separated from the subject which produces them; as distinguished from *fructus percepti*, fruits that have been separated or gathered.

Fructus rei alienæ.—Fruits produced by a subject belonging to another person.

Frugi aut bonæ famæ.—Frugal or of good reputation. *Stirling* v. *Heriot*, M. 369.

Frustra legis auxilium quærit qui in legem committit.—He seeks the aid of the law in vain who is himself acting contrary to the law. The law cannot be invoked by any one in aid of a wrong which he is committing or is about to commit. For example, a thief taking possession by violence of a subject which is not his, cannot seek protection or aid from the law against the violence by which the rightful owner immediately endeavours to recover his property. Nor can damage be claimed by one who suffers injury in doing something he has no right to do, or being in a place where he had no right to be; his wrongful act or his trespass being an answer to his claim. In like manner, no right of action is recognised on an obligation obtained by fraud, at the instance of the person who so obtained it, otherwise the law would be giving aid to a wrong-doer, in enforcing that which he had wrongfully obtained, and enabling him (in violation of another principle of law) to take advantage by his own fraud. On the same principle, one of the parties to a mutual contract cannot enforce its obligations against his co-contractor so long as he himself has wrongfully failed to fulfil his part of it. There is a class of cases, however, which may perhaps, be considered as forming an exception to the general rule just stated. Where damage is occasioned by the collision of two vessels at sea, it does not exclude the claim of one of these vessels, that her own neglect or disregard of the rules prescribed for preventing collisions at sea has materially contributed to the damage sustained, if the other vessel has also disregarded the rules. In these circumstances, claims arise in favour of each vessel against the other; the whole damage sustained is put into a slump sum, one-half of which falls on each vessel, irrespective of any consideration as to the extent of blame or fault attributable to each. Accordingly, in such cases, the law does come to the aid of one who has been acting contrary to the law. *The Khedive*, L. R. 5, App. 876.

Frustra petis quod mox restiturus es.—You seek in vain that which you must immediately restore. Compensation or set-off proceeds upon the principle of this maxim, as the defender, if he were decerned to pay the pursuer the sum sued for, could compel him to repay it under a new action. On the principle of this maxim, one partner cannot, in England, sue his co-partners at common-law for a partnership debt. But it is otherwise if the debt be other than a partnership debt, or arises out of what is not a partnership transaction. *Boulter* v. *Peplow*, L. J. 19, C. P. 190. *Sedgwick* v. *Daniell*, L. J. 27, Exch. 116.

Frustra petis quod statim alteri reddere cogeris.—You seek in vain that which you may be compelled instantly to give back to another. Another form of the preceding maxim.

Frustra probatur quod probatum non relevat.—It is useless to prove that which, when proved, is not relevant to the question at issue. Thus to prove, under a criminal indictment charging the prisoner with theft from the person of A, that the prisoner was guilty of stealing something, in exactly the same manner, and at the time specified, from the person of B. would be unavailing, as irrelevant to the charge laid. Formerly, in civil causes, no proof of facts was allowed until the relevancy was disposed of; but it is the frequent custom now to allow a proof of facts without disposing of the question of relevancy. Such proofs are said to be " before answer." As to the meaning and effect of these words, see *Robertson* v. *Murphy*, 6 Macp. 114 ; *Macvean* v. *Maclean*, 11 Macp. 506 ; and *Simpson* v. *Stewart*, 2 R. 673. On the subject of the maxim, see Dickson, § 1935 *et seq.*

Functus officio.—Having discharged his official duty. This is said of any one holding a certain appointment, when the duties of his office have been discharged. Thus a judge, when he has decided a question brought before him, is *functus officio*, and cannot review his own decision. So is an arbiter, when he has issued his decree-arbitral.

Fundo annexa.—Things annexed or attached to the soil. These may be either corporeal, such as houses, trees, &c., or incorporeal, as rights of patronage, right to teinds, &c. All things thus attached to the soil are considered heritable, and pass with the lands to the heir. Trade fixtures are dealt with exceptionally, for although they are regarded as moveable in a question between landlord and tenant, yet if they have been erected in connection with a lease to which the heir succeeds, such fixtures are regarded as heritable, and descend, along with the lease, to the heir. *Brand's Trs.* v. *Brand*, 2 R. 258, reversed H. L., 3 R. 16. *Photoglyptic Printing Co.*, 31 Scot. L. Rep. 569.

Fundus instructus.—Land already provided with certain necessaries.

Fur famosus.—A thief habit and repute ; a common thief.

Furiosi nulla voluntas est.—An insane person has no will. It is on this account that an insane person cannot bind himself in civil obligations, enter into contracts, or dispose of his property. These acts all require the intelligent exercise of mind and will, of which an insane person is not possessed. Nor can he be punished for criminal offences committed during insanity ; such acts, to be criminal, require the *mens rea*, which cannot exist where there is no mind at all, or only a mind so diseased as to be unable to distinguish between right and wrong. The acts of an insane person are not always without effect. For example, it has been held that where a policy of insurance declared that the same should be void in case the assured should die by his own hands, and the assured having drowned himself at a time when he was not capable of judging between right and wrong, the policy was thereby voided. *Borrodaile* v. *Hunter*, L. J. 12, C. P. 225. The same question was again discussed in *Clift* v. *Schwabe*, L. J. 17, C. P. 2, and the decision repeated. In the latter case the policy was declared void if the assured should "commit suicide," and it was maintained that suicide, being a felony, could not be committed by an insane person. The Court, however, held that the terms of the policy included all cases of voluntary self-destruction whether felonious or not. In the still later case of *Horn*, L. J. 30, Ch. 511, where the policy contained no provision against suicide by the assured, and the assured committed suicide in a state of temporary insanity, it was held that the policy was not thereby voided. See Bell's Prin. § 523.

Furiosus absentis loco est.—An insane person is regarded as an absent person. In the absence of his intelligence the man is not there, and a curator is appointed to take charge of his affairs, just as a factor is appointed to look after the affairs and protect the interests of a person who, through absence from this country, is unable to do so for himself.

Furiosus solo furore punitur.—An insane person suffers the punishment of his insanity only : that is, he cannot be punished for his acts during insanity, whatever they may be, as in such circumstances he is not responsible for his acts. The insanity, however, in order to exculpate an act criminal in itself, must amount to an incapacity to distinguish between right and wrong, for if the person on whose behalf insanity is being pleaded knew that his act was one which he ought not to do, he will be punishable. See a valuable exposition of the law on this subject in *M'Naghten's* case, 10 Cl. & F. 200 ; see also Macdonald, 11 *et seq.*

Furtum.—Theft. The Romans distinguished between *furtum manifestum*—*i.e.*, the case where the thief was caught in the act, or in the place where the theft was committed, or before he reached the spot to which he intended to convey the stolen property; and *nec manifestum*, where none of these circumstances had place. This distinction is similar to that once regarded in Scotland as infang thief and outfang thief, a distinction long ago abolished.

G

Garba.—A sheaf or handful of corn. Ersk. B. 2, T. 10, § 13. See *Decimæ garbales*.

Generalia specialibus non derogant.—General statements or provisions do not derogate from special statements or provisions. On the other hand, *specialia derogant generalibus*,— special provisions derogate from general. Where a deed contains provisions of a general nature, and also others which are special, the latter may limit the application of the former, but the special are never limited or explained by the general. This rule applies whether the deed be unilateral, as, for example, a deed of settlement, or a contract to which there are several parties. One of the best illustrations, perhaps, of the two maxims just given may be found in the rules adopted in construing the meaning and effect of deeds of submission. Where there is a submission to an arbiter of all disputes between the parties, and especially of certain enumerated points of difference, the special enumeration is held to control the general reference so as to admit under the latter only questions or differences of the same character as those specially mentioned. The reader will find some valuable observations by Lord Westbury on the rule expressed by this maxim in the case of the *Earl of Kintore*, 4 Macq. 522. See *Enumeratio unius*, &c.

Generalia verba sunt generaliter intelligenda.—General words are to be understood in their general sense. Where the words of a conveyance or of an obligation are quite general, without any adjected restriction or limitation, they are to be taken in their broad and general sense, for "that which is generally spoken shall be generally understood" (Broom, 647). Such general terms may, however, be qualified, so that, for example, the general conveyance may be made a conveyance only in trust; or the obligation rendered prestable only on the fulfilment of a certain condition. In like manner the maxim *generalis regula generaliter est intelligenda* (a general rule is to be understood generally) imports that a general rule is to be understood as applying to the general case, without excluding the consideration or effect of an exception to the rule, if that can be shown, in the particular circumstances, to be admissible. Thus the rule *pater est quem nuptiæ demonstrant* is a general rule, and applies to all children born in wedlock. But the rule is understood generally, for it is quite competent to show that a child born in wedlock is nevertheless illegitimate. The rule is general, but it is not absolute.

Generalis clausula non porrigitur ad ea quæ antea sunt comprehensa.—A general clause is not extended to those things which have been previously narrated or described. Suppose that A by his settlement conveys to a person therein named his lands of B and C, and also the stock held by him in certain banks or railways, and after other enumerations of parts of his estate, adds a general clause of conveyance, " and generally all estate, heritable and moveable, of whatever kind and wherever situated, belonging to me at the time of my death;" the general conveyance would not extend to the subjects specially conveyed—that is, the general clause would be regarded as conveying something other and beyond that which had been specially conveyed. Nor, in the general case, does a general conveyance evacuate or supersede a prior special destination. *Glendonwyn*, 8 Macp. 1075, affd. H. L. 11 Macp. 33; *Gray*, 5 R. 820.

Genus nunquam perit.—The class never perishes. Where a specific subject has been sold but not delivered, the sellers' obligation to deliver is discharged if the article (through no fault of the seller) has ceased to exist. On the other hand, when the subject of sale is a quantity of goods of a certain description or class (such as a hundred quarters of wheat, or a hundred tons of pig-iron), the destruction of the sellers' goods (which he had intended to deliver in fulfilment of his contract) will not discharge his obligation. As the class never perishes, he must deliver to the buyer goods of the quantity and description sold.

Gestio pro herede.—Behaviour as heir. Such behaviour incurs a passive title, rendering the person so conducting himself universally liable for his ancestor's debts and obligations. It consists in intermeddling with the ancestor's estate, by granting leases, drawing rents, disponing part of the property, and, in short, by the commission of such acts as an heir alone should, or could, competently perform. Such acts, however, to incur such a passive title and its liabilities, must be performed *animo gerendi* (with the intention of acting as heir), for any act whereby the *gestor* did not take any advantage, or any act inadvertently performed, and not followed up by subsequent interference with the estate, will not incur the passive title. This article, however, must be read in connection with the provisions of the Act 37 & 38 Vict. c. 94, § 12, whereby an heir's liability for his ancestor's debts has been materially restricted.

Gleba.—The glebe, or piece of ground given in addition to their stipends to the ministers of the Established Church. As to the rights which a minister now has over the glebe, see *Decimæ debentur*, &c.

Gleba terræ.—Clod or piece of earth. Proprietors of land *pro indiviso*, such as heirs-portioners, have a right of property in every piece of the land over which the joint right extends.

Grammatica falsa non vitiat chartam.—Grammatical error does not vitiate a writing. See *Mala grammatica*, &c.

Granum crescens.—Growing grain.

Grassum.—A sum paid in anticipation of rent, or a fine paid for a lease of lands during a term of years. Thus, in feu-contracts and leases, it is often stipulated that a double of the feu-duty or rent shall be paid every nineteenth year, over and above the payment for that year. Such an additional payment is called a *grassum*.

Gratia mandatarii.—For the sake of the mandatory. In the general case, a mandate, being for the benefit of the mandant, may be recalled by him at pleasure. Mandates, however, which are granted solely for the sake (or advantage) of the mandatory, such as the mandate contained in the registration clause of a deed, whereby the granter gives authority for its registration, are not revocable. Such also was the character of the mandate contained in a precept of sasine, which was not revocable by the granter, and which might be acted upon after the death, not only of the granter, but also of the grantee. All mandates *in rem suam* are granted for the benefit of the mandatory, and are irrevocable. As to whether a cheque is to be regarded as of the nature of a mandate *in rem suam* of the payee, and, therefore, not subject to be recalled or countermanded, see *Waterston* v. *City of Glasgow Bank*, 1 R. 470.

Gratis dictum.— An observation or remark without foundation, either on reason or former authority; differing from *obiter dictum*, which is a remark incidentally made, but not essential to the determination of the question at issue.

H

Habeas corpus.—The name given to a certain writ in England, and according to Blackstone " the most celebrated writ in English law." There are various writs of *habeas corpus,* but the most important of them all is that under which the legality or illegality of a prisoner's detention is determined. For the history of this writ, and the law applicable to it, the reader is referred to Blackstone, iii. 138 *et seq.;* and as to its equivalent in Scotland, see *De libero homine,* &c.

Habili et competente forma.—In a habile and competent manner.

Habili modo.—In the manner competent. Thus the habile mode of proving the existence of a debt which has undergone the triennial prescription is by writ or oath of the debtor; or, of a disputed trust, by the oath or writ of the trustee.

Habilis causa transferendi dominii.—A habile or sufficient title for transferring the property. The word *causa,* in the sense in which it is here used, has been already explained. See *Causa et modus,* &c. A habile or sufficient title for the purpose of transferring property is one which includes both the power and the intention to convey. Thus when one sells a subject and delivers it to the buyer, there is a transference of the property to the buyer, the seller's power to sell, and his intention to transfer his right, being a sufficient title to complete the transference, and to vest the buyer with the full right of property in the subject sold. But where there is either no power or no intention to convey, there can be no habile or sufficient conveyance—no habile or sufficient title by which the conveyance is effected. For example, where lands were conveyed by a vassal to his superior, by resignation *in* *favorem* of the vassal's disponee, such conveyance transferred the subjects to the superior only to the effect of enabling him to give them out again to the new vassal; the property not being transferred to him (to the effect of transferring the ownership) by the vassal's surrender of the lands. In such a conveyance there was no cause or title in respect of which the superior could retain the lands. On the contrary, the cause as expressed, pointed to his conveying them to the new vassal, the disponee; and there being on the part of the resigner no intention to reinvest the superior with the lands resigned, the law held that the fee of the property continued vested in the resigner during the period intervening between the resignation and the completion of the disponee's feudal title. Where there is no habile cause or title for conveying, there can be no conveyance.

Hac voce.—Under this word or phrase; used by way of reference, and generally written *h.v.*

Hæredes alioqui successuri.—Heirs entitled otherwise to succeed. See *Alioqui*, &c.

Hæredes nati et facti.—Heirs born and made. The former is heir by virtue of his birth and consequent relationship to the deceased, and is called heir-at-law; while the latter is only heir by appointment, that is, an heir of provision. Heirs are divided into two great classes — namely, those who are heirs *provisione legis* (by provision of the law), and those who succeed *provisione hominis* (by the provision or appointment of the testator); the former corresponding to the *nati*, the latter to the *facti* of the phrase. All included in the latter class are known as heirs of provision.

Hæredes necessarii.—Necessary heirs. A class of heirs under the civil law, who had no choice in taking up the succession or rejecting it, and were generally slaves appointed in this character to preserve the good name of their master after death. The sale of a deceased's effects for the payment of his debts affected his *existimatio*, or reputation, and often inferred infamy, to avoid which an insolvent master appointed his slave his heir, so that when the effects were sold, they were regarded as the property of the heir, not of the testator, whose name was thus preserved unblemished. There are no such necessary heirs in the Scotch law.

Hæredes proximi et remotiores.—Heirs nearer, and more remote.

Hæredes sui.—This name was given in the civil law to those persons who were under the power (*sub patria potestate*) of the deceased at the time of his death. Just. Inst. B. 2, T. 19, § 2.

Hæredibus et assignatis quibuscunque.—To heirs and assignees whomsoever. These are the terms of a simple destination, and in any question regarding the interpretation of such a destination will be held to mean the heir-at-law.

Hæreditas.—Succession; inheritance. This includes the whole estate of the deceased, whether heritable or moveable, but is frequently used as signifying merely heritage as opposed to executry. *Hæreditas* is defined in the civil law as the succession to the entire estate of the deceased. D. B. 50, T. 17, § 62.

Hæreditas ex dimidio sanguine non datur.—Succession is not recognised through the half-blood. This maxim no longer expresses the law of England, but is still a rule of our law in reference to the succession to real property. See *Frater fratri*, &c.

Hæreditas jacens.—A succession which the heir has not entered upon or taken up, which, still lying in the right of the deceased, is liable to be attached by the diligence of creditors for the deceased's debts.

Hæreditas nunquam ascendit.— Succession never ascends. This was at one time a rule of English law, which did not recognise the right of succession in ascendants of the direct line; a rule which will be found illustrated in Broom, 527. This rule was altered by the Act 3 & 4 Will. IV. c. 106. In Scotland, failing descendants, collaterals succeed, and failing collaterals, ascendants; but the succession ascends only to the father and his relations, to the exclusion of the maternal line. Bell's Prin. § 1667.

Hæreditas paterna.—A succession descending upon the heir from or through his father, in contradistinction from that derived through his mother, or through collaterals.

Hæres.—Heir. An heir is one who succeeds to the estate of a deceased person, either by force of legal rule or private provision; and the name is given as well to one who succeeds to moveables as to one who succeeds to heritage, although the former is generally, and more correctly, termed executor. The term heir is generally qualified or explained by some other term joined to it. Thus heir-at-law expresses at length what is most frequently understood by the term heir, and is the name given to the person succeeding according to the legal rules regarding succession. Heir of provision is one who succeeds to a certain right provided to him under a certain deed; and heir by destination or of entail, is one who is called to the succession only on the failure of another who is called to it before him.

Hæres actu.—Heir by appointment. Erskine uses this phrase in treating of the rights of a child under the marriage settlement of its parents. Where such settlement confers a certain *jus crediti* on the heir of the marriage, the child of the marriage is not deprived of its right, although its father should deprive it of the character of heir, by the nomination of some other person to his succession. "From these observations it follows, that though the rights which thus create a proper credit be granted to *the heir* of the marriage, that appellation is to be understood only *designative*, for marking out that the person to whom the right is granted stands in such a relation to the deceased as gives him a right to serve to him if he should think fit; but there is no necessity that he be *hæres actu* to his father (that is, heir to his father, through his father's act, deed or appointment), for he is the proper creditor." Ersk. B. 3, T. 8, § 40.

Hæres est eadem persona cum defuncto.—An heir is the same person with the deceased—*i.e.*, the deceased person to whom he succeeds. See *Eadem persona*, &c.

Hæres factus.—An heir who has been made or constituted heir: as distinguished from *hæres natus*, an heir who succeeds in respect of birth or relationship. See *Hæredes nati*, &c.

Hæres fiduciarius, or **fidei-commissarius.**—An heir in trust; a trustee. This name is given to the person or persons appointed by the testator's settlement to succeed to his estate, in order that they may fulfil the purposes of the testator's will. They are termed heirs because they succeed to the estate of the deceased; and fiduciary heirs, because the succession devolves upon them in trust for the fulfilment of the provisions of the settlement.

Hæres hæredis mei est hæres meus.—My heir's heir is my heir. A destination to heirs, on the principle of this rule, includes not only the immediate heirs of the granter, but the remoter heirs succeeding through them. Thus a grandson is the heir of his grandfather, because he is the heir of his father who was the immediate heir.

Hæres in mobilibus.—Heir in moveables. Executors are so called because they succeed to the moveable estate of the deceased.

Hæres legitimus est quem nuptiæ demonstrant.—He is the lawful heir whom the marriage (of his parents) indicates or points out. Legitimacy is an essential qualification of an heir-at-law, and this maxim imports the presumption that children born in wedlock are legitimate; consequently the eldest son born in wedlock is presumably the father's heir. This presumption, however, may be overcome regarding which, see *Pater est*, &c.

Hæres succedit in universum jus quod defunctus habuit.—The heir succeeds to the entire estate which the deceased had.

Hinc inde.—" A technical expression used in Scotch legal phraseology, to signify on either side, or on this side and the other, as connected with a particular process, account, or transaction. Thus the claims of parties *hinc inde*, signifies their reciprocal claims against each other, as at a particular time, or in a particular process or suit." Bell's Dict. *h.v.*

Hoc intuitu.—In this prospect or expectation. Deeds granted *intuitu matrimonii* are of no avail if the marriage never takes place, and simply because they were executed in the expectation of an event, which, as a condition, had failed.

Hoc loco.—In this place.

Hoc nomine.—In this name; under this character. See *Eo nomine*.

Hoc ordine.—In this order.

Hoc titulo.—Under this title; frequently used by way of reference in law books, and often written *h.t.*

Homicidium in rixa.—Manslaughter committed in a quarrel or brawl. Such crime amounts only to culpable homicide, and the punishment being in the discretion of the judge, varies according to the particular circumstances of each case. It is not punished capitally, because this crime lacks the previous malice essential to the crime of murder.

Honeste vivere.—To live honourably, or morally. This is one of the fundamental maxims of law, as given by Justinian. *Honeste* included more than mere obedience to the rules of law; for *non omne quod licet honestum est* (everything permitted by law is not morally right). It included all social and moral obligations, whether they could be enforced at law or not. See *Alterum non lœdere*.

I

Id certum est quod certum reddi potest.—That is regarded as certain (or fixed) which can be made certain. See *Certum est*, &c.

Id non agebatur.—Literally that was not done. Stair uses this phrase in the following passage, which serves to illustrate it. In treating of the liability of executors for the full value of the subjects given up in their inventory, he states that they are entitled to value the subjects in certain cases at the value put upon them by the deceased, but "otherwise executors are comptable according to the ordinary prices ; seeing *id non agebatur* by the price (that is, by the deceased's valuation) to gift to the executor." Stair, B. 3, T. 8, § 62. The meaning of the words as they occur here is this : the deceased, when he valued the subjects, did not intend to depreciate their value for the purpose of benefiting the executor,—this was not in his consideration at all—this was not what he did (*id non agebatur*) by the valuation ; therefore, the executor is bound for the true value of the subjects.

Id quod nostrum est, sine facto nostro, ad alium transferri non potest.—That which is ours cannot be transferred to another, without our act. See *Quod meum est*, &c.

Id quod prius fuit voluntatis, postea fit necessitatis. —That which was at first a matter of choice, becomes afterwards a matter of necessity. On this rule is founded the obligation of a tutor or curator, having once accepted the office, to hold it, and fulfil its duties. To accept the office depends upon the free will of the person accepting, but having accepted, to perform the duties of that office becomes a legal obligation. So also an arbiter having accepted office cannot resign, but must pronounce his decree-arbitral. Formerly testamentary trustees who had once accepted office could not resign unless specially authorised or permitted to do so by the deed under which they were appointed. But this was altered by the Act 24 & 25 Vict. c. 84, and gratuitous trustees can now resign their office at pleasure if there be no provision to the contrary in the deed of appointment, subject to the limitation imposed by § 10 of the Act 30 & 31 Vict. c. 97, which provides that no sole trustee shall be entitled to resign until he has assumed new trustees, or a judicial factor on the trust estate has been appointed by the Court. M'Laren, ii. 226 *et seq.*

Id solum nostrum quod debitis deductis nostrum est.—That only is ours which remains to us after deduction of debts. An heir succeeding to the whole estate of his ancestor, succeeds to it less the burdens which affect it, because debts, &c., belonged to others, and were no part of the deceased's possession. The estate of a rebel or criminal falling as escheat to the Crown, is also, according to Stair, subject to the deduction of just debts.

Id tantum possumus quod de jure possumus.—We can do that only which we can lawfully do. This has reference to contracts in themselves unlawful, or having unlawful conditions thereto attached. Such contracts and conditions cannot be enforced, for they are considered as legally impossible,—not capable of being entered into or imposed, and consequently of no legal effect.

Idem agens et patiens non potest.—The same person cannot both do and submit (in reference to the same matter). The same person cannot, for example (at least he cannot in the same character), be both the pursuer and the defender of an action; he cannot be both creditor and debtor in the same obligation, for whenever the debtor in an obligation acquires the creditor's right, or *vice versa*, the obligation is extinguished *confusione*. So a servitude becomes extinguished when the dominant and servient tenements become vested in the same person; no man has a servitude over his own land, for any previously existing servitude which he held merges in the greater right of property which becomes his when he acquires the burdened lands. There is a practice, however, which forms a kind of exception to this general rule, which is of considerable practical importance. Where lands are bought, which at the time are burdened with debt, it is not unusual for the purchaser to take an assignation to the debt rather than a discharge, and thus, in a fashion, he becomes his own debtor and creditor at the same time. The purpose of this mode of dealing with the secured debt is to preserve it as a separate estate in the purchaser, in order that he may be enabled to make it good against the lands in the event of his being evicted from the lands or his title thereto being successfully challenged. This is only resorted to when the title to the lands is doubtful: where the title is clear, all burdens are generally discharged.

Idem est non esse et non apparere.—That which does not appear (*i.e.*, is not produced or proved) is the same as that which does not exist. See the explanation of this maxim given under another form, *De non apparentibus*, &c.

Idoneis argumentis.—By suitable, or sufficient, arguments. Hume, i. 260.

Ignoramus.—We ignore. The word formerly indorsed on a bill laid before the grand jury (in England) when they ignored the bill. It is not now used. See *Billa vera*.

Ignorantia eorum quæ quis scire tenetur non excusat.—Ignorance affords no excuse in reference to those things which one is bound to know. Thus when any one offends against the law, it is no excuse that he did not know the law, since every one is presumed to know and bound to know what the law provides. "The law is administered upon the principle that every one must be taken conclusively to know it without proof that he does know it" (per Tindal, C. J., in M'Naghten's case, 10 Cl. & F. 210). But there are matters of fact also, ignorance of which cannot be pleaded in excuse. If a merchant enters into a contract to purchase goods, the quantity, quality, or price of which is, by contract, agreed to be ascertained by reference to a certain standard, he cannot refuse to implement his contract on the ground that he did not know what the standard was. He was bound to know that with which he was dealing; and if he did not know, should have informed himself before entering into his bargain. Again, where a charterer engages to discharge or load a vessel according to the custom of a certain port, his obligation is absolute, and he cannot plead ignorance of the custom in answer to a claim arising out of the non-implement of his contract. In like manner, the shipowner or shipmaster who agrees to such a charter cannot refuse to implement it, on the ground that the ship, according to such custom, would be detained for an unusually long period, and that if he had known this he would not have entered into the charter. The parties in all such cases are bound to know what it is they are binding themselves to do, and ignorance of what they ought to know will not excuse them from the performance of their obligation.

Ignorantia facti.—Ignorance of a fact; and used in opposition to

Ignorantia juris.—Ignorance of the law. Where any payment has been made or service performed on an error in fact, restitution can be enforced; not so where the error was one in law. On the latter point our law seems scarcely settled, although as a general rule error in law is not admitted as a ground on which restitution may be enforced. See *Condictio indebiti*.

Ignorantia juris neminem excusat.—Ignorance of the law excuses no one. Every one is presumed to know the law, and therefore a plea of ignorance will not excuse a breach of it. Ignorance, when not plainly culpable, may induce leniency, as where a law newly promulgated, and the provisions of which are not yet generally known, has been broken. See *Ignorantia eorum*, &c.

Impedimentum rebus agendis.—A hindrance to the transaction of business. "It was not found relevant to elide death-bed, that the defunct was in strength and ability to have come to kirk and market; nor that the defunct put on his clothes daily, and that any disease he had was but lent (mild), and not *impedimentum rebus agendis*." Stair, B. 3, T. 4, § 28.

Imperitia enumeratur culpæ.—Unskilfulness is reckoned as a fault. In the hiring of skilled labour, the employer is entitled to rely on ordinary skill, and damage arising from the want of it may be recovered from the person employed. Mere error in judgment, in a professional man, is not sufficient to found a claim for damages, if he should be shown to be wrong, unless in acting on his own judgment he has departed from the common rule or practice observed in like cases. Bell's Prin. § 153-54.

Imperium merum.—The name given in the civil law to the power conferred on judges of executing sentences on criminals; sometimes called the *jus gladii*. Dig. L. 2, T. 1, l. 3.

Imperium mixtum.—The name given to the authority possessed by judges in civil matters; called *mixtum* because it conferred power to declare the law (*juris dictio*), and also the power of enforcing their decisions. Dig. *ut supra*. See *Inhærere jurisdictioni*.

Impossibilium nulla obligatio est.—There is no obligation to perform what is impossible: impossibilities give rise to no obligation. See *Lex non cogit*, &c.

Impotentia excusat legem.—Inability excuses the non-observance of the law. Where a person cannot possibly perform what the law orders him to do, or does that, under invincible necessity, which the law forbids, such non-performance or violation of the law will not be treated as an offence, for *lex non cogit ad impossibilia*. The inability, however, must be absolute, and not in any way brought about by the person who pleads it. What will be held as amounting to the inability or necessity referred to in the maxim, may be learned from the judgment delivered by Sir W. Scott (Lord Stowell) in the case of the "*Generous*," 2 Dodson Adm. Rep. 323. That case arose out of a breach of the revenue laws, and after remarking upon the inflexible character of those laws, the learned judge proceeded—" It is not the private opinion of the judge upon the policy (of those laws) that is to guide his public judgment; he must follow where the law leads in a general unbending course. But the law itself, and the administration of it, must yield to that to which everything must bend—to necessity. The law in its most positive and peremptory injunctions is understood to disclaim, as it does in its general aphorisms, all intention of compelling to impossibilities, and the administration of laws must adopt that general exception in the consideration of all particular cases. In the performance of that duty, it has three points to which its attention must be directed; in the first place, it must see that the nature of the necessity pleaded be such as the law itself would respect, for there may be a necessity which it would not. A necessity created by a man's own act, with a fair previous knowledge of the consequences that would follow, and under circumstances which he had then a power of controlling, is of that nature. Secondly, that the party who was so placed used all practicable endeavours to surmount the difficulties which already formed that necessity, and which, on fair trial, he found insurmountable. I do not mean all the endeavours which the wit of a man, as it exists in the acutest understanding, might suggest, but such as may reasonably be expected from a fair degree of discretion and an ordinary knowledge of business. Thirdly, that all this shall appear by distinct and unsuspected testimony, for the positive injunctions of the law, if proved to be violated, can give way to nothing but the clearest proof of the necessity that compelled the violation."

In acquirenda possessione.—In the course of acquiring possession.

In alode.—Allodial subjects; which were lands held independent of any superior, and burdened with no feudal homage or service.

In alternativis electio est debitoris.—Where there is an alternative, the election lies with the debtor. Thus, where in a contract of sale it is stipulated that the goods shall be paid for on delivery either in cash or by approved bill, it is in the option of the purchaser (who is debtor in the obligation) to adopt which of the alternatives he pleases; the creditor has no choice. On the same principle, if one who is debtor in two or more different debts to the same creditor, makes a payment to his creditor to account, that payment is appropriated *pro tanto* in extinction of whichever of the obligations the debtor pleases; he has the choice of the debt to which it is to be applied, and the creditor cannot appropriate the payment unless it has been made as an indefinite payment, that is, not appropriated towards any particular debt.

In ambigua voce legis ea potius accipienda est signi-

ficatio quæ vitio caret, præsertim cum etiam voluntas legis ex hoc colligi possit.—Where the language of a statute is ambiguous, that interpretation is to be preferred which involves no injustice (or inequity), especially when this can be gathered from the statute to have been the intention of the law. Dig. B. 1, T. 3, § 19.

In ambiguis orationibus maxime sententia spectanda est ejus qui eas protulisset.—In ambiguous expressions (*i.e.*, in construing or interpreting ambiguous expressions) the meaning or intention of him who used them is chiefly to be regarded. Dig. B. 50, T. 17, § 96.

In apicibus juris.—In the subtleties of the law. See the opinion of Lord Meadowbank in the case of *Harvie*, 12th December, 1811, F. C.

In arbitrio alieno.—According to the judgment of another. Legacies are said to be so bequeathed when their distribution and extent are left to the judgment and discretion of persons other than the testator. Thus a testator may (and such a case is not unfrequent) bequeath large sums of money to be divided among certain charities, as his trustees may think proper. "It is at the best doubtful whether, by will, a general and unlimited power of distribution, after the testator's death, can be given to another; but if distinct limits are appointed for the exercise of the power, it will be effectual." Bell's Prin. § 1862. As to the limits within which such a power will be regarded as effectual, see the case of *Cobb's Trs.*, 9th March, 1894, and cases there cited. This phrase is sometimes written: *In arbitrio tertii* (According to the judgment of a third person).

In arbitrio judicis.—In the discretion or decision of the judge. "Discretion, when applied to a court of justice, means *sound* discretion *guided by law*. It must be governed by rule, not by humour; it must not be arbitrary, vague, and fanciful, but legal and regular." Per Lord Mansfield in *Rex* v. *Wilkes*, 4 Burr. 2539. See also per Lord Halsbury (L. C.) in *Sharp* v. *Wakefield*, L. R. App. C., 1891, p. 179.

In articulo mortis.—At the point of death; on deathbed.

In æmulationem.—Emulously; with a desire to injure

or annoy; or acting wantonly, so as to produce injury or annoyance.

In æmulationem vicini.—To the injury or annoyance of a neighbour. A proprietor must use his property so as not to injure the property of another. If the act done is necessary to the improvement, or adds to the value of his subject, the right to perform it falls within his right of property, and may not be interfered with. But if the act be unnecessary, or not advantageous, and be performed wantonly, to the injury or annoyance of his neighbour, he may be compelled to desist. Ersk. B. 2, T. 1, § 2.

In æquali jure melior est conditio possidentis.—Where the right is equal, the position of the possessor is the better. If two persons have an equally good title to the possession of a subject, the position of the person actually in possession is obviously the better of the two, for he has not only title but possession; and one who holds upon a good title cannot be compelled to surrender his possession except upon the production of a better title than his own. It is difficult to conceive, however, of two persons having a title equally good to the same subject at the same time: *duo non possunt in solido unam rem possidere.* The maxim under explanation has reference probably to joint rights, concerning which see *In re communi*, &c.

In æquo.—On equity. Natural law is founded upon strict equity and justice; positive law is founded *in bono* or *utili*, for the profit and advantage of men.

In bonis.—Among the goods of a person; and property, the right to which has vested, is said to be *in bonis.*

In bonis defuncti.—Among the goods of the deceased; property vested in the deceased.

In campo.—In the field—*i.e.,* before the court, and maintaining, or having an opportunity of maintaining, conflicting interests. Stair, B. 4, T. 20, § 16.

In casu extremæ necessitatis omnia sunt communia.—In cases of extreme necessity all things are common. Broom, 2 (note *a*).

In causa.—In the cause or process; sometimes signifying, on the merits of the cause.

In civilibus ministerium excusat, in criminalibus non

item.—In civil matters agency (or service) excuses, but not so in criminal matters. If one enters into a civil contract avowedly as agent for another, while in point of fact he holds that position, he binds his principal and not himself to performance; and in like manner that which a servant does in the course of his employment and on his master's instructions, binds the master, and makes him, not the servant, directly responsible for the consequences. It is held to be the master's own act, performed by him through another, and the servant or representative is excused or exculpated on that ground. But a different rule is applied where the act done is criminal. If a master order his servant to commit an assault, or a theft, the servant is not bound to obey such an order—he is bound to disobey; but if he does perform that which the master ordered, he will be personally responsible for the consequences. If a master sends his servant to the bank with a forged bill or cheque, and the servant in ignorance utters it as genuine, he will not be held guilty of crime, not because of his master's order, but because he was ignorant of the forgery, and had no felonious intention; the *mens rea* was wanting. If he uttered the forged bill on his master's order, in the knowledge that it was a forgery, the fact that he was a servant obeying orders would not afford him any defence or excuse.

In claris non est locus conjecturis.—Things that are clear (unambiguous) do not admit of conjecture or construction. Of course, when a statement is clear, its meaning appears from itself; it is only when ambiguity exists, that construction or conjectural meaning is admitted.

In clientela.—Standing in the relation of client to patron. "There was formerly a kind of bondage in Scotland, called Manrent, whereby free persons became the men or followers of those who were their patrons and defenders; and therefore these were rather *in clientela* than in bondage." Stair, B. 1, T. 2, § 12.

In commendam.—In trust. In former times, when a vacancy occurred in a benefice or living, the bishop of the diocese frequently appointed some one as steward, to levy the fruits during the vacancy. The person thus appointed, being a mere trustee, was called *commendator*, and he was bound to account for the fruits and others levied and received by him. When, however, the benefice was conferred *in perpetuam commendam*, it operated as a gift, and the commendator appropriated the fruits without being liable to account therefor. This power of appointment in the bishop was limited.

In commercio licet decipere.—Deception is permitted, or lawful, in trade. It has already been stated that fraud or wilful deception will be a sufficient ground for the reduction of any contract or bargain to which it gave rise (see *Dolus*); and that would seem to be at variance with this maxim. The deception, however, to which this maxim refers, consists in the exaggerated encomiums pronounced by a dealer on his goods, his endeavour to induce a belief of their value being greater than it really is, their being peculiarly adapted for a certain market, &c. In such matters the purchaser must be on his own guard, and if he allows himself to be deceived he has no legal remedy.

In communi forma.—In common form.

In computo.—In computation.

In confinio majoris ætatis.—Having nearly attained majority. Acts done and obligations undertaken by persons of such an age will in some cases be binding upon them, notwithstanding their plea of minority; and especially so, if they have stated themselves to be of full age; or perform acts affording reasonable grounds for inferring this. See *Deceptis*, &c.

In confinio minoris ætatis.—Having nearly attained minority.

In consequentiam.—As a consequence, or necessary result.

In consimili casu consimile debet esse remedium.—In similar cases the remedy ought to be similar.

In contractis tacite insunt quæ sunt moris et consuetudinis.—Contracts are held as containing, although not expressed, those conditions which practice and custom have imported into such contracts. There are many implied conditions of contracts. A contract of sale by sample contains an implied condition that the bulk shall be equal to sample; and this is a condition binding on the seller, although not expressed. It is an implied condition, further, that the price is to be paid on delivery; and if payment is not to be so made, that must be expressed so as to overcome the implied condition. But if in a certain trade or business the uniform custom is to allow credit for a certain time, or to give a certain discount, parties are held in their contracts to deal with each other according to the custom of the trade, and the purchaser will be entitled to credit or discount unless it is specially otherwise provided. In short, the regular custom of trade is supposed to be followed, and tacitly to form part of all contracts entered into in pursuance of that trade. Further illustration of this maxim may be obtained by a consideration of the conditions or warranties implied in the contract of marine insurance, for which reference may be made to Arnould, ii. 636 *et seq.*

In conventionibus contrahentium voluntas potius quam verba spectari placuit.—In contracts, the intention of the contracting parties is to be regarded rather than the words in which the contract is expressed. This rule must be read and applied with caution. If the contract is clearly expressed, and free from ambiguity, the intention of parties can only be ascertained from the language in which that intention has been expressed. It would be contrary to all rule to allow the plain expression of a contract to be modified or contradicted by an allegation that any one of the contracting parties intended something different from the ordinary meaning of the language used. There may arise questions, however, in which the rule of the maxim can be applied, as, for example, whether a condition of the contract was or was not a condition precedent—whether a certain clause was merely representation, or amounted to warranty, &c. The reader will find an instructive case on this matter in *Behn* v. *Burness*, 32 L. J. Q. B. 204. See *Non quod dictum*, &c.

In corporibus sed non in quantitatibus.—In separate and distinct subjects, but not in things estimated in quantities. This phrase is used by Stair (B. 3, T. 5, § 9), in reference to the character of heirship moveables, which consisted of the best of certain moveables belonging to the deceased, to which the heir had right. Under such right the heir claimed the best articles of furniture, the best horse, yoke of oxen, plough, &c.; but heirship moveables did not include wine, money, corn, &c., because they are fungibles, and are estimated in quantities. The claim to heirship moveables was abolished by 31 & 32 Vict. c. 101, § 160.

In criminalibus humanior interpretatio accipienda est.—In criminal matters the more benevolent (or humane) interpretation is to be received. This rule is applied in the construction of penal statutes which are construed as against an offender, not in the most severe and stringent, but in the most humane sense which they can reasonably bear. The same rule is applied in the consideration of the proof adduced against a prisoner under a criminal charge. Where the prisoner's conduct, or the circumstances attending the commission of the alleged crime, are reasonably consistent with the theory of the prisoner's innocence, he is entitled to the benefit of that interpretation or construction; a prisoner can only be found guilty when the facts proved against him are conclusive of his guilt.

In criminalibus non est argumentandum a pari ultra casum a lege definitum.—In criminal matters it is not allowed, by argument from analogy, to go beyond the case defined (or limited) by law; in other words, penal statutes are not to be extended by analogy to cases which the law itself does not enumerate or provide for.

In criminalibus sufficit generalis malitia intentionis cum facto paris gradus.—In criminal matters, a general malicious intention, with an act of corresponding degree or character, is sufficient (to constitute crime). To constitute crime there must be both intention and act; but there may be crime where the criminal did something which he did not intend. Take the case that A intends to murder B, and with that intention shoots at C by mistake, who dies: A is guilty of the murder of C. There was no intention to injure C, but there was the malicious intention to murder somebody, and an act performed of a character calculated to carry the intention into effect. Hume, i. 180. Again, where an attempt is made to procure the abortion of a pregnant woman, and she dies in consequence of the means used for that purpose, the crime is murder: there was no intention to commit murder, but there was general malicious intention to commit a crime, and an act performed in pursuance of that intention, which resulted in death.

In cursu diligentiæ.—In the course of doing diligence. The word diligence is here used in its broadest sense, including more than is usually understood by it. It includes not only personal diligence, arrestments, &c., but also adjudications, confirmations before the commissary, and generally all judicial proceedings by which property is attached or transferred.

In cursu rebellionis.—In the course of rebellion; or, during the time anyone was held to be a rebel. All persons were formerly regarded as in rebellion against the Crown who had been put to the horn for non-fulfilment of a civil obligation; their whole moveable estate fell to the Crown as escheat; they might be put to death with impunity; and lost all their legal privileges. If the denunciation remained unrelaxed for year and day (which was the time known as the *cursus rebellionis*), the rebel was esteemed *civiliter mortuus*, and his heritage reverted to the superior, under the casualty of liferent escheat. Where the denunciation was for treason, the whole property, heritable and moveable, fell to the Crown. Denunciation for civil obligation and its consequences were in effect abolished by the Act 20 Geo. II. c. 50. By the Act 1 & 2 Vict. c. 114, it was provided that a registered execution of charge should have the effect of a denunciation; but that effect was merely to accumulate the debt and interest into a principal sum, bearing interest, and also to subject the debtor to personal diligence. The only proper denunciation that now exists is that which may proceed on a sentence of fugitation pronounced by the Justiciary Court.

In damno vitando.—In endeavouring to avoid damage or injury.

In Dei nomine.—In the name of God; the solemn invocation with which, in former times, certain official writs began.

In detrimentum animi.—To the injury of the soul. Upon this ground persons were debarred from calling in question any deed or act which they had made oath they would never question,—such, for example, as the judicial ratification of a deed made by a wife outwith her husband's presence. (Stair, B. 1, T. 17, § 14.) No such reason now operates as a bar by way of personal exception to the reduction of a deed. See *Extra præsentiam*, &c.

In diem.—He is called a creditor *in diem* whose debt is due but not yet prestable. The debt is called *debitum in diem*. See Ross, L. C. (L. R.) i. 288 *et seq.*, as to the right of a creditor *in diem* to do diligence in security of the debt.

In disjunctivis sufficit alteram partem esse veram.— In disjunctives it is sufficient that either part be true. The most familiar illustration of this maxim is found in the common direction in deeds of settlement for payment of provisions to a child " on attaining majority *or* being married." If either condition be fulfilled, it is enough, and the provision becomes payable. Again, leases are sometimes declared terminable at the pleasure of the landlord, if the tenant should be sequestrated, or become notour bankrupt, or cease to reside on his farm, or assign the lease to another without the landlord's consent. If any of these disjunctives be true, that is, if any one of these events happen, it is sufficient to entitle the landlord to put an end to the lease. In criminal indictments the prosecutor frequently sets forth disjunctively the weapon by which the panel had committed an assault upon another; and it is sufficient to warrant a conviction if the prosecutor proves that the assault was committed by means of any one of the weapons so named.

In dote æstimata.—When the dowry or tocher was valued. Under the civil law the *dos* was restored by the husband to the wife, or her relations, on the dissolution of the marriage. During the marriage he was only entitled to its fruits, and in the general case, could not dispose of the *dos* itself. If, however, a fixed value was put upon the *dos*, the husband was entitled to dispose of it, being in such case bound to make payment of the fixed value when the marriage was dissolved.

In dubio.—In doubt or uncertainty; in a doubtful case.

In dubio pars mitior est sequenda.—In a doubtful case, the most favourable—*i.e.*, the most equitable view, is to be followed. There are several maxims and phrases to the same effect in different words as suitable to the different cases to which they are applied. Thus—

In dubio pro innocentia respondendum est.—In a doubtful case, the answer or decision should be in favour of innocence. On this maxim is founded a prisoner's right to the benefit of any doubt in his case, the presumption of his innocence being favoured until he is proved guilty. And—

In dubio pro possessore respondendum est.—In a doubtful case the decision should be in favour of the possessor. In a question of disputed right the possessor of the subject must be held to have the right to it, until his opponent can show a better title. Instances of these phrases need not be multiplied, as those already given will afford a sufficient explanation of their general meaning.

In dubio sequendum quod tutius est.—In a doubtful case that course is to be followed which is the safer.

In duriorem sortem.—To the debt which it was the debtor's interest to have first discharged; that debt "which bound him fastest, or to which a penalty was adjected." Indefinite payments were so applied under the civil law. See *Durior sors*.

In eodem negotio.—Having reference to the same transaction; arising out of the same matter or business.

In essentialibus.—In the essential parts. An error in the essential parts of a deed, such as its solemnities, is fatal.

In executione rei judicatæ.—In execution of a thing, or right, already judicially determined.

In facie ecclesiæ.—Before the church; according to the rules, or under the approbation of the church. Regular marriages are said to be so solemnised.

In faciendo.—In doing. Obligations *in faciendo* are for the performance of some act, and, as it is regarded as indivisible, where two or more persons are bound by such an obligation, each is bound for complete performance.

In facto præstando.—In the performance of some act or deed. The phrase is similar in import to the preceding one. See *Ad factum præstandum*.

In facto proprio.—Concerning a person's own act.

In favorem.—In favour of. A resignation *in favorem* was one made into the hands of a superior in favour of the purchaser who was to become the new vassal. Entry with a superior in this manner is now incompetent. 37 & 38 Vict. c. 94, § 4.

In favorem vitæ libertatis et innocentiæ omnia præsumuntur.—All things are presumed in favour of life, liberty, and innocence, or (as the maxim may also be rendered) the presumption is always in favour of life, liberty, and innocence. (1) According to the civil law, life was presumed for a hundred years from the date of birth, and this view seems to have been adopted by Stair (B. 4, T. 45, § 17). The presumption in favour of life for a hundred years after birth was not, in later years, regarded in the law of Scotland as a hard and fast rule, but gave way to circumstances which clearly indicated that death had taken place at an earlier period. The presumption in favour of life, however, was always difficult to overcome,— so difficult that many cases occurred where death, beyond reasonable doubt, had happened, and where, notwithstanding, the court did not feel itself at liberty to declare that death had taken place, or to distribute a succession on that ground. The hardships arising from this state of the law led to the passing of the Act 54 & 55 Vict. c. 29, which now regulates the law of Scotland in this matter. (2) The presumption in favour of liberty is only directed against the personal liberty of any subject being invaded without good grounds, although proof of guilt is not necessary to warrant apprehension and imprisonment for the purposes of investigation or inquiry. No prisoner, however, should be committed for trial except upon a *prima facie* case of guilt made out against him, and considered by the committing magistrate. (3) The presumption in favour of innocence lays the *onus* of proving guilt on the accuser. Every one is presumed innocent until guilt has been established.

In fictione juris semper æquitas existit.—Equity always exists in legal fiction; or, legal fiction is always consistent with equity. See *Fictio juris.*

In fieri.—In course of completion.

In fine.—Towards the end or conclusion. Used by way of reference.

In forma delicti.—In the form of a delict; or under the character of a delict. Certain prosecutions not strictly criminal must be pursued in some measure as if they were. Thus " prosecutions for offences against the game laws must be *in forma delicti.*" Bell's Prin. § 955.

In forma pauperis.—As a pauper, or in the character of a pauper. A person having a just or probable cause of action, but who is unable to bear the expense of a litigation, is entitled to the benefit of the poor's roll, and that exempts him from the necessity of paying agent or counsel the usual fees, and also exempts him from payment of the ordinary fees attendant upon the procedure of an action at law. Such a person is said to sue *in forma pauperis.*

In forma specifica.—In the specified form; or, in the manner specified. See *Per equipollens.*

In foro contentioso.—In a contested action. A decree is said to be granted *in foro contentioso* where the action in which it is pronounced has been litigated, and parties fully heard on the merits of the case. But it is not necessary that parties should be fully heard to make the decree pronounced in the case a decree *in foro.* " Where defences have been lodged, the decree is still *in foro*, though they may not have been insisted in." Shand, i. 311. So also when defences have been stated, but the defender fails to appear at some diet, or fails to obtemper some order of court, the decree pronounced against him in default is still a decree *in foro. Forrest* v. *Dunlop,* 3 R. 15. By the Court of Session Act, 1868, § 24, certain decrees in absence are declared entitled to all the privileges of a decree *in foro* on certain conditions. The reader is referred to the clause.

In foro contradictorio.—A phrase similar in meaning to the preceding one.

In fraudem.—In defraud of; with fraudulent intention. Thus a bankrupt is held to have acted *in fraudem* of his creditors when he grants preferences within sixty days of his bankruptcy, and such deeds are reducible on that ground.

In fructu.—Among the fruit. Whatever a *bona fide* possessor may have gathered of the fruits of his possession remains absolutely his. This applies strictly to those things which are the fruits or produce of the subject possessed, and will not extend to any part of the original subject of which he may have disposed, such part of the subject not being *in fructu.*

In graviorem causam.—This phrase is similar in meaning and application to the phrase *in duriorem sortem*, which see.

In gremio.—In the body of. Any clause, or condition, or restriction set forth in a deed, is said to be *in gremio* of it. The phrase is a common one, and has no technical meaning.

In gremio juris.—In the body of the right—*i.e.*, of the deed constituting the right. Clauses thus inserted are binding upon singular successors, but otherwise (unless they are duly recorded so as to be binding) they have not this effect. For example, a conveyance in security, properly expressed, entitles the debtor under it to demand his reinvestment in the subject conveyed on his making payment of the debt in security of which it was granted, no matter into whose hands it may have passed. *In gremio* of the conveyance, such a right is reserved to him. But if the conveyance is *ex facie* absolute, and there is no back letter or bond recorded qualifying the absolute disposition, a singular successor will be entitled to retain the subject in a question with the debtor, there being nothing *in gremio juris* of the creditor or on record, preventing him disponing the subject absolutely to any purchaser.

In hæreditate jacente.—In the estate of a person deceased, which has not been entered upon or taken up by his heir. See *Hæreditas jacens.*

In hoc statu.—In this position; in the present state of matters.

In iis quæ sunt meræ facultatis nunquam præscribitur.—Prescription does not run against a mere power or faculty to act. Rights of different kinds may be lost or acquired through prescription; but the mere power or faculty of doing something, the essence of which is, that it may be done at any time, cannot be so lost. Such are, for example, an heir's power to enter upon a succession, a faculty to burden lands, the power of building on one's own property, the right to levy and exact feu-duties and casualties of superiority, although in this last case arrears may be lost by prescription.

In infinitum.—Without limit : for ever.

In initialibus.—In the preliminary stage. Questions put to a witness *in initialibus* are those put to test his competency before his examination in chief is commenced. Initial examinations, formerly very common, are now very rare, because recent changes in the law affecting evidence have abolished almost all the restrictions formerly existing as to the persons who may competently be adduced as witnesses.

In initio litis.—At the outset of the suit. All preliminary defences affecting the pursuer's title, the relevancy of the summons, competency of the action, &c., should be set forth at this stage of the process, and if subsequently stated, will not entitle the proponer to expenses.

In integrum.—Entirely ; to the fullest extent. See *Restitutio*, &c.

In ipso termino.—At the very end ; on the last day. A decree-arbitral may be pronounced by the arbiter *in ipso termino*—*i.e.*, the very day on which his office of arbiter ceases ; and so prescription may be interrupted *in ipso termino*—*i.e.*, the last day of the prescriptive period.

In judicio possessorio.—In a possessory action. A possessory action is one in which a question of possession, apart from the question of right of property, is determined. Such an action may either be for acquiring, or retaining, or recovering possession ; and uninterrupted possession for seven years entitles the possessor to a possessory judgment. For the effect of such a judgment see Ersk. B. 4, T. 1, § 50.

In jure.—In right. Certain subjects consist *in jure* (termed in the civil law *res incorporales*), such as mere rights of superiority, rights of patronage, &c. ; and although they are rights of property as really as any other, they are by this name distinguished from those subjects of property which are corporeal and tangible, such as houses, lands, &c.

In jure non remota causa sed proxima spectatur. —In law, the near (or direct) cause is regarded, not the remote cause. See *Causa proxima*, &c.

In lecto.—On death-bed. See *Ex capite lecti*.

In lecto ægritudinis.—Literally, on a bed of sickness ; but the phrase has generally the same signification as the preceding one—*i.e.*, death-bed. It may be taken sometimes, however, in its literal signification; for "the weakness occasioned by extreme illness, such as childbirth pains, is a relevant ground for reducing a bond or a discharge." Bell's Dict. *v. Lectus.*

In liberam baroniam.—Into a free barony. In former times, many persons holding certain feudal rights from the Crown were called barons, but in the strict legal sense, the title was only due to him whose lands had been erected or confirmed by the king *in liberam baroniam*. The advantages conferred by the right of barony were considerable. Such a right conferred on the baron both civil and criminal jurisdiction within his barony; and under the clause of union contained in his charter, he was enabled to take infeftment in the whole lands and rights of the barony in, what was at that time, an easy and inexpensive mode. The jurisdiction of barons was abolished by the Jurisdiction Act (20 Geo. II. c. 43), except to a very limited extent: in effect, such jurisdiction is entirely abolished, although it was insisted in and given effect to in the case of *Tulloch*, 12 S. 754.

In liberam regalitatem.—Into a free regality. Regalities were originally feudal rights of lands granted by the king, to which were attached extensive jurisdiction. In civil matters, Lords of Regality (the title conferred on those holding such grants, although commoners) had the same jurisdiction as a sheriff; but in criminal matters their jurisdiction was more extensive, as it included even the four pleas of the Crown; they were not, however, competent judges in a case of treason. These jurisdictions were abolished by the Act 20 Geo. II. c. 43.

In libero sochagio.—In free soccage. Soccage was one of the ancient tenures by which lands were held in Scotland. Under it the vassal was bound in return for the land bestowed upon him, to render agricultural services to his superior. This was intended in some measure to prevent the waste and ruin to land which was almost inevitable on account of vassals being called away to render the military services for which for the most part lands were granted.

In liege poustie.—See *Liege poustie.*

In limine judicii.—At the outset of the suit. See *In initio litis.*

In linea recta.—In the direct line. Heir-of-line is synonymous with heir-at-law; and, consequently, in former times a disposition by a vassal to his heir-of-line did not incur the casualty of recognition, because his conveyance only carried the lands to him who would have succeeded to them by force of law.

In litem.—In the suit; or, regarding the subject of the suit. The oath *in litem* was that which a pursuer was entitled to emit in his own cause, in two classes of cases. "1*st*, Where there is full proof that the defender has been engaged in some illegal act, as spuilzie, or the like; and, 2*dly*, In the case of losses which a party is entitled to recover under the edict *nautæ, caupones,* &c. In either case, the oath *in litem* is conclusive as to the quantities lost; but in so far as regards the price or value put on the articles, it is subject to modification by the Court." (Bell's Dict. *voce* Evidence.) The peculiarity of the oath *in litem,*—being that of a pursuer bearing testimony in his own favour, and therefore limited to the cases mentioned, where no other proof could be obtained,—no longer exists. All persons, whether pursuer or defender, may now, in the general case, be examined as witnesses in their own actions; the oath *in litem,* as a special proceeding, may therefore be said to be entirely at an end.

In loco facti imprestabilis subest damnum et interesse.—Damages come in the place of an act which cannot be performed. See *Loco facti,* &c., and *Lex non cogit,* &c.

In lucro captando.—In endeavouring to make gain; or to gain an advantage.

In majorem cautelam.—For greater security; in the exercise of greater caution. Thus, where contravention of the condition of an entail operated as a forfeiture of the contravener's right, the question might arise whether this forfeiture did not also exclude the heirs succeeding in and through him. To obviate this difficulty, Erskine says "a clause is generally inserted in the deed *in majorem cautelam,* that the contravener shall forfeit only for himself, but not for his descendants." (B. 3, T. 8, § 31.) Such a precaution, while a very prudent one, now appears to be scarcely necessary. "The penal consequences of an act of contravention seem to be confined to the contravener, unless it is otherwise expressed." Duff's Feud. Con. 376, and cases there cited.

In majorem evidentiam.—For more sure evidence. Earnest was formerly given for more sure evidence of the completion of a bargain between the contracting parties; as also were arles given by a master to a servant at the time of hiring, for the same purpose. Neither of these customs are now observed, or at least are very rarely so.

In mala fide.—In bad faith; deceitfully; dishonestly. A possessor *in mala fide* is one who holds possession of a subject, in the knowledge that it is not his own, on a title which he knows, or has reasonable ground for believing to be a bad one. Such a possessor is bound not only to restore the subject to the true owner, but also all the fruits and profits which he has reaped during his occupancy. He is further liable in what are called violent profits—*i.e.*, those fruits or profits which the subject was capable of producing, and which, by proper care and diligence, the possessor might have reaped.

In maleficiis voluntas spectatur non exitus.—In delicts (or crimes) the intention is regarded, not the result. This maxim expresses a sound rule in criminal law, but read literally, might mislead. It is undoubtedly true that intention is essential to the commission of crime; for where there is not the *mens rea* there can be no offence. See *Actus non facit*, &c. But the result is necessarily regarded by the law, for without result there would be no crime; intention does not of itself constitute crime, unless it is followed by some act. See *Cogitationis pœnam*, &c. The maxim may be safely read as meaning that in cases of alleged crime the intention of the doer of the act is first to be considered : the intention must not only have preceded the act in point of time, but it precedes it also in point of importance.

In medio.—The property or money held by the pursuer in an action of multiplepoinding is called the fund *in medio*, because it is, or may be, subject to the claims of all the claimants, and as yet belongs to none of them. It is thus common to them all, and forms the centre or substance of the litigation.

In meditatione fugæ.—Meditating flight ; intending to leave the country. According to our older law, a debtor leaving Scotland might be apprehended at the instance of his creditor, and detained until he found caution *de judicio sisti*. He was considered *in fuga* if about to leave Scotland, although his departure was not proved to be for the express purpose of evading his creditor's claims. To warrant this procedure, however, the debts claimed required to be of such an amount as could be enforced, when decree was obtained, by imprisonment. But as imprisonment for civil debt has now been almost entirely abolished, the *fugæ* warrant has all but disappeared in practice ; and it has been decided that the apprehension of a debtor as *in meditatione fugæ* is incompetent where the claim on which it proceeds cannot be enforced by personal diligence. *Hart* v. *Anderson's Trs.*, 18 R., 169. The *fugæ* warrant, when competent, could be obtained against a foreigner (except in particular circumstances) as well as against a native. But leaving the country in fulfilment of duty, or public service, as in the case of a sailor, or soldier, was not considered *fuga*. Bell's Com. ii. 449 *et seq.*

In modum adminiculi.—As an adminicle of evidence. Hume, ii. 324.

In modum pœnæ.—By way of fine or penalty. Interest may almost be said to be exacted from a debtor *ex lege*, as a fine or penalty, when he is *in mora* in the payment of his debt. "Where a feu-duty is prestable in grain, the superior is entitled to such grain, of the kind stipulated, as the vassal's industry and skill enable him to raise on the lands ; and in the event of non-delivery, he may exact the highest fiars prices *in modum pœnæ*." Duff, Feud. Con. 83.

In modum probationis.—In the form, or, by way, of proof. Documents previously in process, as productions, are frequently put in by a party at a jury trial, as part of the proof on which he rests his claim for a verdict. Such documents are said to be given in, *in modum probationis*.

In modum simplicis querelæ.—By way of summary complaint.

In mundo.—Papers written "*in mundo,*" are what are usually termed extended, or clean copies. See for an example of the use of the phrase, Ross, L. C. (L. R.) ii. 94.

In nudis finibus contractus.—In the bare terms or limits of a contract. Parties are said to be *in nudis finibus contractus* when the terms merely of the contract have been agreed upon, and nothing has been done by either party in consequence of, or in dependence upon it. In some cases a party may be entitled to resile from his contract while it remains in this condition.

In nudis terminis.—This phrase does not admit of literal translation. It signifies a right, title, contract, &c., in the simple condition as when granted without being clothed or fortified by any subsequent act. It may be explained or illustrated by a quotation from Erskine, in which it occurs. In treating of the nature and effect of inhibition, he says :— " It is agreed by all, that proper rights of lands, such as charters or dispositions, may be secured by inhibition against the deeds of the inhibited, though they continue *in nudis terminis* of personal deeds, without actual seisin " (B. 2, T. 11, § 9). The phrase is similar in import to the preceding one, *In nudis finibus,* &c.

In obligatione.—Under an obligation ; by way of obligation.

In odium.— In detestation. A donation by a husband to a wife is, on her being divorced for adultery, revoked by the operation of the law, *in odium* of her guilt ; but it seems doubtful whether this effect follows from the commission of the offence, unless divorce is sued for and decree obtained. Fraser, ii. 952.

In odium corrumpentis.—In detestation of the person corrupting or bribing. Hume, ii. 377.

In odium spoliatoris omnia præsumuntur.—All things are presumed against a thief in detestation of his crime. The maxim, although thus literally rendered, is applied in all cases of wrong-doing ; and for an explanation of the maxim in this general sense, see *Omnia præsumuntur contra spoliatorem.*

In omnibus pœnalibus judiciis et ætati et imprudentiæ succurritur.—In all cases involving penal sentence, both the age and want of experience of the offender are taken into account in favour of the offender. Such want of age or experience are inconsistent with any very determined purpose and intention, and are taken into account in mitigating a sentence, which otherwise, and in the case of a more advanced offender, might be severe.

In pari casu.—In a similar position. While a minor can obtain restitution against his own acts or transactions with one of full age, obligations entered into between him and another minor are binding, because they are *in pari casu*, the one being as able to act for his own interest as the other.

In pari causa potior est conditio possidentis.—In an equal case (*i.e.*, where the claimants are in a similar position), the possessor is in the better position. When one is in possession of a subject, he is not bound to cede possession to any one showing as good a title to it as that on which he possesses. The claimant or challenger must show a better title than the possessor, for the law presumes right to possess where possession is held. This maxim is sometimes rendered: *In pari causa possessor potior haberi debet;* where the claimants are in a similar condition (as regards their rights) the possessor ought to be held the stronger.

In pari delicto potior est conditio possidentis—(defendentis).—In equal delict, the position of the possessor (or the defender) is the stronger. Where a claim arises, or is based upon a delict in which both parties were equally concerned, the person resisting the claim is in a stronger and better position than the person making it. In illustration of this, suppose the case of two persons engaged in a smuggling transaction, and that the smuggled goods are in the possession of one of the parties. His position who holds possession of the goods is the stronger, because his co-adventurer cannot either recover any part of the goods or their value. If the latter was to raise an action for delivery of part of the goods or their price, his action could not be successful if the other pleaded that the goods or the money in question were the result of an illegal transaction, for *ex pacto illicito non oritur actio.* See *Ex dolo non oritur,* &c.

In patiendo.—In permitting, or enduring. Servitudes

consist merely *in patiendo,* and consequently the servient proprietor cannot be called upon to do anything in support of the dominant proprietor's right. The proprietor having right of way through another's ground, must himself maintain the road; if his right be that of leading water (*aquæ ductus*) through another's property, he must maintain the pipes, &c., necessary for that purpose.

In patrimonio principis.—In the patrimony of the prince or sovereign; a phrase synonymous with *Inter regalia,* which see.

In pendente.—In suspension; not vested. The fee of heritable property is held never to be in this position. See *Dominium non potest,* &c.

In periculo constitutus.—Standing in danger (of life). Hume, i. 225.

In perpetuam commendam.—In perpetual trust. A right so granted was equivalent to a gift. See *In commendam.*

In perpetuum.—For ever. Land so granted descended on the death of the grantee to his heirs; but in the earlier periods of the feudal system, when grants of land were given in return for service, they were generally restricted to the life of the grantee himself. See *Beneficium.*

In pessima fide.—In the worst faith; dishonestly.

In petitorio.—In a petitory action. A petitory action is one in which something is sought to be decreed by the judge in respect of the pursuer's right thereto. Almost all actions are of this character. In an ordinary action the person who claims or sues is said to be *in petitorio:* he is seeking something.

In placito.—In a suit; or, forming the subject of a depending litigation. Fraser, Par. & Ch. 447. See *Minor non tenetur,* &c.

In pœnam.—As a penalty or punishment. See *In modum pœnæ.*

In possessorio.—In a possessory suit. See *In judicio,* &c.

In potestate patris.—Under the power of the father. Children are subject to their father's power, and their property is subject to his administration during their minority. As this power is conferred by the law, so on cause shown the father can be deprived of it. It is very limited in comparison with the *patria potestas* of the civil law.

In potestate viri.—Under the power of the husband. The husband is the legal guardian of his wife, and as such, may regulate her place of residence, must be a party consenter to any action she institutes (unless it be against her husband), and to deeds which she grants disposing of her estate, &c. Formerly a husband, as guardian of his wife, had the administration *stante matrimonio* of her property; but this right of administration has now been abolished, 44 & 45 Vict. cap. 21. Judicial separation or divorce puts an end to the husband's guardianship.

In præsentia dominorum.—In presence of the Lords. The letters I.P.D. (representing the words of the phrase) are added to the signature of the presiding Judge adhibited to any interlocutor of the Court of Session, to indicate that he has signed it in presence of the other judges, so as to dispense with the necessity of their signatures being also adhibited. A hearing *in presence*, is a hearing of counsel on a certain cause before the whole Court.

In privato patrimonio.—Among private property or patrimony. Private patrimony is that which one has or acquires for himself in his private and individual capacity, as opposed to that which he holds in a public or official character.

In procinctu.—Girt for battle. Wills executed by soldiers before entering upon a campaign were privileged in many respects under the civil law. Even their nuncupative testaments were under such circumstances held valid. No such privilege is known in Scotch law.

In proximo gradu.—In the nearest degree. Children are heirs of their father in the nearest degree, and grandchildren, when they represent their father, are in the nearest degree to their grandfather.

In publica custodia.—In the public custody. Deeds and others held by an official for the public benefit, such as the records of Court, the records of Sasines, and other writs, &c., are said to be so held.

In publicam vindictam.—For vindicating public right, or public justice. See *Ad vindictam*, &c.

In puram eleemosynam.—In pure charity. Church lands were sometimes so gifted, the difference between them and other church lands being, that for lands gifted in pure charity, no return was made but prayers and supplications for the granter, and masses to be performed after his death; while other ecclesiastical fees in mortmain were held by the tenure of ward for the performance of military services by substitutes.

In quantum locupletiores facti sumus, ex damno alterius.—In so far as we have been enriched to the loss, or by the damage, of another. In some cases persons are bound in restitution to this extent. Thus, one for whom in his absence another has acted (*negotiorum gestor*), must repay anything expended by that other on his (the absent person's) property, or on his behalf, for he has thereby been enriched at the other's expense. So also an heir, although not liable for his ancestor's delict, if he has been enriched thereby, must restore to the injured person whatever he has acquired through the delict.

In quantum lucratus est.—In so far as he has gained or profited. An executor who takes up a succession in moveables, with the benefit of inventory, while not universally liable for the debts of the deceased, is liable for those debts in so far as he has been benefited by the succession. Such is also now the measure of an heir's liability for the debts of his ancestor. See *Minor tenetur*, &c.

In quantum valeat.—For what it is worth.

In quibus inficiando lis crescit.—In which the suit (or the sum sued for under it) increases by denial. The Romans had a class of cases which were partly *rei persecutoriæ*, and partly penal, in which, if the defender denied the pursuer's statement, he was, on its being proved, subjected in the double, triple, or quadruple value of the thing or sum claimed. Thus, where one sued another for wrongful damage (*injuria*), and the defender denied that it had been inflicted or occasioned, he was held liable for double value on the damage being proved. So also a depositary with whom a subject has been deposited in some urgent necessity occasioned by an accident, such as fire, &c., was held liable in double value, if, on restitution being sought, he denied that the deposit had been made.

In re communi melior est conditio prohibentis.—In common property the condition of the one prohibiting is the better. A subject held in common by several proprietors cannot be altered or interfered with in any way except in so far as such interference is warranted by the common use, unless with the consent of the whole proprietors; not even if the proposed alteration should have the effect of enhancing the value of the subject. Therefore, in an action regarding any alteration on a common subject, the condition of the person prohibiting or opposing such alteration is better than that of the person desirous of and endeavouring to effect it.

In re mercatoria.—In, or connected with, a mercantile transaction. All writings *in re mercatoria* are privileged, and are held valid and binding, although wanting the solemnities common and necessary to ordinary deeds. Bank cheques, mandates, guarantees, &c., are included in this class. So, also, are bills and promissory notes, which are in themselves probative, and constitute the debt to which they refer. This privilege has been given to these documents, because of the rapidity with which, in most cases, they have to be prepared, and the immediate use to which they have to be put, and also because, from the necessity of the case, they are generally prepared by those who are not supposed to be acquainted with the formalities and solemnities of deeds.

In re propria.—In a subject belonging to one's-self; in one's own business or affairs.

In rebus litigiosis.—In things rendered litigious. All subjects are considered litigious which have been made the subject of a contested lawsuit, or have been attached by legal diligence, such as inhibition, adjudication, or arrestment; but inhibition or adjudication only renders the lands thereby affected litigious from and after the date of the registration of such diligence. (31 & 32 Vict. c. 101, § 159.) Subjects in this position cannot be disponed or assigned to a purchaser, even if the purchase be an onerous one, for litigiosity is "an implied prohibition of alienation to the disappointment of an action or of diligence, the direct object of which is to attain the possession, or to acquire the property, of a particular subject." (Bell's Com. ii. 144.) Any such sale or conveyance may be reduced on this ground.

In rem suam.—Regarding one's own property; in one's own affairs. A procuratory *in rem suam* is a mandate authorising certain acts, in the carrying out of which the procurator alone has any interest or advantage. Such mandate cannot be recalled by the mandant, nor does it fall upon his death. The ordinary assignation of a debt is an example of this, in which the assigner makes over to the assignee "his whole right, interest, and title in the premises, with power to sue for and discharge the debt assigned," and so on. This procuratory or mandate is *in rem suam* of the assignee. So also is the power given to the disponee in an heritable bond, in virtue of which he may sell the subjects conveyed in security, if his debt be not paid.

In rem suam tutor fieri non potest auctor.—A tutor cannot act or transact for his own behoof; that is, he cannot so act in reference to anything in which his ward or his ward's estate is concerned. See *Auctor in rem,* &c. See also the illustrations given of the application of this principle in Fraser, Par. & Ch. 260.

In rem versum.—Employed in one's own matter; used to a person's advantage. A tutor or curator holding in his hands money belonging to his ward, without investing or lodging it in bank, and neglecting thus to employ it for the advantage of the ward, is liable in the highest rate of interest. No action lies against a curator or guardian for the price of goods furnished to a minor which were unnecessary, and not *in rem versum.* Again, a debtor paying a debt to a curator, who has assumed the office without any title to do so, or whose appointment is not complete (as, for example, where the curator has been appointed by the Court, but not having lodged the necessary bond of caution, has not obtained an extract of his appointment), is liable in repetition on the failure or death of the curator, if the debt so paid has not been *in rem versum* of the minor.

In retentis.—Evidence taken to lie *in retentis* is that which, in certain circumstances, is taken to be held back or laid aside, until the proper time arrives for adducing it. Such evidence is allowed to be taken at any stage of the process, on the application of either party, where there is any danger of its being lost through the extreme old age of the proposed witness, or his severe indisposition rendering life precarious, or where the witness is about to leave the country.

In rigore juris.—According to strict law.

In rixa.—In a quarrel or altercation. Defamatory words spoken *in rixa*—*i.e.*, in the course of an angry altercation—are "not actionable, when there has been no repetition, or attempt to spread the scandal after the parties have cooled down." Smith on Reparation, 192.

In rixa per plures commissum.—An offence committed in the course of a quarrel in which several persons were engaged. Hume, i. 273.

In sacris.—In sacred matters. The Church Courts have supreme jurisdiction in such matters, which involve questions of ecclesiastical discipline, scriptural doctrine, &c. *Lockhart*, 13 D. 1296. This phrase must be carefully distinguished from *Circum sacra*, which see.

In solidum.—For the whole. Where there are several co-obligants bound *in solidum*, each is liable in full payment or performance, and the creditor may choose which of the obligants he will sue. Every person whose name appears on a bill, whether as acceptor or indorser, is liable in full payment of its contents, although he may after payment do diligence against the others for relief. Those who in a joint obligation are not bound for the whole, but only for their share, are said to be liable *pro rata*.

In solutum.—In payment or extinction.

In spe.—In hope, or expectation. See *Spes*, &c.

In stipulationibus cum quæritur quod actum sit, verba contra stipulatorem interpretanda sunt.—In stipulations (or obligations), when any question arises as to the obligation undertaken, the words of the stipulation (or obligation) are to be interpreted against the creditor in the obligation. Under the civil law, in obligations constituted by stipulation (see *Stipulatio*), the person who undertook the obligation was called the *promissor*, while he in whose favour the obligation was granted was called the *stipulator*. If any question arose as to the character or extent of the obligation, in consequence of ambiguity in the language in which it had been expressed, such ambiguity was interpreted in favour of the *promissor*, and against the *stipulator*, the reason for which was *quia stipulatori liberum fuit verba late concipere;* because the stipulator was free to use language so broadly conceived as to cover the obligation which he was then taking from the *promissor*. If there was any ambiguity, it was from the fault of the *stipulator*, who proposed the words in which the obligation was to be constituted, the *promissor* merely acquiescing therein; the consequences of the fault or ambiguity, therefore, were visited on the *stipulator*. In principle, the maxim holds good in Scotland; for if a contract or obligation is ambiguous, it is construed in the manner least burdensome to the debtor.

In stirpes.—Literally, among, or according to, the stocks. Succession *per stirpes* is distinguished from succession *per capita* (according to the heads, or number of persons). To illustrate this, suppose a testator to die leaving grandchildren by two sons, one of whom had left one child, the other eleven. If the testator directs his succession to devolve upon his grandchildren *per stirpes*, it would be divided into two shares, being the number of persons (or stocks, or roots) from whom the children were descended,—one share would go to the one grandchild representing his father, the other share would go equally to the eleven grandchildren representing theirs. But if the succession was directed to be distributed *per capita*, the twelve grandchildren would succeed to the estate equally.

In subsidium.—In aid of. Proper cautioners are only bound *in subsidium* of the original debtor, and consequently (where they have the right of discussion) they cannot be called upon for payment until the debtor has been discussed. They only come to the aid or assistance of the debtor when he has been shown to be totally incapable (or so far as he is incapable) of discharging his own obligation. Cautioners are now regarded more in the character of co-debtors than mere cautioners, and have no right of discussion unless it has been specially reserved to them.

In suo.—In reference to one's own affairs. Any one

acting for himself, in reference to his own affairs, or for his own interest, acts *in suo*.

In suo genere.—Of their own kind or class. Writings *in re mercatoria* are complete and binding deeds of their kind, although deficient in the ordinary solemnities.

¶ **In suo hactenus facere licet quatenus nihil in alienum immittit.**—One may use what is his own as he pleases, so long as he does not invade the rights of others; or, a man may do what he likes (carry on any operation he pleases) on his own property, so long as he does not send anything on the property of another (his neighbour). With regard to this maxim, and for cases illustrative of it, see Smith on Reparation, 359 *et seq.*, where the reader will also find some cases on the limitation to which the general rule is subjected.

In suo ordine.—In his order. A cautioner who is entitled to the benefit of discussion can only be called upon, for fulfilment of the obligation which he guaranteed, in his order—that is, after the principal creditor has been discussed. So, also, an heir can only be made liable for the moveable debts of his ancestor, after the executor who succeeded to the moveable estate has been discussed, and where the moveable estate has proved insufficient to meet those debts.

In tantum.—To that extent.

In tempus indebitum.—At an undue time.

In terminis.—In express terms.

In testamentis plenius testatoris intentionem scrutamur.—In (the construction of) wills we are chiefly to seek for the intention of the testator. This maxim is sometimes expressed thus—

In testamentis plenius voluntatis testantium interpretantur.—Wills are to be interpreted according to the purpose and intention of the testators. On the subject of the construction of wills in which there is uncertainty or ambiguity, see M'Laren, i. 318; and Broom, 554.

In thesi.—In the particular case, which has occurred; in opposition to *in hypothesi*, a case which might be supposed.

In toto.—Entirely; wholly.

In transitu.—In transit; during conveyance. If a purchaser of goods becomes bankrupt before they are delivered, the seller has the right of stopping them *in transitu*. If, however, delivery has been made to the purchaser, either actually or constructively, the goods are no longer *in transitu*, and the creditor's right to stop delivery ceases. It is not delivery in this sense, that the goods have been delivered to a third person, such as a shipmaster, for conveyance to the purchaser; *secus* if the shipmaster is the agent of the purchaser to receive the goods. On the law of stoppage *in transitu*, see Bell's Prin. § 1307 *et seq.*; Bell's Com. i. 223 *et seq.*; and 56 & 57 Vict. cap. 71, §§ 44-46.

In turpi causa potior est conditio possidentis.—In any claim or obligation arising out of an immoral consideration, the condition of the possessor (or defender) is stronger. If a bond or obligation is granted as the price or consideration of illicit intercourse, it cannot be enforced; and the position of the defender (who is the possessor of that which by the obligation he bound himself to pay) is stronger than that of the person seeking to enforce the claim, because his defence to the claim is stronger than the ground on which the claim is based, and will prevail against the claim. On the same ground, if the obligant has paid the amount of his obligation, he cannot claim repetition; the person who has got possession of the money is then in the stronger position.

In tuto.—In safety.

In utero.—In the womb; unborn. "It is a good objection to service claimed by a collateral heir, that the deceased has left a widow suspected to be with child, so long as there are hopes of her delivery." Duff's Feud. Con. 467. Whether a child *in utero* will succeed equally with its brothers and sisters born at the time when the succession opens, depends upon the terms of the destination. On this subject see the case of *Wood* v. *Wood*, 23 D. 338, and cases there cited and commented on. See also M'Laren, i. 651 *et seq.*

In valorem.—For the value; or, according to the value. An executor confirmed by the commissary is only liable for the deceased's debts *in valorem* of the inventory given up, or rather of the estate realised by him.

In viridi observantia.—A practice, custom, or law which is still in full observance is said to be *in viridi observantia*.

Inædificatum solo cedit solo.—Anything built on the

ground belongs to the ground. On this principle the proprietor or purchaser of land has right to everything built thereon. There are, nevertheless, exceptions to the rule, and nice questions may arise out of them. Thus, in cases between landlord and tenant, the tenant is not entitled, on quitting possession, to remove fixtures. But where he has built on the ground an edifice, for the purpose of protecting machinery necessary for carrying on his business, both the machinery and the house will be regarded as accessories of trade, and will not fall to the landlord. Even these, however, so long as attached to the soil are reckoned *partes soli*, subject to the tenant's right to remove them; if that right is not exercised or is renounced, the fixtures are held to belong to the owner of the soil. *Brand's Trs.*, 2 R. 258, revd. H. L. 3 R. 16. *Photoglyptic Printing Company*, 10th March, 1894. Where one builds upon ground, in the belief that the ground is his own, while in reality it belongs to another, the building so erected belongs to the true proprietor of the land; but the builder will be entitled to claim from him its value, in respect of his *bona fides*. It has been a controverted question, however, whether one who builds upon another's ground *in mala fide* is entitled to any recompense for the value of his building. Stair held that he was—" He who even *mala fide* buildeth upon another man's ground, or repaireth unnecessarily his house, is not presumed to do it *animo donandi*, but hath recompense by the owner *in quantum lucratus.*" (Stair, B. 1, T. 8, § 6.) In support of this view the authority of the civil law and Cicero are quoted; and Mr. Brodie, the editor of Stair, maintains the soundness of the view contained in the text. (Brodie's Stair, 203, Note *b*.) But Erskine (B. 3, T. 1, § 11) doubts "whether this is, or ought to be, held as the law of Scotland," and it may now be regarded as settled, that according to our law any one building *in mala fide* on the property of another has no claim for recompense. *Barbour* v. *Halliday*, 2 D. 1279. See also the opinions delivered in the case of *Buchanan* v. *Stewart*, 2 R. 78, in which the authority of the case of *Barbour* is recognised.

Incerto patre.—From an uncertain father. Bastards are said to be so descended. They do not succeed to their reputed father *ex lege,* nor is any tie of relationship between them and their father's relatives admitted by the law. "A bastard is in the eye of the law *filius nullius.* Not only has he no father, but no proof can give him a father—nothing can do that but marriage between his mother and his putative father." *Corrie* v. *Adair,* 22 D. 900.

Inchoatum. — Inchoate; commenced; imperfect. An arrestment may be called inchoate diligence until perfected by furthcoming : or a poinding, until perfected by sale.

Incidenter.—Incidentally.

Incommodum non solvit argumentum.—Inconvenience does not answer an argument; does not deprive an argument of its force ; that is, an argument is not the less sound, nor less entitled to prevail, merely because giving effect to it might result in inconvenient consequences. See *Argumentum ab inconvenienti,* &c.

Incrementa.—Additions. All land that is gained by the sudden recess of the sea or river, or gradually and imperceptibly through its changes, becomes the property of the riparian proprietor, as the *incrementa* of his original property.

Indebiti solutio.—The payment of something not due. Money paid under the erroneous belief of liability therefor, may be recovered. There is a distinction to be observed between the cases, where the payment has been made under an error in law and an error in fact. This has been pointed out above. See *Condictio indebiti.*

Indemnis.—Free of loss or damage.

Index animi sermo.—Language is the index of the purpose ; expression indicates intention.

Induciæ legales.—Days of grace allowed in legal proceedings for the performance of some act. Thus a defender in an action before the Court of Session is allowed an *induciæ* of seven or fourteen days, according to circumstances, after service of the summons, before entering appearance to defend. An *induciæ* of fifteen days must elapse between the service of an indictment and the prisoner's being called upon to plead. In the usual case a debtor is allowed an *induciæ* of fifteen days to fulfil a charge of payment on a decree before diligence can proceed, &c.

Inest de jure.—It is implied in the right. The right to

build upon land does not require to be expressed in the titles, for *inest de jure*—it is inherent, according to law, in the right of property. For the contrary reason, restrictions on the exercise of the full right of property must be expressed. *Inest de jure* applies to any right which the law recognises, or infers to exist under certain circumstances, unless that right has been taken away by private paction. *Moir's Trs. v. M'Ewen*, 7 R. 1141.

Infamia facti.—Infamy arising from general bad character, which may affect, when proved, the credibility of a witness, but affords no ground for excluding his testimony.

Infamia juris.—Infamy arising from a legal conviction for crime. This at one time disqualified all persons as witnesses against whom it could be proved, but the disqualification (except where the infamy arose from a conviction for perjury or subornation) was removed by the Act 1 Will. IV. c. 37. Exclusion of evidence on account of the infamy of the proposed witness has been entirely abolished by the Act 15 & 16 Vict. c. 27.

Infantem innocentia concilii tuetur.—Innocence of design protects an infant (from criminal punishment). "No authority has ever maintained that a mere infant, one who is under seven years old, is in any case liable to any sort of punishment." Hume, i. 35; Macdonald, 11. Children of such tender years are regarded as not capable of the *mens rea*, owing to immaturity of will.

Infantiæ proximus.—Next to infancy. A child is said to be next to infancy until it arrives at the age of seven years, and during this period the mother is, in the general case, entitled to the custody of it.

Infeudatio. — Infeftment; investiture. "The (original) meaning of the word *infeftment*, so frequently used in relation to feudal conveyancing, differs considerably from that of *sasine*. Infeftment was originally employed to denote those deeds, whether charter or sasine, disposition sasine and confirmation, or other titles of investiture, whereby a feudal right is completed. It still occasionally bears the same meaning, but more generally denotes the ceremony of infeftment. The word sasine often occurs in the latter sense,—to give sasine, meaning the same as to give infeftment; but it usually means the instrument of sasine, and never the whole title or investiture." (Duff's Feud. Con. 57.) "The word (*infeudatio*) is frequently used for the charter alone in the *Regiam Majestatem* and the other old books of our law." (Ersk. B. 2, T. 3, § 18.)

Infra præsidia.—Within the walls ; under protection. This phrase is used in reference to ships taken during war, and signifies that the prize has been brought within the ports, fleets, or under the batteries, of the captors, and has thus been brought completely within the power of the captors. Formerly, the mere bringing of the prize *infra præsidia* vested the property of the prize in the captor; but the rule now is that no property vests in the captor "until the vessel has been carried into the port of the belligerent state, or of an ally in the war, and is condemned by a court of competent jurisdiction exercising its functions within the same country." Maclachlan, 18. As to the rights of salvors in the case of recapture, see Bell's Prin. § 445.

Ingenui.—The name given among the Romans to free persons, who had been born free and had never lost their freedom, as distinguished from *libertini*, persons who had obtained freedom by manumission.

Inhærere jurisdictioni.—To be necessarily connected with jurisdiction. The Roman magistrates were invested both with the *imperium merum* and *imperium mixtum;* the former was the power under which they inflicted punishment upon criminals ; the latter the power under which they enforced, by subsidiary punishment, the fulfilment of a civil sentence or award. As a judge's authority would be practically *nil* unless he had the power of enforcing his decision, the maxim was observed *Imperium mixtum inhæret jurisdictioni*—the mixed power of enforcing their sentences and of punishing for their non-fulfilment, was inherent in their jurisdiction. In short, the *imperium merum* was the simple power of enforcing the primary sentence in criminal cases, while the *imperium mixtum* included not only the power of enforcing civil awards, but also of punishing those who refused obedience to such awards. See both of these phrases, *supra*.

Inimicitia capitalis.—Deadly enmity : strong and deep-rooted hostility.

Initialia testimonii.—The initial or introductory part of the deposition of a witness. See *In initialibus.*

Initium non finis operis nomen imponit.—The commencement, not the end of the thing done, affords its name (or, fixes its character). This phrase may be illustrated by a reference to the case of *Galloway* v. *Craig,* 4 Macq. 267, where the question was whether a policy effected over the life of a husband was to be regarded as a provision for the wife, or as a donation made by the husband. If the former, the wife was entitled to it as against her husband's creditors, he having become bankrupt ; if the latter, the creditors took the proceeds of the policy under the revocation of the donation implied in bankruptcy. It was held that the policy was effected by way of provision ; that its character as a provision was then impressed upon it ; and that the emerging circumstances of the husband did not change that character, or give it another.

Initium possessionis.—The beginning or origin of the possession : the right or title in respect of which possession was first had.

Injuria.—Injury or damage wrongously inflicted ; any wrongful act. See *Damnum absque,* &c.

Injuria non excusat injuriam.—A wrong does not excuse a wrong. No one is entitled to take the law into his own hands, and therefore no one is entitled to commit a wrong in return for a wrong inflicted on himself ; if he does commit such a wrong, the wrong which he had suffered will not excuse or exculpate him from the consequences of his wrong-doing. Abstractly, this is quite a sound principle, but the law does admit the consideration of provocation given or wrong inflicted in mitigation of the penalty imposed on him who under such circumstances commits a wrong. In some cases the law even allows the one injury to be set off against the other. See *Compensatio injuriarum.*

Injuria non præsumitur.—Wrong is not presumed. Just as in criminal matters guilt is never presumed, so in civil cases no one is presumed to have done a wrongous or injurious act. It must be proved by him who complains of it.

Innocuæ utilitatis.—That act which is useful to the person who does it, and which is not detrimental to the rights or interests of another, is an act *innocuæ utilitatis:* it is useful, and at the same time harmless. *Morris v. Bickett,* 2 Macp. 1089.

Innovata lite dependente.—Innovations or alterations during the dependence of the suit. Referring to interference with a subject after it has been rendered litigious. See *Pendente lite,* &c.

Inops concilii.—Destitute of advice.

Inspectio corporis.—An inspection of the person. In some cases such a proceeding is allowed, and the result of such inspection received as proof ; as, for example, in criminal prosecutions for child murder and concealment of pregnancy. It is only admitted, however, in cases of the most urgent necessity. *Davidson,* 22 D. 749. See *De ventre,* &c.

Instantia perit.—The instance falls or perishes. When a defender puts up protestation against the pursuer for not enrolling, or not insisting, the instance perishes, and the process is dismissed. This does not in any way affect the merits of the pursuer's case, who is entitled to cite the defender again for the same claim. In the same way, in a criminal indictment, where the prosecutor does not insist in his libel, at the diet to which the prisoner has been cited, *instantia perit,* but the prosecutor may have the prisoner recommitted, and serve him with a new indictment.

Institor.—The person to whom the immediate management of a shop, business, or undertaking has been committed by the master or owner, and for whose acts in that capacity the master is liable. See *Actio institoria.*

Instruit concilio.—He furnishes with advice or counsel. Hume, i. 278.

Instrumenta noviter reperta.—Instruments newly or subsequently discovered. See *Ex instrumentis,* &c.

Inter conjuges.—Between spouses.

Inter conjunctas personas.—Between conjunct persons. By the Act 1621, c. 18, all conveyances or alienations between conjunct persons, unless granted for onerous causes, are declared, as in a question with creditors, to be null and of no avail. Conjunct persons are those standing in a certain degree of relationship to each other, such, for example, as brothers, sisters, sons, uncles, &c. These were formerly excluded as witnesses on account of their relationship, but this as a ground of exclusion has been abolished.

Inter eosdem.—Between the same persons.

Inter naturalia (feudi).—Among the things naturally arising from a feu ; such as the payment of the feu-duty, the rendering of the stipulated services to the superior, &c. These are binding upon all heirs and singular successors. Regarding the question of how far stipulations not *inter naturalia* are binding upon singular successors, see Bell's Prin. § 861.

Inter regalia.—Among the things belonging to the Sovereign. Among these are rights of salmon fishing, mines of gold and silver, forests, forfeitures, casualties of superiority, &c., which are called the *regalia minora*, and may be conveyed to a subject. The *regalia majora* include the several branches of the royal prerogative, which are inseparable from the person of the Sovereign.

Inter rusticos.—Among rustics or illiterate persons. Deeds or obligations granted *inter rusticos* are not judged of by the same strict rules as those prepared by professional men with all the usual technicalities, and containing all the necessary solemnities. They are dealt with more according to equitable principles than rules of strict law.

Inter virum et uxorem.—Between husband and wife. See *Donatio inter virum*, &c.

Inter vivos.—Between living persons. An ordinary deed importing obligation or conveying property is called a deed *inter vivos ;* as distinguished from a will bequeathing moveables, or a deed conveying heritage, to take effect only on the granter's death, which is called a deed *mortis causa*.

Interest reipublicæ, ne quis re sua male utatur.—It is for the interest of the State that no one shall use his property improperly. On this maxim, the law interposes to prevent any one using his property wantonly to the injury of his neighbours, or of the public generally. Thus where the use to which property is put creates a nuisance, it may be interfered with, and the nuisance removed ; or where a proprietor without benefiting himself uses his property to the injury of his neighbour, he is presumed to be acting *in æmulationem vicini*, and his proceedings may be interdicted. The statute 39 & 40 Geo. III. c. 98 (known as the Thellusson Act) may be taken in illustration of this maxim. By it a restraint is imposed upon all trusts, deeds or wills, whereby the profits or produce of real or personal estate is directed to be accumulated, and the beneficial enjoyment thereof postponed beyond twenty-one years. Such accumulation and postponement are obviously impolitic, and therefore the law regards the testator's direction to accumulate in this manner as *pro non scripto*. See the application of this statute in the case of *Lord*, 23 D. 111. A more recent illustration than the Thellusson Act will be found in the Act 31 & 32 Vict. c. 84, § 17, which prohibits the constitution of liferent rights in moveable estate beyond certain limits there specified.

Interest reipublicæ ut sit finis litium.—It is for the interest of the State that there should be an end of lawsuits. On this principle, when a question has once been fairly tried and determined between two parties, the law does not permit them to raise another suit involving the same question. It is upon the same principle that some of the limitations of actions are based; as, for example, the limitation that action cannot be raised upon a cautionary obligation after seven years, or upon a bill after six years. On this subject see Broom, 343. This maxim is sometimes expressed thus: *Interest reipublicæ componere lites*—It is for the interest of the State that lawsuits should be adjusted, or settled.

Interim dominus.—Proprietor in the meantime. A widow is *interim domina* of terce lands after her service, and in virtue thereof may either possess them herself, or let them out to tenants.

Interpretatio chartarum benigne facienda est ut res magis valeat quam pereat.—Charters (or deeds) are to be interpreted liberally, so as rather to validate than nullify the transaction. See *Benigne faciendæ sunt*, &c.

Interpretatio viperina.—" That construction which has been much condemned, and which the doctors called *interpretatio viperina*, because it destroyed the text." Per Cleasby, B. in *Gray* v. *Carr*, L. R. 6 Q. B. 531. See *Benedicta est*, &c.

Intervertere possessionem.—To invert or alter the possession. Thus one who receives a subject as a depositary, and thereafter conceals it with a view to its felonious appropriation, inverts the character of his possession: he changes the possession of a depositary into the possession of a thief. But where one who is a mere depositary advances money to the depositor on the security of the deposit, he changes also the character of his possession from that of a depositary to that of a pledgee; in this latter case, however, he is not said to invert the possession, but *mutare causam possessionis*—to change the ground or title in respect of which his possession is held.

Intra familiam.—See *Extra familiam*.

Intra fines commissi.—Within the limits of the trust or duty committed. An agent or servant will bind his principal or master by all acts performed within the limits of the mandate or duty committed to him; but for acts beyond those limits the master is not bound; the servant must answer for such acts himself. The principle upon which a master or principal is liable for the acts of his servant or agent, is, that the master is doing those acts himself by the hands of another. But if that other does acts which were not authorised, they cannot be called the acts of the principal, much less so if the acts were not only unauthorised, but contrary to instructions. Cases do arise, however, in which a principal is bound for the acts of an agent, although these acts were not authorised; as, for example, where the act falls within the ordinary presumed mandate of an agent in a particular business, and no notice has been given that the agent's mandate has been limited. See *Qui facit per alium*, &c.

Intra triduum.—Within the space of three days. It was formerly a rule of our law that a seller was entitled to the restitution of goods delivered to, but not paid for by, the purchaser, if the latter became bankrupt within three days of the transaction. This was founded upon the presumption that his impending bankruptcy must have been known to the purchaser, and that he was guilty of fraud in not communicating it. This rule was overturned, and the doctrine of stoppage *in transitu* (which had long previously existed in the English law) introduced in its place, for the first time by the decision of the House of Lords in the case of *Allan, Stewart & Co.*, 23rd December, 1790, M. 4949.

Intuitu matrimonii.—In the prospect of marriage. Deeds granted between the spouses in the prospect of marriage, are considered onerous, if the marriage follows.

Intuitu mortis.—In the prospect of death.

Intus habet.—The law " presumes, till accounting, that the tutor *intus habet*, or, in other words, that he hath in his own hands as much of the pupil's money unaccounted for as will balance the claim he has against the pupil." (Ersk. B. 1, T. 7, § 32.)

Inurit labem realem.—Brands it with a real defect. Theft has such an effect on the thing stolen, for it attaches such a real defect to the subject, that no possession, for whatever length of time, nor onerosity in acquiring it, can possibly make the possession good, or sufficient to resist the demand for restitution, if made on the part of the rightful owner. Forgery also has this effect, for although in the case of a bill the plea of no value would be good if stated against the original holder, it cannot be successfully maintained against an onerous indorsee; yet if the signature be a forgery, this attaches such a real defect to the bill, that it may be maintained against any one suing on it, no matter what may be the character in which he sues. See *Labes realis.*

Invecta et illata.—Literally, things brought or carried in, and commonly used to signify a tenant's furniture and plenishing, over which the landlord has a right of hypothec.

Inverso ordine.—Contrary to rule; erroneously.

Invito beneficium non datur.—A benefit is not given, or conferred, on one who is unwilling (to receive it). As any one may renounce a benefit or right conferred upon him, so any one may decline to accept the benefit: it cannot be made his against his wish. If A leaves a settlement, whereby he makes B his heir and sole executor, to the exclusion of his (A's) own children, that does not of necessity make B the heir or successor in point of fact. He may decline the succession, in which case it will be distributed as an intestate succession. Again, the law confers upon a minor the right to challenge all deeds granted or contracts made by him to his lesion during his minority. But a minor may decline to take advantage of this legal privilege, and fulfil his obligation, although it may be very much to his disadvantage : he cannot be compelled against his will to plead his minority. Or one may have an unquestionable claim of damages against another for breach of contract, on account of slander, for personal injury, or any other cause, which the law will give effect to if urged ; but he cannot be compelled to enforce such a claim. See *Cuique licet juri*, &c.

Invito debitore.—Without the consent, or against the wish of a debtor. A creditor may assign or discharge his debt *invito debitore*.

Invito superiore.—Without the consent or against the wish of the superior. It was for a long time a doubtful question whether a vassal could, *invito superiore*, renounce his feu, to the effect of freeing himself from the payment of future feu-duties, or future performance of those services in return for which he held his feu. It was ultimately decided that he could not ; and the same rule applies to a disponee who has adopted the feu right. *Hunter*, 13 S. 205. Where the lands are burdened with payment of a ground-annual, the conveyance of the lands does not free the original vassal from his personal obligation to pay the same, nor does it impose a personal obligation on the disponee to pay it. *Millar*, 1 Macq. 345 (reversing the judgment of the Court of Session) ; and *Gardyne*, 1 Macq. 358. The personal obligation of the original vassal remains, and the lands are liable for his fulfilment of that obligation into whose hands soever they may have come. See also the cases of *Dundee Police Com.*, 11 R. 586 ; and *Aiton*, 16 R. 625.

Ipso jure.—By the law itself.

Ipsum corpus.—The thing itself. Under the contract of commodate, the borrower must return the very subject borrowed, and if it should have perished through no fault of his, no liability for the subject or its value attaches to him. Under *mutuum* it is different ; for there the borrower is liable, whatever happens, for the equivalent of the thing borrowed. Again, where a testator bequeaths a legacy of a specific object—*ex. gr.*, a ring, a piece of plate, a certain picture, &c., the *ipsum corpus* must be delivered to the legatee, and if it perishes, the legacy falls, and the legatee has no claim for its value. On the other hand, specific legacies suffer no diminution, as other legacies do, where the estate of the deceased is insufficient to meet all the legacies he may, by his testament, have directed to be paid.

Is qui dolo malo desiit possidere, pro possessore habetur.—He who has fraudulently ceased to possess is still held to be the possessor. The true owner of a stolen subject is entitled to recover it wherever it can be found, and any one in possession of it is bound to restore it, even although he acquired it *in bona fide,* and for a fair price. If such possessor has again sold it, still *in bona fide,* he is only liable to the owner in that which he has received for it, in excess of that which he himself paid. But if, knowing the true owner, the possessor of such a subject has fraudulently quitted possession, that he might not be called upon to restore it, he is held by law to be still the possessor, to the effect of rendering him liable for its value.

Is qui omnino desipit.—He who is altogether void of reason. The definition of a fatuous or insane person, as distinguished from one who is merely of weak intellect.

Iter.—One of the rural servitudes, importing a right of way on foot or horseback, in favour of the dominant owner through the servient proprietor's lands; sometimes termed the *jus eundi.*

J

Jacere telum voluntatis est; ferire, quem nolueris, fortunæ.—To throw a dart or weapon is a matter of will ; but that it strike a person whom you have no wish or intention to strike, is a matter of chance. This phrase is quoted by Erskine from Cicero, while treating of the principle that malice or dole is essential to the commission of crime. " If a huntsman who aimed a dart at a roe or a buck should casually kill a man who happened to be passing by, chance alone is to be blamed, not the huntsman." (Ersk. B. 4, T. 4, § 5.)

Jactus lapilli.—The throwing down of a stone. One of the modes under the civil law of interrupting prescription. Where one person was building on another's ground, and in this way acquiring a right by *usucapio*, the true owner challenged the intrusion and interrupted the prescriptive right by throwing down one of the stones of the building before witnesses called for the purpose.

Jactus mercium navis levandæ causa.—The throwing of goods into the sea for the purpose of lightening the ship ; jettison. When a ship, either through perils of the sea, or other cause, has been disabled from performing her voyage in safety, and goods are thrown overboard to ensure the safety of the ship and remainder of the cargo, the loss thus sustained has to be borne by the owners of the ship and cargo *pro rata :* this loss is called General Average. " The law relating to General Average regards ship and cargo together as one combined adventure, comprising a variety of interests all exposed to the perils of the sea, and equally concerned under a common danger in the averting of a total loss ; and it prescribes, in case of the sacrifice of part for the preservation of what remains of the common adventure, that the loss accruing by reason of the sacrifice shall be assessed upon the value of what remains together with the value of the thing sacrificed, in order to recoup the loser, and place him once more on a footing with his co-adventurers." (Arnould, ii. 812.) This equitable rule of law is borrowed by us from the civil law (*Lex Rhodia de jactu*), and is adopted, under several modifications, by all the commercial countries in Europe.

Jactus retis.—The cast of a net. This may form the subject of a valid sale, although a mere *spes*.

Judex non reddit plus quam quod petens ipse requirit. —A judge cannot give more than the petitioner (or suitor) himself asks. The matter upon which a judge can alone decide, as between the parties to a suit, is that which has been submitted to him on the pleadings or claims. If he goes beyond this, he is outwith his jurisdiction, and outwith his jurisdiction a judge has no power whatever. Consequently, if a judge decerns for more than the pursuer or claimant seeks, his decree is ineffectual, and may be reversed or set aside on the ground that it has gone *ultra petita*.

Judex tenetur impertiri judicium suum.—A judge is bound to communicate (or give the benefit of) his decision: or, less literally, a judge is bound to fulfil the duty of his office, and give judgment in any case competently brought before him. "It must never be forgotten, that in cases in which jurisdiction is competently founded, a court has no discretion whether it shall exercise its jurisdiction or not, but is bound to award the justice which a suitor comes to ask." Per L. J.-C. Inglis in *Clements* v. *Macaulay*, 4 Macp. 593.

Judicatum solvi.—That the sum decerned for will be paid; that the decree will be implemented. This is a species of caution formerly required of all defenders in maritime actions, although it cannot now in ordinary circumstances be required of any defender domiciled in Scotland. The cautioner in such an obligation is bound in payment or fulfilment of whatever may be decerned for, and he is not liberated from the obligation by the death of the principal debtor. It is a kind of caution not frequently required. Under the civil law this caution was required of any defender who remained in possession, during the suit, of the subject which gave rise to the dispute. The cautioner was there liable to pay whatever was contained in the *condemnatio*, and he also guaranteed that the defender should use no fraud.

Judices dati.—Judges given or appointed. Under the second system of legal process among the Romans with which the civil law has made us acquainted, the system, namely, of the *formulæ*, all cases were first brought before the Prætor. The real question between the parties was settled and defined by him, and sent for judgment under his instructions to the judge appointed, who might be chosen by the parties. This judge was called the *judex datus*. The question to be decided, and the instructions of the Prætor thereanent, were contained in the *formula*, and beyond it the *judex* could not go without invalidating his decision. The *formula* of the civil law bears a strong resemblance to the issue of the present day, and a copy of it may not be without interest to many. It ran thus (Gaius, B. 4, § 40-43)—"Let N. be the judge. Whereas Aulus Agerius sold a slave to Numerius Negidius; if it appears that N. N. ought to give (or is due) A. A. ten thousand sesterces, let the judge condemn N. N. to pay the ten thousand sesterces to A. A.; if it does not so appear, let the judge acquit him." If the defender pleaded an exception, then (instead of the last clause here given) the *formula* concluded thus—"Unless the obligation was extorted through fear," or, "was obtained through fraud," as the case might be. See *Ope exceptionis*.

Judices pedanei.—A class of inferior magistrates among the Romans who had jurisdiction in cases not exceeding in value three hundred *solidi*. They differed from the ordinary *judex* in this, that they determined both the law and the fact, and cases sent to them by the superior magistrates were not accompanied by any *formula*.

Judicia posteriora sunt in lege fortiora.—Later judgments are stronger in law. This maxim expresses the principle on which precedents are used and applied in legal arguments. If a question of law has been decided in several cases affirmatively, but in a later case has been negatived, the latter decision is to be taken as expressing the rule, and is binding upon all judges who are inferior to the judges by whom that decision has been pronounced. Such decision, however, does not preclude the judges who pronounced it, or others of co-ordinate jurisdiction, from a reconsideration of the question involved, or from reversing that decision if they think proper in any subsequent case in which the question arises. In illustration of this maxim, the reader may refer to the cases of *Crawford* v. *Beattie*, 24 D. 357 ; and *Virtue* v. *Pol. Com. of Alloa*, 1 R. 285.

Judicia summaria.—Actions entitled to summary discussion and decision ; actions in which only objections or defences can be heard which admit of instant verification. Ross, L. C. (L. R.) i. 359.

Judicis est judicare secundum allegata et probata.—It is the part (or duty) of a judge to decide in accordance with what has been alleged and proved. In deciding a case, the judge has first to consider what the pursuer who asks decree has averred, and then to what extent the averments have been established by proof. What has not been averred cannot be competently proved ; and what has not been proved is as if it had not been averred. The force of the maxim lies in the last word of it : the judge is only to proceed in giving judgment on what has been proved in the case, and is not to proceed to any extent on information, however sound or reliable, of which he has otherwise become possessed. " All questions of law may be decided by the judge on his own knowledge ; but as regards questions of fact, he cannot proceed on his own private knowledge, but must decide according to the evidence adduced." (Mackenzie, Rom. Law, 315.) There are cases, however, in which the judge may satisfy himself as to the matter of fact in dispute by the evidence of his own senses, and he may proceed to give judgment on that evidence without requiring any other. See *Lex non requirit*, &c.

Judicis est jus dicere non jus dare.—It is the part of the judge to enunciate, not to give or make law. Judges, as such, have no power of legislation, and their power is limited to the mere administration of that which has already been declared law by the proper authority. The power vested in the judges of the Supreme Court, in virtue of their *nobile officium*, of pronouncing what has not hitherto been held as law, is no violation of this maxim. In exercising that power, they merely exercise a certain discretion in the equitable administration of justice, and it has only reference to the particular case before them. They have no such discretion where the law is clear and fixed, nor do such decisions in equity form absolute precedents.

Judicio sisti.—To be forthcoming in answer to the suit. This is a species of cautionary obligation, under which the cautioner binds himself that the principal shall appear at all diets of court, when his presence shall be required by his opponent. In case of failure, the cautioner becomes liable for the amount contained in his bond of caution, which is generally the amount of the debt sued for. The cautioner may free himself of his obligation at any time by producing the principal in court (after due intimation to the other party), and stating that he will be no longer liable for his appearance. The principal will then require to find another cautioner, to prevent his being personally detained. This kind of caution is required of persons apprehended as *in meditatione fugœ;* but is most frequently used in the cases of persons apprehended on a criminal charge, who are liberated on finding caution, to the extent of a certain sum, for their appearance to answer to that charge when preferred against them.

Judicium a non suo judice nullius est momenti.—A judgment pronounced by a judge in a matter not falling within his jurisdiction is of no effect. See *Factum a judice,* &c.

Judicium semper pro veritate accipitur.—A judgment is always accepted as true. Any judgment pronounced by a competent court upon a question submitted to it for decision is conclusive, as between the parties to the suit, both of the fact and the law involved. It may be that through a deficiency of evidence the real truth has not been ascertained, or that through a mistaken view of the value or import of the evidence, or the law applicable, the court has arrived at an erroneous conclusion. Yet if judgment is pronounced, that judgment must be taken as correctly ascertaining the truth of the matter in dispute. While this is so, as regards the parties to the action in which the judgment has been pronounced, the judgment, so far as questions of law are involved, may be challenged by other parties in subsequent cases. There is one case which might appear to be an exception to this rule, but it is not really an exception. Suppose an action raised upon a bill, the defence to which was that the bill was a forgery, and that the court held the bill to be genuine, and gave decree. This, although a pure judgment on matter of fact, would not be sufficient to preclude the Justiciary Court trying the same question, and on the jury finding that the bill was a forgery, punishing the forger. Here, however, the second question of fact does not arise between the same parties; for in the civil action the question was between the holder of the bill and an obligant thereon; while in the criminal process the question was between the holder of the bill (assuming the holder to be the forger) and the Crown for the public interest. In short, a judgment is held to express the truth upon a disputed question between the parties to the dispute, and cannot by them be questioned, either on the ground of its being untrue in fact or erroneous in law. But it has not the same conclusive character as against others than the parties to that dispute. See the distinction drawn between a *judicium*—a sentence or judgment pronounced by the court as the result of its own consideration of the matter in dispute, and a decree pronounced of consent of parties in respect of a compromise. *Jenkins* v. *Robertson*, 5 Macp. (H. L.) 27. See *Res judicata pro*, &c.

Jura eodem modo destituuntur quo constituuntur.—Rights are abandoned or discharged in the same manner as that by which they are constituted. Thus a contract, with the rights and obligations arising out of it, depending upon the consent of parties (as in sale), may be abandoned or discharged by mutual consent; but a bond for money, or any right which requires to be constituted by writing, must be discharged in writing. An exception to the last illustration may be found in the case of rights constituted by bill or promissory note, which, although constituted by writing, may be abandoned or discharged by the mere delivery of the document of debt, without any written discharge of it. Such documents are *in re mercatoria*, and privileged.

Jura fixa.—Immoveable (*i.e.*, heritable) rights.

Jura sanguinis nullo jure civili dirimi possunt.—Rights of blood cannot be destroyed by the provision of the civil law. No law can destroy blood relationship, and therefore rights which depend upon or arise from such relationship are equally indestructible.

Juramento.—By oath. A limited kind of proof, which, however, may be resorted to in most cases by either of the parties under the form of a reference to the oath of the opponent. It is always a matter in the discretion of the Court whether a reference to the oath of a party is to be sustained or refused. This subject was fully discussed in the case of *Longworth* v. *Yelverton*, 3 Macp. 645, where the proposed reference was refused. This judgment was affirmed by the House of Lords, 5 Macp. 144, L. R. 1 Scot. Ap. 218. See *Scripto vel juramento*.

Juratores.—Jurors; so called on account of their being required to swear (*jurare*) that they will give their verdict according to the evidence laid before them.

Jure accretionis.—By right of accretion. Accretion is a mode of validating a right or title in the person of the possessor, by some act on the part of that possessor's author, and it may be illustrated by an example familiar to all who are acquainted with the former rules of conveyancing. If A, having only a personal title to lands, disponed them to B, granting precept for infeftment, any infeftment following upon that precept was invalid, because the warrant on which it proceeded flowed *a non habente*. But if A subsequently feudalised his title by infefting himself, this subsequent act, *jure accretionis*, validated the precept which he had granted to A, and the infeftment which followed upon it. Such accretion acts *retro*, and validates the deeds otherwise invalid, as of their own respective dates.

Jure devolutionis.—By right of devolution. See *Jus devolutum*.

Jure officii.—By right of office. Hume, ii. 131.

Jure proprietatis.—By right of property; or, as proprietor. Bell's Prin. § 997.

Jure proprio.—By his or their own proper right.

Jure sanguinis.—By right of blood. An heir succeeds

to hereditary titles, &c., *jure sanguinis*, and no service is necessary to vest him with the right to them.

Juri sanguinis nunquam præscribitur.—No prescription runs against a right by blood. This maxim, taken from the civil law, imports "that the right of relationship, being a personal right, is not lost *non utendo*. It is not to be understood, however, that one cannot, by prescription, establish his right to a subject which another claims in virtue of his right of relationship. Thus, after the lapse of the vicennial prescription of retours, the party served, although not the true heir, may exclude him. All that is meant is, that if no other heir has been entered, the right of blood is not lost by the negative prescription, but that a person may enter heir to his predecessor, although he died centuries ago." Bell's Dict. *h.t.* See *Alexander*, 4 Macp. 741.

Juris divini.—Of divine right; consecrated to God. Churches, communion-plate, &c., are said to be *divini juris*, and, so long as dedicated to sacred purposes, cannot be the subjects of commerce, or be applied to the uses of private property.

Juris executio non habet injuriam.—The execution of the law inflicts no wrong. See *Executio juris*, &c.

Juris privati.—Of private right. All private property is so termed, as opposed to property held for the public benefit. Property held by a corporation for behoof of its members, however numerous, is reckoned *juris privati*, because it partakes of the character of a private trust.

Juris publici.—Of public right. All property held for the benefit of the people generally, and of which they are entitled to the common enjoyment, is said to be of public right. Such are navigable rivers, the sea-shore, &c., held by the Crown for the public behoof. All other rights of a similar character are *juris publici*.

Jurisdictio contentiosa.—Contentious jurisdiction. The Romans divided jurisdiction into two branches, voluntary and contentious, the distinction between which cannot be better explained than by quoting the words of Erskine on this subject—" Voluntary (jurisdiction) was that which was exercised in matters that admitted of no opposition. Contentious had place in all questions truly debatable, which were in their nature capable of receiving a judicial discussion. A decree, therefore, upon a point which might have been the subject of dispute, though, in fact, pronounced in absence of, or without opposition from the defender, was *jurisdictionis contentiosæ*. The essential differences between the two were, that voluntary jurisdiction might be exercised by any judge, and upon any day, and in any place; whereas acts of contentious jurisdiction must have been performed *pro tribunali*, or in Court, and upon a lawful day, and by that judge alone who was competent to the cause. The judicial ratifications of women clothed with husbands may be accounted *voluntariæ jurisdictionis* by the law of Scotland ; for they may be proceeded in by any judge, even *extra territorium."* Ersk. B. 1, T. 2, § 4. See also upon this subject the observations of Lord Deas in the case of *M'Millan*, 22 D. 324.

Jurisdictio emanata.—A jurisdiction proceeding from the constitution of a Court: a jurisdiction inherently possessed by a Court, although not specially conferred. The right of every Court to punish those who are in contempt of its authority, is an example of this inherent jurisdiction. In *Ledgerwood* v. *M'Kenna*, 7 Macp. 261, it was questioned whether Justices of the Peace, acting under the Nuisances Removal Act (1856), had power to decern for expenses in a complaint brought before them, seeing that the statute did not specially confer upon them the power of awarding expenses. The Lord Ordinary was of opinion that "it might be fairly held that they had, by virtue of a power inherent in all judicial tribunals," and this view was supported by the Court.

Jurisdictio in consentientes.—Jurisdiction in a judge over parties by virtue of their consent : prorogated jurisdiction.

Jurisdictionis fundandæ causa.—For the purpose of founding jurisdiction. See *Arrestum*, &c.

Jurisdictionis voluntariæ. — Of voluntary jurisdiction. See explanation of voluntary jurisdiction, and wherein it differs from contentious jurisdiction, above, *Jurisdictio contentiosa*.

Jurisprudentia.—Jurisprudence ; or, a knowledge of the law. Jurisprudence is defined by Justinian in his Institutes, as "the knowledge of things divine and human; the science of the just and of the unjust."

Jus.—This word signifies either law or legal right. In the civil law it is used to signify the unwritten law established by custom (derived from *jubeo*), while *lex* signified the written law (from *lego*).

Jus accrescendi.—The right of accrescence. This phrase is used, although rarely so, by Scotch law writers, to signify the right of accretion, by which a title, formerly invalid or challengeable, is fortified by some supervening right acquired by the author who granted it. That right is more correctly expressed by the phrase *jus accretionis*. The present phrase is one borrowed from the civil law, and may be rendered (being the signification which it bears in the law of England) the right of survivorship. It has reference to the rights of co-legatees, some of whom under the civil law had the right of succeeding to the share of a co-legatee on his failure, others of whom had not. This right depended on the terms of the will; and while it would occupy too much space to state and illustrate here the rules on which such rights depended, yet they may be briefly mentioned. Co-legatees were said to be conjoined, either (1) *re*, (2) *re et verbis*, or (3) *verbis*. They were conjoined *re*, where the same subject was bequeathed to each, but bequeathed in separate and distinct sentences of the same testament; as where the testator provided: "I leave my house Z to A;" and in the same testament also provided: "I leave my house Z to B." In such a case it depended entirely upon the peculiar mode in which the thing was bequeathed, whether the heir was bound to give to one of the legatees the subject itself, and to the other the full value of it, or only bound to make delivery of the subject to the legatees jointly. But (apart from any question with the heir) it is evident that on the failure of any of the legatees so joined, there could be no room for the *jus accrescendi*, since to each legatee the whole subject was bequeathed. So, a surviving legatee taking the whole on the failure of his co-legatee, rather avoided a diminution than received an addition to his legacy; and on this account his right was termed by some civilians, the *jus non decrescendi*. (2.) Some legatees were conjoined *re et* *verbis*—*i.e.*, both as regards the subject of the legacy, and in the same sentence or provision of the testament. " I leave my house to A and B," is an instance of such conjunction; and under such a provision, on the failure of one of the legatees, the whole subject became the property of the other, by virtue of his *jus accrescendi*. (3.) There was no additional right accresced to the survivor on the failure of a co-legatee joined with him only *verbis*. In such case, the legatees were only conjoined in so far as their legacies were bequeathed in the same sentence; as where the testator provided, " I bequeath such a piece of land to A and B, each to have a half." Here there was no unity of interest between the legatees: their legacies, although bequeathed in the same sentence, were distinct and separate bequests, and, therefore, between such legatees there was no room for the application of the *jus accrescendi*. Correctly speaking, the *jus accrescendi* only applied in the cases of joint legatees who were conjoined *re et verbis*. For the law of Scotland on this subject, see M'Laren, i. 677 *et seq.*

Jus accrescendi inter mercatores, pro beneficio commercii, locum non habet.—For the benefit of commerce, there is no right of survivorship among merchants: that is, there is no right of survivorship among the members of a mercantile partnership. Although they hold jointly the property of the firm, the share of each partner, on his death, goes to his representatives like any other part of his estate, unless the articles or contract of the copartnery has otherwise stipulated. In England the presumption in the general case at common law (but not, it would appear, in courts of equity) is that property held jointly is held with the right of survivorship, entitling the survivor to the whole property on the death of his co-proprietors (*Crossfield* v. *Such*, 22 L. J. Exch. 325); but in the case of partners this rule has no application. *Buckley* v. *Barbour*, 20 L. J. Exch. 114. The law of England with regard to the rights of joint-tenants will be found in Smith on R. and P. Prop. 241 *et seq.* See also Paterson's Compend. 53 *et seq.* This presumed right of survivorship is not known in Scotland. Where property is held jointly, the holders of it are presumed to have equal interests; and on the death of any one of them, his share descends to his heirs, if it be not otherwise expressly provided either by destination or by contract.

Jus accrescendi præfertur oneribus.—The right of accrescence (or, right of survivorship) is preferred to burdens. This maxim (used in the English law) states, in effect, the principle that one of two proprietors having a joint right in the subject with a sole right in the survivor, cannot at his own hand burden or affect the subject held by them, so as to affect the right of his joint proprietor who survives him. "If one joint tenant grants a common or a way, or makes a charge, as distinguished from an alienation, it is good as against himself; but if he dies in the lifetime of the other, it does not affect the survivor; for *jus accrescendi præfertur oneribus.*" (Smith on R. and P. Prop. 245.) In like manner, the maxim *Jus accrescendi præfertur ultimæ voluntati* (The right of accrescence is preferred to the provisions of a will) expresses the rule that what the joint proprietor (or joint tenant as he is called) could not do by any act or deed during his lifetime, he cannot do by any provision in his last will or testament. In Scotland the rule is the same. One joint proprietor cannot burden the subject held jointly, if there be a destination of the whole subject to the survivor.

Jus actionis.—A right of action.

Jus ad rem.—The right to a subject; a personal right. See *Jus in re.*

Jus agendi.—The right of acting, or of taking action. This right is spoken of as distinguished from the *jus exigendi;* the former being the power which one has to take action to preserve his right, the latter the power of adopting proceedings to enforce or recover his right. See the two rights contrasted in Napier, 204.

Jus antiquum.—The old law. The old Roman law was so called.

Jus apparentiæ.—The right of apparency. In ordinary phraseology an heir-apparent is the person upon whom a certain succession would devolve *ab intestato;* as, for example, the eldest son is heir-apparent to his father. Technically, an heir-apparent is one to whom the succession has already opened, but who has not completed his title to his predecessor's estate, either by service or precept of *clare constat.* His right of apparency entitles the apparent heir to draw the rents of the estate, and pursue for them if necessary. He is also entitled to defend his ancestor's title if challenged, and was formerly entitled to reduce death-bed deeds. The acts or deeds of an heir-apparent are not effectual as against the estate or the next heir, unless he shall have possessed on his apparency for three years.

Jus aucupandi.—The right of hunting—*i.e.*, the right of seeking and killing game.

Jus civile.—The civil or Roman law. Law was divided by Justinian (Inst. B. 1, T. 1, § 4) primarily into two branches, public and private. The *jus publicum* (or public law) had reference to the constitution of the state, its relations with its members, civil administration, and, among the Romans, it regulated religious worship; while the *jus privatum* (or private law) regulated the reciprocal rights and duties of individuals. The latter was subdivided, in reference to the sources from which it was derived, into three branches — (1) The *jus naturale*, or natural law taught by nature to all animals; (2) the *jus gentium*, or law of nations, being the law established by natural reason among all men, and acquiring its name because of its observance among all civilised nations; and (3) the *jus civile*, or civil or municipal law, being that which any state constitutes for itself, differing from the two preceding branches in this, that while they are common to and binding upon all persons, the civil law is only obligatory upon the citizens of that country where it has been constituted or set up. *Jus civile*, occurring in works on Scotch law, invariably refers to the civil law of Rome. It will be observed that the signification attached by Justinian to the title *jus gentium* is entirely different from that which now attaches to it. With him it signifies those principles of right dictated by reason to all men (which modern writers term *natural law*); with us, the *jus gentium* signifies those rules which form the basis of one nation's dealings with another, or international law.

Jus constitui oportet in his quæ ut plurimum accidunt non quæ ex inopinato.—The law ought to be established to meet those cases which most frequently happen, not those which arise unexpectedly. Dig. B. 1, T. 3, § 3. See *Ad ea quæ frequentius*, &c.

Jus coronæ.—The right of the Crown; under which the Sovereign is entitled to claim those things which are regarded as *inter regalia*.

Jus crediti.—The right of credit—*i.e.*, the right of a creditor. This signifies the right in a debt or obligation vested in a creditor. The phrase is used frequently in contradistinction to a mere *spes* or expectancy; the one being a right which can be made effectual by legal process, while the other cannot. For example, when property is conveyed in trust for behoof of certain beneficiaries, although the trustee is legally vested in the property, yet the beneficiaries have a *jus crediti* therein which cannot be affected by the trustee's debts or deeds, and under which they can compel him to administer in terms of the provisions of the trust-deed.

Jus delatum.—A transferred right.

Jus devolutum.—A devolved right. When a church living or benefice became vacant by the death of the incumbent or otherwise, the patron (prior to the abolition of patronage by the Act 37 & 38 Vict. c. 82) was bound to present to the presbytery a fit person to supply the cure within six months of the vacancy occurring. In the event of the patron's failure so to present, the right of presentation devolved upon the presbytery, and this right was called the *jus devolutum*. By the cited Act, the right to appoint a minister to a vacant church is vested in the congregation, but that right must still be exercised within six months after the vacancy has occurred, otherwise the presbytery may appoint *tanquam jure devoluto*.

Jus domino proximum.—A right very near, or nearly equal to, that of absolute property. Such a right is enjoyed by one who holds lands in feu, for he is entitled to sell the subjects, or alter or use them in any way he thinks proper. And yet the property is not absolutely his—that is, he does not hold the property so absolutely as did the superior from whom he acquired, because the land is burdened with the feu-duty payable to the superior, and to this extent the absolute right of property is restricted. Similar to the right of a feuar under our law, was that of the *emphyteuta* under the civil law.

Jus et norma loquendi.—Style of language. Ross, L. C. (C. L.) i. 103.

Jus ex injuria non oritur.—No right arises from a wrongful act. The rule of this maxim applies solely to the wrong-doer. No one can set up his own wrongful act as the basis of a claim or right, just as no one can take benefit by his own fraud. But a right to compensation or reparation arises out of the wrongful act to the person injured, on account of the wrong which has been done.

Jus exigendi.—The right of demanding or enforcing fulfilment. A creditor may have an unquestioned *jus crediti*, and yet not have the *jus exigendi*, for a debt may be due and yet not be exigible. For example, where a testator directs his testamentary trustees to pay a certain legacy, which he has unconditionally bequeathed to the legatee, six months after his (the testator's) death, the legacy vests on the death of the testator, and the legatee acquires then the *jus crediti*, but he cannot enforce payment of the legacy until after the expiry of the six months; he acquires the *jus exigendi* when the debt has become prestable. See *Jus agendi*.

Jus gentium.—The law of nations; international law. For the different signification attaching to this phrase under the civil law, see *Jus civile*.

Jus gladii.—Literally, the right of the sword; the name given in the civil law to the right or power of executing criminal sentences.

Jus incorporale.—An incorporeal right. In the civil law rights were divided into corporeal and incorporeal, a division adopted by the law of England, but not much regarded in the law of Scotland. The subject of a corporeal right is that which may be seen and handled, as a horse, a house, land, &c., while the subject of an incorporeal right is one that does not fall under the senses, as a right of superiority, &c. The phrase *jus incorporale* is sometimes used to signify an incorporeal personal right as distinguished from such a right which has been feudalised. Thus, in speaking of a right of patronage, Lord Medwyn said (*Lord Advocate* v. *Graham*, **7** D. 198)—"If a patronage has never been feudalised, but has always been held and transmitted as a *jus incorporale*, a personal title will be sufficient for its conveyance, and a personal title with possession will be good under the Act 1617 to secure the right in the disponee." "If once feudalised, it loses its character of a *jus incorporale*, and it can only be acquired afterwards by a title habile for conveying a feudal subject."

Jus individuum.—An indivisible right. Such rights are those which can only be exercised by one person, as the right of superiority. Heirs-portioners each possess a *jus individuum* in the lands to which they succeed, as each has a right not to an equal portion of the lands, but an equal right in every portion of them.

Jus in re.—A right in a thing; a real right. This kind of right is generally spoken of as opposed to a *jus ad rem*, —a personal right—which merely implies a right to demand delivery or possession of a subject, without enabling the holder of it to vindicate possession against all and sundry. The difference between the two rights may be simply illustrated. No one possessed of the *jus in re* in any subject can be deprived of his right of property therein, except with his consent or by legal process. If it should be stolen from him, he may claim it wherever he may find it, even if in the hands of a *bona fide* purchaser. Or, if one purchase from another certain goods and pay the price thereof, he thereby acquires a *jus in re* in the goods bought, which cannot be defeated by the seller's creditors on his bankruptcy, although the goods are still in the seller's custody. This was not so previous to the passing of the Mercantile Law Amendment Act (1856), for until then, no right, other than a personal right in the sold goods, passed to the buyer until delivery was made. As to the change introduced by the Mercantile Law Amendment Act, see *Dans et retinens*, &c. A *jus in re*, therefore, is such a real right in the subject itself as cannot be defeated. A *jus ad rem*, on the other hand, is a mere right to sue for fulfilment of an obligation without any right to vindicate possession of the actual subject. Thus, if B engages and binds himself to make delivery to A of a certain subject, which, however, in violation of his obligation he sells and delivers to C, the right of A being merely a *jus ad rem*, he cannot recover the subject from C, and can only sue B for the delivery, and on failure in that, for damages on account of breach of contract. Such a right, therefore, is merely personal, and is not absolute but defeasible.

Jus in re inhæret ossibus usufructuarii.—The real right of a liferenter is inseparable from himself. A liferenter may assign the benefits arising from his liferent (if it is not an alimentary liferent) to another, but he cannot assign the right itself. Such an assignation can only have effect during the liferenter's lifetime. It is like a mandate by the liferenter authorising the assignee as mandatory to receive and discharge the liferent, but falls by the death of the mandant. The interest of a liferenter, so far as and where it is assignable, may be attached by the diligence of the liferenter's creditors. See *Ossibus inhæret*, &c.

Jus mariti.—The right of a husband. The *jus mariti* was that right by which the husband acquired to himself absolutely the personal property of his wife (Fraser, i. 676). The marriage operated as a conveyance of the wife's moveable estate to her husband, and vested him, farther, with the uncontrolled power of administration of the estate known as the goods in communion. This is no longer the law of Scotland. See the Acts 40 & 41 Vict. c. 29 ; and 44 & 45 Vict. c. 21. See also *Communio bonorum*.

Jus meræ facultatis.—A right of mere power: a right to do or not to do something, the non-exercise of which does not diminish the right. See *Res meræ*, &c.

Jus nobilius.—The nobler or superior right. Where a debt is made heritable by being secured upon land, it does not become moveable by the subsequent granting of a personal bond of corroboration or bond of cautionary. This may make the debt more secure, but does not alter its character,—the subsequent obligation being considered an accessory of the heritable right, which in such a case is the *jus nobilius*.

Jus non decrescendi.—The right of not suffering diminution. See *Jus accrescendi*.

Jus non patitur idem bis solvi.—The law does not suffer the same thing to be paid twice. Any such repetition of payment will found an action for restitution. A payment may be made under an erroneous belief of obligation therefor, and yet the person paying it have no claim for restitution. This may happen in a variety of cases, but it cannot happen where the debt has been twice discharged. This maxim is sometimes written, *Jus non patitur ut idem bis solvatur.* See *Bona fides non patitur,* &c.

Jus novum.—The new law. The more modern Roman law was so called as distinguishing it from the older law, which was termed the *jus antiquum.*

Jus obligationis.—A right of obligation, or personal right. Similar to a *Jus ad rem,* which see.

Jus pascendi pecoris.—The right of pasturing cattle. This is one of the rural servitudes whereby the proprietor of the dominant tenement is entitled to pasture a determinate number of his cattle on the grass grounds of the servient tenement. The right may be acquired by express grant, or by prescription.

Jus persequendi in judicio quod sibi debetur.—The right of suing before a judge for that which is due to us; being the definition of an action, given by Justinian in his Institutes (B. 4, T. 6, Pr.) Proceedings before a *judex* were said, by the Romans, to be *in judicio,* while those before the Prætor or other magistrate were said to be *in jure.*

Jus pignoris.—The right of pledge. A creditor, with whom any subject has been pledged by his debtor in security of his debt, is entitled, under his *jus pignoris,* to retain that subject until the obligation, in security for the fulfilment of which it was given, has been fulfilled. If, however, the creditor has lost possession of the pledge, his *jus pignoris* will not entitle him to recover it. *N. W. Bank and Others,* 21 R. 513.

Jus prætorium.—The Prætorian law, or law of the Prætors. This consisted of the edicts which it was the custom of each Prætor to publish on his entering office, declaring the rules on which he would proceed in various given cases; and also of the perpetual edicts which were held as forming part of the common law. (See *Edictum perpetuum.*) The Prætorian law was sometimes termed the *jus honorarium,* or honorary law, because it was made or promulgated by magistrates *qui honores gerebant* (who bore magisterial honours), the word *honores* signifying offices entitling the holders of them to certain external marks of dignity.

Jus præventionis.—A right of preference. Where two Courts are equally competent to judge in a certain cause, that Court which exercises the first act of jurisdiction has a preferable right of jurisdiction to judge in it, to the exclusion of the other. This right is said to arise *jure præventionis*, because the court first exercising jurisdiction prevents, or comes before, the other court. See the Act 31 & 32 Vict. cap. 96, § 4.

Jus publicum privatorum pactis mutari non potest.—The public law cannot be changed by bargain or agreement between individuals. See *Conventio privatorum*, &c.

Jus quæsitum.—An acquired or vested right.

Jus quæsitum tertio.—A right vested in, or acquired by, a third party. Where, in a contract between certain parties, a stipulation or provision is made in favour of a third, who is not a party to the contract, the right thus created is called a *jus quæsitum tertio*. Thus, under an antenuptial contract, where certain provisions are made in favour of trustees for behoof of the children of the marriage, without any power reserved to the spouses to alter their contract, a *jus quæsitum tertio* is created in favour of the children. So also in a trust-settlement, such a right is created in favour of the beneficiaries, for whose behoof the trustees are appointed.

Jus regale.—A royal right, or right belonging to the sovereign. See *Jus coronæ*.

Jus relictæ.—The right of the widow. This phrase signifies only the right which the widow has in the moveable estate of her deceased husband, and is never applied to any of her other rights. The *jus relictæ* entitles the widow to one-third of her deceased husband's moveable estate where there are children of the marriage existing, and one-half of that estate where there are no children. This right cannot be defeated by the husband's testament; nor is it presumed to be discharged by other provisions which the husband may have made in favour of his widow.

Jus representationis.—The right of representation; or that right by which a son or other relative succeeds to the rights and privileges of a person deceased. By this right the son of an eldest son succeeds to the estate of his grandfather in preference to the grandfather's surviving younger sons, because, in virtue of this right, the grandson representing his father, is regarded as *eadem persona* with him, and, by the law of primogeniture, is preferred to the succession. Formerly the right of representation was only permitted in successions to heritage, but it was extended to moveable succession by the Act 18 Vict. cap. 23 (1855).

Jus respicit æquitatem.—The law pays regard to equity. All law is based upon equity in its broadest sense, and regard is had to equity in all legal decisions. But when a law is clear it must be applied, even where the results may appear in any particular case to be hard or inequitable : it does not give place to equity, or what may seem to be so.

Jus retinendi et insistendi.—A right of retention, and of insisting or suing. Seamen have these rights in reference to the recovery of their wages,—the right of retention or lien over the ship in security, and the right of proceeding against both the owner and the ship for payment. Even where the ship has become a wreck, the seaman's right of lien exists over what may remain of it.

Jus sanguinis nunquam præscribitur.—A right by blood never prescribes. Thus the heir to a title never loses his right to the title through prescription or lapse of time : a child's right to aliment, and the parents' obligation to provide it, never prescribe, although the right and obligation may be otherwise extinguished. See Napier, 635.

Jus sibi dicere.—To declare the law for himself—*i.e.*, to take the law into one's own hand. Where any one in the lawful possession of a subject has been deprived of it by violence or other illegal means, he is not entitled to take the law into his own hands, and, by violence or other illegal means, repossess himself of it. If he should do so, he will, in any competition regarding it, be ordered *ante omnia* to restore it to the person from whom he took it, even were he in a position instantly to instruct his sole right to it. While, however, the law forbids any one to recover by violence, it does not forbid a possessor retaining by violence what is attempted to be taken from him violently. Such retention cannot be said to be *jus sibi dicere.*

Jus singulare.—A singular right ; that is, a right acquired otherwise than by succession. See *Titulo singulari*.

Jus superveniens auctori accrescit successori.—The supervening or subsequently acquired right of an author accresces to his successor. This maxim is borrowed from the civil law, and is the basis of the Scotch law doctrine of accretion. See *Jure accretionis*.

Jus tertii.—The right of a third party. Where any one in an action at law propones pleas, or advances arguments, which he has no title or interest to maintain, he may be met by the reply that such pleas are *jus tertii* to him. Thus, where a tenant assigns a lease, in which assignees and sub-tenants are expressly excluded, although the landlord, for whose benefit this restriction has been introduced, may object to the assignation as a contravention of the terms of the lease, it is *jus tertii* to the creditors of the tenant to object thereto upon that ground.

Jus utendi et abutendi.—The right of using and consuming. This is the essential characteristic of property. A proprietor has the right not only of enjoying the use of what is his, but may so use it as to consume it entirely. In this respect his right differs from the following—

Jus utendi fruendi.—The right of using and enjoying : that is, a mere liferent. A liferenter has the right of using and enjoying the subject over which this right is constituted, and can gather and consume its fruits. But such use and enjoyment must always be consistent with the full preservation of the subject. It is the proprietor alone who has the *jus abutendi*. Where lands in which the minerals are being wrought on lease are left in liferent, the liferenter seems to be entitled to the rents, if it is plain that this was the intention of the granter of the liferent. (Bell's Com. i. 61.) But a liferenter is not entitled to the rents of a mineral field not worked or opened up until after the testator's death. *Campbell's Trs.*, 9 R. 725, *Baillie's Trs.*, 19 R. 220.

Justitia.—Justice ; defined by Justinian to be " the constant and perpetual desire to render every one his due." (Inst. B. 1, T. 1, Pr.)

Justo tempore.—At the right time; in due time. *Gardner*, 3 R. 713.

L

Labes realis quæ rei inhæret.—A real defect which attaches to the thing. There are some objections to a contract or a document of debt which can only be urged effectually by certain parties against certain others, but a real defect is one that can be pleaded by any one. Thus, where the drawer of a bill pursues the acceptor for the amount contained in it, the acceptor may plead successfully in defence that the bill was granted without value for the drawer's accommodation: but such a defence could not be successfully maintained (in the ordinary case) against an onerous indorsee. The objection is personal, and constitutes no real defect in the bill itself. But the defence that the alleged document is a forgery is good against any holder, whether he be an onerous holder or not; it is a real defect, which renders the bill void. Again, where a debtor binds himself, along with a cautioner, in a personal bond for a sum of money therein mentioned, both principal and cautioner are free, if it can be shown that the principal obligation was obtained by force or fraud; and that, even where the cautioner is bound as full debtor, and no force or fraud has been used in obtaining his obligation. The force or fraud used is a real defect vitiating the principal obligation, and when it falls, the accessory obligation falls also. Theft, also, constitutes a *labes realis* in the title of any one holding the subject stolen, no matter how honestly he may have acquired it; and on this defect, which attaches to it until it return to his possession, the true owner may vindicate his right, and recover his subject wherever it can be found.

Læsio pietatis.—A breach or violation of filial duty. Conditions which involve such a violation are regarded in some cases as *contra bonos mores*, and held not binding.

Thus, in the case of *Fraser*, 11 D, 1466, a condition attached by a father to a provision made by him in favour of his child, to the effect that she should cease to reside with her mother, who was of irreproachable character, involving as it did a breach of filial duty, was regarded as *contra bonos mores*, and therefore held *pro non scripto*. A different view seems to have received some favour (although the question was not actually decided) in the case of *Reid*, 5th March, 1813, F. C. In that case a settlement had been made by an uncle upon his nephew, on the condition that he should not reside with his mother, or any of her relations, nor should she reside with him. The legatee objected to this, as involving a *læsio pietatis*, contrary to law and morality, and which he could not obey without violating the established order of nature ; but the court declined to decide the general question, as the legatee had signified an intention of taking up a separate establishment, if this was necessary to entitle him to take benefit under the settlement. The distinction between the cases seems to be this :—A father is bound to provide for his child, and to that provision he has no power to attach an illegal or immoral condition; but an uncle, being under no legal obligation to provide for a nephew, may attach what conditions he pleases to any provision he may make for him, leaving it as a matter in the option of the legatee to accept or refuse that provision.

Lapsus bonis.—Reduced in worldly circumstances ; in straitened circumstances. The phrase applies to a person in pecuniary difficulties, but scarcely amounts to insolvency. It means a person now poor, who had at one time been otherwise.

Lata culpa æquiparatur dolo.—Gross fault is held as equivalent to fraud. This is to be applied only to questions of civil liability; for while fraud, in the usual acceptation of that term, will render the person guilty of it liable to criminal prosecution for fraud, *culpa lata* will not. Thus if the depositary under a contract of deposit, is guilty of gross fault or carelessness, in consequence of which the deposit is lost, he will be civilly liable to the depositor for its value, in the same manner as if he had fraudulently disposed of the subject. So also trustees, who have, through their gross fault or negligence, allowed the property entrusted to them to be lost or deteriorated, are liable to the beneficiaries in restitution or compensation, just as if they had wilfully defrauded them. Regarding the different degrees of *culpa* recognised in our law, and the diligence for which certain persons are responsible, see *Culpa*. See also *Culpa lata*, &c.

Lato sensu.—In a wide sense; in a more comprehensive sense.

Latori præsentium.—To the bearer of these presents. Written obligations and personal bonds for payment of money or delivery of goods, made payable to the holder without inserting the name of any creditor, were at one time very common. Lord Stair, in treating of such deeds, says: "The conveyance of bonds or other writs, wherein the name of the creditor or acquirer is left blank, have become of late very frequent, and have occasioned many debates as to the conveyance of such rights, and the effects thereof; as, first, whether the leaving the name of the creditor or acquirer blank be warrantable, or a fraudulent conveyance, to conceal and keep in the dark to whom the right belongeth, that creditors may not know to affect it by legal diligence: the reason ordinarily given for taking writs in that way is, to shun the trouble of assignations, translations, or intimations thereof, as they pass from hand to hand, according to that tenor of obligation, frequent in other places, whereby the debtor obligeth him to pay and perform such things *latori præsentium;* by which he is obliged to pay to none but to him from whom he may get up the bond, and may safely pay to any that hath it." (B. 3, T. 1, § 5.) The frequency with which such deeds were used for fraudulent purposes, gave rise to the Act 1696, c. 25, which declared that no bond, assignation, disposition, or other deed, subscribed and delivered blank in the creditor's name, should be valid. From the rule of this statute were exempted the indorsations of bills of exchange and the notes of any trading company, such as banking companies, and the principle of this exemption has been since extended to cheques, &c. In the case of *Bovill* v. *Dixon*, 16 D. 619, the question was raised whether an ironmaster's warrant or scrip-note, binding himself to deliver the quantity of iron therein mentioned " to the party lodging this document with me," was of the nature of the obligations struck at by the Act 1696. It was held by the Court of Session to be a document granted *in re mercatoria*, transferable without indorsation, and not falling within the provisions of the statute; and that decision was repeated in the case of *Dimmack*, 18 D. 428. The decision in *Bovill's* case was confirmed on appeal by the House of Lords, 3 Macq. 1, but upon a special ground. The Lord Chancellor (Cranworth), in delivering his opinion observed—" If the question had turned exclusively upon the validity or invalidity of this document, I am bound to say that I should not have concurred with the Court of Session. I think that the document is invalid. The effect of such a document, if valid, is to give a floating right of action to any person who may become possessed of it. Now I am prepared to say that this cannot be tolerated by the law either of Scotland or of England." " I have no hesitation in saying that, independently of the law merchant and of positive statute, within neither of which classes do these scrip-notes range themselves, the law does not, either in Scotland or England, enable any man by a written engagement to give a floating right of action at the suit of any one into whose hands the writing may come, and who may thus acquire a right of action better than the right of him under whom he derives title." On this subject the reader may also refer to the cases of *The Commercial Bank* v. *Kennard*, 21 D. 864, and *Connal* v. *Loder*, 6 Macp. 1095.

Legatum generis.—A legacy of a subject of a certain class. Where the testator bequeathed to the legatee a subject of a certain kind or class without specifying it so as to distinguish it from other subjects of the same class belonging to him, as, for example, where he bequeathed a horse, a yoke of oxen, a slave, &c., the legacy was called among the Romans *legatum generis*. In some cases of this kind the legatee had the right of choice, but the general rule was that the heir could not be compelled to give the best nor the legatee to accept the worst subject of the class mentioned. Such a legacy conferred no *jus in re* on the legatee, but merely a personal right to recover, or *jus ad rem*.

Legatum generis perit hæredi, legatum speciei perit legatario.—A general legacy perishes to the heir, a special legacy perishes to the legatee. A special legacy, being a legacy of a specific subject, can only be enforced against the heir or executor so long as the thing bequeathed exists. If it perishes (through no fault of the heir or executor) the loss falls on the legatee. He had right to the specific object alone, and not to any equivalent: if the specific subject has ceased to exist, he cannot compel delivery. On the other hand, a general legacy, *ex. gr.*, of a sum of money must be paid by the heir or executor if there are funds to meet it. The estate may suffer diminution by losses, or it may not realise as much as was expected, but the provision to the heir or executor himself must bear the loss; in a word, it may reduce the residue, but the legatee must be paid. By way of compensation the law provides, that if the estate is not sufficient to pay all the legacies, they must, so far as they are general legacies, suffer proportionate abatement. But the special legatee is entitled to his special legacy without abatement or contribution.

Legatum liberationis.—Legacy of a discharge. This is a legacy of that which the legatee may be owing the testator at his death. It frees him from his liability for payment of any sums belonging to the testator which may be in his hands at that time properly as debtor, but gives him no right to retain the testator's money which he may happen to have merely passing through his hands, or with him on temporary deposit.

Legatum nominis.—Legacy of a debt. Such a legacy gives the legatee the full right to the debt so bequeathed, and carries with it the right to enforce payment. This kind of legacy, however, is generally bequeathed to the debtor himself, in which case it operates as a discharge.

Legatum per universitatem.—A universal legacy; so called because under it the legatee succeeds to the *universitas* or whole moveable estate of the deceased, in so far as it was at his disposal, or to the reversion or residue after satisfying expenses, debts, and other legacies.

Legatum quantitatis.—A legacy of quantity, or, of so much. This is the name given in the civil law to that which we call a general legacy. It is a legacy, not of a special article or debt, but indefinite, of so much money or other moveables of a particular description; such as a legacy of £100. A special legacy is one of a particular subject clearly distinguished from the rest of the testator's estate, as, for example, a legacy of a certain watch, or ring, &c. General legacies abate with the inadequacy of the fund out of which they are to be paid; but a special legacy depends only on the existence of the thing bequeathed, and suffers no abatement if there be enough besides to pay the debts and expenses. A special legacy confers upon the legatee a *jus ad rem specificam*.

Legatum rei alienæ.—Legacy of a subject not belonging to the testator, but belonging to some other person. Where a testator bequeaths a subject not his own, erroneously believing it to be his, it is no legacy (*Traquair* v. *Martin*, 11 Macp. 22); but if he bequeath it knowing it to be the property of another (*res aliena scienter legata*), the legacy must be made good by purchasing and delivering the subject to the legatee, or otherwise satisfying him. If the subject cannot be purchased, the value of it must be paid to the legatee. These rules are borrowed from the civil law.

Legatum universitatis.—A universal legacy, or legacy of the testator's whole estate. See *Legatum per*, &c.

Legis constructio non facit injuriam.—Legal construction inflicts no wrong. See *Constructio legis*, &c.

Legitima potestas.—The lawful power. The phrase *liege poustie* is supposed to be derived from these words. Erskine says: " The term properly opposed to death-bed is *liege poustie*, by which is understood a state of health; and it gets that name because persons in health have the *legitima potestas* or lawful power of disposing of their property at pleasure." (B. 3, T. 8, § 95.)

Legitima remedia.—Legal or lawful remedies.

Legitima successio.—Legal succession, or, succession according to the rules of law. An heir-at-law takes up the succession of an ancestor who has died intestate according to these rules, and this is called the *legitima successio*. Bastards may succeed to their mother or reputed father by destination, but they are excluded from their succession by the rule of law. They have no *legitima successio;* and formerly they had not even the power of disposing *mortis causa* of what was their own property. This power was conferred on them by the Act 6 Will. IV. c. 22.

Legitimo modo.—In legal form ; in the manner prescribed by law.

Legitimum tempus restitutionis.—The legal period for restitution ; or the time within which, according to the rules of law, restitution may be claimed. Such, for example, is the *quadriennium*, during which deeds executed in minority may be reduced by the granter on the ground of minority and lesion, and restitution *in integrum* claimed against any act which he may have committed to his own prejudice. The *quadriennium* is an example of a *legitimum tempus* restricted to a certain period ; and the right of the owner of a subject which has been stolen to claim restitution of, and recover that subject whenever and wherever he may find it, may be taken as an example, on the other hand, of a right to insist on restitution, which is laid under no restriction in point of time.

Lenocinium.—Pandering to licentiousness ; the technical name given in law to the conduct of a husband in pandering to, or conniving at, the infidelity of his wife. It includes any act on the part of the husband which is likely to result in unfaithfulness on the part of the wife, or which exposes her to pollution. It affords a good defence to an action for divorce at the instance of the husband, and was given effect to in a case where the husband had "caused, prompted, or hounded" the person with whom his wife had committed adultery to attempt to seduce her, although the husband averred that his acts were merely intended to test his wife's chastity. This defence was likewise sustained in a case where the wife averred that her husband had committed such indecencies towards her as invited others to seduce her. *Mackenzie*, M. 333. For circumstances which were held not to amount to *lenocinium*, see the case of *Donald*, 1 Macp. 741. On the other hand, see the case of *Marshall*, 8 R. 702.

Leonina societas.—A leonine partnership—*i.e.*, a partnership in which one of the partners bears all the loss, while another receives all the profit. It was so termed by the civil jurists because the partner receiving all the profits was receiving the lion's share. Such an arrangement was not recognised in the civil law as partnership, nor is it recognised in ours. According to our law, to plead that a partnership is *leonina societas*, is to plead that it is illegal and void.

Leviora delicta.—The lighter delicts. These include crimes of the less heinous character, such as breach of the peace, petty larceny, &c., and all those which may be tried summarily; they are called the lighter delicts in opposition to those of a more serious character, the guilt of which must be determined by a jury.

Levis exceptio excusat a spolio.—A slight defence excuses from the consequences of spuilzie. Spuilzie is the taking away of moveables without either the consent of the owner or legal warrant. The person so depriving another of his lawful possession is liable not only in restitution of the subject taken, but also in violent profits, although action for the latter prescribes in three years. As spuilzie is not presumed, a slight defence is held sufficient to elide its consequences, such as that the person taking the subject had reasonable grounds for believing the subject to be his own, or that his appropriation was unintentional, or that the subject was returned immediately, &c. Spuilzie is the same as theft, except that the criminal intent, which is essential to the latter, is not essential to the former. Theft is the *nomen juris* used in criminal proceedings arising out of the act, spuilzie when the act is considered *ad civilem effectum*.

Lex commissoria.—The term applied to a condition which under the civil law might be adjected to a contract of sale, whereby the seller was entitled to regard the sale as null if the price of the subject sold was not paid by a certain day. See *Pactum legis*, &c.

Lex contractus.—The rule or law of the contract. Parties to a contract may make any stipulations regarding it or its fulfilment which they may think proper, and the law will enforce them, provided they be not illegal or *contra bonos mores*. Thus, although it be the general rule of law that the lessee of a subject is not liable for its value if it perish by accident, but that such loss shall be borne by the owner or lessor, yet the parties may validly stipulate to the contrary, and the law will enforce such a stipulation, for that is the *lex contractus*. In like manner, although it is the general rule that a feuar is entitled to support for his feu, yet he may contract with his superior not to claim damages for any injury done to his feu or buildings thereon by the removal of support in consequence of the superior or his tenant working the minerals underneath the feu. *Buchanan v. Andrew*, 11 Macp. 13 (H. L.), reversing the judgment of the Court of Session, 9 Macp. 554. The *lex contractus* includes all provisions or stipulations in a contract by which the reciprocal rights and obligations of the parties thereto are determined.

Lex domicilii.—The law of the domicile. Personal contracts, or deeds relating to moveable property, are interpreted and enforced according to the law of the place where the contracting parties, or the granter of the deed, had their domicile at the time of contracting or granting, and that without regard to the place where the contract is to be executed, or where the moveables are situated. Thus a conveyance of moveables situated in Scotland, granted by a domiciled Englishman, will be construed and given effect to according to the law of England; and so, likewise, a contract entered into between Scotchmen domiciled in Scotland, for the performance of certain works in England, will be enforced according to the law of Scotland. While it is the general rule that the law of any country will acknowledge and enforce contracts lawfully entered into in some other country, yet the rule admits of exception in cases where the contract is at variance with the morals or general policy of that country in which it is sought to be enforced. Thus in some countries polygamy is permitted, and the several contracts of marriage entered into by the husband recognised. Such contracts are not recognised in countries where polygamy is forbidden, nor would the rights of any but the first wife be enforced against the husband, since the law acknowledges none other than the first married to be a wife at all. Again, contracts concerning and deeds conveying heritable property must be in accordance with the law of the country where the heritage is situated, because it would be contrary to good policy to admit of the administration of a law different from that held and administered where the property is placed. This rule, although generally recognised and acted upon, must now be read subject to what was decided in the case of *Studd*, 8 R. 249, which appears to sanction an exception to the general rule. The *lex domicilii* rules with respect to the person and personal rights, but immoveable and heritable rights are regulated by the *lex rei sitæ*.

Lex feudi.—The rule or law of the feu; that by which the feudal title is determined and regulated. Where two separate titles to the same subject concur in one person, that title which is the chief one, or under which he is bound to hold, is the one by which his right is regulated. "If the seller possess on a fee-simple apparency, and likewise as having right under the entail, the entail, although not feudalised, being the title on which he is by law bound to possess, will be regarded as the *lex feudi*, the regulating title." (Duff, Feud. Con. 180.) See a further illustration of this given under the phrase, *Accessorium sequitur naturam*, &c.

Lex fori.—See *Lex loci*, &c.

Lex loci actus.—The law of the place where the act was performed.

Lex loci contractus.—The law of the place where the contract was made. Where contracts are entered into in one country, performance and fulfilment of which are to be made in another, questions frequently arise as to the rules by which those contracts are to be construed and performance enforced. It cannot be said, however, that the decisions upon such questions have always been in harmony: some authorities maintaining that the law of the place where the contract is to be performed (*lex loci solutionis*) governs the construction of the contract, while others are of opinion that the law of the place where the contract is made does so. The reader will find the principal authorities on this subject cited or referred to in *Valery* v. *Scott*, 3 R. 965; Addison on Cont. 194 *et seq.*; and Story, Con. Law, § 242 *et seq.* It may, however, be stated generally, that while the *lex loci solutionis* is always of importance in such a question, the construction and interpretation of a foreign contract depends upon the law of the place where the contract is entered into. (*Jacobs*,

L. R. 12, Q. B. D. 589.) Thus if a contract be entered into, or obligation undertaken, in England, founded upon a *nudum pactum*, where no valuable consideration was given, the Courts of Scotland would not give effect to nor enforce such an obligation, because, by the law of England, a *nudum pactum* confers no right, and can sustain no action. In such a case the judgment would proceed upon the rule of the *lex loci*, for, by the law of Scotland, the plea of *nudum pactum* would not be held a good defence in reference to a Scotch contract. Again, in Scotland, no bill or promissory note can bind the obligant therein, unless it be duly stamped; but the law of Scotland does not, on that account, refuse to enforce the obligation contained in an unstamped bill or promissory note granted in a country by the law of which no stamp is necessary. While, however, the construction of a contract is determined by the *lex loci contractus*, the mode of procedure for its enforcement must be regulated by the *lex fori*,—the law of the country to whose Courts application has been made to compel fulfilment. Accordingly a Scotch creditor cannot proceed in England against an English debtor on a bill by summary diligence, as he would against his debtor in Scotland, but must raise action on the bill, according to the forms of procedure in England, either before the Supreme or County Courts. "In Scotland this rule has been carried so far, that although we admit the solemnities required in the execution of foreign contracts, the *proof*, by witnesses, that an English bond was truly executed, although necessary in England, has been held unnecessary when the bond was sued upon here, in respect no such proof is required in the case of a Scotch bond; and on the same principle, it was decided that a debt contracted in England, though proveable there by parole evidence, could not be so proved when it was sued for in Scotland." (Thomson on Bills, p. 157, and cases there cited.) The *lex loci* thus determines the meaning, intent, and measure of the obligation, the *lex fori* the mode of procedure by which fulfilment of that obligation is to be enforced. This distinction is well brought out in the case of *Don*, 2 S. & M'L. 682, in which the House of Lords (reversing the decision of the Court of Session) held that the bill sued on (which was a foreign bill) was subject to the sexennial prescription of the *lex fori,* and not to the rules of prescription according to the *lex loci,* in respect that prescription affects not the right itself, but the legal remedy for enforcing it.

Lex loci solutionis.—The law of the place where the money is to be paid or the obligation fulfilled.

Lex neminem cogit ad vana seu inutilia peragenda.—The law compels no man to do that which is futile or fruitless. See the opinion of Willes, J., in *Bell* v. *Mid. Ry. Co.;* 30 L. J. C. P. 280.

Lex neminem cogit ostendere quod nescire præsumitur. —The law compels no one to disclose (or make known) what he is presumed not to know.

Lex nil frustra facit.—The law does nothing in vain; that is, the law does not perform acts or pronounce decrees which are useless or without practical effect. So, the law will not grant an interdict where no trespass has been committed or threatened, merely for the purpose of preventing by anticipation an event which may never happen. Nor will the Court pronounce a decree of declarator of an abstract fact upon which no right depends, and upon which no legal conclusion or consequence can follow; any more than it will declare a right to exist which no one has questioned. For illustration of this, see *Gifford* v. *Traill,* 7 S. 854. *Lyle* v. *Balfour,* 9 S. 22. *Mag. of Edin.* v. *Warrender,* 1 Macp. 887.

Lex non cogit ad impossibilia. — The law does not compel the performance of what is impossible. The performance of an act may be rendered impossible from any of four causes—(1) From the nature and character of the act itself, (2) from the act of God, (3) from the act of the law, and (4) from circumstances (not falling within any of the two preceding classes) emerging after performance of the act had been stipulated or contracted for. With regard to the first, it may be said in a word that the present maxim applies. If parties agree or stipulate for the performance of what is plainly impossible, and beyond the power of man to perform, there is no obligation for its performance. Such impossible conditions, and the contract to which they are attached, are held null; they are regarded as not having been seriously intended or relied on by the parties, and the rule regarding them is *impossibilium nulla obligatio est.* (2.) The second class, including things rendered impossible by inevitable accident (called *damnum fatale*), against which ordinary prudence and foresight could not have provided, or human skill have prevented, is in many cases covered by the rule of law expressed in the maxim. Thus if a landlord lets to a tenant a subject which is destroyed by fire, or blown down by a tempest, he cannot be compelled to give the tenant possession, nor is he liable in damages for failing to do so. But a person may so contract as to make himself liable for damages on account of non-performance of his obligation, even although that performance has been rendered impossible by the act of God. " By the common law of England a person who expressly contracts absolutely to do a thing, not naturally impossible, is not excused for non-performance because of being prevented by the act of God, or the King's enemies." (Per Willes, J., in *Lloyd* v. *Guibert*, L. R. 1, Q. B. 121.) So, a consignee bound under charter-party to discharge a cargo within a certain time, is liable in demurrage after the lay-days have expired, even where the delay in discharging has arisen from tempestuous weather which prevented the possibility of discharging. *Thiss* v. *Byers*, L. R. 1, Q. B. Div. 244. (3.) Of those acts, performance of which is excused on the ground that performance has been rendered impossible by the act of the law, a good example will be found in the case of *Baily* v. *De Crespigny*, L. R. 4, Q. B. 180. In that case the defendant had demised certain premises to the plaintiff for a long term of years, and undertook that neither he nor his assigns should, during the term, permit any building to be erected " on a paddock fronting the demised premises." Some years after entering into that bargain a railway company took the paddock under the powers conferred by an Act of Parliament, and built upon it. The action was thereupon raised to enforce the defendant's obligation, but the Court held that the defendant was discharged from his obligation by the Act of Parliament, which compelled him to assign the ground, and authorised the buildings to be erected by the company, and thus put it out of the power of the defendant to fulfil his obligation. (4.) The impossibilities of this class are not covered by the maxim, and will not excuse non-performance of an obligation. "There can be no doubt that a man may by an absolute contract bind himself to perform things which subsequently become impossible, or to pay damages for the non-performance, and this construction is to be put upon an unqualified undertaking, where the event which causes the impossibility was, or might have been, anticipated and guarded against in the contract, or where the impossibility arises from the act or default of the promissor." (Per Hannen, J., in *Baily* v. *De Crespigny, supra.*) Thus if one undertakes to deliver certain goods or stock on a given day at a certain price, he will not be excused from the performance of his obligation, because at the time specified the article or stock is not procurable, and cannot, therefore, possibly be delivered; that being a contingency against which the obligor could and should have provided. Impossibility of performance may arise from a fifth cause—namely, the act of the obligant himself. But in such a case the impossibility could not be pleaded in excuse of non-performance. One who puts it out of his own power to fulfil his obligation is held to be both able and bound to fulfil. See *Impotentia excusat,* &c.

Lex non favet votis delicatorum.—The law does not favour the wishes of the fastidious. Broom, 379.

Lex non requirit verificari quod apparet curiæ.—The law does not require that to be proved which is apparent to the Court. Where the question before the Court turns upon whether a deed has been erased or not, the Court may determine this, without the evidence of experts, upon an examination of the writ. If there is difficulty in determining whether there has been an erasure, the Court may order a proof; but if the erasure is apparent, no proof is necessary. *Hamilton* v. *Lindsey-Bucknall,* 8 Macp. 323. So, again, the Court may determine for itself whether a deed is stamped, or whether it is duly stamped.

Lex patriæ.—The law of one's country. This phrase is synonymous with *lex domicilii,* that being regarded as a person's country in which he has fixed his residence. Moveable rights and moveable succession are regulated by the law of domicile, and not by the *lex rei sitæ*,—that is, the law of the place where the subjects in which the rights exist are situated. So, if a domiciled Scotchman die leaving moveable property in England or elsewhere abroad (even if the whole of his moveable property should be so situated), his succession will, nevertheless, be regulated by the law of his domicile. See *Lex domicilii*.

Lex posterior derogat priori.—A later statute derogates from a prior. If two statutes are passed which are inconsistent with or repugnant to each other, the later in date prevails: it derogates from the authority of the former in so far as the inconsistency between them is concerned, but no further. Even if, in the same statute, there are inconsistent or repugnant clauses, the later clause rules, and the earlier is disregarded, except where the earlier clause is in accordance with the general spirit and intention of the Act, and the later is not. This maxim will be found sometimes expressed thus: *Leges posteriores priores contrarias abrogant*,—Laws later in date abrogate prior contrary laws. Broom, 27. See *Cum duo inter se*, &c.

Lex rei sitæ.—The law of the place where the property or subject is situated. Moveable rights, as we have seen above, are regulated and determined by the law of the domicile; but immoveable or real rights are determined by the law of the place where the subject or property is situated. Thus a contract entered into in England, according to the laws of England, will be enforced in Scotland; or a testament executed in England, conveying moveables situated in Scotland, will be held a valid conveyance, although not according to the forms observed in Scotland in such conveyances. But a deed affecting or conveying Scotch heritage, wherever executed, must, to be effectual, be framed according to the requirements of the law of Scotland; and therefore a deed executed in England conveying Scotch heritage, if not so framed, although executed according to the form by which heritage in England is validly conveyed, will be ineffectual in Scotland. See, however, the case of *Studd*, referred to under the phrase *Lex domicilii*.

Lex rejicit superflua, pugnantia, incongrua.—What is superfluous, repugnant, incongruous, the law rejects. In dealing with the construction of deeds or statutes, the law disregards what is mere surplusage in langauge, and rejects any construction which is incongruous or repugnant to the general spirit and intention of the deed or enactment. Such a course is only open to the Court when the deed or statute is open to construction through ambiguity or obscurity. When the deed or statute is unambiguous and clear, the law rejects or disregards no part of it: every word has its proper meaning and effect given to it.

Lex Rhodia de jactu.—The Rhodian law regarding property thrown overboard, for the sake of lightening the ship. The general rule of this law, as stated in the Pandects, is "that if goods have been thrown overboard for the purpose of lightening the ship (the loss thus occasioned), shall be made good by the contribution of all, because it was done for the general behoof." (Dig. B. 14, T. 2, l. 1.) See *Jactus mercium*, &c.

Lex semper dabit remedium.—The law will always afford a remedy. There are many wrongs which cannot be reached or remedied by legal action, but for every wrong of which the law can take cognisance it affords a remedy. Thus, against trespass it gives an interdict; against wrongs done to the person or good fame of any one, it gives damages and vindication of character; against loss by fraud it gives restitution, &c. The *remedium* of the maxim includes more than the popular term "remedy" in the sense of reparation. It means also the right of action and diligence which it affords to enable any one to enforce a right which is being withheld. So that whether the wrong arises from an injury inflicted or a right withheld, the law affords a remedy.

Lex semper intendit quod convenit rationi.—The intendment of a law is always in accordance with reason. Hence, in construing a statute that interpretation will be more readily accepted which is reasonable than one which is otherwise; and what is reasonable in the circumstances will be gathered from the purpose and spirit of the enactment. It would afford a strong argument against any proposed reading or construction of a statute, that it was in itself absurd or out of harmony with ordinary reason and good sense.

Lex spectat naturæ ordinem.—Law regards the order or course of nature.

Lex talionis.—The law of retaliation; by which a person was made to suffer as punishment for his offence, the same injury as that which he had inflicted, or attempted to inflict, upon another. It was "a rule of the judicial law of Moses, directing the punishment to be analogous to the crime,—an eye for an eye, and a tooth for a tooth. Thus, if one swore falsely that another was guilty of a capital crime, the swearer was himself punished capitally. This law does not seem ever to have been established in any civilised state. It was at one time attempted to introduce the *lex talionis* into England, in the case of malicious accusations; it being enacted by statute 37 Edw. III. c. 18, that such as preferred any suggestions to the King's Great Council should put in sureties of taliation. But after one year's trial this punishment of taliation was rejected, and imprisonment adopted in its stead." Bell's Dict. *h.v.*

Liberatio nominis.—The discharge of a debt. From a very early period the Romans kept *tabulæ* or family-ledgers, in which the paterfamilias entered his assets and liabilities, his expenses and receipts. As the creditor put down in his *tabulæ* the *name* of his debtor, the word *nomen* came to signify a debt; but the mere insertion of the debtor's name and debt in the creditor's ledger did not prove the obligation. Where the debtor had made an entry in his ledger corresponding to that made by the creditor in his, the two together constituted the obligation; the two entries having the same effect as if the parties had entered into a stipulation. In cases, however, where there was only the creditor's entry, he was allowed to prove the debt in the usual way, and the entry in his ledger was received as an adminicle of evidence. In order to secure the accuracy of this ledger, which was, in fact, a perpetual record of the family estate, a note was taken of the various transactions of the day in a waste-book, called *adversaria*, which was destroyed once in three months. The *adversaria* was of no weight in a court of law, where entries made in the *tabulæ* were alone regarded. Gaius calls debts by the name of *nomina transcriptitia*, a name arising from the fact of the debts being transcribed from the *adversaria* to the *tabulæ*.

Liberis nascituris.—To children yet to be born. Certain legal rights can, under this destination, be secured to children yet unborn, and such a destination is almost universally to be found in marriage contracts. Where lands are conveyed to a husband in liferent, for his liferent use allenarly, and to his children *nascituri* in fee, such a destination confers a fee on the father fiduciary for his children, of which he is bound to denude in favour of his children when the time arrives at which they can demand this. In like manner, a conveyance by a father to his children in life at the time *nominatim,* and to those *nascituri,* constitutes an absolute fee in the children named to their own share, and a fiduciary fee in the shares allotted to the children yet to be born. Such conveyances, if properly made and perfected, cannot be affected by the subsequent acts or deeds of the father, but give the children a preference over all their father's posterior deeds, even although onerous.

Libertini.—Freed men. Persons who had been slaves but were freed from slavery were called, among the Romans, *libertini,* in opposition to *ingenui,* persons born free, and who had never lost their freedom. The modes in which a slave might be manumitted or enfranchised according to the provisions of the civil law were numerous; it might be done—*ex. gr.,* by the master declaring before five of his friends that he bestowed freedom on the slave, or by publicly calling the slave "son"; or a master might bequeath liberty to his slave in his testament, either expressly, or by implication, as by nominating him his heir.

Liege poustie.—A phrase used in the Scotch law (which, although not a Latin phrase, is said to be derived from the Latin *legitima potestas*), to signify that state of health in which a person might legally and effectually dispose *mortis causa* or otherwise, of his heritable property, as contradistinguished from the term "death-bed,"—a *liege poustie* conveyance being one·not challengeable by the heir on the ground of death-bed. This condition of health the granter of a deed was held to have enjoyed, if at the time of granting it he was not affected by the disease of which he died, or if, after executing it, he attended kirk or market unsupported, or survived for sixty days. Reduction of a conveyance *ex capite lecti* is now abolished, 34 & 35 Vict. c. 81.

Ligia et non ligia.—Liege and non-liege. A liege-fee is that held directly of and under the Crown, while a non-liege is that held of a subject superior. Erskine, when treating of the division of feus (or fees) according to the practice of Scotland, says:—"Fees are also divided into *ligia* and *non ligia*. In a liege-fee the vassal owes absolute fidelity to his immediate over-lord without exception, which is the case of all fees granted by sovereigns; whereas in those granted by subjects, a reservation is always implied with respect to the highest or liege lord; since no subject can at his pleasure throw off the obedience he owes to his sovereign. The obligations resulting from a liege-fee affect not only the lands granted by the sovereign, but the whole other estate of the vassal; for the person of the vassal is, in that kind of fee, subjected to the liege lord, and of consequence, all his estate, even his moveables *quæ sequuntur personam*. And hence our forfeitures have had their rise; the effect of which, when they fall upon a delinquency against the liege lord, reaches to the offender's moveable estate as well as to his heritable." (B. 2, T. 3, § 12.) Crown vassals are designated, in the older writers on Scotch law, *vassalli ligii*.

Linea recta semper præfertur transversali.—The direct line is always preferred to the collateral. This is a rule of law regarding the order of succession. So long as any person exists in the direct line of descendants, he is preferred as heir to all others. Although both descendants and ascendants are included in the term "lineal," the rule expressed in the maxim only applies to lineal descendants, for after them collaterals succeed before ascendants. Bell's Prin. § 1647-1661.

Lis alibi pendens.—A suit elsewhere depending. It is a good preliminary defence to any action, that there is already depending before a competent court another lawsuit between the same parties regarding the same subject or dispute. The other action must, however, be depending before a competent court in Scotland, as it has been decided that another suit pending before an English court does not give rise to this plea, and raises no bar to a similar action being tried in Scotland, if the parties are subject to the jurisdiction of the Scotch courts. The English courts observe the same rule of rejecting the defence of *lis alibi pendens* in Scotch courts. Bell's Dict. v. *Lis pendens.* Shand, i. 201. *Cochran* v. *Paul,* 20 D. 178. It has become not unfrequent in practice, where an action has been raised in Scotland by any one having a depending suit in England against the same defender, and in reference to the same subject-matter, to sist the action in Scotland until the previously depending suit in England has been determined, but this is a matter entirely in the discretion of the court. See the case of *Wilmot,* 3 D. 816, and other cases collected in Shaw's Digest, i. 745, v. *Foreign.* Where an action is depending before the Sheriff or other inferior court, and a similar one is raised before the Court of Session, the plea of *lis alibi* cannot be obviated by appealing the former *ob contingentiam.* *Greig,* 13 S. 635. The effect of this plea is to throw out the action in which it has been successfully maintained. As to what is regarded as a depending action, in reference to this plea, see the cases of *Aitken* v. *Dick,* 1 Macp. 1038, and *Kennedy* v. *Macdonald,* 3 R. 813.

Lis est sopita. Lis est finita.—Synonymous phrases, signifying that the suit is sopited or brought to a conclusion. These phrases mean, not merely that the lawsuit or action is at an end, but that the subject-matter of it, that is, the question regarding which the parties were at issue, is finally determined. This is usually said where the one party has referred the whole matter in dispute to his adversary's oath. Such oath, when explicitly given, is decisive of the cause, and no evidence whatever is admissible to impugn the deposition of the party to whom the reference is made. The clearest evidence of his having committed perjury cannot affect the decision of the cause, which must be decided according to the import of the oath ; and while in such circumstances the person so foresworn may be punished criminally, yet as regards the civil suit, *lis est sopita.*

Lis pendens.—A depending process or suit; an action in the course of being litigated; litiscontestation. This phrase is sometimes used technically to express a preliminary objection to the suit in which it is advanced.

For the nature of this plea, and its effects, see *Lis alibi pendens*.

Litem suam facere.—To make the suit his own. By the civil law, a judge was said to make that suit his own, in which, under the influence of corruption, malice, favour, or fear, or even through ignorance of the law, he pronounced an erroneous judgment. He was said to make the suit *sua*, because, being responsible for his decision, he took upon himself the risk of the suit. The party injured by the erroneous judgment had an action for indemnity against the judge who pronounced it, the amount of which was determined by the judge before whom such action was tried. In Scotland no action lies against an inferior judge in respect of any decision pronounced by him contrary to law; although an action is competent if malice or corruption can be proved against him. But, "the supreme judges of the realm are not amenable to their own or any other tribunal, for anything said or done in a judicial capacity. Where there has been abuse of their high office, the remedy is by petition to the House of Commons, or complaint to the Queen in Council." Smith on Rep. 206. See *Haggart* v. *Hope*, 1 S. 49, affd. H. L. 2 Sh. App. 125.

Litis contestatio.—Litiscontestation. This phrase is borrowed from the civil law, and was the term applied to a ceremony which took place before the magistrate before he delivered the *formula*, under which the question in dispute was to be tried by the *judex*: the ceremony consisted in both parties to the suit calling witnesses (*contestatio*) to the fact that the *lis* or lawsuit had begun. "In the Roman system of civil process the time when a contested right was to be considered as really made the subject of litigation was very carefully marked. It was very necessary that this should be clearly ascertained. The claimant in whose favour the ultimate decision was given was entitled to all that accrued to the thing claimed from this moment; and when once a point had been submitted to litigation, it could not be again litigated, both parties surrendering all their interest into the hands of the Court, which assigned to the successful claimant such a fresh interest in the thing claimed as might appear to be due to him. This time was marked by each party, at the end of the proceedings before the magistrate, calling bystanders to witness that they submitted the matter to the decision of the judge. This was called the *litis contestatio.*" (Sandars' Justinian, Introduction, § 105.) At a later period, when the magistrate and the *judex* were no longer different persons, the *litis contestatio* was fixed by the commencement of the trial. According to Stair (B. 4, T. 39, § 1), litiscontestation in a Scotch action takes place only when an order for proof has been pronounced; but Bankton (B. 4, T. 25, § 5) says that "litiscontestation properly is made by the defender's compearance, and objecting to the pursuer's claim or libel, or proponing peremptory defences against it." And certainly, according to present practice, the effects of litiscontestation, so far as it has any effect in our law, follow (whether the name may be strictly applicable or not) whenever the parties have stated their respective claims and pleas before the Court, and have fairly submitted for judgment the question upon which they are in dispute. After that has taken place, neither party can withdraw from the suit without the leave of the Court, although a pursuer has the statutory right of abandoning his action on payment of the expenses previously incurred by the defender. Any decree pronounced after litiscontestation is a decree *in foro,* even although it may have been pronounced in respect of absence or default. Litiscontestation has with us this further effect, that after this has taken place an action will transmit to and against heirs, which otherwise would not have so transmitted. Ersk. B. 4, T. 1, § 70. See *Actio contra defunctum,* &c.

Litis ordinatio.—The rule or form under which a suit is instituted and carried out.

Locatio.—The contract of location or hiring. Under this contract one party agrees to give the temporary use of a certain subject, or to perform certain services, to the other, in return for which the other party binds himself to make payment of a certain stipulated hire. The person who binds himself to furnish the subject or give the service is called the *locator* or letter; he who binds himself to pay the consideration is called the *conductor* or lessee. These names are those generally applied to the parties to this contract in the civil law, although in particular forms of the contract, the lessees had special names, as *ex. gr.*, the hirer of a house was called *inquilinus*, of a farm, *colonus*. There are three principal kinds of this contract—1. *Locatio rei;* when one person lets a thing and another hires it, as, for example, when one lets and another hires a horse. The duty of the locator under this form of the contract is to provide and deliver the subject, that of the lessee being to use the subject for the specified purpose agreed upon, and to pay the consideration. If the conductor uses the subject for a purpose other than that agreed upon, he must make good any damage thereby occasioned (*Seton*, 8 R. 236); but if, in the using of the subject, he adheres to the terms of his contract, he is not liable for any damage, or for the total loss of the subject (unless where this has been occasioned by his fault), according to the rule, *res perit suo domino*. 2. *Locatio operarum;* the form of the contract where one person lets his services, and another hires them, whether it be for common labour, as of a domestic servant or a workman, or skilled labour, as of a physician or lawyer. Here the obligation of the locator is to do the work stipulated, in the manner and at the time agreed upon, while that of the conductor is to pay the consideration. In the hiring of skilled labour, the locator is bound to bestow attention, art, and skill, on the act or services to be performed, and the want of that skill on his part, on which the conductor was entitled to depend, will render him liable for the consequences arising from that want, because *imperitia culpæ enumeratur*. 3. *Locatio operis* is the name given to that form of the contract of location where one person contracts for the performance of a particular piece of work, and another contracts to do it, as for example, the building of a house. See the case of *M'Intyre*, 2 R. 278, as to the non-liability of the locator to make good part of the work performed by him but destroyed by a *damnum fatale*. The contract for the conveyance of goods, called the *locatio operis vehundarum mercium* (one of the forms of the *locatio operis*), is that under which a carrier contracts for the safe delivery of goods committed to him. His duty is to deliver the goods according to order; and, in the ordinary case, he is liable for their value if lost, under the provisions of the edict *nautæ caupones,* &c. He is not liable if the loss has been occasioned by what are known as the acts of God, or of the Queen's enemies, except in the special case of the goods perishing through accidental fire, in which case the carrier has been declared liable for the value of the goods by statute (19 & 20 Vict. c. 60, § 17). The contract of location gave rise, under the civil law, to the actions *directa* and *contraria,* and, under our law, gives rise to similar actions. See *Actio.*

Locatio navis.—The letting or hiring of a ship. When a ship is chartered for a certain voyage in return for a certain freight, the contract is *locatio vehundarum mercium,* and this is the most common kind of contract between the owner and freighter of a vessel. Under this contract the shipmaster and crew are the servants of the owner, who is responsible to the freighter or others for their acts. But if the contract be *locatio navis* (or, as it is sometimes called, *locatio navis et operarum magistri et nauticorum* — the letting or hiring of the ship, as well as the services of the master and crew) the charterer becomes, for the time, practically the owner of the vessel and the employer of the master and crew. In the language of the law of England, such a contract amounts to a demise of the ship; and under it the charterer incurs the responsibilities of ownership. The distinction is well brought out in the judgment of the Lord Ordinary in the case of *Mitchell* v. *Burn,* 1 R. 900, where the authorities on the subject are collected.

Locator.—Lessor. The person who, in the contract of location, provides the subject or the services to be given on hire, and receives the consideration therefor.

Loco facti non præstabilis, vel non præstiti, succedit damnum et interesse.—Damages come in the place of an act which cannot be, or has not been, performed. The non-performance of a contract subjects the party failing to a claim of damages at the instance of the other party to it, whether the failure arises from a refusal or inability to perform. Thus if A and B enter into a contract whereby A binds himself to deliver a certain commodity to B, and thereafter refuses to make delivery, he will be liable in damages. Even where A is unable to procure the commodity contracted for, he is liable in damages, because B was entitled to rely upon delivery, and to make his arrangements accordingly. A will also be liable in damages, in the event of his having disabled himself from fulfilling his contract by selling or delivering the commodity to some other purchaser. The different circumstances of each case would determine the amount of the damages to be awarded, but damages to some extent would be due in each. See the case of *E. of Galloway* v. *Stewart*, 24 D. 93, reversed H. L. 3 Macp. 73. See also *Lex non cogit*, &c.

Loco parentis.—In the place of a parent. Tutors appointed to children, by the will or testament of their father, stand *in loco parentis* to the pupils. They have the control of the pupils' persons (although in the general case this faculty is not exercised where their mother, or other near relative, is surviving), as well as the administration of their estate. The office of tutor falls on the children attaining minority, when they acquire a *persona standi* which they could not previously have, and are entitled to perform certain acts for themselves, which until then could only be performed by their tutors on their behalf.

Loco rerum immobilium.—In the place or position of immoveable things. This phrase is used by Erskine (B. 3, T. 9, § 4) in reference to the question whether the shares of trading companies, or of the public stocks of any country, are to be regarded as moveables, and dealt with, in questions of succession, according to the law of the domicile; or as immoveable, and subject to the rules of the *lex rei sitæ*. He says—" A question having been moved whether debentures granted for money lent to the public in Ireland, and secured to the creditors by an Act of the Irish Parliament, were to be held *loco rerum immobilium* (*i.e.*, as of the character of immoveables), it was adjudged that they were not, but that they descended as proper moveables *secundum legem domicilii*."

Loco tutoris.—In the place of a tutor. The Court of Session is in the practice of appointing, on application made for such appointment, a factor *loco tutoris* on the estates of pupils not having tutors. Such an appointment places the factor in the same position towards the pupil, both as regards his person and the administration of his estate, as if he held the office by virtue of relationship and was tutor-at-law, or had received the appointment of tutor from the pupil's father under his testamentary settlement, the only difference being that the office of a tutor appointed by the Court is not gratuitous. The duties and obligations pertaining to the office of factor *loco tutoris*, and the forms to be observed in applying for their appointment, were originally laid down in an Act of Sederunt of 13th February, 1730, but applications of this kind having become very numerous, and it having " been found that the existing regulations and the present means of enforcing them, are imperfect and insufficient for preventing in many instances the occurrence of great irregularity in the conduct of such factors," an Act was passed for the " better protection of the property of pupils," &c. (12 & 13 Vict. c. 51), which now regulates the procedure for the appointment of the factor, as well as the duties the performance of which is incumbent upon every one holding such office.

Locupletari cum damno alterius. — To be enriched through the damage or injury sustained by another. It is an equitable rule of law that no one shall be so enriched, and accordingly, any one acquiring gain through damage inflicted on another is liable in restitution. So an heir (who in the general case is not bound by nor responsible for the delict of his ancestor) is liable in restitution to the person injured, if he has been enriched by the act or delict which occasioned the injury. Penal actions raised against the ancestor transmit against the heir if he has taken any benefit from the delict on which they are founded. See *In quantum locupletiores*, &c.

Locupletior aliena jactura.—Richer through the loss, or at the expense of another. Ross, L. C. (L. R.) iii. 147. See *Nemo debet ex alieno*, &c.

Locus contractus.—The place of the contract ; *i.e.*, the place where the contract was entered into. See *Lex loci contractus*.

Locus delicti.—The place of the delict, or where the delict was committed. The commission of a delict or crime invests the judge within whose territory it has been committed with an exclusive jurisdiction *quoad* it over the person guilty of it. " The common law considers crimes as altogether local, and cognisable and punishable exclusively in the country where they are committed. No other nation, therefore, has any right to punish them, or is under any obligation to take notice of or to enforce any judgment rendered in such cases by the tribunals having authority to hold jurisdiction within the territory where they are committed. Hence it is that a criminal sentence of attainder in the courts of one sovereign, although it there creates a personal disability to sue, does not carry the same disability with the person into other countries." (Story, Con. of Laws, § 620.) It is immaterial in such a case to inquire to what country the offender belongs, or to what jurisdiction in civil matters he is amenable; for criminal jurisdiction arises *ratione delicti*. In all criminal libels or indictments the *locus delicti* must be clearly set forth, and with as much precision as the circumstances will admit of. The alleged offender is entitled to this, because he may be able to prove that at the time when the offence was committed he was elsewhere than at the libelled *locus;* and where the *locus* is stated, it is necessary, to warrant a conviction, that the place be proved as set forth in the libel.

Locus pœnitentiæ.—Place or opportunity for repentance, or change of intention. So long as a bargain remains uncompleted by the parties to it, each of them has an opportunity of resiling therefrom, and this opportunity is called the *locus pœnitentiæ*. A great variety of cases might be given in illustration of this. For example, if one party making an offer, which if accepted by the person to whom it is addressed would constitute a completed contract, changes his mind before acceptance, or after the time allowed for acceptance has expired, he has the power of resiling from his offer, so as not to be bound by it. Again, if two persons, having a dispute, agree to enter into a submission of the subject of it to an arbiter chosen by them, either may resile from this agreement before the deed of submission has been executed;

or if a landlord agree to give a certain lease of lands to one desirous of becoming his tenant, he may resile from this agreement before the lease has been granted. So long as the bargain or agreement remains incomplete, there remains this power of resiling, for until then the final assent is held not to have been given. The power of resiling may, however, be barred by *rei interventus*, which is the occurrence of some act or circumstance on the faith of the uncompleted bargain being completed. Thus if the landlord who agreed to give the lease allowed the tenant to enter on possession of the lands in pursuance of the verbal arrangement, he has no longer the *locus pœnitentiœ*, but is bound to complete his bargain by granting the stipulated lease. Homologation, which is an act approbatory of a preceding engagement (and similar in principle to *rei interventus*), also bars the power of resiling. Thus if, in pursuance of the agreement to submit, the parties have appeared before the arbiter, and been heard on their respective claims, neither of them can resile on the ground that the submission has been informal or incomplete, for, by their appearance, they have homologated the informal or incomplete agreement, and are held as having departed from all objection thereto.

Locus regit actum.—The place governs the act. An act done or contract made is to be construed, and its effect and validity determined, by the law of the place where the contract was made or act performed. For an instance of the use of this maxim, see *Lloyd* v. *Guibert*, L. R. 1, Q. B. 119. See *Lex loci contractus*.

Locus rei sitæ.—The place where the subject is situated. See *Lex rei sitœ*.

Locus solutionis.—The place of payment or performance.

Luce clarius.—Clearer than light.

Luce meridiana clariores.—Clearer than the light at mid-day. "In occult crimes, where criminals study the greatest privacy, and which hardly admit of a direct proof by witnesses, as adultery, incest, forgery, presumptions are sustained as evidence, from the necessity of the case. But because of the severity of the conclusion in criminal trials, the circumstances which constitute the presumptions ought, in the style of the doctors, to be *luce meridiana clariores*, so strong and violent as to carry full conviction to every unprejudiced mind." (Ersk. B. 4, T. 4, § 99.) This phrase is most frequently written *Luce clarius*.

Lucratus.—Gained; acquired; enriched. This word imports only clear gain, or profit. When, therefore, it is said that an executor, with benefit of inventory, is liable for the deceased's debts in so far as he is *lucratus*, it does not mean that he is liable for debts to the extent of the sum which the estate yielded, but to the extent of that sum, less all the expenses attendant upon its realisation. If a person honestly, and for an onerous consideration, purchases an article which has been stolen, and thereafter sells it for a higher price than that paid by him for it, he is liable to the true owner for the amount of the excess in the sum received over that which he paid,—that being the extent to which he is *lucratus*. See *In quantum lucratus*, &c.

Lucrum cessans, aut damnum emergens.—Gain ceasing, or damage arising. For damage of either kind, the person causing it is liable. An instance of the former may be found in the damage sustained by a wife through the culpable homicide of her husband, for thereby she is deprived of that pecuniary support which her husband afforded, and which, on his death, ceased; while the second may be instanced by the case of a person severely injured by assault, or otherwise, from which arises the expense attendant upon his recovery, the loss of work, &c.

Ludere in extremis.—To play or make sport on deathbed. See *Nemo præsumitur ludere*, &c.

Luito cum persona qui luere non potest cum crumena.—Let him pay in his person who cannot pay out of his purse. A phrase rarely used, which has its illustration in the ordinary sentence of imprisonment, on failure to pay a fine, or money penalty. In England, before imprisonment for civil debt was abolished, the imprisonment of a debtor was held to be satisfaction of the debt; the debtor thus paid in his person what he could not pay in money.

M

Magister navis.—The master of a ship; whose acts as master bind the owners. See *Exercitor*.

Magistratus majores.—Superior magistrates. "It would seem that by the Roman law, none but the *magistratus majores*, or supreme courts, had a power of reviewing their own definite judgments. And though by our customs several inferior judges, as sheriff-deputies, commissaries of Edinburgh, and bailies of boroughs, may review interlocutory judgments pronounced by themselves, till decree be extracted in the cause; yet no inferior court has an implied right of reviewing any definite sentence of its own, so as, without special statutory powers, to suspend or set it aside, after it hath, by the clerk's giving forth an extract, become a decree. From that period the judge's right of cognition ceaseth; whereas our supreme civil court can review, not only the decrees of inferior judges, but their own." (Ersk. B. 1, T. 2, § 6.) This power of review must now be understood in a more limited sense than that seemingly indicated by Erskine. All the judges of the Court of Session have not the power of reviewing their own decisions. The Lords Ordinary cannot do so, although their judgments may be reviewed by either Division of the Inner House; nor can the judges of either Division review a judgment pronounced by them, in the case in which it is pronounced. They may review it to the effect of overturning or disregarding it in any subsequent case, but when a definite judgment has been pronounced in a cause, the supreme, alike with inferior judges, become *functi officio* as regards it. *Cuthill* v. *Burns*, 24 D. 849. This rule, however, does not preclude the Court from correcting *de recenti* a clerical error, or *error calculi* in a signed interlocutor, and in the case of *Harvey* v. *Lindsay*, 2 R. 980, the Court cancelled an interlocutor dismissing an appeal as incompetent, on the ground that the interlocutor had been pronounced and signed under an error in point of fact, induced by the parties.

Majorennitati proximus.—Near majority. Minors are restored by our law *in integrum*, against any deed granted, or obligation undertaken by them to their lesion during minority, and it will not bar their right to this privilege that they were near majority when the deed or obligation was granted. The obligations of a minor are, however, binding upon him, if at the time of incurring them he represented himself to be major, and his appearance warranted a belief in his statement, as otherwise he would be taking benefit from his own fraud. The fact of a minor's being near majority is chiefly of importance in redarguing the presumption of law that the person who contracted with him was taking advantage of his youth and inexperience. See the case of *Wilkie*, 12 S. 506, where the minor was near majority, but the privilege of his minority was denied him; and the case of *Dennistoun*, 12 D. 613, where the privilege was given effect to.

Majori minus inest.—The greater includes the less. A conveyance of the principal subject carries with it all its accessories to the grantee, although not expressly enumerated. Thus a disposition of heritable property is held to convey not merely the property, but also the lesser rights attached to it, such as servitudes; and an assignation, in like manner, to a personal debt, carries the interest due upon it, as well as all action competent for its recovery. So also under an indictment charging murder, a verdict of culpable homicide may competently be returned; the latter being less than and covered by the former and greater charge. This phrase is sometimes written, *Majus includit minus.*

Majus dignum trahit ad se minus dignum.—The more worthy draws to itself that which is less worthy. Less literally, this maxim may be rendered: The lesser right follows the greater, or, in the words of another maxim, The accessory follows the principal. Thus a right of servitude follows the right of property in the dominant tenement, because the greater right of property draws to itself all the lesser rights involved in it. The assignation of a debt, on the same principle, confers also the right to sue for and enforce it.

Majus et minus non variant speciem.—Greater and less do not alter the kind. An obligation or a right are not altered or affected by the circumstance that much or little depends upon its enforcement. In short, consequences do not affect the right to enforce. See an example of the use of this maxim (which sufficiently illustrates its meaning) in the case of *Pullar,* 3 R. 1176.

Mala demonstratio.—Erroneous description. See *Falsa demonstratio,* &c.

Mala grammatica non vitiat chartam.—Grammatical error does not vitiate a writing or deed. If the meaning be clear and intelligible, and the substantial facts expressed, no account is taken of grammatical inaccuracies. *Mackintosh,* 4 S. 190; and *M'Ghie,* 5 S. 758. In the latter case the word "*dici*" in the notary's docquet to a sasine was spelt "*disi,*" but the objection stated on this, among other grounds, was repelled. See *Falsa grammatica,* &c.

Maledicta expositio quæ corrumpit textum.—That is a bad exposition (or interpretation) which corrupts the text; or, it is a bad construction which sets aside the text, or brings it to nought. This is a rule of construction, and is the converse of the rule *Benedicta expositio,* &c., which see. Where deeds or statutes are, through ambiguity or other obscurity, open to construction, that construction will prevail which is most in accordance with the spirit and purpose of the writing construed, and which will at same time rather preserve it and render it effectual, than destroy or render it nugatory. It is plainly inadmissible to construe any writ in such a manner as to render it meaningless, so long as any other construction is possible: for persons who execute deeds are supposed to have intended to do something, and not to have executed their writ with no meaning and for no purpose. The writ may be ineffectual to do what was intended—but that is a judgment upon its effect, when construed, rather than a legal construction of it.

Malitia capitalis.—Deadly malice: "bitter and deep-rooted malice." Dickson, § 1761.

Malitia supplet ætatem.—Malice supplies the place of

age. A child still in pupilarity committing a crime is not amenable to the ordinary punishment inflicted upon adults for its commission, because the law presumes that the child acts in ignorance, and that there is thus wanting the criminal intention which forms the essence of every crime. If, however, this intention can be proved, that supplies the defect in age, and takes away the legal presumption in the pupil's favour. See the case of *Fulton*, 2 Swinton, 564, where a boy under the age of fourteen was convicted of the crime of rape, and had sentence of transportation. This presumption in favour of the pupil has place *a fortiori* in crimes created by statute, where the offence committed is a *malum prohibitum*, not a *malum in se*, and where, consequently, the criminal character of the act is not so obvious.

Malitiis hominum non est indulgendum.—Indulgence is not to be shown to the malicious desires of men. This may be best explained by quoting a passage from Erskine, in which the phrase occurs—" As all servitudes are restraints upon property, they are *stricti juris*, and so not to be inferred by implication. Neither does the law give them countenance, unless they have some tendency to promote the advantage of the dominant tenement. No man, therefore, who has not acquired an interest in his neighbour's grounds by an antecedent right of pasturage, can, by any stipulation, restrain him from pasturing on his own property as many cattle as he shall think fit to set upon it ; for *malitiis hominum non est indulgendum*. Upon this ground the Roman law required, towards the constitution of a servitude, vicinity in the dominant and servient tenements." (B. 2, T. 9, § 33.) Upon the same ground our law will prohibit any proprietor putting his property to any use which is not for his own advantage, but is merely *in æmulationem vicini*.

Malum in se.—Bad (or wrong) in itself. This name is given to any wrongful act, the culpability of which arises from its being contrary to the law of nature or the rules of morality, and which may form the subject of indictment. Formerly all serious offences against morality were punished criminally, as, for example, blasphemy and adultery ; but now offences against morality merely, which do not violate the declared and recognised laws of the land, are not made the subject of criminal prosecution. The acts falling under this general designation, as the name implies, must be wrong in themselves, such as murder, theft, perjury, &c., and not merely rendered illegal by statutory enactment.

Malum prohibitum.—A wrongful act, because a prohibited act. Such acts are distinguished from the *mala in se* in this respect, that these being opposed to morality and law, are wrong in themselves, while *mala prohibita* are not criminal in themselves, but become illegal by virtue of their prohibition. Thus salmon-fishing cannot be regarded at any time as in itself an illegal act, but by virtue of statutory enactment it is rendered so during a specific period of the year; and by the Public House Act (1853) certain practices were declared illegal which had not previously been considered so, but were, on the contrary, universal in their adoption by the persons in that particular trade.

Malum regimen.—Bad or unskilful (medical) treatment. In cases of homicide it is sometimes pleaded in defence that the deceased died, not from the effects of the act which the prisoner is charged with committing, but in consequence of unskilful medical treatment. As to the effect of such a defence, see Hume i. 184.

Malus animus.—Bad intention: which along with the overt act to carry the bad intention into effect constitutes crime. Hume, i. 23.

Malus usus est abolendus.—Bad custom or usage is to be abolished. Custom or usage long enough continued has the force of law; all common law is the result of usage. But to have this effect, the custom must not, in its origin, be contrary to reason, nature, or right; and if, in course of time, it should become so, then the custom must yield. Broom, 921. See *Communis error*, &c.

Mandatarius terminos sibi positos transgredi non potest. —A mandatory cannot go beyond the limits prescribed to him by the mandate. A mandatory is one who acts on the authority of another (called the mandant), and that not for his own, but for that other's behoof. As the mandatory's authority for acting is the mandate which the mandant has given, he is bound to observe its terms, and cannot effectually do anything which exceeds the limits of the authority so given. All that a mandatory does within the authority of the mandate is binding upon the mandant, but anything done in excess of the limits of the mandate binds the mandatory only. So, again, the mandatory can only seek relief from obligations undertaken, or reimbursement of expenditure made on the authority of the mandate, or in the proper pursuance of its object: the mandant is not liable in any other relief or reimbursement than this, because beyond this it was not authorised. Not only must the mandatory observe the limits of his mandate, but so must also those with whom he deals in that character, if they desire to have the mandant responsible to them; for although they may be acting in the best faith, and relying upon the statements and representations of the mandatory, yet, if the thing done is beyond the power conferred by the mandate, the mandant is not responsible. In general agency, an agent may act so as to bind his principal to third parties in a matter not authorised by the principal (Bell's Prin. § 219); but agency is not merely mandate: it is more. The contract of mandate is gratuitous, and the mandatory can claim no recompense for his actings: when the contract ceases to be gratuitous, it becomes agency. Testamentary trustees may be taken as examples of what are, in the strict sense, mandatories: but the contract of mandate has now been almost superseded by agency or factory.

Mandatum nisi gratuitum nullum est.—It is not mandate unless it be gratuitous. See above.

Manifesta probatione non indigent.—What is manifest needs no proof. See *Lex non requirit*.

Manu aliena.—By the hand of another. Formerly, when sasines were necessary to complete a feudal right, those given *propriis manibus* required no antecedent precept, while those given *manu aliena*, that is, by the hands of another than the person from whom the right proceeded, required such an authority to warrant the sasine, and to make it effectual. The words of this phrase are also frequently to be found in the long docquet which the notary required at one time to append to the instrument of sasine. It was customary for him there to state, although not essential to the validity of the deed, that the instrument had been written *manu mea* by his own hand, or *manu aliena* by the hand of some other person. The long docquet was abolished along with the old form of instrument by the Act 8 & 9 Vict. c. 35, and the instrument of sasine was, by the Titles to Land Act (1858), declared unnecessary, and the conveyance itself allowed to be recorded instead. The last-mentioned Act was repealed, but at same time practically re-enacted by the Titles to Land Consolidation (Scotland) Act, 1868.

Manu militari.—By military aid. "By our present practice, since the union of the two kingdoms in 1707, where one opposes by violence the execution of a decree, or any lawful diligence, which the civil magistrate is not able by himself and his officers to make good, application is made to the military for assistance, who enforce the execution *manu militari.*" (Ersk. B. 4, T. 3, § 17.)

Manu propria.—By one's own hand.

Maritagium.—The casualty of marriage. Under the feudal system the superior was entitled to this casualty on the marriage of the heir who succeeded to the estate. If the heir was a female, the superior was entitled to select for her a husband, and she could not refuse the person so selected without forfeiting her estate, or at least as much as the match was estimated to be worth. In the case of a male heir, the superior was also entitled to this casualty, which varied in value in different cases, but was generally equal to the tocher which the heir received. The casualty was excluded if the heir married during the lifetime of the ancestor, because during his life the heir was not the superior's ward, and the superior had, consequently, no right to dispose of the heir in marriage. This casualty of superiority was abolished by the statute 20 Geo. II. c. 50.

Materna maternis.—The goods acquired through the mother descend to those connected with her. "In the Roman law, where a person died leaving half-brothers, both consanguinean and uterine, a distinction was taken as to his succession between what he had derived from his father and what he had derived from his mother. The former went to his brothers-consanguinean, the latter to his brothers-uterine, on the maxim *paterna paternis, materna maternis.* And, generally, the principle of the maxim applied to any competition between relations on the father's and mother's side. This rule has no place in the law of Scotland, where the half-blood uterine, and in general all the relations by the mother's side, are excluded from succeeding." Bell's Dict. *h.v.* This last sentence must be read as now modified by the Act 18 & 19 Vict. c. 23, which gives, in certain circumstances, the half-blood uterine the right of succeeding to the one-half of the moveable estate of an intestate. See *Frater fratri uterino*, &c.

Matrimonia debent esse libera.—Marriages ought to be free. Full and free consent is essential to the contract of marriage, and force or fraud will have the same effect in nullifying it as it would have in the case of any other contract. The force founded upon for that purpose must, however, have been such as the person pleading it could not have withstood. The mere force of parental influence, or threat of parental displeasure, disinheritance, &c., is not sufficient; nor would fraudulent misrepresentations as to wealth, rank, &c. In application of the principle of this maxim certain restraints put upon marriage are regarded as null; and obligations or bonds granted in consideration of bringing about a certain marriage are also held null as interfering with the freedom by which the consent to marry ought to be characterised. See *Conditio illicita*, &c.

Matrimonium ipsum.—Marriage itself. Present consent alone is essential by the law of Scotland to constitute marriage; but the consent, to have this effect, must not refer to a ceremony to be celebrated at a future date. Thus, in a marriage-contract, where the parties consent to take each other as lawful spouses, and bind themselves to solemnise the marriage, the consent does not constitute marriage, but merely an obligation to marry, from which either party may resile. The consent must be given with the view of constituting marriage at the time when it is given. Ersk. B. 1, T. 4, § 5, with Lord Ivory's note. 139. "Nor will a written declaration of marriage, found in one's repositories after death, or so framed as to be effectual only after death, be a legal constitution of marriage." Bell's Prin. § 1515. See *Consensus non concubitus*, &c.

Media concludendi.—The grounds of action; those allegations or grounds on which the pursuer of an action seeks to have decree pronounced in terms of the conclusions of his summons. When the allegations so made are insufficient, or are such that, being admitted or proved, the conclusions libelled would not follow according to law, the summons is said, technically, to be irrelevant.

Media sententia.—A middle view or opinion. This phrase is quoted by Bell (Prin. § 1298) from the Institutes of Justinian, who settled the controversy regarding specification which took place between the rival factions of jurists, the Sabinians and Proculeians, by adopting the *media sententia.* To state very briefly the nature of this controversy, and the view taken by the Roman Emperor, and now adopted by our law, will be the most satisfactory manner in which to explain and illustrate the present phrase. The Proculeians held that specification, by changing the form of the raw material, changed its nature, and replaced it by something quite new, and that, therefore, the maker of the new article was the owner of it, and not the person to whom belonged the material of which it was made. The Sabinians, on the other hand, were of opinion that the material retained its original nature, and continued to subsist, notwithstanding its change of form, and that, accordingly, the new article belonged to the proprietor of the material. Neither of these extreme views were adopted by Justinian, who followed a middle opinion, based upon this distinction : " If the thing made can be reduced to its former rude materials, then the owner of the materials is also considered the owner of the thing made; but if the thing cannot be so reduced, then he who made it is the owner of it." (Just. Inst. B. 2, T. 1, § 25.) The distinction sanctioned by Justinian, decided the question according to the fact of there being or not being a really new thing made. If there was, then the reasoning of the Proculeians held good, and the maker became the owner by a species of occupation, *quia quod factum est, ante nullius fuerat* (because that which was made had not previously belonged to any one). If the thing made was only the old materials in a new form, then it belonged to the owner of the materials, in accordance with the opinions of the Sabinians. The opinion of each school, therefore, was admitted where the facts were in accordance with it. The rules of our law upon this matter follow the *media sententia* of Justinian, and will be found stated in Bell, *supra*. The reader will find an instructive case upon the subject in *Wylie & Lochhead* v. *Mitchell*, 8 Macp. 552. It may just be noted, with regard to the two great schools of Roman jurists above mentioned, that they took their names from those of their leaders, both of whom flourished in the time of Augustus; the distinguishing feature between them being, that the Proculeians, the disciples of Proculus, endeavoured to enlarge the principles of the Roman law, and did not hesitate to make such innovations as they conceived a more liberal philosophy and reason to require; while the Sabinians, the disciples of Sabinus, adhered with scrupulous fidelity to the legal doctrines as they had been handed down to them.

Medio tempore.—In the meantime. (Stair, B. 1, T. 6, § 45.)

Meditatio fugæ.—The intention of absconding. See *In meditatione fugœ*.

Medium concludendi.—The ground on which the conclusions of a summons are based : the ground of action.

Medium filum fluminis.—The middle line of the river. This is the imaginary line or *thread* drawn down the centre of a private river, which forms the boundary of the property belonging to riparian proprietors on the opposite banks. See *Ad medium filum*.

Medium impedimentum.—A mid-impediment; which is defined to be "anything which intervenes between two events, and prevents, *quoad* the former event, the retrospective operation of the latter." (Bell's Dict. *h.v.*) The term mid-impediment is most frequently used in the language of Scotch law-writers, to indicate that obstacle which in certain circumstances (under the rules of conveyancing formerly existing) prevented a disponee whose holding was base from having it made public by confirmation. To illustrate this, take the following case: A disponed to B certain lands to be holden *a me*, on which B was duly infeft; thereafter A disponed the same lands to C with a similar holding, who was duly infeft and obtained confirmation from the superior. The lands in such a case were vested in C to the exclusion of B, although

B's sasine was first on record, because B's right was imperfect, and could not come into competition with the right of C, until confirmed, and confirmation was rendered impossible or ineffectual by the *mid-impediment* occasioned by the confirmation in favour of C. But for that mid-impediment B might at any time have rendered his right complete and indefeasible by confirmation. The result, however, would have been different if the holding in B's right had been alternative (*a me vel de me*), for in that case his sasine on the *de me* precept would have vested him indefeasibly with the property, while C's prior confirmation would only have created in his favour a mid-superiority. This form of mid-impediment cannot now occur, since, by the Act 37 & 38 Vict. c. 94, confirmation by the superior has been abolished, and every proprietor duly infeft in his subjects is held to be, by such infeftment, duly entered with the superior. This mid-impediment of former days gave rise to many nice questions, and the reader may be referred on the subject of it to Menzies' Lectures, 637, and Duff's Feud. Con. 221-23. The term will, however, be also found used otherwise than in connection with the subject just referred to. For example, it was at one time questioned whether an intervening marriage of one or both of the parents formed a mid-impediment to the legitimation *per subsequens matrimonium* of children born prior to that marriage. It was held that it did not. Fraser, Par. & Ch. 37.

Melior est conditio possidentis vel defendentis.—The condition of a possessor or of a defender, is better. The condition of a possessor of a subject concerning the right to which there is a dispute, is better than that of the person challenging the right of possession, and claiming the subject. The advantage of the possessor consists in this, that he requires to show no title, while the challenger must do so, and even then the possessor is preferred to the subject, unless the challenger can show a better title than that on which the possessor holds. The condition of a defender is better than that of a pursuer, because the whole *onus* of proving his case lies on the pursuer. See *In re communi*, &c.

Meliorem conditionem suam facere minor potest, deteriorem nequaquam.—A minor can make his condition better, never worse. A minor entering into a contract which is to his disadvantage, can be restored against it; he is not bound by obligations which would have the effect of diminishing his estate. This rule proceeds upon the necessity and propriety of protecting a minor against his own inexperience or folly, and also *in pœnam* of those who would take advantage of his inexperience. If, however, the bargain or contract is advantageous to the minor, he may enforce it; and in that case the person contracting with him cannot have the bargain set aside on the ground of the minor's minority. The minor may, however, in some cases lose this privilege, regarding which, see *Majorennitati proximus.* See also *Minor tenetur,* &c.

Melius est ut decem noxii evadant quam ut unus innocens pereat.—It is better that ten guilty persons should escape than that one innocent person should perish or suffer.

Mendicatorie.—Supplicatingly. Stair, B. 1, T. 12, § 2.

Mens rea.—Guilty purpose; criminal intention. See *Actus non facit,* &c.

Mens testatoris in testamentis spectanda est.—In the construction of wills, the intention of the testator is to be regarded. This is the leading rule in the construction of all testamentary writings. They are supposed to express the intention of the testator, and to that intention the Courts are bound, and always ready to give effect. This holds true, however, only in those cases where the will is open to construction; for if the expression be clear, and free from ambiguity, it will be given effect to, although it may appear from the deed that the provision so expressed is not in harmony with the general scope or intention of the deed. Words, again, which have a technical signification attached to them by law must be received as if used in that sense; it is not permissible to argue that the testator did not know of the technical meaning, or that he had an intention other than that which the technical meaning conveys. "I agree that this is a question of intention, to be collected from the words of the trust-disposition; but if certain words are employed which have obtained a known and settled meaning by law, we are not at liberty to look behind them in order to discover some other intention in the mind of the testator different from their legal import." (per Lord Chelmsford, in *Ralston* v. *Hamilton*, 4 Macq. 418). In a word, where the deed is clearly expressed the Court will hold that the testator's intention was that to which expression has been given; but where doubt may fairly be entertained as to the meaning of the deed, or any of its clauses or provisions, the testator's presumed intention, gathered from the rest of the deed, will prevail over any other construction. On this subject see the case of *Finlay* v. *Mackenzie*, 2 R. 909.

Mera facta quæ in meris faciendi finibus consistunt.— Mere acts, which consist merely in bare performance. For an explanation of this phrase, see Fraser, Mas. & Ser. 38.

Merx et pretium.—Goods, and a price. These two things are necessary to every valid contract of sale, namely, the commodity to be sold, and the determinate money price to be paid therefor. It is not a sale, but barter, where anything other than money is given in exchange for the commodity.

Messis sementem sequitur.—The crop follows the sower —*i.e.*, the sower is entitled to reap the crop. This maxim is applied to cases of *bona fide* possession, and on the principle of it, it is held that a person who sows a crop on lands of which he is in possession, and of which he has reason to believe himself the proprietor, is entitled to reap that crop, although it is discovered in the meantime that another person has a preferable title to the land, and he (the sower) has been dispossessed. The executor of a deceased person is entitled also on the principle of this maxim to reap the crop which the deceased sowed.

Metus causa.—Through fear. If the consent of a party to a deed or contract has been extorted through fear, he may reduce either on that ground. But the fear must be a just fear, and such as, in the circumstances, the person could not withstand. See *Ex capite metus*.

Metus perjurii.—The fear of perjury. On this ground the evidence of the parties to a cause, and that of their relatives, was formerly excluded. It was feared that their own, or their relatives', interest in the result of the cause might lead them to give false evidence, in order to bring about a favourable decision. This, however, is no longer law. The desire to obtain all the light possible on the facts in dispute, has overcome the *metus perjurii.*

Miles.—A soldier; but this name was also given anciently to all vassals, who held lands under the obligation of rendering military service to their superior therefor. Ersk. B. 2, T. 4, § 2.

Minor meliorem conditionem suam facere potest deteriorem nequaquam.—A minor can improve or better his condition, he cannot make it worse. See *Meliorem conditionem,* &c.

Minor non tenetur placitare super hereditate paterna.—A minor is not bound to defend at law his right to his ancestor's heritage; when that right is challenged by one who claims the heritage on a title preferable to that which existed in the minor's ancestor. During minority the minor is not even bound to declare whether he will take up the succession, but is allowed six months after he has attained majority to deliberate whether he will do so or not. "This privilege is limited to proper feudal heritage, and does not extend to leases, however long the period of endurance. Nor does it apply to the settling of marches, nor to the division of land, nor to a possessory action, nor to an action at the instance of the superior for feu-duties or casualties, nor where the action has been commenced in the lifetime of the ancestor. In order to entitle the minor to state this plea, he must be served heir and infeft; and his infeftment, when produced, supersedes all further production till he be of age. It is the heir of investiture alone who can plead the privilege; and it cannot be pleaded to support the fraud of the ancestor, nor to oppose the effect of the ancestor's obligation, nor in opposition to a minor suing for reduction on the head of minority and lesion." (Bell's Dict. *v. Minor.*) *Placitare* signifies to be a party to a suit, from *placitum,* a vocable of the middle ages for suit or process. Ersk. B. 1, T. 7, § 43.

Minor tenetur in quantum locupletior factus.—A minor is bound to the extent to which he has been enriched or benefited. A minor on attaining majority has the privilege of reducing any deed granted, or obligation undertaken, and of repudiating any transaction entered into with or for him, if the same has been to his lesion. But if he has been benefited thereby, his privilege is excluded, for it would be obviously unjust to allow him to reap the advantage, and thereafter repudiate the transaction which conferred it. This would be directly opposed to the maxim, *Nemo debet ex alieno damno lucrari*. The measure, therefore, of the minor's benefit or lesion is the measure of his privilege. If he has been altogether benefited by the transaction, his privilege is altogether excluded, but if he has suffered lesion, he can plead his privilege to the effect of being restored against that which caused it, and to the extent of the injury inflicted.

Minus est actionem habere quam rem.—Literally, it is less to have a right of action than to have the thing; which means that a mere right of action or *jus ad rem* is a lesser right than one in the thing itself or *jus in re*. The distinction between the two rights has already been pointed out under *Jus in re*.

Minus solvit qui tardius solvit nam et tempore minus solvitur.—He pays too little who pays tardily (*i.e.*, delays payment), for owing to the very delay too little is paid. This is the principle on which, under the civil law and our own, interest is exigible from a debtor who does not pay his debt when it is due. Obviously, he who pays a debt after it is due is paying less than the creditor is entitled to demand. The creditor is entitled to his money when it is due, that he may put it to his own use and profit; and so long as the payment is delayed, such use and profit is withheld from the creditor; indeed, is being reaped by the debtor. The creditor is thus getting, and the debtor is paying less than is due, if payment be delayed or withheld after payment becomes exigible.

Misera est servitus ubi jus est vagum aut incertum.—" Obedience to law becomes a hardship when that law is unsettled or doubtful" (Broom, 150). Laws are enacted to meet those cases which most frequently happen, and so as to preserve the rights and promote the interests of the great body of the people. It cannot, however, but happen that a measure passed for the general advantage will sometimes bear hardly upon individual interests, and that the application of the strict rules of law will result in hardship to some.

The endeavour to do something by which that hardship may be mitigated is natural, although it may not be wise ; hard cases are said, on this very account, to make bad law. A variable or uncertain law makes the rights of parties determinable by that law necessarily uncertain—resulting in frequent litigation, and even worse consequences. It is not possible—at least it is difficult and painful—to render obedience when the command is not clear ; if what constitutes the offence be not well defined, no one can tell when he has offended, or know how to avoid offence. It has been well said with regard to the rules of law that "when once established and recognised, their justice or injustice in the abstract is of less importance to the community than that the rules themselves shall be constant and invariable." Per Lord Chancellor Westbury in *Ralston* v. *Hamilton,* 4 Macq. 405.

Mitiores pœnæ nobis semper placuere.—Literally, lighter punishments are always more pleasing to us ; *i.e.*, it is more pleasing to inflict a light than a severe punishment. Stair, B. 2, T. 11, § 31.

Mitiori sensu.—In the sense or meaning more favourable to the obligant ; that is, in the sense imposing the least burden or obligation.

Mobilia sequuntur personam.—Moveables follow the person. By a legal fiction, moveables are always regarded as having no locality of their own (*Mobilia situm non habent*), but as being situated in that place where their owner has his domicile. Thus if a Scotchman having moveable property situated in Scotland be domiciled in England at the time of his death, the succession thereto will be regulated by the law of England ; and on the same principle a deed of transference of moveables executed according to the law of the domicile will be held effectual to convey moveables situated in a country where such a mode of conveyance would not be effectual. The payment of succession duty on personalty is also settled upon the principle of this phrase ; for if the deceased be domiciled within the kingdom at the time of his death, the duty is exigible without regard to the place where the personalty is situated, but if he be domiciled outwith the kingdom, no duty is exigible, although the whole of his moveable estate should be situated within it.

Mobilia situm non habent.—Moveables have no locality; that is, they are not regarded as having any locality of their own different from that of the domicile of their owner. "It is a clear proposition, not only of the law of England, but of every country in the world whose law has the semblance of science, that personal property has no locality. The meaning of that is not that personal property has no visible locality, but that it is subject to that law which governs the person of the owner. With respect to the disposition of it, with respect to the transmission of it, either by succession or by the act of the party, it follows the law of the person." Per Lord Loughborough, in *Gill* v. *Worswick*, 1 H. Bla. 690. See also *Goetze* v. *Aders*, &c., 2 R. 153.

Moderamen inculpatæ tutelæ.—The limits of inculpable defence. This phrase signifies that degree of self-defence which any one may legally use, although it should occasion the death of the aggressor, without subjecting himself to the charge of murder or homicide on that account. The rules of our law regarding inculpable homicide will be found in Hume, i. 227 *et seq.*

Modica differentia.—A slight or moderate difference. Stair (B. 3, T. 8, § 62), in treating of the office and duty of an executor, and of the value put by him upon the effects of the deceased which he is required to give up by inventory to the commissary, says—"It may be questioned here whether these things can be called *male appretiata* which are appreciated by the defunct himself? Doubtless *modica differentia* is not to be regarded; but if the price be considerably to the lesion of creditors, legatars, or others, as being a half or third within the just price, they may be repreciated."

Modus.—Manner or mode. The *modus* of an indictment is that part of it which contains the narrative of the commission of the crime; the statement of the mode or manner in which the offence was committed.

Modus et conventio vincunt legem.—The form of the agreement and the agreement itself overcome the law. This is equivalent to stating that parties, by an agreement duly entered into, may renounce, diminish, or increase their respective rights at common law; indeed, so long as the parties abstain from illegal contract, or such agreements as the law cannot recognise, they may make what bargains they please, and the law will enforce fulfilment. In illustration of the maxim, take the following cases : A debtor is, at common law, liable for interest on the amount of his debt from the time when it becomes payable until it is actually paid. But if both debtor and creditor agree that in no circumstances shall interest be payable, their agreement overcomes or sets aside the common law rule ; and the creditor gets less than the common law would have given him. Again, the common law holds him liable in damages who is guilty of breach of contract, and the measure of the damages awarded against him is the loss actually arising from or suffered through the breach. But parties to a contract may stipulate that in the event of a breach of contract, the party in fault shall pay to the other a certain sum in name of liquidated or conventional damage ; and payment of that sum will be enforced, if liability for it be incurred, without any inquiry as to the extent of actual loss, and even although it should be admitted that it exceeds the loss. In that case the creditor in the obligation gets more than the common law would have allowed him, because the common law has been overruled by the agreement. By the rules of common law an agent acting for a disclosed principal binds the principal and not himself ; but he may so contract as to make himself personally liable, the rule of law notwithstanding. These illustrations, which might be multiplied, are sufficient to show the meaning and force of the maxim.

Modus habilis.—A habile or competent mode. See *Habili modo*.

Modus legem dat donationi.—The manner in which a donation is given regulates the gift; or, in other words, a donor may attach to his gift such conditions as he pleases. A donor may stipulate that in a certain event the gift is to be returned, and if the donation is accepted on such terms, the common law rule that a donation is irrevocable will give way to the condition of the gift. This also illustrates the maxim *Modus et conventio vincunt legem*. The principle of the maxim also applies to legacies. In *Reid* v. *Coates*, 5th March, 1813, F.C., an uncle made a provision in favour of his nephew on condition that he should not reside with his mother, and although no decision was pronounced on the question whether that was an illegal condition, the rubric bears that such a condition "is lawful in a settlement by an uncle on his nephew." Such a condition was held illegal in the case of a provision by a father in favour of a daughter, and was disregarded. (*Fraser* v. *Rose*, 11 D. 1466.) The distinction between the two cases seems to be that in the latter the father was bound to make a provision for his daughter, and could not encumber it with an illegal condition, whereas the uncle was under no such obligation, and could make his gift dependent upon such conditions as he pleased, the donee or legatee being entitled to decline the provision if the conditions attached to it were distasteful. In *Ommaney* v. *Bingham*, 3 Paton's Ap. 448, a father had made a certain provision for his daughter, but by a codicil he declared that if she married a certain person she should forfeit that provision. In that case the daughter having married the prohibited person, it was held to be a good revocation. The Court of Session (whose judgment was reversed) had held the revocation invalid, on the ground that it was *contra libertatem matrimonii*, and therefore null; but the House of Lords distinguished between such a condition in a testamentary writing and a similar condition attached to a bond of provision.

Modus tenendi.—The manner of holding : that is, the the tenure by which lands are held. See *A me*, &c.

Modus transferendi dominii.—The form of transference of property. Lawyers distinguish between the *titulus* and the *modus transferendi*, the former being the will or intention to convey, and the latter being the overt act by which that intention is expressed and the real right transferred. See *Causa et modus*.

Modus vacandi.—The manner in, or the act by which the property became unoccupied or ownerless. This phrase scarcely admits of literal translation, but its meaning will be clearly understood 'from the following quotation, where it occurs. In treating of the *quæquidem* clause in the charter of resignation, Mr. Menzies says—" Its office here is to express the *modus vacandi*—*i.e.*, to show how it is, and for what purpose, that the fee, having been formerly given out by the superior, is again in his hands. It bears, therefore, that the lands formerly pertained heritably (*i.e.*, by a completed infeftment) to the former vassal (granter of the disposition), holden by him of the granter of the charter as immediate lawful superior thereof, and were resigned by him, by virtue of the procuratory of resignation contained in a disposition (which is identified by its dates), granted by him to the disponee, in the hands of the granter of the charter as superior in favour and for new infeftment of the same to be granted to the disponee."—Menzies' Lectures, 626.

Moliturae.—Multures; which were the portions of grain given to the miller in return for his grinding the rest. Where lands were thirled to a certain mill, the miller was entitled to the multures out of the astricted grain, although it was not brought for grinding to his mill, and this alike where the thirl had carried his grain to another mill, or had sold it unmanufactured. For the history and description of the different kinds of multures, see Ersk. B. 2, T. 9, § 18 *et seq.*

Mora.—Delay. This word signifies technically undue or culpable delay, and subjects the person against whom it can be charged to the consequences which arise from it. A debtor is said to be *in mora* if he does not pay his debt when it is due, and is thereafter, consequently, liable to the creditor in interest, which is held at common law to be the loss which the creditor suffers by the delay. Should the creditor suffer real loss by the debtor's delay, he will be entitled to decree against the debtor therefor. *Mansfield*, 14 S. 585. On the same principle, a borrower in commodate, or a lessee in hiring, although in the general case not liable for damage to the subject lent or hired will be liable for such damage if he has been guilty of *mora* in the redelivery of the subject, after the purpose for which it had been obtained is fulfilled, and that even where the damage has arisen from accident. Again, *mora* on the part of a creditor in beginning or completing diligence against his debtor's estate or person, will free cautioners from their obligation to him. See *Ex mora*, &c.

Morandae solutionis causa.—For the purpose of delaying, or postponing payment. In construing a will the question frequently arises whether legacies there bequeathed vest on the death of the testator, or do not vest until the day specified as the date of payment. In the case of *Burnets*, M. 8105, the question arose whether a legacy left " to be paid when he (the legatee), is sixteen years of age " vested *a morte testatoris ;* the legatee having predeceased the term specified. It was held that it did so vest, the court being of opinion that the bequest itself was absolute and the time specified only *morandœ solutionis causa*. But see the case of *Omey*, M. 6340, the decision in which seems to be opposed to the one just stated. The later decisions on this point appear to be somewhat conflicting, but the tendency now is to hold the legacy as vested, and that uncertainty in the time attaches to the date of payment merely, unless the terms of the deed be such as clearly to indicate a different intention on the part of the testator. On this point see the cases quoted in Menzies' Lectures, 495. See also M'Laren, ii. 1 *et seq.*

Morbus sonticus.—A serious sickness or malady; defined by Stair as a mortal sickness. It was at one time necessary to prove a *morbus sonticus* in reducing a deed on the head of death-bed, but this in later times (and before death-bed as a ground of reduction was abolished) was not so. It was sufficient ground of reduction if the testator had been affected by the disease of which he died when he executed the deed, and did not survive the execution of it sixty days, or attend kirk or market, although the disease was not of the class generally known as mortal. This phrase is now applied to incapacitating diseases. *Laird*, M. 3315.

More burgi.—According to the custom in burgage-holdings. Burgage-holding was the tenure by which lands situated in a royal burgh were held of and under the Crown. The titles (and the manner especially in which an heir's title was completed) to burgage subjects were at one time different from the ordinary title to lands held feu, but they have been assimilated by the recent statutes affecting land rights. The distinction between burgage tenure and feu has been abolished by the Act 37 & 38 Vict. c. 94; but writs affecting land, which immediately prior to the commencement of that Act were held burgage, are still recorded in the burgh register of sasines.

Morte donantis donatio confirmatur.—A donation is confirmed or established by the death of the donor. Ordinary donations being absolute and irrevocable, need no confirmation; but this phrase applies to the case of a donation between husband and wife, which is revocable at any time. The donor may revoke the donation during lifetime, or by *mortis causa* deed, but failing revocation by himself or herself, the death of the donor confirms the donation, so that it cannot be revoked or called in question by the donor's heirs. See *Donatio inter virum,* &c.

Morte legatarii perit legatum.—By the death of the legatee, the legacy perishes, or lapses: that is, the death of the legatee during the lifetime of the granter of the legacy. This is the rule where the legacy is granted to the legatee individually, as "I bequeath to A B:" but when the legacy is bequeathed to "A B and his heirs," the latter words import a conditional institution of the heirs, who would take the legacy notwithstanding A B had predeceased the granter. Legacies to a class of persons do not lapse if any of them survive the testator.

Morte mandatoris perit mandatum.—A mandate falls on the death of the mandant. As the mandatory's authority originated in the mandate, so that authority is at an end when the source from which it proceeded has ceased to exist. Yet if the mandatory be ignorant of the mandant's death, and proceed thereafter to the performance of certain acts in terms of the mandate, such acts will bind the mandant's heir. On the principle of this maxim, precepts of sasine, being mandates by the granter authorising the infeftment of his disponee, were at one time ineffectual to warrant sasine after the granter's death. To remedy the inconvenience thence arising, it was enacted (1693, c. 35) that such precepts should continue in full force, notwithstanding "the death of the granters or parties to whom they are granted, or both." See *In rem suam.*

Mortis causa.—Deeds made in contemplation of death are so called, because the prospect of death is the cause which induces their execution. Wills disposing of moveables, and dispositions of heritage, to take effect only after the granter's death, are called *mortis causa* deeds, in opposition to deeds taking effect during the life of the parties, which are termed *inter vivos.* As *mortis causa* deeds are of no avail until the death of the granter, they may be recalled or altered by him at any time during his life, and that even where they contain a renunciation of his right to revoke.

Mortis causam tribuerunt.—They did that which occasioned the death. Hume, i. 183.

Mortuus sasit vivum.—The dead ancestor invests the living heir. A maxim of the English law which signifies that the moment a man dies his real estate vests in his heir-at-law, without any service or other legal proceeding being taken by the heir to establish his right. Prior to the year 1874 this rule was not recognised in Scotland except in the case of leases which vested in the heir *ipso jure* without service or other title. On the contrary, the rule of Scotch law was *nulla sasina, nulla terra*,—no infeftment, no land; and until the heir completed a feudal title to his ancestor's estate in habile form, the lands were said to be *in hœreditate jacente* of the deceased. If the heir died without making up a title, it was not his heir but the ancestor's heir who succeeded to the estate. But a change upon this rule was introduced by the Act 37 & 38 Vict. cap. 94, which provided (§ 9) that a personal right to every estate in land descendible to heirs should, without service or other procedure, vest, or be held to have vested, in the heir entitled to succeed thereto, by his survivance of the person to whom he was entitled to succeed, and that such personal rights should be of the like nature, and be attended with the like consequences, and be transmissible in the same manner as a personal right to land under an unfeudalised conveyance. An heir has now, therefore, by mere survivance a personal title to his ancestor's estate; and to this extent the rule of the English law expressed in this maxim has become the law of Scotland.

Multa impediunt matrimonium contrahendum, quæ non dirimunt contractum.—Many things hinder the contraction of a marriage, which do not detract from its validity when contracted. There are not many cases illustrative of this maxim to be found in the law of Scotland, but the following may be taken as an example. If, at the time of entering into the marriage either of the parties be insane, such marriage would be null. Insanity before marriage,—that is, at the time when the contract is entered into,—effectually hinders or impedes its contraction, because insanity prevents the party so affected giving that consent which is essential to marriage. But the fact of one of the parties becoming insane after marriage will not affect its validity if otherwise valid.

Multa in jure communi contra rationem disputandi pro communi utilitate introducta sunt.—Many things have been introduced into the common law with a view to public utility (or for the public convenience) which are inconsistent with sound reason—*i.e.*, which cannot be logically defended.

Multa non vetat lex quæ tamen tacite damnavit.—There are many things which the law does not forbid which yet it has tacitly condemned.

Munera publica.—Public offices. Among the Romans there were certain offices regarded as public duties, which no citizen (unless he could plead certain specified excuses) could refuse to accept of and fulfil; and among these were included the offices of tutor and curator. These offices are voluntary by the law of Scotland, and their acceptance, as well as the performance of the attendant duties, cannot be imposed upon any one against his own wish. But if the office has been once accepted and acted upon, the tutor or curator cannot resign it. He must perform the duties of his office until it expires through the death, attainment of minority or majority, as the case may be, or it may be through the marriage of the ward, and he will be liable for the consequences of his neglect, as well as the consequences of his actings and intromissions. The office of High Sheriff of a county in England is somewhat similar to the *munus publicum*, for no one elected to that office can decline to accept it, except under a heavy pecuniary penalty. It is in the option, however, of the Sheriff elect either to take the office or to pay the fine.

Municipia.—Free towns. These were towns or cities (particularly in Italy) dependent upon Rome, the citizens of which possessed the right, and certain of the privileges, of Roman citizenship. They were governed by their own laws, called *leges municipales*, and hence the term municipal law came to signify the law of any free state.

Mutare causam possessionis.—To change the title or ground of possession. See *Nemo potest sibi*, &c.

Mutatis mutandis.—Things being changed which are to be changed. This phrase, and the use of it, may best be explained by an example. A proprietor of an estate feus his lands, and the feu contracts all contain the same general clauses, the same obligations on the feuars, confer the same rights. In such a case two of the feu-charters are said to be the same *mutatis mutandis*, that is, they are the same, if (or when) the name of the disponee, the particular description of the lands feued, and other such-like particulars which are peculiar to each, be changed. The reader will find another example of the use of this phrase in Hume, ii. 181.

Mutua petitio.—A counter claim; or a claim set up by a defender in answer to one made against him by a pursuer. Ersk. B. 4, T. 2, § 11.

Mutuum.—A species of loan. The loan of mutuum is that contract under which the borrower receives certain articles which perish in the use, as wine, corn, &c. (known technically as fungibles), in return for which he binds himself to give the lender an equal quantity of a subject similar to that borrowed. It differs from loan in commodate, in respect that under that contract the borrower is bound to return, not an equivalent, but the *ipsum corpus* of the thing borrowed. There is this further difference, that in commodate any deterioration of the subject lent, or its total loss, if not occasioned by the fault of the borrower, must be borne by the lender; whereas, in mutuum, all the risk lies with the borrower. Both of these contracts of loan are necessarily gratuitous, for if anything was given or paid in return, it would become location.

N

Nævi materni.—Moles or other natural marks on the person. Dickson, § 262.

Nam scire debet cum quo contrahit.—For one ought to know with whom he contracts: a man ought to know about the person he deals with. See *Quisque scire debet*, &c.

Nasciturus.—Yet to be born. Lands are frequently disponed by marriage-contracts to the children *nascituri*, and if properly fenced, such destination carries the fee to the children, leaving it meanwhile as a fiduciary fee in the person of their father for their behoof. Another common form of destination is to children *nominatim* and to others *nascituri*, which vests the fee in the children named, for their own share, and with a fee in trust for those not yet born.

Natis et nascituris.—To children born and to be born. A form of destination frequently used in conveying heritage to children of a marriage.

Nativi.—Bondmen or slaves, by whom anciently, in Scotland, the lands were laboured. They resembled in some respects the *adscriptitii* of the Romans; but they could not be sold by their master. They acquired an immunity from their servitude by residing for a year together in any royal burgh without challenge on the part of their master.

Natura negotii.—The nature or character of the transaction.

Naturale est quidlibet dissolvi eo modo quo ligatur.—It is natural that any obligation should be discharged by a similar mode to that by which it was constituted. "So verbal obligations are discharged verbally, and consensual obligations (or contracts) are discharged by consent." Dig. B. 50, T. 17, § 35. See *Eodem modo*, &c.

Naturalia feudi.—Those things which naturally belong to

a feu grant. Such, for example, is the obligation on the part of the granter of the feu to warrant it against eviction to the grantee. "By the *naturalia feudi* is understood whatever arises from the nature of the contract; and so is deemed part of it, though it should not be expressly provided for. In this they differ from the essentials of a feu, that they may receive an alteration from the will of the parties without destroying the feudal contract; but such will must be properly expressed in the grant or contract itself." (Ersk. B. 2, T. 3, § 11.) Among the *naturalia* of a burgage grant were the watching and warding in return for which the lands were held.

Nautæ, caupones, stabularii.—Literally, carriers by sea, innkeepers, stablers. These are the first words of an edict issued by a Roman prætor, which is well known as the edict *Nautæ, caupones,* &c. By it such persons as those described were rendered liable for the goods and effects of travellers lodging at their inns or for goods entrusted to them for carriage and delivery, where the goods were lost or damaged. To render them liable, it was not necessary to prove fault or negligence on their part, as this was presumed. This stringent rule was enacted because such persons by their position had unusual facilities for committing theft, or inflicting injury on the effects committed to their care, without incurring the same risk of detection. To maintain that the goods were stolen from them was no valid defence, for otherwise it would have been an easy matter for them to arrange with dishonest men, a plan by which they should share in the booty without subjecting themselves in any civil liability. This rule has been adopted by the laws of England and Scotland, as well as by most of the nations of modern Europe. With us its provisions apply to all common carriers whether by sea or land, innkeepers, stablers, &c. "The rule is, that common carriers, innkeepers, and stablers are responsible for the loss of things committed to their charge, although no neglect can be proved, if such loss do not arise from natural and inevitable accident, the act of God, or of the King's enemies." (Bell's Prin. § 235.) But this rule has been rendered, in one particular, still more stringent by the Act 19 & 20 Vict. c. 60, which provides that carriers shall be liable to the owners for the value of goods which perish through accidental fire. There are a variety of circumstances in which the responsibility thus imposed is removed from the innkeeper, &c., altogether, or limited in its extent, for which reference may be made to Bell's Prin. § 236, and the authorities there quoted.

Ne conjuges mutuo amore se invicem spolient.—Lest spouses through their mutual love should impoverish one another. This is the ground stated in the civil law as that on which donations between husband and wife were held as invalid or ineffectual. (Dig. B. 24, T. 1, § 1.) The rule prohibiting inter-conjugal donations was said to be introduced for the purpose of preserving the marriage relation in its purity, as an agreement subsisting by affection, and not maintained (for the husband could dissolve the marriage by simply giving the wife a letter of divorcement and leaving her) by purchase or by gift from one party to another. At a later period in the history of the civil law (under Septimius Severus), the strictness of this rule was relaxed, and donations between husband and wife were held valid if not revoked by the donor before his death. This is now the law of Scotland. See *Donatio inter virum*, &c.

Ne dominia rerum sint incerta, neve lites sint perpetuæ. —Lest the ownership of things should remain uncertain, or lawsuits never come to an end. The rules of prescription are founded upon the principle of this phrase, for it has been deemed impolitic to allow a right of property to be disputed after a certain time, or to allow actions to be raised at a period when the parties to the transaction out of which it arises may all be dead, and the circumstances of the transaction entirely forgotten, or most imperfectly remembered. Accordingly, by our law, undisputed possession of a subject for forty years does not merely raise a presumption of right, but confers a right of property. Under the provisions of the Act 37 & 38 Vict. c. 94, § 34, undisputed possession of a subject for twenty years, after 1st January, 1879. will have the same effect as the former prescription of forty years; and if possession has been had after that date for thirty years no allowance or deduction is to be made "on account of the years of minority or less age of those against whom the prescription is used and objected, or of any period during which any person against whom prescription is used or objected was under legal disability." (As to the effect of the clause first referred to, see *Buchanan*, 9 R. 1218 ; and *Hinton*, 10 R. 1110.) A right of action must be exercised within the same period (some actions within a much shorter, as, for example, an action arising out of tutorial accounts, which prescribes in ten years), otherwise the action will be excluded. The distinction between a proper prescription, and that which (although generally so called) is merely a limitation, must be borne in mind. Prescription extinguishes the claim and action arising therefrom, while a limitation merely limits the mode in which the claim may be substantiated, or the legal remedy enforced. Thus the forty years' prescription, *ipso jure*, extinguishes the debt and bars action for it, and this defence is sufficient of itself to throw the action out of court. On the other hand, the triennial prescription (commonly so called, but more correctly a limitation) merely confines the pursuer to the necessity of proving the debt claimed by the debtor's writ or oath. The septennial prescription of cautionary obligations is a proper prescription because after the lapse of seven years the cautioner is entirely free from his obligation. The plea of *res judicata* is founded upon the principle expressed in the latter part of this phrase. If a question has once been finally determined in an action, the parties to that action cannot have the decree opened up and the question reconsidered on the ground either of pleas proponed and repelled, or pleas competent and omitted.

Ne fictio plus valeat in casu ficto quam veritas in casu vero.—A legal fiction cannot avail more in the fictitious case than the truth would if the case really happened. A legal fiction is an equitable presumption that a certain proposition is true, or that some particular thing has taken place. The meaning of the maxim is that a legal fiction is never to be carried in its effect beyond that which would follow if, instead of its being a fiction, it really was the fact: the law to be applied on the presumption to be co-extensive with that which would be applied if the facts were as the law presumes them to be. For an example of the use of this maxim, see Ross, L. C. (L. R.) i. 368.

Ne mutuato amore invicem spoliarentur.—Lest they should be impoverished by each other through their mutual affection. See *Ne conjuges*, &c.

Ne urbs ruinis deformetur.—Lest the city should be disfigured by ruinous houses. All questions relative to the building, repairing, or taking down of houses, fall properly within the jurisdiction of the Dean of Guild, and such alterations or new erections can only proceed on his warrant. He has power to order the repair or demolition of ruinous buildings; and payment of the expense incurred by repairs made upon his order is secured by a tacit hypothec over the building on which such repairs are made. This power, however, only extends over buildings the insufficiency of which threatens the safety of the lieges. If the building be sufficient and safe, it need scarcely be added, the Dean of Guild has no power to order alteration or repairs, simply because it disfigures the city. He may refuse his warrant for the erection of a house where the proposed plan is not in accordance with the prescribed form and character of building on that particular plot of ground, but this proceeds upon the fact that the builder proposes to violate certain restrictions by which he is bound, and not because his building would disfigure the adjoining range of buildings.

Nec cum sacco adire debet.—He (a debtor) is not bound to go about with a money-bag. This phrase means that a debtor cannot be expected to carry with him as much money as will meet his obligations, and that therefore a reasonable time for paying his debt must be allowed him after requisition has been made; and so Stair, in treating of the time of performing obligations, uses this phrase (quoting from the Pandects, B. 46, T. 3, § 105), where he says—" If money be required, if the debtor offer within twenty-four hours, it would not infer delay; for it is not his part to carry a sum of money about with him, nor to have it ready at each instant, *et nec cum sacco adire debet.*" B. 1, T. 17, § 18.

Nec manifestum.—Not manifest. Theft was so called in the civil law when the thief was not caught in the act, or before he had reached the place whither he was conveying the stolen property. See *Furtum*.

Necessitas facit licitum quod alias non est licitum.—

Necessity makes that lawful which otherwise would not be lawful. Killing a person in self-defence, and as the only means of protecting one's own life, falls within the rule of this maxim; such homicide is excused by the absolute necessity which leads to it, and by that necessity only, for if it be possible to escape from the assailant's violence otherwise than by killing him that course must be adopted. To cut away cables or masts, or to throw goods overboard in a storm for the safety of the crew and ship, are quite lawful when necessary: but if there was no necessity, such conduct would be criminal.

Necessitas inducit privilegium.—Necessity introduces privilege; or necessity brings the privilege into play. The observations on the preceding maxim show how necessity, and necessity only, gives rise to a privilege which otherwise would not exist. The same illustrations also serve to explain partly the following :—

Necessitas inducit privilegium quoad jura privata.—Necessity gives rise to privilege so far as private rights are concerned. This maxim introduces a limitation of the general rule by restricting its application to matters of private right. Necessity will not excuse an act which is contrary to or directed against the commonwealth; for while a man is entitled to defend his own rights against invasion, and to defend them, as we have seen, by acts which in other circumstances would amount to crime, yet in a question with the State the individual is bound rather to suffer the wrong than do violence to the commonwealth : *privilegium contra rempublicam non valet.* Thus a man will not be excused for stealing bread although he was morally compelled to the act by his own absolute want or that of his wife and children. Or again, if a wife under threats of personal violence on the part of her husband commits a crime on his instigation, she will still be responsible for her act. In neither of these cases can necessity be effectually pleaded as a defence: in both cases the suffering and violence should have been endured rather than the offence have been committed.

Necessitas publica major est quam privata.— Public necessity is greater than private; that is, the necessary requirements of the public good are stronger, and prevail against private or individual necessity or right. The public necessity for the preservation of good order and suppression of crime prevails (as we have seen above) over the private necessity of the man who steals bread to preserve his life. But in civil matters this maxim has also application; as, for example, where the legislature authorises a railway company or other public body to take land compulsorily for the formation of their works, in which case the public necessity prevails over the private wish, necessity, or right of the proprietor.

Necessitas quod cogit defendit.—The necessity which compels, defends, or excuses (that which was done under the necessity). See *Necessitas facit licitum*, &c.

Necessitate juris.—By necessity of law: arising necessarily from the nature or effect of legal rules. In illustration of this, reference may be made to Erskine, where, in treating of what is carried by an adjudication directed against the *hæreditas jacens* of a deceased debtor, and of its effects as regards rents which have become due after the debtor's death, but before the decree of adjudication is pronounced, as opposed to the effect of an ordinary adjudication, which carries no rents due previous to the date of the decree, he says—" But rents incurred after his death cannot be said to have belonged to him, since they did not even exist at his death, and are truly a rent grown out of his heritable estate since his death, which, for that reason, would have accrued to his heir if he had entered. As, therefore, by the heir's renunciation of the debtor's succession, the adjudger comes in the heir's place, these rents must, *necessitate juris*, be carried by the creditor's adjudication against the *hæreditas jacens*, though fallen due previously to the date of it, there being no other method known in law by which they may be affected by diligence." B. 2, T. 12, § 48.

Necessitate precepti sed non necessitate medii.—This phrase (occurring in Stair, B. 1, T. 4, § 6) scarcely admits of literal translation. It means that the consent spoken of by Stair is necessary as an act of obedience to the law, but not necessary as an essential to the validity of the contract; that minor children should obtain the previous consent of their parents to their marriage, but that the want of such consent will not invalidate the contract after it has been entered into. With us the consent of parents is in no way necessary to the validity of a marriage entered into between minors; in England a different rule prevails, for the parents' consent is essential to the marriage of persons still in minority.

Negotiorum gestor.—The name given to any one who manages the affairs, or acts for the behoof of another in his absence without his knowledge, and without having any mandate authorising such acts or interference. The office is gratuitous, and the *negotiorum gestor* can claim nothing as recompense for the trouble or labour he may have been put to. He is entitled, however, to recover all expense incurred or outlaid by him in the course of his actings, and to interest on all money paid out; while, on the other hand, he is bound to account for all sums of money that may have come into his hands during that period. In the ordinary case, he is liable in that degree of diligence which a prudent man bestows on his own affairs; but when his interference takes place under the pressure of great necessity, where immediate interference is necessary, he will only be liable for *culpa lata*.

Nemine contradicente.—No one saying otherwise; without contradiction.

Nemo ad littus maris accedere prohibetur.—No one is prevented from having access to the sea-shore. The sea-shore—being the land which lies between high and low water mark—is *res publica*, and as such is vested in the Crown in trust for the subject. No one, therefore, can be prevented from having access to the shore, or from walking thereon, or using it for such purposes as are lawful. At same time no one can insist on gaining access to the sea-shore through private lands, for that would be trespass.

Nemo agit in seipsum.—No one acts against himself; no one can pursue an action against himself. See *Idem agens et patiens*.

Nemo cogi potest præcise ad factum, sed in id tantum quod interest.—No one can be compelled to fulfil his obligation absolutely, but only in so far as the creditor in the obligation has an interest to compel performance. The meaning of this maxim is that contracts are not to be enforced judaically; and that what amounts practically to performance will be sufficient. For example, if A undertakes to deliver to B a cargo of fish to be shipped at a certain port, but ships them at a different port from that named, B cannot refuse to accept delivery on the ground that the contract had not been fulfilled *præcise*. The bargain was for a cargo of fish, and that being offered to B, he has no interest to ask more. But it would be otherwise if it could be shown that the fish generally shipped at the port named in the contract were better than those shipped at the actual port of loading—that the naming of the port of shipment in the contract amounted to a representation of quality —or that fish shipped at the one port brought a better price in the market than fish shipped at the other—for in these circumstances B had an interest in enforcing shipment at the particular port named; he suffered loss by the non-fulfilment of the precise terms of the contract. While every one is bound to fulfil his contract, fair fulfilment will be sufficient— the creditor in the obligation not being entitled to insist on the observance of minute particulars in which he has no real interest whether they be observed or not. The principle of this maxim requires, however, to be applied with great caution. See the case of *Webster* v. *Cramond Iron Co.*, 2 R. 752; and *Bowes* v. *Shand*, L. R. 2, App. C. 455.

Nemo cogitationis pœnam patitur.—No one suffers punishment on account of his thought or intention. A maxim taken from the civil law (Dig. B. 48, T. 19, § 18). See *Cogitationis pœnam*, &c.; *Actus non facit*, &c.

Nemo contra factum suum venire potest.—No one can go against his own act. When an act has once been performed which is binding on the actor, he cannot at will depart from that act or lawfully do anything contrary to it. Thus if one has submitted a question to arbitration, he cannot resile therefrom nor validly do anything to prevent the submission proceeding. An agent who enters into a contract on behalf of his principal cannot subsequently depart from his contract on the ground that he had no authority from the principal to enter into it. That might be a good defence in the mouth of the principal, but would not be available to the agent. So, again, in pleading: where a party in the Court of Session maintained that a certain street was a private street, he was not allowed to maintain on appeal that the street was a public street. *Campbell*, L. R. 2, Sc. Ap. 4. One who grants a permission may, however, withdraw it without violating the rule of this maxim. The two acts are of a contrary nature, but the doing of the one implied the right to do the other at pleasure.

Nemo dat qui non habet.—No one gives who has not : one who has no title cannot confer a title. The same maxim is sometimes expressed—

Nemo dat quod non habet.—No one can give what he has not got. On the subject of both these maxims, see *A non habente*, &c., and *Nemo plus juris*, &c.

Nemo debet bis puniri pro uno delicto.—No one should be punished twice for the same offence. Punishment once suffered, the crime is extinguished, and a second punishment cannot follow. An offence may, however, entail the necessity of answering for its consequences in more courts than one ; the offence may incur both civil and criminal consequences. Culpable homicide may be punished by the sentence of a criminal tribunal, and it may still form the subject of a civil action of damages. The one punishment, however, is *ad vindictam publicam*—on account of the violation of the public law—the damages decerned for civilly are the compensation due for private injury. In one sense the crime is one — namely, the culpable homicide of a certain person, but in another sense the offence is twofold—(1) against the State, and (2) against private individuals.

Nemo debet bis vexari si constat curiæ quod sit pro una et eadem causa.—No one ought to be molested twice, if it appears to the Court that it is for one and the same matter. It is upon this principle that, in Scotland, a prisoner cannot be called upon to answer, or be tried, twice for the same offence. If a prisoner has once been put upon his trial, and the jury sworn, he must have a verdict for or against him ; and if the trial breaks down through the want of an important witness or other cause, the verdict in the prisoner's favour frees him from all further trial for the same offence. He is said technically to have "tholed an assize." But if the trial is stopped " by some unforeseen accident, such as the illness of the juryman or of the accused, or proved to be a nullity in consequence of some defect for which the prosecutor was not responsible, such as a person having personated a juryman, or the like, the plea of *res judicata* will not be sustained" (Macdonald, 462). Generally speaking, the same principle holds in England. " It has been urged upon us that according to the law of England no man ought to be put in peril twice on the same charge. I entirely agree. But we must apply that great fundamental maxim of the criminal law according to its true meaning. It means this : a man shall not twice be put in peril after a verdict has been returned by the jury, that verdict being given on a good indictment, and one on which the prisoner could be legally convicted and sentenced. It does not, however follow if, from any particular circumstance, a trial has proved abortive, that then a case shall not be again submitted to the consideration of a jury, and determined as right and justice may require." (Per Cockburn, C. J., in *Winsor* v. *The Queen*, L. R. 1, Q. B. 311.) In *Winsor's* case the " particular circumstance " which led to the necessity for the second trial was, that on the first trial the judge had discharged the jury, they being unable to agree upon a verdict. In Scotland, where a verdict may be returned by a majority, this could not have happened. This maxim is applied *in civilibus* as well as *in criminalibus*, and an instance of such application will be found in the case of *Wood* v. *Gray*, L. R. App. C. (1892), 576.

Nemo debet esse judex in propria causa.—No one ought to be a judge in his own cause. This maxim includes not only those cases in which the judge appears directly as a party, but those also in which he has an interest. In the case of *Borthwick* v. *The Scottish Widows' Fund*, 2 Macp. 595, a question arose which was sent to the whole Court for opinion, when six of the judges declined on the ground that they had policies of insurance effected over their lives with the defenders' society. Such a ground of declinature has now been removed by the Act 31 & 32 Vict. cap. 100, § 103. The interest of relationship to one of the parties is a sufficient ground of declinature. *Camp-*

bell v. *Campbell*, 4 Macp. 868. On the subject of the declinature of a judge, either by a party or the judge himself, see Bell's Dict. *v. Declinature.* As regards the law of England on the disqualification of judges through interest, see the case of *Wildes* v. *Russell*, L. R. 1, C. P. 722, and cases there cited.

Nemo debet ex alieno damno lucrari.—No one should be enriched out of the loss or damage sustained by another. A maxim of the Roman law, founded upon equity, the principle of which has been adopted by the Scotch law. Upon this principle the *negotiorum gestor* recovers that which he has expended on behalf of one who is absent, and unable to guard his own property or manage his own affairs. This maxim also finds application in the case where one builds a house upon ground which he believes to be his own, but which ultimately proves to be the property of another. In such case the owner of the ground takes the house as an accessory to his land, but he is bound to indemnify the person building *bona fide*, to the extent at least to which he has been benefited by the other's labour and outlay. This maxim is expressed in various forms, as follows: *Nemo debet locupletari aliena jactura: Nemo debet ex aliena jactura lucrari: Nemo debet locupletari ex alterius incommodo;* all meaning, no one should be enriched at another's cost or loss. One other form of the maxim is used by Erskine (B. 1, T. 7, § 33)—*Nemo locupletandus est cum detrimento alterius*— who quotes it as the ground on which an exception is founded to the general rule, that a minor is not bound by contracts or engagements entered into by him during minority; and the following passage may be quoted as affording an additional illustration of the principle of the maxim to those above given: "This rule obtains, contrary to the nature of contracts, both from the favour of minors, to whom the law has not denied the power of making their condition better, though they cannot make it worse, and *in pœnam* of those who would impose upon their weakness. But it is to be received with the two following exceptions: First, minors are effectually obliged, by their own acts and deeds, and even by bonds of borrowed money granted by them, though without the consent of their curators, for all sums that have been profitably applied to their use, in which case the maxim holds, *Nemo locupletandus,"* &c.

Nemo ejusdem tenementi simul potest esse hæres et dominus.—No one can at the same time be heir to and proprietor of the same subject. The two characters and titles are inconsistent: the expectancy of the heir ceases when the possession as proprietor commences.

Nemo ex alterius facto prægravari debet.—No one should be burdened by the act of another. Therefore, no one is entitled to act *in æmulationem vicini;* and no one can be burdened by obligations incurred by another in his name without his authority or sanction. But there are cases in which one man's act may create a burden upon another quite lawfully. One acting lawfully in the exercise of his own right may do that which may be burdensome to another. As where one by building or other operations on his own land makes his neighbour's tenement less secure; or again, where one by uninterrupted use of another's property in a certain way acquires a right of servitude over that property. The latter burden is recognised as much *in pœnam* of the proprietor who neglects to look after his own interests, as in virtue of the actual use which has created the burden.

Nemo ex proprio dolo consequitur actionem.—No one can pursue an action based upon his own wrong-doing; no one acquires a right of action through his own fraud. See *Ex dolo non oritur,* &c.

Nemo ex suo delicto meliorem suam conditionem facere potest.—No one can improve his condition by his delict; no one can take advantage by his delict. Delict or crime being unlawful, no one can thereby acquire any right which the law can recognise: the source being tainted, all that proceeds from it is equally so. A thief cannot enrich himself by that which he steals, for the rightful owner may recover it; the forger, in like manner, is bound to repay all that which by his forgery he had temporarily gained.

Nemo hæres est viventis.—No one is the heir of a person still alive. "I do not think anybody can fulfil the part of a man's heir during that man's lifetime. A man's heir has no existence until he dies, and it never can be ascertained till he dies who will be his heir. It depends upon a variety of circumstances." (Per Lord Pres. Inglis in *Todd* v. *Mackenzie,* 1 R. 1210.)

Nemo habetur agere dolose qui jure suo utitur.—No one is held to act wrongfully (or fraudulently) who acts in the exercise of his right. See an illustration of this maxim in Fraser, ii. 1009.

Nemo jus sibi dicere potest.—No one can declare the law for himself; no one is entitled to take the law into his own hands. See *Jus sibi dicere.*

Nemo mori potest pro parte testatus pro parte intestatus. —No one can die partly testate and partly intestate. This rule is not in observance: a man may validly dispose of part of his estate by testament, leaving the remainder to be distributed according to the ordinary legal rules regulating succession.

Nemo patriam in qua natus est exuere nec ligeantiæ debitum ejurare possit.—No one may cast off his native country or abjure the obligation of allegiance. Broom, 75.

Nemo plus juris ad alium transferre potest quam ipse habet.—No one can transfer to another a greater right than he has himself. To illustrate this rule, take the case of a *bona fide* purchaser of a stolen article, and that whether purchased from the thief directly or from some one acquiring from him. Such a purchaser has no title to the thing purchased, which he can put in competition with the real owner, because the person from whom he acquired had no title, and (according to the maxim) his author could not give him a better right or title than he himself possessed. There are important exceptions, however, to the rule. For example, in the case of an accommodation bill indorsed for value by the drawer, the indorsee may have a better title or right than the indorser. As against the drawer and indorser, the acceptor could have pleaded that he had received no value; but as against the onerous indorsee, no such defence can be maintained (unless the bill has been indorsed after it became payable, 19 & 20 Vict. c. 60, § 16). A bill granted for a gaming debt affords no action or right to the drawer, but if indorsed for value to an indorsee who knew nothing of the cause of granting, the fact that it was granted for money lost at gaming does not affect the rights of the indorsee. In both of the cases just noticed the indorsee acquires a right from the indorser greater or better than the latter had; to this extent better, that the right as transferred is not open to exceptions pleadable against it before transference. So, again, possessors of moveables who have lawfully come into possession, may in some cases give a better title than they have; their own title may be that of mere factor or agent,—not proprietor,—but they may sell so as validly to vest the purchaser *in bona fide* with a right of property. See on this subject Bell's Com. i. 519 *et seq.*

Nemo plus juris tribuit quam ipse habet.—No one can bestow or grant a greater right (better title) than he has himself. Another mode of expressing the preceding maxim.

Nemo potest esse simul actor et judex.—No one can be at the same time both pursuer and judge (of the same action). See *Nemo debet esse judex*, &c.

Nemo potest immittere in alienum.—No one can throw or place anything on the property of another. This phrase regards the absolute right of property which every proprietor has in the subject of which he is possessed, *a cœlo usque ad centrum*. Without the servitude of stillicide duly constituted no one is entitled so to build his house that the eaves-drop or rain flow shall fall therefrom on his neighbour's property. Nor can any one support his house by building against or upon the gable of his neighbour's house, without a legal right so to do, acquired by permission or otherwise. See *A cœlo*, &c.

Nemo potest mutare consilium suum in alterius injuriam. —No one can change his design (or alter that which has been concluded, or determined upon), to the injury of another. When a bargain has been finally closed, neither party can go back upon it at his own hand, or decline to carry it out: and the maxim may be taken as expressing this rule. But the maxim, in its primary sense and application, has reference to enactments, and expresses the rule that laws, once determined and acted upon, should not be changed to the detriment of vested rights, acquired on the faith of the then existing law.

Nemo potest renunciare juri publico.—No one can renounce a public right. Any one can renounce a private right conceived in his favour, and so effectually renounce it as never after renunciation to be able to resume or claim it. But a public right, being conceived for public benefit, cannot be renounced. Thus the right to walk on the sea-shore, the right to exercise the elective franchise, &c., are public rights, and no one can, by any renunciation of these rights, preclude himself from exercising them if so disposed.

Nemo potest sibi mutare causam possessionis.—No one can of himself change the title or ground of his possession. This rule is taken from the civil law (Dig. B. 41, T. 2, l. 3, § 19), and signifies that no possessor, whose possession commenced upon one title, can alter it by afterwards ascribing it to another. In Scotland this rule is not absolute in its application, for a possessor holding upon several titles may ascribe his possession to that one which is surest and least liable to challenge. In such case, however, the title founded on must be an original right, and not merely an accessory to some other. See the case of *Robertson* v. *D. of Athole*, Ross, L. C. (L. R.), i. 208, where Lord Hermand is reported to have said that the maxim expresses " good Roman law, but very bad Scots law." See upon the subject of this maxim, Napier, 182 *et seq.*

Nemo potest nisi quod de jure potest.—No man can do anything except what he can do lawfully : or, that is not considered to be within the power of any one which he cannot lawfully perform. No one can defeat his children's claim of legitim,—that is, no one can by deed *mortis causa* distribute his moveable estate effectually is such a manner as to disappoint his children's succession to that part of the estate to which the law has declared them entitled. But a man may during his lifetime give away or otherwise dispose of his whole moveable estate, for the law allows a man to do what he pleases with his own, and thus practically defeat his children's claim for legitim. In the latter case he is acting in conformity with the law, and his act is effectual : in the former, his act would be contrary to law, and ineffectual.

Nemo potest sibi debere.—No one can be his own debtor. Where the creditor succeeds to the place of his debtor, or where a debtor acquires the rights of his creditor, the debt is extinguished *confusione;* so that the right of creditor and obligation of debtor cannot exist in the same person at the same time.

Nemo præsumitur alienam posteritatem suæ prætulisse. —No one is presumed to have preferred another's offspring to his own. This is a legal presumption which holds with regard to testamentary writings. A will executed by a person who at its date had no issue is held to be revoked by the birth of his posthumous child, or by the birth of a child shortly before his death : the presumption being against the idea of intentional disinheritance. In the language of the maxim, he is not presumed to have preferred others to his own offspring. This presumption may, however, be redargued. See *Si sine liberis,* &c.

Nemo præsumitur donare, vel suum perdere.—No one is presumed to give in donation, or to lose what is his. See *Donatio non præsumitur.*

Nemo præsumitur ludere in extremis.—No one is presumed to trifle, or make sport, at the point of death. Accordingly, when one by his will, or *mortis causa* deed (which is regarded as the expression of a man's will and intention at the extreme moment of his life, whatever its date may be), bequeaths as a legacy a subject which is not his, in the knowledge that it is not his, this places the executor under an obligation to procure and deliver the subject of the legacy to the legatee, or otherwise satisfy the legatee thereanent. The testator is presumed to have seriously intended this, and not merely to have been perpetrating a practical joke. On the same principle, when impossible conditions are adjected to a legacy or bequest, the legacy holds good, as seriously intended to be made while the condition is disregarded. Impossible conditions adjected to contracts have, on the other hand, the effect of annulling the contract. The parties to a contract are regarded as not serious when they make their bargain conditional on impossibility. See *Conditio illicita,* &c.

Nemo præsumitur malus.—No one is presumed to be bad—*i.e.,* guilty of any particular offence with which he may have been charged. Thus it is that no number of previous convictions, even if they be for the same description of crime, are allowed to weigh against a prisoner on his trial, although they will and do aggravate his punishment on his being found guilty. He must be proved guilty of each offence, independently of what his previous character may have been.

Nemo punitur pro alieno delicto.—No one is punished for another's crime. A crime infers punishment only upon the person guilty of it.

Nemo rem suam amittit nisi ex facto, aut delicto suo, aut neglectu.—No one loses what is his, except by his own act, his delict, or his neglect. As a general rule, a right of property can only be lost in one or other of these three modes—(1) By the proprietor's own act, such as sale, gift, abandonment, &c. Under this head must also be included all legal diligence proceeding upon the civil act or obligation of the proprietor, by virtue of which his right of property is transferred from him to another in fulfilment of his obligation. (2) By delict or crime, on which escheat of goods follows; and (3) By neglect, in consequence of which the thing perishes. See *Quod meum est*, &c.

Nemo sibi esse judex vel suis jus dicere debet.—No one should be judge for himself (in his own case) or declare the law (*i.e.*, pronounce judgment) in his own affairs. See *Nemo debet esse judex*, &c.

Nemo tenetur ad impossibilia.—No one is bound to perform impossibilities. See *Lex non cogit*, &c.

Nemo tenetur edere instrumenta contra se.—No one is bound to produce writings against himself. This rule admits of very limited application in our law, and, indeed, can only be said to have application at all in criminal prosecutions. In such cases the panel is not bound, and cannot be called upon, to produce any document which will injure his defence, or aid the prosecution, any more than he can be called upon to give parole evidence in support of the case laid against him. It is different, however, in civil actions, for there either party may be called upon and compelled, at the instance of the other (in the discretion of the Court), to produce any document in his possession tending to support the case of his opponent. The parties to a suit can not only be adduced by each other as havers, but may also (under the provisions of the recent Evidence Acts) be adduced as witnesses.

Nemo tenetur jurare in suam turpitudinem.—No one is bound to depone to a matter involving his own disgrace. No panel can be required to swear, either in affirmation or denial of the charge laid against him, nor can any one be compelled to answer a question in the course of his deposition as a witness in a civil suit if the answer will or may involve him in a criminal prosecution. This, however, is the limit to which the rule now extends; formerly the limits of its application were much more extended. A witness, formerly, might be asked, but was entitled to decline answering any question which involved even his shame or moral degradation, for it was thought that to compel witnesses to speak to their own shame was likely to result in very frequent acts of perjury. Accordingly, in the case of *King*, 4 D. 590, a witness was held entitled to decline answering a question to the effect of, Whether she had "frequently been found fault with, by various persons in whose service she was, for listening at doors and windows, and telling lying stories?" But the *metus perjurii*, on which this rule was founded, has been overcome by the obvious principle of justice, which entitles each party to a suit to elicit any fact from his adversary's witness reflecting on that witness's character or credibility. The rule now is, as already stated, that no witness can decline to answer a question put to him, no matter what disgrace it may involve, if it does not infer criminal prosecution. A witness has been held entitled, however, to decline answering a question which involves an admission of the guilt of adultery on his part, because, although no criminal prosecution has been raised on account of this crime for a century, it still stands on our books as a point of dittay. *Stephens*, 2 Swinton, 348. *Don*, 10 D. 1046. See the Act 37 & 38 Vict. c. 64, § 2. Reference may also be made to a valuable exposition of the limits of this rule in Taylor on Evidence, § 1453 *et seq.*

Nemo tenetur prodere seipsum.—No one is bound to appear against himself. One of the rules of evidence, which must be read in connection with the following maxim and with what has already been said under the preceding.

Nemo tenetur seipsum accusare.—No one is bound to accuse or criminate himself. This phrase is akin to the preceding one. No one is bound to answer any question, or produce any document, tending to involve him in criminal prosecution ; but the rule goes no further. See the observations on *Nemo tenetur jurare*, &c.

Nexus.—A bond, tie, or fetter. An arrestment is said to impose a *nexus* upon the subjects arrested, because it imposes a legal restraint on the arrestee from parting with the custody of them. The reader will find this word frequently used in the civil law to signify a man free born, but who had been reduced to slavery on account of debts which he could not pay.

Nexus realis.—A real bond, or fetter ; *i.e.*, any bond or fetter attaching to real or heritable property, and which restricts the owner's exercise of the absolute rights of property. Servitudes are so designated by our older writers ; for an example of which, see Stair, B. 4, T. 45, § 17. An inhibition is a *nexus realis*, placing a restriction, as it does, on the owner's right of disposing of his property ; so also is an adjudication.

Nigrum nunquam excedere debet rubrum.—Literally, the black should never go beyond the red : the text of a statute should never be read in a sense more comprehensive than the rubric or title. This rule (given by Sir George Mackenzie, in his works, vol. ii. p. 139) does not hold. The rubric is not a part of a statute ; it is never submitted to nor considered by the legislature, and it never receives the sanction or approval of the legislature : it is a mere index, and may be right or wrong. The rubric can never be read as modifying or explaining the text of the statute. But where a clause in a statute is ambiguous, and open to construction, the title and preamble of the Act (which in themselves, although parts of the statute, have no practical or operative effect) may be read as throwing light upon the intention of the legislature, and so serve to clear away the ambiguity, and lead to a reasonable and proper construction of that clause which is doubtful.

Nihil agitur si quid agendum superest.—Nothing is done if anything still remains to be done ; or, in other words, an incomplete proceeding is equivalent to none at all. This maxim applies only to those cases where something requires to be done completely before it can be done effectually or done at all. Thus, to complete the feudal transference of heritage from a seller to the purchaser, there must not only be a conveyance, but that conveyance must be recorded. The mere granting of the conveyance would be held as nothing (in competition with another purchaser whose conveyance was first recorded), so long as anything remained to be done to make the purchaser's title complete. So, again, a verbal bargain as to the sale of heritage, although finally agreed upon, is nothing so long as that agreement is not reduced to writing. The law requires all such bargains to be written so as effectually to bind the parties, and until everything is done which the law requires, nothing is held to be done. Compare these cases, however, with one to which the maxim would not apply. If A contracted to build a house for B, and after it was half finished he became bankrupt, and was thus rendered unable to fulfil his contract, it would not be held that nothing had been done because something remained to be done before the contract could be regarded as fulfilled or completed. If the maxim was applied in that case, A's creditors could recover nothing for the work actually performed. But that is not so. A's creditors would be entitled to recover a part of the price proportionate to the work performed; at all events, they would be entitled to recover payment for the work done, according to the *quantum meruit*.

Nihil consensui tam contrarium est quam vis atque metus.—Nothing is so contrary to consent as force and fear. Consent, to be regarded as consent at all, must be freely given; there can be no such thing in law as a forced consent. Consequently, when force and fear are used to constrain or enforce consent, it is not consent; and any deed or obligation obtained through force and fear may be reduced on that ground. See *Ex vi aut metu*.

Nihil facit error in nomine cum de corpore constat.—An error in the name is of no importance, so long as it is clear as to the subject meant; or, if there be no doubt about the thing referred to, an error in naming it is of no moment. See *Falsa demonstratio*, &c.

Nihil fit a tempore quamquam nihil non fit in tempore.

—Nothing is done by time, although everything is done in time. A prescriptive right is commonly said to be acquired by lapse of time; the maxim, however, more correctly states both the fact and the law. *By* time nothing is gained; the right is gained, not by lapse of time merely, but through the person against whom the prescription is running failing to do anything to protect his right *in* time. By use or possession in or during a certain time the right is acquired, not by the time having elapsed simply. Napier, 216.

Nihil in lege intolerabilius est eandem rem diverso jure censeri.—Nothing in law is more intolerable than that the same matter should be determined according to a different law (or, varying rule). Cases similar in circumstances should be determined by the same principles, and not one view of the law adopted in one case, and another view adopted in another case where the same question is involved.

Nihil novit.—He knows nothing. Under a reference to oath, a defender may swear that he knows nothing of the matter referred, and so obtain absolvitor; but such an answer would not avail any defender in regard to a *factum proprium*. In regard to such a matter, an answer of *nihil novit* would, in the general case, be regarded as simply an evasion, and be treated as an admission of the debt. But where an action is raised for a prescribed debt against the heir or testamentary trustee of the alleged debtor, who knows nothing personally of the debt or the transaction out of which it is said to have arisen, such a defender may on reference depone *nihil novit*, and such an answer is negative of the reference. See the interlocutor of the Lord Ordinary (Cockburn) in *Auld* v. *Aikman*, 4 D. 1487, and the case of *Cullen* v. *Smeal*, 15 D. 868.

Nihil perfectum est dum aliquid restat agendum.—Nothing is performed (*i.e.*, completely or effectually performed) while anything remains to be done. See *Nihil agitur*, &c.

Nihil præscribitur nisi quod possidetur.—Nothing is prescribed except that which is possessed; that is, a prescriptive right acquired by possession or use is limited strictly to that which has been used or possessed. Thus, use and possession of a certain road as a path or road for foot-passengers only, would not confer a right to use that road for carriages, carts, or driving cattle; there had been no use or possession of that road for such purposes, and therefore no prescriptive right to such use. Again, a proprietor may acquire by the necessary possession or use of a subject adjoining his own, a right of property in such subject as part and pertinent. If the possession has been solely had by him, and his possession was such as a proprietor would exercise, he acquires a prescriptive right to the subject used as his own, to the exclusion of all others: his possession had been possession as proprietor, and the prescriptive right acquired makes him proprietor. But if he used the adjoining subject along with others, prescription would only confer upon him a right commensurate with the use and possession he had enjoyed. See *Tanquam præscriptum*, &c.

Nihil quod est inconveniens est licitum.—Nothing which is inconvenient is lawful. Taken literally, this maxim is erroneous; nothing is illegal simply because it is inconvenient. This maxim, "which is frequently advanced by Sir E. Coke, must certainly be received with some qualification, and must be understood to mean, that against the introduction or establishing of a particular rule or precedent inconvenience is a forcible argument." Broom, 186. See *Argumentum ab inconvenienti*, &c.

Nihil tam naturale est, quam unumquodque eodem modo dissolvi quo colligatur.—Nothing is so natural as that anything (any obligation) should be dissolved, or discharged, in the same manner as that in which it was constituted. See *Eodem modo*, &c.

Nil facit error nominis cum de corpore vel persona constat.—An error in name (or description) does no harm so long as it is clear as to the subject or person meant. See *Falsa demonstratio*, &c.

Nil ligatum.—Nothing is bound; no obligation has been created or imposed.

Nimia subtilitas in jure reprobatur et talis certitudo certitudinem confundit. — Too great subtlety in law is condemned (or disproved), and such certainty confounds certainty; over-refinement in search of certainty confounds the certainty otherwise attainable. Broom, 187. See *Apices juris*, &c.

Nisi aliud convenerit.—Unless something else has been agreed upon ; or, unless it has been otherwise agreed. Ersk. B. 2, T. 3, § 25.

Nisi cum sua conditione et causa.—Except under the terms of the title and the burden of its conditions. Duff, in giving the opinion of Sir Thomas Hope as to the validity and effect of the irritant and resolutive clauses, invented in his time for the protection and maintenance of entails, says : " Of their combined effect he proceeds to give some account ; and he declares his opinion to be, that except in questions with the Crown or the superior, they were valid declarations, effectual against the heirs as conditions of the grant, and against creditors-comprisers, because they cannot have the right " *nisi cum sua conditione et causa.*" Feud. Com. 335.

Nisi malitia suppleat ætatem.—Unless malice supplies the place of age.—See *Malitia supplet,* &c.

Nobile officium.—" The *nobile officium* of the Court of Session does not admit of a precise definition. Generally speaking, it may be said to be the equitable power vested in that Court, whereby it interposes to modify or abate the rigour of the law, and, to a certain extent, to give aid where no remedy could be had in a court confined to strict law." Bell's Dict. *h.v.* Stair, B. 4, T. 3, § 1. Ersk. B. 1, T. 3, § 22. For an example of the exercise of this equitable power, see *Anderson,* 4 Macp. 577.

Nomen juris.—A word employed in legal phraseology, having a recognised technical signification ; as, for example, heritage, conquest, &c. Heritage includes all heritable property acquired by descent, while conquest includes all property of the same character acquired by purchase, gift, or other singular title. " A nominate right is a right possessing a *nomen juris,* the use of which defines its boundaries, and settles the consequences to all concerned. These rights generally receive a *nomen juris,* which are frequently the subjects of contract and of legal discussion ; while other rights, of infrequent occurrence, remain innominate, and must be determined by the application of the law to the circumstances in the particular case. The nominate and innominate contracts illustrate the doctrine. Where two parties enter into a bargain, recognised as a nominate contract, such as sale, the legal rules which regulate its operation are at once understood, and the reciprocal rights of the parties are implied in the mere *name* of the contract. The law supersedes the necessity of special stipulations, and creates an obligation in the one party to perform, and a right in the other to demand, whatever is necessary to the explication of that contract." (Bell's Dict. *v. Nominate*, &c.) " It is equally futile to attempt to interrupt the legal course of succession by words of disinheritance. *Exhæreditation* is not a *nomen juris* by the law of Scotland ; and a writing declaring certain heirs to be disinherited conveys no right to any one. The heir-at-law, therefore, can only be excluded by granting an effectual conveyance to another party." Menzies' Lectures, 693.

Nomen universitatis.—Literally, the name of the whole together ; that is, a name under which many rights of different kinds are included, so as in legal effect to embrace them all as one right. Thus the name Barony is, in our law, a *nomen universitatis*, for it includes not only the lands over which the rights of barony extend, but also the rights competent to the owner of the barony themselves. A conveyance of a barony conveys all the lands which constitute it, although not specially named or described, as well as all rights, such as servitudes, &c., which pertain to them. Formerly, when sasine was necessary to perfect a heritable right, sasine given on any part of the lands of a barony was sufficient to infeft the disponee in the whole, whether they lay discontiguous, proceeded from different superiors, or were held by different tenures. All the rights pertaining thus to a barony were held as expressed in, and conveyed under, that one name.

Nomina debitorum.—Literally, names of debtors ; but signifying in the civil law (and in our law, when used) personal debts. *Nomina* came to signify debts, because the names of the debtors were entered, along with the amount due, in the *tabulæ* of the creditor. See *Liberatio nominis*.

Nominandus.—To be named. When an entailer reserves right to himself in his deed of entail to nominate an heir or substitute by a separate deed of nomination, such heir or substitute is called *nominandus*. To be effectual, it is thought that such a deed of nomination must be recorded in the Register of Tailzies, although this has not been expressly decided. Duff's Feud. Con. 346.

Nominatim.—By name. Heirs *nominatim* are those who are specially called by name to the succession. This name is given in contradistinction to that conferred on a person called to the succession who is not yet born (*nasciturus*), or one to be subsequently named (*nominandus*). The difference between them will be understood at once from the following form of a clause of destination: "I dispone to and in favour of (1) A B, my son, whom failing (2) the heirs-male to be born of his body, whom failing (3) to any person or persons I may appoint by a writing under my hand, all and whole the lands of," &c. In this clause the disponer's son is called *nominatim*, his children, *nascituri*, are called on the failure of their father, and on their failure the disponer calls the heir *nominandus*.

Nomine albæ firmæ.—In name of blench-farm; in return for lands held blench. Blench-holding is one of the tenures by which lands are held in Scotland, and the payment made to the superior in lieu of all other services is generally elusory, such as a penny Scots. This return, in itself of no value, and rarely, if ever, exacted, is yet of importance in so far as it preserves the superior in his right to the casualties of superiority. "Craig informs us that the holding now known by the name of blench was originally called *feudum francum*, because the vassal was free of all feudal services, being bound only by an oath of fealty. It arose when the feudal manners began to give place to a certain degree of industry and civilisation, and superiors who were in want of money were willing to give lands to their vassals at nominal or quit rents, in consideration of a large sum advanced in a single payment." (Duff's Feud. Con. 49.) The extent of land held under this tenure was greatly increased by the Act 20 Geo. II. c. 50, which converted all lands then held ward of the Crown (a holding abolished by that statute) into blench-holding. This tenure is not now adopted in the constitution of an original right.

Nomine damni.—In name of damage; on account of loss.

Interest is said to be due to a creditor in name of damage, or as a recompense for the loss he is supposed to sustain through his debtor's delay in making payment of his debt. Ersk. B. 3, T. 3, § 80.

Nomine dotis.—In name of dowry or tocher.

Nomine feudifirmæ.—In name of feu-farm; on account, or in return for, lands held feu. Feu-holding is now the most common tenure by which lands are held in Scotland, and the return which the vassal is bound to render to his superior for lands so held is called feu-duty. This duty may consist either of a stipulated money payment, of grain, cattle, &c., or of services. The latter, to entitle the superior to exact them, must be of a valuable description, or merely occasional, as *ex. gr.*, attendance with a boat and rowers for the use of the superior and his family; because all services strictly personal and *quasi* military were abolished by the statute 20 Geo. II. c. 50.

Non accipi debent verba in demonstrationem falsam quæ competunt in limitationem veram.—Words ought not to be taken or regarded as erroneous description which suitably express a real limitation. False description or particularisation appended to a bequest or gift does not destroy or invalidate the gift, if it is clear what the granter intended; and this rule applies whether the false description refers to the person to be benefited, or the benefit conferred. But words may be used capable of being regarded either as a false description or as a limitation of the right conferred. Thus suppose that A conveys by his settlement to B "all my property which is situated in Scotland," and died possessed of property situated in Scotland and elsewhere, such a conveyance might be read as a conveyance of the testator's whole property wherever situated, if the words "which is situated in Scotland" were regarded as merely a false or erroneous description of the situation of the property. But according to the rule expressed in the maxim these words would not be so regarded, but would be held to be a limitation of the conveyance to property in Scotland, seeing that the words used were suitable to express such a limitation; and so long as the words competently or effectually express a limitation, the idea of false description is excluded. See some further examples of this in Broom, 642 *et seq.*

Non aliter a significatione verborum recedi oportet quam cum manifestum est aliud sensisse testatorem.—The ordinary meaning of the words ought not to be departed from, except where it appears manifest that the testator understood or used them in another sense. A rule observed in the construction of wills, which can only, however, be safely applied where it appears manifest from the deed itself that the testator did not use the words employed in their ordinary sense. As to whether or not it is admissible to travel out of the deed to show that the testator meant something different from what he has said, see the opinions delivered in the case of *Glendonwyn* v. *Gordon*, 11 Macp. (H. L.) 33. See also what has been said on the maxim *Mens testatoris*, &c.

Non bis idem.—Not the same thing twice. A man cannot be punished twice for the same offence; nor be compelled twice to fulfil the same obligation. See *Nemo debet bis*, &c.; and *Bona fides non patitur*, &c.

Non compos mentis.—Of unsound mind.

Non constat.—It does not hold; it does not appear; that is, it is not to be assumed. Thus it may be argued by one of the parties to a suit, that admitting certain statements made by the other, *non constat* that another statement made by him is necessarily correct. The difference between this phrase and the phrase *non sequitur* is this: the former refers to an unwarranted assumption of fact, the latter to an illogical inference or conclusion.

Non creditur referenti, nisi constet de relato.—The reference is not to be believed, unless the thing referred to is otherwise proved or certain. Thus an instrument of sasine does not prove the existence of the charter, or other warrant, to which it refers; nor a charter of resignation the procuratory on which it proceeds.

Non dat qui non habet.—He does not give who has not See *Nemo dat*, &c.

Non debeo melioris conditio esse quam auctor meus a quo jus in me transit.—I cannot be in a better condition (have a better title) than my author by whom the right to me is transferred. See *Assignatus utitur*, &c. ; and *Nemo plus juris*, &c.

Non debet adduci exceptio ejusdem rei cujus petitur dissolutio.—That cannot be pleaded as exception or defence in bar which is itself in question ; an exception or defence in bar cannot be based upon that right which the action is brought to question or set aside. Thus in *Sandilands* v. *Sandilands*, 10 D. 1091, a defender who resided abroad opposed an order being made upon him to sist a mandatory in respect he was possessed of landed estate in Scotland, but the objection was repelled and the order made, because the action had been brought to set aside his title to that estate. To give effect to the objection would have been to hold that he was proprietor, which was the question the action had been raised to try. So if one brings an action for the purpose of setting aside a sentence of outlawry as illegal or irregular, the sentence itself cannot be pleaded as excluding the person outlawed from being heard.

Non debet alteri per alterum iniqua conditio inferri.—No one ought to be put in an unfair or injurious position by the act of another. See *Nemo ex alterius*, &c.

Non debet cui plus licet, quod minus est, non licere.—It should not be forbidden for one to do the lesser act who may lawfully do the greater. This is the same maxim (in a form less frequently used) as *Cui licet quod majus*, &c., and both may be illustrated by a simple example. He who has the right of property in a subject may do what he will with it so long as he acts lawfully : he may sell, destroy, or give it away in donation. With such unlimited powers as these it would be unreasonable to suppose that he could not exercise the lesser power, of feuing, letting, burdening, pledging, &c., the same subject. The greater includes the less, and therefore he who can sell can let or feu, and he who can destroy may use or pledge.

Non decipitur qui scit se decipi.—He is not deceived who knows that he is being deceived. Fraud or deception, whether arising from actual misrepresentation or improper concealment, will afford a good ground for the reduction of any contract or obligation which proceeded upon, or was undertaken in consequence of, the fraud. But if the misrepresentations are known to be such to the person to whom they are made—if he knows that the person he is contracting with is deceiving him, and in this knowledge goes on with the transaction, he is bound by it, and cannot plead, against the fulfilment of his obligation, that he has been deceived. It is only where the fraud or misrepresentation induces the contract — *dolus dans causam contractui*—that it affords relevant ground for reduction ; but this, of course, cannot be said, where the contract is entered into in the knowledge, and notwithstanding, of the attempted or intended fraud. See *Dolus.*

Non deficit jus sed probatio.—Not the right defective, but the proof of it. Rights when disputed require to be proved, and some require proof whether disputed or not. A person from whom goods have been stolen is entitled to recover them wherever he finds them; but he must prove that the goods are his, and also the mode in which he lost possession. If he fails to establish these points by competent evidence, his claim to the goods cannot be sustained, not because his right to recover was defective, but because his proof was insufficient. Again, A may be the heir of B, but when he seeks to be served heir he must prove his relationship, and his obtaining the service depends upon the sufficiency of his proof. The service may be refused, not because his right to be served heir is defective, but because the proof of his right is so. *Crawford* v. *Royal Bank,* Ross, L. C. (C. L.) i. 229.

Non efficit affectus nisi sequatur effectus.—The intention is of no avail unless some effect follows. Intention to commit crime cannot be punished unless some overt act follows as the effect or consequence of the intention. See *Cogitationis pœnam,* &c.

Non entia.—Things having no existence ; nonentities. Certain writs are disregarded by our law, and treated as if they did not exist at all. Thus a bill or promissory note not duly stamped cannot be looked at by the Court to any effect or purpose whatever. Regarded as a bill, it is *non ens.* Thus, also, " a deed signed by one naturally incapable of consent, as an idiot, or by one whom the law presumes to be such, as a pupil, infers no degree of obligation, and is truly no deed, but a kind of *non ens*, which cannot admit of homologation." Ersk. B. 3, T. 3, § 47.

Non est novum ut priores leges ad posteriores trahantur.—It is no new (doctrine) that prior laws are drawn to later laws; that is, the earlier laws in point of date follow those which are later, and are either confirmed or repealed according as the later laws are consistent or inconsistent with the earlier. See *Lex posterior*, &c.

Non exemplis sed legibus judicandum.—Things are to be judged of (or rights determined), not by examples, but by laws. This maxim means that disputed questions are to be determined according to the principles of law which are applicable not according to previous decision or precedent. A previous decision or precedent is of no weight or authority, if it can be shown to be erroneous, and therefore, in that event, ought not to be followed. A series of consistent decisions upon one question, however, decide the law upon that question, and therefore to follow them in any subsequent case involving the same matter would be applying the law itself, not merely following a precedent.

Non impedit clausula derogatoria quo minus ab eadem potestate res dissolvantur a qua constituuntur.—A derogatory clause does not prevent deeds (obligations, enactments) from being discharged (set aside, abrogated) by the same power as that by which they were constituted (imposed, enacted). A derogatory clause is one by which any person (or authority) deprives himself (at least in terms) of a power which otherwise he had and could have exercised: it derogates from his own proper power and right. Thus a testator may declare his settlement to be his last will, and renounce his right to revoke the same—that is a derogatory clause. So the legislature may pass an enactment declaring that it shall remain in full force and not be repealed for a certain time. The maxim teaches that such derogatory clauses do not prohibit the person or authority from whom they emanated doing that against the doing of which the derogatory clause was passed or made. A testator may at any time revoke or alter his will, notwithstanding of its containing such a clause. Regarding this maxim, see Bankton, B. 4, T. 45, § 62 *et seq.*

Non jus ex regula sed regula ex jure.—The law does not arise from the rule (or maxim), but the rule from the law. Rules of law or legal maxims do not give rise to or make law; rules or maxims are convenient modes of stating briefly and forcibly what the law is, and are only of weight or value in so far as they accurately express the law. The maxim does not give birth to the law which it expresses: the law gives birth to the maxim.

Non liquet.—It is not clear. This phrase is explained by Montesquieu (De L'Esprit des Loix, B. 6, chap. 4), where, contrasting the different modes in which judgments are arrived at in monarchical and republican countries, he says:—"At Rome and in the cities of Greece, the judges did not consult together, each gave his own opinion in one of these three modes—(1) I absolve, (2) I condemn, (3) It is not clear to me (*non liquet*)." This phrase is not applicable to modern practice; the judges in this country are bound to give a decision in every case competently submitted to them.

Non memini.—I do not remember. Where a party to whose oath the resting-owing of a debt, or a payment, is referred, swears that he does not remember receiving the goods charged for, or of his incurring the debt, or of receiving the alleged payment, such oath, as not being evidence of the point referred, may result in decree of absolvitor in his favour, where the whole circumstances tend to the conclusion that the *non memini* is not only an honest answer, but a reasonable one. But if the fact referred is so recent that the deponent cannot be believed to be ignorant of it, or to have forgotten it, he is considered as concealing the truth, and will be decerned against in the same manner as if he had refused to depone. If the party to whose oath reference is made, depones negative of the point referred, there is an end of all proof on the subject—every other proof, however conclusive, is barred. But *non memini* not being equivalent to a denial of the fact, does not exclude the person making the reference from establishing it by proofs originally competent. Dickson, § 1624.

Non numeratæ pecuniæ.—Of money not paid. See *Exceptio non*, &c.

Non obstante.—Notwithstanding: or, not opposing.

Non officiendi luminibus vel prospectui.—Of not obstructing the lights or prospect. This is a servitude whereby the servient proprietor is prohibited from building, planting, or in any way exercising his right of property, so as to intercept the light, or obstruct the prospect, of the dominant tenement. The servitude of light does not necessarily infer the servitude of prospect. If the dominant proprietor is entitled only to the former, the servient proprietor may exercise his right of property in any way he pleases, if he does not thereby intercept the light of the dominant tenement, although his operations should shut out the prospect entirely. This being a negative servitude, can only be constituted by grant, and is strictly construed. *Craig* v. *Gould*, 24 D. 20.

Non omne quod licet honestum.—Not everything which is permitted is honourable, or morally right; that is, there are some things permitted, or rather not prohibited, by the law, which are not honourable or moral in themselves. The distinction drawn by the phrase is between those things which a man is not prevented by the law from doing, and those things which cannot be regarded in ordinary dealing as fair or just. Thus a seller may so laud the character of his wares, or sell them at a price so enhanced or unfair, as to amount to a morally dishonest act, yet the law will not reduce the transaction at the instance of the buyer. Again, a debtor may object that an unstamped obligation granted by him is not binding, because, although given to and accepted by his creditor as a mere acknowledgment of debt with obligation to pay, it must be held by legal interpretation to be a promissory note. Such a plea is neither honest nor honourable, and yet the law must give effect to such a plea, and refuse decree on the document libelled.

Non pars substantiæ sive fundi, sed accidens.—Not a part of the subject or land, but an accident. Servitudes are here described, which being accidents of property, may or may not exist, and are not regarded as essential to the right of property in the land.

Non possessori incumbit necessitas probandi possessiones ad se pertinere.—There is no necessity laid upon a possessor of proving that his possessions belong to him. In regard to moveable subjects, possession implies property, and the possessor is not bound to prove that he possesses lawfully. It lies upon the person challenging the right of possession, whether the subject be heritable or moveable, to show that the possessor has no title : in such a case *melior est conditio possidentis.*

Non potest probari quod probatum non relevat.—That cannot be proved which when proved is not relevant. See *Frustra probatur,* &c.

Non potest rex gratiam facere cum injuria et damno aliorum.—The king cannot grant a favour which occasions injury and loss to others. Take in illustration of this maxim the case of a landed proprietor convicted of treason, whose lands have been forfeited to the king, and by him bestowed upon another. The king may pardon the person guilty of treason, but he cannot divest his donee of the lands so as to reinvest the original proprietor who forfeited them; the pardon is within the king's grace, and he may grant it when and how he pleases, but he cannot in the exercise of his prerogative injure the donee by depriving him of the lands. See Broom, 63.

Non præscribi potest rebus meræ facultatis.—There is no prescription against those rights which consist in the power of doing or not doing a certain thing. For instance, no prescription runs against a proprietor of land to the effect of excluding him from building upon his land, however long he may be in exercising that right. A right *meræ facultatis* is not lost through non-usage. *Gellatly* v. *Arrol,* 1 Macp. 592. Napier, 606. Bell's Prin. § 999.

Non quod dictum est sed quod factum est inspicitur. —Not what has been said, but what has been done, is regarded. In disputes arising out of contracts, the principal question to be determined is, what was the contract or bargain which the parties made; the words in which that bargain was expressed may be regarded, in a certain sense, as a secondary consideration. .The contract may have been expressed in ambiguous terms, its language may be faulty in grammatical construction, or terms may have been used erroneously, which are inapplicable to the circumstances, all of which considerations require that the bargain—what the parties did rather than what they said—should be first ascertained and chiefly regarded in determining their respective rights and liabilities. For example, among uneducated people nothing is more common than the expression that in certain given circumstances a man should "be *entitled* to pay," &c., meaning that in these circumstances he should be *bound* to pay. In *Uhde* v. *Walters*, 3 Campb. 15, an insurance effected over a vessel "to any port in the Baltic" was held to cover the loss by capture of the vessel on a voyage to Revel, a port in the Gulf of Finland, because by universal custom and consent among merchants, the Gulf of Finland, was considered and treated as within the Baltic, although the two seas were treated as distinct by geographers. In that case the words did not express the whole contract between the parties, but what was really done and bargained for prevailed over the mere terms used. The provisions of the Sale of Goods Act, 1893, are declared (§ 61) not to apply to any transaction, by which it is intended merely to operate a security, although the transaction takes the form of a sale. The substance, not the form, of the transaction is thus regarded. This maxim is applied also in questions of construction of wills and deeds. It is to be observed, however, that if words are used in the statement or expression of a contract or other deed which have a well-recognised meaning, and which are not modified or altered by usage of trade, or universal practice in some particular district, the words used will be read in their ordinary meaning, and neither of the contracting parties will be heard to maintain that he intended to express something else than the meaning which the words usually bear. See *In conventionibus contrahentium*, &c.

Non remota sed proxima causa spectatur.—Not the remote but the near (or immediate) cause is regarded. See *Causa proxima*, &c.

Non repugnantia.—An absence of opposition ; or a withdrawal of opposition,—as in a conflict between contending claims. "The concurrence of one as a consenter (in a heritable bond) who possesses a prior security, does not import a conveyance of his right to the creditor, but a *non repugnantia*,—a departure from his preference in a question with this creditor." Duff's Feud. Con. 269.

Non tenetur placitare super hæreditate paterna.—See *Minor non tenetur*, &c.

Non utendo.—By non-usage. Some rights are lost to their proprietor simply through his neglect to use them. Thus servitudes are lost *non utendo* if the owner of the dominant tenement neglect to use his right for forty years together; and the right to vicarage teinds is lost by the neglect of the incumbent to levy them. Generally it may be said that any right may be lost by non-usage which can be acquired by lengthened use. Rights *meræ facultatis* are never lost by mere non-usage.

Non valens agere.—Not able to act.

Non valentia agendi.—Want of ability to act. This and the preceding phrase are descriptive of the condition of those persons who through nonage or other legally-recognised impediment are incapable of defending or protecting their rights, and against whom consequently prescription does not run. See *Contra non valentem*, &c.

Non videntur qui errant consentire.—They do not appear to consent who are in error. The consent which is necessary in consensual contracts or obligations to bind the person consenting must be free and voluntary, not induced by force, fear, fraud, nor given under essential error. Thus a wife who discharges her husband or his representatives of all her legal claims against her husband's estate may reduce the discharge on the ground that at the time she granted it she was labouring under essential error as to the extent of the rights discharged. Again, one who consents to sell a subject of which he believes himself to be the owner, is not bound to fulfil his obligation, if it turns out that he is not the owner and has no power to sell. As to the effect of error upon contracts, see *Consensus in idem*, &c.

Notabilis excessus.—A remarkable or very great excess. Stair, B. 1, T. 4, § 18.

Nova causa obligationis.—A new ground of obligation. Actions containing penal conclusions are, in the ordinary case, considered personal, falling upon the death of the defender, and not transmissible against the heir. If, however, litiscontestation has taken place (that is, if the parties have proponed their respective pleas, or a proof of the facts has been allowed), such actions do transmit. This proceeds upon the principle that the parties are held bound as if by contract to abide by the decision which may be pronounced upon the proof to be adduced,—a contract in which the heir is held to represent his ancestor, although he did not represent him as regards his delict or its penal consequences. Litiscontestation is thus said to impart a *nova causa obligationis*, because it introduces an obligation to abide by the decision, differing essentially from that obligation on which the action originally proceeded, Ersk. B. 4, T. 1, § 70.

Nova debita. — New debts; that is, debts newly or recently contracted, as opposed to old or prior debts. A security granted by a debtor within sixty days of his bankruptcy for a debt contracted before that period is reducible as a fraudulent preference. But security or payment granted in consideration of a *novum debitum*—a debt presently contracted—is not reducible although granted within the sixty days.

Nova constitutio futuris formam imponere debet non præteritis.—A new law ought to impose its conditions on the future, not on the past; that is, laws ought to be prospective, not retrospective. Retrospective legislation is never presumed, and therefore a law will only be applied to cases occurring after its date, unless it appear from the statute itself that it is intended to have retroactive effect. Penal laws are never retrospective; but remedial statutes, which are more liberally interpreted, are sometimes allowed retroactive effect. Upon this subject see the opinions delivered by the consulted judges in the case of *Reid*, 1 Macp. 774.

Novalia.—A term applied to lands recently improved or cultivated. In the beginning of the twelfth century almost all the religious orders in this country were freed by papal exemption from their liability for the teinds properly exigible in respect of the lands held by them. Towards the end of that century the then existing exemptions were very much restricted, and all religious orders except three were declared liable for the teinds payable out of their property. Exemption was, however, then extended to *novalia*,—lands which, having lain waste from time immemorial, had been newly brought into a state of cultivation by the monks by their own labour and at their own expense. It has, on a similar principle, been held that lands gained from the sea by embankments, or gained by the draining of a loch, are not liable for teinds to the titular or patron of the parish. See More's Notes to Stair, ccxxxix.

Novatio.—Novation; which is a mode of extinguishing an obligation already existing by the substitution of a new engagement or obligation by the same debtor to the same creditor in its place. Thus, when a bill is given for the amount of an open account, and the account is in consequence discharged, novation takes place, the obligation being thereafter for payment of the bill, and not the account. Another form of novation is when a new debtor is substituted for the old one, with consent of the creditor; this is generally termed delegation. See *Delegatio*.

Novatio non præsumitur.—Novation is not presumed. The new obligation must bear to be in satisfaction and complete discharge of the one previously existing, or otherwise it will *in dubio* be regarded as merely corroborative of it, or regarded as constituting a separate and additional obligation. Thus where new bills are given in satisfaction of previous bills, unless the latter are delivered up to the debtor, the creditor will be entitled to sue on them should the new bills be dishonoured: the new bills are not presumed to have been given in extinction, but rather in fortification of the previous bills. And so in delegation, the obligation of the new debtor will not be regarded as discharging the obligation of the original debtor, unless this be distinctly stipulated. *In dubio*, the presumption will be that the new obligant is cautioner for or co-debtor with the original obligant, and that the new obligation is granted in corroboration, or in security of that already existing. The legal presumption, may, however, be redargued.

Novodamus.—Literally, we give of new. This name is given to any charter, original or by progress, by which the superior renews to his vassal a grant of lands previously made. It is generally granted to obviate some defect in the previous title, or to supply the place of some deeds necessary to the progress which have been lost. Such a charter secures the vassal against the consequences of a defective title as in a question with the superior, and frees him from liability for arrears of feu-duties or casualties remaining due to the superior, for it implies a discharge of bygone duties. The Act 37 & 38 Vict. cap. 94, by which charters and other writs by progress are abolished, has excepted charters of *novodamus* from its operation.

Noxa caput sequitur.—Punishment follows the person guilty of the crime ; punishment is personal.

Nuda pactio obligationem non parit.—A bare bargain gives birth to no obligation. See *Nudum pactum.*

Nuda patientia.—Mere forbearance or sufferance. In servitudes the obligation of the proprietor of the servient tenement is one of mere sufferance or submission ; he must submit to the exercise of the right which the proprietor of the dominant tenement possesses, but he is under no obligation to do anything by which that right may be maintained or exercised. Thus, for example, the proprietor of the servient tenement over which another has the servitude of way, is not bound to keep the necessary roads in repair, his obligation being simply to permit or suffer the dominant proprietor to exercise his right of passage. Everything required for the exercise or enjoyment of that right must be provided and maintained by the dominant proprietor himself. " Neither can the fiar of a decayed house be compelled by the liferenter to put it in tenantable repair ; because a liferent being a servitude, binds the person burdened no further than to *nuda patientia.*" Ersk. B. 2, T. 9, § 60.

Nudum officium.—The bare office or character, without any of the emoluments or advantages which generally pertain to it. Ersk. B. 3, T. 9, § 26.

Nudum pactum. — A mere paction ; or engagement amounting merely to a promise. In England the phrase is used to signify an obligation for which no valid legal consideration has been given, and one, consequently, which cannot, according to the rules of English law, be enforced.

Nudum pactum est ubi nulla subest causa præter conventionem.—A mere paction is one where no cause or consideration underlies the obligation, where there is nothing but the bargain. " What amounts to a legal consideration, however, is a question liberally dealt with, and generally it is held that the promisor must either obtain some kind of advantage, or the promisee suffer some loss, injury, or inconvenience in respect of the promise. Mere love, affection, friendship, or a sense of moral duty, is not a legal consideration in this sense." (Paterson's Compend. § 441.) The law of England in regard to *nuda pacta* will be found stated in Addison on Contracts, 2 *et seq.* In Scotland no distinction is recognised between *pacta nuda* and *non nuda*. If an obligation is granted, the granter of it can be compelled to fulfil it, or is subjected in damage for non-fulfilment, whether a consideration has been given for the obligation or not. It will, however, be borne in mind that no obligation relating to heritable rights is, in Scotland, effectual unless it has been constituted by writing.

Nudum pactum inefficax ad agendum.—A mere agreement is ineffectual to maintain action. Among the Romans a mere agreement did not in the general case create a civil obligation which could be legally enforced. In most cases, besides the mutual consent, something had to be transferred, certain words to be uttered, or written documents used, before an agreement became obligatory and a contract arose. Without these incidents, an agreement by which one promised to give or to do something, continued a mere agreement without any action attaching; except in the case of contracts constituted by consent alone, such as sale, location, &c. The *nudum pactum* of the Roman law was one which through informality or want of the necessary ceremony gave rise to no legal obligation; and it was immaterial whether the obligation was onerous or gratuitous. The question whether an agreement is *nudum pactum* by the English law, does not depend upon informality, but simply upon whether a legal consideration has been given for the obligation undertaken.

Nulla pactione effici potest, ne dolus præstetur.—No contract can effectually stipulate that fraud or dole is not to be answered for: or, no one can effectually stipulate that he is not to be responsible for his own dole or fraud. Thus in the contract of fire insurance, no one can stipulate that he is to be entitled to the amount of the loss sustained through fire, even although it should appear that he had been guilty of setting fire to the subject insured; or, in marine insurance, that the insurer should be entitled to the amount insured, even if the ship was scuttled by the insurer. These stipulations would be contrary to good policy, which forbids all contracts that might tempt men to commit offences, or, in a manner, offer a premium to crime. By the Act 33 & 34 Vict. cap. 28, § 7, it is provided that an agreement between an attorney or solicitor and his client that the former should not be liable for negligence is wholly void.

Nulla persona.—No person. *Persona* is any being regarded as capable of having rights and undertaking obligations; and hence it includes, in its legal signification, not only mankind, but also such creatures of the law as cities, corporations, &c. On the other hand, all men are not *personæ*; rebels, for example, are not, because they can neither have legal rights nor fulfil legal obligations; neither are pupils, who, on account of their nonage, are deemed incapable of exercising rights or undertaking obligations. A married woman is *nulla persona*, because the law regards her as merged in the person of her husband, and she is held incapable of undertaking any personal obligation. *Persona* originally signified the mask worn by an actor indicative of the character he, for the time, assumed, and so came to signify the different characters or positions a man might hold in his social or public life. Thus the same man might have the *persona patris*, or *tutoris*, or *mariti*; that is, he might be regarded in his character of father, tutor, or husband.

Nulla sasina, nulla terra.—No sasine (or infeftment), no land. This phrase signifies that the fact of infeftment is that by which a right of property in land is to be tested. Until infeftment was taken, there was no feudal, and therefore no indefeasible right in the lands. The absolute character of this rule has been to some extent modified by the provision of the Act 37 & 38 Vict. cap. 94, § 9. See *Mortuus sasit*, &c. The old ceremony of giving infeftment has been abolished, and the instrument of sasine which for a time came in place of the ceremony is now unnecessary. The recording of the conveyance comes in place of sasine.

Nulli res sua servit jure servitutis.—No man's property

is under burden of a servitude to himself: no one can have a right of servitude over his own subject. The right of servitude is a limited right of use, which disappears when the greater right of property comes into existence: the greater includes the less. No one could at the same time and with reference to the same subject, have the limited right of servitude and the unlimited right of property.

Nullius in bonis.—Among the goods of no one; no one's property. See *Res nullius*.

Nullum tempus occurrit regi.—No time runs against the king: the rights of the sovereign are not barred by the lapse of time. The rule expressed in this maxim, if taken in its fullest extent, is certainly not in conformity with the law of Scotland; and it may be doubted whether it expresses the law of Scotland to any extent. By the Act 1617, c. 12, the positive prescription is made effectual against the Crown: and the tendency of opinion has been that the negative prescription runs against the Crown also, although this does not appear to have been ever positively decided. On this latter question the reader may be referred to Ersk. B. 3, T. 7, § 31. Napier, 650 *et seq*. *E. of Fife's Trs.*, 11 D. 889; and *Deans of Chapel Royal*, 5 Macp. 414. As to the extent to which the maxim is still held by the law of England, see Broom, 65.

Nullus commodum capere potest de injuria sua propria. —No one can take advantage (or benefit) from a wrong committed by himself. A wrong is just as illegal as a crime, and cannot be the basis of a legal right; it gives rise to no right of action at the instance of the wrong-doer. Thus a creditor who, taking advantage of his debtor's position, has compelled his insolvent debtor to give him an obligation to pay his debt in full, as the condition of his (the creditor's) acceding to a composition arrangement, cannot recover under that obligation. *Macfarlane* v. *Nicoll*, 3 Macp. 237, and cases there cited.

Nullus videtur dolo facere qui suo jure utitur.—No one appears to act wrongfully (or in dole) who exercises his right; he is not a wrong-doer who does that which he has a right to do. See *Nemo habetur agere*, &c.

Nummi pupillares.—Money belonging to a pupil. It is

provided by the Act 12 & 13 Vict. c. 51, § 5, that if a factor shall keep in his hands for more than ten days a greater sum than fifty pounds belonging to the estate over which he has been appointed, he shall be held liable to the estate " at the rate of twenty pounds per cent. per annum on the excess of the said sum of fifty pounds, for such time as it shall be in his hands beyond the said ten days."

Nunc valent et quantum valuerunt tempore pacis ?—What is the value (of the lands) now, and how much were they worth in time of peace ? This was one of the inquiries directed to be made by the brieve of inquest under the old form of special service; the purpose of which was to fix the value of the lands so that they might bear their proper proportion of public subsidies and taxes, and also that the rights of the superior under his different casualties might be ascertained. See *Antiquus*, &c.

Nunciatio novi operis.—An information lodged respecting a work unwarrantably commenced or threatened by another to one's injury. This was a proceeding under the civil law, whereby one protected his rights against another who had wrongfully invaded or threatened to invade them by some new operation. The person who was being injured went to the ground where the new work was begun or threatened, and there, either by symbolic act (*ex. gr., jactu lapilli*), or by verbal declaration, protested against the further progress of the work. If, notwithstanding this declaration (*nunciatio*), the work was proceeded with, the *nunciator* applied to the prætor for an interdict to have the work prevented if it had not yet been commenced, or its further progress forbidden if it had been commenced. If, however, the work had been completed, the remedy to be adopted for its removal was of a different kind, varying according to circumstances. This is fully explained in the Digest, B. 39, T. 1. In illustration of this form of procedure, reference may be made to Stair, B. 2, T. 7, § 23.

Nunquam concluditur in falso.—" A maxim importing that in actions of reduction-improbation, on the head of falsehood or forgery, any relevant defence may be pleaded, or any additional proof brought forward, however late in the proceedings, provided decree has not been extracted. The application of this maxim has been very much limited in civil proceedings by the introduction of the new forms of process." (Bell's Dict. *h.v.*) Actions of the class referred to are now regulated by the same rules as those which regulate any other action of reduction.

Nunquam crescit ex post facto præteriti delicti æstimatio.—The extent of a past delict is never increased by a subsequent act. The character or enormity of a crime is determined as at the time when it is committed, and no subsequent act on the part of the delinquent can enhance it. He may commit other crimes, and be tried for them all at one time, but each crime must be complete in itself, and one crime cannot be taken as making another previously committed more heinous. This does not prevent the judge, however, from taking into account the whole crimes of which a panel is found guilty in awarding sentence.

Nunquam decurritur ad extraordinarium sed ubi deficit ordinarium.—Extraordinary remedies are never had recourse to except when ordinary remedies are insufficient. Where the ordinary rules and practice of law afford a sufficient protection against wrong, or reparation for injury done, these must be appealed to; they are provided for that purpose. But as the law always affords a remedy, extraordinary remedies will be applied where no ordinary remedy can be found which meets the necessity of the case. As the name implies, however, these extraordinary remedies are only afforded when all ordinary remedies fail. See *Nobile officium*.

Nunquam præscribitur in falso.—A prescriptive right can never be founded upon a falsehood; prescription never runs in favour or in support of that which is criminally false. A title, however invalid, even when proceeding *a non habente*—from one having no power to grant it—may be rendered unchallengeable after the lapse of the necessary period by the positive prescription. But if the title founded upon be a forgery (which is a species of the crime known by the generic term falsehood), it may be challenged at any time, for forgery attaches a *labes realis* to the title which prescription cannot cure. With regard to this maxim, see Napier, 607 *et seq.*

Nuptiales tabulæ.—Marriage tablets. This was a writing among the Romans equivalent to our marriage-contract; and these words are intended to signify marriage-contract when used in Scotch law. *Contra fidem*, &c.

Nuptias non concubitus sed consensus facit.—Not cohabitation but consent makes marriage. See *Consensus non concubitus*, &c.

O

Ob contingentiam.—On account of connection or similarity. Where two actions are depending before the Court at the same time, between the same parties, and involving the same dispute, in which the one decision will dispose of the whole pleas of parties, they may be conjoined *ob contingentiam*, on account of the connection existing between them.

Ob defectum hæredis.—On account of a failure of heirs. A person attainted for treason loses all his civil rights, and his property, heritable and moveable, falls to the Crown. But where a succession to a feu-right subsequently opens up to the attainted person, from which, by his attainder, he is excluded, it falls, not to the Crown, but to the immediate superior, as escheat *ob defectum hæredis*. The heirs of such a person are excluded from all succession to an ancestor, where the propinquity betwixt the ancestor and them is necessarily connected by the attainted person, or where the attainted person would have succeeded to the estate of the deceased, had it not been for his attainder. Attainder thus necessarily results in a failure of heirs. When any one leaving property dies without heirs and intestate, the Crown succeeds as last heir; and although this right of the Crown cannot be said to arise *ob defectum hæredis*, the Crown itself being heir, yet in point of fact, it is in respect of the failure of heirs that the Crown succeeds to such estate as *bona vacantia*.

Ob majorem cautelam.—For greater security; in the exercise of greater caution. See *In majorem*, &c.

Ob metum perjurii.—On account of the fear of perjury; an apprehension on which certain evidence was at one time excluded, or left in the discretion of the witness whether to give it or not. See *Ob reverentiam*, &c.

Ob non solutum canonem.—On account of unpaid canon or feu-duty. By the Act 1597, cap. 250, it was made a statutory condition of all feus that if the feu-duty remained unpaid for two whole years together, the vassal should forfeit his right to the lands, in the same manner as if an irritant clause to that effect was engrossed in his infeftment. This being a penal irritancy requires to be declared by an action, which is still competent to a superior, and is called an action of tinsel of the feu. The vassal may avoid the forfeiture by purging the irritancy (that is, by paying the arrears) at the bar, or at any time before extract. Where the irritancy depends upon the statutory enactment, it is called legal ; but where this is fortified by an express irritant clause inserted in the title, it is called a conventional irritancy.

Ob pias causas.—On account of religious reasons ; on account of dutiful considerations. "If legacies exceed the defunct's own part, then they abate proportionally, unless there be a preference granted by the testator, or a privilege by law, whereof I know none with us, for even a legacy *ob pias causas*—viz., a mortification to a kirk, was found to have no privilege, but it and other legacies suffered proportional deduction, seeing they exceeded the dead's part." (Stair, B. 3, T. 4, § 24.) Provisions made by a son to his father *ob pias causas* are those which proceed from the affectionate regard and natural duty which the son is bound morally to render to his father.

Ob pœnam negligentiæ. — As punishment for negligence. The laws aid those who are careful of their own interests, not those who neglect them. Accordingly, where one allows another to use his subject so that he thereby acquires a right of servitude over it, that right is recognised as much by way of a punishment of the person who allowed such use without interruption, as on account of the actual use itself. See *Vigilantibus*, &c.

Ob publicam utilitatem.—On account of public utility, or for the public advantage.

Ob reverentiam personæ et metum perjurii.—On account of reverence or respect to the person, and the fear of perjury. On these reasons were founded the exclusion of certain persons as witnesses, as well as the right which a witness in certain circumstances had of declining to answer the question put. On account of the former, all persons standing in the position of relationship to the suitor for whom they were proposed to be adduced were excluded as incompetent witnesses, because it was apprehended that the respect or reverence they had, or were supposed to entertain, for their relative would prevent them telling the truth, or the whole truth, or might induce them to tell what was not true. All exclusion on the ground of relationship (unless it be the relation of husband and wife, and that only in criminal cases) has been abolished. The *metus perjurii* was that on which chiefly witnesses were entitled to decline answering any question put to them, where the answer involved a confession of an indictable offence, or of moral delinquency, or shame. In any such circumstances it was feared that the witness would screen his guilt or shame by perjury rather than confess it truthfully, and therefore he was entitled to decline answering any question involving such consequences. The necessity, however, of obtaining such evidence for the due administration of justice, together with the recognised principle that the desire for truth must prevail over the fear of perjury, have overturned this rule, and no witness can now decline to answer any question which may be put to him. There is still an exception with reference to questions, the answers to which involve the confession of an indictable offence. Such questions a witness may still decline to answer ; but this privilege is accorded upon the principle of the maxim *Nemo tenetur seipsum accusare*, and not upon the *metus perjurii*.

Ob turpem causam.—On account of a dishonourable cause, or immoral consideration. An obligation which has been granted on account of an immoral consideration, as, for example, a bond or bill granted as the price of prostitution, cannot be enforced. No action or diligence can be maintained on such a bond or bill, and that whether the consideration appear *ex facie* of the obligation or not. There is a distinction drawn between an obligation granted as the price of prostitution, and one granted subsequent to such a connection as a provision due in honour and justice to a young woman who has been seduced; the latter may be enforced although the former cannot. But even in the latter case, if the connection has been adulterous, action will be denied on the obligation if the woman knew at the time of the connection that the man was married. Although action does not lie upon an obligation granted *ob turpem causam*, yet if it has been implemented, no action will lie, on the other hand, for restitution.

Obæratus.—A person involved in debt. Stair, B. 1, T. 9, § 15.

Obiter dictum.—An opinion given incidentally. In the course of pronouncing their decision in a case before them, judges sometimes give opinions incidentally on points which may have been raised, but, not being essential to the case, have not been fully discussed or weighed. Such opinions are called *obiter dicta*; they are not considered as authoritative, nor would they be received as such by the Court, if the question on which they had been expressed came up at a subsequent period for judgment. They are only of importance commensurate with the reputation of the judge delivering them.

Obligatio literarum.—An obligation constituted by writing; a written contract. Among the Romans contracts were divided into four classes, which took their names from the manner in which they were constituted. Contracts were constituted—(1) *re*, when the delivery of something was essential to their constitution, as in pledge, deposit, &c.; (2) *verbis*, when certain solemn and formal words were necessarily used, as in stipulation; (3) *literis*, when the contract was constituted by writing, as in the case where a debtor became bound for the debt regarding which he had made entries in his *tabulæ* corresponding to those in the *tabulæ* of his creditor (explained under the phrase *Liberatio nominis*); and (4) *consensu*, where consent alone was required, as in sale, partnership, &c. Hence contracts were said to be real, verbal, literal (or written), and consensual.

Obreptione.—By surprise; by deceit; clandestinely.

Obtorto collo.—By the throat. "Absents, because they

are incapable of making a defence, cannot be prosecuted criminally. It was a rule long observed by the Romans, that neither criminal nor civil causes could be tried in absence ; and hence, when a defender would not voluntarily appear in judgment, the only remedy left to the pursuer was to drag him by open force to the Court, *obtorto collo.*" Ersk. B. 4, T. 4, § 83.

Occultatio thesauri inventi.—The concealment of found treasure. Hume, i. 63.

Occupantis fiunt derelicta.—Things abandoned become the property of the occupier, that is, the person who first takes possession of them after their abandonment. Things abandoned by their owner become *res nullius*, and in England fall to the finder or first occupier ; in Scotland (although practically the same rule prevails) the theory is that all such things belong to the Crown. Upon this subject, see *Res nullius*. The term *derelict* is now most frequently used in our law with reference to ships and cargoes that have been abandoned at sea ; and with regard to them the maxim does not apply. Take the case of a ship abandoned at sea in stress of weather, supposed to be in a sinking condition, and that after the abandonment another ship finds it and tows it safely into port : the abandoned ship does not become the property of the salvors, but is the property of the owners at the time of the abandonment (or of the underwriters if abandoned by the owners to them), subject only to the salvor's claim for salvage. If the derelict ship after being brought into port is not claimed by owners or underwriters, it falls to the Crown after satisfaction of the claims for salvage. Again, goods which have been jettisoned do not become the property of the finder ; but that is because goods jettisoned are not considered derelict.

Officium nemini debet esse damnosum.—An office should inflict damage or loss upon no one. The meaning of this maxim is, that no one should be subjected to loss by the discharge of an office or duty. Thus a tutor or curator, whose office is gratuitous, is entitled to be indemnified for all that he has disbursed on behalf of his ward in the performance of the duties of his office during its continuance. So, likewise, a mandatory is entitled to demand from the mandant all reasonable expenses disbursed by him, and the damage sustained by him in the execution of the mandate, even although the management should not have been successful or prosperous. A *negotiorum gestor* is in a similar position; and the fact that he takes the office upon himself (unless his acts amount to needless and officious interference), makes no difference in this respect between him and a regularly authorised mandatory.

Officium virile.—An office of or belonging to a man. The office of tutor or curator among the Romans being a public office, none but a man could fill it, except in certain cases where, by the special authority and permission of the Emperor (C. B. 5, T. 35), women were allowed to assume the office and perform its duties. This, and any other office or duty which a man was appointed to perform, was termed *officium,* or *munus virile.* In Scotland, any one may be named as tutor who is of full age, except a married woman, who, being herself under the curatory of her husband, cannot act as tutor during the subsistence of her marriage.

Omissa et male appretiata.—Things omitted and erroneously valued. See *Ad omissa,* &c.

Omissio eorum quæ tacite insunt nihil operatur.—The omission of those things which are tacitly implied operates nothing; that is, their omission does not operate against their being held, by implication, as expressed. In like manner, their expression operates nothing; for the expression of that which is necessarily implied adds nothing to the nature and extent of the right or obligation which the contract or deed is meant to create. See *Expressio eorum,* &c.

Omne actum ab intentione agentis est judicandum.—Every act is to be judged of by the intention of the doer. It is the intention or purpose which prompts the act that gives that act its character; and it has been already pointed out that the very same act may be criminal or innocent according to the intention of the doer. (See *Actum non facit,* &c.) In addition to the examples already given, the following cases may be taken as illustrative of this maxim. If A and B mutually accept each other as husband and wife, with the intention of making marriage, they thereby become married persons; but if the very same words are used by C and D in frolic, and with no intention of marrying each other, there is no marriage—the intention in each case qualifying the act, making it marriage in the one case, and not in the other. Again, if A offers to sell B his horse for a certain price, and B accepts, the contract is completed; A is bound to deliver the horse and B to pay the price, provided the parties intended to make a contract. But if the offer and acceptance were merely made in jest, with no intention either to buy or sell the horse, there is no contract; here again the intention of parties affords the criterion by which it is to be judged whether a contract was made or not.

Omne jus reale.—Every real right.

Omne majus continet in se minus. — The greater includes the less. See *Non debet cui plus*, &c.

Omne quod in se erat.—All that one had in his power; everything that he could do. Ersk. B. 1, T. 7, § 44.

Omne quod solo inædificatur cedit solo.—Everything that is built upon the ground belongs to the ground. See *Inædificatum solo*, &c.

Omne testamentum morte consummatum est.—Every will (or testamentary writing) is perfected or completed by death. A man's will being ambulatory or revocable so long as he lives, can only be said to be completed when the testator dies, for not until then can it be completed in the sense of being unchangeable and beyond revocation.

Omne verbum de ore fideli cadit in debitum.—Every word sincerely spoken will constitute obligation. This phrase is taken from the canon law, and expresses the difference which existed between its provisions and those of the civil law on the subject of pactions. By the latter mere words or promises had not the effect of constituting a binding obligation, unless some act or deed followed upon the words, or unless they were solemn words (such as those used in *stipulatio*), and recognised by the law as sufficient to constitute an obligation. Such mere words or promises were regarded as *nuda pacta*, were not binding, and gave rise to no action. By the canon law, on the other hand, all words spoken, and promises given, sincerely and in earnest, were regarded as binding, and implement could be enforced by action; and this is the rule followed by the Scotch law.

Omnes licentiam habent his quæ pro se indulta sunt renunciare.—Every one has liberty to renounce those rights which have been granted (or made) in his favour. It does not matter whether the right or privilege is one conferred by the law or by private bargain or deed; no one can be compelled to enforce his rights. The right being conceived in his favour, he may decline to enforce it; he may renounce it. But "the words *pro se* have been introduced into the maxim, to show that no man can renounce a right which his duty to the public, which the claim of society, forbid the renunciation of." Per Lord C. Westbury in *Hunt* v. *Hunt*, 31 L. J. Ch. 175. See *Cuique licet juri*, &c., and *Invito beneficium*, &c.

Omni exceptione major.—Beyond all exception; unexceptionable. This is frequently said of witnesses whose known character places their evidence beyond all suspicion. An instance of the use of the phrase will be found in Ersk. B. 4, T. 2, § 29.

Omnia grana crescentia.—All growing grain. Thirlage, when constituted by writing, differs in its extent according to the terms in which the grant is expressed. It may either be of (1) all growing corns, including barley; (2) of all grindable corns, which is held to mean those corns alone which are ground for use within the thirl, and which the mill is fitted to grind; or (3) of all corns brought within the thirl, which includes all corn brought within it for use or consumpt, although not of the growth of the astricted lands. When the thirlage was of the first of these three kinds, the grant was expressed in the words of the phrase. Thirlage being a monopoly in favour of the miller, and a heavy burden upon landholders and feuars, was never regarded with much favour by the law, and is now almost unknown.

Omnia præsumuntur contra spoliatorem.—All things are presumed against a wrong-doer. The wrong-doing to which this maxim has reference is that which can be so regarded by law, and does not include those acts which, however wrong according to a moral standard, are still within the legal right of the doer. As a general rule, also, the maxim does not apply in criminal cases, where (with very rare exceptions) there is no presumption against the accused, but everything essential to guilt must be proved. But the maxim has application in many circumstances in civil cases. For example, if one of the parties to a suit calls for the production of an agreement or letter or other document in the possession of his opponent, the terms of which are in dispute, and it appears that the party having the custody of the document has wilfully destroyed it, the document will be presumed to have been in the terms alleged by the party calling for it, or at all events it will be presumed to have been in its terms disadvantageous to the destroyer of it. So, also, where goods liable to duty are concealed on board a ship, the person concealing them will be presumed to have concealed them for the purpose of defeating the revenue, and will incur the penalties of smuggling, and the goods will be forfeited. Where articles of value are lent or deposited, and the borrower or depositary refuses to deliver them up, the presumption will be that the article was of the most valuable description of its kind, and his liability for its price will be ascertained according to that standard. See upon this subject the cases cited in Smith's Leading Cases, i. 385 *et seq.*; and Taylor, i. 130 *et seq.*

Omnia præsumuntur legitime facta donec probetur in contrarium.—All things are presumed to have been done according to law until the contrary is proved. This is another form of the following maxim.

Omnia præsumuntur rite et solemniter acta esse.—All things are presumed to have been done duly and in the usual manner; or, all things are presumed to have been solemnly done and with the usual ceremony. This is one of the presumptions of law, and may be illustrated by a reference to the old procedure of giving sasine. If the instrument of sasine, properly authenticated and recorded, set forth that sasine had been given to the disponee upon production of his warrant, by delivery of the usual and necessary symbols in presence of witnesses, the law presumed that sasine was duly given, and that the ceremony usual in such a case had been properly observed. An objection that the ceremony was not observed, or that the prescribed symbols had not been delivered, could not be listened to so long as the instrument of sasine stood unreduced, for it was presumed that everything was duly and solemnly performed. So also, with all notarial instruments, the presumption holds that the notarial act set forth was duly and regularly performed at the right time and place and before the proper witnesses; executions of citation and charge by officers of court, and generally all official acts, are protected by the same presumption. But like other *presumptiones legis*, it may be redargued by proof. This maxim is sometimes written in the briefer form of *Omnia rite acta præsumuntur*.

Omnia quæ jure contrahuntur contrario jure pereunt.—All obligations contracted or imposed by law perish through a contrary law. If one statute imposes a duty or obligation, another statute may discharge it; the same authority which declares "thou shalt" may subsequently declare "thou shalt not." Thus by statute, fishing for salmon is forbidden during a certain period of the year called close time, and an obligation is imposed on all to abstain from fishing during that time. But if another statute was passed restricting the close time, or abolishing it altogether, the latter statute would discharge the obligation which the former had imposed. Again, by the Act 11 & 12 Vict. cap. 36, it was provided that an heir of entail in possession of entailed lands might procure the same disentailed, provided the three nearest heirs entitled to succeed consented to the disentail. These consents were essential, and the disentail could not be procured without them. But the obligation or condition in reference to disentail thus imposed by statute has been taken away by the Acts 38 & 39 Vict. cap. 61, and 45 & 46 Vict. cap. 53, which provide that on payment being made or security given for the value in money of the expectancy or interest of such heirs the consents may be dispensed with. This maxim is the same in principle as, and forms one of the subdivisions of, the more general maxim, *Eodem modo*, &c., which see.

Omnia quæ sunt uxoris sunt ipsius viri.—Everything belonging to a wife belongs to her husband. This maxim will sometimes be found in this form: *Omnia uxoris durante conjugio mariti sunt*—Everything belonging to the wife during the subsistence of the marriage belongs to the husband. In neither form does the maxim now express a rule of Scotch law. Marriage does not now operate as an assignation of the wife's moveable property to the husband, nor does it give him any right in or over such property. What belongs to a wife at the date of her marriage, or is acquired by her during the marriage, remains her own separate estate. See *Communio bonorum.*

Omnis definitio in jure periculosa est.—All definition in law is dangerous. To define or limit either the meaning or application of a law too nicely is dangerous, because in the general case it is impossible to foresee all the circumstances or cases to which that law may be applied, and to define or limit its application beforehand might result in great inconvenience if not injustice. Such definition is further dangerous, because cases may arise in which the definition might require to be modified or abandoned, and in this way decisions on the same law be pronounced not in conformity with each other; and nothing is more desirable than uniformity of decisions on the same law. The cases arising out of the Poor Law Act of 1845 as to the meaning of "continuous residence," afford a striking illustration of both the risks above mentioned as attending definitions in law. The definition referred to in the maxim is that which is put upon a law by the judge administering it, and does not refer to definition or limitation imposed by the law itself. All laws, so far as this is possible, ought to be so defined as to leave no doubt as to the cases to which they are applicable: and further, so as to leave the application of the law as little as possible to the discretion or opinion of the judge. See *Optima est lex,* &c.

Omnis interpretatio præferenda est ut dicta testium reconcilientur.—Every interpretation is to be preferred by which the statements of witnesses are reconciled; that is, where statements made by different witnesses regarding the same matter or occurrence admit of being differently construed, that interpretation or construction of their statements which reconciles them and brings them into harmony with each other will be preferred to any construction which involves contradiction or difference.

Omnis ratihabitio retrotrahitur et mandato priori æquiparatur.—Every ratification operates retrospectively, and is equivalent to a prior order or authority. To ratify or homologate that which has been done without authority has the same effect as if the act had been authorised at the time of its performance. To illustrate this, suppose that A, as agent for B, enters into a contract whereby he undertakes that B shall deliver certain goods, perform certain services, or pay a certain sum, and that at the time he entered into this contract he had no authority, actual or implied, from B to do so. In such a case the contract would not impose any obligation on B. But if, subsequently, B ratifies the contract, his ratification draws back to the date when the contract was made, and he is as much bound to fulfil the obligation which the contract imposes as if A had had B's authority or mandate to enter into it at its date. So, also, where one acts for another in his absence and without authority, subsequent ratification of the acts done will bind the absentee just as if he had previously authorised them. On the subject of ratification and homologation generally, see Bell's Com. i. 139 et seq.

Omnium bonorum.—Of all goods, or effects. A disposition *omnium bonorum* is one by which the granter conveys the whole estate and effects of which he is possessed at the time of granting. Such a conveyance is required of every one obtaining the benefit of the process of cessio, and until it is granted, no extract of a decree can be given which confers upon the applicant that benefit. A conveyance of this description was likewise required from an incarcerated debtor, who sought to be alimented by his creditor under the Act of Grace (1696, c. 32); and if he refused, after being requested, to execute such conveyance, he was entitled to no aliment while so refusing, 6 Geo. IV. c. 62, § 7. It is not very clear whether granting such a conveyance is still a condition of a civil prisoner's receiving aliment (45 & 46 Vict. c. 42, § 8), but as imprisonment for or on account of civil debt is now practically abolished (43 & 44 Vict. c. 34, amended by the statute just cited) the question is not one of much importance. See *Cessio bonorum*.

Omnium contributione sarciatur quod pro omnibus datum est.—That which is given for all is made good by the contribution of all. This is the principle upon which ship, cargo, and freight are liable in general average. Where goods are thrown overboard on a voyage, or other damage is suffered for the good of all concerned, the loss thence arising is made good by the contribution of all for whose benefit the loss was occasioned or sustained. See *Lex Rhodia*, &c.

Onera realia.—Real burdens; which are burdens or encumbrances affecting land, and exigible from it. They are distinguished from personal burdens, which only affect and are exigible from the person upon whom they lie. A single example may illustrate the nature of both. It is a common enough practice, when lands are sold, for the seller not to insist on payment of the full price at the time of the sale, but to allow a part of the price to remain on the lands as a burden. If the balance so left be declared in the sasine (or, now, in the conveyance) to be a real lien and burden affecting the lands themselves, and as such be entered upon the record, it is a burden for which the lands may be attached and sold, into whose possession soever they may come. But if the burden of payment of the remainder of the price be laid upon the purchaser alone, and not upon the lands, then the burden is personal, and a subsequent purchaser from him incurs no liability therefor, the lands not being affected. Again, a testator, in conveying his lands to his heirs, may declare that the conveyance is granted under burden of the payment of certain legacies. If the declaration be in such general terms, it will only impose a personal obligation upon the heir, and the lands would pass to a purchaser from him free of any such encumbrance; but if the testator declares the specified legacies to be real burdens affecting the lands, and this appear from the recorded title, then the lands are answerable for the same, whether they have been disponed by the heir to a purchaser, or been adjudged by the heir's creditors. In the former case, the legacies would be lost in the event of the heir's death or insolvency after having squandered the succession; in the latter, the legacies would be indefeasible so long as the lands remained. Personal burdens, it may be observed, are not binding upon singular successors, but real burdens are; and all that is necessary to constitute a burden real is an explicit declaration that it shall be so, and that such declaration shall appear upon the public records.

Oneris ferendi.—Of bearing a weight or burden. This

was one of the urban servitudes of the civil law, in virtue of which the dominant proprietor was entitled to rest the weight of his house in whole or in part on the wall or property of the servient proprietor. There was this distinction between the servitude *oneris ferendi* and other servitudes, that as the latter only consisted *in patiendo*, the servient proprietor was not bound to do anything to maintain the dominant proprietor's right, while in the former the servient proprietor was bound so to keep and maintain his pillar or wall as to be capable of sustaining the dominant proprietor's buildings which rested upon it. This servitude has been imported into our law, but the distinction between it and other servitudes above alluded to is not regarded. A special contract is with us necessary to render the servient proprietor bound to maintain the support on which his neighbour's property rests.

Onus probandi.—The burden of proving. The general rule is that the party making an allegation must prove it. Thus the burden of proving a claim which is denied lies on the pursuer who advances or maintains it, and on his failure to do so, the defender is assoilzied. The burden of proving, however, sometimes falls on the defender, as, for example, where he admits that he owed the sum sued for, but alleges that it has been paid; in which case the proof of such payment is incumbent upon him. This rule does not apply where there is a legal presumption in favour of the allegation made. So, in the payment of a debt made to a minor himself and not to his curator, action is competent against the debtor for repayment, on the ground that the payment made was to the lesion of the minor. In the ordinary case the minor would be bound to prove the lesion averred; but as the law presumes all such payments to be in lesion, the rule does not apply, and therefore it falls upon the debtor to show that there was no lesion, but that the payment was *in rem versum* of the minor. In some cases very little proof suffices to shift the *onus* from one party to the other, for an example of which see *Williams* v. *Dobbie*, 11 R. 982.

Ope et concilio.—By aid and counsel; equivalent to aiding and abetting, or art and part. Any one aiding and abetting another in the commission of some crime is himself regarded as criminal in that matter. " By *art* is understood the mandate, instigation, or advice, that may have been given towards committing the crime; *part* expresses the share that one takes to himself in it by the aid or assistance which he gives the criminal in the commission of it." "The Roman law affirms that a bare advice, though without doubt it deserves censure, infers no proper crime against the adviser, unless it be also proved that he has given actual assistance. But this doctrine has not been adopted into the law of any other nation." Ersk. B. 4, T. 4, §§ 10, 12.

Ope exceptionis.—By force of exception. An exception is a kind of defence, but the distinction between defences and exceptions is practically disregarded in the practice of our law. In the civil law (where it originated) an exception was a reason set forth by the defender why he should not be condemned to pay or perform that which the pursuer claimed, founded upon some equitable ground, and of which the strict law could take no cognisance. For example, by the civil law no question was made as to how a *stipulatio* arose; its existence, if admitted or proved, was sufficient to entitle the stipulator to action thereon, and decree against the promissor. But many exceptions might be stated by the promissor, on account of which the stipulator could be defeated on equitable grounds, although at strict law he was entitled to judgment. It might be excepted that the stipulation was forced or extorted from the promissor under fear (*exceptio metus causa*), or that the sum for which the promissor had given his obligation had never been paid to him (*exceptio non numcratæ pecuniæ*). When, therefore, an exception was pleaded before the prætor, he inserted it in the *formula* which he sent to the *judex* who tried the case, and as that *formula* directed decree to be given, *except* (or unless) the stipulator had been guilty of the fraud, &c., averred, hence arose the name of exception. Even in the time of Justinian, however, the word came to mean, as it does with us, any defence other than a denial of the right of action, urged by the defender before the magistrate or judge. A single instance may illustrate the distinction between defence and exception, as held in Scotland, although, as we have said, this distinction is practically disregarded. If A, suing B for the price of certain goods ordered by and delivered to him, be met with the statement that the goods were never either ordered or delivered, this is a defence ; but if B, admitting the receipt of the goods, pleads that he has already paid the price thereof to A, this is an exception. For an example of the *formula* of the civil law, see *Judices dati*.

Optima est legis interpres consuetudo.—Custom or usage is the best interpreter of law. See *Consuetudo est*, &c.

Optima est lex quæ minimum relinquit arbitrio judicis, optimus judex qui minimum sibi.—That is the best law which leaves least to the discretion of the judge ; he is the best judge who takes least upon himself. Two maxims already given—*Misera est servitus*, &c., and *Omnis definitio*, &c.—throw light upon the meaning of the present maxim, and may be consulted as in illustration. This maxim approves the statute, which is so clearly expressed and well defined as to leave the judge little room, if any, for the exercise of his own judgment or opinion ; a law so clear, that the rights or duties thereby created may be at once discerned ; while the judge is approved who adheres most to the terms of the law he is administering, and relies as little as possible on his own views of its interpretation, meaning, or intention.

Optima fide.—In the best faith.

Optimus interpres rerum usus.—Custom or usage is the best interpreter of things. See *Consuetudo debet*, &c., and *Consuetudo est*, &c.

Opus manufactum.—Artificial work ; in contradistinction to that which is natural. Thus an embankment or bulwark reared by a riparian proprietor to prevent the inundation of his land in the event of a flood, is *opus manufactum*, as distinguished from the natural bank of the river.

Ore tenus.—By word of mouth.

Origine propria neminem posse voluntate sua eximi manifestum est.—It is clear that no one can of his own will free himself from (the allegiance which he owes to) the country of his birth. Broom, 77.

Ossibus usufructuarii inhæret.—A phrase implying that a right of liferent is a right personal to the liferenter, intransmissible, and ceasing upon his death. A liferent right, which is either legal or conventional, is one which entitles the holder of it to use and enjoy the subject of it during his life. The legal liferents are terce and courtesy; all others are conventional, for the subdivisions of which see Ersk. B. 2, T. 9, § 40 *et seq.* The right of liferent is intransmissible; and although an assignation of a liferent is common enough in practice, yet such an assignation does not convey that right itself, but merely the benefits arising from it. Accordingly an assignee only enjoys the fruits of the subjects liferented during the cedent's life, and not during his own, if he be the survivor. See *Jus in re inhæret,* &c.

P

Pacta dant legem contractui.—The stipulations of parties constitute the law of the contract. The intention of the parties to a contract, and the agreement into which they have entered, is the rule upon which the law will proceed in enforcing fulfilment of the obligations undertaken, even where such agreement is contrary to the general rule of law regarding such contracts. Thus, in the contract of partnership, the rule upon which the law proceeds in regulating the rights and obligations of the partners is, that each partner is entitled to an equal share of the profits, and is liable for an equal proportion of the losses. But if the parties have stipulated that their proportions in the profit and loss shall not be equal, the terms of the contract will afford the rule for its enforcement. So, again, although the rule of law is that the risk attaching to a subject let on hire lies with the locator, yet the law will recognise the risk as lying upon the conductor, if that has been the bargain between the parties. The law refuses to recognise the conditions and terms of a private contract only when they are illegal, against sound policy, or *contra bonos mores*. See *Lex contractus*.

Pactis privatorum non derogatur juri communi.—The common law is not derogated from by the private contract of individuals. This maxim of the civil law imports that no private bargain or arrangement between individuals can validate any contravention of the law, or render that valid and binding which the law declares to be invalid and ineffectual. Thus an agreement not to object to an obligation for a debt incurred at gambling does not validate the obligation or bar objection, because the fixed rule of law is that such obligations cannot be enforced. Nor, in like manner, will such an agreement validate an obligation which proceeds *ob turpem causam*.

An agreement by a married woman, that she will not object, on the ground of her being a wife, to a personal obligation which she has incurred, will not sustain an action brought upon that personal obligation; and a further illustration of this principle will be found in Ersk. B. 2, T. 6, § 50. This maxim may be regarded as in a great measure the counterpart of the preceding one, and applies merely to all contracts which are in themselves illegal, impolitic, or *contra bonos mores*. It is not therefore to be regarded as absolute, for there are some legal provisions which may be derogated from by private bargain. Thus the legal provisions in favour of a widow and children, of which they cannot be defeated by the *mortis causa* deed of the husband and father, may be renounced or discharged in consideration of other provisions made in their favour, or even gratuitously.

Pactis privatorum publico juri derogari nequit.—Another mode of expressing the preceding maxim, not unfrequently used.

Pactum.—A bargain, agreement, or paction. A paction is, in the civil law, defined to be "the consent and agreement of two or more persons in the same matter, or regarding the same thing." Dig. B. 2, T. 14, l. 1, § 2.

Pactum corvinum de hæreditate viventis.—An agreement concerning the succession of one still living. Among the Romans, any agreement on the part of an heir to sell his right of succession during the life of his ancestor was forbidden as *contra bonos mores;* as also was any obligation which was to be discharged by the heir out of the succession of his ancestor, when this had devolved upon him by the ancestor's death. A different rule obtains in Scotland and England, where it is quite lawful for the heir to dispose of his *spes successionis*, or to burden the succession by a post-obit. It is supposed that the Romans called this a corvine agreement (*pactum corvinum*) on account of the eager rapacity of ravens, which prompts them to attack and commence to devour animals weakened and dying before death has actually taken place.

Pactum de assedatione facienda et ipsa assedatio æquiparantur.—An agreement or bargain to grant a lease is equal to the lease itself. If a landlord enters into a missive of lease with one proposing to become his tenant, binding himself to let the lands, and to execute a regular lease at a future period, the missive is as binding, if possession by the tenant followed upon it, as the lease would have been if then executed. *Rei interventus*, if to a sufficient extent, has, in this respect, the same effect as possession. Thus, improvements made upon the land on the faith of such missives, if made in the knowledge of and without obstruction from the landlord, will give effect to an informal or irregular missive, although no possession has followed upon it, where the term of entry does not arrive until after the date of the improvements. Such missives, however, even with *rei interventus*, are not sufficient to secure to the proposing tenant the lands or farm he has taken. For if the landlord should thereafter let the lands or farm, and give possession to another tenant, the first has no preferable claim on which he could deprive the second of possession; he has merely an action to enforce implement of the missives, failing which, for damages on account of breach of the contract thereby entered into. This maxim only applies to those cases where, upon informal or imperfect missives, possession has followed, in which case they are as binding upon both landlord and tenant as a regular lease, seeing that they contain all the conditions of the lease, and that they have been acted upon. The maxim, as here given, is sometimes written with these additional words: "*præcipue si possessio sequatur*"—especially if possession follows.

Pactum de non petendo.—An agreement not to seek;—*i.e.*, an agreement by which the creditor in an obligation binds himself not to seek or to enforce its fulfilment; forming one of the well-known exceptions of the civil law, and thence imported into the law of Scotland. This agreement might either be absolute or temporary: in the former case it operated as a renunciation or discharge, and absolved the debtor from his obligation. If the agreement was merely temporary, its effect was only that of sisting execution upon the creditor's diligence, until the expiry of the time during which the creditor had bound himself not to seek performance. In treating of the defence afforded by this *pactum*, Stair says, "If it be only temporary, for a short time, it does not exclude a decreet, but only the present effect thereof, whereby the decreet is granted conditionally, to pay or perform at the time to which the delay is granted; but it maketh the pursuer liable to the expenses of plea, *plus petendo tempore* (that is, of having sought before the agreed-on time). And, being dilatory, it must be instantly verified; yet, if it be a long delay, it will procure a time to prove it, and will absolve the defender from that process, seeing he is not obliged to lie under the process for so long delay, and therefore a new citation will not revive that process; yet it will not hinder a new process to be raised after the time of delay is past." Stair, B. 4, T. 40, § 31.

Pactum de quota litis.—An agreement for a share of the subject of a law suit. This is an agreement made by an advocate or law-agent to receive, in return for professional services, a portion of the subject of the suit instead of the usual fees. It is regarded as an illegal contract, and is void at common law; and accordingly, in the case of *Johnston*, 9 S. 364, an agreement entered into between an agent and his client, to the effect that if a certain suit was successful, the agent should receive the half of the property recovered, and if unsuccessful, he should charge nothing for his outlay or trouble, was held null, and the action raised upon it dismissed. By the Act 1594, cap. 216, it was enacted, that any member of the College of Justice (extended by practice to practitioners before the inferior courts) who should purchase any property at the time forming the subject of a lawsuit, should be punished by deprivation of office, place, and privilege. The course of decisions has been to sustain the purchase as valid, and to regard the penalty as the only sanction of the Act. In England all such agreements are void, whether made in England or in a foreign country where such agreements would be legal. Addison on Con. 1140.

Pactum de retrovendendo.—An agreement concerning the selling back of a subject. This paction of the civil law was one which could competently be adjected to a contract of sale, and by it the seller reserved right to himself to purchase back within a certain time that which he had sold. There do not appear to be any examples in the law of Scotland of such an agreement being made with regard to the sale of moveables; but there are instances of such agreements in reference to the re-purchase of heritage. The right of pre-emption reserved by a superior is an example of this paction, differing from the agreement of the civil law, however, in this, that it is not limited to a certain time, but may be exercised sooner or later, as the vassal may wish to retain or dispose of the subject, and that the exercise of the right is not dependent upon the will merely of the superior, as it was upon the will of the seller. Another illustration may be found in the right of reversion which the debtor under a wadset had, although there, again, the reverser might redeem his subjects, even after the lapse of the prescribed time, and at any time before declarator of the irritancy.

Pactum de successione viventis.—A bargain concerning the succession of a person still living. See *Pactum corvinum*, &c.

Pactum donationis.—An agreement to give in donation. Such an agreement confers upon the donee no right in the subject agreed to be given, as the donor continues proprietor until delivery. The donor may, therefore, even gratuitously, give and deliver it to another, who thereupon becomes proprietor. This paction, however, according to Erskine (B. 3, T. 3, § 90), confers upon the first donee a *jus ad rem*, in respect of which he may sue the donor for performance, or damages for breach of agreement, if performance be refused or be rendered impossible by the act of the donor.

Pactum illicitum.—An illegal agreement or contract. This term is applied generally to all contracts which are contrary to law, *contra bonos mores*, or opposed to the principles of sound policy. No contract which can be shown to belong to this category can be legally enforced. Such, for example, are contracts entered into or obligations granted *ob turpem causam*, obligations arising from betting or gambling transactions, the *pactum de quota litis*, contracts imposing restraints on marriage, &c. Although such obligations cannot be enforced, yet where they have been fulfilled no action will lie for restitution, for the same illegality which bars the right to enforce, bars also the right to claim restitution when implement has been made.

Pactum legis commissoriæ.—An agreement, under which the seller in a contract of sale was entitled to the benefit of the *lex commissoria*. The *lex commissoria* was the name given to a clause often inserted among the Romans in conditions of sale, whereby the seller reserved right to himself to rescind the sale if the purchaser did not make payment of the price of the subject sold within a certain time. This condition did not make the purchase a conditional one; on the contrary, the sale was regarded as absolute, but subject to be rescinded at the pleasure of the seller if the price was not paid by the time specified; and accordingly, if the subject was destroyed or lost before the arrival of the agreed-on term of payment, the loss fell upon the purchaser. It was necessary for the seller, if he intended taking advantage of his right under this condition, to intimate this to the purchaser as soon as the condition was broken. If he received or claimed any part of the purchase money after the day agreed upon, he thereby waived the right which the *lex commissoria* conferred upon him. It was usual to insert in this clause an agreement, that if the seller had to sell the subject again, the first purchaser (who had failed to make payment) should be liable for any difference which might arise between the price at which he had bought it, and that which it brought at the second sale. The *pactum legis commissoriæ* was intended solely for the benefit of the seller, and could not be enforced against him by the buyer. "The *pactum legis commissoriæ* was reprobated in the civil law, and is not much favoured by us. It certainly would not operate without declarator, and without giving an opportunity of purging." Per Lord President Campbell, quoted in Ross, L. C. (L. R.) i. 163. See, as bearing upon this part of the law of sale, Bell's Com. i. 288 *et seq.*; and the case of *Brown*, 7 R. 427.

Pactum legis commissoriæ in pignoribus.—An agreement giving to the pledgee the benefit of the *lex commissoria* in contracts of pledge. The *lex commissoria* in pledge was a condition attached to the contract, under which, if the pledger failed to redeem the subject pledged within a certain time, his right of redemption ceased, and the pledge became the absolute and irredeemable property of the pledgee. This condition, at one time very common, was, at a later period of the history of the civil law (A.D. 326) declared to be illegal by the Emperor Constantine. In Scotland, under the Pawnbroking Acts, a subject pledged is forfeited if not redeemed within a year, or on certain notice being given by the pledger, within fifteen months; but even after that period, and at any time before the pledge has been sold as forfeited, the pledger has the right of redemption on making payment of the sum advanced, with the interest which may be due thereon.

Pactum liberatorium.—An agreement whereby a real right is departed from or restricted. Such agreements would seem to form an exception to the general rule, that writing must intervene in all that relates to land, in order to bar the power of resiling. Accordingly, it has been held that a mere verbal obligation, followed by no *rei interventus*, agreeing to restrict an infeftment in security, cannot be retracted, and may be proved by the oath of the party restricting; and in the case of *Ker*, M. 8465, a promise to liberate part of the lands burdened with a liferent was sustained without writing. It may be doubted, however, whether such a decision would be followed were any similar question now to arise.

Pactum super hæreditate viventis.—An agreement concerning the succession of a person still living. See *Pactum corvinum*, &c.

Par in parem non habet imperium.—An equal has no power over an equal. An illustration of this maxim is afforded in the following passage from Stair, where it is used to indicate that a Lord Ordinary on the Bills cannot, where the circumstances are unaltered, pronounce a decision upon a bill presented to him different from that already pronounced by the preceding Lord Ordinary on a bill concerning the same subject-matter, and at the instance of the same party. Both of such judges being equal, the one has no power to review or alter the decision of the other. "If a bill hath been presented and refused, the clerk of the bills ought to retain the bill; and if another bill be presented, he ought to show the Ordinary the refused bill, that if the new bill contain new matter of fact, he may pass or refuse it; but if it only contain new arguments of law or reason, urging the former points, he may not pass, but by a meeting of three, or by a report to the Lords; for *par in parem non habet imperium."* Stair, B. 4, T. 1, § 68. On the same principle courts are not bound to follow or regard as precedents the decisions of other courts of co-ordinate jurisdiction.

Paraphernalia.—The name given to those moveables which were properly personal to a wife, and remained her own property, notwithstanding of her marriage, even when (as the law formerly stood) the marriage operated as an assignation of the wife's whole moveable estate to her husband. The term includes a wife's wearing apparel, jewels, all ornaments proper to her person, &c., which were hers before the marriage, and gifts of a similar character from her husband made before or on the marriage-day: it also includes the cabinets or wardrobe in which such effects were kept. Fraser, i. 770 *et seq.* No part of a wife's moveable estate now passes to the husband by virtue of the marriage, 44 & 45 Vict. c. 21.

Parata executio.—A prepared or completed diligence; diligence on which the creditor may instantly proceed to operate so as to obtain payment or fulfilment of an obligation from his debtor. Ersk. B. 3, T. 4, § 15.

Pares curiæ.—Literally, the peers of the court. *Curia* was the place or court where the superior exercised his jurisdiction over his vassals: and those vassals being alike subject to him, and lying under the same obligation to attend his court, were therefore styled *pares* or peers. The *pares curiæ* included all the vassals holding of the same superior. Their presence was, according to the ancient law of Scotland, so essential to the validity of a feudal grant, that it was void without it. Where the superior had no other vassal than the one to whom he was making the grant, the vassals of the neighbouring superiors were admitted to supply the place of the *pares curiæ.* The *pares* had also the power of judging in most cases falling within the jurisdiction of their superior, whether civil or criminal, from whence, says Erskine (B. 2,

T. 3, § 17), "the right which we retain to this day, of being tried in criminal prosecutions by a jury of our *pares* or peers, derives its original."

Pares curtis.—The members of the superior's court; but generally written *pares curiæ*. The term *curtis* is very rarely used in the sense of *court*,—being almost invariably used to signify the whole domain over which the superior exercised jurisdiction, as well as that jurisdiction itself. An example of its being used to signify the superior's domain will be found in Ersk. B. 2, T. 4, § 5.

Pari passu.—In equal grade; equally. When creditors claiming a common fund and competing as to their rights of preference, as in an action of multiplepoinding, are preferred to the fund equally, or share and share alike, they are said to be preferred *pari passu*. Where one of the claimants is preferred to the fund to the extent of his claim before all the other claimants, he is said to be preferred *primo loco*.

Paries oneri ferundo, uti nunc est, ita sit.—The wall for bearing the burden, as it now is, so let it be. These were the words used in the civil law for constituting the urban servitude *oneris ferendi*, under which the servient proprietor was bound to keep the wall on which his neighbour's tenement rested in such a sufficient state of repair as to ensure its supporting the weight laid upon it. See *Oneris ferendi*.

Pars contractus.—Part of the contract. Verbal consensual contracts are binding upon the contracting parties immediately upon their consents being interchanged, and neither of them can afterwards resile from the transaction without subjecting himself to damages for breach of contract. But if it be agreed that their contract shall be reduced to writing, such agreement being *pars contractus*, the contract is not finally entered into, nor does it become binding, until the writing has been executed. The law regards such a stipulation as a reservation of the right to resile, and consequently either of the parties may resile at any time before the execution of the writing. Even in such a case, however, the right to resile is cut off if anything has been done by the parties, or by any one of them in the knowledge and with consent of the other, in dependence upon the contract.

The parties have no power to resile where *res non est integra*.

Pars ejusdem negotii.—A part of the same business or transaction. Where an obligation is undertaken conditionally, it cannot be enforced until the condition be purified, nor can a defence founded on the failure of the condition be disregarded, because the obligation and the condition are *partes ejusdem negotii* and must be considered together as forming the constituent parts of one transaction. In considering whether statements made by a party under a reference to his oath are intrinsic or extrinsic, it is of importance to ascertain whether such statements relate or do not relate to *partes negotii*. If they do, they must be regarded as intrinsic qualifications of the oath, and binding in their effect on the party referring. Thus if the pursuer of an action which has been brought for payment of goods alleged to have been furnished to the defender, refers the question at issue to the defender's oath, and he depones that he bought the goods at the price libelled and received them, but adds that he paid the price to the pursuer, such an addition is intrinsic, and must be received as part of the answer to the question referred; the sale and delivery of the goods, and the payment of their price being parts of the one transaction, namely, the contract of sale between the parties. But if the defender, instead of deponing that he paid the price of the goods, depones that he does not owe the sum sued for because he holds a counter claim against the pursuer, such an addition is extrinsic to the matter referred, and must be set up by the defender *aliunde*, not by his oath on reference. The claim of compensation is not *pars ejusdem negotii* regarding which the reference was made, but part of another and totally different transaction.

Pars fundi.—Part of the ground or soil. All those things which are in the soil, as well as those growing upon it or immoveably fixed to it, are reckoned parts of the soil itself. Such, for example, are houses built upon the ground, trees, minerals, &c.; and these being regarded as parts of the soil, descend to the heir and not to the executor. Further, a conveyance of the land carries all these as parts thereof, although not specially mentioned. Industrial crops are not considered *partes fundi*, and therefore a conveyance of land will not carry them; they belong to the sower. See *Fundo annexa*.

Pars judicis.—The part or duty of the judge. This refers to the duty which the judge is bound by his office to perform, whether it has been urged upon him by any of the parties to a suit or not. Thus if an action is raised for payment of a sum of money due *ob turpem causam*, as, for example, for the wages of prostitution, it is *pars judicis* to dismiss the action whether the defender has appeared to plead this defence or not. In like manner, a judge should refuse decree for those items of an account which are struck at by the Tippling Act, although the defender should not plead the statute, for the judge is bound to carry out the intention of the legislature in repressing an evil, the existence of which is considered as obnoxious to sound policy. It is also *pars judicis* to refuse effect to a deed or document not properly stamped, for he is bound to see that the revenue laws are observed. Everything which a judge should do in his capacity as judge, and without reference to the pleas of parties in the suit before him, is included in the phrase *pars judicis*.

Pars viscerum matris.—Part of the mother's body. This is said of a child which is still *in utero*, the malicious destruction of which cannot be charged as murder, seeing that it had not (although quick) a separate and independent existence. Hume, i. 186.

Parte inaudita.—One party being unheard; a case argued upon the one side, but not on the other. "Ministers lawfully provided to benefices are secured in the enjoyment of the tithes belonging to them against all grants, made or to be made to their prejudice, even in parliament, *parte inaudita*" (Ersk. B. 2, T. 10, § 11); that is, ministers cannot be deprived of their tithes even by an order of parliament until they have been heard in support of their right, or until an opportunity has been afforded them for being heard. Where a decree is pronounced against a defender *parte inaudita*—*i.e.*, without his appearing or being heard on his defence, he may be reponed at any time before implement of the decree.

Parte non comparente.—A party not having appeared. The effect of non-compearance in a civil suit after citation is the same, for the time, as a confession that the sum sued for is resting-owing, and on this implied confession decree is pronounced against the defender. The defender may subsequently be reponed, and elide the presumption raised against him through his non-compearance by proponing a defence, which is not weakened by his previous absence. In criminal prosecutions the effect of non-compearance is different. It raises no presumption of guilt of the specific crime charged, and cannot warrant sentence being pronounced on account of that crime in the absence of the accused. Such absence, however, constitutes the crime of contempt of the Crown, and disloyalty, for which the accused undergoes the sentence of outlawry. See *Fatetur facinus*, &c.

Partes beneficii.—Parts of a benefice, or living. Stair, B. 2, T. 8, § 35.

Partes rei sunt favorabiliores.—The condition of a defender is more favourable (than that of the pursuer). This arises from the fact that the law presumes the claim made upon a defender to be unfounded until the pursuer has substantiated his claim as a just one. Accordingly the defender is not bound to prove his defence until the pursuer has made out his claim, for until then the legal presumption is altogether in favour of the defender. The same presumption holds, if possible, in a stronger degree in criminal prosecutions. The panel is presumed to be innocent until he has been proved guilty, and he is not bound to adduce a single witness tending to prove his innocence until the prosecutor has proved his guilt. If the prosecutor fails in establishing this, no matter how suspicious the circumstances may appear to be, the panel is entitled to an acquittal without any explanation from him regarding those circumstances.

Partes soli.—Parts of the ground or soil. See *Pars fundi*.

Particeps fraudis.—A partaker or partner in the fraud. One who has been a party to a fraudulent transaction can take no benefit under it. Thus if a bill has been obtained through fraud, that will form a valid defence to any action or diligence raised upon it by any one who was a partaker in the fraud.

But if the bill has passed into the hands of a *bona fide* and onerous indorsee, the previous fraud, to which he was no party, will not affect his right to sue for and enforce payment of the sum contained in it. Again, if a creditor on the estate of an insolvent debtor, while appearing to the other creditors to accept of a composition upon his debt equally with them, should arrange with the debtor for full payment of his debt, such an arrangement being one in defraud of the other creditors, cannot be enforced by that creditor who participated in it; and in any action raised upon it, the plea that it proceeds upon a fraud may be successfully maintained, even by the debtor, who was himself equally involved in its perpetration.

Partus sequitur ventrem.—The offspring follows the mother. Accession is one of the modes in which property is acquired, and is either artificial or natural. Artificial accession is that addition to property which is the result of human skill and industry; while natural accession is that which human skill cannot produce, but which proceeds as the result of natural laws. The young of cattle is of the latter class, and belongs as an accessory to the owner of the mother at the time of the birth. The same rule applied, under the civil law, to the offspring of a female slave.

Pater est quem nuptiæ demonstrant.—He is the father whom the marriage indicates to be so. All children born in wedlock are presumed to be the legitimate children of the husband and wife, but this is a presumption which may be redargued. Formerly our law demanded, in order to overturn the presumption of legitimacy, a proof amounting to this, that it was physically impossible for the husband to be the father of the child, in respect either that he was impotent and incapable of procreation, or that he was absent from his wife, and could not possibly have had access to her during the period of gestation, which is fixed by law to be not more than ten nor less than six lunar months before the birth. " It may be mentioned, however, that there is a doubt whether the longer period should be ten *lunar* or ten *calendar* months. Conflicting judgments on this point were pronounced by Lords Gillies and Meadowbank in the only case where the point arose for decision; but the general point was waived by the

Court." (Fraser, Par. & Ch. 11.) The rule of law expressed in this maxim has been considerably relaxed by the more recent decisions upon the point. It may now be regarded as settled that the Court, in deciding whether the child born in wedlock is the child of the husband, will take into consideration, not only such evidence as will tend, in consequence of the husband's impotency or absence, to prove that this is a physical impossibility, but also such evidence of the relative position of the parties, their habits of life and conduct, their statements regarding the point at issue, and, indeed, any competent evidence tending to induce a moral certainty that the child is not the issue of the spouses. This subject underwent full discussion in the case of *Brodie* v. *Dyce*, 11 Macp. 142, where the reader will find the authorities upon the question collected : reference may also be made to Fraser on Parent and Child, 1 *et seq.* It is not sufficient, however, to overturn the presumption of legitimacy that both husband and wife shall declare the child to be that of another than the husband, unless such declaration is corroborated *aliunde*, because it might be their interest at the time to make such a declaration, to the prejudice of the legal rights of the child as their own legitimate offspring. In such case the law constitutes itself the guardian of the child's rights, and requires the clearest evidence of its illegitimacy before declaring it to be so. This maxim has no application in the case of a child born out of wedlock, but whose alleged father subsequently married its mother (*Innes*, 13 S. 1050); nor to a child not born *justo tempore*—i.e., a child "born beyond ten months after the marriage is dissolved, or within six months after it is entered into." Fraser Par. & Ch. 2. *Gardner*, 3 R. 695, affd. H. L. 4 R. 57.

Pater patriæ.—Father of the realm. "In default of tutors-legitim, there is place for tutors-dative ; who were, by the Roman law, named by the magistrates, but with us by the King alone, as *pater patriæ*, in his Court of Exchequer." Ersk. B. 1, T. 7, § 8.

Paterna paternis.—Estate succeeded to through the father descends to the father's heirs. See *Materna*, &c.

Patrem sequitur sua proles.—His offspring follows the father. This has reference only to the right of succession vested in children, who, if their father has not otherwise validly disposed of his property, are entitled to succeed to his estate to the exclusion of all others.

Patria potestas.—This was the name given to that power which, under the civil law, a paterfamilias had over all the members of his family; the family including his wife, children, and grandchildren, as well as those who became members of the family by marriage or adoption. At one time this power was very extensive, for under it the paterfamilias could sell, abandon, or put to death any member of his family; but subsequently it was much limited, and ultimately it gave the paterfamilias scarcely any other right than that of demanding as his own any property which was acquired or succeeded to by a member of the family.

Patrimonio ejus abest.—That which is wanting from a person's estate. Anything which belongs or is due to one person, which is abstracted or retained by another, falls within this description. An article which has been stolen, a debt which is due, expenditure on behalf of another, as by a mandatory or *negotiorum gestor* not reimbursed, are instances of what this phrase includes; they are all wanting, or absent from the creditor's estate—*i.e.*, his estate is *minus* their value or amount. See *Ei abest*.

Patronum faciunt, dos, ædificatio, fundus.—Endowment, building, the lands on which the church is built, constitute the patron. "There stood the like relation betwixt patrons and kirk's patronate, as betwixt patrons and libertines (freedmen), the ground whereof was an eminent good deed done by the patron or his predecessor to that kirk, especially those acknowledged in law, *patronum faciunt, dos, ædificatio, fundus*; signifying the building of the church, or giving of the stipend or of the grounds necessary for the church, churchyard, manse, or glebe, were the grounds for constituting the patronage, which were sufficiently instructed by the custom of the kirks acknowledging such a patron." Stair, B. 2, T. 8, § 27.

Peculium.—Property. A wife's paraphernalia, as also that estate which she possessed as her own, independent of her husband's control, were called her *peculia* in the civil law. Bell (Prin. § 1560) gives this name to all property which by custom or special gift is appropriated to the wife, and that in regard to which the husband, while solvent, has renounced his marital rights. See *Bona castrensia*, &c.

Pendente lite.—During the dependence of the suit. Formerly, if one of the parties to a suit assaulted his opponent during the dependence of the suit, or was accessory to such assault, he was punished by the loss of his cause; but the statutes under which this penalty was inflicted were repealed by the Act 7 Geo. IV. c. 19. Such an assault is now punished in the same way as any other assault; it has no effect on the decision of the suit.

Pendente lite nihil innovandum.—Nothing is to be changed during the dependence of a suit. When a subject once becomes litigious (see *In rebus*, &c.), neither of the parties can affect or prejudice the other's rights by any act done by him in reference to the subject of the suit; all such acts are ineffectual in so far as his opponent is concerned. Thus if a pursuer seeks reduction of a conveyance of lands executed by him in favour of the defender, the defender cannot avoid the consequences of the action by conveying the lands even onerously to another party. Such a conveyance will be ineffectual as in a question with the pursuer's rights, who, if he be successful in the reduction, will be entitled to recover the lands from the purchaser. This maxim "applies only to things done by the debtor or defender in the action, which tend to make the right of the creditor or pursuer worse, but cannot hinder the creditor or pursuer from making his right better, even in competition with another creditor or pursuer." *Massey*, M. 8377; *Donald* v. *Nicol*, 5 Macp. 146.

Pendente processu.—During the dependence of the process or suit. Stair, B. 4, T. 20, § 11.

Pendente tutela.—During the tutory.

Pendentes (fructus).—Hanging fruits; fruits still undetached from the tree. Such fruits must be restored along with the subject of which they are a part to the real owner, when he vindicates his right to the property as against a *bona fide* possessor, because being still pendent they are an accessory of the heritable subject, and go along with the principal. In this respect they differ from the fruits which have been gathered, although not yet consumed; these remain the property of the *bona fide* possessor, for as soon as they are gathered they become a separate moveable subject, and, having come lawfully into the possession of the *bona fide* possessor, are not affected by subsequent proceedings as to the land.

Penuria peritorum.—A want or scarcity of skilled men. It is a question how far a conveyance of moveables, or a deed regulating moveable succession will be sustained when it is improbative or otherwise defective, on the ground that the granter could not obtain skilled assistance in its preparation and execution. In the case of *Crichton*, M. 15952, where a testamentary deed, not holograph, and wanting the name of the writer and designation of the witnesses, was found ineffectual, it was observed from the Bench that an improbative writing had never been sustained as a conveyance of moveable succession, unless where there had been a *penuria peritorum*, as in the case of military testaments made abroad. There does not seem, however, to be any case reported in which a defective or improbative writ was sustained upon that ground.

Penuria testium.—A scarcity of witnesses. Formerly, when persons were disqualified as witnesses on account of relationship and interest, it was customary nevertheless to admit their evidence where the circumstances of the case necessarily involved a scarcity of witnesses. Thus, in an action for separation and aliment at the instance of a wife on account of ill-treatment by her husband, their children (in the general case excluded on the ground of relationship) were admitted to prove or negative the pursuer's averments, as without such admission it might have been impossible to prove the case. The same rule was followed in the case of occult and domestic crimes, where of necessity there was a *penuria testium*. This is now comparatively of no importance, since disqualification of witnesses has been almost entirely abolished. As to what constitutes a *penuria testium*, see the case of *Surtees* v. *Wotherspoon*, 10 Macp. 866.

Per alium stetit.—It was owing (to something done) by another. Hume, i. 382.

Per æs et libram.—By brass (or money) and scales.

Under the older civil law, things (in which term was included everything that could be the object of a right) were divided into *res mancipi* and *res nec mancipi;* the former comprehended lands or houses in Italy, prædial servitudes thereto attached, slaves, and ordinary beasts of burden; while all other things taken separately, and not as a *universitas*, were *nec mancipi*. The property of the first could only be acquired or transferred according to prescribed ceremonies, of which there were two—viz., *mancipatio* and *in jure cessio*. Mancipation consisted of an imaginary sale, and Gaius (who takes the instance of the sale of a slave), describes this ceremony as follows: "*Mancipatio* is effected in the presence of not less than five witnesses, who must be Roman citizens and of the age of puberty, and also in the presence of another person of the same condition, who holds a pair of brazen scales, and hence is called *Libripens*. The purchaser, taking hold of the thing, says: I affirm that this slave is mine according to the Quiritarian law, and he is purchased by me with this piece of money and brazen scales. He then strikes the scales with the piece of money, and gives it to the seller as a symbol of the price." (Gai. i. 119.) Property thus acquired was said to be acquired *per æs et libram*. The *cessio in jure* was a fictitious suit in which the person who was to acquire the subject claimed it before the magistrate, who declared it to be the property of the claimant on the person who was to transfer it acknowledging the justice of the claim. There was no other mode in which the quiritarian ownership in *res mancipi* could be acquired or transferred; if these forms were not observed the property was not transferred. *Res nec mancipi* were transferred by simple delivery. The distinction between *res mancipi* and *nec mancipi*, as well as the ceremonies above explained for the transference of the former, were abolished by Justinian. The ceremony of mancipation was, under the older law, sometimes observed in making a will, where the testator received from the purchaser of the inheritance a piece of money as a symbol of the price; the purchaser being thereby constituted heir.

Per ambages.—In a round-about way; indirectly; or, by evasion. A father cannot by his *mortis causa* deed defeat his children's right to legitim, although he may affect the ultimate value of that right, and even practically defeat it, by gifts or other form of *inter vivos* conveyance. Nor can he defeat this right *per ambages*, as, for example, by the execution of a deed which, according to the tenor of the words used, may appear to be a deed *inter vivos*, while in reality, and as regards its effects, it is a deed *mortis causa*. Again : donations between husband and wife are revocable, and it will not deprive the donor of the power to revoke that the deed or obligation is made, not as a pure donation, but in the form of a gift to some other person, as, for example, the donee's heirs. *Fernie v. Colquhoun's Trs.*, 17 D. 232. "A deed, the only genuine intention of which is to convey a gratuitous right from one of the spouses to the other, though it be granted nominally or in trust to a third party, is, notwithstanding that mask, subject to revocation." Ersk. B. 1, T. 6, § 29. The attempt to do *per ambages* what cannot be done directly is ineffectual. See *Dolus circuitu*, &c.

Per aversionem.—By bulk, or aggregate quantity. Sale *per aversionem* means the sale of a certain subject by the bulk, without any specific statement of its exact quantity, as, for example, all the corn in a certain granary, a certain crop, or all the wine in one's cellar.

Per æquipollens.—By an equivalent. This is used as antithetical to the phrase *in forma specifica*. Where a specified form of action or expression is essential to render a certain act effectual, no equivalent, however intelligible or express will supply the place of the prescribed form. Thus, prior to the passing of the Act 37 & 38 Vict. c. 94, the word "dispone" was essential to every deed intended to operate as a *de presenti* conveyance of heritage. No other word, or number of words, however clear their meaning—such, for example, as "sell," "alienate," "convey," &c.—could supply its place. The word itself was essential, and could not be supplied *per æquipollens*. (*Kirkpatrick*, 11 Macp. 551, affd. on this point, 1 R. (H. L.) 37.) Another illustration may be found in the case where the granter of a deed calls in witnesses to attest his subscription who have not seen him subscribe it. In such case it is essential to the validity of the deed that the granter shall, in the presence of the witnesses, declare the signature to be his. His declaration must be distinct, and have special reference to the signature This declaration cannot be supplied *per æquipollens*, such as requesting the witnesses to subscribe as such, that it is "all correct," that the deed (as in the case of a testator executing his settlement) embodies his wishes or expresses his will, &c. He must declare that the signature is his in express terms, otherwise it will not be held to have been validly executed.

Per capita.—According to the heads, or individuals. Where a testator provides that his estate is to be distributed among the beneficiaries *per capita*, it is divided into as many shares as there are persons called to the succession. In such a succession each individual succeeds in his own right, and the right of representation is excluded. See *In stirpes*.

Per collationem bonorum.—By collation of goods. Collation is a provision of our law by which the heir of a deceased person may, by resigning the heritage to which he has succeeded, claim an equal share of the whole succession of the deceased. It is the interest of the heir-at-law to collate, when the heritable estate of the ancestor is small and his executry great. The heir can never be compelled to collate, but, on the other hand, every heir has not this privilege, for to entitle him to the benefit of collation, it was formerly necessary that he should be of the next-of-kin to the deceased, and consequently one who would have participated in the moveable succession had he not been the heir in heritage. Some changes were, however, introduced into the law upon this point by the Act 18 Vict. c. 23, which see.

Per expressum.—Expressly; in direct terms.

Per fas aut nefas.—By lawful or unlawful means. To determine to attain some end "through fair play or foul;" or to accomplish some object "right or wrong," are familiar equivalents for the phrase *Per fas aut nefas*.

Per incuriam.—Through negligence, mistake, or error.

Per insidias et industriam.—By stratagem and labour. This phrase is antithetical to the preceding one. The present phrase refers to things done intentionally and of set purpose: while a thing done *per incuriam* is done unintentionally—the result of a mistake or blunder.

Per membra curiæ.—By members of the Court. Ersk. B. 2, T. 5, § 81.

Per modum exceptionis.—By way of exception. Where an obligant claims exemption from fulfilment of his obligation, on the ground that it was extorted from him through force or fear, he may plead this ground of exemption in either of two ways; he may proceed by action for reduction of the obligation, or plead it by way of exception or defence in any action brought against him to enforce fulfilment. So also in the case of a bill which the alleged debtor in it avers to be a forgery; he may either reduce the bill upon that ground, or plead forgery by way of exception in the action, or under a suspension of the diligence, raised upon it. The same course is open to one of the parties to a contract, where he has been induced to enter into it by fraud, or where it proceeds *ob turpem causam*. An exception (although the term is frequently used as synonymous with defence) is, properly speaking, only that kind of defence which admits the relevancy of the libel, and that the conclusion would be just if it were not elided by the exception pleaded.

Per modum gratiæ.—By way of favour; as an act of grace.

Per modum justitiæ.—By way of justice; as an act of justice to which one is entitled. "One who is restored to his estate *per modum justitiæ*, against an attainder, either on account of its injustice, or of some legal nullity in the proceedings, recovers his whole estate, though the king should have made a grant of all or part of it over to a donatary, after the forfeiture;" "on the other hand, where one is restored to his estate *per modum gratiæ*, merely in the way of favour, the attainder is presumed to have been legal, and is accounted such in law; for which reason all grants of the forfeited estate made in consequence thereof by the Crown, in the intermediate period between the attainder and the restitution, must stand good." Ersk. B. 4, T. 4, § 107.

Per modum pœnæ.—By way of punishment or penalty. The oath *in litem* of a traveller as to the value of the property lost in an inn, and claimed by him from the innkeeper under the provisions of the edict *Nautæ caupones*, &c., is said to be allowed by way of punishment, as well as on account of its being the best evidence which, in the circumstances, can be adduced. An heir is liable for any sum in which his ancestor, whom he represents, has been found liable by judicial award, except where the award is pronounced by way of penalty or fine on account of a delict committed by the ancestor; for such penalty the heir is not responsible. Nor is a husband liable for any fine imposed in like manner upon his wife. See *In modum*, &c.

Per modum simplicis querelæ.—By way of simple complaint. Erskine refers to this (B. 4, T. 4, § 68) as a mode in which an action of improbation, on the ground of forgery, may be brought before the Court of Session "without any summons, or by a formal summons of improbation." Such a form of proceeding has been altogether unknown in our practice for a very lengthened period.

Per rescriptum principis.—By a rescript or ordinance of the prince. Legitimation of illegitimate children was sometimes effected by an imperial rescript. Under the civil law such rescript was not granted by the emperor, if the father had other legitimate offspring, or if marriage with the mother of the illegitimate children had become impossible by her death, or from any other cause. Where these objections could not be urged, the rescript might be obtained by the father, or even by the children, if their father's testament declared it to be his wish that they should be legitimised. Such a mode of legitimation has been recognised in our law, and has been granted, even where legitimate offspring were still living. The effect of the sovereign's rescript, however, was merely to confer upon the children the *status* of legitimacy; it did not entitle them to succeed to their father. The chief purpose for which such rescripts were obtained in Scotland was to entitle the bastard, where he had no lawful children, to dispose of his heritage or moveables by will; but as the disability thus removed in each case by rescript has been entirely removed by statute, letters of legitimation from the sovereign are now practically worthless, and in practice are unknown. The only mode of legitimation now practically known is that *per subsequens matrimonium*.

Per saltum.—Literally, by a leap; without intermediate

steps. "Signatures and charters of the vassals of kirk lands, where their valuation does not exceed ten pounds Scots, pass by the great seal *per saltum*, without passing any other seal" (Ersk. B. 2, T. 5, § 83); charters of a different description were required first to pass the privy seal. An heir who makes up his title to an ancestor more remote than the one on whose failure he succeeds (as he may do for the purpose of avoiding representation) may be said, in thus passing over his nearer ancestors, to make up his title *per saltum* to the ancestor more remote.

Per se.—By himself, or itself.

Per stirpes.—According to the stocks. Succession *per stirpes* is succession by right of representation, where the estate is divided, not according to the number of persons who take benefit therein, but according to the number of persons called to the succession, and through whom the others (for example, their lawful issue) take their right. See *In stirpes*.

Per subsequens matrimonium.—By subsequent marriage. Children who, at their birth, were illegitimate, become legitimate by the subsequent marriage of their parents. This rule is borrowed from the civil law, where it was introduced by the Emperor Constantine after his conversion to Christianity, with the view of checking the general depravity of manners which the Roman law of marriage was calculated to produce. To render this mode of legitimation effectual, it is essential that the parents should have been under no legal impediment to marry at the date of the procreation of the child or children, and consequently children born of an adulterous intercourse are not legitimated by the subsequent marriage of their parents. It was at one time questioned whether legitimation *per subsequens matrimonium* was barred by the intermediate marriage of either of the parties with another than the parent of the child, but it was decided, according to the opinions of a majority of the whole Court, that such intermediate marriage did not bar legitimation. The reader may consult the instructive case of *Kerr* v. *Martin*, 2 D. 752, where this was decided, and in which the whole authorities on this part of our law are quoted and commented upon. In the same case it was incidentally questioned whether a son thus legitimated would succeed, by right of primogeniture, to his father's estate, to the exclusion of a son born of the intervening marriage; and although the point was not decided, the opinions given were to the effect that he would not. A son, however, who is legitimated, succeeds by right of primogeniture, to the exclusion of those children born after the subsequent marriage of his parents.

Per tacitam reconventionem.—By a tacit renewal of the bargain or contract. Stair, B. 1, T. 6, § 36.

Per tacitam relocationem.—By tacit relocation. Tacit relocation is the implied reletting of a subject, or renewal of a lease, inferred where a landlord, instead of warning his tenant to remove, allows him to remain in possession after the stipulated term of the lease has expired. Parties are then presumed to have entered upon a new lease, upon the same conditions as the former one. Tacit relocation is also understood to take place between master and servant when the parties allow the term of the original engagement to expire without giving the legal warning that the engagement is then to be at an end; but in any case, for however long a period the original lease may have been granted, or term of service agreed upon, tacit relocation has only the effect of binding the parties for a year, and it may be put an end to by either of the parties giving the required warning. Where the original term of service has been for a shorter period than a year, tacit relocation will only renew the contract for a period equal to that for which it was originally entered into; thus the contract of a monthly servant will only be renewed for a month by tacit relocation.

Per universitatem.—Regarded as a whole; in its entirety. Stair, in treating of vicious intromission, and of the extent to which this must be carried in order to render the intromitter liable, says—" The intromission must be universal; not that the intromitter must meddle with all the defunct's moveables, but must meddle *quasi per universitatem*, because heritage is *per universitatem*: as he that meddles with a flock of sheep meddles *per universitatem*; yet many of the flock may be meddled with by others, but what remains being still the flock, he is only said to meddle with the flock. And so intromission with one thing, or some small thing, will not infer this passive title." B. 3, T. 9, § 7.

Per venditionis, donationis, cessionis, vel commutationis titulum.—By the title of sale, donation, cession (assignation), or barter. These terms were used in the older forms of conveyancing, to distinguish lands so acquired from lands acquired either by inheritance or feudal grant. They signify what is now known by the name of a singular title. All persons are now regarded as singular successors in lands who have acquired them by purchase or gift, or in any other character than that of heir.

Per vim legis.—By force of law. The succession to the estate left by an intestate is regulated by legal rules; and persons who succeed *ab intestato* are said to succeed *per vim legis*, in contradistinction to those who succeed under the terms of the testator's will. They are said to succeed—

Per voluntatem hominis.—By the will of man—*i.e.*, the will or purpose of the testator.

Percepti sed non consumpti.—Fruits gathered, but not consumed. See *Possessor*, &c.

Perceptio.—A gathering in, collecting, appropriation. A *bona fide* possessor of lands makes the fruits thereof his own by gathering them, and for these he is not accountable to the real owner, whether they have been consumed or not. The fruits which have not been gathered, but are still *pendentes*, remain the property of the true owner. See *Pendentes fructus*.

Peremptoria litis et causæ.—Decisive of the suit and cause. Defences are either peremptory or dilatory. The latter (now more generally called *preliminary* defences) are those which affect the particular case or process in which they are pleaded, without affecting the pursuer's right on the merits. Such, for example, is any plea founded on informality in the summons, a plea that the pursuer has no title to sue, or a plea declining the jurisdiction of the court; and the effect of any dilatory plea, if sustained, is merely to throw that suit out of court, without prejudice to the pursuer's right to raise and insist in another action (it may be elsewhere) regarding the same subject-matter. A peremptory defence, on the other hand, as its name imports, is decisive of the question at issue between the parties, when it has been sustained. Thus if an action, proceeding on the ground that the defender is resting-owing the sum sued for, be met with the defence of payment, that is a peremptory defence, which, if sustained, has the effect, not merely of dismissing the action, but of assoilzieing the defender, and settling that question between the parties for ever. The pleas of compensation, *res judicata*, prescription, &c., may be given as further illustrations of peremptory defences. Peremptory defences may be briefly defined as those which enter into and affect the merits of the case, while dilatory or preliminary defences are those which do not affect the merits, but some other point to be discussed before the merits of the question at issue are inquired into or discussed. As to the distinction between dilatory and peremptory defences, see the opinion of Lord Chancellor Truro in *Geils* v. *Geils*, 1 Macq. 39.

Perficere susceptum munus.—To perform the duties of an office undertaken. Any one who voluntarily undertakes a certain duty, or accepts of a certain office, cannot of his own will resign it, but must perform all the duties incumbent on him in respect of it. Thus an arbiter, having once accepted of the office, must proceed in the submission until he has pronounced his final award; a mandatory must perform that which, by the mandate he has accepted and acted under, he has been authorised and empowered to do; and so also with a *negotiorum gestor*, tutors and curators, &c. In some of these cases the court will relieve the party of his office and its duties, as in the case of a tutor or curator in whose favour some interest has emerged adverse to the interest of the ward; but the parties cannot of themselves capriciously resign an office of which they voluntarily accepted, until its duties have been performed and its purpose or object attained. Testamentary trustees were formerly subject to this rule, and could not resign their office, after once accepting it, until the purposes of the trust had been fulfilled: but this has now been altered by statute. See *Id quod prius*, &c.

Periculo petentis.—At the risk of the person seeking. All judicial warrants obtained at the instance of a private suitor are granted at his risk. Thus an interdict to prevent the sale of goods is granted to the petitioner entirely at his risk, for it is he who alone can be made liable in the consequences of its use should the party interdicted thereafter show that the application was groundless, and claim damages on account of any loss sustained by him in consequence of the interdict. The judge granting the warrant is not liable for its consequences, however disastrous they may be. In like manner a creditor seeking a warrant for the apprehension of his debtor as *in meditatione fugæ*, obtains it *periculo petentis*, and he, not the judge, will be liable in damages if the debtor can show that the obtaining of the warrant and the using of it were illegal.

Periculum.—Risk, danger, peril.

Periculum rei venditæ nondum traditæ est emptoris.—The risk of a subject sold, but not yet delivered, lies with the purchaser. According to our law, as it formerly stood, the sale of goods not followed by delivery, conferred no right of property in the goods on the buyer. But notwithstanding this, any risk of loss arising from destruction, deterioration, decay, &c., of the thing sold, was with the buyer, this forming an exception to the general rule, *res perit domino*. This rule of law has now however been altered. By the Sale of Goods Act, 1893, it is provided (§ 20) that "unless otherwise agreed, the goods remain at the seller's risk until the property therein is transferred to the buyer, but when the property therein is transferred to the buyer the goods are at the buyer's risk whether delivery has been made or not." All risk attending the subject sold is now therefore with the person in whom is vested the property of the subject. As to the circumstances and conditions under which the property now passes to the buyer under the contract of sale, the reader must consult the provisions of the Act above cited, which has not yet been subjected to judicial consideration. The former law of Scotland as to the buyer's risk in things sold but not delivered will be found fully stated in the case of *Hansen* v. *Craig & Rose*, 21 D. 432.

Perimere causam.—To put an end to, or exhaust the cause. This is the effect of a peremptory defence when sustained, for it not only frees the defender from the particular suit in which the plea is urged, but totally extinguishes the pursuer's right of action upon that claim; it constitutes a *res judicata* between the parties on the point at issue. A dilatory or preliminary defence has only the effect of throwing out of court the particular case in which it has been set up, without prejudicing the pursuer's right to bring a new action. See *Peremptoria*, &c.

Perinde est ac si scriptum non esset.—It is the same as if it had not been written. "When the words of a deed, illustrated by evidence of the surrounding circumstances and of the meaning of any technical words in it, are insufficient to determine the granter's meaning, extrinsic evidence will not be admitted to prove what he intended, and the deed will be void for uncertainty—*perinde est ac si scriptum non esset*. Dickson, § 211.

Persona conjuncta æquiparatur interesse proprio.—(The interest of) a conjunct person is equivalent to a personal interest. This is one of the Baconian maxims, and imports that the interest of a personal or blood relation is equivalent to the interest of the individual. "So, if a man menace me, that he will imprison or hurt in body my father or my child, except I make unto him an obligation, I shall avoid this duress as well as if the duress had been to mine own person." (Bac. Max. reg. 18.) In Scotland the amount of fear or duress which will avoid an obligation thereby obtained depends upon the circumstances of each case, the rule being that such fear or duress only will avoid the obligation as a person of ordinary firmness and resolution could not withstand. For example, a threatened exposure of her child to criminal prosecution, or to public shame on account of some improper act, under which a mother was induced to grant an obligation otherwise not incumbent upon her, would be sufficient in the general case to avoid the obligation. (Bell's Prin. § 12.) Conjunct persons, according to the law of Scotland, are those who are related to each other either by consanguinity or affinity. Bell's Dict. *v. Conjunct*.

Persona dignior.—The more worthy person; the more fitting or suitable person. Where a heritable right is conceived in favour of a husband and wife in conjunct fee and liferent and their heirs in fee, the general rule is to regard the husband, being the *persona dignior*, as the sole fiar.

This rule, however, is not absolute, but is subject to several limitations, arising from the intention of the parties from whom the right flowed, presumed from the special circumstances of each case. Concerning these limitations, see *Cujus hæredibus*, &c.

Persona illustris.—A person of noble birth, or position. Stair, B. 1, T. 4, § 16.

Persona prædilecta.—A person chiefly favoured, or preferred. This phrase signifies one person who, among others appointed with him as colleagues in some office, enjoys the confidence and esteem of the person appointing, more than those appointed with him. Thus a testator not unfrequently appoints among his trustees one who shall be a *sine quo non*—that is, one whose concurrence and consent shall be indispensable to every act of administration under the trust. Such a trustee falls within the description of a *persona prædilecta*.

Persona standi in judicio.—A person or character entitling one to appear in a lawsuit to vindicate his right, and that whether in the character of pursuer or defender. This right is common to all, except those who have been deprived of it by the operation of the law, or those who have never yet attained it. Thus a rebel, who is civilly dead, and deprived on account of his crime of all his legal privileges, has no *persona standi*, and can neither sue nor defend action so long as his legal disability remains unremoved. Nor can a pupil exercise this right, as the law does not confer it upon him until he has attained minority, on account of his presumed inability, through nonage, to exercise it discreetly or to his advantage. The distinction between *persona standi* and *title to sue* must be borne in mind; the former refers to the right which a party has generally to sue or defend action, while the latter refers to the legal interest which a party has to pursue any particular action.

Personæ miserabiles.—Poor or destitute people; such as widows, orphans, paupers, &c. Ersk. B. 1, T. 5, § 30.

Personali exceptione.—By personal exception. A personal exception is one founded upon reasons strictly personal to the party against whom it is urged, and arising from some act or omission of his own. Thus if the indorsee of a bill gives the acceptor time to make payment of the contents beyond the day on which it falls due, in the knowledge and with the consent of the drawer, the drawer cannot afterwards claim exemption from his liability to the indorsee on account of the want of due negotiation. He is barred by personal exception from maintaining any plea on that ground in respect of his consent having been given to the delay. Yet such a plea might be effectual if maintained by a prior indorsee who was no party to the arrangement under which the delay was granted. A superior is barred by personal exception from claiming non-entry duties from a vassal's disponee when the non-entry arises from his own fault, as, for example, where he has not made up his title to the superiority. A personal exception, thus, as its name implies, is one that can only be pleaded as against the particular person, and is founded upon some act of his own; whereas other exceptions, such, for example, as that a bill is forged, may be maintained against any one, however guiltless of the forgery, who holds or does diligence upon the bill.

Personali objectione.—By personal objection. Some persons are rendered incapable of holding certain offices by reason of personal objection. Thus it will be sufficient to exclude one from the office of trustee on a sequestrated estate that he is already trustee upon another estate, the interests of which are conflicting with those of the former. So, also, a candidate for the office of trustee on a sequestrated estate was held ineligible for that office on the ground of personal objection, because he held a commission to act as an occasional sheriff-clerk depute in that county to the sheriff of which the sequestration proceedings fell to be remitted. *Clark,* 10 D. 117.

Pessima fides.—The worst faith; amounting to a moral dishonesty.

Pessimi exempli.—Of the worst example; affording a very bad precedent. Thus, to acquit a man of a crime because he had committed it under the influence of drink, or to allow any one to take benefit under a contract induced by his fraud, would be *pessimi exempli,* as tending to lead others to be dishonest or unfair in their dealings, or to be careless of their habits or their acts.

Pignus.—A pledge ; the contract of pledge. This was one of the real contracts of the civil law, which could only be constituted by the delivery of the subject pledged. It gave rise to the actions *directa* and *contraria*, the former at the instance of the pledger for delivery of the pledge when his debt had been paid or obligation fulfilled; the latter, at the instance of the pledgee for the recovery of any expenses necessarily disbursed by him for the maintenance or preservation of the pledge. The pledgee could not be compelled to give up the pledge until that claim, in security for which he held it, had been satisfied ; if he parted with its possession, his right over it ceased. These rules obtain also in our law. *N. W. Bank and Others*, 21 R. 513. A pledge given voluntarily, and as a matter of contract, is called a *pignus conventionale*, as distinguished from *pignus prætorium*.

Pignus prætorium.—A legal pledge ; a pledge given by the law, or the magistrate who administers it. The right vested in a creditor by adjudication is an illustration of the prætorian pledge. The adjudication does not vest the creditor with an absolute title to the heritage of his debtor, but merely gives him a right which may be defeated by the debtor's making payment of his debt, for the debtor may redeem his lands by payment of his debt at any time before declarator of the expiry of the legal : otherwise the right of the creditor is indefeasible. The right thus vested is really a right of pledge, because the creditor at first only holds the lands in security of the fulfilment of the debtor's obligation, and it is *prætorium* because it is granted by force of law, and not voluntarily by the debtor.

Placuit regi et concilio suo.—It has pleased the king and his council. Ersk. B. 1, T. 1, § 38.

Plagium.—The crime of stealing a human creature, styled in the Roman law the *crimen plagii*. Hume, i. 82.

Plebiscitum.—A law passed in the general council of the Roman people on the motion of a plebeian magistrate—*i.e.*, a tribune. Originally such laws were not binding upon the patricians, but only on the plebeians, and hence their name. At a later period, however (B.C. 286), they were made binding on all Roman citizens ; and the *plebiscita* formed one of the chief portions of the written law of Rome.

Pleno jure.—With full right. A conveyance or presentation *pleno jure* carries the full right with the profits or advantages pertaining to it.

Plenum dominium.—The full right of property. This includes both the *dominium directum* and the *dominium utile* of a subject; but the phrase may also be read as signifying an unrestricted fee.

Pluralis electio duorum numero contenta est.—The choice or selection of a plural number is satisfied (or complied with) by the selection of two. Thus if a truster directed his trustee to carry out some purpose,—*ex. gr.*, to found a hospital, or appoint to a bursary, &c., and to that end directed them to make choice of fit persons to do the work, or assist them in the appointment, or if he directed them to assume into the trust such persons as they might select, the general direction to select *persons* (in the plural number) would be sufficiently complied with if two persons were so selected. To select one person would not be compliance with the direction, but choice of more than two persons is not necessary. The Act 1672, c. 2, requires that a tutor, before entering upon his duties, or in any way exercising his office, shall give up inventories of his ward's estate, with consent of his nearest-of-kin on the father's side and the nearest-of-kin on his mother's side, who shall be majors, and within the kingdom at the time. The statute, however, does not specify the number of the nearest-of-kin who shall be necessarily cited for this purpose, and practice has interpreted the statutory provision as meaning two on each side, according to the rule of law expressed by this maxim.

Plures eandem rem in solidum possidere non possunt.—Two or more persons cannot each have the entire right to the same thing (at the same time). See *Duo non possunt,* &c.

Pluris petitio.—A claim for more than is due. Where a creditor claims judicially from his debtor more than is due, the only effect of such a proceeding is to modify the claim for expenses which he would otherwise have had. It does not affect his right to obtain decree under that action for the sum really due him. It is not considered a *pluris petitio* where a pursuer in an action of damages claims a much larger sum than that which is ultimately awarded him, for in such cases the sum libelled is generally a random sum, sufficient to cover any award which a jury may pronounce. Where an adjudging creditor leads his adjudication for a larger sum than is due him, such *pluris petitio*, if it be material, will have the effect of annulling the adjudication; where the claim made is only slightly in excess of the real debt, its effect is only to reduce the adjudication to a security for principal and interest, without expenses or penalties.

Plus enim valet quod agitur, quam quod simulate concipitur.—That which is done is of more avail than that which is pretended to be done. Thus a donation between a husband and a wife, although clothed in some other form, such as a right in trust conveyed to a third party, may be revoked, for the law regards the real character of the transaction rather than the form in which it is transacted. So also a donation *mortis causa*, in whatever form of words it may be expressed, if its real character be plain, is revocable at any time by the granter. On the same principle, one who has disponed his lands by an *ex facie*, absolute disposition to a creditor, is entitled to insist on a reconveyance if the disposition granted by him was really one in security; the real transaction being, when proved, more regarded than the simulate form in which it is clothed. See *Non quod dictum*, &c.

Plus petendo tempore.—When a creditor pursues for payment of a debt due him before the time at which he is entitled to demand or sue for it, he is said to be seeking his debt *plus petendo tempore*. This takes place, for example, when a creditor, who agreed to give his debtor six months' credit, sues for payment at the end of three, or at any time before the agreed-on term of credit expires; so, also, in the case where the creditor of a person deceased sues the executor before the expiry of the six months allowed to an executor to realise the estate. In such a case the pursuer renders himself liable in the expenses of the defence. See *Pactum de non petendo*.

Plus quam tolerabile.—More than can be borne or endured. A farm tenant is entitled, in certain cases, to an abatement of rent where his crops have suffered extraordinary damage—extraordinary, both in extent and in the cause from whence the damage arises. "Though the tenant should have got possession, and sown his arable grounds, the landlord cannot, by the Roman law, claim any part of the rent of that year if inundation, the calamity of war, the corruption of the air, or the inclemency of the weather, by earthquakes, lightning, &c., hath brought upon the crop a damage *plus quam tolerabile;* but if the loss be more moderate, he may exact the full rent." "These rules have been adopted into the law of Scotland, not only in the opinion of writers, but by our decisions, so far as they have gone in that matter." The risk of the seasons is, however, one of the risks undertaken by the tenant, and therefore it must be an event of such a character as cannot reasonably be supposed to have been contemplated by either of the parties to the lease, or to have entered into their calculations, which alone can warrant the tenant's claim for abatement. Regarding the law on this point, the reader may consult Ersk. B. 2, T. 6, § 41 (from which the above extract is taken), and Bell's Prin. § 1208, with the authorities there cited.

Pœna arbitraria.—Arbitrary punishments, or punishments the extent of which is left to the discretion of the judge and not fixed by rule. These are sometimes termed *pœna extraordinaria*, regarding which, see the following phrase.

Pœna ordinaria.—Ordinary or usual punishments. In some cases the punishment inflicted upon a criminal for the commission of certain crimes is fixed and determined, and in no respect within the discretion of the judge; such, for example, as those in which a prisoner has been found guilty of murder, treason, &c. There are others in which, while the judge has a certain discretion, this is limited to the extent or duration of the punishment, and not to the nature of the sentence. As, for example, when a statute provides that for a certain offence, the offender shall be subjected to imprisonment, not exceeding a certain period, in which case the sentence must be one of imprisonment, but its duration, in the discretion of the judge, may be anything within the prescribed limit. These are instances of the *pœna ordinaria*, the usual punishments attached to certain crimes. But there is another class of punishments, the *pœna extraordinaria*, which are unusual, and regulated by no fixed rule; such, for example, as the punishment for contempt of court, breach of sequestration or interdict, &c.; and in these the punishment is entirely in the discretion of the judge, who may either pronounce on the offender a sentence of imprisonment, inflict a fine, or dismiss him with an admonition. In a word, the *ordinaria* are those imposed according to a recognised and fixed rule, while the *extraordinaria* are not regulated by any determined rule, but lie entirely in the power and discretion of the judge.

Pondere, numero, et mensura.—By weight, number, and measure. These are the tests proposed by our law, by which to ascertain whether a certain subject falls within that class of subjects known as fungibles, which class includes all those things which perish in the using, and which can be estimated generally by weight, number and measure; such, for example, are corn, wine, money, &c. Fungibles may be given in *mutuum*, because there the borrower is not bound to return the identical subject borrowed, but its equivalent in quantity and value; but as fungibles perish in the using, they cannot form the subject of commodate, or of a contract of hiring, for in both these contracts the *ipsum corpus*, borrowed or hired, must be returned to the owner. Fungibles are so called, because they are things which are able to be replaced.

Popularis.—Popular; of or belonging to the people. Certain rights among the Romans were called popular, because they could be exercised by any citizen. Such was the right to demand the exhibition or production of a freeman unjustly imprisoned or detained by another, or demand the removal of a tutor *suspectus:* and the actions by which these rights were enforced were termed *actiones populares*. See *Actio*.

Portio Falcidia.—The Falcidian portion; which was a fourth of the whole estate of a testator reserved to the heir, and of which the testator could not otherwise dispose, deriving its name from the law which conferred this benefit upon the heir. See *Quarta Falcidia*.

Portio legitima.—Legal portion: legitim. Legitim is that portion of the father's moveable estate, as it exists at the time of the father's death, to which every lawful child is entitled; it is called the child's legal portion, because it is conferred upon him by the provision of the law and not the good pleasure of the father; and it cannot be defeated. The legitim which a child can claim is a half of the father's moveable estate, where there is no widow left, and one-third where there is a widow. If there be more children than one, the third or half (as the case may be) is divided equally among the children, but if the eldest son has succeeded to heritage, he is excluded from participation in the legitim except he collate. It has been said that this right cannot be defeated, which is correct, but the statement admits of qualification. By *mortis causa* deed, a father cannot dispose of moveables to the effect of lessening or defeating the child's claim; nor can he by making provisions for his children prevent them claiming their legal rights. But as legitim is a portion of the moveable estate left by a father at his death, he may practically defeat the child's claim by giving away or disposing of his moveable estate during life, provided this be not done by a fraudulent contrivance to disappoint the child without touching the father's own right during his life. *Agnew* v. *Agnew*, M. 8210, and *Hog* v. *Hog*, M. App. v. *Legitim*, 3. Bell's Prin. § 1584. The discharge of a claim for legitim is never presumed; in the general case it must be either expressly discharged, or discharged by the acceptance of a provision in lieu of it. There is some nicety in the questions which have arisen as to the discharge of legitim, but it will be sufficient to refer the reader upon this matter to Bell's Prin. § 1587, and cases there cited.

Portionibus hæreditariis.—In hereditary portions; those portions which descend to heirs-portioners. Ersk. B. 3, T. 8, § 50.

Positus in conditione non censetur positus in institutione.—One placed (or named) in a condition is not regarded as placed (or named) in the destination. "If a man devises land to a stranger after the death of his wife, this does not necessarily infer that the wife should have the estate for her life; it is but declaring at what time the stranger's estate shall commence; and in the meantime the heir shall have the land." Kames' Eq. 177.

Posse comitatus.—The power or force (the constabulary,

&c.) of the county, which the sheriff has a right to call out for the enforcement of legal diligence.

Possessio bona fide.—Possession in good faith. A person is said to possess a subject in good faith when he possesses it in the belief that he does so honestly, that he is entitled to do so, and is ignorant that any other has a better title to it than himself. Such a possessor is entitled to all the fruits of the subject which he has gathered, whether they are consumed or not. This kind of possession is contradistinguished from—

Possessio mala fide.—Possession in bad faith; which takes place when one holds possession of a subject in the knowledge that another is the true proprietor, and that he himself has no good title thereto. Such a possessor is liable to the true owner, not only for the whole fruits yielded by the subject, but for those which it might have yielded, known technically as violent profits. It is often a difficult question to decide at what period of his possession the good faith of the possessor ceased. If the title of the claimant be obviously a good one, and that of the possessor obviously defective, the execution of the summons to try the validity of the latter title will, in the general case, be sufficient to place the possessor in *mala fide;* but the solution of this question will depend upon the particular circumstances of each case. See *Bona fide possessor*, &c.

Possessor in bona fide facit fructus perceptos et consumptos suos.—A possessor in good faith makes those fruits his own which he has gathered and consumed. See the observations on the two preceding phrases, and on the phrase *Pendentes*, &c.

Possidere.—To possess; in the sense of being proprietor, and not merely custodier. The latter kind of possession is signified by the term *in possessione esse*. See *Aliud est*, &c.

Post causam cognitam.—After the case has been made known; after the grounds of action have been inquired into. See *Causa cognita*.

Post contractum debitum.—After debt has been contracted. By the Act 1621, cap. 18, all gratuitous alienations and conveyances of his lands or estate granted by a debtor in favour of any conjunct or confident person, "the same being done after the contracting of lawful debts from true creditors" are declared null. As to the persons who are regarded as conjunct or confident, see Bell's Dict. *v. Conjunct or Confident.* An heir incurs a passive title inferring liability to a certain extent for his ancestor's debts when he accepts gratuitously during his ancestor's life a right to a heritable estate to which he would have succeeded on his ancestor's death. His title to the lands is said to be granted *post contractum debitum*, and it renders him liable for debts contracted by the ancestor prior to the date of the gift. See *Præceptio*, &c.

Post litem motam.—After the action has been raised, or moved in. After this has been done, neither of the parties can perform any act effectually whereby the interests of the other in the subject-matter of the action can be affected. Thus if an action of reduction of a deed has been raised, on the ground of any informality or defect in it, the subsequent rectification of the error, or supplying of the defect, will not take away the grounds of action; the deed will be regarded as it stood at the time when it became the subject of the suit. See *Pendente lite*, &c.

Post tantum temporis.—After so long a time.

Posteriora derogant prioribus.—Subsequent (enactments) repeal prior ones. Any statutory enactment inconsistent with, or opposed to, one which has preceded it, operates as a repeal of the latter, although this should not be expressly embodied in the former. So also a subsequent clause in the same statute will operate as a repeal of a preceding clause, to the terms of which it is opposed. A pure case of the latter illustration seldom, if ever, happens; but where a subsequent clause differs from a preceding one, the earlier will be interpreted so as to make it agree with the provisions of the later clause. See *Lex posterior*, &c.

Potestas gladii.—The power of the sword; that is, the power of executing sentences pronounced in criminal cases.

Potestas maritalis.—The marital power; the power vested in the husband by virtue of the marriage. This power so vested in the husband extends over the person and formerly, the estate of his wife, although, as regards the latter, his power is now practically abolished. (See *Communio bonorum*.) As regards the person of his wife, the husband's curatorial power is so complete, that the wife, in the eye of the law, loses her distinct *persona* altogether. She cannot act by or for herself; all her acts and deeds to her own or her husband's prejudice are ineffectual without his consent. He cannot be deprived of her society on account of any civil obligation she may have come under, even before marriage; so if, at the time of the marriage, the wife should be engaged in service, the husband is entitled to take her away from her master's house, and the latter cannot compel her to remain, although he may have an action against the husband on account of breach of contract.

Potior est conditio masculi.—The condition of the male (*i.e.*, husband) is stronger. This maxim has application in questions arising out of destinations of joint fee and liferent. Thus where a subject is disponed to husband and wife in liferent, and their heirs in fee, the "heirs" are understood to mean the husband's heirs, because his position is considered the stronger or more preferable. The only exception to this rule is where the subject descends through the wife, or from her relations, in which case such a general destination as the one supposed would be held as conferring the fee upon the wife's heirs, or upon the wife herself, if her right was not specially limited to a liferent. See *Cujus hæredibus*, &c.

Potior est conditio possidentis vel defendentis.—The condition of a possessor or of a defender, is stronger; *i.e.*, stronger than the condition or position of the person challenging the possession, or suing. See *Melior est conditio*, &c.

Præbentes causam mortis.—(Persons) occasioning the cause of death. Hume, i, 183.

Præceptio hæreditatis.—A taking of the inheritance in advance; receiving the inheritance before the ancestor's death. This is one of the passive titles known in law, which, if incurred by the heir, renders him in some measure liable for his ancestor's debts. It was introduced to prevent an heir from receiving and enjoying, under a gratuitous disposition *inter vivos* from his ancestor, that heritable estate to which he would be entitled to succeed on the ancestor's death, and of thus avoiding responsibility for his ancestor's debts and other obligations. Accordingly, any heir incurring this passive title renders himself liable for those debts contracted by his ancestor prior to the date of the ancestor's conveyance; and this liability transmits against the heir's representatives, if, after taking possession, he should predecease the ancestor. To incur this passive title, it is necessary that, as regards the subject received, the person receiving it should be heir, *alioqui successurus*, and that the conveyance be gratuitous, the *onus* of proving that it was onerous lying upon the heir. If the heir prove that he has paid money for the right conveyed, it will always be a question for consideration whether the sum paid bears any adequate proportion in value to the subject conveyed; if not, the conveyance will be held to be gratuitous, for the heir is presumed to have paid that sum *dicis causa*, in order to avoid incurring this passive title.

Præcipuum.—A part of an estate which is not subject to the rules regulating its division, and which is paid or given over before division is made. This name is generally applied to that portion of the ancestor's estate which is allotted to the eldest heir-portioner, in addition to that share which she receives equally with the other heirs-portioners. It consists of titles of honour, the mansion-house on the family estate, with the garden and orchard attached to it, &c., and these she takes as her *præcipuum*, without giving any compensation therefor to the other heirs. She has also the right to such subjects as are indivisible, such as rights of superiority, the ancestor's town residence, &c.; but for these she requires to give compensation. The reader will find the word *præcipuum* used in reference to a different right than that of the eldest heir-portioner in Ersk. B. 3, T. 3, § 58; but it needs no further illustration than that given in the text. It may be observed, however, that the word is now rarely, if ever, used to signify anything other than the heir-portioner's right above explained.

Prædium.—Land; real property. This word signifies real property, whether it consist in lands or house property. All servitudes affecting real property are called prædial, and these are divided into rural and urban: the former includes all servitudes connected with the soil such as a right of way, the right of conveying and drawing water, of pasturage, &c.; while the latter includes all those which have a necessary connection with buildings, such as stillicide, *oneris ferendi* (the right of having one's building supported by that of a neighbour), *altius non tollendi* (of not building above a certain height), &c.

Prædium servit prædio.—Literally, land is under servitude to land,—*i.e.*, prædial or real servitudes are not personal rights separate or separable from the land, but attach to the dominant tenement, and pertain to, or may be exercised by, persons only as having right to that tenement. See Napier, 395 and 925; Stair, B. 2, T. 7, pr.

Prædium urbanum.—An urban tenement. This phrase is also used in the civil law writers to signify any building, whether it be within a town or not, in contradistinction to *prædium rusticum*, which signifies the soil. Just. Inst. B. 2, T. 3, § 1.

Prælibatio matrimonii.—A foretaste of marriage. An instance of the use of this phrase will be found in *Gray* v. *Marshall*, 2 R. 908, the circumstances of which case will sufficiently explain and illustrate the phrase.

Præmatura diligentia.—Premature diligence. Stair, B. 3, T. 5, § 22.

Præposita negotiis vel rebus domesticis.—Set over domestic affairs. A wife is presumed from her position to be invested with this *præpositura*, and therefore binds her husband for the price of anything she may purchase which is necessary for the family. It affords the husband no defence to a claim thus arising that his wife used the articles so purchased otherwise than for the benefit of the family, or that he gave her the money to pay for them; tradesmen and others being entitled to rely upon the presumed *præpositura* of the wife in their dealings with her. Where the wife incurs obligations in a manner not strictly falling within her presumed office, such as, for example, by borrowing money, it lies upon the creditor to show that the money was expended upon necessary furnishings, and that it was *in rem versum* of the family. This presumed right on the part of the wife to bind her husband in domestic matters ceases if she abandons her family, or if her husband has put an end to it by inhibition. According to Bell (Prin. § 231), an authority similar to the *præpositura* of a wife "is held to be given to the person placed at the head, or in management of, the domestic establishment." But that statement of the law must be taken now with some qualification, since the decision in the case of *Mortimer* v. *Hamilton,* 7 Macp. 158.

Præpositor.—A person who deputes the management of his business to another; one who confers on another the *præpositura*. The person who receives the delegated authority is called *institor* or *exercitor*.

Præpositura.—The office conferred by a principal on his factor, agent, or servant, under which the latter is authorised to carry on the business of the former, and in respect of which the servant by his acts binds the master in performance of the obligations undertaken in the course of the management of the business intrusted to him.

Præpositus negotiis.—Placed over one's business; intrusted with the charge of certain affairs. The acts and deeds of any one vested with the *præpositura*, if within the nature of the office so conferred upon him, are binding upon the *præpositor* or principal. Thus a master who intrusts to his servant the charge of a certain business, is liable for the obligations incurred by that servant in carrying it on, even where the servant has been unfaithful to his trust; a clerk, who has authority to draw and endorse bills in his master's name, binds the master by such transactions, even where he has embezzled the proceeds of the bills negotiated and absconded; and a factor or agent binds his principal if he acts within the terms of his mandate, although he should so act in defraud of his principal. To bind the alleged *præpositor* in any such case, it must be clear that the acts of the servant were authorised, and this may be proved either by the express terms of the servant's mandate, or by the acknowledgment or homologation on the part of the master, of similar acts of administration and management on the part of the servant.

Præpositus negotiis societatis.—Placed over the affairs or business of the partnership. It is implied in the contract of partnership that each partner is *præpositus negotiis societatis* "to the effect not only of holding possession for the company, and of acquiring property for them in the line of their trade, but also to the effect of entering into contracts for the partnership within the line of the trade which they profess to carry on, and of subscribing the firm, and binding the company in all acts of ordinary administration." Bell's Com. ii. 503. Under this implied authority a partner may bind the firm by an obligation granted by him in the firm's name, although that obligation may have been granted and used for his own advantage exclusively, and even although by the contract of copartnery he has been taken bound not to use or subscribe the signature of the firm. *Bryan*, 19 R. 490. A company is even liable for the fraudulent acts of a partner acting in the line of the partnership. But if a partner grants an acceptance or other obligation in name of the firm, without the knowledge of the firm, for a private debt of his own, the company is not liable to the creditor improperly receiving such an obligation. *Paterson Bros.*, 18 R. 403. On the subject of the powers of partners generally, see Bell's Com. ii. 503 *et seq.*, and cases there cited; and Ersk. B. 3, T. 3, § 20, with Lord Ivory's note, 124.

Præscriptio fori.—An exception to the competency of the court; a declinature of the jurisdiction. *Præscriptio* was originally a kind of defence, and derived its name from the position it occupied in the *formula* sent by the prætor to the *judex* who was to try the case. It was written at the head or outset of the *formula*, and the object of it was to prevent the *judex* inquiring further into the case if the *præscriptio* was proved. The difference between this kind of defence and the *exceptio* was this: the *præscriptio* (which stood at the head of the *formula*) put an end to the case at once, if the statements upon which it rested were true; the *exceptio* (stated in the body of the *formula*) made it requisite to go into the whole matter, in order to see whether there had been fraud, force, &c. As the *præscriptio* was generally founded upon alleged possession for such a length of time as took away the pursuer's right to claim, it ultimately came to signify, as it does now with us, the right which such lengthened possession conferred.

Præscriptio longissimi temporis.—The prescription of the longest period. With us the prescription of the longest period is the prescription of forty years, which has the effect of discharging a debt not sued for within it, &c. ; and this is generally known as the long prescription, in contradistinction to others of a shorter period. Among the Romans the prescription signified by the words of the phrase was of a different character. It was either of a period of thirty or forty years. 1. By possession for the former period, the property of a subject stolen was transferred to the possessor, if his possession began *in bona fide;* and even in the case of the thief himself the lapse of thirty years gave him a valid defence to any action for recovery at the instance of the true owner. The difference in the case of a person possessing *in bona fide,* and of one possessing *in mala fide,* was this, that the latter was only protected by the prescription so long as he retained possession, for if he lost possession he had no action for recovery: this lay with the true owner ; while the former, by the lapse of the prescriptive period, became the true owner, and enjoyed all the rights attaching to ownership. In short, where there was *bona fides* the prescription transferred the property ; where there was *mala fides* it only afforded an exception to any action for recovery. 2. The forty years' prescription was the same as that of thirty years, with this exception, that it applied only when the property in question belonged to the State, the Church, or to a pupil. The Romans had also the prescription *longi temporis,* which applied to immoveable or real rights. Its period was ten years, *inter præsentes*—*i.e.,* where the party possessing and the party challenging the possession lived in the same province, and twenty years *inter absentes*—*i.e.,* where they lived in different provinces. The period of the long prescription (negative), necessary in our law to bar all challenge to a title *ex facie* valid, has been reduced from forty to twenty years by the Act 37 & 38 Vict. c. 94, § 34.

Præscriptis verbis.—In the words before written. The *formula,* under the civil law, sent by the prætor to the *judex* appointed to try the question at issue between two suitors, set out with a statement of the contract under which the respective rights and obligations of the parties arose. Thus in the example of the *formula* already given (see *Judices dati*), the contract between the parties was one of sale. The first question to be decided by the *judex* was whether the contract thus specified had been entered into, and if the facts proved in the course of the investigation did not amount to the constitution of the specified contract, the pursuer was cast in his suit. This rendered it necessary to have an action which would apply to those cases where parties had entered into an innominate contract, that is, into one of those agreements which, while valid as regards the parties, were not known by a special name, and where, consequently, the contract could not be set forth as in the ordinary case. The action provided to meet this want was called the action *præscriptis verbis*, because the formula directed the *judex* to decide for the pursuer, if the circumstances set forth in the words at the head of the formula were proved.

Præsentia corporis tollit errorem nominis, et veritas nominis tollit errorem demonstrationis.—The presence of the subject takes away the effect of error in its name, and the truth of the name takes away the effect of error in description. The first part of this maxim is accepted as expressing a sound rule. If a man by his will left to A B his ruby ring, and left several rings, but among them no ring of that description, the bequest would be invalid, and would carry nothing to the legatee. But if one said to another, I give you this ruby ring as a present, and handed over a diamond ring, the error in the name or description would have no effect in invalidating the gift, because the subject gifted was present, and no difference of opinion or doubt could exist as to the subject which was intended to be given: the subject of the gift was the ring delivered to the donee, whether set with a ruby or a diamond. The second branch of this maxim, however, has not been accepted or recognised as the first branch has been. If the name and description do not coincide, there is no presumption, in the absence of the thing itself, in favour of the one over the other: the truth of the name will depend on the falsity of the description, or *vice versa.* "There is a maxim that the name shall prevail against an error of demonstration; but then you must first show that there is an error of demonstration, and until you have shown that, the rule *veritas nominis tollit · errorem demonstrationis* does not apply. I think that there is no presumption in favour of the name more than of the demonstration." Per Lord Chancellor Campbell in *Drake* v. *Drake,* 8 Cl. 179.

Præsentibus post proximum terminum minime valituris. —These presents being of no avail after next term. Formerly, when an heir was served in general or in special to his ancestor in lands held of the Crown, the next step in making up his title was to obtain a precept from Chancery for his infeftment, proceeding on the narrative of the retour of his service. The effect of this precept was limited to the term of Whitsunday or Martinmas following its date by the words of the phrase. The form of procedure now to be observed in making up a title by service is regulated by the Act 31 & 32 Vict. c. 101.

Præstatio culpa levis.—An obligation or liability for the middle degree of diligence;—*i.e.,* for the diligence and care which a man of ordinary prudence is accustomed to bestow upon his own affairs. See *Culpa.*

Præsumendum est pro libertate.—The presumption is in favour of liberty. Any restriction upon the full and unrestrained enjoyment of property, or in the exercise of the rights of ownership which attach to it, are regarded unfavourably by the law, the legal presumption being, as expressed in the words of the phrase, in favour of the free and unlimited exercise of these rights; and therefore all such restrictions are disregarded where not clearly imposed, and even then are interpreted *stricti juris.* Accordingly, rights of servitude, being burdens and restrictions of the nature referred to, are strictly construed; so also are the restrictive conditions of an entail.

Præsumitur pro legitimatione.—Legitimacy is presumed; the presumption is in favour of legitimacy. All children born in wedlock are presumed legitimate—they are presumed to be the children of the spouses—according to the rule *Pater est quem nuptiæ demonstrant.* It has been stated (Fraser, Par. & Ch. 2) that this rule does not apply to children born within six months after the marriage has been entered into, or ten months after the marriage has been dissolved, and the law as thus stated was approved and followed in the case of *Gardner*, 3 R. 695, affd. H. L. 4 R. 56. But in the case of children born within six months of the marriage, there is a presumption (not so strong or absolute as that expressed by the maxim *Pater est*, &c.) that the husband is the father of the child. The strength of that presumption will be increased or diminished according to the circumstances of each case. The reader will find this subject fully discussed in the case of *Gardner*. Reference may also be made to the case of *Jobson* v. *Reid*, 8 S. 343, where a married woman sued for the aliment of a child to which she gave birth within six months after her marriage, and of which she alleged the defender (who was not her husband) was the father. It was pleaded in defence that the pursuer being a married woman, the presumption was that the husband was the father and the child legitimate. The court ordered an investigation to be made for the purpose of ascertaining certain dates and facts tending to show that the husband could not be the father, in consequence of his absence at sea at the time when the child (which was mature at birth) was begotten; but in ordering this inquiry the Lord President (Hope) remarked—" The child of this woman, though born so recently after marriage, would, but for these proceedings at its mother's instance, have been unquestionably legitimate. The presumption of the law is, that the parents of a child that is born during wedlock are the married parties —a presumption not only supported by favour towards the child, but well founded also in that daily experience which proves that after parties, particularly among the lower orders, have had intercourse, in consequence of which the woman becomes pregnant, a marriage, whether previously promised or not, is the common consequence, and the natural reparation by the father of the injury he has done to the mother of his child." In England the rule is that a child born after the marriage is presumed to be the husband's, without regard to the length or shortness of time intervening between the marriage and the birth. (Weightman, 161.) " With respect to the case where the parents have married so recently before the birth of the child that it could not have been begotten in wedlock, it stands upon its own peculiar ground. The marriage of the parties is the criterion adopted by the law, in cases of antenuptial generation, for ascertaining the actual parentage of the child. For this purpose it will not examine when the gestation began, looking only to the recognition of it by the husband in the subsequent act of marriage." Per Ellenborough, C.-J., in *The King* v. *Luffe*, 8 East, 207. The presumption of legitimacy may be redargued by proof that the husband is not the father, regarding which see *Pater est quem*, &c. The joint statement by the spouses that the child is not their offspring is not of itself sufficient to overcome the presumption. Stair, B. 4, T. 45, § 20.

Præsumptio cedit veritati.—A presumption yields to the truth. Presumptions of law, being merely suppositions of what may be true, and what is held to be true in the absence of proof to the contrary, are overcome or redargued by proof that what is supposed or presumed is not consistent with the real fact; the presumption gives place to the truth when this has been ascertained. This maxim, however, has no application where the presumption is one *juris et de jure*. See *Præsumptio juris*.

Præsumptio hominis vel judicis.—The presumption of the man, or of the judge. This is the opinion or conviction of the judge, arising from the circumstances of the case laid before him. It differs from the *præsumptio juris* in this, that the latter is that arising from statutory provision, decisions, or custom, while the former emerges from the circumstances of each special case, and is frequently strong enough to overcome the legal presumption.

Præsumptio juris.—A legal presumption. This is a presumption fixed by statute, decisions, or custom, in favour of a certain argument or case, but which admits of being redargued by contrary proof. Thus, in moveables, property is presumed from possession; a debtor is never presumed to have given anything in gift to his creditor; a bond or bill found in the debtor's repositories is presumed to have been paid; the husband is presumed to be the father of all children to which his wife gives birth during the subsistence of the marriage, &c. In so far as the *præsumptio juris* admits of being redargued, it differs from the

Præsumptio juris et de jure.—A legal presumption,

amounting to a legal rule. This does not admit of refutation; but the facts on which it is founded being admitted or proved, the presumption receives the weight and effect of a fixed rule of law. Thus a minor with curators is not held bound by any contract into which he may enter without their consent; he is presumed to be incapable of acting for himself, and this presumption cannot be overturned, even where it can be proved that the minor has acted, and is capable of acting with great prudence and care, and advantageously for himself. So also the plea of lesion, as a ground of reduction, will not be sustained if the action of reduction is not brought within the *quadriennium utile*, the law presuming, from the party's silence during that period, that the deed or contract sought to be reduced was not to the minor's lesion,—a presumption which cannot be traversed, even by legal evidence to the contrary. In like manner (before the law of death-bed was abolished), the law presumed a man to be mentally incapable of executing a settlement disposing of heritage upon death-bed; and this could not be redargued by the clearest proof of his mental capacity at the time of executing the settlement, or during the whole period of sixty days before his death.

Præsumptio opponitur probationi.—Presumption is set against proof; or, is opposed to proof, by way of antithesis. Napier, 729, 831.

Præsumptione.—By presumption; *i.e.*, according to the *presumptio juris*.

Præter dotem.—Over and above the dowry or tocher. Ersk. B. 1, T. 6, § 15.

Prævento termino.—By anticipating the term. This name was given to a form of action formerly in use but now unknown in the Court of Session, adopted by a charger against whom a bill of suspension had been presented, in order to force on a discussion of the reasons of suspension. The object of the suspender being not unfrequently to occasion delay, and thus postpone the payment of his debt, it was his interest to get a distant day of compearance assigned in the deliverance on the bill of suspension. As by the forms of court the charger could not insist on having the reasons of suspension discussed until the day on which by the letters of suspension he was cited to compear, he was allowed to bring an action for shortening the term or *induciæ*, and this was therefore called an action *prævento termino*. The present forms of procedure in the Bill Chamber have superseded the necessity for such an action.

Precarium.—A species of the contract of commodate, where the subject is lent, not for a certain time or for a special occasion, but during the pleasure and at the will of the lender. In the civil law *precarium* included everything which one had obtained or extorted from another by prayers and entreaties (*preces*). The person from whom, the possession had been thus extorted could resume possession at any time under the interdict *de precario*; and hence the word *precarius* came to mean uncertain.

Preceptum amissionis superioritatis.—A precept of a lost superiority. A disponee was sometimes unable to complete his right to the lands which he had acquired through the refusal or inability of the superior to give him an entry. In such a case the disponee formerly charged the superior to enter him, or (where this was necessary) to make up his title to the superiority and enter him. On the superior's failure to make up his title or enter as charged, the disponee brought an action of declarator of tinsel of the superiority, in which he called the next superior or over-lord as a party, in order that he might be authorised and ordained to receive the disponee as his own immediate vassal. Where the mediate superior was the Crown, a precept was issued from Chancery on the decree of tinsel, for the infeftment of the disponee, infeftment on which made his title as complete as it would have been had he been infeft on a charter of resignation from his immediate superior. This precept was called the *preceptum amissionis superioritatis*, because its effect was to deprive the superior of his right to the casualties during that vassal's life, although it did not affect his right to the yearly duties. A simpler and more expeditious mode of compelling an entry was introduced by the Act 10 & 11 Vict. c. 48, but entry with the superior is now abolished (37 & 38 Vict. c. 94), and every proprietor duly infeft is deemed to be, as at the date of his infeftment, duly entered with his superior.

Pretium affectionis.—The price of regard. This is the

value attached to it by the owner of a subject, on account of the regard in which he holds it, and apart altogether from its intrinsic value. Thus, heir-looms, gifts from deceased friends, &c., have a *pretium affectionis* attached to them, on account of the manner in which the owner has acquired possession. Damage is never estimated by this standard when the injury has been done without fraud or dole.

Pretium periculi.—The price of the risk; the payment in consideration of which the risk is undertaken. Such is the premium paid on a policy of insurance, either on a life or against fire, which varies in amount according to the nature of the risk. So also the interest paid on money advanced on bottomry or *respondentia* (called generally marine interest) partakes more of the character of a *pretium periculi*, or premium, than of mere interest for the loan of money, because, if the ship on which it is advanced is lost, the lender loses his right to claim the capital sum lent.

Primæ impressionis.—Of first impression. That is said to be a case of first impression which has no precedent; "where never the like action was brought before." Powys, J., in *Ashby* v. *White*, 2 Raym. 944.

Primo fronte.—At first sight; palpably.

Primo loco.—In the first place. When a claimant in an action of multiplepoinding is preferred *primo loco* to the fund *in medio*, he is preferred to the exclusion of all other claimants, who can take no part of the fund until the claim preferred has been satisfied.

Primo venienti.—To the person who comes first. An executor, after having realised the estate of the deceased, is entitled to pay off his debts as they shall be claimed; that is, he is not bound to wait until all the claims against the deceased have been presented for payment, but may pay them as they are presented. It may happen that the executor, having paid all the claims presented in full, is unable to pay one subsequently presented, of the existence of which he was not previously aware. In such a case the executor is not personally liable, because he was entitled to pay away the estate to the creditors first claiming. Bell's Prin. § 1900.

Primus actus judicii est judicis approbatorius.—The first act or step of procedure in a suit is held to be approbatory of the judge. The import of this maxim is, that any objection which can be urged against the judge before whom the action is brought must be stated at the outset, for if the party entitled to take the objection proceeds in the suit without taking it, his proceedings are regarded as an approval of the judge which bars him stating the objection at any subsequent stage of the case. Thus, if a defender propone defences on the merits of the action brought against him, without declining the jurisdiction of the judge, he cannot thereafter decline the jurisdiction. Such objections must be stated *in limine*, or they are held to be waived.

Prior læsit.—First hurt or injured. The law does not regard in so serious a light injuries resulting from an assault made in retaliation, as those resulting from an assault which was unprovoked; the fact that the person assaulting had been first assaulted or injured is to some extent a justification. Hume, i. 262.

Prior possessio cum titulo posteriore melior est priore titulo sine possessione.—Prior possession with a subsequent title is better than a prior title without possession. This was a rule applied in cases of competition for lands where both claimants held a base right to the subject (see *A me*, &c.); the one who had had possession being preferred to one who had not, although the title of the latter was prior in date to that of the former. As all rights are now made public by infeftment, and confirmation by the superior has been abolished, the rule of the maxim has no longer any application in our law; but the student may be referred for further comment upon the maxim to Ross's Lectures, ii. 263.

Prior tempore potior jure.—Prior in date, preferable in right. This is the rule of law on which rights of preference in competitions are decided, the import of which is, that he whose right to the subject claimed has been first completed is preferred, as having the best right, to the exclusion of all others. Thus the conveyance first in date upon the record gives a preferable right to the lands over that afforded by a conveyance subsequently recorded, without regard to the date of the conveyance itself. On the same principle, the first confirmed title to lands held *a me* (so long as confirmation was necessary) was preferred to that subsequently confirmed, although the infeftment last confirmed should have been first recorded. So also the preferences of arresting creditors are decided according to the dates of their respective arrestments and not according to priority in point of time or date of the decree on which the arrestments proceed.

Privæ leges.—Personal laws ; imperial constitutions having reference merely to one person. Under the civil law were included in this class all laws or ordinances which had reference alone to an individual, and did not affect the people generally, and that whether such ordinances were beneficial to the individual (as in the case of imperial rescripts, by which a person was legitimated, a convict pardoned, &c.), or were disadvantageous to him. Such laws, however, in the general case, were passed for the purpose of conferring a benefit, and hence the word privileges. In our law the term is applied to all Acts affecting private, personal, or local interests, such as those authorising the construction of a railway, a road, restitution of family honours, titles of dignity, &c. These are not, in the strict sense, laws, and cannot therefore be recognised by the courts, unless pleaded by the parties having the interest to do so.

Privatis pactionibus non dubium est non lædi jus cæterorum.—It is not doubtful that the private bargains or arrangements of certain persons cannot injure the right of others. As no one can lose a right which he possesses except by the act of the law or his own act, it is clear that such right cannot be infringed or defeated by the acts of others. The kind of right which cannot be so defeated must, however, be borne in mind. Under a father's settlement a child may have right (in popular language) to a certain succession, but during the father's life such a right is merely a *spes* which may be defeated by the father—it is not a right strictly speaking. But if in an antenuptial contract the husband conveys to the children (*nascituri*) of the marriage, or to trustees for their behoof, certain estate or effects as provision for such children, that confers upon the children a right which the father cannot revoke by any subsequent deed or settlement. The right referred to in the maxim is a *jus quæsitum*.

Privatorum conventio juri publico non derogat.— An agreement or bargain between individuals does not derogate from the public law. See *Conventio privatorum*, &c.

Privatum incommodum bono publico pensatur.—Private inconvenience or disadvantage is counterbalanced (or compensated) by the public good. Where the legislature authorises or orders certain things to be done, which in their performance inflict an injury or disadvantage on individuals, the latter have no claim for compensation (unless the legislature has otherwise directed), the public advantage gained by the operation being regarded as outweighing the private inconvenience or loss. In practice, however, the legislature, in ordering or authorising public works, protects private interests by directing that compensation shall be given for all injury or loss occasioned by the operations authorised.

Privilegiatus contra privilegiatum non utitur privilegio. —A privileged person cannot plead his privilege against another privileged person. Thus creditors in privileged debts have no preference over each other. In *Peter* v. *Monro*, M. 11852, the disburser of funeral expenses was not preferred to but ranked *pari passu* with the "furnisher of medicines" to a deceased on her death-bed. Some of the Lords thought the *funerator* preferable, as a dead person must be buried; others thought the furnishing medicines to be no less a debt of humanity, and that *privilegiatus*, &c.; and in this the plurality agreed." " It is the common opinion that the minor cannot defend himself on this privilege (*i.e.*, his minority) against a minor who sues for reduction on the head of minority and lesion; not merely because the pursuer has in that case equal privilege with the defender, but also because the case of the pursuer, who is *in damno vitando*, is more favourable than that of the defender, who is *in lucro captando*." Ersk. B. 1, T. 7, § 46. See further on this subject, Fraser, Par. & Ch. 448, and cases there cited.

Privilegium contra rempublicam non valet.—Privilege does not avail against the State; privilege cannot be effectually pleaded in a question with the State, or against the common weal. See *Necessitas inducit*, &c.

Pro bono publico.—For the public good; for the advantage of the public generally. See *Pro privato*, &c.

Pro confesso.—As having confessed. Where a defender

fails to appear to answer or defend a summons raised and executed against him, he is held *pro confesso*, and therefore decree is pronounced against him; that is, his failure to appear is regarded as a confession of the justice of the pursuer's claim, and on this inferred confession the decree proceeds. In the same way, where one party to a suit refers the point at issue to the oath of his opponent, and the latter fails to appear and depone under the reference, he is held as confessed that his case is unfounded, and that the other party's case is sound, and decree follows in terms of this implied confession.

Pro forma.—As a matter of form; a proceeding purely formal.

Pro gravitate admissi.—According to the gravity of the offence.

Pro hac vice.—Literally, for this turn; for this occasion or service; for the discharge of this duty or office. Some appointments are made for the discharge merely of a certain specified duty, which, being performed, the appointment falls. Thus in the introductory part of a Court of Session summons, it is directed to messengers-at-arms "Our Sheriffs in that part," which is the same as, our Sheriffs *pro hac vice*. They are appointed the sheriffs or officers for the fulfilment of a certain office, namely, the execution of the summons; and on this being done, the authority deputed to them ceases, in so far as regards that particular writ.

Pro indiviso.—In an undivided manner; in common. A *pro indiviso* right is one which gives to several proprietors a conjunct and common right in the whole subjects over which the right extends; and while each has an equal right to the whole, none of the proprietors can claim an absolute right to any individual portion. Heirs-portioners are *pro indiviso* proprietors of the inheritance to which they succeed. They have an equal right to the whole rents and profits of the estate as a *cumulo* sum, but none of them can claim the rent or profit of any particular field or farm as her absolute right. Such a right constitutes a kind of partnership among the proprietors, under which they equally enjoy the profits of the subjects so held, while they equally bear its burdens and responsibilities: but *pro indiviso* proprietors have no presumed mandate as partners have under which they can bind each other to third parties.

Pro loco et tempore.—For the place and time. Where an objection has been taken successfully to the relevancy of an indictment, or anything occurs to induce the public prosecutor to delay proceeding with the trial, such as the absence of an essential witness, &c., he may, before the jury is sworn, move the court to desert the diet against the prisoner *pro loco et tempore*, and this reserves to him the power of indicting the prisoner again for the same offence, at another place and time. The diet cannot thus be deserted where the panel is indicted under the provisions of the Act 50 & 51 Vict. c. 35, § 43 (which now comes in place of the Act 1701, c. 6), for any desertion of the diet in that case amounts to a desertion of the cause *simpliciter*, which frees the panel for ever of all challenge or question touching the offence libelled ; nor can the diet be deserted *pro loco et tempore* in any case after the jury has been sworn to try the cause.

Pro modo admissi.—According to the measure of the offence.

Pro non adjecto.—As not added. In the nomination of testamentary tutors, where a tutor is nominated who is incapable of filling the office through legal incapacity, or otherwise, this will not invalidate the appointment as regards the others. The name of the one incapacitated is regarded as *non adjectus*, while the appointment as regards the others will be sustained. Anything in a deed which is not essential, but mere surplusage, is held *pro non adjecto*, and cannot affect its validity.

Pro non scripto.—As not written. Certain conditions attached to legacies or testaments are disregarded by our law, and are held *pro non scripto*—as if they had not been written, and did not form part of the deed ; but to be thus disregarded, the conditions must either be impossible or illegal. Thus if a testator directed that his heir should succeed, or a legatee receive the legacy bequeathed, only on condition of their committing a theft, or on their committing an assault, &c., the condition would be disregarded as illegal, and the heir or legatee would succeed without fulfilment of the condition. So also, if the condition be one of which the fulfilment is impossible; as, for example, that the heir or legatee should travel over Britain in a day. A distinction was regarded by the civil law between impossible conditions attached to a contract, and such conditions attached to a testament; in the former case they were held to void the contract, in the latter they were held *pro non scripto*. This distinction is also followed in our law. "As an obligation to perform impossible facts is null, so are those granted under an impossible condition; for the adjection of a condition which cannot exist is an evidence that the parties did not seriously intend a bargain. But deeds are construed to be granted absolutely, and the condition is held *pro non scripto*, not only in testaments and legacies, but even in grants *inter vivos*, where the granter of the obligation lies under a natural tie to execute them." Ersk. B. 3, T. 3, § 85.

Pro omni alio onere.—For all other burden. A clause used in charters, the effect of which is to restrict the duties to be rendered to the superior by the vassal on account of the lands held by him, to those expressed in the charter. The clause (called the *reddendo*) generally runs in terms similar to the following :—" Giving therefore yearly the said A (the vassal) and his foresaids, for the lands and others above disponed to me and my foresaids, lawful superiors of the same, the sum of £   in name of feu-duty at two terms in the year, &c., and these *for all other burden*, exaction, demand, or secular service whatsoever, which can be any way exacted for the said lands and others, or any part thereof, in all time coming."

Pro parte.—Partly; as regards a part. Under the civil law a testator could not die intestate *pro parte*, that is, as regards a part of his estate; his succession must have been either wholly testate or wholly intestate. Where a testator appointed a certain person his heir, and conveyed to him certain portions of his succession, but left other portions undisposed of, the law regarded the heir so named as the universal heir, and he succeeded accordingly. A different rule prevails with us; for while our law will give effect to the testator's will, in so far as this has been expressed by a valid instrument, and hold the deceased to be thus far testate, yet if he has left property which is certainly not disposed of by that instrument, the law will dispose of it according to the rules of intestate succession, giving it, not to the person succeeding under the deed, but to the heir-at-law if it be heritage, and to the next-of-kin if it be moveables. Where, however, a testator has left a will purporting to be a conveyance of his whole estate, intestacy as regards any part of that estate will not be readily implied. The presumption in such a case is against intestacy. *Ogilvie's Trs.*, 8 Macp. 427.

Pro parte legitimus, pro parte illegitimus.—Partly legitimate—partly illegitimate. Although it seems anomalous, it is not the less true that a person may be in the position described by this phrase: a short statement will explain how. Children illegitimate at their birth are legitimated by the subsequent marriage of their parents according to the law of Scotland; but this rule does not obtain in England, where children originally illegitimate remain always illegitimate. If the father of a child legitimised as above mentioned dies possessed of heritage in England, the child cannot succeed to it—he is not the heir, because according to English law he is not legitimate; but his personal status of legitimacy is "admitted, and the rights of a legitimate child in part conceded to him. He is there—*pro parte legitimus—pro parte illegitimus.*" Fraser, Par. & Ch. 55.

Pro parte virili.—For the share per man; for one's own share or proportion. Where there are several vitious intromitters with the estate of a deceased, any one of them may be sued by a creditor of the deceased *in solidum*, for the whole debt due to him; but if he calls them all jointly in one summons, each is liable only for his own share of the creditor's claim, which is regulated according to the number of the defenders, without regard to the extent of their several intromissions.

Pro possessore habetur qui dolo desiit possidere.—He is held as the possessor who, for a fraudulent purpose, has ceased to possess. Such a person cannot take benefit by his own fraud, and therefore all the liabilities of a possessor must be borne by him who has fraudulently quitted possession. See *Is qui dolo*, &c.

Pro privato commodo.—For private convenience. This phrase is used in contradistinction to *pro bono publico*, and they may both be illustrated simply. A highway is constructed for the public good or convenience, and every one has a right to use it, while a private road is made for the convenience of the proprietor alone, and no one, without his permission, can use it without trespassing.

Pro quantitate hæreditatis et temporis.—According to the extent of the succession (*i.e.*, the lands succeeded to), and of the time. The casualty of ward entitled the superior to the whole profits of the ward-fee during the minority of the heir, and by the rule of an ancient law he was liable for a proportion of the debts of the deceased vassal, according to the extent of the estate and the length of time the heir was in minority. This was subsequently altered, and he was entitled to the profits of the estate without deduction, nor could his right be affected by any act (such as the constitution of servitudes) of the late vassal. The casualty of ward, and the other casualties proper to ward-holding, were abolished by the Act 20 Geo. II. c. 50.

Pro rata.—Proportionally; for a proportion. Where several debtors are each liable for the whole debt, they are said to be liable *in solidum*, but where each is liable for his own share or proportion only, they are said to be bound *pro rata*. An example of both phrases may be found in the liability of partners; each is liable *in solidum* for the debts of the co-partnery in a question with the creditor, but each is liable only *pro rata* in a question between themselves.

Pro rata itineris.—For the proportion of the journey or voyage. Where a ship, chartered to convey a cargo to a certain port for a specified freight, is prevented from completing the voyage, either through the perils of the sea or hostile power, the master of the ship may tranship the goods, and thus conveying them to their destination, earn his full freight. But if, when the ship has been prevented from proceeding on her voyage, the freighter himself tranships the cargo, the master is entitled to freight *pro rata itineris*, for the proportion of the voyage which he has accomplished. On this subject see Bell's Com. i. 617 *et seq.*; and Abbot, 368 *et seq.*

Pro re nata.—Arising from some particular thing or circumstance. A meeting or proceeding *pro re nata* is a meeting which has been called, or a proceeding taken, in consequence of some emergency, which has rendered it necessary. Thus a *pro re nata* meeting of presbytery is one which has been called out of the ordinary course of presbytery meetings, for the special consideration of some case or circumstance requiring such attention.

Pro servitio burgali.—For burghal service. Burgage subjects were formerly held of the Crown in return for burghal service, which always included watching and warding in the burgh, whether this was expressed in the charter or not. All burgage lands are now held blench of the Crown. The distinction between burgage tenure and feu has been abolished by the Act 37 & 38 Vict. c. 94, § 25.

Pro tanto.—For so much; to account of. Where a defender consigns a certain sum, which he admits to be due, in an action raised against him by his creditor, the latter, obtaining decree for the full sum claimed, is entitled to uplift the consigned money, and impute it *pro tanto* in extinction of his claim. Or where a defender is found liable in a sum sued for, but found entitled to his expenses, he may impute the amount of his expenses in extinction *pro tanto* of his creditor's claim, and obtain a discharge on payment of the balance.

Pro tempore.—For the time being; temporary.

Pro tribunali.—In court; before the judge.

Pro veritate accipitur.—Is held or received as the truth. See *Res judicata pro,* &c.

Pro virili.—For one's own share. This phrase is a contraction for *Pro parte virili.* Ersk. B. 3, T. 9, § 55.

Probabilis causa litigandi.—A probable or plausible ground of action. Any one may raise and prosecute an action, whether he has reasonable grounds for doing so or not, the award of expenses against an unsuccessful litigant being generally a sufficient check upon unnecessary and groundless litigation. But when litigants, unable to afford the expense of an action, apply for the benefit of the poor's roll, either in the Supreme or Inferior Courts, against whom no available award of expenses can be given, it is necessary to ascertain that their ground of action is at least reasonable, so that if it is, they may not be denied the justice to which they are entitled; and if it is not, that their reckless litigation may not be allowed to proceed to the detriment of their opponent. For this purpose the Court appoints certain persons practising before it to inquire into the nature of the action, and the grounds on which it is based, and if they report that the applicant has a *probabilis causa litigandi*, he is admitted to the benefit of the poor's roll; if they report otherwise, the application is refused.

Probandi necessitas incumbit illi qui agit.—The necessity of proving (his claim or contention) lies on him who sues. See *Affirmanti incumbit*, &c.

Probatio probata.—Literally, a proved proof; that is, a proof which is not permitted to be impugned or redargued. Thus the verdict of a jury, where it cannot be reviewed, is called *probatio probata*; and of the same nature is the finding of a Lord Ordinary upon the facts, who, of consent of parties, presides at a trial without a jury, under the provisions of the Act 13 & 14 Vict. c. 36. In the latter case the findings of the Lord Ordinary on the facts are final, unless they proceed upon some erroneous view of the law as to competency of evidence or otherwise.

Probatio prout de jure.—A proof according to law. A proof *prout de jure* includes all the legal means of probation, parole, documentary, and oath of party; although in practice this phrase is understood to signify a general proof of the facts and circumstances of the case in which it is allowed, in contradistinction to a proof which is limited to the writ or oath of the party.

Probatis extremis præsumuntur media.—The extremes being proved, those things which fall within or between them are presumed. See *Extremis probatis*, &c.

Procurationes ad resignandum in favorem.—Procuratories of resignation in favour of the disponee of a vassal. At one time resignation was the only form in which a superior could be compelled to receive as his vassal the disponee of the vassal who had previously held the lands; although at a later period a superior could be compelled to enter a vassal by confirmation. Entry with a superior in either form is now abolished.

Procuratorio nomine.—In the name and character of a procurator. Stair, B. 3, T. 1, § 16. See *Proprio nomine*.

Promutuum.—As if a loan. Where a person, under an erroneous belief of liability, paid a sum of money to another which was not due, the civil law gave an action, the *condictio indebiti*, for its recovery. The sum so paid was regarded as if it had been a loan in *mutuum*, which the lender was entitled to recover, and on account of this was called *promutuum*, or *quasi mutuum*. The action for recovery might be successfully resisted on either of two grounds: first, where the sum paid, although not legally exigible, was one due upon a natural or moral obligation; and second, where the person knew, at the time of paying, that nothing was due, in which case the payment was held to be a donation. A difference existed between the case of money paid upon an error in fact, and that of money paid upon an error in law, regarding which see *Condictio indebiti*.

Propriis manibus.—By one's own hands. Under the old form of infeftment, sasine was said to be given to the disponee *propriis manibus*, when the disponer appeared personally on the ground, and with his own hands delivered to the disponee the usual and necessary symbols, instead of this being done, as was most usual, by another person who acted as the disponer's baillie. This form of infeftment was, perhaps, most frequently adopted in the case of provisions being made to a wife or children, where the husband receiving infeftment in lands he had purchased, at the same time gave his wife infeftment in a liferent right, both of which rights were included in the same instrument. Infeftment *propriis manibus* required no antecedent warrant, for it was unnecessary for an heritable proprietor to grant warrant to a baillie to do that for him which he was to do himself. "It is to be carefully observed that sasines *propriis manibus* are not protected by the Act 6 & 7 Will. IV. c. 33, which exempts sasines from challenge on the ground of erasure. On the contrary, they are expressly excepted from that statute, and justly so, inasmuch as the sasine *propriis manibus* is not like other sasines, merely an attestation of the delivery of possession, but is by its nature an act of alienation, and embraces in itself the warrant as well as the delivery." (Menzies' Lectures, 594.) A vassal, in like manner, was said to resign his lands *propriis manibus* when he delivered the symbol of resignation to the superior with his own hands.

Proprio jure.—By one's own proper right.

Proprio nomine.—In one's own name. When a person sues for a debt due to himself, he sues in his own name and individual character; but where it is not due to himself, but to him for behoof of some other, he sues in that character in which he is entitled to claim it. Thus a trustee or factor does not sue for a trust-debt, or one due to his constituent, in his own name, because to him as an individual, apart from the office with which he has been invested, the debtor owes nothing whatever: he therefore sues in that name and character in respect of which he acquires the title to sue. In the one case, where the money is due to himself, the claimant sues *proprio nomine;* in the other case, where it is due to him in respect of the office he holds, and for behoof of another, he sues *procuratorio nomine.*

Proprium negotium.—One's own affair or business: that which one does in his own name and for his own behoof, as distinguished from that done for behoof of another.

Propter commodum curiæ.—For the advantage of the Court. Stair, B. 4, T. 34, § 3.

Propter curam et culturam.—For, or, on account of, care and cultivation. Ersk. B. 2, T. 6, § 31, and T. 10, § 10.

Propter delectum personæ.—On account of the choice or selection of person. Although, under many mandates, certain steps in fulfilment of the purpose for which the mandate is granted have to be executed by or intrusted to others than the mandatory himself, yet a mandatory cannot delegate the whole of the authority, or the principal parts of his trust, to another, as this would render nugatory the mandant's *delectus personæ,* in exercise of which he chose and appointed his mandatory. See *Delectus personæ.*

Propter eminentiam masculini sexus.—On account of the superiority of the male sex. It is said to be upon this ground that a conveyance to a husband and wife in liferent, and their heirs in fee, is held to constitute a fee in the heirs of the husband. See *Potior est conditio masculi*, which is only another form of rendering the same phrase.

Propter fragilitatem sexus.—On account of the weakness of their sex. Stair, B. 1, T. 4, § 22.

Propter ingratitudinem.—On account of ingratitude. Formerly, when heritable rights were conferred gratuitously by the superior upon a vassal to ensure his fidelity and services, and even where the fee had been conferred for a price, but that inadequate to the value, the superior could revoke the gift and resume the lands on account of the ingratitude of the vassal. Under the civil law all donations could be recalled upon this ground; and this appears to have been at one time a rule of our law, although it does not now seem to be recognised.

Propter majorem securitatem.—For the sake of greater security.

Propter negligentiam hæredis jus suum non prosequentis.—On account of the negligence of the heir in not following up his right. By the early feudal customs, if, on a vassal's death, his heir neglected for a year and day to enter with the superior, his right to the lands was forfeited on account of such negligence, and they reverted in property to the superior. As lands cannot now be deemed to be in non-entry, another form of action has taken the place of the former action of declarator of non-entry, regarding which and its effects, see the Act 37 & 38 Vict. c. 94, § 4, subsection 4.

Propter quod fecerunt per alium.—On account of what they have done by another. The acts of a servant performed within his ordinary duty, and on his master's instructions, are regarded as the acts of the master himself, and render the master responsible for the consequences. Thus where a coachman by careless or faulty driving injures any one, the master must answer for it; or where workmen leave an obstruction on the highway, or in a place where any one has a right to go, and some one falls over it and receives injury, the master of the workmen is responsible for the injury so inflicted. Again, where an agent enters into contracts, or grants obligations within the terms of his agency or mandate, the principal is bound to fulfil them. In these cases, the master or principal, acting through another, is held liable on account of that which the other has done : it is regarded as his own act, for *qui facit per alium facit per se.*

Propter rem ipsam non habitam.—On account of not having had in possession the thing itself. Where one party to a contract binds himself absolutely to deliver to another a certain subject, and fails to fulfil this obligation, he is liable in the damages occasioned by his failure. Such damage may arise from several sources, and among others, from the mere want of possession of the subject agreed to be delivered, because by such a want of possession the buyer may have been unable to take advantage of a good market, a rise in prices, &c.

Prorogatio de loco in locum.—A prorogation (of jurisdiction) from one place to another. The consent of parties cannot confer any jurisdiction upon a judge outwith his own territory, and in this sense, as regards the power of the judge, there can be no such prorogation as that expressed by the phrase. But there may be such prorogation as regards the interest of the parties, and this takes place where a defender, not subject to the jurisdiction of the judge before whom he is cited to appear, acquiesces in the jurisdiction, and lodges peremptory defences.

Prorogatio de tempore in tempus.—Prorogation (of jurisdiction) from one time to another. There can be no prorogation of the jurisdiction of a judge where his jurisdiction is vacated or its term expired. In another sense, however, such prorogation is known with us; as in the case where parties to a submission, having agreed to abide by any decision pronounced by an arbiter within year and day, afterwards prorogate the arbiter's jurisdiction to a period more remote. Such prorogation, to be effectual, it need scarcely be observed, must be agreed upon, and the minute embodying it executed before the expiry of the original term. If not, a new submission alone would confer jurisdiction on the arbiter, and be binding on the parties.

Protectio trahit subjectionem et subjectio protectionem.—Protection gives rise to (or produces as a consequence) subjection, and subjection to protection. This maxim expresses the counterpart obligations of a ruler and the ruled. An Englishman is subject to the laws of his country, and owes allegiance to his sovereign, and so long as he yields obedience to the one, and is loyal to the other, he is entitled to the protection which the laws or his sovereign can give him. The protection of the sovereign renders the subject bound to submission and loyalty—the loyalty of the subject puts upon the sovereign the duty of protection. The same rule applies to persons resident temporarily in a country other than their own. So long as they are in that country they must respect and obey its laws and ruler, receiving in return the protection which such laws or ruler can afford.

Protestatio contraria facto.—Protestation inconsistent with one's conduct while protesting. Stair, B. 4, T. 40, § 39.

Prout de jure.—According to law. A general proof of facts and circumstances is called a proof *prout de jure*, in contradistinction to a proof limited to the writ or oath of party. See *Probatio prout*, &c.

Provisio hominis non tollit provisionem legis.—The provision made by an individual does not take away or abrogate the provision of the law. By legal provision a widow is entitled to a certain part of her deceased husband's moveable estate, and so are the children; and no testamentary provision of the husband or father can deprive them of this legal right. If by his will or settlement the deceased has made certain provisions for his wife and children, they may receive the benefit of such provisions without in any way prejudicing their claim to that which the law entitles them to (*M. of Breadalbane* v. *Chandos*, 14 S. 309, affd. 2 S. & M'L. 377), and should the deceased's provisions be declared to be in lieu of legal rights competent to his widow and children, they have the option of either accepting these provisions, and renouncing their legal rights, or of declining the provisions, and insisting on their *jus relictæ* and legitim respectively. What the law declares certain persons entitled to, they cannot be deprived of by private arrangement, unless they are parties consenting to it. The reader may occasionally find this maxim expressed thus:

Provisio hominis tollit provisionem legis, but this merely applies to the case where the conventional provision is declared to be inclusive or in lieu of the legal provision, and is so accepted.

Provisione hominis.—By the provision or appointment of an individual. Heirs who succeed, through the provision or appointment of the testator, to that to which they would not have succeeded by force of law, are said to succeed *provisione hominis*. All heirs who so succeed are called heirs of provision.

Provisione legis.—By provision of the law. Heirs who succeed according to the rules of law regulating succession, without the consent or appointment of their ancestor, are said to succeed *provisione legis,* and are known as heirs-at-law.

Provisione tenus.—As far as the provision goes : to the extent of the provision.

Proximus pubertati.—Near puberty; having nearly attained the years of puberty, but still in pupilarity.

Puberes.—Minors; persons who have attained the age of puberty, which with us is 14 years in males and 12 in females.

Publica vindicta.—The defence or protection of the public interest; the legal punishment by which the public safety and interest are protected. See *Ad vindictam,* &c.

Punctum temporis.—Point of time.

Pure.—Purely; unconditionally. Obligations are either *pure* or *in diem.* Performance of the former is immediately prestable, because performance is at once due, it being burdened with no condition; while performance of the latter can only be insisted upon when that day arrives, or that condition is fulfilled, on which the obligant has bound himself to implement his obligation. When a condition has been fulfilled, it is said, technically, to have been purified.

Q

Qua.—As; in the character of. Thus, a widow is said to be decerned executrix to her deceased husband *qua* relict, and a creditor appointed to the office of executor is said to be decerned executor-dative *qua* creditor. So also, where a trustee sues for a debt due to the trust, he sues, not as an individual, but *qua* trustee.

Quacunque via datur.—In whatever way it is conceded: whichever way you take it. Ross L. C. (C. L.) iii. 940.

Quadriennium utile: Is the name given to the period of four years, commencing from the attainment of majority, during which an action of reduction may be brought by a minor, on the ground of lesion, of any deed granted or contract entered into by him during minority. If no such action is brought within this period, the law presumes that the deed or contract was not to the prejudice of the minor; and this being a *præsumptio juris et de jure*, cannot be redargued by the clearest legal evidence to the contrary.

Quæ ab initio non valent ex post facto convalescere non possunt.—Things invalid from the beginning cannot be made better (or valid) by subsequent act. This maxim refers to those things or deeds which are in themselves invalid, and can never, under any circumstances, be otherwise. Thus a conveyance of land not duly tested, or otherwise defective in the necessary solemnities, where the defect is apparent on the face of the deed, can never be made good or valid by subsequent act. But there are cases in which a deed or contract, at one period invalid, may be made valid by subsequent act. Both these classes have been noticed already under the maxims *Confirmatio est nulla*, &c.; and *Confirmatio omnes supplet*, &c.

Quæ accessionum locum obtinent extinguuntur cum

principales res peremptæ fuerint.—Those things which hold the place of accessories are extinguished when the principal has been destroyed (or discharged). The most familiar example of the application of this rule is the extinction of a cautioner's obligation when the principal obligation, to which it was merely accessory, has been discharged or otherwise extinguished. A mortgage of a vessel earning freight carries with it the freight to the mortgagee if he intervene by taking possession, or by an act equivalent to taking possession, before the freight becomes payable (*Rusden* v. *Pope*, L. R. 3, Excheq. 269); but the right to the freight reverts to the owner when the mortgage is discharged. Interest as an accessory belongs to the creditor in the debt; but when the debt is discharged the right to interest ceases. See *Accessorium principale*, &c.

Quæ cadit in virum constantem.—That which would overcome a man of firmness and resolution. Stair, B. 4, T. 40, § 25. See *Ex vi*, &c.

Quæ cadunt in non causam.—Those things which we lose on the cessation of the title on which we held them. (Stair, B. 1, T. 7, § 7.) Thus, for example, the right of the assignee of a liferenter to the fruits and benefits of the liferent falls on the liferenter's death, because the title on which he holds them necessarily expires.

Quæ cohærent personæ a persona separari nequeunt.—Things which adhere to the person (*i.e.*, purely personal rights) cannot be separated from the person. Thus titles of honour are so personal that they cannot be separated from the person entitled to them for the time: a nobleman may convey his lands to his son, and in some cases may cede to him during his own life the right to entailed lands which otherwise the son could only succeed to on his father's death; but he cannot confer upon him his title, which must remain his during his lifetime; it cannot be separated from the person. A provision made in favour of any one, which is declared to be strictly alimentary, and not affectable by the debts or deeds of the person in whose favour the provision is made, is strictly personal, and cannot be separated from the person either by the act of the person or the operation of the law. The right to sue for a divorce is purely personal, and cannot be separated from the person; no one but the injured spouse can raise such an action.

Quæ functionem recipiunt.—Things which perform the office or supply the places of others. This is the Latin definition of that class of things known in our law as fungibles, which alone can form the subject of a contract of *mutuum*. This class includes all things which may be estimated generically by weight, number, or measure. See *Pondere, numero*, &c.

Quæ non fieri debent, facta valent.—Things which ought not to be done are held valid when they have been done. Some acts prohibited by law are, by virtue of such prohibition, essentially null, and never can be validated by the private agreement of the parties interested. For example, no obligation or contract arising *ob turpem causam* can bind the parties, or be enforced against them, even where they may have expressly waived any defence or objection upon that ground; nor can those obligations be validated by private agreement which are declared by the law to be null, because they are contrary to the good morals or sound policy of the country; yet, if such an obligation has been fulfilled, no action for restitution will lie on account of the invalidity of the obligation. There are, on the other hand, some acts prohibited by the law which will be regarded as valid and binding after their actual performance. Thus, the Act 1594, c. 216, prohibits the purchase, by a member of the College of Justice, of anything which forms the subject of a lawsuit at the time when purchased, and that under the penalty of deprivation of office. The Act does not, however, declare the sale invalid, and therefore, while such a contract of sale is prohibited, it has been the rule in our practice to sustain the sale, but punish the purchaser in the manner prescribed. In short, this maxim applies to all legal prohibitions, where the sanction is the punishment of the doer, and not the nullity of the act done.

Quæ non mente sed manu tenentur.—This phrase is used by Stair (B. 1, T. 5, § 6), when treating of the obligations incumbent upon parents as regards their children. It scarcely admits of literal translation, but means those duties which arise from affection, as opposed to those which arise from legal provision; those obligations which are natural, performance of which lies in the option of the parent, as opposed to those which are civil, performance of which may be enforced by legal process.

Quæ non recipiunt functionem.—Things which do not perform the office, or supply the place of others; all things not falling within the description of fungibles. See *Quæ functionem*, &c.

Quæ perimunt causam.—(Pleas) which take away the ground of action. The effect of peremptory defences, when sustained, is to take away the pursuer's ground of action altogether. The defender is then entitled to be assoilzied, and to plead *res judicata* if the same question be raised in a new suit at the instance of the same party, or his representative. See *Perimere causam*.

Quæ sapiunt delictum.—Things which partake of the character of delict. "The Lords lately found, that these passive titles, *quæ sapiunt delictum*, should not be competent after the intromitter's death." Stair, B. 3, T. 6, § 5.

Quæ sequuntur personam.—Which follow the person. This refers to moveable property, which, by a legal fiction, is supposed to be always with the owner. On this ground succession to moveables is regulated; and deeds affecting moveables are interpreted and judged of according to the law of the domicile. See *Lex rei sitæ; Mobilia sequuntur*, &c.

Quæ servando servari nequeunt.—Things which cannot be preserved uninjured by keeping. Erskine states it as one of the powers conferred upon a general mandatory, that he may and ought to sell such of the mandant's moveable goods as are of a perishable nature. Where there is a dispute as to the right to some subject which, from its nature, is liable to perish entirely, or suffer very material deterioration by being kept, our courts are in the practice, on the motion of either party, of ordering it to be sold, and the proceeds of the sale consigned to abide the issue of the cause. For example, such a course would be followed where a quantity of grain formed the subject of the dispute, as it might perish or be deteriorated in value, either intrinsically or by the fall of the market prices, if kept until the action was decided.

Where the subject is not perishable, there is no reason for ordering it to be sold, and such order would not be pronounced except of consent of parties. This course is, however, sometimes followed, as perhaps it is most frequently done, where the right to live cattle is in dispute, because the expense of maintaining them is so serious, that their whole value or more might be thus expended before the rights of parties were settled.

Quæ singula non prosunt juncta juvant.—Things which, taken singly, or one by one, are of no avail, afford help or benefit when taken together. Thus in a reduction, if the pursuer sought to reduce a deed on the ground of circumvention, the jury might not think the acts proved to have been used sufficient to overcome the will of, or to deceive the granter; or, if he sought to reduce on the ground of facility, the jury might not think that the granter was facile or of weak mind, and sustain the deed. But if both of these grounds were libelled as reasons of reduction, it might be seen how the circumvention, in an ordinary case insufficient, was in this particular case sufficient to deceive the granter on account of his facility, and these grounds thus taken together be sufficient to reduce the deed, while taken singly they would have been insufficient. But this maxim is applicable to almost every case that arises, for there are few in which the whole facts or circumstances considered together and as a whole do not form the basis of the decision. Each individual circumstance may be of little or no importance in itself, and yet acquire the greatest possible importance from the circumstances out of which it arose, or which followed it; and that is the import of this maxim. This maxim is sometimes written, *Quæ singula non valeant, juncta juvant.*

Quæ solum Deum habent ultorem.—Crimes or wrongs which can only be punished by God. Stair, B. 1, T. 3, § 4.

Quæ sunt in patrimonio nostro.—Things which form part of our possessions; things held by us in property. Stair says that slavery reduces the slave from the category of persons to the position of a mere subject of possession similar to any other part of the proprietor's inanimate property. This was the position held by the slave under the civil law, where he was treated of not as a *person*, because persons had rights and incurred obligations neither of which belonged to a slave, but as *res*, a thing in which persons had rights.

Quæ sunt temporalia ad agendum, sunt perpetua ad excipiendum.—Those things which afford a ground of action if raised within a certain time, may be pleaded at any time by way of exception. Some rights of action can only be exercised within a certain prescribed time, within which, if they are not exercised, the right falls; but that which would have been the ground of action may be pleaded as an exception, even after the lapse of the prescribed period. An illustration of this maxim will be found in Ersk. B. 1, T. 7, § 32.

Quæ transeunt per commercium.—Things which pass or transmit through commerce. "Vitious intromission being penal, is not to be sustained against any as representing the intromitter, when no action is intended against the intromitter in his own life; after which no other can be able to clear the title of his intromission with moveables *quæ transeunt per commercium;* and so the defunct might have bought them *bona fide.*" Stair, B. 3, T. 9, § 14.

Quædam etsi honeste accipiantur inhoneste tamen petuntur.—Things which may be accepted honourably, may yet be things which cannot honourably be asked. This phrase is quoted by Bankton (B. 4, T. 3, § 4), in reference to advocates' fees, from Dig. B. 50, T. 13, l. 1, § 5.

Quæquidem.—The name given to that clause in charters by progress which immediately followed the dispositive clause. In it the granter's title was deduced, so as to show the manner in which he had acquired, and the link or links in the progress by which he was connected with the vassal who was last publicly infeft. The name was taken from the first word of the clause as it stood in the old Latin form. Regarding the nature and import of the clause, see *Modus vacandi.*

Quæritur.—It is questioned: the question is raised. See an example of this in Stair, B. 3, T. 8, § 41.

Quæstio voluntatis.—A question of intention.

Qualificate.—Qualifiedly; under qualification. This word is also used, in its more strictly etymological sense, as meaning, made like to, or made such as. When a bargain is made or deed granted *qualificate*, it is made or granted not absolutely, but in a qualified manner, or subject to qualification or condition. An instance of the use of the word in the second sense will be found in the case of *Clark* v. *Stirling*, 3 D. 737, where this passage occurs: "A parish is held to be *qualificate* vacant, when by the concurring opinion of all concerned, including the presbytery, there is necessity for the appointment of an assistant and successor." In such a case the parish, although not actually vacant, is, by the circumstances in which it is placed, made like to a vacant parish. The phrase *"qualificate* vacant" might be rendered "constructively vacant:" this, however, while quite an equivalent expression, could not be called a translation.

Quamdiu sustinuit istam furiositatem.—How long he has laboured under that insanity or madness. This was one of the clauses of the old brief issued for the cognition of an insane person, by which the inquest was directed to inquire into and fix the date at which the insanity commenced. The effect of their finding was retrospective, for by the Act 1475, c. 66, it was enacted that no alienation made by the fatuous person after the time fixed by the inquest as the commencement of his distemper should be valid. In like manner, no obligations granted by him after that date were binding, although granted before he was cognosced.

Quamprimum.—As soon as possible; forthwith.

Quamvis non potuerit dare.—Although he had not been able to give or administer it. Hume, i. 180.

Quando aliquid conceditur, omnia concessa videntur, sine quibus hoc explicari nequit.—When anything is granted (or conferred), all things necessary for the explication (*i.e.*, treatment, development, use) of that thing appear also to be granted. A sheriff has a very limited jurisdiction in questions of heritable right, but he may competently deal with questions in which he has no jurisdiction where this is necessary for the explication of a jurisdiction which he has: thus, he cannot determine upon the validity of a lease where this is questioned, nor can he decide upon competing titles whether the one is valid and the other invalid, but he may incidentally decide that a lease is valid in a question of sequestration for the rent due under it, or that a title is a good and valid title in a question of removing. The sheriff, having jurisdiction in such cases, has also impliedly right to determine whatever is necessary to enable him to exercise that jurisdiction. This maxim is also applied in cases where the question concerns the extent of a private grant or the rights implied in a certain grant ; concerning this see *Cuicunque aliquis,* &c.

Quando aliquid mandatur, mandatur et omne per quod pervenitur ad illud.—When anything is ordered (or authorised) to be done, everything is ordered (or authorised) by which performance of the order may be attained. For example, a client giving his law-agent authority to recover payment of a certain debt, authorises thereby all lawful and usual procedure by which such recovery may be made ; and a power conferred upon a judge to punish for a certain offence, confers power upon him to order the apprehension of a person charged with that offence.

Quando aliquid prohibetur, prohibetur et omne quod devenitur ad illud.—When anything is forbidden, everything which amounts to the forbidden thing is forbidden also. This maxim (which is the counterpart of the preceding maxim) means that when the law has forbidden the doing of anything directly, it equally forbids the doing of it indirectly, and that mere device or colourable evasion will not protect the doer from the consequences of his act. Actions arising out of alleged infringements of patent rights afford frequent opportunities for the application of this maxim. It is seldom that a patented machine or process is openly and avowedly used without the permission of the patentee ; most generally the patent right is invaded under the colour or pretext that something else is being used than that thing which has been patented. But where it is shown that it is really the patent right which is being invaded, the colour or pretext used to cover the invasion will not screen the person using it from the consequences of the infringement. The law, again, forbids any creditor bargaining for or taking from the bankrupt debtor a preference over the other creditors. It is immaterial what form the preference assumes, for if it be really, and in its essence, a transaction of preference, it will be set aside.

Quando duo jura in una persona concurrunt æquum est ac si essent in diversis.—When two rights concur (or are vested) in one person, it is the same as if they belonged to different persons. This rule must be read with some caution when applying it as the law of Scotland. If the rights are separate and distinct from each other, the rule may be read absolutely. Thus, if one man possesses several heritable subjects, acquired by different titles, his rights in them are, of course, the same as if they were each held by a separate person; but when the two rights refer to the same subject, the rule must be qualified. For if a debtor succeeds to his creditor, and thus becomes debtor and creditor in the same obligation, the obligation is extinguished *confusione*,—the rights of debtor and creditor concurring in the same person, do not remain the same as if vested in different persons. In the same way a superior who succeeds, or acquires right, to the estate of his own vassal, does not remain superior and vassal in the same subject, as two different persons would, but the lower right of the vassal is merged in the higher right of the superior. It happens sometimes, however, that the purchaser of a heritable subject, which is burdened with debt at the time of the purchase, takes an assignation to the debts so secured rather than a discharge: this is most frequently done where the title to the subjects is in any way doubtful. The purpose of keeping up the debts by assignation rather than extinguishing them by discharge, is to preserve to the purchaser the rights of a creditor heritably secured in the event of his title as proprietor being questioned or reduced. In such a case this maxim would apply, and the rights of the creditor would not be merged or lost in the higher rights of ownership; the reduction of his title as owner, would bring his lesser right as creditor into operation. Erskine lays it down (B. 2, T. 9, § 37) that servitudes may be extinguished *confusione* " when the same person becomes owner both of the dominant and servient tenements," and adds that " a servitude thus extinguished revives not, though the right of the two tenements should be again divided, unless the servitude be constituted *de novo*." But Bell (Prin. § 997) is of opinion that the doctrine of Erskine " must be taken with some limitation. Wherever a separation or disunion may be anticipated, the effect seems to be to produce rather a combination of the two rights, as if the proprietor had divided himself into two persons with a *suspension* rather than an extinction of the servitude. Nor would it in such a case seem to be necessary, on a subsequent separation of the tenements, to constitute the servitude *de novo.*"

Quando jus domini regis et subditi concurrunt, jus regis præferri debet.—When the right of the king and of a subject concur, the right of the king ought to be preferred. See Broom, 69. As to the rules of preference between the king and a subject when their rights conflict, see Bell's Com. ii. 51.

Quando lex aliquid alicui concedit, conceditur et id sine quo res ipsa esse non potest.—When the law confers a right on any one, it also confers that without which the right conferred cannot exist (or be enjoyed). See *Cuicunque aliquis,* &c., and *Quando aliquid conceditur,* &c.

Quando plus fit quam fieri debet, videtur etiam illud fieri quod faciendum est.—When more is done than should have been done, that appears to have been done which was to be done: in other words, when something has been done in excess of what was authorised or proper, the act is valid so far as authorised, and only invalid *quoad* the excess. Take the case of a provision to the children of a family, with a power of apportionment to the father: the father under the power to appoint, may divide the amount or the estate provided according to his own will, but he cannot add conditions to the appointment, nor give any part of the estate to persons who are not objects of the power. If, in apportioning the estate, the father should adject such conditions, or allot a portion to some one not an object of the power, the apportionment is not thereby rendered invalid. So far as authorised it is good: the apportionment will hold although the conditions will be disregarded, and that portion allotted to persons not entitled to share will be held as not apportioned at all, *Macdonald,* 2 R. (H. L.) 125. Again, take the case of an agent having authority to transact for and bind his principal to a certain extent: the fact that the agent goes beyond his authority will not entirely free the principal, who will be bound by his agent's actings to the extent to which they are authorised :—the agent's going beyond his authority does not vitiate that which he did within it.

Quando res non valet ut ago, valeat quantum valere potest.—When a thing is not valid as I do it (or, as I use it), it may still be valid to some extent. Thus, if A grant a conveyance to B in consideration of a certain sum instantly paid therefor, the deed may be ineffectual as a conveyance, through informality or want of title in the granter, and yet be quite valid as proof of the payment of the price or consideration. Again, a bill or promissory-note without a date is invalid as a warrant for summary diligence, but quite valid as the basis of an ordinary action for payment of the amount for which it has been accepted or granted. As to the application of this maxim in England, see Smith's Leading Cases, ii. 530 *et seq.*

Quandocunque.—At whatever time; at any time.

Quandocunque defecerit.—At whatever time he died. Ersk. B. 3, T. 8, § 44.

Quanti minoris.—The action *quanti minoris* has been explained above. See *Actio quanti*, &c.

Quantum.—How much; the extent. Ersk. B. 2, T. 5, § 49.

Quantum et quale.—How much and of what kind; the extent and quality. It is not unusual for parties to a submission to agree that, in the event of no final decree-arbitral being pronounced, the proof taken in the course of the submission shall be received as legal probation *quantum et quale* (*i.e.*, to the same extent and as of the same quality or effect) in any after-submission or process at law between the same parties regarding the same matter.

Quantum meruit.—As much as he has earned; value. Where services are rendered on hire, but without any specific arrangement being made as to the rate of the hire, there is an implied obligation on the part of the employer to pay a fair remuneration according to the extent and quality of the work done; and so the court has frequently decerned in cases where the amount of the remuneration was disputed, for such sums as they deemed the services to be worth. See the case of *Sinclair*, 9 S. 487. Many professional men are remunerated for their services according to the *quantum meruit*, where indeed it would scarcely be possible to fix any specific payment, as the amount of the service cannot be ascertained until it has been rendered. Architects in preparing plans, civil engineers for examinations and surveys, &c., may be taken as instances. See on this subject, Fraser, Mas. & Serv. 135 *et seq.*

Quantum nunc valent.—How much they (the lands) are now worth. See *Antiquus et*, &c.

Quantum valeat.—Whatever value it may have; for as much as it is worth. Where the competency or relevancy of evidence which has been tendered is doubtful, it is frequently admitted *quantum valeat*—that is, it is not totally rejected, but its value as evidence is left open for consideration.

Quantum valuerunt tempore pacis.—How much they (the lands) were worth in time of peace. For an explanation of this phrase, see *Antiquus et*, &c.

Quarta Falcidia.—That fourth of a testator's estate which, by the *Lex Falcidia*, he was prevented disposing of to the prejudice of the heir. By the law of the Twelve Tables, a testator was permitted to bequeath his whole estate in legacies; but at a later period it was found to be necessary, for the sake even of testators themselves, and in order to ensure the carrying out of their intentions, that this power should be placed under certain restrictions. The great essential of a testament under the civil law was that there should be an heir formally and validly appointed; if he accepted, he was bound to fulfil its directions, and he also became liable for the testator's obligations; but if he declined the character of heir and renounced the succession, the testament fell, the deceased was regarded as having died intestate, and the estate was distributed according to the rules regarding intestate succession. When, therefore, the testator left the whole, or almost the whole of his estate in legacies, the heir generally declined entering upon the succession, because by entering upon it he took no real benefit, while he incurred liability for the testator's obligations; and thus the intentions of the testator were frequently frustrated. To remedy this certain laws were passed, the first of them being the *Lex Furia*, which forbade almost every one receiving by legacy more than 1000 *asses*; but this law failed to effect the object it had in view, for a testator, by multiplying the number of legatees, might still have exhausted the whole of his estate. The *Lex Voconia* was then passed, which prohibited the testator bequeathing to any one a sum greater than that left to the appointed heir; but this law also failed; for, by distributing his goods among a great many legatees, giving to none of them more than the sum left to the heir, the testator had the means of reducing the heir's portion to a sum so small, that it was insufficient to induce him to undertake the office and responsibilities of heir. Lastly the *Lex Falcidia* was passed, by which the testator was prohibited bequeathing in legacies more than three-fourths of his estate, so that the heir (or heirs, if there were more than one) should receive at least one-fourth of the testator's succession. This sum reserved to the heir was called, after the law which created it, the Falcidian quarter or portion. Justinian introduced some changes in the law on this point, for he enacted, that if those entitled to the *quarta* (namely, those who were appointed the heirs under the testament) were more than four in number, they should be entitled to a half instead of a fourth; but if less than four, then they should be entitled to a third.

Quarta Trebellianica.—This was the fourth which an heir in trust was entitled to retain out of the succession when transferring it to that person to whom, by the testament, he was directed to transfer it. There existed considerable similarity between this and the *Quarta Falcidia*; the one being applied in the case of legacies, the other in the case of *fideicommissa*. If the testator directed the heir to transfer the whole, or almost the whole of his estate to some other person, the heir frequently refused to accept his appointment, as it brought him little or no benefit, and inferred considerable liability. To prevent the will falling on the heir's refusal, it was enacted, in the time of Justinian, by the *Senatus-consultum Trebellianum* (so called because it embodied the provisions of a previous *senatus-consultum* of that name, along with others touching the same point of law), that where the heir voluntarily accepted the character and fulfilled the directions of the testator, he might retain a fourth of the succession without being made liable for any charges beyond those attaching to the portion he so received. If the heir refused to take up the succession and transfer it as directed by the testament, he could be forced to do so, in which case he was not entitled to retain any portion whatever, nor did he incur any responsibility, which was transferred entirely to the person receiving the estate.

Quarum natura est ut aliæ aliarum ejusdem generis rerum vice fungantur.—The character of which is that their place may be supplied by other things of the same kind. This is a description of that class of things known in our law as fungibles. See *Pondere, numero,* &c.

Quasi ex contractu.—Arising as if from contract. See *Ex quasi,* &c.

Quasi ex delicto.—Arising as if from delict. See *Ex quasi,* &c.

Quasi feudum.—A kind of fee or heritable right; and, generally, that kind of heritable right which arises in money when heritably secured. See *Feuda pecuniæ.*

Quem nuptiæ demonstrant.—Whom the marriage indicates or points out. See *Pater est,* &c.

Quem sequuntur commoda eundem et incommoda sequuntur.—He who reaps the benefits must also bear the disadvantages. On the principle of this maxim, an heir who succeeds to his ancestor's estate is liable for his ancestor's obligations; for as he takes the advantages or benefits conferred upon him by the succession, he must also bear the disadvantages with which the estate is burdened. So also formerly, the purchaser of goods still undelivered, and in the seller's custody, bore the loss or disadvantage arising from deterioration, because he reaped the benefit which might arise through accretion or otherwise.

Querela inofficiosi testamenti.—The complaint against an inofficious testament. A testament was considered *inofficiosum* under the civil law when, although validly and formally executed, it violated by its terms those duties which affection and natural obligation made incumbent upon the granter; as, for example, when the testator appointed a stranger as his heir, to the exclusion of his children and other relatives. Such a testament could be set aside by the testator's relatives by the action known as the *querela inofficiosi testamenti*, which proceeded upon the presumed insanity of the testator at the time of executing it. It is not known at what date this action was first introduced, but it is treated of by Justinian in the following terms: "Since parents often disinherit their children, or omit them in their testaments without any cause, children who complain that they have been unjustly disinherited or omitted have been permitted to bring an action for setting aside the inofficious document, on the supposition that their parents were not of sane mind when they made their testament. This does not mean that the testator was really insane, but that the testament, though regularly made, is inconsistent with the duty of affection the parent owes." (Just. Inst. 2, T. 18, Pr.) This action was first competent to children, and if there were no children, or if they declined to sue, then to the testator's parents, and failing them, to his brothers and sisters, although the latter only had right to insist in this action where the heir appointed was a dishonourable person. The *querela* could only be adopted as a last resource, and when no other mode of procedure remained by which the relatives might vindicate their right to the succession, and it required to be brought within five years after the heir's entry. It need scarcely be observed that in our law it forms no valid objection to a testament or settlement that it violates natural duty or obligation.

Qui acquirit sibi acquirit hæredibus.—He who acquires for himself acquires for his heirs. When any one by a singular title acquires subjects and takes the title simply to himself without mention of his heirs, it descends nevertheless to his heirs, failing any other disposal of it by the disponee or person who acquired. In the same way a destination to A, whom failing to B, will carry the property to A's heirs past B, if A succeeded and took under that destination. When property becomes vested in a person, it goes on his death to his heirs, either according to his own provision, or, failing any such provision, according to the legal rules regulating succession. See *Qui providet*, &c.

Qui alterius jure utitur eodem jure uti debet.—He

who exercises the right of another ought to exercise the same right. This maxim imports that the right of an assignee is the same as the right of the cedent, not different in character or extent, and admits of being exercised only in the same way. As a general rule this is quite accurate, although there are cases in which the right of an assignee is greater than the right of the cedent. See *Assignatus utitur*, &c., and *Nemo plus juris*, &c. But this maxim will find more direct application in such a case as that of an agent using the rights of his principal, where the right exercised can never be greater in extent or character, or be used differently, from the mode in which or the extent to which the principal could exercise it himself.

Qui approbat non reprobat.—One who approbates cannot reprobate. A person is said to approbate and reprobate a deed when he seeks to take an advantage or benefit conferred upon him by one portion of it, while he seeks to disregard or dispute the validity of another portion which imposes some restriction upon the benefit, or burdens it with a condition. This is not permitted by our law, which requires that any person taking benefit under a deed must take it with the conditions or burdens which the deed attaches to the benefit. Thus, if the settlement of a father makes certain provisions in favour of his children, declaring that such provisions are inclusive or in lieu of their legal rights, the children accepting such provisions are barred from claiming their legal rights: they cannot take the advantage conferred on them by the deed, except upon the condition under which that benefit is conferred. *Bonhote*, 12 R. 984. Nor can an heir approbate his ancestor's settlement in so far as it conveys the estate to him, and reprobate it in so far as it imposes burdens upon the estate, or charges the heir with the payment of certain legacies. This doctrine of approbate and reprobate is known in English law phraseology as the doctrine of election. There are some cases, however, in which an heir or beneficiary is not put upon his election whether he will accept the benefit with its conditions or burdens, or reject it altogether: it sometimes happens that the beneficiary is entitled to take the benefit and disregard the conditions attached to it. In *Fraser* v. *Rose*, 11 D.

1466, a father by his trust settlement made a provision for his daughter exceeding what she would have been entitled to *ex lege*, but added to it the condition that she should not reside with her mother, declaring that if she did so, she should forfeit the provision. The Court held the daughter entitled to disregard the condition as *contra bonos mores*, and found her entitled to the provision made for her by the deed. Other examples of the right to take without regard to the attached conditions will be found in the cases of *Churchill*, L. R. 5, Eq. 44, and *M'Donald*, 1 R. 794, reversed H. L., 2 R. 125. See also on the subject of approbate and reprobate generally, M'Laren, i. 475 *et seq.*

Qui cedit et retinet nihil agit.—One who cedes or transfers, and yet retains, does not transfer effectually. See *Dans et retinens*, &c.

Qui cedit foro.—One who stops payment, or becomes bankrupt. See *Cessio fori*.

Qui consulto dat quod non debebat presumitur donare. —One who gives deliberately to another what he does not owe, is presumed to give it as a donation. Where any one pays another that which he does not owe him under an erroneous belief of obligation, he is entitled to recover it under the *condictio indebiti*. But where the payment is made deliberately, and in the full knowledge that it is not due, no action for recovery will lie at the instance of the payer, because in such cases the law presumes donation, and donations *inter vivos* (except between husband and wife) are not revocable.

Qui cum alio contrahit vel est vel debet esse haud ignarus conditionis ejus cum quo contrahit.—He who contracts with another either is not or ought not to be ignorant of the condition of him with whom he contracts. See *Quisque scire debet*, &c.

Qui facit per alium facit per se.—Where one does a thing through the instrumentality of another, he is held as having done it himself. On this principle a master is liable for the consequences of any act done by his servant in the ordinary course of his duties. Thus, if a coachman, while driving his master's carriage, should, through recklessness or inattention, inflict an injury upon a foot-passenger by driving over him, or otherwise, the master is responsible for the injury so inflicted. But a distinction is recognised between the case where the injury is inflicted upon a stranger, and that where the injury is inflicted upon a fellow-servant engaged in the same common employment with the one occasioning the injury. As the master has the selection of those whom he employs, he is responsible if he selects an improper person; and he is presumed to be an unfit or improper person to fulfil the duties for which he was engaged, if in the performance of them he, through carelessness, recklessness, or incompetency, inflicts damage upon another not in the same service. But a servant is supposed to be aware of the perils to which he exposes himself, not only from his own want of care, but also from the want of care of those necessarily employed with him, and the law presumes that he contracts upon that footing. He is not, therefore, entitled to recover from the master damages for injury inflicted through the carelessness of a fellow-servant. The question of the master's liability or non-liability for the injury done to one fellow-servant through the fault of another gave rise to much controversy, and that the master was not so liable was first definitely settled as the law of Scotland in the case of the *Bartonshill Coal Company*, 3 Macq. 266. Out of this controversy another arose as to what constituted common employment, and who were fellow-servants in the sense employed in the decision just cited. It was for some time considered that fellow-servants in this sense only included servants of the same grade, and that consequently a foreman or manager was not to be considered as the fellow-workman of those who were under him, and subject to his orders. But it came to be settled that all persons under the same master, (*Johnson* v. *Lindsay*, L.R. App. C., 1891, p. 371), engaged in the same common employment, were fellow-servants or fellow-workmen, and that injury or damage done to one of them through the fault of another was an injury for which the master was not responsible if he had exercised due care in the selection of his servants for the different situations to which he had appointed them, and had furnished them with adequate materials and resources for the work. The reader will find an instructive account of the different decisions bearing upon this question in Fraser, Mas. & Serv. 197 *et seq.* The rule thus established, that a master was not responsible to an inferior servant for injury occasioned through the fault of a superior servant, gave rise to a great deal of public dissatisfaction, the result of which was the passing of the Act 43 & 44 Vict. c. 42, by which (to describe its effects generally) an employer is made responsible to his workmen for the conduct of those servants to whom he delegates his authority. The reader will find the Act analysed and commented on in Fraser, Mas. & Serv. 215 *et seq.* There is another class of cases in which the person for whom work is done is not answerable for the faults of those who do the work—those cases, namely, where the performance of the work is intrusted to an independent contractor. "Although, therefore, a person has ordered or directed a particular thing to be done, yet if he does not employ his own servants and workmen to do it, but intrusts the execution of the work to a person who exercises an independent employment, and has the immediate dominion and control over the workmen engaged in the work, he is not responsible for injuries done to third persons from the negligent execution of the work." Addison on Torts, 93. See also Smith on Reparation, 135 ; *Grant* v. *West Calder Oil Co.*, 9 Scot. L. Rep. 254 ; and *Taylor* v. *Greenhalgh*, L. R. 9, Q. B. 487. This maxim has application also in questions arising out of the commission of crime, but here its application is very limited. If a master orders his servant to steal, or to commit any act which is obviously a crime, it will infer his punishment as having been act and part engaged in the criminal act ; but it will not be regarded as his act alone ; it involves also the servant, who will not be absolved from the mere fact that he was obeying an order, which it was clearly his duty to disobey. But if one person gets another to commit an act for him which is criminal, but not obviously so, the doer of the act if he had no guilty knowledge, is guilty of no crime, but the person for whom he did it is, and must bear the punishment attached to its commission. Thus, if A forges a bill, and gets B, ignorant of its being a forgery, to utter it, B is guilty of no crime, while A is guilty both of forgery and uttering.

Qui hæret in litera hæret in cortice.—Who holds by

the letter, holds by the bark : " He who considers merely the letter of an instrument goes but skin deep into its meaning." Broom, 685. The law rather regards the substance of deeds than the mere words in which they are expressed, and accordingly the leading inquiry in cases of construction arising from ambiguity or dubiety is, what did the parties intend, or what did they do, rather than what did they say. *M'Bain* v. *Wallace*, 8 R. (H. L.) 106. In many cases, no doubt, the words used are of the last importance, but this arises from the fact that it is only from the words of the instrument that the intention and purpose of the granter can be ascertained ; it is not permitted to go outside of the deed to ascertain this. See *Non quod dictum*, &c.

Qui in utero est, pro jam nato habetur, quoties de ejus commodo quæritur.—A child in the womb (yet unborn) is held as already born in any question which may arise touching its rights or interest. Accordingly, it is sufficient to bar any service at the instance of the nearest heir to a person deceased if the deceased's widow has been left pregnant. While there is thus the probability of a nearer heir through the widow's delivery than the heir seeking to be served, he is held not entitled to the character of nearest heir, the law regarding him in the meantime as excluded by the child *in utero*, in the same way and to the same effect as if that child was already born. It is also settled in our law that a child born after the period at which the vesting of a right falls to be determined, but proved by the period of its birth to have been *in utero* at that time, is entitled to the rights of an existing person from the period of its conception. On this subject see M'Laren, i. 644, and cases cited.

Qui jure suo utitur neminem lædit.—He who uses his own rights does wrong to no one. No one can do a legal wrong inferring responsibility for its consequences, if he only does what he is fully entitled to do—if, in the words of the maxim, he exercises his right. The exercise of a right may result in loss or injury being inflicted upon another, but that is no reason why the right should not be exercised, provided it be exercised with prudence and care, and not done emulously. An illustration of this will be found in the case of *Andrew* v. *Buchanan*, 9 Macp. 554, reversed in the House of Lords, 11 Macp. 13, where a superior was found entitled to work minerals reserved to him under a feu granted by himself, although the result of his workings might be seriously to damage the buildings on the feu—the feu-contract being in such terms as to confer upon him the right to work the minerals without being responsible for the damage which might thereby be occasioned. Another illustration of this maxim may be found in the right which a proprietor of land has to build up to the very verge of his property, although he thereby destroys his neighbour's lights. Bell's Prin. § 965.

Qui jure suo utitur nemini facit injuriam.—He who uses his own right does wrong to no one. Another form of the preceding maxim.

Qui jure suo utitur non potest dici fraudem committere.—He who uses his own right cannot be said to commit a fraud, or to act fraudulently. See *Nemo habetur agere*, &c.

Qui jussu judicis aliquod fecerit non videtur dolo malo fecisse quia parere necesse est.—He who has done something by order of a judge does not appear to have acted fraudulently (or improperly), because obedience (to the order) is necessary. Improper motive for the performance of an act cannot be attributed to any one who performs the act not voluntarily, but upon the order of a judge to which he is bound to render obedience. The same rule applies where the act is performed on the order of a superior, where the duty of the person receiving the order is simply obedience without the right to question the propriety of the order itself; the necessity of obedience frees the performer of the act ordered from the consequences of the act, for which otherwise he might have been made answerable. Several examples of this have been given under the maxim *Ejus nulla culpa*, &c.

Qui justus esse debet.—Who was bound to be just. Ersk. B. 2, T. 4, § 3.

Qui non cadunt in constantem virum vani timores sunt æstimandi.—Those are regarded as groundless fears which are not sufficient to overcome a man of ordinary firmness and resolution. Such fears do not afford any ground for setting aside the deed or obligation which they are said to have induced. See *Quæ cadit*, &c., and *Ex vi*, &c.

Qui non improbat approbat.—He who does not reprobate, approbates. See *Qui approbat*, &c.

Qui non negat fatetur.—He who does not deny, admits. This rule is invariably applied in pleading, where a statement not denied is held to be admitted, if opportunity of answering the statement has been given. But see the case of *Pringle v. Bremner*, 5 Macp. (H. L.) 55, where the defenders' averment that they had a certain warrant was answered thus—"Reference is made to the alleged warrant for its terms;" and the answer was held not to amount to an admission of the existence of the warrant alleged. See *Qui tacet*, &c.

Qui non obstat quod obstare potest facere videtur.—He who does not hinder what he can hinder appears to do it; that is, any one who knows of an act, or sees it performed, which he can prevent, and does not prevent, is regarded as if he did the act himself. One standing by and seeing a crime committed, which he could prevent but does not, may incur the penalties which attach to the commission of the crime. See *Culpa caret*, &c. But the rule expressed by the maxim does not admit of very general application. A person may know that another is trespassing on his property or otherwise invading his right without preventing him, and yet may afterwards object to the act, and claim relief from its consequences, or damages for the wrong done. "But then it is said that Mr. M. saw and well knew of the operations now complained of, and notwithstanding remained silent. That may be so. Suppose Mr. M. in 1853 did not think fit at once to challenge these operations, and, although knowing them to be illegal, yet perhaps not wishing to quarrel with his neighbours, said nothing about it, does it follow that his singular successors are debarred from challenging the illegal operations? I think that a party may stand by and see an illegal act done without challenging it for many reasons, but still with no intention of consenting." "In interference with rights of property, is it sufficient to bar an injured party that for a number of years he has been silent? Certainly not." Per the Lord Justice-Clerk (Inglis) in *Cowan v. L. Kinnaird*, 4 Macp. 241. The acts referred to in the preceding quotation were acts that the person referred to might have prevented by interdict, and against which his singular successors were restored.

Qui non prohibet quod prohibere potest assentire videtur.—He who does not prevent (or prohibit) what he can prevent is regarded as assenting. Another form of the preceding maxim.

Qui potest et debet vetare, jubet si non vetat.—He who can and ought to forbid, orders if he does not forbid. This maxim differs from the two immediately preceding maxims in this very important particular—it introduces the *duty* of the person having power to forbid or prohibit to exercise that power. The effect of not prohibiting in those cases where one has the power of prohibiting has already been pointed out, but in the cases to which the two preceding maxims have application, the exercise of the power is in the option of the person possessing it; the present maxim deals with the case where there is no option, but where the possessor of the power is under obligation to exercise it. In this latter case, one who can and ought to prohibit a certain thing, and fails in his duty by not prohibiting, is clearly in the same position, as regards the consequences of the act, as if he had given the order for doing the thing himself. Take the case of soldiers ordered by their officer to fire upon a mob, where the order was not warranted by the circumstances—where, in a word, the order was illegal. The soldiers would incur no blame, their duty being obedience to the order given: the officer who gave the order would be answerable. But if the order was given in the presence of a superior officer, whose duty laid upon him the obligation of forbidding such an order being issued, but who stood by without interfering, and failed thus in his duty, he too would be responsible for the order just as if he had issued it himself.

Qui prius jus suum insinuaverit præferetur.—He is preferred whose right has been first recorded. Of two conveyances of the same subjects and by the same party, that one is to be preferred in a competition of rights which is first upon record, even where it is last in date. It is preferred to the effect of giving the party in whose favour it is the full right conveyed by the disposition, and that to the entire exclusion of all others. So also, when two assignations are granted of the same debt, that which is first intimated is preferable, even although it may have been executed and delivered of a later date than the other. The verb *insinuare* is used in law language to signify recording, or intimation, but most frequently the former. An instance of its being used in the former sense will be found in Just. Inst. B. 2, T. 7, § 2 ; and for an instance of the latter, see Menzies' Lectures, 251. See *Prior tempore*, &c.

Qui providet sibi providet hæredibus.—He who provides for himself provides for his heirs. A provision made in favour of a man without mention being made of his heirs is a provision in favour of heirs not the less if the man takes. So a lease for a period of years in favour of A B, is a lease in favour of the heirs of A B should the lessee die during the currency of the lease. See *Qui acquirit*, &c.

Qui sentit commodum sentire debet et onus.—He who reaps the benefit should also bear the burden. Any one acquiring a right must undertake its corresponding obligations—with the advantages the disadvantages must also be taken. Thus one who succeeds to the estate of another must meet that other's debts and obligations. This maxim has already been explained under another form. See *Cujus est commodum*, &c.

Qui sibi vigilavit.—Who has looked after his own interest.

Qui suum recipit licet a non debitore, non tenetur restituere.—He who receives that which is his own (or that which is due to him), although it be not from his debtor, is not liable in restitution. When a payment is made to any one by another under the erroneous belief that he is bound to make it, restitution, as we have seen above, can be insisted on under the *condictio indebiti*. But where, on the other hand, the payment is really due, the receiver cannot be compelled to restore it simply because the person paying it was not himself the proper debtor in the obligation. For example, if a creditor is pressing a debtor for payment of his debt, and a friend of the latter, in the expectation of receiving the amount from him at a future period, in the meantime settles the creditor's claim, he cannot insist on restitution by the creditor of the sum so paid, in the event of his failing to obtain reimbursement from the debtor.

Qui tacet consentire videtur.—He who does not object is held as consenting; silence implies consent. Mandate may either be express or tacit; the former, when given expressly in words or in writing; the latter, when it is inferred from facts implying it. Thus where a party in the knowledge that certain law proceedings are being taken in his name, takes no steps to disclaim them, he is held from his silence to have authorised them; his silence implies that he consents to their being taken. Silence does not always imply consent, where the silence has reference to some interference with rights of property. *Cowan* v. *Kinnaird*, 4 Macp. 241. This maxim has frequent application also in questions of proof, for it is competent (and very common in practice) to adduce evidence of statements made in the presence of one of the parties, which, if he did not deny them at the time, are regarded as true statements of fact. His silence, in such a case, implies an admission of the statement; he is held as consenting to it by his silent acquiescence. See *Qui non negat*, &c.

Qui totum dicit nihil excipit.—He who says everything excepts nothing. The meaning of this maxim is that where what is said is general in its character, exceptions are not presumed, but the contrary. Thus if a statute makes a general provision, it cannot be maintained that that general provision does not cover some particular case on the ground of an implied exception: the general provision will be held applicable to every case which it covers, if no exception be provided for in the statute. In the same way a general conveyance of his estate by a testator, or truster, carries the whole estate; and it cannot be maintained that the conveyance covered everything except some particular thing of which special mention by way of exception has not been made.

Qui utuntur communi jure gentium.—Who use the common law of nations. Stair, B. 3, T. 1, § 12.

Qui vult consequens velle videtur et antecedens.—He who desires the consequence seems also to desire what preceded it: one who desires, or seeks, the effect must be regarded as consenting to the cause. "He which granteth the consequent, or that which followeth, is thought also to grant the antecedent, or that which goeth before." Fraser, i. 310.

Qui vult decipi decipiatur.—Let him be deceived who wishes (or, is willing) to be deceived. Deception, either by actual misrepresentation or improper concealment of material facts, will void the contract thereby induced: this is a general rule. But when the deception is known at the time of the contract by the person who is intended to be deceived, and who nevertheless goes on with his bargain, it will not afford a ground for setting the bargain aside. Nor will deception afford ground for setting aside the bargain where it lay upon the contracting party to satisfy himself as to the real state of matters before making the contract; for in that case he failed in his own duty, and being willing to be deceived (that is, not taking the steps he was bound to take to discover the deception), the law will not then come to his aid. But it is otherwise if the party contracting and bound to inquire was put off his enquiry by statements made by those who were deceiving him. *Venezuela Ry. Co.* v. *Kisch*, L. R. 2 Eng. and Ir. App. 99. *Reynell* v. *Sprye*, 21 L. J. Chan. 633. See *Non decipitur*, &c.

Quia alimenta liberis non debentur nisi in subsidium. —Because aliment is not due to children except in aid. Parents are bound to aliment their children, but that only where such aid or assistance is necessary. A child earning its own subsistence has no right to aliment; and where a child has separate estate, the produce of which is sufficient for its maintenance, the parent is not bound to aliment. The parent is entitled to apply the produce of such estate towards a child's maintenance and upbringing, and is only bound to provide aliment to the extent to which the child's own estate is insufficient for that purpose. The fee of such estate may be applied so far as necessary—it is only when a child can do nothing or provide nothing for itself that the parent's obligation emerges. Fraser, Par. & Ch. 102.

Quia emptores.—The English statute of 18 Ed. I. c. 1, so called because these are its introductory words. The object of this statute was to abolish subinfeudation, and to render the disponee upon infeftment at once the vassal of his author's superior. It was at one time thought that the provisions of this statute had been at an early period imported into the law of Scotland by the Act 2 Rob. I. c. 24, but modern lawyers deem it very doubtful whether that Act is authentic; at all events, there is no reason for believing that it was ever observed. See *Alienatio feudi.*

Quia ita lex scripta est.—Because the law is so written; because such is the tenor of the statute law. In the case of *Kilpatrick*, M. 12061, where an heir repudiated his father's bond on the ground that it was null, in respect it was wanting in the legal solemnities, not having the writer's name, "the Lords thought it in a court of conscience a good and sufficient bond, but, as our law stood, it was null, though it was both unmannerly and unneighbourly to propone this nullity, yet, being proponed, the Lords behoved to sustain it, though hard, *quia ita lex scripta est.*"

Quia succedunt in universum jus quod defunctus habuit.—Because they succeed to every right which the deceased had. This is given by Stair as the reason why "heirs-in-law are called universal successors." B. 3, T. 4, § 23.

Quia surrogatum sapit naturam surrogati.—Because the substitute partakes of the character of the thing for which it is substituted. Stair, B. 2, T. 2, § 14. See *Surrogatum,* &c.

Quibus deficientibus.—Whom failing—*i.e.,* failing in the sense of having succeeded and died, and differing in that respect from—

Quibus non existentibus.—Whom failing; in the sense of never having existed. Thus if the dispositive clause of a deed be conceived in these terms: "To A, whom failing, to B," and A succeeds, but afterwards dies, the succession opens up to B on what is technically known as the failure of A, that is, his death; this is an example of the first of these two phrases. But if the disposition be by A "to B, failing heirs of A's body," B succeeds in the event of A having no heirs, on their failure, or non-existence. At the time when sasine was necessary to complete a feudal title, it was of great importance, in making up the successor's title, to regard the exact terms of the dispositive clause, for it depended upon it whether the successor was a conditional institute or a substitute : if the former, his title was completed by infeftment on the disposition ; if the latter, he required a service to connect himself with the succession. In the two instances which have been given above of a dispositive clause, the first is an example of that clause conferring upon B the character of substitute, while the second confers upon him the character of conditional institute. There is, perhaps, no nicer question in conveyancing than that of conditional institution and substitution, nor one requiring more care and ability properly to solve. The late Professor More states the distinction between them thus : " The distinction between substitution and conditional institution seems to turn upon this—whether, *under the deed*, any person could possibly intervene between the granter and the person who is *nominatim* called, because the mere possibility of such intervention seems to be held sufficient to create a case of substitution. Where there is a proper conditional institution, the deed will entirely fall and be evacuated if the condition should not be purified ; but where there is a substitution the deed subsists, and the substitute may claim under it at any time till the destination in his favour shall be altered." More's Notes on Stair, cccxxvii. On this question reference may be made to the very instructive case of *Fogo*, 4 D. 1063, where the point was considered by the whole court under a remit from the House of Lords.

Quicquid plantatur solo cedit solo.—Everything planted in the soil belongs to the soil. Whatever is natural to the soil, or planted there either for ornament or use, which is intended to be permanent, goes with the soil ; the owner of the soil is the owner of everything planted in it. This does not include, however, ordinary crops, which belong to the sower. See *Inædificatum solo*, &c.

Quicquid solutum solvitur secundum modum solventis ; quicquid receptum recipitur secundum modum recipientis. —Everything paid (or discharged) is paid according to the intention of the payer: everything received is received according to the intention of the receiver. This is the rule which regulates the application of payments made by a debtor to one who is his creditor in several obligations. The debtor paying the money is entitled to appropriate the payment to any of his debts or obligations held by his creditor at the time the payment is made; and if the payment is so appropriated, that appropriation cannot be departed from or varied by the creditor. But the creditor may refuse to accept a payment according to the debtor's appropriation, and desire it to be appropriated in some other way, and if the creditor's view is acceded to, that regulates the appropriation. The right of appropriation lies first with the debtor, thereafter (in the event of no such appropriation) with the creditor. If neither appropriate the payment at the time it is made, the law allows the creditor to appropriate it to which obligation he pleases any time before action; after action the law appropriates the earliest payments towards extinction of the earliest debt. These are general rules, regarding which, and the exceptions to them, see Bell's Prin. § 563.

Quid actum est.—What has been done; or, that which has been done.

Quid juratum est.—What has been sworn; or, that which has been deponed to. In judging of the import of evidence, two questions generally arise for the consideration of the judge—namely (1) What have the witnesses said? and (2) How far is their statement true, and to be relied upon? But in considering the effect of the oath of one of the parties emitted under a reference, the only question for decision is that expressed in the words of the phrase, What has been deponed to? It must be taken as true in so far as it bears upon the question at issue, and cannot be rebutted by any evidence whatever, because the reference proceeds upon a *quasi* contract that the parties shall abide by, and have their dispute settled according to its terms. As to the special cases in which proof may be allowed even after reference, see *Non memini*.

Quid juravit.—What he has sworn. See above.

Quid juris.—What is the law? A form of interrogatory often used in putting a doubtful or difficult case.

Quid pro quo.—Something given in return for something else. Thus, in the contract of sale, the price paid for the commodity, or in location the hire paid for the loan, is the *quid pro quo.*

Quid valet nunc.—What it is now worth. See *Quantum nunc.*

Quilibet est rei suæ arbiter.—Every one is the judge of his own affairs; or, each one may do as he pleases with his own. See *Quisque est,* &c.

Quilibet juri pro se introducto renunciare potest.—Any one may renounce a right which has been introduced for his own advantage. For example, a minor may renounce the right which the law affords him of reducing any deed granted by him to his lesion in the course of his minority, or of refusing implement of an obligation undertaken by him by contract during that period: a widow or children may renounce their respective rights in the moveable goods of the husband or father, either in consideration of a provision made in lieu of it, or gratuitously, without any consideration: a liferenter may (if the liferent is not strictly alimentary and declared not to be assignable) renounce his liferent and disburden the subject over which that right has been constituted in his favour. See *Cuique licet juri,* &c., and *Omnes licentiam habent,* &c.

Quilibet titulus excusat a spolio.—Any kind of title excuses from the charge and consequences of spuilzie; that is, any reasonable or probable excuse for the alleged act of spuilzie will be sufficient to elide its consequences. See *Levis exceptio,* &c.

Quisque est rei suæ moderator et arbiter.—Each one is the manager and disposer of his own affairs, or of his own property; every one may dispose of that which is his, according to his own discretion and pleasure. The maxim holds good in every case where positive law has not placed a restriction upon the exercise of the rights of property. An example of such restriction may be found in the rule of law which forbids the wanton exercise of those rights to the detriment of a neighbour. See *Interest,* &c.

Quisque renuntiare potest pro se introducto.—Every person can renounce (a benefit or right) introduced for his own advantage. See *Quilibet juri,* &c.

Quisque scire debet cum quo contrahit.—Every one

ought to know with whom he contracts : every one ought to know about the person he deals with. Some obligations are neither binding nor prestable, because of the position of the person granting them, and this phrase expresses the rule of law on which action is refused even to a *bona fide* holder of such an obligation. Thus in the case of a debt incurred by a married woman for goods furnished to her without the consent of her husband and not necessary to her, no action will lie against her husband for the amount, because the seller should have known the position of the person with whom he contracted, and that, being a married woman, she could not validly enter into the transaction. So, in dealing with a minor, it will be no defence to an action for reduction of the contract at his instance that the fact of minority was not disclosed and was not known, for the contracting parties should know who and in what position the parties are with whom they contract ; but the case might be different if the minor gave himself out to be of full age, and the person with whom he contracted had no reason for doubting the assertion. Thus, also, any one who had honestly purchased, and for a fair price, a stolen subject, cannot resist restitution thereof on the ground that he was ignorant of the theft, for he was bound to know with whom he was dealing, and to have satisfied himself of the seller's right, and in not doing so he takes all the risk and hazard upon himself. See for further illustration, Stair, B. 2, T. 5, § 15.

Quisque utitur jure auctoris.—Every one exercises the right of his author, that is, the person from whom the right is derived. See *Assignatus utitur*, &c., and *Nemo plus juris*, &c.

Quivis præsumitur bonus donec probetur contrarium.—Every one is presumed good (or innocent) until the contrary is proved. This is one of the oldest law maxims, and has been called "The golden rule of lawyers."

Quo animo.—With what intention.

Quoad civilia.—As regards civil rights and benefits. See *Quoad sacra*.

Quoad creditorem,—debitorem.—As regards the creditor, —debtor.

Quoad excessum.—As regards the excess. Where a husband makes a postnuptial provision in favour of his wife commensurate with his circumstances and natural duty, it is not subject to revocation by him as a donation. But if the provision be immoderate, it may be revoked *quoad excessum,* in so far as it is excessive. In the same way the creditors of an insolvent husband can set aside any such postnuptial provision in so far as regards any excess in that provision not warranted by the husband's social position or by the state of his affairs at the time of making it. Such a provision, although strictly speaking gratuitous, and therefore a donation, is not regarded in the same light as an ordinary donation *inter virum et uxorem,* because, as it proceeds upon a natural obligation, it is considered in some measure onerous, at least to the effect of depriving the husband of his right to revoke.

Quoad fiscum.—As regards the fisk, or the rights of the Crown. See *Fiscus.*

Quoad maritum.—As regards the husband; in so far as the husband is concerned.

Quoad mobilia.—As regards moveables, or moveable estate.

Quoad non executa.—In so far as regards the acts not done. In the event of an executor-dative, who has been appointed by the Commissary to realise and administer the estate of a deceased, dying after the performance of certain acts of administration, but before the whole duties of his office have been fulfilled, another executor may be appointed *quoad non executa; i.e.,* with regard to those duties not fulfilled, and those acts of administration yet to be performed.

Quoad potest.—In so far as one is able; to the extent of one's power.

Quoad reliquum.—As regards the remainder, or balance. When a debtor, in an action brought against him by his creditor, pleads compensation to a certain extent of the debt sued for, *quoad* the sum due to him (if his plea be admitted or sustained), the creditor's right of action falls; but *quoad reliquum,* after making deduction of the sum pled in compensation, the creditor's right of action remains.

Quoad sacra.—As regards sacred things, religious duties and observances. " It sometimes happens that lands, where they lie at too great a distance from the church to which they originally belonged, are, by the Commission-court, annexed *quoad sacra* to another parish, the church whereof lies at a lesser distance from these lands. By annexing *quoad sacra* is understood that the inhabitants of the annexed lands are, for their greater conveniency in attending divine service, brought under the pastoral care of the minister of the church to which they are annexed. But such annexation affects only the inhabitants; the lands continue in all civil respects part of the old parish; and therefore they remain burdened with the payment of the stipend to that church from which the inhabitants were disjoined." Ersk. B. 2, T. 10, § 64. Lands may thus be *quoad sacra* in one parish, but *quoad civilia* (as regards the civil rights of the minister, his temporalities, &c.) may be held as belonging to another. It has been decided that the right to proclaim the banns of marriage belongs to the parish *quoad sacra*, and the fees payable therefor to the Session-clerk of that parish. *Hutton* v. *Harper*, 2 R. 893, affd. H. L. 3 R. 9.

Quoad ultra.—As regards the rest. This phrase is of very frequent use in pleading. A defender admits a certain part of the pursuer's statement and *quoad ultra* denies it; that is, he denies everything beyond that which he has specifically admitted.

Quoad valet seipsum.—As regards its real value; in so far as it is worth.

Quoad valorem.—As regards the value; to the extent of the value. "Other heirs, not being heirs-portioners, are liable for the defunct's debt *in solidum*, except heirs-substitute in bonds, who are only liable *quoad valorem* in the sums in these bonds." Stair, B. 3, T. 5, § 16. This quotation from Stair, although illustrating this phrase, must now be read (as expressing the law of Scotland on the subject of an heir's liability for his author's debts) subject to the provisions of the Act 37 & 38 Vict. c. 94, § 12.

Quocunque.—In whatever way; in any way.

Quod ab initio non valet in tractu temporis non convalescit.—That which is invalid from the beginning does not become stronger (valid) by lapse of time. See *Quæ ab initio*, &c.

Quod ædificatur in area legata cedit legato.—That which is built upon ground bequeathed accrues to the legacy (*i.e.*, belongs to the legatee). This is a particular rule falling within the more general one, *Inædificatum solo, solo cedit*. A legacy or gift of land carries to the legatee or donee all that is built upon it; and in the case of a legacy or bequest it is immaterial that the building has been put upon the ground subsequent to the date of the bequest. Where land is bequeathed and subsequently built upon, and no change made on the bequest itself, the law presumes that the legator meant the land to go to the legatee with all the advantages possessed by an owner.

Quod approbo non reprobo.—What I approbate I do not reprobate. See *Qui approbat*, &c.

Quod constat curiæ operæ testium non indigit.—What is clear to the Court does not need the aid of witnesses. See *Lex non requirit*, &c.

Quod fieri debet facile præsumitur.—That which ought to be done is easily presumed. The law always presumes that any act has been properly and effectually done, performance of which is required by law. For example, it is required in order to the due execution of a deed that the instrumentary witnesses to it should either see the granter subscribe, or hear him acknowledge the subscription previously adhibited to be his. The legal presumption therefore is, if the deed be *ex facie* regularly tested, that the witnesses were present and saw the subscription, or heard it duly acknowledged. Such a presumption may be redargued, but that can only be done by the clearest contrary evidence; for in the case of *Cleland*, 1 D. 254, the Court unanimously sustained the challenged settlement, although both instrumentary witnesses expressly deponed that they neither saw the granter sign it nor heard him acknowledge his subscription. See *Omnia rite*, &c. But no deed is now deemed invalid or denied effect because of any informality of execution. 37 & 38 Vict. c. 94, § 39.

Quod fieri debet infectum valet.—What ought to be done avails although not done. A thing which ought to be done by a person for his own behoof will not avail him if he neglects the duty of doing it. But there are acts which require to be done by one person for behoof of another, the failure to perform which does not take away the advantage which would have been conferred had the thing been done. A good illustration of the rule expressed by this maxim will be found in the case of *M'Kellar* v. *Livingston*, 23 D. 1269, where a bankrupt was held entitled to the benefit of a renewed personal protection against diligence which his creditors had resolved should be granted, although the trustee on his estates had failed to present the petition to the sheriff for such renewed protection, which the statute directs. See in further illustration of this maxim the case of *Love's Trs.*, 7 R. 410.

Quod fieri non debet factum valet.—What ought not to be done avails if it is done. This maxim is of limited application, and is never applied where the thing improperly done affects the rights or interests of third parties. An illustration of this maxim will be found, however, in the case of a member of the College of Justice purchasing (contrary to the provisions of the Act 1594, c. 216) property which at the time forms the subject of a lawsuit. Such a purchase is forbidden under pain of deprivation of office, place, and privilege; but the course of decisions has been to regard the purchase as valid, the only penalty incurred being that provided by the statute, which, while forbidding such a purchase, does not declare it invalid when done. For further illustration, the reader is referred to Broom, 182 *et seq.*

Quod initio vitiosum est non potest tractu temporis convalescere.—That which is radically defective at the beginning cannot be made better (*i.e.*, the defect cannot be cured) by lapse of time. See *Quæ ab initio*, &c.

Quod juris in toto idem in parte.—That which is law as regards the whole, is so as regards a part; the law which governs or prevails in reference to the whole right, applies to every part of that right. Ross, L. C. L. R. ii. 411.

Quod meum est sine facto meo vel defectu meo amitti vel in alium transferri non potest.—That which is mine cannot be lost to me or transferred to another except by my own act or neglect. Where there is once ownership in a subject, that right cannot be lost by the person possessing it except by his own act or his own default. By his act the owner may deprive himself of the rights of ownership, as, for example, when he sells the subject, gives it away, barters it for something else, or wilfully abandons it: by his default, where without interference or interruption he allows another to exercise the rights of ownership over his property for more than forty years. The rights acquired by prescription are generally of this nature, and are based upon the neglect of the real owner to defend his own rights as much as upon the advantage taken of that neglect by the person acquiring. But the mere fact of loss of possession, either through the felonious act of another or through accident, does not deprive the owner of a subject of the right of property in it, and accordingly he may vindicate his right, and claim the subject, wherever or in whose hands soever it may be found. If the subject has been stolen from its owner, the theft attaches as a *labes realis* to the title of any one acquiring it even onerously; and persons finding property which has been accidentally lost, and not restoring it to the owner if he is known, or to the police authorities if the owner is not known, but retaining it in their own possession, are by such acts held to be guilty of theft. It is proper here to notice, that while no one can be deprived of his ownership except as above explained, his right may in certain circumstances be burdened without his act, and even against his will. Thus where one has intrusted to another, as his agent or factor, certain subjects for sale, the agent may pledge such subjects for his own debt then instantly incurred (not for an antecedent debt) or for advances then made to him; and the owner of the subjects can only recover them under payment of the debt or advances for which they were pledged. This liability for an agent's acts is regulated by the Factors Act (52 & 53 Vict. c. 45, extended to Scotland by 53 & 54 Vict. c. 40), regarding which reference may be made to Bell's Com. i. 521 *et seq.*, and cases there cited. There is one mode, certainly, by which the rights of ownership may be lost to the owner and transferred to another without the consent or act of the owner, and that is by the operation of legal diligence. Moveable property may be so transferred by arrestment and furthcoming, by poinding and sale; while heritage may be transferred by adjudication. This may, however, properly enough, be regarded as a loss of ownership arising from the default of the owner, inasmuch as such legal diligence proceeds upon the default or neglect of the owner, to fulfil his obligations.

Quod meum est sine me alieni fieri nequit.—That which is mine cannot become the property of another without my act. See what has been said on the preceding maxim.

Quod natura omnia animalia docuit.—That which nature has taught to all animals. This is the civil law definition of the law of nature. Just. Inst. B. 1, T. 2, Pr.

Quod naturaliter inesse debet præsumitur.—That is presumed which ought naturally to be. The rules of succession proceed upon this maxim; and accordingly when a father dies without disposing of his estate, the law presumes his will and desire in regard to it to be that which, from natural duty and affection it ought to be, namely, that his children should succeed, and the estate is therefore distributed among them.

Quod non in cœtu nec vociferatione dicitur, id infamandi causa dictum.—That which has been said, not in a public assembly nor by way of violent outcry or abuse, is held to have been spoken for the purpose of defaming. The essence of defamation, as a ground on which obligation for damages in consequence thereof is founded, is the intention to defame by the defamatory or libellous expressions used; and this intention, or *animus*, as it is technically called, is inferred from the words themselves, and from the circumstances in which they are used. Thus if any one should go about volunteering the statement that a person formerly his servant was a thief, such a statement, being gratuitous and uncalled for, would be regarded as defamatory and actionable, because no other reason could be assigned for it being made than that the person making it was actuated by the malicious desire, the *animus*, of defaming his former servant. But if the statement is made to one inquiring after the servant's character before employing him, or one otherwise personally interested in his honesty, the former master may (assuming always that it is the fact) tell of the servant's dishonesty without incurring any liability for damages on that account:

in that case there is no *animus defamandi*. Again, if one person in a passion should use very intemperate and libellous language towards another whom he had never previously met, or, having known, had never previously maligned, malice in such a case would hardly be presumed, and if, when the passion had subsided, an apology was offered as publicly as the offence had been perpetrated, no action for damages would lie. In each case, as has been said, the existence of malice, or its non-existence, will be very much inferred from the peculiar circumstances out of which the action has arisen. M'Donald v. Rupprecht, 21 R. 389.

Quod non apparet non est.—That which does not appear does not exist; that which does not appear or is not proved is regarded as not existing. See *De non apparentibus*, &c.

Quod nullius est id ratione naturali occupanti conceditur.—That which is the property of no one is by a reasonable rule conceded to the person taking possession of it. See the two following maxims.

Quod nullius est fit domini regis.—That which is the property of no one becomes the property of the sovereign. This rule applies properly to land and real rights, which, when vacant, are held to belong to the Crown. It proceeds upon the feudal principle that all real rights are vested in the sovereign, who can only be divested of those rights on their being specially vested in another. It applies also to moveable subjects the right of property in which has been abandoned by the owner, and also to treasures hid in the ground the owner of which is not known. See *Res nullius*.

Quod nullius est fit occupantis.—That which is the property of no one becomes the property of the person finding or taking possession of it. This rule applies strictly to those things which have never previously been occupied or held in property by any one. Thus wild beasts become the property of the hunter who takes or kills them, and game becomes the property of the person taking it, even although his pursuit of the game has been unlawful. A poacher, therefore, who has been caught in the act of taking the game, while he may be punished for the violation of the law, cannot be deprived of the game which he has taken, unless the confiscation of it is made part of the penalty, as it is his own by the mere fact of first occupancy. This rule is extended in England to the case of money found upon the street or road, which becomes the property of the finder if the former owner cannot be discovered. See *Res nullius* and *Occupantis fiunt*, &c.

Quod nullum est nullum producit effectum.—That which is nothing produces no effect; that which is regarded as null, and in itself equivalent to nothing, can legally have no effect whatever. For example, so long as the word "dispone" was essential to a deed of conveyance, any deed wanting that word was radically defective and null, although containing other words importing conveyance: such a deed, being regarded as no conveyance at all, could have no effect, and give rise to no right. So a marriage, although regularly celebrated before the Church, between parties incapable of marrying each other, is not a marriage, and neither gives the parties to it the rights of spouses nor their children the *status* of legitimacy.

Quod pure debetur præsenti die debetur.—That which is due purely or unconditionally, is due now. When performance of an obligation is conditional on the occurrence of some event, or where payment of a debt is only exigible on a day yet future, performance cannot be demanded of the one until the condition has been purified, nor can payment be insisted on of the other until the arrival of the specified day. But if the obligation be unconditional, and the debt presently due, performance and payment are due and prestable at once.

Quod remedio destituitur ipsa re valet si culpa absit.—That which is without remedy avails of itself, if there be no fault (in the party seeking to enforce it). An executor creditor is allowed to retain out of the executry funds "so much as will pay himself before any other creditor whose debts are of equal degree. This, be it observed, is a remedy by the mere act of law, and grounded upon this reason, that an executor cannot, without an evident absurdity, commence a suit against himself as representative of the deceased to recover that which is due to him in his own private capacity; but having the whole personal estate in his hands, so much as is sufficient to answer his own demand is, by operation of law, applied to that particular purpose." Broom, 215.

Quod salvum fore receperint.—That which they received (on the understanding) that it would be safe; that which they received for safe custody. The liability of shipowners, innkeepers, and others falling within the provisions of the edict *Nautæ, caupones*, &c., for restitution of things lost, is limited to the value of those things which had been intrusted to them for safe custody or safe delivery. If the traveller makes himself specially the guardian of his own property, the innkeeper's liability for loss ceases. See *Nautæ, caupones*, &c.

Quod semel placuit in electionibus amplius displicere non potest.—That which has once pleased in a matter of election cannot afterwards displease; or, less literally, one who has once exercised his right of election cannot go back upon it and again elect. An heir has his choice either to take the heritage or to collate: if he has once exercised his choice, he must abide by it—he cannot take the heritage, and afterwards insist on collating; or if he has once consented to collation, cannot thereafter decline to collate and insist upon taking the heritage to himself. So, again, if a deed is once approbated, it cannot be reprobated; or if reprobated, cannot be approbated. Insurers have the option of paying the amount insured or reinstating the loss: if they elect to reinstate, they cannot afterwards decline to do so, and offer the amount insured instead; while conversely, if they elect to pay the amount insured, they cannot afterwards decline to do so, and offer reinstatement. *Inglis' Trs.*, 14 R. 740; *Scarf* v. *Jardine*, L. R. 7, App. C. 360.

Quod statim liquidari potest pro jam liquido habetur.—That which can at once be rendered liquid is held as liquid. A liquid debt is one that is already constituted, such as by decree, bill, &c. This maxim has reference to the plea of compensation, in treating of which Erskine says— "Though the aforesaid Act (1592, c. 143) requires that all grounds of compensation be instantly verified; yet, by our uniform practice for near a century, which seems grounded on the Roman law, if a debtor in a liquid sum shall plead compensation upon a debt due by his creditor to him, which requires only a short discussion to constitute it, sentence is delayed *ex æquitate* against the debtor in the clear debt, that he may have an opportunity of making good his ground of compensation, according to the rule *Quod statim*, &c. Agreeably to this, compensation has not only been admitted where the debt was offered to be proved instantly by writing, or by the oath of the party; but the extract of the pursuer's decree hath been superseded for some months, where the liquidation of the debt required a proof by witnesses." (B. 3, T. 4, § 16.) See *De liquido*, &c.

Quod tibi fieri non vis alteri ne feceris.—Do not that to another which you would not that another should do to you. Stair, B. 1, T. 1, § 1.

Quodammodo jurisdictionis voluntariæ.—Belonging in some measure to voluntary jurisdiction. Ersk. B. 1, T. 2, § 28.

Quodque dissolvitur eodem ligamine quo ligatur.—Any obligation is discharged in the same manner as that in which it was imposed. See *Eodem modo*, &c.

Quomodo constat.—How does it appear; how is it shown.

Quomodo desiit possidere.—In what way he ceased to possess, or, lost possession. One who has lost possession of a moveable subject, when claiming it from another in possession of it, is bound, in support of his claim, not only to prove his previous possession, but also to show how that possession ceased, as, for example, that it was stolen from him, or that he lost it accidentally, or that he gave it to another in loan who had lost it, &c.

Quorum bonorum.—The name of one of the interdicts known in the civil law, and deriving that name from the introductory words of the *formula* appropriate to it. When a testator's will was defective, so as to be ineffectual according to the strict civil law, or where it was *inofficiosum*, the prætor, in the exercise of his equitable jurisdiction, gave possession of the goods of the deceased to that person whom he deemed to have the best right thereto. The *bonorum possessio* granted by the prætor was not, as the name implies, a real and actual possession, but was a right conferred by him upon the person to whom it was given to succeed to the deceased, and take or recover possession of his estate—a right which the strict civil law could not confer—and it was under this interdict that such person *enforced* his right to possession. For example, children who had been passed over by an inofficious testament, not being heirs, properly so called, had no right to the succession such as the civil law could recognise ; but under this interdict they recovered the inheritance from the person who held it under the testament. This interdict was the one granted where possession had never been previously had. See *Unde vi.*

Quorum usus consistit in abusu.—The use of which consists in consuming them. Fungibles are of this character; and because they perish in the using, can consequently, never be the subjects of a liferent right, which is a right to use and enjoy a subject during life, without destroying or consuming its substance. Money, although a fungible, may be the subject of a liferent right. On the subject of liferent rights, see Ersk. B. 2, T. 9, § 40 *et seq.* ; Bell's Prin. § 1042 *et seq.* ; *Rogers,* 5 Macp. 1078.

Quot articuli tot libelli.—As many points of dispute as libels. Ersk. B. 4, T. 1, § 65.

Quot generationes tot gradus.—As many generations, so many degrees. In regulating intestate moveable succession, the nearness of degree in relationship is very important, the nearest of kin excluding all who are more remote, unless they have the privilege of representation. Thus, until the passing of the Act 18 Vict. c. 23, the children of a deceased succeeded to his moveable estate to the entire exclusion of grandchildren—because they were nearer in degree. This was an example of the phrase, showing that the degree depended on the generation. Nearness of degree is not now, however, tested in this manner. Children exclude nephews or nieces, although they are, in one sense, of the same generation : they are not on that account of equal degree. This maxim was specially used by the Civilians to distinguish their method of computing degrees of propinquity from that of the Canonists. The difference between these methods may be shortly stated : it had reference only to collateral relationship, for, in so far as concerned the ascending and descending lines, they were alike. According to the civil law, the method of computing the degree of relationship between two persons was this : starting from one of the persons, you proceeded upwards till the common stock or ancestor was reached, and then down to the other person, each generation (excluding the common ancestor) being reckoned a degree, and hence the maxim. Thus brothers stood to each other in the second degree ; ascending from the one brother to the father, and thence down to the other brother, there were two persons generated (the two sons), and consequently two degrees. Again, a nephew stood to his uncle in the third degree : ascending from the nephew to his father, then his grandfather, then descending to the grandfather's other son (the uncle), there were three generations—viz., (1) the nephew, (2) his father, and (3) his father's brother (his uncle). According to the canon law, the collateral line was divided into equal and unequal, the former being that where collateral relations were removed at an equal distance from their common ancestor, as brothers and cousins-german : the unequal where they were unequally removed, such as uncle and nephew. In the equal collateral line the method adopted was to count from the common ancestor down to the persons to be connected, and the number of persons intervening between each of those persons and the common ancestor corresponded with the degree of relationship in which those persons stood to each other. Thus, brothers stood in the first degree to each other, because it was but one step from the common ancestor to each ; cousins-german stood to each other in the second degree, because between each cousin and the common ancestor (the grandfather) there were but two steps, the cousin and his father. In the unequal collateral line the number of degrees was found by counting the number of persons farthest removed from the common stock. Thus an uncle and a nephew stood in the second degree, because the nephew who was farthest removed stood in the second degree to his grandfather, the common ancestor of him and his uncle. For a fuller explanation of this matter, reference may be made to Bankton, B. 1, T. 5, § 38 *et seq.;* Ersk. B. 1, T. 6, § 8 *et seq.;* Fraser, i. 105 *et seq.*

Quota.—A share or proportion.

Quoties in verbis nulla est ambiguitas, ibi nulla expositio

contra verba fienda est.—Where there is no ambiguity in the words used, no construction of them contrary to their ordinary meaning is admissible. This is a rule of construction of universal application. Where the words used in a deed or statute are plain and unambiguous, they must be read and applied according to their ordinary meaning. Construction is only allowed where there is ambiguity.

Quovis tempore.—At whatever time ; at any time.

Quum principalis causa non consistit ne ea quidem quæ sequuntur locum habent.— When the principal no longer exists those things which follow it cease also to have place. See *Quæ accessionum,* &c.

R

Rapina.—Robbery; theft committed by violence.

Ratihabitio mandato comparatur.—Ratification is equivalent to mandate. An act subsequently ratified is equally binding as if it had previously been authorised. See *Omnis ratihabitio*, &c.

Ratio decidendi.—The reason of a decision; the ground on which a decision proceeds. At one time judges were not bound to state the grounds on which they decided the cases before them, but a different rule now prevails. Sheriffs and sheriff-substitutes are now bound to set forth, in any interlocutor disposing in whole or in part of the merits of the cause (and in certain other interlocutors specified in the statute), or in a note appended to and issued along with it, the grounds on which they have proceeded. This was rendered imperative by the Act 16 & 17 Vict. c. 80, § 13. In practice the provisions of this statute are regarded by the Judges of the Supreme Court, as well as by inferior judges.

Ratio scientiæ.—The reason or ground of knowledge. When a witness has spoken definitely to a certain fact, it is of importance to ascertain his *ratio scientiæ*, that is, the grounds on which his knowledge of that fact to which he has spoken is based. If he knows nothing of the matter from his own personal knowledge, but has acquired his information from the statements of some third party, his *ratio scientiæ* is hearsay, and such evidence is valueless. If, on the other hand, he has acquired the knowledge from personal observation; if he has seen the act performed, or heard the words uttered, regarding which his testimony is being given, his evidence is then of the most valuable and decisive character. This phrase is frequently written *Causa scientiæ*.

Ratione bonorum.—On account of property.

Ratione causæ.—By reason, or on account of, the nature of the case. When a judge is declined, on account of his incompetency to deal with the special question at issue, he is said to be declined *ratione causæ*. On this ground sheriffs, and other inferior judges, may be declined in questions of heritable right (except in those cases provided for by the Act 40 & 41 Vict. c. 50), the Court of Session may be declined in criminal cases, &c.

Ratione contractus.—By reason of the contract. By entering into a contract, the contracting parties may, in certain cases, render themselves amenable to the jurisdiction of a judge to whose jurisdiction they would not have been amenable had the contract not been entered into. Thus, a foreigner, for the time being domiciled in Scotland, entering into a contract there with a Scotchman for the performance of certain works or services to be performed in Scotland, renders himself amenable to the jurisdiction of the Scotch courts in any question arising out of the contract, for the parties in the circumstances are presumed to have had the law and the courts of Scotland in view as the *forum* before which any question arising out of the contract was to be decided, and a jurisdiction thus founded is said to arise *ratione contractus*. But to make an action on the contract competent before the Scotch Courts, and the decree in such an action available, it is necessary—(1) that the foreigner be, at the date of the action, personally present in Scotland, and personally cited if he has not at that time resided for the period necessary to constitute a domicile for citation; or (2) that he has effects lying in Scotland which have been attached by arrestment.

Ratione delicti.—On account of the delict. The commission of a crime or delict vests the judge within whose territory it has been committed with an exclusive jurisdiction *quoad* it. He may try the offender, and punish him according to the law of the land where the offence was committed. A foreigner committing a crime in Scotland is amenable to the criminal jurisdiction of Scotland, and to no other; for if he should escape, he cannot be put on trial or punished for the crime in his own country. Erskine gives the reason for founding criminal jurisdiction against the delinquent in the place where the crime has been committed in the following passage (B. 1, T. 2, § 23)—"This appears to be the most natural and rational course of criminal trials, because those under whose eye the offence was committed will be most effectually deterred from a wicked course of life by seeing the criminal also punished, and the just resentment of the person injured, and his friends, will be most amply satisfied." See *Locus delicti.*

Ratione domicilii.—On account of domicile. Domicile is the basis on which civil jurisdiction is most frequently founded; it subjects the person to the jurisdiction of the judge in whose territory he resides, and reasonably so, since he at the same time enjoys the protection of that judge.

Ratione habita.—Regard being had. In the case of the *Caledonian Ry. Co.* v. *Turner*, 12 D. 406, the question being raised whether a person furth of the kingdom, but possessed of heritable property therein, was bound to sist a mandatory, the court intimated an opinion that it could not be laid down as a general rule that every litigant proprietor furth of Scotland must sist a mandatory, but that the question must be decided in each case *ratione habita* of the value of the heritage, and of the whole circumstances of the case.

Ratione incidentiæ.—By reason of the incidence; on account of being incidentally connected with. Ersk. B. 4, T. 4, § 46.

Ratione originis.—On account of one's origin or birth. It was at one time supposed that the jurisdiction to which one was rendered amenable by the fact of his birth, and which vested in the judge of the territory in which he was born, was one which attached for ever, and could not be voided, even by departure from the place of nativity *animo remanendi;* and Erskine, in treating of this, says—"The reason of which decision seems to be that those who are born within the kingdom, though they should be afterwards settled abroad, without an intention of returning home, cannot shake themselves loose from the obligations naturally due by them, either to the laws or to the courts of their mother-country." This doctrine, if ever purely held, has been exploded, except, possibly as regards the exceptional case mentioned by Lord Kames, of a man being guilty of treasonable practices against the sovereign of his native land, who cannot plead his departure from his country as freeing him from the natural loyalty due to his sovereign. Reference may be made to note 28, by Lord Ivory, appended to Erskine, B. 1, T. 2, § 19, in which he fully reviews the decisions upon this point of law.

Ratione privilegii.—On account of privilege. Formerly, members of the College of Justice were only amenable to the jurisdiction of the Supreme Courts, and therefore could decline the jurisdiction of any inferior judge on account of their privilege. Such privilege has been abolished, and no similar privilege now exists but that which a nobleman has, of declining to be tried on a charge of treason before any other judicatory than the House of Lords.

Ratione rei sitæ.—On account of the position of the subject or property. A foreigner is subject to the jurisdiction of the Scotch Courts if he has either heritable or moveable property situated in Scotland. In the case of moveable property, which may be removed from the jurisdiction, arrestment of it for the special purpose of founding jurisdiction is necessary before the foreign owner of it can be called upon to answer to any action raised against him in the Scotch Courts. No antecedent procedure, such as arrestment, is necessary where the subject is heritable. See *Arrestum*, &c.

Ratione subjectæ materiæ.—On account of the subject-matter; according to the subject-matter.

Ratione suspecti judicis.—On account of the judge being suspected. A judge may be declined where, from his personal interest in the issue of the suit, or his relationship to either of the parties, he might be disposed to favour one of them, and deal partially. Such a declinature on the part of a suitor is unknown in practice; but the judges, in cases where the declinature might be urged, are in the habit of declining to adjudicate therein *ex proprio motu*.

Re infecta.—The thing not having been done; the act not having been performed.

Re, verbis, literis, consensu.—By the thing, by words,

by writing, by consent. Contracts were divided among the Romans into four classes, according to the manner in which they were constituted—namely, into real, verbal, literal or written, and consensual. Regarding the constitution of the different contracts, see *Obligatio literarum*.

Rebus integris.—Matters being complete. Where an arrangement or agreement has been entered into with reference to some contract, and, in some cases, even where a bargain has been made, but nothing done in consequence of or in dependence upon it by the parties, matters are said to be complete, so that either of them may resile: the parties are still in the positions respectively occupied by them before contracting. If, however, *rei interventus* has followed upon the agreement, the parties are barred from resiling, because *res non est integra*. The rule by which it is judged whether matters are or are not complete is this: whenever anything has taken place on the faith of the bargain or agreement, which cannot be recalled, and parties put in the same position as before, then it is understood that matters are not complete, and there is no longer *locus pœnitentiœ*. Thus where two parties enter into an agreement regarding the conveyance of land, either may resile before they have entered into written missives, or before the conveyance is completed. But if, on the faith of the agreement, possession has been given, or the price paid, or improvements executed, &c., *res non est integra*, and neither can resile. A mandatory may resign his office after acceptance of it *rebus integris*—that is, provided he has not already executed part of the acts performance of which is authorised by the mandate; but if he has entered upon the office, and performed part of the duty, he cannot resign without consent of the mandant until he has fulfilled the whole.

Rebus ipsis et factis.—By the facts and circumstances themselves. Consent to marriage is sometimes inferred from facts and circumstances, as where the parties are habit and repute husband and wife, and address each other by these names respectively.

Rebus sic stantibus.—Matters so standing; in the existing state of matters.

Receptator.—A resetter ; a receiver of stolen goods

Reconventione.—By reconvention. This is a mode by which courts of law are enabled to determine questions arising by way of counter claim or compensation, in which, otherwise, they would not have jurisdiction. Thus, if a foreigner raises an action before the Scotch Courts against a Scotchman or other person subject to the jurisdiction of the Scotch Courts, the latter is entitled to raise a counter action against the foreigner before the same court, if the counter action relates to or arises out of the same transaction or contract, out of or concerning which the question in the first action has been raised. Suppose that an Englishman pursues a person resident in Scotland for the contract price of certain goods sold and delivered, the defender in that action may, before the same court, raise and insist in an action against the Englishman pursuing, for damages on account of breach of that contract. In the ordinary case the Englishman would not be subject to the jurisdiction of the Scotch Courts, and the person claiming damages against him for breach of contract would require to enforce that claim in the courts of the Englishman's domicile. But when the Englishman seeks the aid of the Scotch Courts in enforcing his rights under the contract, he is bound to submit to the same court the determination of all questions regarding his liability under the contract. The first action is called the *actio conventionis*, the action by which the defender is convened to answer the pursuer's claim ; the second action is called the *actio reconventionis*, being that by which the pursuer is called into court again, or reconvened to answer to the defender's counter claim. " Reconvention is not, in any proper sense, a source or foundation of jurisdiction." " In its most simple and obvious form, reconvention is nothing but a mere unrestricted application of the principle of equity, which is the foundation of the law of compensation." " Reconvention, then, I conclude, as it existed in the law of Rome, and as it has generally been received by the nations of modern Europe, is a rule devised entirely for the protection of a defender, and for the speedy determination of counter claims—that the claims must either arise *in eodem negotio* or be *ejusdem generis*—and that the rule will apply only where the two claims, the *conventio* and the *reconventio*, may be tried simultaneously, and terminated either by a single sentence, or by two sentences contemporaneous or nearly contemporaneous." Per Lord Justice-Clerk (Inglis) in *Thompson* v. *Whitehead*, 24 D. 331. The reader is referred to the opinion just quoted from for an exposition of the principles which govern the application of this rule. Reference may also be made to the case of *Morrison* v. *Massa*, 5 Macp. 130 ; *Longworth* v. *Yelverton*, 7 Macp. 70 ; *Allan*, 31 Scot. L. R. 698.

Reddendo.—That clause in a charter which sets forth the payment to be made, or service to be rendered by the vassal to the superior, in return for the lands held by the former of the latter. It follows the *tenendas*, which expresses the nature of the tenure by which the lands are held. The name is taken from the first word in the clause, as it stood in the old Latin form.

Reddendo singula singulis.—By applying or assigning each to each. A phrase similar in meaning has already been explained. See *Applicando singula*, &c. The reader will find an illustration of the phrase, additional to what has been already given, in Fraser, Mas. & Serv. 474.

Regalem habens dignitatem.—Having royal dignity. Ersk. B. 2, T. 5, § 64.

Regalia.—Royal rights pertaining to the Crown ; things belonging to the Sovereign. The rights of the Sovereign which pertain to the Crown, apart from those enjoyed as an individual, are divided into *regalia majora* and *regalia minora*. The former include those rights which are inseparable from the person of the Sovereign, such as the prerogative of pardoning criminals ; the latter consist of those rights attached to the Crown which may be conferred by gift, or otherwise, upon a subject, such as salmon-fishings, forfeitures, casualties of superiority, &c.

Regiam Majestatem.—The books of the Majesty ; the title given to a collection of ancient laws, said to have been compiled by the order of David I., King of Scotland. Its authenticity as a Scotch performance on the order of King David is seriously doubted, many learned writers inclining to the opinion that it is a compilation from the ancient laws of England made under Edward I., "with the artful design (as Sir Walter Scott thinks) of palming upon the Scotch Parliament, under the pretence of reviving their ancient jurisprudence, a system as nearly as possible resembling that of England." A reference to the different writers who have taken part in this controversy will be found in Bell's Dict. *h. v.*

Regula regulans.—The regulating or governing rule.

Rei depositæ proprietas apud deponentem manet; sed et possessio.—The right of property in a thing deposited remains with the depositor, and also the possession. Deposit is either proper or improper.—1. Proper, where the subject is deposited for mere preservation, and to be specifically returned, as in the case of plate lodged with a banker for greater security; in such case, according to the above maxim, the right of property in the deposit never passes from the depositor, and he may vindicate his right to the *ipsum corpus* at any time; the civil possession of the deposit also remains with the depositor. 2. Improper, where fungibles are deposited for the return of an equal quantity, as money with a banker, where the property in the deposit is transferred to the depository, and the depositor becomes a mere creditor. In the latter case the present maxim does not apply.

Rei interitus.—The destruction of a thing.

Rei interventus.—The intervention of a thing or act. *Rei interventus* is the technical name given to any act done in consequence of or on the faith of a hitherto uncompleted bargain, the effect of which is to bar objection on the ground of the bargain being incomplete, and to take away the *locus pœnitentiæ*. For cases illustrative of this, see *Locus pœnitentiæ. Rebus integris.*

Rei persecutoriæ.—The name given to a class of actions under the civil law, and explained *supra*, page 14.

Rei suæ providus.—Careful of his property, or prudent in its management. Interdiction, whether voluntary or judicial, can only be recalled or removed by an interlocutor of Court, and it affords a good ground on which to apply for the removal of the restraint imposed by interdiction that the interdicted has become *rei suæ providus*.

Rei vindicatio.—An action under the civil law by which the owner of a subject claimed the subject itself; a real action, as opposed to *condictio*, which was a personal action under which delivery of the thing itself could not be enforced, but its value might be recovered. The *vindicatio* was only competent to the true owner against the possessor for the time being. For an illustration of the application of this action in the Scotch law, see Ersk. B. 3, T. 3, § 34. See *Condictio*.

Reipublicæ interest ut sit finis litium.—It is for the public interest that there should be a known termination of pleas; *i.e.*, a termination beyond or after which the decision in a suit should be final and unquestionable. "The Lords have never reduced or altered their decreets upon alledgeances, either in fact or law, which were proponed and repelled therein; and if they should so do, there could be no end of pleas. For if they could alter the first time, by admitting that which they did repel, or by repelling that which they did sustain, there is nothing could secure the lieges, but that they would return again to their first judgment, and back from that to the second, without end; and thereby no man could, with security and confidence, call anything his own; therefore custom hath so secured that point, 'proponed and repelled,' that it is an unbrangeable foundation of all the securities of the nation. All nations have been earnest and anxious that there might be a known termination of pleas" (Stair, B. 4, T. 1, § 46). The phrase may also mean that it is for the public interest that there should be a fixed and determinate time beyond which a right of action should cease; and upon this ground, action is with us denied for a debt or on an obligation which is not brought within forty years. Various reasons combine to make this rule not only politic but just; after a period of forty years all those persons may have died, or all trace of them lost, who could have supported the case of the defender, and rebutted the claim of the pursuer; the witnesses for the pursuer after such a period, would in all probability speak from mere recollection, and the proof thus afforded by them would amount more to a proof of indistinct impressions than to a proof of facts—a kind of proof on which it would be hazardous to disturb rights which had remained undisturbed for forty years.

Reipublicæ interest, voluntates defunctorum effectum sortiri.—It is for the public interest that the wills of deceased persons should receive effect. In construing a testament or will, the intention of the testator is that which is chiefly regarded, and in questions involving such construction, the court gives effect to this intention where it can be ascertained. The court will not, however, adopt that as the testator's intention which is not warranted by the terms of his deed, even although he should have used words and clauses in ignorance of their legal effect, the mere use of such terms raising a presumption of knowledge on his part of their technical meaning and effect. See *Ralston* v. *Hamilton*, 4 Macq. 397.

Relegatio.—Banishment. The *relegatio* of the civil law was much similar to the punishment of transportation formerly imposed under our law on criminals. It was rarely a perpetual banishment, and did not deprive the exile of his citizenship (*civitas*), nor of his rights as one of a family (*familia*). In this respect it differed from deportation, under which the condemned lost all his civil rights, and even when recalled was only restored to his civil rights for the future, unless in the special case where the emperor granted absolute restitution (*per omnia*), which had the effect of reinstating him in his original position.

Rem pupilli salvam fore.—That the pupil's estate would be safe, or be preserved. All tutors, except those appointed by the will of the pupil's father (testamentary tutors) require, on entering upon their office, to find caution for their intromissions with the pupil's estate, and that they will act faithfully in the performance of their duties as tutors. Testamentary tutors are exempt from this, "because the confidence which the father places in them by the nomination creates a presumption that he was well assured of their probity and diligence." Ersk. B. 1, T. 7, § 3.

Remediis prætoriis.—By prætorian remedies. Those were termed prætorian remedies under the civil law which arose from the provisions of the Prætor's Edict, and had no place in the strict civil law. Thus the *bonorum possessio* was the prætorian remedy under which a child was enabled to succeed to its father, where, by the *capitis diminutio* or otherwise, he was by the strict law rendered incapable of succeeding. All the prætorian interdicts, and many of the exceptions pleadable in defence to an action, were of the class of prætorian remedies.

Remedium extraordinarium.—An extraordinary remedy; one out of the usual order of legal remedies, and not resorted to except in cases of great necessity, and where ordinary remedies cannot be resorted to.

Remissio injuriæ.—Forgiveness of the offence; condonation. It affords a good defence to an action of divorce on the ground of adultery, that the injured spouse was fully aware of the other's unfaithfulness, and in such knowledge forgave the offence. Such forgiveness, or condonation, as it is most frequently termed, may either be express, as in the case where a verbal or written forgiveness is given; or implied, as where the injured spouse continues to cohabit with the adulterer after knowledge of the offence, or delays raising an action of divorce for a period so lengthened as to import acquiescence. When adultery was tried criminally, the forgiveness of the injured spouse did not exempt the adulterer from punishment; but as that offence gives rise now only to the civil remedy of divorce, it may, like all other civil rights, be abandoned or discharged.

Remotis testibus.—The witnesses being absent. Ersk. B. 3, T. 2, § 7.

Remoto impedimento actio emergit.—The hindrance or obstacle being removed, the right of action emerges. A good right of action may exist, and yet the person possessing the right may be hindered from exercising it. Thus no action can be brought against an heir concerning the heritage of his ancestor for six months after the ancestor's death—the heir has that time allowed him to deliberate whether he will enter upon the succession. When that time has elapsed, the creditor may exercise his right of action, the obstacle in the way of exercising that right being then removed. So, also, an executor cannot be sued for a debt due by the deceased for six months, which is the time allowed to him to realise the executry estate. The maxim may also be illustrated by the case of a bankrupt, who after his discharge and reinvestiture, may sue for recovery of debts due him before his bankruptcy, which he could not do during the dependence of the bankruptcy.

Renovatio.—A renewal. In treating of the rights which churchmen had over their lands, Erskine mentions that no clergyman could dispone any part of the lands of his benefice without the consent of his bishop and the majority of the chapter; but, he adds, "this incapacity did not strike against their power of receiving the heirs of vassals; for though the entry of heirs be a *renovatio*, it is not an *alienatio feudi*." (B. 2, T. 10, § 5.) The distinction here taken is between a mere renewal, in a feudal sense, of a grant already made; and a new disposition or original grant of benefice lands. The one act was within the power of the holder of the benefice, because it did not in any degree impoverish or lessen its value; while the other, as it affected the Church generally, being a conveyance of Church lands, and also affected whoever should subsequently succeed to the living, could only be done by the holder with consent of the bishop and majority of the chapter in that see.

Reo absente.—The defender being absent.

Reo præsente.—The defender being present.

Res accessoria sequitur rem principalem.—An accessory follows the principal. See *Accessorium principale*, &c., and *Quæ accessionum*, &c.

Res aliena.—The property or subject belonging to another.

Res aliena scienter legata.—The property of another knowingly bequeathed;—*i.e.*, a subject bequeathed by a testator in the knowledge that it does not belong to him, but is the property of some other. When a testator bequeaths what he knows does not belong to him, his executor is bound to make good the legacy to the legatee, either by purchasing and delivering the thing itself, or, where this cannot be done, by paying him the value of it. A different rule prevails where a testator bequeaths a subject belonging to another, under the erroneous belief that it is his own; in such case the legacy falls.

Res alienari prohibita.—A thing which cannot be alienated; a subject the alienation or assignation of which is forbidden.

Res communes.—Common things; defined in the civil law as things the property of which belongs to no one, but the use to all, such as air, light, running water, &c.

Res fit inempta.—The subject is regarded as unbought. Where the *pactum legis commissoriæ* is attached to a contract of sale, the contract becomes void, and the subject regarded as never having been bought, if the price is not paid by the day fixed upon. The seller can then recover the subject if it still remains in the hands of the purchaser, but if it has passed into the *bona fide* possession of others, he has only a personal action for the price.

Res gesta.—The thing done; the whole transaction or circumstance. This phrase, which is of very frequent occurrence, signifies not only an act performed, but everything said or done at the time bearing upon or having reference to it. Thus it includes all statements made immediately before or immediately after any particular act so nearly connected with it in point of time as to be inseparable parts of the whole transaction, and incapable of omission from any narrative or testimony professing to be an account of it. Statements offered in evidence, which would otherwise be excluded as hearsay, are received when they form part of the *res gesta*, and the following passage from Hume in support of this doctrine may be given as an illustration of that which this phrase is held to include. He says (Vol. ii. 406, note)—"Very often words uttered to a witness are a substantial part of the *res gesta* told by such witness; are the cause and motive why the witness himself has proceeded to do a certain thing; and he cannot relate truly and intelligently what he did, without mentioning why and how he came to conduct himself in that way. Put the case that John finds James lying wounded and bleeding on the highway, and James tells John that he has been fired at with a pistol and robbed, and that the robber is dressed so and so, and has robbed him of such and such articles, and has gone off by such and such a road. Now, here, if John in consequence pursues by that road and takes a man dressed as has been told him, and on a search the articles mentioned and a pistol bearing marks of being recently fired are found on him, certainly this verbal information from John is a link and circumstance of the fact, is an act in the progress of the business, and equally admissible as the rest of the story." In this case John's *act* was to run after and apprehend a certain man, but the information on which he proceeded (although of the nature strictly of hearsay as evidence), the intention and motive on which he acted, all form constituent parts of his whole interference in the matter ; they are all parts of the *res gesta*. Reference may be made further on this point to Dickson on Evidence, §§ 92, 1381.

Res integra.—The matter is entire or complete. In certain cases, parties may resile from agreements entered into, so long as *res integra*—*i.e.*, so long as the matter remains on the mere agreement, and nothing has been done by either party in consequence of and in dependence upon it. But if any act has followed upon the agreement, then *res non est integra*, and resiling is barred. See *Rebus integris*.

Res inter alios acta, aliis neque nocet, neque prodest.— A thing done, or a transaction entered into, between certain parties cannot advantage or injure those who are not parties to the act or the transaction. A co-debtor thus cannot be affected by the admissions or pleas of his co-debtor in an action founded on their joint obligation, but to which he has not been called as a party ; nor does the decision in that action render the question as between him and the creditor *res judicata*. On the other hand, while he cannot be injured by that decision, neither can he be advantaged by it. So, again, where a creditor inhibits his debtor, he alone can take advantage by the inhibition ; for should the debtor alienate his lands notwithstanding the inhibition, it is a good and valid conveyance if not reduced by the inhibiting creditor. The inhibition being a *res inter alios acta*, cannot be pleaded by any of the inhibitor's co-creditors, who are third parties. The effect of all legal process is regulated by this maxim ; it cannot injure, but neither can it avail any who were not parties to it. On this point see the opinions delivered in the House of Lords in *Jenkins* v. *Robertson*, 5 Macp. 27. See *Judicium semper*, &c.

Res inter alios acta aliis non nocet.—A thing done by or between certain parties does not injure others (who were not parties to the thing done). This is another form of the preceding maxim; the maxim is also to be found expressed as follows—

Res inter alios acta alteri nocere non debet.—A thing done by certain persons, ought not to be injurious to another who was not a party to the thing done.

Res ipsa loquitur.—The thing itself speaks; or, the thing done, or the transaction, speaks for itself.

Res judicata.—A case, or matter decided; a final judgment. A point or question becomes *res judicata* when it has been so decided by the Supreme Court as conclusively to settle it, and so as to prevent the same question being again raised by the same parties or their representatives; but there can be no *res judicata* so long as the decision is subject to review. This plea, when stated and substantiated in a defence, prevents the judge from inquiring into the merits of the case. Such final decision cannot affect others than those who were parties to the action in which it was pronounced except in so far as that decision constitutes a precedent.

Res judicata inter alios, aliis neque nocet neque prodest. —A case or matter, finally settled between certain parties, can neither injure nor benefit others. See the observations on the preceding maxim, and also on the maxim *Res inter alios*, &c.

Res judicata pro veritate habetur (or accipitur).—A case (matter or question) decided is held (or received) as true; the rule, according to Erskine, that all final sentences are considered in law as grounded upon truth and justice. This maxim has universal application within the country in which the judge who pronounces the decision has jurisdiction; his decision must be taken as sound and just, and cannot be inquired into. But " where the obtainer of a decree given forth in one state demands the execution of it by an action brought before the Court of another state, that Court, who are not bound to interpose their authority to it *ex necessitate*, but only *ex comitate*, have a right, previously to their interposition, of inquiring into the merits of the question in dispute, that they may form a judgment, whether there be sufficient ground, either in law or in equity, for awarding execution upon the decree." Ersk. B. 4, T. 3, § 4. This statement, however, must now be read with some modification since the passing of the Judgments Extension Acts, 31 & 32 Vict. c. 54, and 45 & 46 Vict. c. 31. See *Judicium semper*, &c.

Res litigiosa.—A subject which has been rendered litigious. See *In rebus*, &c.

Res meræ facultatis.—A matter of mere power; a mere faculty. Such, for example, is the right which a proprietor has of building upon his own property, or which any one has of walking upon the seashore, or sailing upon the sea, or on any navigable river. It is a right which may or may not be exercised at the pleasure of him who holds it; and such rights are never lost by their non-exercise for any length of time, because it is of their essential character that they may be used or exercised at any time. See *In iis quæ*, &c.

Res non est integra.—The matter is not entire or complete. See *Rebus integris*.

Res nullius.—A subject which is the property of no one. There are two distinct classes of subjects included in the name *res nullius*, those, namely—(1) which are in their original state, and have never had an owner; and those (2) which have belonged to some one who had lost or abandoned their possession. Subjects of the first class, such as pebbles on the seashore, wild animals, fish in the sea, &c., belong to the person who first finds or captures them, by the title of occupancy; but those of the second class, such as abandoned heritable rights, treasure trove (which consists of coin, gold, silver, plate, &c., hidden in the earth, the owner of which is unknown), belong to the sovereign. In England things found in the street or road and not hidden in the earth, belong to the finder; but with us in theory a different rule prevails; in practice, however, our rule is the same, the subject so found becoming the property of the finder, if, after due public inquiry by advertisement, &c., the owner cannot be found. But if property found on the street or highway be appropriated by the finder without any attempt being made on his part to discover the true owner, such appropriation constitutes the crime of theft. There is this difference to be observed between the right which an occupier has to that which had never been appropriated before being taken possession of by him, and the right which a finder has to a subject lost by its true owner, that the mere occupancy in the former case gives an indefeasible right to the subject occupied, while in the latter the true owner may recover his lost subject from the finder any time within the years of prescription. *Res nullius* among the Romans signified those subjects which were not and never could be the property of any one, such as things consecrated to God, temples, the ground on which they were built, burial-places, &c. See *Quod nullius*, &c.

Res perit suo domino.—A thing perishes to its owner. The meaning of this maxim is, that the loss consequent upon the deterioration or destruction of a subject must be borne by the owner, unless such loss has been occasioned by the fault of another. Thus, when a subject is hired out, any deterioration it may suffer, or its total loss, falls upon the owner and not upon the person hiring it, so long as the hirer uses it for the purposes for which it was hired, and (if not destroyed) returns it on the expiry of the stipulated period. All accidental loss falls upon the owner. In like manner goods committed to a common carrier for transit and delivery perish to their owner, if they are damaged or destroyed by storm, tempest, the Act of God, the Queen's enemies, &c.; but if they perish or are damaged through accidental fire, the carrier is responsible—the loss falls upon him. 19 & 20 Vict. c. 60, § 17. This maxim has been explained in the House of Lords to mean, that the interest which each has in a subject perishes to the *dominus* of that interest, as well as the corporeal thing to its *dominus*. *Bayne*, 3 Dow, 233.

Res publicæ.—Subjects belonging to the public; property of public right. Such are the seas, seashores, navigable rivers, highways, harbours, &c., which are exempted from commerce, and either belong to the public, or are vested in the sovereign for behoof of the community.

Res religiosæ.—Sacred things. Among the Romans any sepulchre or burial-place was regarded as sacred, and was exempted from commerce. With us the phrase includes all things which have been consecrated or set apart for the service of God, such as churches, communion-cups, &c.; and these are exempted from commerce, and cannot be applied to the uses of private property while they continue in that state. Under certain circumstances, they may, however, be disposed of, and others substituted for them; regarding which see Ersk. B. 2, T. 1, § 8. *Russell*, 10 R. 302.

Res singulorum.—The property of individuals.

Res sua.—One's own property.

Res sua nemini servit.—No one can have a servitude over his own property. The owner of a subject cannot have a servitude over it, because that, being a minor right, is merged in his paramount right of property, and all his acts in reference to the subject, or the uses to which he puts it, are attributed to this paramount right. So if the servient owner should acquire the dominant tenement, the servitude previously existing is extinguished *confusione;* and Erskine lays it down that "a servitude thus extinguished revives not, though the right of the two tenements should be again divided, unless the servitude be constituted *de novo.*" (B. 2, T. 9, § 37.) Bell objects to this doctrine as being too broadly stated, and observes "that if, in the exercise of the right, or otherwise, the owner has indicated no intention of extinguishing the servitude, it would, on separation of the tenements, revive." Bell's Prin. § 997.

Res universitatis.—Subjects belonging to a corporate body, such as a borough, a hospital, a university, &c., as opposed to *res singulorum*, the property of individuals.

Rescripta.—Rescripts. One of the kinds of imperial ordinances or constitutions under the civil law; by these the Emperor gave instructions for the decision of some case which had arisen, and which had been referred to him for instructions. See *Decreta*.

Reservatio ut et protestatio non facit jus sed tuetur.—Reservation and protest do not make a right, but protect it. In a feu-charter the superior generally reserves to himself the right to the minerals in the lands feued: such reservation does not give him the right to the minerals, which is already his at the date of the charter, but it protects that right to him, which without reservation would pass by the general conveyance of the lands to the vassal. Again, take the case of a riparian proprietor discharging offensive matter from his works into the stream so as to pollute it, and who, if allowed to do so uninterruptedly for forty years, would acquire a prescriptive right so to pollute the stream which could not be questioned: a lower heritor, entitled to interdict such pollution of the stream, but indisposed to enter upon a litigation at the time, may preserve his right to question and interdict the pollution of the stream by serving an instrument of interruption and protest on the person whose operations are objected to. Such an instrument does not confer the right upon the lower heritor to interdict the pollution of the stream—that right belongs to him as a lower heritor at common law—but it prevents the currency of prescription, and so protects his right.

Resoluto jure concedentis resolvitur concessum.—The right of the granter having ceased, the right granted determines. Or, as the maxim is sometimes expressed—

Resoluto jure dantis, resolvitur jus accipientis.—The right of the giver having ceased, or become void, the right of the receiver ceases also. The right of an assignee in the general case is only co-extensive with that of the cedent, and therefore any defect or limitation in the title of the former attaches to the title of the latter. So if a liferenter assigns the benefit of his liferent, on his death all the right of the assignee ceases, as the period of his life was the limit of the cedent's right. "Though a donation between man and wife," says Erskine (B. 1, T. 6, § 32), "is not null, yet the donee holds it under the tacit condition that it shall fall in the case of revocation; so that the donee's right continues pendent upon the donor's will during his life. The donee cannot therefore alienate the subject, nor charge it with any burden to the prejudice of the donor; and consequently the donor returns, upon his revocation, to the full property of the subject, free from the consequences of all the intermediate deeds granted by the donee, even to his creditors or singular successors." In such case the donee's right having ceased by revocation, all the rights he or she have granted *quoad* the donation also cease. Where also the right or title of the granter or disponer is reduced, the title of the disponee ceases

—the cedent's title being set aside, all rights flowing from him are necessarily regarded as proceeding *a non habente*, and invalid. But this maxim is generally applied to those cases where the right of the original granter was only of a temporary or defeasible nature.

Respondeat superior.—Let the master answer, or be responsible. According to this maxim a master is civilly responsible for the acts of his servant committed or done in the performance of his master's orders, or in the course of the ordinary employment for which he was engaged. The master's liability proceeds upon the ground that, as he has the selection of those admitted to his employment, he ought to be responsible for the results, if through want of due inquiry or otherwise, he selects an unfit or improper person. He is thus, as it were, only made responsible for his own want of care. The tendency of recent decisions has been to narrow the application of this rule: and a master is not now in every case held responsible (as he once was) for the injury inflicted by his servant upon a fellow-servant engaged in the same common employment. See *Qui facit*, &c.

Respondentia.—The name given to a security granted over the cargo contained in a ship for a loan advanced in contemplation of a particular voyage. It is of the same nature as bottomry, only in bottomry the security is granted over the ship itself. If the cargo perishes through the perils of the sea, or superior force of an enemy, the lender loses all claim for the repayment of his money; and in consideration of the risk thus undertaken he is allowed a higher rate of interest than usual, which is called *fœnus nauticum*, or marine interest.

Restitutio in integrum.—Entire restitution; restoration to one's former condition. A minor is entitled to entire restitution against all acts done by himself, or others on his behalf, during his minority, which have been to his lesion. The effect of such restitution is to place him in the same position *quoad* each particular transaction, as if it had never been entered into. This right must be judicially claimed by the minor, by challenging the deed or transaction complained of before the expiry of the *quadriennium*—the four years following his attaining majority—otherwise his claim to restitution is barred. Where a contract is entered into under essential error on the part of one or both of the contracting parties, the contract will be set aside, but only on restitution *in integrum* being made, and the parties restored to the same position in which they were before the contract was made. Thus if the contract was for the sale of land, and on the faith of the contract being a valid one the purchaser has proceeded to build upon or otherwise improve the estate, the seller can only have the contract set aside and the lands restored to him on making repayment to the purchaser of the price paid by him, with interest thereon, as well as of the whole sums expended by him on the improvement of the estate. *York Buildings Co.* v. *Mackenzie*, 3 Paton, 378, 579. *Gilmour* v. *Hart*, 3 R. 192.

Retenta possessione.—Possession being retained. A sale of moveables without delivery was formerly of no effect whatever in passing the property of the subject sold to the purchaser; but the absolute character of this rule was somewhat relaxed by the provisions of the Mercantile Law Amendment Act (1856). That Act has now been repealed, in so far as it affected the law of Sale, and property in things sold but not delivered, is held, in some circumstances, to pass to the buyer. 56 & 57 Vict. c. 71. The rule, however, still holds in the case of moveables assigned in security, but retained in the possession of the assigner. Such an assignation without delivery confers no preferential right on the assignee: the moveables so assigned but retained in the possession of the assigner are subject to the diligence of the assigner's creditors, and on his bankruptcy pass to his trustee. See *Dans et retinens*, &c.

Retractus feudalis.—A recall of the feu; or (as used in Erskine, B. 2, T. 12, § 27) more correctly, a repurchasing of the feu right. This was the privilege which a superior had of paying off the debt due to the appriser or adjudger of his vassals' lands, and taking a conveyance to the adjudication in his own favour. Where the debt exceeded the value of the lands, the superior was only bound to make payment to the extent of the value in return for the conveyance; and this privilege he could only exercise before the expiry of the legal. It is a privilege now unknown in practice.

Retro.—Backward. Some acts have, as regards their legal consequences, a retrospective effect. Thus the subsequent marriage of their parents has the legal effect of legitimating illegitimate children as from the date of their birth; the subsequent confirmation of a disponee's sasine who held upon an alternative holding, had the effect of confirming that sasine as from its own date; and where a disponer's title is invalid or defective at the time of granting the disposition, and is afterwards validated by a supervening right, that supervening right accrescing to the disponee validates his title as from the date of it being granted. All these are said in legal phraseology to operate *retro*.

Reus.—Defender or defendant. *Actor.*—Pursuer or plaintiff.

Rex non potest peccare.—The king can do no wrong. Broom, 52.

Rex nunquam moritur.—The sovereign never dies. See *Collegium*.

Rex statuit per commune concilium.—The king has enacted by his Common Council. Ersk. B. 1, T. 1, § 38.

Ripæ muniendæ causa.—For the purpose of fortifying or protecting the bank of the river. A navigable river being public property, no one is entitled so to build upon its banks as to obstruct the navigation, or the right of the public to walk there. But a riparian proprietor may build upon the bank, for the purpose of fortifying or protecting it, where a change in the channel from natural causes, threatening an encroachment on his lands, becomes imminent, or where, from a flood or otherwise, he has reason to apprehend damage to the banks and to his adjoining property. Even in such cases, however, his operations must not interfere with the navigation of the river, or obstruct the enjoyment of the public rights; nor is he entitled to make such erections as will divert the course of the stream in times of flood, or throw the same upon the lands of an opposite proprietor. The reader may compare the judgments pronounced in the cases of *Menzies* v. *E. of Breadalbane*, 3 W. & S. 235; and *Tennent* v. *E. of Glasgow*, 1 Macp. 133.

Rustica et urbana.—Rural and urban. Prædial servitudes are subjected to this division, rural and urban: the former including all the servitudes affecting the soil, although the land burdened should be situated in a city—such as right of way, pasture, aqueduct, &c.—and the latter, all servitudes affecting buildings, although they should be situated in the country—such as stillicide, *oneris ferendi*, &c.

S

Sacramenta puberum sunt servanda.—The oaths of minors are to be kept inviolate. On the principle of this maxim minors were barred, according to the rules of our older law, from challenging or repudiating any deed or transaction entered into or granted by them during their minority, which they had sworn never to call in question. As minors, however, could as easily be induced to ratify upon oath obligations undertaken by them to their lesion as they could be induced to grant them, this rule has long been abolished, and by the Act 1681, c. 19, the elicitors of such oaths were declared infamous. By that statute it was made competent to any kinsman of the minor to pursue an action for setting aside such transactions, lest the minor should be indisposed to sue for reduction in his own name of a deed or transaction which he had sworn never to question. The minor himself is the only person now entitled to sue such an action, unless he should die within the *quadriennium,* in which case the right of action transmits to his heir.

Salus populi suprema lex.—The welfare of the people (or, the public welfare) is the highest law. Private or individual rights and interests must always give place to the public welfare. So, where a railway or public road is to be made, the private rights of the owners of land over which it is to pass have to give way before the public advantage to be conferred by the new works. So also the house of a private proprietor may lawfully be destroyed or injured for the purpose of checking a fire which might otherwise spread to the injury of the town : the public welfare justifying what would otherwise be an illegal and unjustifiable interference with private property.

Salus reipublicæ suprema lex.—The welfare of the

State (or, the public welfare) is the highest law. This maxim is akin to the preceding maxim, and implies it. Wherever the interest of the State comes into conflict with the rights of individuals, the former must prevail and the latter yield. Where, for example, lands are needed on which to erect fortifications, bulwarks, breastworks, &c., for the preservation or defence of the kingdom against enemies, these lands must be yielded up by the private proprietor. Society is based upon the principle expressed by this maxim; the common weal is the first and highest consideration, on account of which, and the benefits thence arising, all individuals consent to the restriction of rights and liberties which otherwise might have belonged to and been enjoyed by them without restriction.

Salva substantia.—The substance being saved; the subject being preserved without being diminished. The right of a liferenter is only to the fruits, profits, or revenues of the subject liferented, and he cannot encroach upon the capital of the subject itself. He cannot do anything by which the subject may be endangered or deteriorated in value, except in so far as the deterioration may arise from the mere tear and wear of ordinary use to which his liferent entitles him. A right of liferent, therefore, cannot be constituted in a subject which necessarily perishes in the use; it must be a subject which can be used *salva substantia*.

Salvam fecit totius pignoris causam.—He furnished the means of saving the whole pledge, or subject on the security of which the loan was granted. (Bell's Prin. § 456.) It is upon this ground that the bottomry creditor whose bond is last in date is preferred to others holding bottomry bonds over the same ship, contrary to the ordinary rule *prior tempore potior jure*. To his loan is to be attributed the safety of the common subject of pledge; because, but for the money advanced by him, the ship would have been unable to prosecute and complete her voyage. He having thus afforded the means of preserving the pledge for the benefit of other creditors as well as himself, is preferred.

Salvo beneficio competentiæ.—Saving the benefit of a competence; the benefit of a competence being reserved. See *Beneficium competentiæ*.

Salvo jure cujuslibet.—Saving or reserving the right of all others. This was a saving clause formerly to be found in charters of confirmation, the effect of which was to reserve to the superior, and all others whomsoever, their rights in or concerning the lands confirmed, in so far as those rights might otherwise be prejudiced by the confirmation. In the case of *Forbes*, M. 6517, it was held in respect of this clause, that a superior, by granting confirmation, was not thereby precluded from the benefit of inhibition affecting the property which he had previously used. This clause did not, however, reserve the superior's right to casualties or duties due at the time of confirmation; these required to be expressly reserved, as the delivery of a charter by progress presumed the discharge of all prior casualties and duties. In almost all the later Scottish Parliaments the last Act of the session was generally one entitled *Act salvo jure cujuslibet*, the purpose of which was to secure the rights of third parties against the effects of private Acts or ratifications.

Sanæ mentis.—Of sound mind.

Sancire.—To confirm; to forbid under pain of punishment. "That part of the law which inflicts the punishment upon disobedience is called its *sanction*, from *sancire*, to confirm; because it is that which gives the enactment full force and authority, and chiefly preserves it from being violated by perverse men, who would disregard the true grounds of obedience." Ersk. B. 1, T. 1, § 5.

Sapiens naturam delicti.—Partaking of the character or nature of a delict.

Sciens et prudens.—Wittingly; in full knowledge. "If one who makes a gratuitous grant shall *sciens et prudens* (*i.e.*, in the full knowledge of what he is doing, intentionally), bind himself in absolute warrandice, he ought both in law and equity to be tied by his obligation." Ersk. B. 2, T. 3, § 27.

Scientia utrinque par pares contrahentes facit.—Equal knowledge on the part of both makes the contracting parties equal. Where a subject is sold, the purchaser having an opportunity of examining the subject, his eye is his merchant, and he cannot have the contract set aside on the ground of fault or defect where the defect is patent. But it is otherwise if the purchaser has no opportunity of examining the subject for himself, and buys on the representation of the seller. Where the defect is latent, the purchaser will not be barred from reducing the contract by the fact of personal examination, if the seller knew of the defect and concealed it; but if the seller was ignorant of the defect, and sold without warranty, the risk lies with the purchaser. Where both parties are equally aware of the defect, or equally ignorant of it—that is, in the words of the maxim, where the knowledge of both the contracting parties is equal regarding the subject of the contract, neither having in that respect an advantage over the other—the contract will stand whatever defects may afterwards be discovered; their equal knowledge puts them on a perfect equality, so that if the subject turns out of greater value than was supposed, the seller cannot claim restitution, or if it turns out to be less valuable, the buyer must bear the loss without redress.

Scintilla juris.—Spark of law. "I cannot see that there is even *scintilla juris* for such an opinion" (Hume, i. 455); that is, that there is not only no authority for the opinion, but no seeming authority, or appearance of law to support it. This phrase is used in English law to signify a doctrine of a very intricate and technical description which at one time obtained there in reference to the law of real property. With regard to this doctrine, it is sufficient to refer the reader to Wharton, *h. v.;* Stephen's Com. i. 368, note *u*; Williams on R. Prop. 307; Smith on R. and P. Prop. i. 266; and 23 & 24 Vict. cap. 38, § 7.

Scire debes cum quo contrahis.—You ought to know with whom you contract. See *Quisque scire,* &c.

Scire et scire debere æquiparantur in jure.—To know a thing, and to be bound to know it, are regarded in law as equivalent. Ignorance of the law does not excuse any violation of it, because every one is bound to know the law of the place where he resides; and this obligation to know is regarded as equivalent to actual knowledge. Thus an Englishman coming to Scotland and commencing business as a spirit-dealer would not be exempted from the penalties incurred by a violation of the Public Houses Act on the ground that no such law prevailed in England, and of his ignorance of its existence here. He is bound to know the law, and would be held as knowing it in any prosecution which might arise out of his violation of its provisions.

Scribere est agere.—To write is to do, or, to act. " For instance, although mere words spoken by an individual not relating to any treasonable act or design then in agitation do not amount to treason, since nothing can be more equivocal and ambiguous than words, yet words of advice and persuasion, and all consultations for the furtherance of traitorous plans, are certainly overt acts of treason ; and if the words be set down in writing, this writing, as arguing more deliberate intention, has been held to be an overt act of treason, on the principle that *scribere est agere.*" Broom, 312. See also Macdonald, 221.

Scripta litera manet.—A writing remains. See *Vox emissa,* &c.

Scripto.—By writing. A proof *scripto* is a proof by written documents. See observations on following phrase.

Scripto vel juramento.—By writ or oath. In some cases the law allows a party to prove his case only in this limited manner, by the writ or oath, namely, of his opponent. Thus a debt which has undergone the triennial prescription, can only be proved by the writ or oath of the alleged debtor ; the resting-owing of borrowed money can only be proved in like manner ; and the existence of an alleged trust, as in a question between the truster and the trustee, can only be proved (according to the provisions of the Act 1696, cap. 25) by the writ or oath of the latter.

Se defendendo.—In defending one's self ; in self-defence. Every one is entitled to defend his life in the way most likely to secure that end, whenever it is in danger through the violence of others. Even homicide is justifiable, and infers no punishment, where a person, in the necessary defence of his own life, kills one who has attacked him ; but, to justify such a proceeding, it is necessary to show that there was no other way of escape except by the death of the assailant. A woman is entitled, in defence of her chastity, to kill a man who attempts to commit a rape upon her, if there be no other way of escaping from the threatened violence.

Secundum allegata et probata.—According to that which

has been alleged and proved. The decision, in every case, must proceed upon the allegations of the parties, and the proof adduced in support of them, and not upon the private knowledge of the judge, however accurate and extensive that may be. A decision, which is not in terms of the conclusions of the action, may be overturned on review, or reduced upon that ground; and this holds especially in regard to decisions which award more than that concluded or prayed for. See *Judicis est judicare*, &c.

Secundum bonum et æquum.—According to that which is good and equitable.

Secundum chartam conficiendam.—According to a charter to be granted. See *Secundum tenorem*, &c.

Secundum legem domicilii, vel loci contractus.—According to the law of the domicile, or of the place where the contract was entered into. See *Lex domicilii. Lex loci*, &c.

Secundum materiam subjectam —According to the subject-matter.

Secundum tenorem chartæ confectæ.—According to the tenor of a charter already granted. In the earlier stages of feudal conveyancing the vassal was most generally infeft upon a precept granted by the superior for that purpose, before the charter was executed which conveyed the lands. In such case the precept of sasine or possession bore to be "according to the terms of a charter to be granted;" and such precept was of itself a valid title when followed by possession. Where the precept of sasine was granted with reference to a prior charter of the lands, it bore, in the words of the phrase, to be " according to the tenor of a charter already granted." See Duff's Feud. Con. 43.

Secundum vires hereditatis.—According to the extent of the succession; that is, the value of the estate succeeded to. The liability of an heir for the performance of his ancestor's obligations and payment of his ancestor's debts was not, formerly, measured by the extent of the succession, if he entered as heir simply, and without adopting any of the modes prescribed in law by which his liability might be limited. If the heir entered upon the succession generally as heir, he was liable for the whole of his ancestor's debts and obligations, however inadequate his ancestor's estate might be to meet them; but he could restrict his liability by serving heir with the benefit of specification. This rule as to an heir's liability was altered by the Act 37 & 38 Vict. c. 94, which provided (§ 12) that an heir should not be liable for the debts of his ancestor beyond the value of the estate to which he had succeeded; and that if the heir intromitted with the ancestor's estate, and afterwards renounced the succession, he should only be liable for the ancestor's debts to the extent of such intromission.

Secundum vires inventarii.—According to the extent of the inventory. An executor who makes up his title to a deceased person in the usual form, and gives up an inventory of the whole of the deceased's moveable estate to the commissary, is only liable for the deceased's debts to the extent of the value of the estate so given up. But where an executor intromits with the moveables of the deceased without a title, he renders himself liable *in solidum* for the deceased's debts, however these may exceed the value of the deceased's moveable estate. See *Beneficium inventarii*.

Sed quære.—But inquire; or, look into the matter. This phrase is used to indicate a doubt of the soundness of a doctrine laid down, or decision cited, and to suggest the propriety of further consideration of it, before accepting it as conclusive or sound.

Sede vacante.—The benefice being vacant. Stair, B. 4, T. 24, § 7.

Semel baro semper baro.—Once a baron, always a baron. To entitle an heir to claim heirship-moveables (a right which is now abolished), it was necessary that his ancestor should, at the time of his death, have been a baron, a burgess, or a prelate; every one being considered a baron in this matter who, at his death, was vest and seised in lands, houses, or annual rents furth of land not being a mere liferent. If the ancestor was infeft during his life, the presumption, as expressed in the phrase, was that he was undenuded, and therefore a baron at the time of his death, and that heirship-moveables were consequently due to the heir. The effect of this presumption was to throw the burden of proving on the person opposing the heir's claim; but it could be elided by a contrary proof.

Semel civis semper civis.—Once a burgess always a burgess. This was not presumed, and therefore it lay upon the heir claiming heirship-moveables, on the ground of his ancestor being a burgess, to prove that he was so at the time of his death.

Semel prelatus semper prelatus.—Once a prelate always a prelate. See observations on preceding phrase, which apply also to this.

Semiplena probatio.—A half proof. In actions of filiation, a pursuer was formerly entitled, on adducing a *semiplena probatio*, to her oath in supplement to prove that the defender was the father of her child. A *semiplena probatio* was such a proof as induced, not merely a suspicion, but a reasonable belief that the pursuer's case was well-founded, and consisted generally of a proof of opportunity for connection, acts of familiarity on the part of the defender towards the pursuer, &c. ; in addition to this, the pursuer was entitled, as already mentioned, to her oath in supplement to complete her proof, because in such cases it was rarely possible to obtain direct evidence of the alleged connection, except from the woman herself. The leading case on this point is that of *Craig*, 14th June, 1809, F. C. This kind of proof is not now recognised, since the pursuer in such an action, under the recent Evidence Acts, is entitled to adduce herself as a witness in support of her own case ; and, in judging of the proof, the Court will not consider whether, without the woman's own evidence, there is what would formerly have been held a *semiplena probatio*, completed by the woman's oath, but will decide upon the whole case as presented by the record and proof, as they would in any other kind of action. *M'Bayne*, 22 D. 738 ; *Young*, 20 R. 768.

Semper in dubiis benigniora præferenda.—In doubtful matters the more liberal view is always to be preferred. This is a rule of construction, and as applied to deeds, it imports, that where the words used are doubtful or ambiguous, the most liberal interpretation is to be given to them, so as to carry out what from the deed itself appears to have been the intention of the maker of it. See *Benignior sententia*, &c. But the maxim has a wider application than in the construction of deeds : it applies, as a general rule, where doubt exists, whether that doubt concerns the meaning of a word, the intention with which an act was done, or the guilt or innocence of an accused. In all cases of doubt, the preference is to be given to the most liberal and charitable view which the words, act, or circumstances will admit of. It is in the application of this maxim that an accused always obtains the benefit of a doubt concerning his alleged guilt.

Semper in obscuris quod minimum est sequimur.—In matters which are obscure (doubtful, or ambiguous), we follow that which is least ; or, we adopt that interpretation which is least doubtful. In construing deeds or statutes, where ambiguity or obscurity exists in the language used, that interpretation is adopted which accords most with the general scope and purpose of the Act or deed. The obscurity is diminished by the light so afforded, and is thus less obscure than an interpretation which derives no such aid.

Semper præsumitur pro negante.—The presumption is always in favour of the person denying. When a defender denies the allegations of a pursuer, the presumption is in his favour to the effect of requiring the pursuer to prove his averments ; and when an accused pleads not guilty, the presumption is in favour of his defence until the prosecutor proves the charge made. The presumption goes no further than laying the *onus probandi* upon the person affirming. See *Affirmanti incumbit*, &c.

Semper pro legitimatione præsumitur.—The presumption is always in favour of legitimacy. See *Præsumitur pro legitimatione*.

Semper specialia generalibus insunt.—Special things are always included in general. A general conveyance by a testator of his whole estate includes every special or individual asset of which he is possessed or to which he is entitled : a conveyance of land in general terms includes all the special rights pertaining to the ownership of that land, although not specially enumerated ; and a general prohibition of any act or class of acts includes every mode by which that act may be performed or brought about.

But when the special rights or acts are enumerated, such special enumeration may derogate from the generality of the conveyance or prohibition. See *Generalia specialibus,* &c.

Senatus-consultum.—A resolution of the Roman senate, having the force of law, and forming one of the great sources of the civil law. There is a difference of opinion among historical writers as to whether the Senate had the power of directly enacting laws during the period of the Republic; but there is no question that they exercised this power in the time of the Emperors. Justinian, in his Institutes (B. 1, T. 2, § 5), states as the reason why this power was conferred, that "when the Roman people was so increased that it was difficult to assemble them together to pass laws, it seemed right that the Senate should be consulted in the place of the people." Regarding the historical controversy above alluded to, reference may be made to Smith's Dict., *h. v.*

Sententia contra matrimonium nunquam transit in rem judicatam.—A judgment against marriage never passes into a final determination of the question: a sentence against marriage never acquires the force of a *res judicata.* This maxim does not express a rule of Scotch law: a judgment pronounced upon a question of marriage is as much *res judicata* as any other judgment. If A brings a declarator of marriage against B, the decision of that action is a final determination of the question between them as to whether there was or was not a marriage. Such a decision would not, however, prevent the children of the alleged marriage subsequently raising the question of their legitimacy, and endeavouring to establish it on the ground that the marriage really took place. The former decision would not be *res judicata* against them, but that proceeds upon the ground that they were not parties to the preceding action of declarator, and not upon the rule expressed by the maxim.

Sententia contra minorem indefensum lata nulla est.—A decision pronounced against an undefended minor is null. Where a minor is without a curator he is said to be undefended, even although he should appear in the cause and defend it for himself. In such a case, it is the interest of the party pursuing to have a curator *ad litem* appointed to the minor, as otherwise any decree obtained against him is reducible on the principle of this maxim. A decree obtained against a minor upon an edictal citation of tutors and curators was reduced, he having had no tutors and curators, and a curator *ad litem* not having been appointed. *Bannatyne,* 14th Dec., 1814, F. C.

Sententia interlocutoria revocari potest, definitiva non potest.—An interlocutory judgment may be recalled, a definitive judgment cannot. As a rule, judges cannot recall or review any judgment pronounced by themselves. But a distinction is drawn between judgments which are merely interlocutory and those which definitely determine any question submitted for their decision : the former may be recalled by the judge pronouncing them, the latter cannot. Thus, a judge may recall an interlocutor sisting process, for that is purely interlocutory, while he cannot recall an interlocutor decerning against the defender as libelled, ordaining the defender to find caution, &c. ; for these are *quoad* him definitive upon the question so decided.

Sententia voluntatis.—The purpose or determination of the will. This is the chief thing to be considered in the interpretation of testamentary writings, namely, the purpose or intention of the testator in executing the deed.

Separatim.—Separately ; apart from anything already advanced or pleaded.

Separatio tori.—A separation as to the marriage-bed. This was all that was allowed to the injured spouse in cases of adultery by the canon law, for marriage being regarded by it as a sacrament, was indissoluble. See *A mensa,* &c.

Separatum tenementum.—A separate tenement ; a subject held on a distinct title appertaining to itself. Stair, B. 2, T. 3, § 26.

Seriatim.—One by one ; one after the other.

Series rerum judicatarum.—A succession of decisions deciding some particular principle. A single decision is not regarded as definitely settling the principle enunciated in it, and may be gone back upon and reversed. But when a principle has been established or recognised by a succession of decisions, it becomes properly a precedent which will not be disturbed. Uniformity and consistency of decision with regard to the same principle can alone give certainty; and certainty is of more importance than the consideration whether the rule determined was, at the first, the most convenient, or even the most just, abstractly considered. "It must be remembered that the rules which govern the transmission of property are the creatures of positive law, and that when once established and recognised, their justice or injustice in the abstract is of less importance to the community than that the rules themselves shall be constant and invariable." Per Lord Chan. Westbury in *Ralston* v. *Hamilton*, 4 Macq. 405. At the same time, a rule supported by a *series judicatarum* may be upset, if the rule is found to be contrary to law.

Sermo index animi.—Language is the index of the purpose; expression indicates intention.

Servate terminos quos patres vestri posuere.—Preserve (or observe) the boundaries or landmarks which your fathers have placed. This was the answer given by Lord Pitfour to the doubt raised whether there was any good reason for giving a husband a right of courtesy in his wife's heritage acquired by succession and not in that acquired by conquest. He was of opinion that there was no good reason for the distinction, but agreed that it was a fixed point not to be touched. (Bell's Com. i. 60.) (The phrase is quoted, but not quite accurately, from the Vulgate, Prov. xxii. 28.) That landmark has now been removed by the abolition of the distinction between heritage and conquest. 37 & 38 Vict. c. 94, § 37.

Servitia solita et consueta.—Services used and wont. This was at one time the common return made by vassals to their superiors for lands granted to them; and where special services were not specified, the words of the phrase implied military services.

Servitii præstatio.—The performance of services.

Si aliquid sapit.—If he knows anything; if he is not altogether void of reason. Ersk. B. 1, T. 7, § 48.

Si antecedit ictum licet non congressum.—If it precedes the blow, although not actually joined or connected with it. In treating of the malice necessary to constitute murder, Hume points out, in the words of this phrase, that it is not necessary that the malice or wicked purpose should be conceived at the moment the fatal blow is struck, but is sufficient to constitute the capital offence if it has been entertained at any time prior to the blow : it is not necessary that the malice and blow should meet at the same time, or be almost simultaneous, but only that the malice should have existed, even if it should be of old date. Hume, i. 254.

Si constet de persona.—If it be clear or certain who is the person meant. See *Falsa demonstratio*, &c.

Si deprehendatur.—If captured or apprehended.

Si deventum sit ad actum maleficio proximum.—If it approaches an act bordering upon crime ; or, if the act has gone so far as just to fall short of crime. Sir George Mackenzie, in his Treatise on Criminal Law (Part 1, T. 1, § 4), lays it down that an attempt to commit a crime, if it borders on or approaches near to the crime itself, should be punished as severely as if the crime had been perpetrated ; because such attempt is a lesser degree of that very crime to which it so nearly approaches, and because the state cannot be otherwise secure from the person who has evinced such a wicked and mischievous disposition. Mere attempt to commit a certain crime, although still punishable with us, rarely *per se* forms the subject of an indictment, but it is frequently libelled as an aggravation. The attempt to commit murder by the discharge of loaded fire-arms is sometimes libelled as a substantive charge ; and by statute (10 Geo. IV. c. 38) it is rendered a capital offence, but the prosecutor has the power of restricting the pains of law. In Scotland, capital punishment is now only inflicted for murder, but in England the capital sentence for attempting to commit murder was carried into execution so lately as in the case of *Martin Doyle*, who was executed for that crime at Chester, on 27th August, 1861.

Si duo in testamento pugnantia reperiuntur ultimum est ratum.—If two clauses (or provisions) are found in a will inconsistent with each other, the last is sustained. See *Cum duo inter se*, &c.

Si ingratum dixeris omnia dixeris.—If you affirm that one is ungrateful, in that you include every charge. Ingratitude was recognised among the Romans as a good and sufficient ground for revoking a donation *inter vivos ;* and some writers on the feudal law, it would appear from Stair (B. 2, T. 11, § 9), have maintained that ingratitude was a sufficient ground to warrant the superior in revoking his grant, and taking possession of the lands,—an opinion with which Stair does not agree.

Si institutus sine liberis decesserit.—If the institute should die without issue. See *Si sine liberis,* &c.

Si malitia suppleat ætatem.—If malice supplies the want of age. This phrase occurs in Ersk. B. 1, T. 6, § 2, where, in treating of the invalidity of a marriage entered into by pupils, he says: "The canon law, indeed, affirms that a pupil may enter into marriage where there is an ability to procreate or conceive; or, as it is expressed by some doctors, *si malitia suppleat ætatem.*" This rendering of *malitia* is not common. For an explanation of the most usual application of the phrase, see *Malitia supplet,* &c.

Si minor se majorem dixerit.—If the minor has said that he is major. "Restitution (on the ground of minority and lesion) is excluded *si minor se majorem dixerit,* as where the minor's bond bore expressly that he is major, and the creditor knew not he was minor by his aspect or otherwise, nor did fraudulently induce him to insert his majority." Stair, B. 1, T. 6, § 44. See *Majorennitati,* &c.

Si non jure seminis, saltem jure soli.—If not by right of seed, at least by right of soil: if not as sower of the seed, at least as proprietor of the soil. Fraser, Par. & Ch. 2.

Si parcere ei sine suo periculo non potest.—If he could not spare him except at his own peril, or, at the risk of his own life. Hume, i. 220.

Si petatur tantum.—If asked only. In blench holdings, where the return for the lands is generally elusory, that return is for the most part due and payable *si petatur tantum;* and this clause, by universal practice, has been interpreted to mean, if asked only within the year (*si petatur intra annum*). If the duty is not demanded within the year, the vassal is not liable for it. Such elusory duties are in themselves of no value, but they reserve the superior's rights to the casualty of relief, and the rights which now take the place of the casualty of non-entry.

Si quidem in nomine cognomine prænomine legatarii testator erraverit cum de persona constat nihilominus valet legatum.—If a testator has made an error in the name or title of the legatee, the legacy will nevertheless be valid if it appear clearly who was the person meant. See *Falsa demonstratio*, &c., and *Constat de persona*. The words *nomen, cognomen,* and *prænomen* used in the maxim, are used merely to show that it makes no difference in what part of the name or title the error occurs,—the effect is the same, if it be an error which still leaves no doubt as to the person intended to be benefited. Among the Romans the *nomen* was the name of the individual, the *cognomen* the name of his family, and the *prænomen* the name also belonging to the individual, but placed before the *nomen*. Thus Marcus Tullius Cicero : Tullius is the *nomen*, Cicero the *cognomen*, and Marcus the *prænomen*. The *prænomen* included also any title which preceded the name, as *Imperator*.

Si sine liberis decesserit.—If he shall have died without children. This is an implied condition, borrowed from the civil law, which, in certain cases, our law holds as attached to *mortis causa* dispositions of moveable or heritable estate, conveying such estate beyond the disponer's own children. If at the time of executing the conveyance the granter should have no children, but after his death a posthumous child should be born to him, the conveyance will be ineffectual to carry the succession past the child, in whose favour it is presumed a new conveyance would have been granted had its father survived. The same presumption holds where a father conveys to his child, whom failing, to a stranger, if the child should die leaving lawful issue ; for in that case the child's issue would succeed, to the exclusion of the stranger substitute. If, however, the conveyance being granted, and a child thereafter born to him, the granter should survive the birth of his child a considerable time without revoking this conveyance, or executing a new one, the presumption will not hold ; and in any case, the presumption may be redargued by proof. The presumption in favour of the child is always stronger where the conveyance is not merely a partial conveyance of the estate, but a universal settlement. See the case of *Elder*, 31 Scot. L. R. 594; and also M'Laren, i. 257 *et seq.*

Si sit admodum grave.—If it be very heinous. Hume, i. 86.

Si sit incompos mentis, fatuus et naturaliter idiota.—If he is of unsound mind, fatuous, and naturally an idiot. This is the inquiry which the jury have to answer from the evidence laid before them under a brieve of idiotry. Ersk. B. 1, T. 7, § 50.

Si sit incompos mentis, prodigus, et furiosus, viz., qui nec tempus nec modum impensarum habet, sed bona dilacerando profundit.—If he is of unsound mind, wasteful, and furious (*i.e.*, mad)—viz., one who has no regard to the seasonableness or measure of his expenditure, but squanders his estate foolishly. This is the inquiry addressed to the jury in a brieve of furiosity. See Ersk. *ut supra.*

Si sit legitimæ ætatis.—If he is of lawful age. Ersk. *ut supra.*

Si vidua manserit et non nupserit.—If she should remain a widow and not marry. It is not illegal to stipulate that a widow's provision should cease or be restricted in the event of her entering into a subsequent marriage. M'Laren, i. 589. See *Conditio illicita*, &c.

Sibi imputet.—Let it be imputed to himself. In treating of the liability of cautioners, Erskine uses this phrase in reference to the cases where, and as the reason why, the cautioner still remains bound, although the principal debtor may go free of his obligation—" Thus a cautioner in an obligation, where the debtor's subscription is not legally attested, or a cautioner for a married woman, or for a minor acting without his curators, is properly obliged, though the debtor himself should get free, by pleading the statutory nullity, or his own legal incapacity. The reason of this is obvious : *sibi imputet* (*i.e.*, let it be imputed to himself as the consequence of his own act—let him blame himself), who interposed in such a case. As the cautioner is presumed to know the debtor's condition, the plain language of his engagement is, that if the debtor take the benefit of the law, he, the cautioner, shall make good the debt." B. 3, T. 3, § 64.

Sibi invigilare.—To watch for themselves; to be careful of their own interest. Stair, B. 3, T. 3, § 20.

Sic utere tuo ut alienum non lædas.—So use your own property as not to injure that of another. This maxim of the civil law contains the only restriction laid upon the otherwise unlimited right which a proprietor has of using his property according to his own pleasure. Even where the use to which a proprietor puts his subject is injurious to his neighbour, yet if it be for his own advantage, and not merely a wanton or malicious act intended to injure, such use cannot be interfered with, for *utitur suo jure*. But, on the other hand, an act of a proprietor done *in æmulationem vicini*, may be interdicted.

Silva cædua.—This is the name given "to a wood, which, on being cut, stoles out again for another cutting, so as, by proper management, to yield a yearly profit" (Bell's Dict. v. *Sylva*). A liferenter, who has no right to cut down the timber on the estate liferented, even where it has been planted by himself, is entitled to the *silva cædua*, because that is regarded as a part, not of the estate itself, but of its revenue or profits.

Simplex commendatio non obligat.—A mere recommendation does not bind—*i.e.*, does not infer an obligation. Where goods are sold by sample, or without the buyer seeing any of the goods which he purchases, he is entitled to rely upon the statements of the seller as to the character and quality, and he will be entitled to repudiate the transaction, or claim damages, if the seller's statements should be false, or calculated to deceive. But where the goods are inspected by the buyer, he has no such remedy; for in that case his eye is his merchant, and he is bound to satisfy himself. In the latter case, the mere commendation of the seller of the goods he is disposing of, or boastful representations of their quality or value, infers no obligation or warrandice that they are what he represents them to be (Bell's Prin. § 111), and the buyer can only claim compensation, or resile from his contract, where the defect, subsequently discovered, was one in the knowledge of the seller at the time, and one which he, the buyer, could not have discovered from careful inspection. This maxim may also be taken as expressing one of the rules of law concerning guarantees. A mere letter of introduction, or one conceived in general terms, recommending a certain person as worthy of confidence, and to whom credit in mercantile transactions may be safely given, is regarded as a mere recommendation, not inferring any liability as against the person writing such a letter. But when it goes beyond this, and specifies a sum as the limit to which credit may be given, " or when it applies specially to a transaction, or dealing, or course of dealing, in which credit is necessary, and is accompanied by an assurance of safety, it will be held as a guarantee." Bell's Prin. § 280; Bell's Com. i. 389. See *Dolus*.

Simul et semel.—At one and the same time.

Sine animo remanendi. — Without the intention of remaining. Said of a person who has left the country temporarily, and intending to return; as exemplified in the case of a sailor entering upon a foreign voyage, but without the intention of remaining in the foreign country.

Sine animo revertendi. — Without the intention of returning. Said of a person who has left this country with the intention of settling in another.

Sine cura et cultura. — Without care and culture. Natural fruits, which grow without the care or culture of man, pass as pertinents of the land to the purchaser, although not mentioned in the conveyance; not so industrial fruits, which, being the result in some measure of artificial or human labour, require to be specially conveyed.

Sine decreto.—Without a decree. Ersk. B. 1, T. 7, § 17.

Sine fraude. — Without fraud; honestly; in good faith.

Sine pacto.—Without a bargain or agreement.

Sine quibus funus honeste duci non potest.—Without which the funeral cannot be decently conducted. All expenditure for such things as are necessary to the decent and becoming interment of a deceased person are included under the term funeral charges or expenses, and form a preferable claim upon the deceased's moveable estate. Such charges, of course, vary according to the rank and circumstances of the deceased.

Sine quo non.—Without whom nothing can be effectually done. In appointing trustees for carrying out the testamentary purposes of his settlement, a testator sometimes appoints one of his trustees to be a trustee *sine quo non*. The effect of this is, that if the trustee so named should die, or decline to accept, the nomination falls; without him there can be no trust. Where such trustee accepts the office, his concurrence is essentially necessary to every act of the trustees under the trust, so as to make it valid and effectual. But if the trustee is declared by the testator to be a *sine quo non* during his survivance, the effect is somewhat different; for while, in the event of his non-acceptance, the whole nomination falls, yet if he accept and afterwards die, the other trustees may validly fulfil the purposes of the trust. The same rules apply to the nomination of tutors or curators and the like, where any one of the nominees is named *sine quo non*.

Sine vi aut dolo.—Without force or fraud.

Singuli in solidum.—Each for the whole. Where there are several co-obligants in one obligation, each bound in full performance, they are said to be liable *singuli in solidum*; and where each is liable only for his own proportion of the debt, they are said to be liable *pro rata*. See *In solidum. Pro rata*.

Sive tota res evincatur sive pars habet regressum emptor in venditorem.—Where the subject sold has been evicted in whole or in part, the purchaser has recourse against the seller. In all sales the seller gives an implied warranty of his title; and if the subject be subsequently evicted from the purchaser *ex defectu juris*, the purchaser has recourse for the loss thereby sustained against the seller, and that whether the eviction has been entire or partial. Bell's Prin. § 121-22. A seller may protect himself against such recourse by expressly stipulating that he shall not be responsible for such eviction, or by only granting simple warrandice, that is, against his own future act or deed.

Societas.—The contract of society or partnership.

Socii.—Partners; associates.

Socius criminis.—An associate or accomplice in the commission of a crime. Complicity involves the same punishment as actual commission. A *socius* is a competent witness for the Crown; and the seemingly least guilty of the culprits is sometimes taken in this character where there is not sufficient evidence without his testimony to lead to a conviction.

Socius mei socii meus socius non est.—The partner of my partner is not my partner. If A and B are partners in one concern, and B and C are partners in another, A and C are not partners, although they are both partners of B.

Sola superviventia.—By mere survivance. There are some rights which require no legal process to confer them upon those who succeed to them, but which vest by mere survivance: such, for example, are the rights to titles of dignity descending to a son, a widow's *jus relictæ*, children's legitim, &c., which require neither service nor confirmation. Leases, which are heritable, vest in the heir without service; and by the Act 37 & 38 Vict. c. 94, § 9, a personal right to heritable estate descendible to heirs vests in the heir entitled to succeed by mere survivance.

Solatium.—Compensation; indemnification. This word indicates the compensation given by the law for injury done to the feelings of any one; while *damages* generally signifies the compensation awarded for pecuniary loss sustained, or bodily injury inflicted. Thus where a man has been killed through the fault or negligence of another, the widow and children of the deceased are entitled, not only to damages on account of his death, and consequent removal of the pecuniary support he afforded, but also to *solatium* on account of their wounded feelings. *Solatium* was given even where "the death of the sufferer, instead of being a loss to his family, might be regarded as a benefit, on account of his bankruptcy and dissipated habits." *Brown*, 26th February, 1813, F. C.

Solertia.—Shrewdness; craftiness. See *Dolus*.

Solo animo.—By a mere act of the mind; by mere intention or design. The law takes no cognisance of that which is merely mental or intentional, until the design or intention finds expression in some overt act. Thus the mere intention of acquiring a domicile does not constitute one unless the intention be followed by actual residence; nor does the intention to commit theft subject the person so intending to punishment, unless it be followed by the act of felonious appropriation.

Solus cum sola in loco suspecto.—A man alone with a woman in a suspicious place, or in suspicious circumstances.

Spe numerandæ pecuniæ.—In the hope or expectation of the money being paid. Where one grants an obligation in the expectation of being paid the money in return for which it is granted, but does not receive it, he may resist any action founded upon that obligation by the *exceptio non numeratæ pecuniæ*. So, also, where one delivers a conveyance which acknowledges receipt of the consideration price, and discharges the disponee, this does not exclude his action for the price, if the disponee, on receiving delivery, refuses payment; the disponee is still liable *ex dolo*, the deed having been delivered *spe numerandæ pecuniæ*.

Specialia generalibus derogant. — Special provisions derogate from general. See *Generalia specialibus*, &c.

Species facti.—The particular character of the thing done. The peculiar circumstances attending any act or transaction are termed the *species facti*. Thus in libelling a theft, the public prosecutor avers that the prisoner, on a certain day and at a specified place, feloniously appropriated a certain thing then in the lawful possession of a certain person; and that (where the crime is aggravated by housebreaking) he did so by entering a house in a certain specified manner. Or in libelling a murder, he must aver the time, place, and manner in which the crime was perpetrated, as by assaulting the deceased with a lethal weapon, by administering a certain poison, &c. These constitute the *species facti* of the crime. Again, in a civil action for damages on account of slander, the pursuer must state the slanderous words used by the defender, as well as the place where, and the persons in presence of or to whom, they were used. Such allegations constitute the *species facti* on which the action is founded.

Spes obligationis.—The hope or expectancy of an obligation yet to emerge. Conditional obligations are not prestable until the condition be purified; but though that should not happen during the creditor's life, the right under the obligation descends to his heir, who may claim performance after the condition has been purified. The heir, in such a case, succeeds to a *spes obligationis;* a *spes* because the condition may be purified, and only a *spes* because it may not. Children who have rights under the marriage-contract of their parents of which they cannot be defeated, are to a certain effect creditors of their father, from whom their right flowed, and upon whom the obligation of making good such rights or claims is imposed. " But the term creditors, as applied to them, has been condemned as improper ; and a happier definition of a right, which has no analogy in law, has been found in designating it a *spes successionis in obligatione,* as contradistinguished from the ordinary right granted by a simple conveyance of a *spes successionis in destinatione."* Fraser, ii. 1406.

Spes recuperandi.—The hope of recovery ; or, the hope of regaining possession.

Spes successionis.—The hope or expectancy of a succession. Any one who has a right to succeed to certain lands, either from his natural position or from the terms of a deed, but whose right, at same time, is one which may be defeated, is said to have a *spes successionis.* Thus the eldest son of a landed proprietor has the hope of succeeding to his father's estate, and will succeed unless his expectation is defeated by his father's act ; and so, also, a substitute called to a succession under a simple destination, has the hope or expectancy of succeeding, but merely the hope, since the institute may defeat it by altering the course of the succession. Such a *spes* may, by our law, form the subject of a sale ; but it cannot be adjudged, nor is it carried by the bankruptcy of the person having the *spes* to the trustee on his estates for behoof of his general creditors. *Trappes* v. *Meredith,* 10 Macp. 38. *Reid* v. *Morison,* 20 R. 510. See *Pactum corvinum,* &c.

Spes successionis in destinatione.—A hope of succession under a destination.

Spes successionis in obligatione.—A hope of succeeding to a right under an obligation now existing.

Spoliatus ante omnia restituendus.—A man despoiled is to be restored to his possession first of all ; a maxim importing that spuilzied goods must be restored before any discussion takes place as to who is the rightful owner of them. No one is entitled by violence to possess himself of that even which is his own, so long as it is in the lawful possession of another. Any one so dispossessed may recover the subject on proving that he was in the lawful possession of it, and the allegation of a preferable right on the part of the true owner, although instantly verified, will not be received as a sufficient answer to the demand for restitution. In such an action the subject must *ante omnia* be restored to the person from whose possession it was violently taken, and the condition of parties being thus restored, they may have the question of their respective rights discussed and settled.

Spoliatus debet ante omnia restitui.—A person despoiled ought to be restored (to his former condition of possession) first of all. Another form of the preceding maxim.

Spondeat superior.—Let the master answer or be responsible. See *Respondeat*, &c.

Spondet peritiam artis, et imperitia culpæ enumeratur.—He is responsible for skill in his profession, and want of such skill is regarded as a fault. Where one employs skilled labour, such as the services of a physician or lawyer, he is entitled to rely on the person so employed having and exercising ordinary skill; the person so employed professes to possess, and is responsible for such skill, and the want of it is regarded as a fault which subjects him in damages for whatever consequences may arise from his deficiency. See *Imperitia*, &c.

Sponsalia de futuro.—A promise or engagement to marry; betrothal. Such promises to enter into a marriage at a day still future constitute no binding tie between the parties. Either may resile from the engagement, although, in the general case, the party doing so subjects himself in damages on account of breach of promise.

Sponsiones ludicræ.—Literally, obligations come under in jest; obligations by which the parties did not seriously intend to bind themselves. This name is given in our law to all obligations incurred by betting, gaming, &c., which are void at common law, and sustain no action.

Sponte.—Spontaneously. Natural fruits are said to spring up *sponte*, in contradistinction to industrial fruits, which are the result of care and culture bestowed upon them.

Spreta authoritate judicis.—The authority of the judge being disregarded ; in despite of the authority of the judge. Stair, B. 1, T. 9, § 21.

Spreta inhibitione.—In contempt of an inhibition ; in disregard of an inhibition.

Spurii.—Bastards. The civil law distinguished between *naturales*, who were illegitimate children sprung from a marriage not considered lawful, or from concubinage as recognised by the law ; and *spurii* (or *vulgo concepti*, as they are sometimes termed) who were the offspring of illicit intercourse. *Legitimi* were the children born of a lawful marriage.

Squalor carceris.—" This term means merely the strictness of imprisonment which a creditor is entitled to enforce with the view of compelling the debtor to pay the debt, or disclose any funds which he may have concealed. It does not imply (as it did with the ancient churchmen, from whom the term is derived) anything loathsome or unhealthy in the imprisonment in Scotland, which is indeed less close than in England." Bell's Dict. *h. v.*

Squalor morbi.—The dregs of disease. Stair, B. 3, T. 4, § 28.

Stabit præsumptio donec probetur in contrarium.—The presumption will stand until the contrary is proved. A general rule, importing that any one in whose favour there is a presumption will get the benefit of it until the presumption has been redargued by a contrary proof.

Stante matrimonio.—The marriage being still extant ; during the subsistence of the marriage. The personal obligations entered into by a married woman during the subsistence of the marriage are not binding upon herself, nor can she be subjected to personal diligence thereon during that period.

Stare decisis.—To stand upon decisions ; to abide by precedents.

Stare enim religioni debet.—For he ought to abide by his solemn obligation or undertaking : he is bound to abide by the oath. In the passage in Hume (i. 373) from which this phrase is taken, the author is dealing with the question of perjury committed under a reference to oath of party :

which perjury, although proved, does not affect the general rule that what a party swears on reference must, so far as that case is concerned, be taken as true. The party referring is bound to abide by the quasi-contract involved in a reference, that whatever is sworn shall be regarded as decisive. The use of *religio* in this sense is rare; it has been translated here " obligation," because that word expresses the meaning which attaches to it in the phrase; and this translation has some warrant in the fact that many scholars are of opinion that *religio* comes from the root *ligare*, to bind.

Status.—Position; condition; rank. By the subsequent marriage of its parents, an illegitimate child acquires the *status* of legitimacy.

Stillicidium.—Stillicide; being that servitude by which a servient owner is obliged to receive on his property the eavesdrop which falls from the dominant owner's house. When the water does not fall in scattered drops, but is collected on the house in a spout, and so discharged upon the servient tenement, the servitude is called *flumen*.

Stilus curiæ.—The form of court; a matter of legal form, and not essential. Stair, B. 3, T. 3, § 22.

Stipulatio.—Stipulation; the mode by which, under the civil law, a verbal obligation was constituted. It consisted of a question by which one of the contracting parties (called the stipulator) asked the other whether he would promise to give or do something, and of the answer of the other party (who was called the promissor) that he did so promise. The following example of a stipulation will illustrate this:— *Quinque aureos dare spondes?* (Do you engage to give me five *aurei?*); *Spondeo* (I engage). Such question and answer completed the obligation, and bound the promissor in payment or performance. Previous to the reign of Leo, certain words required to be used, than which none other would bind the parties; but a constitution enacted by him (A.D. 469) rendered the use of these special words as a solemnity unnecessary. Thereafter a stipulation might be entered into in any words, if they clearly expressed the intention of the parties, but it was still required that they should retain the form of a direct question and answer. An action arising out of an obligation so constituted was said to arise *ex stipulatu*.

Stipulatio sponsalitia.—The stipulation of betrothal; being the manner in which, under the civil law, espousals were entered into. This stipulation was entered into by the future husband on the one part, and the person who gave the woman in marriage on the other part; but it appears to have belonged to the older law of Rome. At a later period the *sponsalia* seem to have been merely an interchange of consent between the future spouses.

Stricti juris.—According to strict right. Some rights with which the law has to deal are regarded strictly, and the exercise of them limited to that alone which the express terms of their constitution warrants. Such rights, for example, as servitudes, monopolies, &c., are regarded *stricti juris*, because they are restrictions upon the free exercise of the rights of property, or on public commerce; they are limited to the express terms of the grant or deed which constitutes them, and no extension of the right or its exercise can be inferred or implied. The express words of the constitution, strictly interpreted, afford the criterion according to which the extent of the right is to be judged. Warrandice is also regarded strictly, and nothing is covered by the warranty beyond that which it clearly expresses. Under the Roman law there was a class of actions known as *actiones stricti juris*, as opposed to *actiones bonæ fidei;* these have already been explained. See *Actio.*

Strictissimæ interpretationis.—According to the strictest possible interpretation; according to the most literal rendering. All statutes imposing penalties, conferring personal privileges, restraining natural liberty, prescribing solemnities, &c., are so interpreted.

Strictissimi juris.—A phrase, more emphatic, but of much the same meaning and application as *stricti juris;* it is often used, however, in the same sense as the preceding phrase.

Sua potestas.—That natural power which a man has over his own person. A man is said to be *suæ potestatis* when it is meant that he enjoys freedom from any restraint.

Sua sponte.—Of one's own free-will; voluntarily; according to one's own discretion.

Sub colore officii.—Under colour of a certain office; or under pretence of an official proceeding. "The Ecclesiastical Courts appear to have exclusive jurisdiction in sacred matters, subject to the control and correction of the Court of Session, when, *sub colore officii,* they violate the law of the land." Ersk. Prin. 69.

Sub cura mariti.—Under the care or curatory of the husband. So long as a wife is under her husband's care or power, all personal obligations entered into by her without his consent are void.

Sub cura uxoris.—Under the care or curatory of the wife. Fraser, i. 155.

Sub dominio.—Under dominion; belonging to or in the property of any one. Hume, i. 81.

Sub modo.—Under condition or restriction. A conveyance in trust is one *sub modo,* because it conveys, not for the purpose of vesting the subject conveyed in the disponee merely, but to vest him in order that he may fulfil certain purposes and perform certain duties. He is therefore vested under restriction of the uses to which he may apply the subject conveyed.

Subfeudum.—A sub-feu—*i.e.,* a feu held of and under one who himself holds, in the character of vassal, the lands he sub-feus.

Sublato principali tollitur adjunctum.—The principal being taken away, the adjunct or accessory is taken away. Another mode of expressing the rule that an accessory follows the principal. See *Accessorium principale,* &c.

Subreptione vel obreptione.—By deceit or surprise.

Subsequente copula.—Carnal intercourse having followed; with subsequent carnal intercourse. A mere promise or engagement to marry at a future period does not constitute marriage, because the parties, by delaying the marriage, are supposed not to have given that final and determinate consent which is necessary to its constitution. But where such promise or engagement is followed by carnal intercourse permitted on the faith of it, the law presumes the final consent to have been given at the time of the connection, and that the marriage was then consummated. Such a marriage is said technically to have been contracted by promise *subsequente copula.* See the case of *Monteith,* 6 D. 934, where all the previous cases upon this point of law were reviewed. See *Consensus non*, &c.

Subsidiarie.—Subsidiarily. Proper cautioners are only bound in payment to the creditor of that debt which they have guaranteed, when the principal debtor has been discussed, and his estate has proved insufficient to meet the claim. They are only bound *subsidiarie*, in aid of the principal debtor, when he is unable to satisfy the demand of his creditor. Cautioners had at one time the benefit of discussion *de jure*, but this was abolished by the Mercantile Law Amendment Act (1856), which provided that, to entitle cautioners to such benefit, they must specially stipulate for it in their bond of caution. Parents, also, are only liable for aliment to their children *subsidiarie*, that is, are only bound to provide that which the child cannot provide for itself. If the child has a separate estate sufficient for its own maintenance and upbringing, the parents are not bound to aliment him at all. See *Quia alimenta*, &c.

Substitutio exemplaris.—This was the mode in which, under the civil law, heirs could be appointed to a minor who was insane. It was competent to any ascendant of the minor, maternal or paternal, to appoint, by an instrument, the person who should succeed to the minor's estate in the event of his dying without recovering his reason. The heir appointed, however, required to be one of the minor's descendants if he had any; if he had none, then one of his brothers; and failing brothers, the choice of the testator (or person appointing) was unrestrained. This form of substitution was introduced by Justinian, whose constitution will be found in the Code, L. 6, T. 26, l. 9; and is referred to in the Institutes, B. 2, T. 16, § 1. See also Stair, B. **3**, T. 8, § 19.

Successio prædilecta.—A selected or preferred succession —that is, a succession where the persons called to it are called by the choice of the testator; not a succession *per vim legis*, where the successors are called according to the legal rules.

Successor titulo lucrativo post contractum debitum.— A successor under a lucrative (gratuitous) title after debt has been contracted. An heir who succeeds to his ancestor's estate is liable for that ancestor's obligations; but this liability might be elided, if there were no legal provision to the contrary, by the heir receiving, during his ancestor's life, the whole estate in gift. To prevent this, the law provides that any heir receiving gratuitously, during his ancestor's life, that to which he would have been heir *alioqui successurus*, shall be liable for the debts due by his ancestor as at the date of the gift. The acceptance of such gift renders the heir liable under the passive title known as the *præceptio hereditatis*. Where the heir acquires the estate by *bona fide* purchase from the ancestor, no liability attaches to him for his ancestor's debts; the liability only arises where the estate has been transferred gratuitously.

Sui juris.—Persons who are independent of the control of others as regards their legal acts, and who can validly contract, and bind themselves by legal obligation, without the consent of another, are called *sui juris*—that is, they can contract, &c., as of their own right. See *Alieni juris*.

Sui potens.—Able of himself to do anything, to enter into contracts, to grant obligations, &c. This phrase is the same in meaning as the preceding one; this form of expression, however, is rarely used.

Summa necessitate.—In extreme necessity.

Summo jure.—In the highest right; the greatest right which a certain title can confer. Ross, L. C. (L. R.), i. 218.

Summum jus, summa injuria.—Extreme right is extreme injury; a maxim appealed to when it is contended that the complete enforcement of a right cannot be granted to one party without inflicting upon the other some wrong from which the law is bound to protect him; an equitable restraint on the strict enforcement of a legal obligation.

Suo nomine.—In one's own name. See *Proprio nomine*.

Suo periculo.—At one's own risk. See *Periculo petentis*.

Super aliquam partem fundi.—Upon any part of the land. In lands erected into a barony, sasine given under the old form, upon any part of the lands, was sufficient to vest the disponee feudally in the whole, except in the case where the charter or a clause of union specified a particular place as that at which sasine was to be given. In such case sasine required to be given at the appointed place, otherwise only the portions contiguous to that where sasine was actually given, and held of the same superior, were carried by the infeftment.

Super attentatis aut innovatis lite dependente.—Concerning those things attempted to be done, or alterations made, during the dependence of the suit. Stair, B. 4, T. 3, § 25. See *Pendente lite*, &c.

Super eisdem deductis.—Upon the same grounds or arguments. Stair, B. 4, T. 52, § 43.

Super jure naturæ alendi liberos.—On the ground of natural law, which obliges parents to aliment and support their children. Upon this ground parents are liable not only to aliment their children, but also for necessaries which have been supplied to the children by others. It lies on the furnisher of the goods, however, to show that they were necessaries.

Superflua non nocent.—Superfluities do not injure. Any verbiage in a deed which is merely superfluous does not render the deed less effectual than it would otherwise have been; it is held *pro non scripto*, and disregarded in the interpretation of the deed. The following passage from Ersk. B. 2, T. 3, § 21, contains an illustration of this maxim—"Charters begin with the name and designation of the granter, who is the proprietor of the lands disponed. Where there is an uncertainty in whom the property is vested, the grantee may desire that, for his security, every one who has a claim to the subject may concur in granting this deed; for though the right can be transmitted only by the true proprietor, yet the concurrence of another who is supposed to have also a title to it, is, without vitiating the charter, held as superfluous." See *Utile per inutile*, &c.

Supersedere.—A sist. When creditors voluntarily agree to supersede or sist diligence against their debtor for a certain period, such an agreement is called a *supersedere;* and the same name is given to any judicial act by which creditors are restrained from doing diligence. A creditor who commits a breach of the *supersedere*, whether it be voluntary or judicial, is liable to the debtor in damages.

Supplendo vices.—By supplying the place; or, by coming in place of.

Suppressio veri.—The suppression or concealment of the truth. See *Expressio falsi.*

Supra citatum.—Above cited ; used by way of reference, and generally written *sup. cit.*

Surplusagium non nocet.—Surplusage does no harm. See *Superflua non,* &c.

Surrogatum.—A thing which comes in place of another ; a thing substituted for another.

Surrogatum capit naturam rei surrogatæ.—A thing substituted takes the nature or character of that for which it is substituted. The reader will find an instance of the application of this maxim in the case of *Stainton's Trs. v. Dawson,* 6 Macp. 246. This maxim is sometimes written as follows—

Surrogatum sapit naturam surrogati.—A thing substituted partakes of the nature or character of that for which it is substituted. Stair, B. 2, T. 2, § 14.

Suum cuique tribuere.—To give to every one that which is his own. See *Alterum,* &c.

Sylva cædua.—Wood that can be cut without injury. See *Silva,* &c.

T

Tacere per quadriennium utile.—To be silent throughout the four years after majority. During the four years succeeding his attaining majority, any one may reduce a deed granted by him to his lesion in the course of his minority, but if the four years be allowed to elapse, no challenge of the deed upon that ground can be effectually maintained. It is then held *præsumptione juris et de jure* that the deed was not to his lesion, and such presumption cannot be traversed by the clearest proof. If the deed has been granted in pupilarity, it does not require to be challenged during the *quadriennium* or at any other period ; it is null from the beginning because a pupil is incapable of contracting or binding himself.

Talis qualis.—Such as it is. Where, in the purchase of heritable property, the purchaser agrees to accept of the seller's title as it stands at the time of the sale, without requiring any further title or remedy of real or supposed defects, he agrees to take it *talis qualis*—such as it is without challenge. A *talis qualis* proof is a proof such as the peculiar circumstances admit of, and which in those circumstances cannot be made better ; it is not a complete proof, nor such as would in ordinary circumstances discharge the *onus* laid upon a party requiring to prove his averments, but it is the best proof obtainable. Dickson, § 1304.

Tam facti quam animi.—In deed as well as in intention. Both intention, and the act proceeding upon that intention, are necessary to every act which can be regarded as effectual in law. Thus mere residence is not sufficient in the general case to constitute domicile where such residence is merely temporary, and where there is no intention or design on the part of the resident to acquire a domicile ; on the other hand, mere intention to acquire, without the residence indicative and in pursuance of that intention, will not constitute domicile. There must be *animus et factus*—the intention, and the overt act expressive of it. So also the mere taking possession of another's goods without felonious intent does not constitute the crime of theft, any more than does felonious intent without the act of appropriation; both are necessary to the constitution of the crime.

Tanquam bonus vir.—As an honest or honourable man. An agricultural tenant is bound to labour his farm "honestly and *tanquam bonus vir*, during the whole stipulated term" of his lease (Bell's Prin. § 1222); that is, he is bound to use his farm only for the purposes for which it was let, to grow such crops as will not waste or unduly impoverish the soil, and in every respect to take care of and cultivate the farm as if it were his own subject.

Tanquam dominus.—As owner; as in the character of proprietor.

Tanquam in libello.—As if alleged in the libel. Ersk. B. 2, T. 3, § 32.

Tanquam interim dominus.—As proprietor in the meantime; as the temporary owner.

Tanquam jure devoluto.—As if the right had devolved; as in the case of a devolved right. See *Jus devolutum*.

Tanquam optimum maximum.—At its best and fullest; a right undiminished either in point of quality or in point of extent. Conveyance of an estate *tanquam optimum maximum* implies that the right conveyed is one of full ownership throughout all the boundaries of the estate. Ersk. B. 2, T. 3, § 31.

Tanquam quilibet.—Like any other person. "The sovereign, when he grants a charter, not in consideration of the granter's services, as sovereign *jure coronæ*, but *tanquam quilibet*, for a just price, must be liable to the common rules" regarding warrandice. Ersk. 2, T. 3, § 27.

Tantum concessum quantum scriptum.—So much is granted as is written; the writing is the limit of the grant. When a right to lands or other right is conferred by charter or other writing, the right so conferred is limited by the terms of the grant; the right cannot be extended beyond or made to include more than the grant expressly confers. Thus a deed conferring a liferent limits the right to a liferent; a conveyance of an acre cannot be founded on as giving a right to more; a bounding charter confines the right thereby granted within the limits or boundaries there specified.

Tantum et tale.—So much and of such a kind; both as regards quality and extent. When a purchaser accepts a subject from the seller *tantum et tale* as it stands in the person of the latter, he accepts it with all its advantages and all its faults; he comes precisely into the right and place of the seller: if the subject or the right sold turns out to be more valuable than was thought, the purchaser has the advantage; if otherwise, he bears the loss. When a subject is sold *tantum et tale*, there is no warrandice on the part of the seller, except simple warrandice. See the *N. B. Ry. Co.* v. *Lindsay*, 3 R. 168. Bell's Com. i. 298. The effect of sequestration is to vest the trustee with the rights of property *tantum et tale* as they stand in the person of the bankrupt. *Heritable Reversionary Co.*, 18 R. 1166. Revd. H. L. 19 R. 43.

Tantum operatur fictio in casu ficto quantum veritas in casu vero.—A legal fiction operates to the same extent and effect in the supposed case as the truth does in a real case. See the observations made on the counterpart of this maxim, *Ne fictio plus valeat*, &c.

Tantum præscriptum quantum possessum.—There is only prescription in so far as there has been possession. The extent of a servitude constituted by grant is regulated by the express terms of that grant although partial possession only may be given, so that the dominant owner may exercise his right to its full extent when he thinks fit. But a servitude acquired by prescription is limited to the use or possession which the acquirer had; his possession affords the criterion by which to judge of the measure of his right. The same rule applies where one acquires by possession a piece of ground lying contiguous to his property, as a pertinent to his lands: his prescriptive right only covers that which he has possessed as a pertinent.

Temerarium perjurium super assisam.—Rash perjury on an assize. A rash and inconsiderate verdict returned by jurors is so described (Hume, i. 413), and it is termed *perjury* because it is contrary to the oath which the jury take that they will "well and truly try the cause and a true verdict give." It is, however, improperly termed perjury, for breach of an oath of promise is not perjury.

Temere jurantes super assisam.—Persons swearing rashly upon an assize; jurors returning a verdict rashly, inconsiderately. Stair, B. 3, T. 5, § 43.

Temere litigare.—To litigate rashly or without reasonable ground.

Tempestive.—Timeously; at the proper time.

Temporanea ad agendum sunt perpetua ad excipiendum. —Things which at a certain time (or, for a limited time) afford a ground of action may be used by way of exception at any time. See *Quæ sunt temporalia*, &c.; and for further illustration of this maxim, see Napier, 153, 602, 605. This maxim is sometimes written *Temporalia ad agendum*, &c.

Tempus continuum.—Time running on without interruption, whether it be time in which a legal right may be exercised or not. See *Tempus utile*.

Tempus deliberandi.—Time for deliberation; that period, formerly a year, but now restricted to six months, which an heir has after a succession has opened up to him to deliberate as to whether he will take up or renounce such succession. The *tempus deliberandi* is now of no practical importance. See *Damnosa*, &c.

Tempus ex suapte natura vim nullam effectricem habet. —Time, in its own nature, has no effectual force; time, taken by itself, has no force, or produces no effect. This maxim applies only to those cases in which rights are said to be acquired or strengthened by lapse of time, not to those cases in which by lapse of time rights are lost or extinguished. The mere abstinence during forty years to enforce a claim or payment of a debt extinguishes the debt; and the mere lapse of six years in like manner extinguishes a bill as a ground of debt. But where rights are to be acquired they need more than lapse of time. Thus to acquire right to an adjoining piece of land as a pertinent requires uninterrupted possession and use for twenty years on a title which conveys parts and pertinents (*Buchanan*, 9 R. 1218): the lapse of time alone would confer no right, nor would the possession alone give the right: the two must be combined—there must be possession of a certain kind, and for a certain time. In like manner, in acquiring a servitude otherwise than by grant, there must be use and possession, and also lapse of time—time without the use would confer no right.

Tempus mortis inspiciendum.—The time of the death is to be regarded, or looked to. In considering the rights conferred by a *mortis causa* deed, the time of the testator's death rather than the date of the deed is to be regarded, the testator's death being the time at which rights conferred by such a deed become effectual. Accordingly, a legacy bequeathed to a person who predeceases the testator lapses and becomes ineffectual, because at the time of the testator's death no such legatee is in existence, his being in existence at the date of the deed being immaterial, as no right to the legacy then vested. See *Lord* v. *Colvin*, 23 D. 111.

Tempus utile.—Time which can be used; a time which is available for exercising legal privileges or rights; and so differing from *tempus continuum*, which is time running on continuously, whether available for such a purpose or not. See observations on *Anni continui* and *Anni utiles*.

Tenendas.—That clause in a charter which sets forth the nature of the tenure by which the lands are held; as, for example, whether it be feu, blench, burgage, &c. The name is taken from the first word in the clause as it stood in the old Latin form.

Tenor est qui legem dat feudo.—It is the contents (of the charter or deed of grant) which gives the law to the feu-right: or, the contents of the charter regulate the right thereby conferred. If a superior grants a feu, it is by the terms of the charter granting the right that the respective rights and obligations of the superior and vassal are regulated. The law cannot interfere to modify or enlarge such rights and obligations, for *quoad* them the parties have made a law for themselves in the charter. See an instructive illustration of this in the case of *Andrew* v. *Buchanan*, 9 Macp. 554, reversed in H. L. 11 Macp. 13.

Termini habiles.—Sufficient grounds. Thus the fact of possession of a certain kind, and the continuance of that possession for a certain length of time, are the *termini habiles* on which to base a prescriptive right; a summons is said to be irrelevant when it does not contain *termini habiles* warranting the conclusions, &c.

Termini sanctorum.—The limits or precincts of a sanctuary. Among the Romans, churches and altars dedicated to the gods afforded protection to those who had been guilty of the smaller delinquencies, but not to those chargeable with the grosser crimes of murder, &c. In Scotland we have no sanctuary affording protection to those guilty of anything which may be punished as a crime, but (prior to the abolition of imprisonment for civil debt) the sanctuary of Holyrood afforded protection against personal diligence on account of civil debt. The debtor had only protection, however, so long as he remained within its limits, for he might be apprehended if he went beyond them, except on Sunday, on which day no civil process or diligence can be executed.

Terminus a quo.—Literally, the point from which. An example of the use of this phrase will be found in the following passage, where, treating of the summary diligence which may proceed upon a bill, Bell says—"The protest must be registered in the books of a competent court within six months from the date of the bill, in case of non-acceptance; or six months from the date of payment, in case of non-payment; and it would seem that in a case where protest has been taken at once for non-acceptance and non-payment, the day of payment will be the *terminus a quo* in reckoning the six months." Bell's Prin. § 344.

Terminus ad quem.—The point to which; that point at which a calculation ends; or that point or conclusion to which an argument tends.

Tertia.—A third; the widow's terce.

Tertia rationabilis.—A reasonable third; used in reference to the widow's terce by Stair, B. 2, T. 6, § 17.

Tertium quid.—A third thing having a character and qualities distinct from those of either of its two component parts. Thus where, by the confusion of liquids or commixture of solids, the subject produced is of a character different from that of either of its component parts, it is called a *tertium quid*.

Testamenti factio.—The power of testing or of making a

mortis causa settlement. Among the Romans this phrase included not only the power of testing in regard to one's own property, but also of taking any benefit under the testament of another. See *Factio testamenti*.

Testatio mentis.—The expression of a testator's will or mind; a testament.

Testibus non testimoniis credendum est.—Credence is given to the witnesses, not to their testimony; that is, the weight to be attributed to evidence depends upon the character and credibility of the witness more than upon the probability or improbability of his statements. The value of the evidence given is commensurate with the honesty and truthfulness of the witness; evidence as to an improbable fact spoken to by a witness above all suspicion deserves and receives more weight than the evidence of a doubtful or incredible witness regarding a fact in itself very probable. This maxim is rarely used, but the principle it expresses is constantly being applied.

Testimonia ponderanda sunt, non numeranda.—Testimonies are to be weighed not numbered. This rule imports that more regard is to be paid to the character of the evidence adduced in support of a case than to the number merely of the witnesses who give it; for the evidence of two respectable and credible witnesses is of more value than that of a dozen witnesses of notoriously abandoned and profligate character.

Tigni immittendi.—One of the urban servitudes of the civil law, under which the dominant owner was entitled to insert a beam into the wall of the servient tenement for the purpose of supporting his own.

Titius hæres esto.—Let Titius be my heir. This was the form under the civil law by which, in his testament, the testator appointed his heir. The nomination of an heir was the great essential of a testament under the civil law; wanting this, there could be no valid testament.

Titulo lucrativo, qui titulus est post contractum debitum.—By a lucrative (*i.e.*, gratuitous) title, which title is subsequent to the contraction of debt. See *Successor*, &c.

Titulo singulari.—By a singular title. Any one acquiring heritage by purchase, gift donation, &c., or in any other way than by succession, is said to hold or acquire under a singular title; persons so acquiring are called singular successors. See *Per venditionis*, &c.

Titulo universali.—By a universal title. An heir who succeeds to the estate of his ancestor is said to acquire or hold such succession by a universal title.

Titulus transferendi dominii.—The cause, or intention of conveying property; the *modus transferendi* being the overt act by which that intention is carried out and the real right transferred. See *Causa et modus*, &c.

Tota re perspecta.—The whole matter being clearly had in view; the whole matter being considered or regarded. This phrase is sometimes written *Tota materia perspecta*.

Toties quoties.—As often as; for each time.

Toto genere.—In their whole character; in every respect; entirely.

Tractus futuri temporis.— A tract of future time. "Rights which have a *tractus futuri temporis* are also heritable. These are rights of such a nature that they cannot be at once paid or fulfilled by the debtor, but continue for a number of years, and carry a yearly profit to the creditor while they subsist, without relation to any capital sum or stock; *ex. gr.*, a yearly annuity or premium for a certain term of years." Ersk. B. 2, T. 2, § 6.

Traditionibus et usucapionibus, non nudis pactis, transferuntur rerum dominia.—Rights of property are transferred by delivery, and by prescription founded on lengthened possession, not by a mere agreement or paction. A paction was regarded as *nudum* under the civil law where it was not binding in respect either that the parties had not finally agreed upon the matter, or that it had not been entered into with the usual and necessary solemnities. Such pactions transferred no right in that which formed the subject of the paction; real rights could only be transferred or conveyed by actual delivery or lengthened possession of the subject itself. With us a mere agreement to sell or deliver may constitute a *jus ad rem*, but does not, in the general case, confer a real right, or *jus in re*. But with reference to this see the Sale of Goods Act, 1893. See *Nudum pactum*.

Trado tibi ecclesiam.—I deliver this church or living to you. The form of words sometimes used by a patron in presenting an incumbent to a vacant cure.

Transeunt cum universitate.—They transmit with the whole estate. When an estate is transmitted in its entirety, its burdens transmit along with it. Thus a husband who, by the marriage, was formerly vested with the wife's moveable estate, was also thereby rendered responsible for her debts; and an heir who succeeded universally to his ancestor, was liable for the whole of his ancestor's debts and obligations; they transmitted with the estate. But an heir is now only liable for the whole of his ancestor's debts, if the estate is sufficiently large to meet them: he is not liable for his ancestor's debts and obligations in so far as these exceed the value of the succession; (37 & 38 Vict. c. 94, § 12) and as marriage no longer operates as an assignation to the husband of the wife's moveables, he is not now liable for her antenuptial debts, beyond the extent to which he is *lucratus* by the marriage. (40 & 41 Vict. c. 29.)

Transit terra cum onere.—The land passes with its burdens. When lands are conveyed, whether gratuitously or for onerous considerations, the disponee who gets the land becomes liable for the obligations incumbent on the owner. He who reaps the advantages bears also the disadvantages; and therefore he who has the land, with its rents and profits, must bear the burden of all those payments and duties exigible from the land or its owner. See *Qui sentit commodum*, &c. It need scarcely be observed that the owner of land is responsible for all the burdens attaching to it or the ownership thereof, whether he reaps advantage from the land or not.

Triennalis pacificus possessor beneficii est inde securus. —The undisturbed possessor of a benefice for three years is thereafter secure from challenge. "This rule gives not right to the Church, but prefers one churchman to another, if he continue to possess three years without interruption, though he could not defend himself by his right." Stair, B. 2, T. 1, § 25.

Tutius est rei incumbere quam personæ.—It is safer to rely upon a subject than upon a person; that is, a real security is safer than a personal security, or a real right better than a personal right.

Tutius semper est errare in acquietando quam in puniendo, ex parte misericordiæ quam ex parte justitiæ.—It is safer to err in acquitting than in punishing, to err on the side of mercy than of justice. This is just another mode of expressing the maxim that it is better ten guilty men should go unpunished than that one innocent man should suffer unjustly. See *Melius est*, &c.

Tutor ad litem.—A person appointed by the Court to protect the interest of a pupil in an action to which he is called as a party. A person appointed to protect the interest of a minor, or married woman, or other person above pupilarity, but not considered capable of protecting his or her own interest in a suit, is called a *curator ad litem*.

Tutor datur personæ.—A tutor is appointed to the person;—*i.e.*, to take care of the person of his ward; and in this respect differs from a curator, who is (*datur rei*) appointed to take care of and preserve the ward's estate.

Tutor in rem suam auctor fieri non potest.—A tutor cannot act for his own behoof—*i.e.*, in any matter where his interest conflicts with that of his ward. He cannot purchase any part of the ward's estate (except, according to Erskine, at a public auction), nor do anything directly or indirectly which would result in benefit to himself and injury to his ward. See *Auctor in rem*, &c.

Tutor incertus dari non potest.—An uncertain person cannot be given or appointed as tutor. A father has power to name any person he pleases to be tutor to his pupil children, but he must be named, and not left uncertain. He cannot delegate this power; it must be personally exercised. Accordingly, where a father conferred on the trustees under his settlement a power to assume new trustees, and appointed his trustees, "named, or to be named or assumed," tutors to his pupil children, it was held that the appointment of assumed trustees as tutors was invalid. *Walker* v. *Stronach*, 2 R. 120.

Tutor præsumitur intus habere, ante redditas rationes. —A tutor is presumed to have funds in his own hands until his accounts have been rendered;—*i.e.*, he is presumed, before the rendering of his accounts, to have as much of the property of the ward in his own hands as will extinguish any claim he may have against the ward, until this presumption is redargued by his showing on reckoning with the ward that it is not so. See *Intus habet*.

Tutor rem pupilli emere non potest.—A tutor cannot purchase the estate, or that which is the property of the pupil his ward. Erskine (B. 1, T. 7, § 19) states, as an exception to this general rule, that a tutor may purchase the estate of his ward if it be exposed for sale by public auction; and the principle on which such an exception proceeds is this; that in a private purchase of his ward's estate the tutor might exercise his influence over the ward, to his own advantage and to the lesion of the pupil, but in a public sale, where any one may compete for the subject exposed, there is no room for such private influence. Whether such an exception to the general rule would now be given effect to may be doubted. *York Buildings Co.* v. *Mackenzie*, 3 Paton, 378.

Tutores testamentarii, legitimi, et dativi.—Testamentary tutors, tutors-at-law, and tutors-dative. Testamentary tutors are those appointed by a father in his will to the guardianship of his pupil children; tutors-at-law are those who have the office of tutor by force of legal rule on account of their relationship to a pupil, such as a paternal uncle; and tutors-dative are those appointed by the Court on an application for their appointment.

Tutorio nomine.—In the name or character of tutor.

Tutus accessus non fuit.—There was no safe access. Stair, B. 2, T. 12, § 26.

Typographum.—Impressed by means of a die or type, as distinguished from *chirographum*—written with the hand. Stair, B. 4, T. 42, § 3.

U

Uberior titulus.—The fuller or more unlimited title.

Uberrima fides.—Good faith of the most full and copious character; a phrase similar in meaning, but more emphatic than *optima fides*.

Ubi aberat animus fœnerandi.—Where the intention of taking a usurious interest was wanting. Usury is the taking or stipulating for a higher than legal interest in return for the loan of money. Formerly a contract which stipulated for usurious interest was null, and the lender stipulating for it was liable in certain penalties; this liability, however, was not incurred where the lender had no intention of exacting usury, for here, as in other offences, the *animus* was essential to the commission of the offence. All the usury laws have been repealed by the Act 17 & 18 Vict. c. 90, and any rate of interest is now regarded as legal, and may be exacted, if the parties to the loan have agreed upon it; where there has been no agreement specifying the rate of interest, the legal interest, five per cent., is presumed to be the return due for the loan. Even under the old law a greater than the fixed legal rate of interest could be validly stipulated for where the risk was unusually great, as in bottomry and respondentia.

Ubi aliquid conceditur, conceditur et id sine quo res ipsa esse non potest.—When anything is granted (or, right conferred) that also is held as granted without which the right or grant cannot exist (or, be enjoyed). See *Quando aliquid conceditur*, &c., and *Quando lex aliquid*, &c.

Ubi cessat remedium ordinarium, ibi decurritur ad extraordinarium; et nunquam decurritur ad extraordinarium ubi valet ordinarium.—Where ordinary remedy is wanting (or, is not available), recourse is had to extraordinary remedy; and extraordinary remedy is never had recourse to where the ordinary remedy is available. The name "*extraordinary remedies*" implies necessarily that they are of a kind not usually resorted to. Under the Roman law the extraordinary remedies were those applied by the prætor in the exercise of his equitable jurisdiction, and were only given when the strict law afforded no remedy, or where from the circumstances of the case such remedies were not available. See *De minimis*, &c. The Supreme Court of Scotland, in the exercise of its *nobile officium*, also affords remedies where the common law affords none. See *Nobile officium*.

Ubi damna dantur victus victori in expensis condemnari debet.—Where damages are awarded, the unsuccessful party ought to be found liable in expenses to the successful party. As a rule an unsuccessful litigant is always found liable in costs to his successful opponent; but in this the Court can and does always exercise its discretion. Success in the litigation does not necessarily infer, as matter of absolute right, a right to the expenses of the suit. By the Act 31 & 32 Vict. c. 100, § 40, it is provided that where the pursuer in any action of damages recovers less under the verdict of the jury than five pounds, he shall not be entitled to expenses unless the presiding judge certifies that the action was brought to try a right besides the mere right to recover damages, "or that the injury in respect of which the action was brought was malicious; or, in the case of actions for defamation or libel, that the action was brought for the vindication of character, and was in his opinion fit to be tried in the Court of Session." In the House of Lords, formerly, expenses were never given to a successful appellant when the judgment appealed against was reversed, but that is not now the rule. Expenses there, as in other courts, generally follow success.

Ubi defunctus habuit domicilium.—Where the deceased had his domicile. Executors-dative must be confirmed in that county where the deceased had his domicile, and if domiciled furth of Scotland, but possessed of moveable estate here, the confirmation must be taken before the Commissary at Edinburgh. The place of the deceased's domicile is of importance in a question relating to the succession duties payable on personalty; for if the deceased had his domicile in Great Britain, the duty is exigible although the whole of his moveable estate should be situated abroad; while, on the other hand, if the deceased had his domicile furth of the kingdom, no duty is exigible, even where the whole of his moveable estate is situated within it.

Ubi dies cessit, licet nondum venerit.—In the case where the time has arrived at which money has commenced to be due, although that time has not arrived at which it may be exacted. Money may frequently be due and yet not be prestable; as, for example, where a legacy is bequeathed to one still in minority, and made payable on his attaining majority; the legacy in such case becomes due to him on the death of the testator, but payment cannot be demanded until the arrival of the time fixed by the testator as the date of payment; so also rent becomes due from the date of entry, but is not prestable until the arrival of the stipulated term. See *Dies cedit*, &c.

Ubi dolus dedit causam contractui.—Where fraud gave rise to the contract. Where a contract is founded upon fraud, or where one of the parties has been induced to enter into a contract upon the misrepresentations or falsehood of the other, it may be reduced upon that ground. The distinction, however, between *dolus* and *solertia* must be regarded, for the latter will not vitiate the contract which it has induced. See *Dolus*.

Ubi eadem est ratio ibi idem est jus.—Where there is the same reason there is the same law. All laws are founded upon some reason, that is, are enacted to meet some particular case or class of cases: and wherever the reason exists that law is applied. For example, certain documents are privileged to the effect that they are held binding and probative although not executed with the formalities or solemnities generally required to make a deed either probative or binding. Documents or writs *in re mercatoria* are so privileged: and, therefore, wherever a document can be brought within that category, its privilege is admitted; the reason for giving the privilege being shown to exist in reference to that particular document, the same law is applied as would be applied to all documents of that class. Again, by the Act 30 & 31 Vict.

c. 101, certain specified trades are put under regulation, and subjected to certain restrictions, as are also trades or manufactures other than those enumerated if they are "injurious to health;" whenever, therefore, it is established before the proper tribunal for deciding upon that question that a manufacture is injurious to health, that manufacture will be subjected to the statutory restrictions, because the reason or ground for such restriction being there, the law will be applied. This maxim is sometimes written *Ubi eadem est ratio ibi eadem est lex.*

Ubi id non agebatur.—Where that was not done. See *Id non*, &c.

Ubi lex deest, prætor supplet.—Where the law is wanting or deficient, the Prætor supplies the deficiency. All the prætorian remedies of the civil law proceeded upon this rule. Where the strict law would have condemned the promissor in a stipulation, and could afford him no relief from his obligation, even where he had been defrauded, the Prætor supplied this want in the strict law and gave an *exceptio*, which was given effect to if substantiated. The strict law took no account of equity, but this was supplied by the Prætor: and his equitable jurisdiction was somewhat similar to (although more extensive in its application than) that power vested in the judges of our Supreme Courts, known as the *nobile officium*. See *De minimis*, &c.

Ubi jus ibi remedium.—Wherever there is a right there is a remedy. *Remedium* includes more than is usually included in the English term *remedy*: it means right of action as well as remedy. Thus where one's right is invaded or destroyed, the law gives a remedy by interdict to protect it, or damages for its loss; and where one's right is denied the law affords the remedy of an action for its enforcement. Wherever, therefore, a right exists there is also a remedy—that is, an action to enforce it, to protect or replace it. See *Lex semper dabit*, &c.

Ubi onus ibi emolumentum.—Where the burden is, there is the profit or advantage. Advantages and disadvantages go together; and where one has a right he must bear its corresponding obligations. See *Cujus est commodum*, &c. This maxim is sometimes written *Ubi emolumentum ibi onus*

—where the advantage is, there is the burden or disadvantage.

Ubi verba conjunctiva non sunt sufficit alterutrum esse factum.—Where words are not conjoined, it is enough that one or other (of the things required) should be done. To illustrate this, suppose a testator directed his heir to give to a certain legatee " my gold watch *and* my signet ring," the obligation thus imposed could only be discharged by the heir delivering to the legatee both of the articles specified : here the words are conjoined, and both must be observed. If, however, the words were " my gold watch *or* my signet ring," the heir fulfils his obligation by delivering either: the words are not conjoined, and compliance with one or other of the directions is sufficient fulfilment. Where, again, a provision to a daughter is made payable on her attaining majority *or* being married, she is entitled to payment on the happening of either event, as it is dependent on either event, not both, that the right becomes prestable.

Ultima voluntas testatoris est perimplenda secundum veram intentionem suam.—The last will of a testator is to be fully carried out according to his true intention—that is, the real intention and purpose of a testator, as expressed in or gathered from his will, are to receive full effect. See *In testamentis plenius*, &c.

Ultimo loco.—In the last place. The claimant in a multiplepoinding, who is preferred *ultimo loco*, can only take that which remains of the fund *in medio*, after all the other claimants have been satisfied.

Ultimum tempus pariendi.—A time beyond or after which a child may not be born. The length of the period of gestation being a purely medical question, and varying according to medical experience, the law fixes no precise time beyond the date of connection or conception within which the child must be born, so as to be held the result of such connection. The rule is different as applied to questions of legitimacy, and questions of mere paternity or filiation ; concerning which, see Fraser, Par. & Ch. 12 *et seq.*

Ultimus hæres.—Last heir. The sovereign succeeds as last heir, both in heritage and moveables, to every subject dying intestate and without lawful heirs entitled to take up the succession. Where heritage so devolving upon the sovereign is held of a subject superior, it is necessary to interpose a donatory, because the sovereign cannot hold of a subject. When there are relatives of the deceased existing, but who cannot succeed according to the legal rules regulating intestate succession, it is usual for the Crown, on application made, to confer the estate upon them. The Crown, or Crown's donatory, is liable for the debts and obligations of the deceased to the extent of the value of the estate, but no further. The right of the Crown as *ultimus hæres* is rather a caduciary right than a right of succession; the Crown cannot succeed as conditional institute under a destination to "heirs." *Torrie* v. *Munsie*, 10 S. 597.

Ultra fines compromissi.—Beyond the limits of the submission or reference. See *Ultra vires compromissi*.

Ultra fines decreti.—Beyond the limits of the decree; beyond the terms of the judgment.

Ultra fines mandati.—Beyond the limits of the mandate. As a mandatory's authority arises entirely from the mandate, so the limit of that authority is prescribed by its terms. Anything, therefore, which a mandatory does in excess of the power conferred upon him, being unauthorised, is not binding upon the mandant. But where a general mandate or factory is granted, all acts falling within, or usually understood to fall within, such a mandate, are binding upon the mandant as in a question with third parties, even although they have been excepted from the general authority, leaving the mandant his relief as against the mandatory for the consequences of such acts. Thus a tenant is entitled to pay his rent to his landlord's factor, and the receipt of the latter will be binding upon the landlord, even if the power of uplifting and discharging rents has been excepted in the factory granted, because such a power is presumed to be a part of the factor's authority. It will be different if the landlord specially intimates to the tenant that such power has not been conferred, or has been withdrawn.

Ultra petita.—Beyond that which was sought. A judgment or decision is said to be *ultra petita* when it awards more than was sought or sued for in the petition or summons; and the same thing is said of a sentence when it is not conform to its grounds and warrants. This affords a good ground for the reversal or reduction of such a decree.

Ultra valorem.—Beyond the value.

Ultra vires.—Beyond the power; in excess of the authority. An act performed by a mandatory not authorised by the mandate in his favour, is said to be *ultra vires* of the mandatory; and it is *ultra vires* of the court to alter a final decision which it has pronounced.

Ultra vires compromissi.—Beyond the force or import of the submission; beyond the authority conferred by the submission. Arbiters are limited in their acts and in their power by the terms of the submission under which they are appointed, and if in their proceedings or decree-arbitral they go *ultra vires compromissi*—*i.e.*, if they decide any point not referred, or give an award of greater amount than the submission warrants, such decision or award may be reduced upon that ground. Where that part of the decision which is in excess of the power conferred upon the arbiters can be separated from the rest, the decision will only be reduced *quoad excessum;* but when this cannot be done, the decision will be reduced entirely. The leading cases upon this point will be found collected in Menzies' Lectures, 411.

Ultra vires inventarii.—Beyond the extent in value of the inventory; or beyond the value of the estate given up in the inventory. "The executor is, in the judgment of law, a trustee, appointed either by the deceased or by the judge, for executing the testament, and therefore is not subjected to the debts of the deceased *ultra vires inventarii*, beyond the value of the inventory." Ersk. B. 3, T. 9, § 41.

Una cum multuris omnium terrarum intra parochiam. —Together with the multures of the whole lands within the parish. Stair, B. 2, T. 7, § 19.

Unaquæque gleba servit.—Every part of the land is subject to the servitude. Where a servitude exists over a certain subject, every clod of the earth composing it (according to this rule) is affected by it. The servient proprietor, therefore, cannot alter or interfere with any portion of the subject, however small, if such alteration will affect or interfere with the dominant owner's right. Yet as servitudes are limitations of the rights of property, they must be used in the way least burdensome to the servient tenement, and any attempt to use them in *æmulationem* will be prevented.

Unde vi.—One of the prætorian interdicts under the civil law, and deriving its name from the introductory words of the *formula* appropriate to it. The prætorian interdicts were divided into three classes, according to the nature of the object to be attained by them; they were granted either for acquiring, retaining, or recovering possession of a subject. Of the first class, the interdict *quorum bonorum* may be taken as an example; of the second, the interdict *uti possidetis*; and of the third, *unde vi*. The interdict *unde vi* was that granted to any one who had been violently dispossessed of a subject, in order that he might recover its possession. To entitle him to this interdict, it was necessary that he should have been dispossessed by violence, and that he should have been in actual possession at the time of the violence being committed. It was no answer that the person committing the violence was the true owner, and that he who had actual possession was an intruder or unlawful possessor, because no one was entitled to vindicate his right by force. This interdict was at one time granted only where the subject sought to be recovered was immoveable, but at a later period its application was extended also to moveables.

Unico contextu.—In one connection; that is to say, by one and the same act; or by an act performed in connection with another, and at the same time. This may be best explained by an example of its use. When there are more parties than one to a deed, it is not essential to the validity of its execution that they should subscribe *unico contextu*—*i.e.*, it is not necessary for them to subscribe at the same time and place. But where (as was formerly required) two notaries subscribed for a person who could not write, it was necessary that they should subscribe *unico contextu* at the same time and place, and before the same witnesses. The subscription of one notary, or a justice of the peace, is now sufficient. 37 & 38 Vict. c. 94, § 41.

Universitas.—Literally, the whole. The *universitas* of an estate, heritable or moveable, is that estate in its entirety, without limitation or deduction. Among the civilians *uni-*

versitas is used as signifying a separate body, such as a city or trade guild.

Universum jus. — The entire right. When an heir succeeds to the entire right of his ancestor, heritable and moveable, he is called a universal successor.

Unum quid.—One thing. This implies that several things are, for some purpose, taken and considered as one. Thus heritage and moveables, separate and distinct rights in themselves, and regulated by different rules of law, may be so conveyed by a testator to trustees as to constitute his whole estate a *unum quid*—*i.e.*, one right which his trustees must deal with as one, and not as separate real and moveable rights.

Unumquodque eodem modo dissolvitur quo colligatur.—Anything (that is, any obligation) is discharged in the same manner as that in which it was constituted. A verbal obligation may be verbally discharged; but an obligation requiring writing in its constitution requires, in the general case, a written discharge. See *Eodem modo*, &c.

Unusquisque debet esse gnarus conditionis ejus cum quo contrahit.—Every one ought to be acquainted with the condition of the person with whom he contracts. See *Quisque scire*, &c.

Usque ad sententiam.—Until the pronouncing of judgment. "Though an executor cannot, in the general case, sue the debtors of the deceased till he be confirmed, because it is the confirmation which gives him the *jus exigendi;* yet executors who are unwilling to be at the charge of confirming doubtful debts may even, before confirmation, sue for payment, if they obtain a licence from the Commissary for that purpose. These licences are never granted till he who applies for them has obtained a decree decerning himself executor. They are intended merely to save expense, where there is danger of getting nothing by the confirmation; and for that reason they do not include a power to the pursuer to insist for a decree against the debtor; they are only granted *usque ad sententiam*." (Ersk. B. 3, T. 9, § 39.) Such a procedure as that here detailed, of suing upon the licence of the Commissary before confirmation, is now unknown in practice. An executor may sue the debtor of the executry estate according to present practice, without confirmation; it is enough if he produces his confirmation before extract.

Usucapio.—Usucapion; or the acquisition of property by lengthened possession, a right under the civil law similar to that conferred by the positive prescription of our law. To found this right, it was necessary, according to the older law, that the party acquiring it should have been in the *bona fide* and unchallenged possession of the subject for one year if it was a moveable, or two years if immoveable, and situated in Italy; the *dominium* of immoveables, situated in the provinces, could not be acquired by usucapion at all. But this was somewhat altered by Justinian, who enacted that, to acquire moveables by usucapion three years' possession should be necessary; and that immoveables, wherever situated (for he abolished the distinction previously existing between immoveables situated in Italy and in the provinces), should be acquired by "possession of long time;" that is, possession for ten years (*inter præsentes*) where the person acquiring and the person challenging his right resided in the same province, or for twenty years (*inter absentes*) where they resided in different provinces. See *Præscriptio longi*, &c.

Usucapio constituta est ut aliquis litium finis esset.—Usucapion was instituted that there might be an end of lawsuits; the right of property conferred by lengthened possession was introduced, or made law, in order that after a certain term no question should be possible concerning the ownership of the property. See *Usucapio*.

Usura.—Interest; usury.

Usura manifesta.—Direct or manifest usury. A creditor was guilty of this when he stipulated for a higher than the legal rate of interest, or even when he took interest before it was due, although no higher than the legal rate, as, for example. when he accepted a year's interest before the year had expired. The punishment of usury was declared, by the Act 1597, c. 251, to be escheat of moveables, the annulling of the usurious contract, and forfeiture of the principal sum lent and interest due upon it to the Crown or its donatory. All the usury laws have now been repealed. See *Ubi aberat*, &c.

Usura velata.—Covert usury; as where a creditor stipulated for usurious interest by adding it to the principal sum, and thus making it appear as a part of the original loan.

Usus.—Use. One of the civil law personal servitudes, which conferred upon the person entitled to it the right to use the subject, but to use it merely. He had the *nudus usus*, the bare use; and while he enjoyed any advantages which the use conferred, he could not avail himself of anything which the subject produced. Thus where the subject over which the right was given was a dwelling-house, the *usuarius* was only entitled to use it personally, and could not, like a *usufructuarius*, gain profit to himself by letting it to another. But where the subject was one of which the bare use would be of no benefit to the *usuarius*, the rigour of this principle was somewhat abated, and he was allowed to gather and enjoy certain of its fruits, but that only to a limited extent. He might take, for example, such fruits as were necessary for the subsistence of himself and family; if the subject of the servitude was a flock of cattle, he might take a moderate quantity of the milk, &c. The *usuarius* was the person entitled to the right of *usus*.

Usus fit ex iteratis actibus.—Usage arises from repeated acts; repeated acts constitute usage. A right acquired by use cannot be acquired by a single act; the acts must be repeated before they are held to amount to use. Thus to acquire a right of passage by use, the road must be traversed frequently, and those acts of use must extend over a certain period of time: the fact that one person or several persons have each gone once or twice over the road would not amount to such use as is necessary to constitute the servitude. In like manner the custom or usage of a certain port or locality must not only be general, but constantly observed in reference to the same matter, or matters of the same kind, before that usage will be regarded as binding, or be admitted to modify or interpret contracts, &c. See *Consuetudo debet esse*, &c.

Ususfructus.—This was one of the personal servitudes of the Roman law, which might be constituted over a moveable or an immoveable subject. It conferred upon the person entitled to it (called *usufructuarius*) the right to use the subject, and also to gather the whole fruits or produce thereof; he could also sell or let his right, but only so as to give the purchaser or hirer a right co-extensive with his own. If the subject of the usufruct perished, the right perished. As to the modes in which such a right was terminated, and generally concerning this right itself, see Just. Inst. B. 4, T. 4. Usufruct is in most respects similar to the right known in our law by the name of liferent. They differ in this respect, however, that a liferent with us, as the name implies, confers upon the liferenter the right during his whole lifetime, whereas a usufruct under the civil law might be constituted for a shorter period, even for a single day. The right known in Scotland which bears the nearest resemblance to the civil law usufruct, is that which confers upon the person in whose favour it is made a right to use and enjoy a certain subject or estate until the occurrence of a certain event, as, *ex. gr.*, until the liferenter marries, or until the death of another person occurs, or on a widow so long as she remains unmarried. This (although commonly called a liferent) is not properly a liferent, as it may cease during the lifetime of the person enjoying it: it is, more correctly, a right of use and enjoyment under the condition or for the time specified. The terms *ususfructus causalis* and *ususfructus formalis* appear to have been used in Scotland at one time (although now obsolete), the former to indicate that kind of right which while called a liferent was in reality a fee, the latter to indicate a proper liferent along with a fiduciary fee. Thus where a conveyance was granted to A in liferent and his children unborn or unnamed in fee, this conferred the fee upon A, and gave only a *spes* to his children; this was the *ususfructus causalis* (Ross, L. C. L. R. iii. 603). But where the conveyance was in favour of A for his liferent use allenarly, or under restrictive words of similar signification, and to his children to be born in fee, this conferred a liferent upon A with a fiduciary fee for behoof of the children: this was the *ususfructus formalis.* (Ross, *sup. cit.* 643.)

Ut continua mentis alienatione omni intellectu careat.—So that he is utterly devoid of intelligence through continued mental alienation. Hume, i. 37.

Ut nihil illi desit.—That nothing may be wanting to him; that he may not lose.

Ut prosint ad veritatem indagandam.—That they may

avail or be of service, for investigating the truth. Hume, ii. 341.

Ut res valeat potius quam pereat.—That the thing may avail (or, be valid) rather than perish. This is sometimes written *Ut actus valeat*, &c. See *Benigne faciendæ sunt*, &c.

Ut sortiantur effectum.—That they may receive effect. "By the Roman law, if one bequeathed a subject which he knew did not belong to himself, the legacy had this effect—that the heir must have either purchased it for the legatee, or paid its value to him if it could not be purchased; for all testamentary deeds ought to be so explained *ut sortiantur effectum*; and unless the legacy had been interpreted in this manner, it could have had no effect." Erskine, B. 3, T. 9, § 10.

Ut supra.—As above. A common mode of reference to a preceding passage.

Ut voluntas testatoris sortiatur effectum.—That the will of the testator may receive effect. On the death or declinature of the trustees appointed by a testator in his trust-settlement, the Court, on application to that effect, is in the practice of appointing a judicial factor, by whom the purposes of the testator may be carried into effect.

Uti mos est in feudifirmis.—As is the custom in feu-holdings. Ersk. B. 2, T. 5, § 48.

Uti possidetis.—One of the prætorian interdicts under the civil law, deriving its name from the introductory words of the *formula* appropriate to it. This interdict was one of that class which were given for the purpose of retaining or defending possession of the subject in dispute; and it was granted only where the possession was not vicious, as in a question with the person claiming it. Possession was said to be vicious when obtained *vi aut clam aut precario*,—by force, or clandestine means, or by importunate entreaty. Possession so obtained could not be defended by the interdict *uti possidetis*. Natural possession was not required to found this interdict; it was sufficient if there was civil possession. See *Unde vi*.

Uti quisque rei suæ legassit, ita jus esto.—As any one disposes of his own property by testament, so let the law be. This was the rule of the Twelve Tables regarding the disposal of property by testament. Previous to this, the effect of any will not made before the *comitia curiata*, which was convoked twice a-year for the purpose of making wills, was very uncertain : the rule of the Twelve Tables was intended to take away this uncertainty, and to give effect to any will which was intelligible and clear. It has been maintained by some, that the Twelve Tables (by the provision now under explanation) first gave the right to a Roman citizen to dispose of his own property according to his pleasure ; but this position does not seem to be well founded. The controversy on this point will be found treated of in Smith's Dict. *v. Testamentum.*

Utile per inutile non vitiatur.—The useful is not vitiated, or rendered invalid, by the useless. This maxim is the same in effect as one already noticed, namely, *Superflua non nocent.* The rule expressed by both is this, that a deed or writing otherwise valid and effectual is not to be invalidated by the addition of something that is not necessary to the deed, something that is useless or superfluous. Thus it has already been shown that where a legacy is left to a certain person regarding whose identity there is no doubt, the addition of something by way of description of the legatee, which is useless, or may even be false, is immaterial ; the legacy is valid notwithstanding. See *Falsa demonstratio,* &c. Care must be taken, however, rightly to distinguish between what is useless in the sense of this maxim, and therefore immaterial, and what was unnecessary in itself, and yet has been made a part or condition of the grant or conveyance, and therefore cannot be set aside as mere surplusage. Of this latter class many illustrations will be found in those cases which have arisen as to the validity of entails. The case of *Horne* v. *Rennie*, 15 S. 372 (the Balliliesk case), reversed in the House of Lords, 3 S. & M'L. 142, affords a good example. In that case the entail validly set forth the cardinal prohibitions ; but the irritant and resolutive clauses ran as follows : "And in case the said A B, or any of the heirs of tailzie before mentioned, shall contravene or fail in performing any part of the premises, *particularly* by neglecting," &c., then such contraventions were not only declared void in themselves, but the contravener's right under the entail was declared forfeited. The enumeration in the irritant and resolutive clauses covered all the prohibitions of the entail except the prohibition against alienation: the entail was set aside on the ground that the prohibition against alienation was not duly fenced. Now if the entailer had been satisfied with the general terms of the irritant and resolutive clauses as expressed before the word "particularly," and had omitted the special enumeration which followed, the entail would have been valid: the clauses would have applied to contravention or failure to perform "any part of the premises." In one sense, therefore, the enumeration was useless; it was not necessary, for the deed was complete without it. But as the entailer had added this special enumeration, it was treated as derogating from the general clause which preceded it, and having been made part of the deed as expressing specifically the conditions of the grant in favour of the heirs of tailzie, could not be regarded as useless or immaterial. The result was, that that which was for all practical purposes useless, and might have been with perfect safety omitted, being insufficient and incomplete in itself, had the effect of vitiating that which was otherwise valid and effectual. Some very apposite observations on this subject were made by Lord Gillies in the case of *Adam* v. *Farquharson* (the Finzean entail), 2 D. 1172. See *Abundans cautela*, &c. See also Ross, L. C. (L. R.) ii. 27.

Utiliter et equivalenter.—Duly, and with equal effect. Stair, B. 3, T. 2, § 5.

Utiliter impensum.—Usefully expended.

Utitur jure auctoris.—He uses or exercises the right of his author. A disponee exercises the right of his author in the subject disponed; that is to say, he possesses all the rights *quoad* it which his author possessed, and is subject to all the objections or obligations concerning it to which his author was liable. See *Assignatus utitur*, &c.

Utitur jure communi.—He uses the common law. Ersk. B. 2, T. 3, § 27.

Utitur jure privato.—He uses or exercises his own private right.

Utitur jure suo.—He uses or exercises his own right. The exercise of rights of property on the part of a proprietor, so long as not exercised *in œmulationem,* cannot be interfered with, even where they are injurious in their effects to the adjoining property. In such case the proprietor is only doing that which he has a right to do, *utitur jure suo.* See *Qui jure suo,* &c.

Uxor non est sui juris sed sub potestate viri.—A wife is not in her own right (that is, she cannot act independently), but is under the power of her husband. A wife, during the subsistence of her marriage, has no *persona* in law; she is merged in her husband, and therefore cannot undertake obligations, or enter into contracts so as to bind herself without the consent of her husband. This rule is absolute as regards moveable estate; but if a wife has heritable estate from which her husband's rights are strictly excluded or have been validly renounced, she may, without her husband's consent, sell and convey the estate to another, or she may leave it by will as she pleases. A wife cannot sue without her husband's consent, in the general case; but she can sue her husband, in which case the Court appoints her a curator *ad litem.* As to the difference effected on a wife's position by her separation from her husband, see Fraser, i. 636 *et seq.,* and the Conjugal Rights (Scotland) Amendment Act, 1861, 24 & 25 Vict. c. 86. In *M'Crorie* v. *Cowan,* 24 D. 723, an opinion was expressed by a majority of the whole court that *stante matrimonio* a married woman could not have a parochial settlement apart from her husband, whether he had one in Scotland or not; but it has been decided that a deserted wife can have or acquire for herself such a settlement *stante matrimonio.* "If we are to regard her as a deserted wife, I think that she is in the same position as if she had lost her husband by death, to this effect, that she became *sui juris* from the time when the husband's desertion was ascertained." Per Lord Pres. Colonsay in *Mason* v. *Greig,* 3 Macp. 716; *Carmichael* v. *Adamson,* 1 Macp. 452; *Palmer* v. *Russell,* 10 Macp. 185; *Johnston* v. *Wallace,* 11 Macp. 699. This rule was first applied in cases where the deserting husband had no settlement in Scotland, leaving it for a time an open question whether the same rule would be applied in the case where the deserting husband had such a settlement. It has now been decided that the same rule applies in both cases. *Craig* v. *Simpson & Greig*, 3 R. 642.

Uxor sequitur domicilium viri.—A wife follows the domicile of her husband. As the wife's person is merged in that of her husband, she cannot during the marriage have any other domicile than that of the husband. Stair, B. 1, T. 4, § 9. Fraser, i. 583. This rule, however, seems to admit of some modification in cases of divorce, regarding which, see *Shields* v. *Shields*, 15 D. 142; *Jack* v. *Jack*, 24 D. 467; and *Pitt* v. *Pitt*, 1 Macp. 106, reversed in the House of Lords, 2 Macp. 28.

V

Valeat quantum.—For as much as it is worth; for whatever value it may have. See *Quantum valeat*.

Valens agere.—Able to act. A person is said to be *valens agere* when, from age and position, he is able to protect his rights against the invasion of them by others : against such a person not protecting his rights prescription runs, while prescription does not run against one who is *non valens agere*. See *Contra non valentem*, &c.

Valentia agendi.—The power or capacity of acting. This phrase expresses the same thing as *valens agere*.

Valere seipsum.—To be of its own value. In the retour of a special service, it was formerly necessary to specify the value of the lands, in order that the right of the superior, under his casualties, might be ascertained; but " because annual rents arising out of lands had no distinct valuation or extent, therefore they were said, in the *valent* clause of the retour, *valere seipsum*—*i.e.*, the annual rent itself was accounted the retoured, and consequently the non-entry duty." (Ersk. B. 2, T. 5, § 38.) The *valent* clause in a retour was that which specified the value of the lands according to the old and new extent.

Vani timores sunt æstimandi quæ non cadunt in constantem virum.—Those are regarded as groundless (empty) fears which are not such as would overcome a man of ordinary firmness and resolution. See *Ex vi*, &c.

Vassalli ligii.—Vassals holding immediately of the Crown. See *Ligia*, &c.

Vassallo et quibus dederit.—To the vassal and to whomsoever he shall have given it. In the earlier period of the feudal system, and after feudal grants had become the absolute property of the vassals, descending to their heirs and irrevocable on the part of the superior, there was still a restriction placed upon the vassal's power of conveying the subject of the grant to a singular successor. Unless with consent of the superior, he could not convey more than the half of the grant without incurring the casualty of recognition, which was a forfeiture of the whole fee; nor could a superior be compelled to receive as vassal one who had acquired right under a conveyance to which he, the superior, was not a consenter. If the original grant had been destined to the vassal, "and his heirs and assignees whomsoever," this only bound the superior to receive the proper heirs of the vassal and not his assignee; but if the destination bore to be to the vassal "*et quibus dederit*," this was construed as a consent on the part of the superior to alienation, and under which he was bound to receive as vassal his vassal's disponee. This distinction, at one time of much importance, was practically abolished by the Act 20 Geo. II. c. 50, which introduced a mode by which either an heir or disponee could force an entry from the superior. Duff's Feud. Con. 62.

Vassallo faciendo superiori quod de jure facere oportet.—Upon the vassal performing that to the superior which, according to law, he ought to perform. Ersk. B. 3, T. 8, § 79. See *Faciendo domino*, &c.

Vel faciendo vel delinquendo.—Either by doing something, or by leaving something undone; either by act or omission.

Venditio corporis.—A sale of a specific thing: as distinguished from

Venditio generis.—A sale of goods of a class or kind. Where the subject of sale is a quantity of goods of a certain kind, as a hundred quarters of wheat, a hundred tons of pig iron, a hundred yards of cloth, this is called a *venditio generis*, as distinguished from a sale of a specific subject, as of a certain vase, or picture, or cargo *ex* a certain vessel, which is termed *venditio speciei* or *venditio corporis*. In the former case the seller's obligation is fulfilled if he delivers to the buyer the stipulated quantity of any goods answering the description; in the latter, the seller's obligation is only fulfilled by delivering the specific thing sold. See *Genus nunquam*, &c.

Venditio nominis.—The sale or conveyance of a debt. See *Liberatio nominis*.

Venditor nominis tenetur præstare debitum subesse non vero debitorem locupletem esse.—The seller of a debt is bound to warrant that the debt is due, but not that the debtor is able to pay it. When one sells to another a debt or personal claim, it is implied that the debt or claim exists; the purchaser is not buying a debt which is merely fictitious; and therefore, if it turns out that the claim assigned or sold has no existence, the purchaser can demand back the price paid. But the seller does not warrant that the debtor will pay, or is able to pay the debt; of that the purchaser takes his risk, unless there be some special bargain or warranty in reference to that matter.

Venditio speciei.—A sale of a specific thing. See *Venditio generis.*

Verba accipienda sunt secundum subjectam materiam.—Words are to be accepted (or, understood) according to the subject-matter with which they deal. This may be illustrated by a case falling within the scope of the foregoing maxim, *Venditor nominis tenetur,* &c. Suppose a creditor assigns his debt, and adds in his assignation "and I warrant this." These words would be interpreted to mean that the creditor warranted that the debt was due, and also that he had a title to assign it: it would not, on account of its general terms, be held to imply a warranty that the debtor was good for the amount, or that he would pay the debt, because taken in its connection with the subject-matter of the assignation, it would be limited to the warranty which, in such circumstances, a seller or cedent is bound as well as supposed to give.

Verba chartarum fortius accipiuntur contra proferentem.—The words of charters (or, writings) are understood in the sense most burdensome to the granter, or the person using them; a deed is to be construed most strongly against the granter. See *Ambiguum placitum,* &c.; *Verba sunt interpretanda,* &c.

Verba cum effectu accipienda sunt.—Words are to be understood in a sense which will give them some effect. In construing deeds, contracts, or writings, the words used are to be read in such a manner as is consistent with giving them some effect; they are supposed to mean something and to be intended to have some effect from the fact of their having been used. If two interpretations or constructions of the words are possible, that one is preferred which will enable the words to be read as meaning something rather than that which would make them useless and insensible. In short, they are to be read *ut res valeat potius quam pereat.*

Verba debent intelligi cum effectu ut res magis valeat quam pereat.—Words ought to be read (or, understood) as of some effect, so that the matter (deed, contract, &c., in which the words are used) may rather be of avail than perish. See what has been said in the preceding article; and also Bell's Com. i. 456, note 5, with case there cited in illustration of this maxim.

Verba generalia restringuntur ad habilitatem rei vel personam.—General words are confined to the fitness of the thing or person; general words are confined in their construction and application by the consideration of their aptitude to the matter or the person concerning which or whom they are expressed. This is in effect another mode of saying that words are to be understood according to the subject-matter with which they deal. See *Verba accipienda sunt,* &c., and illustration there given. "All words, whether they be in deeds or statutes, or otherwise, if they be general, and not express and precise, shall be restrained unto the fitness of the matter and the person." Bac. Max. reg. 10. See the case of the *West London Ry. Co.* v. *L. & N.-W. Ry. Co.,* 22 L. J. C. P. 117, where this maxim was applied in restricting the effect of certain general words used in an agreement between two railway companies; it being held that the general words might have received a different interpretation if used in other circumstances, or by parties in a different position from those who used them.

Verba illata inesse videntur.—Words brought in (by reference) are regarded as present: or, words imported by reference are held as incorporated. See *Verba relata,* &c.

Verba ita sunt intelligenda ut res magis valeat quam pereat.—Words are so to be understood (or, are to be read in such a sense) as will make the matter (to which they refer) effectual and valid rather than destroy it. See *Verba debent intelligi,* &c.

Verba jactantia.—Empty, vain, bragging words; words not seriously spoken nor with the intention of binding the person using them to their truth. If two persons declare themselves to be man and wife, and do so seriously before witnesses, such a declaration will constitute a valid and binding marriage; but when such declarations are made in jest, and amount to mere *verba jactantia*, they constitute no contract. Again, it is a crime if one challenges another to fight a duel, but this crime will not be committed by the use of boastful or defiant words (*verba jactantia*), however much they may tend to bring about a duel, if they do not amount to an actual challenge.

Verba posteriora propter certitudinem addita ad priora quæ certitudine indigent sunt referenda.—Words subsequently added for the purpose of giving certainty or clearness are to be referred to those previous words which (through their own ambiguity) require to be made certain or clear. It is quite common to find in deeds or statutes a clause followed by the words " that is to say," which again are followed by an explanation or paraphrase of what had gone before. These explanatory clauses, according to the maxim, are to be held as referring to and explaining those prior clauses which need explanation, and not clauses which are clear in themselves. It will always depend upon the terms of the explanatory clause itself, and its position, and indeed upon a consideration of the whole deed or statute in which the explanatory clause appears, whether it applies to and overrides the whole deed or statute, or only a portion of it, and if the latter, what portion.

Verba relata hoc maxime operantur per referentiam ut in eis inesse videntur.—Words referred to operate in respect of the reference in the same way as if they had been incorporated; a reference to certain words (or, things) has the effect of importing the words (or, things) referred to into the deed referring to them. The most familiar example of this is found in pleadings where a document is referred to by description without giving any detail of its contents,—the reference to it importing the whole document into the pleading as effectually as if it had been recited at length. Again in conveyances, where lands are conveyed under the burdens set forth in a sasine or conveyance already upon record, the reference to the recorded deed in which the burdens are detailed has the same effect as if the whole burdens were repeated instead of being merely referred to. So also, where a person purchases a bill of lading which sets forth that the captain of the vessel is to deliver the cargo on being paid freight "as per charter party," the purchaser is only bound for the freight according to the charter party; but if the bill of lading imposes on the consignee the obligation of "paying freight and all other conditions as per charter party," this has the effect of importing the whole conditions of the charter party into the bill of lading so as to make the purchaser thereof liable for the fulfilment of the whole conditions of the charter. As illustrative further of this maxim, see the observations by Lord Chancellor Westbury, in the case of *E. of Kintore*, 4 Macq. 520.

Verba solennia.—Solemn or formal words; words essential to validity. The word "dispone" was at one time of this character, and no conveyance of lands was effectual if this word was not used. The necessity for this word was abolished as regards deeds of a testamentary nature by the Act 31 & 32 Vict. c. 101, § 20, and as regards all conveyances of land by the Act 37 & 38 Vict. c. 94, § 27.

Verba sunt interpretanda contra proferentem.—Words are to be interpreted against the person using them. This is one of the rules observed in the interpretation of writs. Where the person using common words is vulgar and illiterate, they are interpreted according to the general acceptation of such words among people of the same class as himself; but if he uses technical words and formal expressions, they are construed according to their technical meaning and signification; the using of them raises the presumption of knowledge on his part of their meaning. See *Verba charturum*, &c.

Verbatim et literatim.—Word for word, and letter for letter; an exact copy.

Verbis standum ubi nulla ambiguitas.—One must abide by the words where there is no ambiguity. This maxim expresses a rule of construction. Where the words of a deed or statute are ambiguous, it becomes necessary, in order to ascertain their meaning and intention, to consider the circumstances in which the deed or statute originated, the object it had in view, the evil it was intended to correct, or the right it was intended to confer, &c.; and in the light thus afforded an interpretation or construction is put upon the ambiguous words or phrase. But where there is no ambiguity, and the meaning of the words used is plain and distinct, that meaning must be given to them; construction is not permitted where the expression is clear. See the observations made on the maxim *Ex antecedentibus*, &c., and cases there referred to.

Verborum obligatio.—An obligation constituted *verbis;* a verbal obligation. This was one of the classes of contracts among the Romans, which included all contracts or obligations in the constitution of which certain solemn and formal words were necessarily used. For an example, see *Stipulatio:* see also *Obligatio*, &c.

Veredictum.—Verdict.

Vergens ad inopiam.—Approaching to want or insolvency. When a debtor is clearly *vergens ad inopiam*, a creditor may legally resort to certain measures, for the purpose of protecting his interests, which would not otherwise be competent to him. Thus if the debtor be bound under a bill, the creditor may, in consideration of his debtor's circumstances, obtain a precept of arrestment on the bill before it becomes due, on which he may arrest any funds due to his debtor. As this proceeding is only allowed, however, as a protective measure on the part of the creditor, he cannot, by action of furthcoming or otherwise, render the arrested funds available to himself until the bill falls due. Heritable property may be adjudged under the same circumstances in security, but being merely a security, it cannot by the lapse of any length of time become an irredeemable right. The fact of the debtor's being *vergens ad inopiam* will be inferred from different circumstances in different cases, and the proof of that fact will also, necessarily, be varied.

Veritas convicii.—The truth of the accusation. In actions for damages and solatium on account of libel, the *veritas convicii*, or truth of the alleged libel, is a defence competent to the defender, and may be proved by him if he has sufficiently averred it so as to entitle him to an issue upon that point.

At one time it was held that the truth of the accusation did not justify the person who made it so as to free him from liability for damages, but it is now conclusively settled that the *veritas convicii* is a good defence to a claim of damages for slander. The reader will find the whole cases on this subject reviewed in the opinion delivered by the Lord Justice-Clerk (Inglis) in *Mackellar* v. *D. of Sutherland*, 21 D. 222. It is conceivable, however, that this defence would not be sufficient in all cases. Thus, suppose that A had been convicted of the crime of theft many years before, and had subsequently been living an honest life, and that B unnecessarily raked up this old charge, alleging that A was a convicted thief, the malice of such a proceeding would scarcely be sufficiently answered or absolved by the truth of the fact.

Veritas convicii an excusat?—Does the truth of a libel excuse (its publication)?

Veritas convicii non excusat a calumnia.—The truth of the charge does not excuse from slander. This is no longer a rule of Scotch law. See *Veritas convicii*.

Veritas nominis tollit errorem demonstrationis.—Truth in the name takes away (or, destroys the effect of) error in description. See *Præsentia corporis*, &c.

Versans in illicito.—Engaged in some unlawful occupation; performing an illegal act.

Vestita viro.—Clothed with a husband. A married woman is said to be *vestita viro*, and so long as this coverture exists her person cannot be attached on civil diligence, unless that diligence proceeds upon a decree *ad factum præstandum*, for the performance of some act which she is bound to perform, and which cannot be validly performed except by herself, *ex. gr.*, to enter the heir of her vassal, to produce or exhibit as a haver writings in her own custody, &c.

Vestitus et mundus muliebris.—A woman's wearing apparel and ornaments. These are all included in a wife's *paraphernalia*.

Vi aut clam aut precario.—By force, by stealth or other clandestine means, or by importunate entreaty. Possession of a subject obtained by any of these means was regarded in the civil law as vicious, and could not be defended by the prætorian interdict *uti possidetis*; the formula appropriate to that interdict expressly excepted from its benefit any possession so obtained.

Vi aut metu.—By force or fear. See *Ex vi*, &c.

Vi statuti.—By force of statute.

Via.—One of the chief rural servitudes of the civil law, which entitled the dominant owner to a right of way through the servient owner's property. It included both *iter* and *actus*, so that the dominant owner had the right of passing either on foot or horseback, and also of driving a vehicle, cattle, or beast of burden, along the servient tenement.

Via actionis.—By way of an action; by means of an action.

Via facti.—By means of an act; by personal act. "The course of both the positive and negative prescription may be broken off or interrupted by a protestation taken against the possessor, that his possession shall not hurt the right of him who protests. This is called, in common speech, *civil interruption*, because it is attended with no violence; and in our statutes it gets the name of an interruption *via facti*; because it is founded on the extrajudicial deed of him who interrupts." Ersk. B. 3, T. 7, § 40.

Via juris.—By means of law, or legal process. Interruption of prescription by judicial proceedings is called interruption *via juris*; while interruption by means of an extrajudicial act is said to be *via facti*.

Via trita via tuta.—An oft-trodden path is a safe path; a common mode is a safe mode. In the hiring of skilled labour, it is one of the obligations of the persons whose services are hired, to act skilfully—that is, to act according to the best of his skill whatever that may be. He must act according to the rules adopted and recognised in his profession, and he will be answerable for the consequences of any deviation from those rules. But if he acts according to rule, he is not responsible—he has adopted the ordinary mode of dealing with such a matter, and that protects him from the consequences. Bell's Prin. § 154.

Vicarius non habet vicarium.—A substitute has no substitute—that is, one who is himself only the substitute of another cannot substitute another in his place, and delegate to him his substituted authority. See *Delegatus non potest*, &c.

Vice versa.—Conversely.

Vicecomes.—The ancient name of the sheriff.

Vicecomitatus.—A sheriffdom or shire.

Vicem fructuum obtinere.—To obtain or hold the place of fruits. This is said of interest, which is regarded as the fruit or produce of money. Interest is therefore a part of a liferenter's right, who is entitled to the whole produce of the estate liferented *salva substantia*. In respect of the character thus given to interest, Erskine says " that a *bona fide* possessor is as strongly entitled to retain interest as natural fruits;" but this seems not to be without doubt. See Ersk. B. 2, T. 1, § 26, with notes appended by Lord Ivory and a previous editor.

Victus victori in expensis damnandus est.—The unsuccessful party is to be found liable in expenses to the successful party. The civil law rule regarding the expenses of a lawsuit. See *Ubi damna dantur*, &c.

Vide infra.—See below. Used by way of reference.

Vide supra.—See above. Used by way of reference.

Vidi scivi et audivi.—I saw, knew, and heard. These words formed part of the long doquet which the notary was formerly in use to append to an instrument of sasine; they imported that he was personally present on the ground when sasine was given, and that the facts attested in the instrument he knew to be true from his having seen and heard them done and said. These words were essential to the validity of the instrument, and their want has been held fatal. The long doquet was abolished, along with the ceremony of giving infeftment then in use, by the Act 8 & 9 Vict. c. 35.

Vigilantibus non dormientibus jura subveniunt.—The laws help or assist those who are watchful of their rights, not those who are careless of them. On this maxim preference is given in competition to rights which have been first perfected, and to diligences which have been first used; those who have been most watchful of their rights, and careful to use the legal means for securing them, being best entitled to the benefits which the law confers or affords. Prescription is founded in part upon this principle; for rights are cut off by prescription as much *in pœnam* of the neglect of the creditor to enforce his claim as a presumption of abandonment or discharge. A creditor, therefore, who fails to claim or enforce his right for forty years loses that right altogether; and one who carelessly allows another for forty years to hold possession of his land, or to use part of it as a common passage or road, without interfering to protect his rights, must thereafter lose his right to the land in the one case, and in the other submit to the servitude so acquired.

Viis et modis.—By ways and means. Dickson, § 957.

Vim vi repellere omnes leges omniaque jura permittunt. —All laws, written and unwritten, permit force to be repelled by force. Where any one is placed in peril through the violence of another, he is entitled to protect himself by violence; a man is entitled to protect by force the property of which another endeavours to deprive him by force; a woman is entitled to defend her chastity if that is threatened by a man attempting a rape upon her, and that even to the extent if necessary of taking the life of the man assaulting her. The violence, however, which the law permits is strictly violence used in defence; it does not permit any one to recover by violence that which has been lost or taken by violence. In all cases, too, the violence must be only such as is necessary, for, exceeding that, it becomes culpable. See *Moderamen inculpatœ,* &c.

Vinco vincentem, ergo multo magis vinco te.—I conquer your conqueror, therefore much more do I conquer you. This is a rule applied to questions of preference in competitions, concerning which see Ross, L. C. (L. R.) i. 267, and Bell's Com. ii. 76.

Vinco vincentem, vinco te.—Conquering your conqueror, I conquer you. Another form of the preceding maxim.

Vinculum personarum ab eodem stipite descendentium. —The bond uniting persons descended from the same stock. Bell's Prin. § 1647.

Vindicatio.—The name given in the civil law to a real action, as opposed to *condictio,* a personal action. It was competent only to the owner for recovery of the thing claimed itself, and only competent to him as against the person then in actual possession. It applied alike to things corporeal and incorporeal, and therefore might be the form of action adopted for recovery of a slave, or of a right of usufruct or servitude. It is common for the Latin jurists to speak of a person being able to vindicate a thing as a mode of asserting that he is the owner, the test of ownership being whether the supposed owner could or could not claim the subject by *vindicatio.* See *Condictio.*

Viri feroces.—Fierce, impetuous, passionate men. Stair, B. 4, T. 40, § 25.

Vis aut metus qui cadit in constantem virum.—A force or fear sufficient to overcome a man of firmness and resolution. Force or fear, if libelled as a ground of reduction of a contract or obligation induced by such means, must, to be effectual, be of the character described in this phrase; but it is always a question of circumstances what amount of force, or what threats superinducing fear, amount to the description here given. It must, however, be a force or fear which the person subjected to it could not at the time, and in the peculiar circumstances, withstand; and the bodily and mental condition of the person influenced, the particular nature of the influence used, and the whole surrounding circumstances, are taken into view in considering whether the force or fear was or was not sufficient to overcome his will. See *Ex vi,* &c.

Vis major.—A greater or superior power. In reference to the subject treated of in the preceding phrase, *vis major* signifies actual personal violence; generally, however, it takes its literal signification.

Vis major naturæ.—The superior force of nature. This phrase comprehends the force of the elements, or force arising from natural causes which are irresistible, such as a violent gale of wind, an earthquake, &c.

Vitium reale.—A real defect. Where there is a real defect in the title to a subject, heritable or moveable, it affects all singular successors or subsequent possessors. It is inseparable from the subject itself, and therefore the most perfect *bona fides* will not remedy the defect. See *Labes realis,* &c.

Viva voce.—Orally.

Voces signatæ.—Marked or formal words; technical

words which are essential, and which cannot be supplied *per æquipollens;* or, ordinary words used in a special technical sense. This phrase is similar in import to *Verba solennia,* which see.

Volenti non fit injuria.—To one consenting no wrong is done. The import of this maxim is, that that which would amount to wrongous injury, subjecting the doer of it in damages to the person injured, loses this character, if the person suffering the disadvantage or injury consents to the performance of the act. Thus it was supposed to inflict an injury upon a superior if his vassal disponed more than half of his lands, and in the event of his doing so the superior recovered the whole lands as forfeited under the casualty of recognition. But if the superior consented to the alienation of the vassal's lands, the casualty of recognition was not incurred, because no wrongous injury was supposed to arise to the superior from an act to which he was a willing and consenting party. To break down a neighbour's fence or wall, to build upon his land, or to do anything inflicting damage upon him, entitles him to reparation, because such acts are wrongous and illegal; but if his consent to the act has been obtained, this takes away that which was wrongous in it, and at the same time takes away all claim for reparation on account of it. *Injuria* signifies, not injury or damage, merely, but injury or damage wrongously inflicted, and giving rise to a claim for reparation. In actions of damages, this maxim has often been urged in defence where the damage arose or was occasioned by a danger seen, or known to the person injured, to exist. Going into a seen or known danger was regarded as a voluntary running of the risk which that danger threatened, and so, on the principle of this maxim, no wrong was done to the person who willingly encountered the danger. This view, however, has been materially modified by the decision of the House of Lords in *Smith* v. *Baker,* L. R. App. c. 1891, 325.

Voluntariæ jurisdictionis.—Of or pertaining to voluntary jurisdiction. See *Jurisdictio contentiosa.*

Voluntas donatoris in charta doni sui manifeste expressa observetur.—The intention of the granter, clearly expressed in the writing by which the grant is made, is to be observed.

Every one who has power to grant or give in donation may (as it is his own voluntary act dealing with what is exclusively his own) impose such conditions on the grant as he thinks fit. Such conditions, therefore, are to be observed by the donatory or other person on whom they are imposed, if he takes any benefit under the deed. Further, in construing such a deed and its conditions, effect is to be given to the obvious intention of the granter; but that intention must be gathered from the deed itself, and not extraneously. Where the intention of the granter is clearly expressed, it must be observed and given effect to in terms: provided, of course, the intention and conditions are such as the law will recognise. Compare the case of *Reid* v. *Coates*, 5th March, 1813, F. C. with *Fraser* v. *Rose*, 11 D. 1466.

Voluntas est ambulatoria usque ad mortem.—A will is ambulatory until death takes place; a will is revocable at any time during the lifetime of the testator. This maxim is sometimes written thus: *Voluntas testatoris est ambulatoria usque ad extremum vitæ exitum:* the will of a testator is ambulatory until the last moment of life. See *Ambulatoria est,* &c.

Voluntas reputatur pro facto.—The intention is regarded as the act; the will is taken for the deed. This rule has scarcely any (if any) application in legal questions. Broom, 310 *et seq.* See *Cogitationis pœnam,* &c.

Voluntas testatoris.—The will or intention of a testator. In the interpretation of a will or settlement, the intention of the testator, as it can be gathered from the whole strain and purpose of the deed, is to be chiefly regarded. Where technical terms are used, however, they must bear their technical signification, and evidence that the testator did not understand them, or that his intention was different from that which they technically express, cannot be received.

Voluntatis non necessitatis.—A matter of choice, and not of necessity.

Votum captandæ mortis alienæ.—An earnest desire for the death of another. Under the civil law, any paction by an heir concerning his ancestor's estate during that ancestor's life was ineffectual, and held as invalid; nor could an heir, during his ancestor's life, sell his *spes successionis.* Such transactions were regarded as *contra bonos mores*, as inducing or likely to induce, an undue or improper desire for another's death. This rule does not prevail with us, for a *spes successionis* may form the subject of a valid sale. See *Pactum corvinum*, &c.

Vox emissa volat—litera scripta manet.—A word spoken flies away—a writing remains. This phrase expresses the advantage which writing has over verbal communications as matter of evidence. The spoken word may be forgotten, misunderstood, or misrepresented: the document speaks for itself, and is always the same.

Vox signata.—A marked word: a technical word. See *Voces signatæ*.

Vulgo quæsiti.—Bastards; frequently called in the civil law *vulgo concepti*. See *Spurii*.